ILLUSTRATORS OF CHILDREN'S BOOKS

ILLUSTRATORS

of

Children's Books

1744 - 1945

Compiled by

BERTHA E. MAHONY

LOUISE PAYSON LATIMER

BEULAH FOLMSBEE

THE HORN BOOK INC. BOSTON

1947

To

WILLIAM D. MILLER

Preface

THIS book could hardly have come into being without the help of Louise P. Latimer, Director, Work with Children of the Public Library of the District of Columbia, Washington. We knew that Miss Latimer had been building there, for thirty years, a collection of illustrated books and books on illustration. We had used the 1929 revised edition of *Illustrators, A Finding List*, concerned with books in print, compiled by her and published by F. W. Faxon in Boston. In the spring of 1944 we asked her if she would join us in making *Illustrators of Children's Books*. Encouraged by the support of Miss Clara W. Herbert, Librarian, and by the enthusiasm of the Children's Department staff, Miss Latimer agreed to contribute Part III, "A Century and a Half of Illustration," in bibliographies.

Although there were centuries of early illustrated books when no credit was given to the artist, we have chosen to look back, in the book as a whole, two centuries to the first children's book published by John Newbery in 1744 at Saint Paul's Churchyard, London. Miss Latimer's bibliographies, however, begin with the earliest children's book for which the illustrator can be identified.

A large proportion of the books listed have been long out of print, but the collection in the Children's Department of the Washington Public Library contains examples of the work of all but nine of the over eight hundred illustrators included in Part III.

The Washington Public Library's generous loan of books from this collection with the privilege of holding them in Boston for the necessary time has facilitated the selection of the pictures representing the work of illustrators of earlier periods and has made possible the desired care in plate-making.

The editors wish to acknowledge their indebtedness to other Libraries: — To the New York Public Library for the loan of books from which pictures were selected and plates made to illustrate the chapter, "Foreign Picture Books." To the Boston Public Library for many courtesies shown us by the Children's Room, the Fine Arts and the Rare Book Departments. To the Boston Athenaeum and the Fine Arts Museum Library for superlative working conditions over a long period of time and the unfailing courtesy and helpfulness of their assistants. To the American Antiquarian Library of Worcester and to the Keeper of the Library in the Victoria and Albert Museum, London.

For the design used on the cover paper we are indebted to the artist, T. M. Cleland, and to Mr. Elmer Adler for the loan of the original drawing made by Mr. Cleland for *The Colophon*, Part Eleven; also to Mr. Adler for permission to quote from two numbers of that publication. To Marguerite MacKellar Mitchell our heartfelt thanks for the generous loan of her studio at "Sunny Fields" in Weston where the designer of the book planned and completed a large part of her work in sympathetic surroundings. To Anne Carroll Moore, Alice M. Jordan, and Louise Seaman Bechtel our thanks for the reading of these pages in manuscript and for many helpful suggestions along the way.

A special note of thanks is due to the publishers of children's books from which a large part of the illustrations were drawn, and about which full information as to title, author, illustrator and publisher may be found in the Bibliographies. In the few instances of illustrations reproduced from books not included in the Bibliographies, such information has been given in Notes, on page 520.

To Mr. Frank Weitenkampf the editors wish to record their cordial thanks for his patience and helpfulness in discussing various aspects of this book in its earliest stages. To Mr. Sinclair Hamilton for his courtesy in permitting us to make such generous use of his article on "Early American Illustrating," in the *Princeton University Library Chronicle* for April, 1945. To Mrs. Edmund Lester Pearson for permission to quote from *Books in Black or Red* by Edmund Lester Pearson. (Macmillan. New York. 1923. Now out of print.) To Mr. Albert A. Achorn, of the Lincoln Engraving Company, for his painstaking care with the making of the plates for the book. To Mr. Thomas Todd, Treasurer of The Horn Book Inc., and printer of the Magazine and of other books published by The Horn Book Inc., who has taken a personal as well as a professional interest in the printing of *Illustrators of Children's Books*.

B. E. M.

Contents

Introduction

In his introduction to the *Fairy Tales* of Hans Christian Andersen translated by H. L. Braekstad, and illustrated by Hans Tegner, Edmund Gosse tells of hearing Andersen himself read aloud a new fairy tale, "The Cripple," now little known. They sat in a bright room looking out on the sound filled with ships, "like a flock of wild swans," Andersen said, and across to the white towns of Malmö and Landskrona sparkling on the Swedish coast, with the sunlight falling on Tycho Brahe's island.

The story tells of a gardener and his wife who have five children, the eldest of whom, a fine boy, is a bedridden cripple. "The parents, worthy, narrow people, live engrossed in their materialistic interests, and when someone . . . gives the cripple a book, they say ungraciously to one another, 'He won't get fat on that.' But it is a book of fairy tales, and the boy's whole spiritual life is awakened by the vistas they open for him in every direction. He finds two simple and direct parables which he reads over and over again to his parents, and their hearts, too, are humanized and melted. Finally, a little dark bird, like the Emperor of China's nightingale, is presented to him, and in a supreme nervous effort to save its life the cripple regains the use of his own limbs."

This story, which expresses the power of the imaginative to extend and to quicken the vision of men, is true also of the illustrator's drawings. No sooner did man begin to observe and meditate upon the wonder and mystery of nature and life than he began to tell his own stories; and these in time became folk and fairy tales, myths, legends, and hero tales. Storytellers must have been active as early as men made drawings on the walls of caves or on tools.

The art of storytelling, and the art of drawing to illustrate the story, have always stimulated each other. There lies before me now a letter describing the part played by his grandfather's stories in the making of one of our well-known illustrators; "handed-down-word-of-mouth stories of the old Frontier," told night after night to small boys listening before the fire. Stories coming down from one generation to another, or from ages long ago to the present, through the storyteller's art, have not only nourished the creative gift in illustrators, but have also been the subject of much of their work, as the reader will see by referring to the bibliography on page 451 of this book. Notice the artists who have made drawings for the *Bible*, for the stories out of Greek mythology, for Aesop's *Fables*, Grimm's *Fairy Tales*, the tales of Andersen, and *Arabian Nights*.

Just as the storyteller has taken pleasure in presenting every phase of human life, so the artist has felt the urge to reproduce nature and life in an endless variety of forms. Sometimes he has tried to realize and set down things just as they are. Sometimes his effort has been to realize and record things as they appear to be. As in literature, so in drawing, there is the realistic and there is the purely imaginative. There is the fable, the parable, the allegory and the symbol — forms as important as ever to us today, and inherent in the work of poet and artist.

The dragon, for example, appears again and again in story and picture. Both help us to recognize the species when the dragon appears in our time in the form of tyranny or other evils. The heroes who, in the literature of earlier times, rid the world of evil giants, Gorgons or dragons — David, Perseus, St. George — all have their descendants in our life today, but it is through our imaginative vision that we apprehend them. Truth comes to us in many forms through story and picture.

One of today's poets, Paul Engle, reviewing a new edition of *Arabian Nights*, expressed the heart of the matter when he wrote, "For there is truth at symbolic level, and this is the highest kind of literary truth, the kind you get in the great books. A story may be true to the clothes people wore, the food they ate, the kind of language they spoke, and yet be wholly wrong and untrue in its presentation of their human nature. And a story may be fantastic in setting and remote in fact, and yet be wholly true to its people. This is the real truth. It is the strength of the *Arabian Nights*. Truth in Bagdad is still truth in Berwyn."

The same stories and books have attracted artists in one period after another because of these universal truths which pervade them. The hope of the world lies in those things which are universal. Pictures, like music, speak a free world language. "There is life and death, brother, and the wind on the heath." In nature the wind scatters the seeds to create new plants. In human life, the restless, adventurous, inquisitive and acquisitive, conquering spirit of man scatters and blends to create new designs or to perpetuate old forms. As in literature, there are artists who initiate, who depart from old forms and express things in a new way; there are those who follow and imitate; and there are the masters who instinctively select the best out of the past and carry it toward perfection;

then the cycle of effort starts over again, sometimes only after perfection has deteriorated into decadence.

The effect of the work of earlier artists can often be clearly traced in those who follow. Dürer's influence is seen in Howard Pyle's drawings, and Howard Pyle's in Robert Lawson's. Some illustrators have been influenced by the art of a country — as Walter Crane by the art of China and Japan; Edmund Dulac and Kay Nielsen by the art of Persia, India and China. The folk art of their native countries, its color and form, is reflected today in the work of a number of artists whose home is now America.

Art is like a world river, able to touch all countries, sometimes turned in direction by this or that land shape; sometimes slowed, sometimes quickened; sometimes even forced underground; but never ceasing in movement or being.

The unbroken thread of pictorial art which links the work of all artists everywhere throughout history constitutes tradition. A young illustrator expresses it elsewhere in this book when he writes, "Children's books and all types of books for me have been affected by most primitive art forms, from the African Congo cave drawings and sculpture through the fine work done in primitive German Bible illustrations, their excellent sense of design; the imagination and daring of French children's books; the fine reality, texture and tactile approach of Russian children's books; and the wonderful unexplored work of the early American primitives and the more refined Audubon."

Perhaps the reader of *Illustrators of Children's Books* will ask, "How do you happen to include such artists as Dürer and Holbein the Younger in a book on children's illustrated books?" For answer the reader is directed to Anne Eaton's opening chapter and to Louise Latimer's introduction to the bibliographies of Part III. In Miss Eaton's chapter he will learn how recent are honest books of entertainment for children. But children have always found their pleasure where they could, creating it for themselves at need, and of course they have enjoyed pictures wherever they have found them.

We have endeavored to present suggestive chapters of what has happened in illustrated books for children in England and America since John Newbery made his first book in 1744. And because, as we have intimated above, the illustrative art of England and America cannot be separated from that of other countries, we have included a chapter on foreign picture books as used in a children's library. These chapters are written for the layman, not the advanced student of art or graphic arts history. They are intended to be suggestive only; points of departure for further reading and study, and the making of other books on the subject. Biographical material on artists no longer living is to be found in various reference books. *Illustrators of Children's Books* presents, therefore, brief information about living illustrators — Part II. The bibliographic section, Part III, provides a basis for wide examination of the illustrative work of those who have made history in the field of children's books.

And so we come to the two purposes of this book. The first is to show that art in children's books is a part of all art, not an isolated special field. In every period the greatest artists have shared in it. The second purpose is to invite to further reading and study, to wider examination of picture books and illustrated books of the past and present, and to more conscious effort to understand all that is involved in fine bookmaking, for thus is pleasure in books increased; and thus is created a book public discerning in its appreciation, capable of judging pictures and format as well as text; the kind of public that encourages artists to greater heights and advances the bookmaking arts.

The work of the artist — like that of the writer, poet, musician — enlarges the understanding and vision of men and quickens their imagination. And imagination is best quickened in childhood. In patient effort and with periods of joy and delight, in spite of all the discouragements life in the world presents, the artist goes on trying to better today his best of yesterday. Always he tries to see "beauty with keener perception and subtler understanding" and to serve it. That is why the artist sees what other men cannot see. The every existence of artists, with their unceasing effort toward perfection in their work, would seem a hope and a promise to the world; a symbol of man's spiritual struggle toward the source of truth, goodness, mercy and beauty; evidence that the struggle is the very heart of life. These creative people who use their talents for children's books are blessed, and far more important than they realize, for they are helping to build that "World Republic of Childhood" which, rightly built, will one day bring into being the ideal Republic of the World.

"Yes," Paul Hazard wrote, "children's books keep alive a sense of nationality; but they also keep alive a sense of humanity. They describe their native land lovingly, but they also describe faraway lands where unknown brothers live. They understand the essential quality of their own race; but each of them is a messenger that goes beyond mountains and rivers, beyond the seas, to the very ends of the world in search of new friendships. Every country gives and every country receives — innumerable are the exchanges — and so it comes about that in our first impressionable years the universal republic of childhood is born."

BERTHA E. MAHONY

PART I. HISTORY AND DEVELOPMENT

¶In this partye conteyneth & repayteth another beste whiche is of dyuers coloures of spottes as white/black/grene/blew & yelowe/lyke as it were paynted/and is called pã there/ and there cometh out of his mouthe so swete a sauour & brethe/that th e bestys go folowynge after it for the sweteneβ of his body / saue the serpent/to whom the swete smell greueth/ in suche wyse that ofte the serpent deth/and whan this beste is otherwhyle so fylled and full of venyson that he hath taken & eaten/He slepeth thre dayes hole without awakynge/and whan he awaketh/he geueth out of his mouth so swete a sauour and smell/that anon the bestes that fele it seche hym/This beste hathe but ones yonge fawnes/   And whan she shal fawne/She hathe suche dystresse and angwysshe that she breketh with her naples and renteth her matrice in such wyse that her fawnes come out/And neuer after whan the matrice is rente and broken they engender ne brynge forthe fawnes/There is a maner of mares that cõceiue of the wynde/and ben in a contrey named capadoce/but they endure not but thre yere.

From a page in " Myrrour of the Worlde," translated
from the French and printed by Caxton in 1481

I. Illustrated Books for Children Before 1800

ANNE THAXTER EATON

*A Little Pretty Pocket-Book: first Worcester
edition, 1787*

Stones.   XII.   *Lapides.*

Sand, 1. *and* Gravel, 2.	*Avena*, 1. & *Sabulum*, 2.
is Stone *broken into bits.*	*est* comminutus *Lapis.*
A great Stone, 3	*Saxum*, 3.
is a piece of	*est pars*
a Rock *(or Crag)* 4.	*Petra (Cautis)* 4.
A Whetstone, 5.	*Cos*, 5.
a Flint, 6. *a* Marble, 7. *&c.*	*Silex*, 6. *Marmor*, 7. *&c.*
are ordinary Stones.	*sunt* Lapides *obscuri.*
A Load-stone, 8.	*Magnes*, 8.
draweth Iron to it.	*adtrahit ferrum.*
Jewels, 9.	*Gemmæ*, 9.
are clear Stones, as	*sunt* Lapilli *pellucidi, ut*
The Diamond *white*,	*Adamas* candidus,
The Ruby *red*,	*Rubinus* rubeus,
The Sapphire *blew*,	*Sapphirus* cæruleus,
The Emerald *green*,	*Smaragdus* viridis,
The Jacinth *yellow*, &c.	*Hyacynthus* luteus, &c.
And they glister, being cut in	*Et micant ungulati.*
fashion of the Nails of ones	
hand.	
Pearls, *and* Unions 10.	*Margaritæ & Uniones*, 10.
grow in Shell-fish.	crescunt in Conchis.
	Corals

Orbis Pictus, the first picture book planned for children:
fifth edition, London, 1705

Illustrated Books for Children Before 1800

The Newbery
facsimiles
issued in honor
of the Father of
Children's
Books

IN 1944, a facsimile of a famous eighteenth-century book for children, *A Little Pretty Pocket-Book*, was published in honor of John Newbery who, two hundred years before, was responsible for the appearance of this first "juvenile"; and in 1945, a second eighteenth-century book for children, *Mother Goose's Melody*, appeared in facsimile. These two little volumes must have started, for many lovers of children's books, a train of thought leading well into the past and far away from the gay and sumptuous volumes crowding the shelves in the children's departments of bookshops today. These same booklovers think gratefully of Frederic Melcher, who brought about the publication of these facsimiles, not alone for the sake of the endearing miniature volumes themselves, but for the reminder that even a superficial survey of children's books of the past is rich in interest. Not only do books written for boys and girls in the years before 1800 open for us a door leading into the world of our ancestors, but, grave and austere as these little volumes are, compared with the exuberance of modern books for children, they offer a very real charm, like that of northern woods and pastures after the opulent vegetation of the South; as Elinor Wylie puts it: —

> the look austere, immaculate
> Of landscapes drawn in pearly monotones
> . . . .
> A thread of water, churned to milky spate
> Streaming through slanted pastures fenced with stones.

Early illustrated
books treasured
by children

To know that the little books of the seventeenth and eighteenth centuries, with their tiny woodcuts, were dearly treasured by boys and girls gives them a touching appeal. That they were treasured we know: Leigh Hunt, in *The Town*, published in 1848, tells how much the pictures in the books of his boyhood meant to him, badly drawn as they were; and the name that we find inscribed in labored, childish handwriting on the flyleaf or title page of some small volume that has managed to survive is another proof that these books were cherished by their youthful owners.

Schoolbooks of the 7th Century

However, for the real beginning of books for children we must look further back than the eighteenth, the seventeenth, or even the sixteenth century. The first books for children were Latin schoolbooks of the seventh century, such as *De Septenario, de Metris, Ænigmatibus, ac Pedum Regulis* (which began with a discourse on the mystical significances and virtues of the number seven, especially as used in Scripture); the school texts of the Venerable Bede (672), and of Alcuin who followed Bede and was a resident of Charlemagne's court; and the famous *Colloquy* of Ælfric, compiled for the boys of the monastery school at Winchester when Ælfric was teaching there at the end of the tenth century. This book of simple questions and answers on subjects of everyday life, with an interlinear Anglo-Saxon gloss for the convenience of the teacher, since the pupils when young in years rarely handled their lesson books themselves, presents in words a succession of vivid pictures of life in the England of the period.

Early Caxtons, unillustrated

Naturally, however, because books in manuscript were rare and costly, we look in vain for the beginning of illustration in books for children until the invention of printing. Even then the idea of pictures for children made headway very slowly. Caxton did not entirely neglect young people but printed, with them in mind, two editions of *The Book of Courtesy* and also *The Booke whiche the Knyght of the Tour made to the enseynement and techyng of his doughters*, by Geoffrey de la Tour-Landry. This work Caxton himself translated "at the request of a noble lady which has brought forth many noble and fair daughters, which be virtuously nourished," and in his preface Caxton advises "every gentleman or woman having children desiring them to be virtuously brought forth to get and have this book." Times and customs change, and of this volume E. Gordon Duff remarks in passing that "in these days the book would be considered anything but suitable for young persons, or for the matter of that, for their elders." When printed in Switzerland, *Der Ritter vom Turn* was adorned with woodcuts, but Caxton, in England, printed it, as well as *The Book of Courtesye*, unillustrated.

Caxton's Æsop illustrated, 1484

The book from Caxton's press most in line with children's own spontaneous interest was, of course, Æsop's *Fables*, printed in 1484, and one would be glad to think that the "lytyl Johns" and also the "lytyl" Joans of those days may have managed to regale themselves on the 185 clear and lively woodcuts which this volume contains.

The Bestiaries

The bestiaries, which date from the fifth century and which combined the

The Caxton Æsop, 1484

Der Ritter vom Turn, 1493

features of a natural history and Æsop's *Fables*, were used by the monks to teach spiritual truths to the people, and the descriptions they contained of fabulous creatures must have fascinated any child who heard them read or expounded, or who caught a glimpse of these animals in an illuminated manuscript. Who could fail to be delighted by the interesting possibilities of " The Panther Attracting Animals with Its Fragrant Breath "; " the Yale (or Eale) with Movable Horns "; or " the Mother Bear Licking her Cubs into Shape "? All of these were included in an English bestiary of the twelfth century. Edward Topsel's *History of Four-Footed Beasts* (1658), from which Walter de la Mare took the illustrations he used in his *Animal Stories*, published in 1939, though purporting to be a natural history, contains cuts of dragons and unicorns and other creatures as strange and remarkable as those of the bestiaries.

Rhymed treatises of the 15th Century

In volume 32 of the " Original Series of the Early English Text Society," Frederick J. Furnivall has edited in delightfully human fashion *The Babees' Boke; or a Lytyl Reporte of how Young People Should Behave; Stans Puer ad Mensam* (The Page Standing at the Table); Simon's *Lesson of Wysedom for all Manner Children* and others of the rhymed treatises (so popular in the fifteenth century) which aimed to set forth the whole duty of children, instructing them in many subjects from Latin grammar to religion, but dealing chiefly with manners and behaviour. Dr. Furnivall included at the end of the volume a selection of scenes of daily life, having to do chiefly with feasting and serving, which were chosen from manuscripts and tapestries of the twelfth to fifteenth centuries. These pictures, stiff and quaint, yet strangely real, of groups and individuals engaged in such matters as washing before dinner with basin and ewer; dining, with steward and servants bringing in an imposing array of dishes; or of a king being served at table; a lady and gentleman feasting in private on a large pasty; or a fifteenth-century countess sitting beside her canopied bed, while two little dogs play beneath it, not only furnish a glimpse into the past, but suggest the kind of woodcut which might well have graced the rhymed treatises designed for fifteenth-century youth, had the matter of pictures for young people been considered important.

Horn-books and battledores

Illustrated or not, however, these rhymed treatises, like the Latin grammars, were too rare and costly to put freely into children's hands. It was with the invention of the horn-book, toward the end of the sixteenth century, that provision was made, for the first time, for children to handle their own books. Here was something less perishable and less precious: a sheet containing the alphabet

THE
HISTORY
OF
Four-Footed Beasts.

The *ANTALOPE*.

THE *Antalope* called in Latin *Calopus*, and of the Grecians *Analopos*, or *Aptolos*: of this beast there is no mention made among the Ancient Writers, except *Suidas*, and the Epistle of *Alexander* to *Aristotle*, interpreted by *Cornelius Nepotius*. They are bred in *India* and *Syria*, neer the **Countrey of** River *Euphrates*, and delight much to drink of the cold water thereof: Their **breed.** body is like the body of a *Roe*, and they have horns growing forth of the crown of their head, which are very long and sharp; so that *Alexander* affirmed they pierced through the shields of his Souldiers, and fought with them very irefully: at which time his company slew as he travelled to *India*, eight thousand five hundred and fifty; which great slaughter may be the occasion why they are so rare, and seldom seen to this day, because thereby the breeders and means of their continuance (which consisted in their multitude) were weakned and destroyed. Their horns are great and made like a saw, and they with them can cut asunder the branches of Osier or small trees, whereby it cometh to passe that many times their necks are taken in the twists of the falling boughs, whereat the Beast with repining cry, bewrayeth himself to the Hunters, and so is taken. The virtues of this Beast is unknown, and therefore *Suidas* saith, an *Antalope* is but good in part.

B

Of

mounted on an oblong piece of wood with a handle, and covered with transparent horn. There was usually a hole in the handle so that it could hang from the child's girdle. The sheet, made first of vellum, later of paper, contained a large " criss-cross," or Christ's cross, from which the horn-book was called " the Christ-cross row " or " Criss-cross row." This was followed by the alphabet in large and small letters, the vowels, and the combinations of vowels and consonants in the form of a table. Then came the exorcism, " In the Name of the Father and of the Son and of the Holy Ghost," then the Lord's Prayer, the whole concluding with the Roman numerals. Variations in form and materials have been described exhaustively in Tuer's two-volume *History of the Horn-book*, and Beulah Folmsbee's *Little History of the Horn-book* tells with great charm and many illustrations of this first lesson book for children in the English-speaking world.

A horn-book

The horn-book's limited space precluded pictures; these, however, found a place in the battledore, a development of the horn-book, first appearing in 1770, or possibly earlier. It was made of cardboard, in three leaves which folded together. Along with its alphabets and numerals (it contained no religious teaching) and easy reading lessons, it included little woodcuts to illustrate the latter.

The battledore, though it contained the first pictures to be put into the child's own hands, was not the first picture book planned for children. That title belongs to the *Orbis Pictus*, or " The World in Pictures," written by Comenius in 1657 in Latin and " High Dutch," and translated into English by Hoole in 1658. In his preface, the kindly author declares that his purpose is to " entice witty children " and expresses the hope that by this book " scare-crows may be taken away out of wisdom's gardens." Each object in the picture was given a number and the name of the object was then given in Latin and in the vernacular.

The many editions of Orbis Pictus

This book was translated not only into English but into French, German, Italian, Russian, Polish, Dutch and Czech, and many editions were published. From family records (see Gladys Scott Thomson's *Life in a Noble Household, 1641–1700*), we know that when William Russell, fifth earl of Bedford, employed a Cambridge graduate, the Rev. John Thornton, as tutor for his seven younger children—four boys and three girls—that tutor ordered several copies of the English translation as soon as it was available, and either because these copies were so much used, or else because they were so badly treated, Mr. Thornton found it necessary to replace them several times.

In the book bills quoted by Miss Thomson we may read what seem today the very modest prices paid for *Orbis Pictus* and other textbooks provided for the boys and girls. Incidentally, it makes this tutor and his charges very human figures to note that, whereas for the other children Bibles costing three shillings and sixpence, or at most seven shillings and sixpence, were provided, little Lady Diana, the next to the youngest, and clearly Thornton's favorite, had one " of fair minion print " costing twelve shillings and sixpence.

The pictures in the one hundred and fifty chapters of the *Orbis Pictus*, each chapter dealing with a particular subject, must have delighted children of long ago at the same time that they gave them their first general idea of the outside world. Something of the genial quality of the author seems to infuse these small but graphic woodcuts which have a charm today for the reader who allows himself to enter the world they portray. The well-furnished house which

Two battledores

the *Orbis Pictus* shows us is a cheerful, comfortable dwelling with stoves and mirrors, a bath, and clocks called " dials." The meadow, too, of another chapter, with trees and haycocks, mushrooms and strawberries, and a waving cornfield against the hills in the background, is a pleasant spot. A table heaped with jewels, of which all the colors are mentioned, as well as the fact that they " glister being cut into corners," no doubt charmed young readers, while the study, " a place where a Student apart from Men sitteth alone . . . whilst he readeth Books . . . and picketh all the best things out of them into his own Manual, or marketh them in them with a dash, or a *little star*, in the Margent," his candle at hand for sitting up late and a snuffer to put it out when his work is ended, takes us straight into the life of a household of nearly three hundred years ago.

During Puritan times, a note of deepest gloom made its way into books written for children. Sin and its punishment was the prevailing theme. James Janeway, about the middle of the seventeenth century, produced one of the most famous of these admonitory volumes in *The Token for Children, An Exact Account of the Conversion, Holy and Exemplary Lives and Joyful Deaths of Several Young Children.* In America, Cotton Mather and other writers were

Puritan times and the note of gloom

no less zealous with their *Godly Young People Their Parents' Joy*, and *Young People Warned, the Voice of God in the Late Terrible Throat Distemper*. Sometimes, though not always, these volumes were "adorned with cuts," highly moral in tone, though not, as one might fear, entirely devoted to death-bed scenes.

In *Adam's* Fall
We Sinned all.

Thy Life to Mend
This *Book* Attend.

The *Cat* doth play
And after flay.

A *Dog* will bite
A Thief at night.

An *Eagles* flight
Is out of fight.

The Idle *Fool*
Is whipt at School.

New England Primer, 1727

In comparison with these titles, the little *New England Primer*, of which a good many copies exist today, seems positively gay and sprightly with its binding of blue paper-covered boards. In the *Primer*, besides the alphabet, were found the Lord's Prayer, the Creed and the Catechism, some of Watts's Hymns, John Cotton's "Spiritual Milk for American Babes" and the famous "Dialogue between Christ, Youth, and the Devil." Each letter of the alphabet was accompanied not only by a rhymed couplet, or triplet, but also by a tiny woodcut.

Luckily, however, there slipped into the lives of these Puritan children, on both sides of the Atlantic, a gayer note. For while Janeway and the Mathers, Nathaniel Crouch and many others in England and America were presenting Biblical and moral instruction with tireless energy—thus, for instance, Abraham Chear, a contemporary of Janeway:—

When by spectators I am told
    What beauty doth adorn me,
Or in a glass when I behold
    How sweetly God did form me—
Hath God such comeliness bestowed
    And on me made to dwell,
What pity such a pretty maid
    As I should go to Hell!

the chapmen and peddlers were carrying on a lively trade in ballads. Indeed, an entry in Cotton Mather's journal notes his concern lest manners and morals be corrupted by the foolish songs and ballads disseminated in this fashion.

Ballads and the chapbook

These ballads—stories in verse about Guy of Warwick, Adam Bell, Bevis of Southampton, Robin Hood and many more—must have delighted children almost more than their elders when they were passed about by word of mouth. After the printing press came into existence, these ballads formed many of the chapbooks—little cheaply made, crudely illustrated booklets which were very popular in the seventeenth and eighteenth centuries—and undoubtedly boys and girls took for themselves what they liked, as they have always done, even though

Chapbook: Robinson Crusoe

Chapbook: Sir Richard Whittington

Chapbook: Two Children of the Wood

Chapbook: Sir Bevis of Hampton

Chapbook: True Tale of Robin Hood

it was written for their elders. It was only natural that "The Babes in the Wood," "Tom Thumb," "Jack the Giant Killer," and other stories still found in favorite fairy tale collections, should please youthful readers. They were illustrated, too, to add to their popularity with their public: here was Robinson Crusoe landing on his island; Robin Hood and Little John shooting a stag; Dick Whittington sending his cat to sea; stiff and crude, to be sure, but nevertheless illustrations to make the story more vivid and exciting.

Chapbook: Tom Thumb

After the zeal for saving the souls of juvenile readers had somewhat subsided, the chapbook was accepted and regularized as a suitable form for juveniles and was issued freely by the publishers of children's books. Just at the end of the eighteenth century, J. Lumsden and Son, whose "Toy-Book Manufactory" was in Glasgow, printed *The Famous History of Whittington and His Cat, Adorned with Copperplates* which contains four delicately engraved scenes from the hero's life and has an interesting trick cover with reversible pictures.

Chapbook: Jack the Giant Killer

In the middle of the eighteenth century, we come upon the most striking and delightful figure in the early history of children's books—John Newbery, described by Goldsmith in *The Vicar of Wakefield* as "the philanthropic bookseller of St. Paul's Church-

John Newbery at the Bible and Sun

yard who has written so many little books for children." He published, of course, even more books than he wrote, and a long list of little books, gay with gold and flowered paper, bear the imprint of the Bible and Sun in St. Paul's Churchyard.

In 1744 was published the book already mentioned—*A Little Pretty Pocket-Book* "Intended for the Instruction and Amusement of Little Master Tommy and Pretty Miss Polly, with an agreeable Letter to read from Jack the Giant Killer, as also a Ball and a Pincushion, the use of which will infallibly make Tommy a good Boy, and Polly a good Girl. Price of the Book alone, 6d., or with a Ball or Pincushion, 8d. To the whole is prefixed a letter on Education addressed to all parents, guardians, and governesses, etc. wherein rules are laid down for making children strong, healthy, virtuous, wise and happy."

Another of Newbery's books was *Nurse Truelove's New Year's Gift, or the Book of Books for Children*, "adorned with cuts and designed as a present for every little boy who would become a great man and ride upon a fine horse, and to every little girl who would become a great woman and ride in a Lord Mayor's gilt coach. Printed for the author, who has ordered these books to be given gratis to all little boys and girls at the Bible and Sun in St. Paul's Churchyard, they paying for the binding which is only 2 d. each book." Newbery obviously believed in making his books serve more purposes than mere entertainment; indeed, being a dealer in patent medicines as well as a bookseller, he contrived to make one part of his stock in trade advertise the other. Thus in *Goody Two-Shoes,* little Margery's father was " seized with a violent fit of fever in a Place where Dr. *James's* Powder was not to be had, and where he died miserably." Many of Newbery's books were reprinted in America and the very advertisements taken over, edited to suit an American public.

Little Goody Two-Shoes, edition of 1766

One of Newbery's most famous books is *The History of Little Goody Two-Shoes Otherwise called, Mrs. Margery Two-Shoes* (third edition 1766). It has been attributed to Goldsmith and is sometimes called the first real children's story because of its humor and naturalness. It also marks a step in advance in the art of book illustration for children, for the pictures were made with the story in mind and dovetailed into it. Very shortly a master of the woodcut and the first great illustrator of children's books, Thomas Bewick, was to carry this principle still further.

It was in 1767 that young Thomas Bewick, the first genuine artist to make picture books for boys and girls, entered upon his career. Born of small farmer stock at Cherryburn on the Tyne, twelve miles west of Newcastle, he was, in this year so important to children's books, apprenticed to a Newcastle engraver of doorplates, teaspoons, letterheads and whatever else was needed. Woodcuts, which were used only in broadsides and chapbooks, and were considered unimportant, were turned over to Bewick. Here the young artist and workman made his experiments, devising a new type of graving tool, developing the use of the " white line " and of the end-grain block. Though Bewick did not invent either of these processes, it was his masterly use of them, and the delicacy of the effects he obtained, that caused others to use them and brought back the popularity of the woodcut for book illustration.

The Bewicks, Thomas and John

After Thomas Bewick had been made a partner in the firm and his younger brother John taken on as an apprentice, he decided to make his first book for

*Thomas
Bewick's
first book
for children*
children, using the experience he had gained in making cuts of animals for alphabet books and books of fables while he was an apprentice. This book, *A Pretty Book of Pictures for Little Masters and Misses: or, Tommy Trip's History of Beasts and Birds*, is not only notable as an example of admirable workmanship, but one detects in it genuine sympathy with childhood and the pleasure taken by a really great artist in using his skill to delight children. Just who wrote the text is uncertain, but the verses which accompany the woodcuts have been attributed to Goldsmith. Though the author, whoever he was, no doubt approached his subject with a more serious attitude than did Hilaire Belloc in his *Bad Child's Book of Beasts*, the reader is sometimes reminded of the latter by such lines as:

THOMAS BEWICK : *Tommy Trip's
History of Beasts and Birds*

> The Bison though neither
> Engaging nor young,
> Like a flatt'rer can lick you
> To death with his tongue.

Tommy Trip was followed in 1784 by *Select Fables of Æsop and Others*, illustrated by Thomas Bewick and his brother John, and in 1792 appeared another juvenile book, *The Looking-Glass for the Mind* (an adaptation of a French book by Berquin called *L'Ami des Enfants*). This had cuts by John Bewick who, if he showed less strength at times than his brother, had a delicacy of line and imagination that gave his figures of children and his interior scenes an irre-sistible charm. Little Adolphus and Little Anthony in lace collars and tiny coat-tails, and the homes in which they lived, must have delighted children who like the feeling that, as they turn the pages, they are really entering a house and going from room to room. This taste Walter de la Mare and Harold Jones remembered when they made their *This Year: Next Year* in 1937, a book which gives the reader the feeling that here is a whole house and its surroundings to wander through, to live in for a year, watching from the windows the change of seasons, beginning with the tulips of spring and ending with December's snow.

Gay's *Fables* (1779); *Select Fables* (1784); *General History of Quadrupeds* (1790); *The History of British Birds* (1797-1804) and *The Fables of Æsop* (1818) are Bewick's great works, but he was responsible for the woodcuts in a long list of lesser volumes, any one of which is worth attention. The reader

THOMAS BEWICK : *History of Quadrupeds*

THOMAS BEWICK : *History of Quadrupeds*

THOMAS BEWICK : *Fables of Æsop*

JOHN BEWICK : *Looking-Glass for
the Mind*

THOMAS BEWICK : *Gay's Fables*

interested in book illustration cannot do better than to study the woodcuts of this great artist, especially the smaller ones and the vignettes. Here one finds truth to nature, and humor; a sense of beauty, a love of detail and skill in using it. That Bewick was a lover of nature we know at once, for here is the outdoor world in every season—wind and cold, sun and rain. The carefully decorative leaf or feather shows a feeling for abstract design; and, small as the vignettes are, they tell with exquisite precision many a story, grave or gay.

The best known juvenile publisher in America, Isaiah Thomas of Worcester, brought over many of Newbery's books, editing them for an American public. Besides publishing in this country *The Little Pretty Pocket-Book* and *Mother Goose's Melody*, already mentioned, Thomas brought out an American edition of *Goody Two-Shoes* with a frontispiece sometimes attributed to Bewick—though on this point authorities are divided. *The Looking-Glass for the Mind*, copied from John Bewick, was published by Durell in 1795, and was the work of Alexander Anderson, the most famous of our early wood engravers. It may be said to mark the beginning in this country of engraving in the Bewick method.

Thomas Stothard

As the end of the century approached, illustrators of children's books were ceasing to be anonymous. In 1789, Thomas Stothard, a well-known English painter, designed a frontispiece for the third volume of John Day's *Sandford and Merton* (published by Stockdale, opposite Burlington House, Piccadilly) which shows the reconciliation between Harry and Tommy, supervised by Mr. Barlow, against a charming country background. John Day's famous story properly belongs to the didactic period in children's literature which was to reach its height in the early nineteenth century when writers in England as well as in France were deeply influenced by the writings of Rousseau.

John Flaxman

Another artist, just at the turn of the century, was making pictures that, though intended for adults, have pleased children for more than two hundred years. John Flaxman's drawings for the *Iliad* and the *Odyssey*, so strong, so simple, so full of radiant life, have that same swift, clear-cut action which makes Homer's stories a never-failing source of delight to boys and girls.

William Mulready

An illustrator whose early work, at least, can be claimed by the eighteenth century, is William Mulready, who was born in 1786 and who began illustrating books before he was twenty. In 1806, in the *Gentleman's Magazine* in London, there appeared a set of verses with the title " The Butterfly's Ball, and the

Grasshopper's Feast, said to have been written by William Roscoe, Esq., M.P. for Liverpool, for the use of his children, and set to music by order of their majesties, for the Princess Mary."

To many readers of today, this rhyme, beginning

> Come take up your Hats, and away let us haste,
> To the Butterfly's Ball, and the Grasshopper's Feast.
> The Trumpeter Gad-Fly has summon'd the crew,
> And the Revels are now only waiting for you.

is familiar. It still appears in anthologies, and grandmothers of present-day children sometimes recall the tune. Its long life proves the wisdom of John Harris, publisher of children's books and successor to John Newbery, who decided that *The Butterfly's Ball* would be popular with children and published it in book *The Butterfly's* form in 1807, with fourteen hand-colored pictures, for twelve of which Mul- *Ball* ready made the original pen and brush drawings. The rhyme may not be poetry, but it has the lively fancy and tripping measure children of any century enjoy, and in its gaiety and conspicuous absence of any effort to inform and instruct, it was a foretaste of the children's books that were to appear in the second half of the nineteenth century.

The spirited drawings, with their touch of Puckish mischief—the young bee, all good humor as he " brings honey to sweeten the feast," the drooping snail, fatigued by " her journey the length of an ell," the airy dragon-fly, the mushroom for table with a water-dock leaf for cloth, and the rest—give Mulready the right to take his place among the artists of fairyland, where the ranking names are Walter Crane, Richard Doyle and Arthur Rackham.

Apparently the world was ready and waiting for this new attitude toward children in the books prepared for them, for within a year the enterprising publisher of this little book had sold twenty thousand copies. Many editions were published; it was reissued by its original publisher—Wilbur Macey Stone notes— as late as 1816. Later it was pirated by other publishers. In 1870, McLoughlin Brothers reprinted it for American children.

The success of *The Butterfly's Ball* called for more books of the same kind *Successors* and there were published in rapid succession, during the years 1807–1808, *to The* *The Peacock at Home*, by Mrs. Dorset, born Catherine Anne Turner; *Butterfly's Ball* *The Lion's Masquerade, a Sequel to The Peacock at Home*, also by Mrs. Dorset; and *The Elephant's Ball* and the *Grand Fete Champetre*, " by W. B."—all with pictures by Mulready. The drawings for *Tales from Shakespeare*, by Charles and Mary Lamb, published by Godwin in 1807, were attributed to Mulready. There were other imitations with slightly varied titles, such as *The Lion's Parliament and the Lioness's Ball; The Fishes' Feast, with a Mermaid's Song; The*

WILLIAM MULREADY : *Lion's Masquerade*

Lobster's Voyage to the Brazils, illustrated with Elegant and Appropriate Engravings; The Rose's Breakfast; The Council of Dogs; Lady Grimalkin's Concert and Supper and *The Cats' Tea Party* —all amply illustrated, though not by Mulready, and the quality of the illustrations was uneven.

Dame Wiggins of Lee

According to strict chronology, an 1823 book belongs to the nineteenth century, but *Dame Wiggins of Lee and Her Seven Wonderful Cats*, that wellknown rhyme later made famous by John Ruskin, still bears, in the illustrations for the original edition—those vigorous but stiff and angular woodcuts—the earmarks of the 1700's. Philip James in his *Children's Books of Yesterday* (*Studio*, Autumn Number, 1933) writes, as a caption for an illustration from the original edition — *Dame Wiggins of Lee and Her Seven Wonderful Cats. A Humorous Tale. Written Principally by a Lady of Ninety* (1823): "Tuer relates that the authors of this very popular book were R. S. Sharpe and Mrs. Pearson—the lady of ninety—and that the illustrations were by R. Stennet. The blocks were also used in an edition of *Dame Trot and Her Comical Cats*."

However, an edition of this work published in 1885 becomes a link between the older illustrated books for children and the flowering of children's book illustration in the nineteenth century, for Ruskin persuaded his friend Kate Greenaway to try her hand at some additional illustrations while he himself wrote several new stanzas. Of the drawings made by Miss Greenaway, Ruskin wrote to her in a letter, " The cats are gone to be woodcutted just as they are— they can't be better." In his Preface, Ruskin explains that he would not allow Miss Greenaway to subdue the grace of her first sketches to the formality of the earlier work. Thus this slim volume—which was published by George Allen in 1885, with a title page reading *Dame Wiggins of Lee and Her Seven Wonderful Cats; a Humorous Tale, Written Principally by a Lady of Ninety. Edited, with additional Verses, By John Ruskin, LL.D., and with New Illustrations by Kate Greenaway. With Twenty-Two Woodcuts*—is a visible link between the early days of children's book illustration and its modern development.

William Blake

Before the eighteenth century closed, a great name in the history of illustrated books for children was to appear, a name that seems to belong neither to the eighteenth century, nor to the centuries to come. Alone and unique, William Blake stands out, a solitary figure, lighted by the soaring flame of imagination, his work—both poems and drawings—glowing with the intense joy his inward vision brought him. One who has once seen the *Songs of Innocence* and the *Songs of Experience* in the original editions, or in facsimiles of those editions, as Blake's own hand inscribed them, will feel ever after that poems and pictures make a whole that should never be divided. In drawings and text alike we are conscious of the sense of upspringing life, of freshness of vision; of spiritual energy which, for all its force, is perfectly controlled. For children to be exposed to Blake at the right time will be for some, at least, a rare and never-to-be-forgotten experience.

Songs of Innocence

It may well be that the power of these books to stir the emotions comes in part from the fact that Blake not only conceived the idea, wrote the poems and drew the designs, but actually carried out with his own hands the entire book-making process. When the *Songs of Innocence* were written and the designs to illustrate them completed, Blake had practically no money, so that how to get them before the public was a problem that occasioned long and anxious thought. Blake himself believed that it was solved only when his dead brother Robert appeared to him in a vision and suggested the technical way in which a facsimile of poem and design could be made. Out of the ten shillings which was all the

WILLIAM BLAKE : *Songs of Innocence*

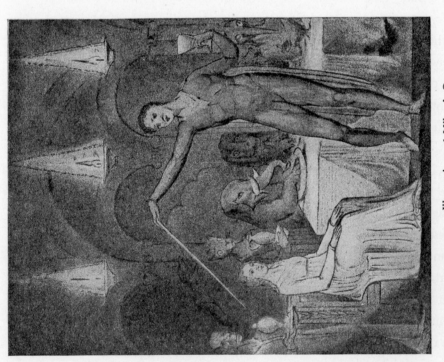

WILLIAM BLAKE : Illustrations of *Milton's Comus*

money the Blakes had in the house, one shilling and tenpence was spent on
materials. Blake then copied the poems and outlined the designs and marginal
decorations on the copper with an impervious liquid, the remainder of the plate
was eaten away with acid, and from the outline of the letter and design that was
left on the plates Blake printed off his facsimiles with brown, yellow or blue for
his ground color, using red for the letters. Each page was then colored by hand
according to the original drawing.

Blake ground and mixed his colors himself on a piece of marble with carpenter's glue for a binder. He applied the colors with a camel's-hair brush. He
taught his wife to take off the impressions and to help in tinting them from his
drawings, a task which she seems to have found a labor of love. The plates were
small, under five by three inches; the number of engraved pages in *Songs of
Innocence* was twenty-seven. These were bound up in boards by Mrs. Blake
and made a small octavo volume. When *Songs of Experience* was ready, the two   *Songs of*
series were bound together in one volume, each with its own title page and a   *Experience*
general title page added. As one of Blake's biographers has said, never before
was a man so literally the author of his own book, for the poet and his wife were
responsible for every step—the writing, designing, printing, engraving, even the
making of the colored inks; everything, in short, but the paper.

After looking at Blake's designs for the *Songs of Innocence* and the *Songs
of Experience*, it comes as something of a surprise to find this artist confining
himself within the bounds of the didactic story for children, a type of book just
beginning to be popular. But Blake was poor, and as potboilers he accepted
commissions from Johnston the publisher. One such commission was to illus-
trate Mary Wollstonecraft's *Original Stories from Real Life*. In editing a reprint   *Original Stories*
of this, E. V. Lucas made the statement that in this kind of employment Blake   *from Real Life*
was uniformly below himself. Melville Lewis, writing in the *Booklover's Magazine*, in 1902, was even more emphatic. "It is astonishing," he says, "that
Johnston the publisher should have given the commission to Blake, who was in
no sense of the word an ingratiating illustrator of narratives of real life for young
eyes. Anything more out of place than some of Blake's illustrations to this volume (i.e. *Original Stories from Real Life*, by Mary Wollstonecraft) it is difficult to conceive. Mrs. Mason, with little Mary on one side, and littler Charlotte
on the other, standing at the door, with arms stretched out above the heads of
the children, exclaiming, ' Look what a fine morning it is. Insects, birds, animals
all enjoying existence,' is humorous in a way never intended by artist or author.

Prim and sententious Mrs. Mason is accompanied, not by children, but by two infant Madonnas, one peacefully grateful for the blessings of a beneficent Providence, the other ecstatically delighted."

Blake's illustrations for Comus

Another set of Blake's illustrations which, though not planned for children, would speak directly to boys and girls because of their high spirits, their fancy and humor, are those he made for Milton's *Comus*. So charming are they, so full of fun and gaiety, that it seems a pity they are so little known. There is a copy of the book in the Boston Museum of Fine Arts and Elizabeth Luther Cary reproduces some of the drawings in her *The Art of William Blake*. Small as these reproductions are, they indicate the charm of the originals. To quote Miss Cary: " The drawings of the revelers at table, the fiery lion, the mild-faced elephant, the long-beaked solemn bird, the cat serving with bristling mustachios, is filled with the atmosphere of fairyland as quaint, as spontaneous as the poetry of Christina Rossetti when she transmits the reality of the animal world into romance. In fact these eight designs, unimportant as they are in the sum of Blake's works, leave the spectator idly wishing that he had oftener indulged himself in this frankly childlike idealism, so unlike are they to the work of any other illustrator and so expressive of the enchanted mood which he awakened in his early poetry by such lines as the familiar ' Piping down the valleys wild.' "

The close of the century

With Blake, book illustration for children before 1800 closes in a blaze of glory. Blake had no descendants in a direct line, yet perhaps his belief in the importance of childhood, his compassion and tenderness for children, may have been the forerunner of the interest in the child for himself—not merely as a prospective adult—and of the effort to understand children, which were to characterize the century to come.

THOMAS BEWICK : *History of Quadrupeds*

II. Illustrators of the Nineteenth Century in England

JACQUELINE OVERTON

GEORGE CRUIKSHANK : *Grimm's Popular Stories*

DANIEL MACLISE : *Story of the Norman Conquest*

THOMAS STOTHARD : *Pilgrim's Progress*

EDITOR'S FOREWORD

"FAIRY missals" are words which have been applied to William Blake's first hand-made copies of *Songs of Innocence* and *Songs of Experience*. Something of their flowerlike beauty can be seen in the facsimile editions reproduced from originals in the British Museum and published here in 1926 and 1927. The reproductions of the tiny octavo pages of the thirty-two originals (five inches high by three wide) are placed in the facsimile editions upon large octavo pages for better preservation.

Miss Eaton has told us that the children of England had, toward the close of the eighteenth century and at the opening of the nineteenth, books illustrated by William Blake, Thomas and John Bewick, Thomas Stothard, John Flaxman and William Mulready. It is hard to realize today how rare at that time were such pictures made expressly for particular scenes and happenings in texts. These fine artists were pioneers in this movement.

This was a period when the engraver was as important as the artist. William Blake himself engraved many of John Flaxman's drawings, doing all of the *Odyssey*. Other Flaxman drawings were engraved by Piroli. Stothard, too, was fortunate in having fine engravers transfer his drawings to copper plates — James Heath, Schiavonetti, Bartolozzi among them. His drawings for *Pilgrim's*

Importance of the early engravers

27

Progress in 1788, and for Samuel Rogers' *Italy* in 1830, and *Poems*, 1834, are usually considered his best work.

There were during this period, and until 1856, a considerable number of "Annuals" and "Keepsakes" and "Christmas Books" for which many artists listed in the bibliographies of this book made pictures — Turner, Etty, Stanfield, Maclise, Cattermole and others. Able designers of the day also contributed to the "Annuals" and to the endless editions of "poets," "novelists," and "essayists."

GEORGE CATTERMOLE : *Master Humphrey's Clock*

Among these designers one finds such well-known names as Cipriani, Angelica Kauffman, Smirke, Corbould and others.

With the passing of the "Annuals" and "Keepsakes," copper and steel engraving passed too. From this time on, one hears less of the engraver and more of the artist, though the engravers came into their own again in the 'Sixties and 'Seventies — the Dalziels, the Whympers, Swain, Linton, and Evans. The art of wood engraving, revived by the Bewicks, now became the favored method of reproduction. In 1832 the *Penny Magazine* came into existence, in 1841 *Punch*,

and in 1842 the *Illustrated London News*. For these magazines outstanding artists began to draw directly on the wood block, or for engraving on wood. The journal *Once a Week* started in 1859, and in 1869 the *Graphic* — both stimulating and offering new opportunities to artists. *Good Words for the Young* (1868-'77), *Aunt Judy's Magazine* (1866-1885), and *Little Folks* (1871-1932?) all published good drawings.

Edward Lear's *Book of Nonsense* and Mary Howitt's translation of Hans Christian Andersen, both published in 1846, were important happenings in the history of children's literature and in the history of pictures for children's books, for through them nonsense and fantasy gained honorable estate.

There was an Old Man of Marseilles,   whose daughters wore bottle-green veils;
They caught several Fish,   which they put in a dish,
And sent to their Pa' at Marseilles.

EDWARD LEAR : *Book of Nonsense*

But, alas, in America an important figure was an enemy of fairy tales. Samuel Griswold Goodrich was more familiarly known as Peter Parley. Peter Parley's books owed something of their origin to England, for Samuel Goodrich, born in Ridgefield, Connecticut, in 1793, had been influenced by Hannah More's *Moral Repository* and in 1823 went to the British Isles and visited Hannah More and Sir Walter Scott. In 1827 he brought out in Boston the first of his informational books, the *Peter Parley Tales*. These books were imported into England and widely pirated there.

But fortunately for children, a rival author and editor appeared upon the scene with a more imaginative and broader vision toward children and their books. This was Henry Cole, later to become Sir Henry Cole, who used the name "Felix Summerly" when, in 1841-9, he brought out "Felix Summerly's Home Treasury of Books, Toys, Pictures, etc., purposed to cultivate the Affections, *Fancy, Imagination and Taste of Children*." (The italics are ours.) In his prospectus, Henry Cole announced that there were old songs and tales of the

*Felix Summerly
and the
Home Treasury
volumes*

past which appealed to these aspects of a little child's mind, aspects just as important as their understanding. There was also need for the creation of new fairy tales and ballads. He stated that the conductor of these new books "purposes to produce a series of works, the character of which may be briefly described as anti-Peter Parleyism. . . . *All will be illustrated, but not after the usual fashion of children's books, in which it seems to be assumed that the lowest kind of art is good enough to give first impressions to a child.*" (Our italics.) Sir Henry Cole's printer and publisher was Joseph Cundall. The *Home Treasury* volumes were illustrated by well-known artists — J. C. Horsley, C. W. Cope, T. Webster and Mulready.

The Moxon Tennyson

Tennyson's Poems, commonly called the Moxon Tennyson, with drawings by Mulready and Millais for the "Idylls," and Rossetti and Holman Hunt for the

C. W. COPE : *Divine and Moral Songs*

Arabian Nights, Book of British Ballads

romance poems, was published in 1857. The Lane translation of the *Arabian Nights* with William Harvey's pictures appeared in 1839-41. The "Abbotsford" edition of the Waverley novels came in 1842-46 with nearly 2000 wood engravings. The *Book of British Ballads* was published in 1843 with the work of a number of artists represented — Gilbert, Tenniel, Birket Foster, Harrison Weir

JOHN GILBERT : *Courtship of Miles Standish*

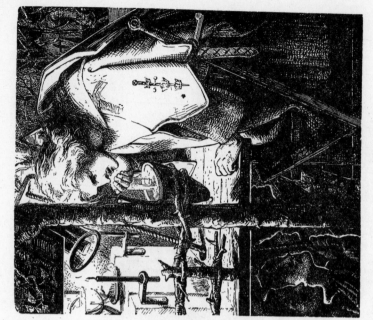

D. G. ROSSETTI : *Tennyson's Poems*

HOLMAN HUNT : *Tennyson's Poems*

J. E. MILLAIS : *Parables of Our Lord*

J. D. WATSON : *Robinson Crusoe*

G. H. THOMAS : *Parables from Nature*

and John Absolon among them. Sir John Gilbert's *Shakespeare* was brought out *Shakespeare,*
from 1856 to '58 in parts. The books of this time are too many to mention and *Pilgrim's*
yet one cannot let go unmentioned editions of *Pilgrim's Progress* illustrated by *Progress,*
G. H. Thomas, 1857, C. H. Bennett, 1859, and J. D. Watson, 1861. The *Parables* *Parables of Our*
of Our Lord by Sir John Millais, 1864; Lord Leighton's drawings for *Romola* in *Lord, Romola*
1862, an ideal illustrator for this book because of his love of Italy.

   This foreword owes much to F. J. Harvey Darton's *Children's Books in
England* — Five Centuries of Social Life, and quotations not otherwise assigned
are from it. Reviewing the changes in point of view toward children and their
books which took place during the first twenty-five years of Queen Victoria's
reign, from 1837 to 1862, Mr. Darton mentions the relegating to an inferior
place of "useful knowledge" books, an exchange of ideas and pictures of juvenile
life between England and America, the coming of the boy's and girl's book without explicit morals, and the lively re-telling of Anglo-Saxon folk tales, legends
and hero stories. And what was perhaps the most important of all — the acceptance of fairy stories as "a permanent and honorable possession," and of nonsense,
"the joy of being silly, inconsequent and innocently hilarious." These changes
produced a new spirit in authors and artists.

   Miss Overton presents two groups of illustrators who expressed this new
spirit in their work and are still the children's very own — trail-blazers for all the
illustrators of children's books who were to follow them.

                                                                B. E. M.

WILLIAM HARVEY : *One Hundred Fables*

Within the illustration:

Hop o'my Thumb & the Seven League Boots

The Father proposes to lose the Children !!!

They leave Hop'o my Thumb and his Brothers in the Wood

George Cruikshank

GEORGE CRUIKSHANK : *Hop-o'-My-Thumb and the Seven-League Boots*

Illustrators of the Nineteenth Century in England

THE ARTISTS WHO WORKED IN BLACK AND WHITE

IN a charming article, "Children's Books and Their Illustrators," written by Gleeson White and published in the Winter Number of the English *Studio* for 1897–98, Mr. White points out that it was not until the beginning of the nineteenth century that illustration for children came into its own as we recognize it today. Discovering then "that the children possessed the right to be amused, the imagination of poets and artists addressed itself at last to the most appreciative of all audiences, a world of newcomers, with insatiable appetites for wonders real and imaginary."

In George Cruikshank we discover the first English artist who dared combine lively imagination and high good humor with fine drawing when he undertook to illustrate books for children. What fun to have been behind the shoulder of a child of the 1820's who picked up the English edition of *Grimm's Fairy Tales*[1] and saw for the first time George Cruikshank's illustrations for them! Looking back over the hundred and more years that have passed since then, we see *Grimm's Popular Stories* as the first picture book for children in our modern sense. *George Cruikshank and Grimm's Popular Stories*

Little Rumpelstiltskin with his spindling legs and tall hat adorned by a chicken feather; the gardener's boy in his breezy flight across country on the fox's brush; the Bremen town musicians; was ever so rowdy a party as this found before in a book for children? After the solemn pictures that had been pointing the morals and adorning the tales previously offered to boys and girls, how they must have reveled in "The Elves and the Shoemaker"; the elves prancing in high glee as they try on their new clothes, while the old shoemaker and his wife watch the performance from behind a curtain. Of all the illustrations which Cruikshank made for Grimm's stories (and he did several series of them—all alive with his own robust appreciation of the quaint old German folk tales), "The Elves and the Shoemaker" remained his favorite.

Perhaps this fairy picture and others that have such a ripeness about them had their beginnings when, as a boy of twelve, he turned to and helped his

37

overworked artist father make designs for nursery tales, Valentine and Twelfth Night Characters. "The earliest job in the way of etching for which he was employed and received payment was a child's lottery picture; this was in 1804." From that time on "anything was acceptable; headings for songs and halfpenny ballads, illustrations for chapbooks; designs for nursery tales, sheets of prints for children . . . a dozen the sheet and a penny the lot, rude cuts, broadsides, etc."[2] Of course none of these early attempts were signed.

GEORGE CRUIKSHANK : *Life and Surprising Adventures of Robinson Crusoe*

So Cruikshank began his apprenticeship early; it was all the teaching he ever had and the London in which he was born in 1792 held him all the rest of his days. According to one of his biographers, Frederic G. Stephens, he never set foot out of England except on one occasion "when he got as far as Boulogne, in which amphibious, half-English place he stayed one day." Next to this his most extended trips seem to have been to Brighton and Margate. He was a Cockney to the core and "cared little and knew less about what went on or was to be seen and heard of beyond the sound of Bow Bells. Dr. Johnson did not love his Fleet Street with more ardour than Cruikshank."

Sketches by Boz

The streets of London with their sights and sounds and smells and crowds and strange individuals were what fascinated him and he gave them back in the pages of Dickens' *Sketches by Boz;* in "London Characters," "Mornings in Bow Street," "Sunday in London" and the masses of other illustration which he executed in his own exaggerated style and with his own particular twist, for Cruikshank was a born caricaturist. Like Hogarth he could not resist poking fun at the modes and manners and fads of his day, nor refrain from hitting off the political events of his time. His cartoons, which appeared in newspapers and in periodicals and as broadsides, present a panorama of national events covering a decade and more. Always deadly in earnest with his humor, he drove home truths with his clever, satirical etching-needle, and neither high nor low, great or small were safe from him. The wonder is that his publishers were always daring enough to print them.

Comic Almanacks

"Mornings in Bow Street," a collection of twenty-one designs, appeared in 1825 and made all London laugh, and his *Comic Almanacks*, which appeared yearly from 1835 to 1853, were something to be treasured in their day and are priceless now. What a delightful picture book his series of etchings, "Home for the Holidays," would make today, and how boys, especially, would revel in the horseplay of the two groups called, "London Nuisances" and "The Sailor's Progress."

In his book *Etching and Etchers*, Philip Gilbert Hammerton says: "Art with a great social and political purpose is seldom pure, fine art; artistic aims are usually lost sight of in the anxiety to hit the social or political mark; and though the caricaturist may have a great natural faculty for art, it has not a fair chance of cultivation." But in Cruikshank, he says, there is an artist within and behind the caricaturist; an artist with an exceptional endowment. "In the best of his etchings he carries one great virtue of the art to perfection—its simple frankness. He is so direct and unaffected that only those who know the difficulties of etching can appreciate the power that lies behind this unpretending skill; there is never, in his most admirable plates, the trace of vain effort."

Punch and Judy

It took George Cruikshank to preserve for us quite seriously the antics of Punch and Judy as he had watched them on many a street corner in London as a boy. The dialogue of the *Tragical Comedy or Comical Tragedy of Punch and Judy*, for which the pictures were made in 1828, was written by Payne Collier. In 1925 it was republished by Washburn and Thomas, of Cambridge, with a delightful note about the artist and the circumstances surrounding the making of the book.

Comic Alphabet

The Comic Alphabet was a panorama of twenty-four little colored etchings in which Cruikshank indulged his sense of fun to the full. Could one forget the exceedingly indigestible Nightmare which N stands for, or see V and U without remembering the Very Unpleasant predicament of the fat gentleman in the lemon-yellow waistcoat running away from the bull?

Oliver Twist

Cruikshank was Dickens' first illustrator. An early series of etchings for the *Sketches by Boz* appeared in 1836, a later series in 1839. Then came twenty-five illustrations for *Oliver Twist*—perhaps the most widely known of all Cruikshank's work. "He brought to life Fagin the Jew, that immortal scamp the Artful Dodger, that beadle of beadles, Mr. Bumble, whose very name has given a word to our language. In Bill Sykes he outdid himself and produced a portrait so vigorous, true and original that it is thought by many to be Cruikshank's masterpiece."[3]

There seems to have been no limit to the books he found time to illustrate (not always with equal success, however): Shakespeare, Scott, Irving's *History*

*of New York from the Beginning of the World to the End of the Dutch Dynasty,
Robinson Crusoe, Don Quixote*—it is impossible even to mention them here
with the exception of those that have a direct bearing on his illustration for
children.

*Cruikshank
and Punch*

One naturally associates the name of George Cruikshank with that genial,
gifted group of men that started *Punch*, but as a matter of fact, though he was
an intimate friend of many on its staff, and of its editor, Mark Lemon, no drawing of his ever appeared between the covers of that well-loved and widely
known periodical "except once indirectly for its advertisement page in 1844
announcing his *Table Book*, in which appeared the portraits of Gilbert Abbott
À Beckett (his literary editor), Thackeray, and himself."[4]

In spite of urging he firmly refused all offers from *Punch* for a variety of
reasons, but mainly, one suspects, because his mighty rival, John Leech, was so
prominent in its pages. "Leech, the very life and soul of the undertaking—
Mr. Punch incarnate." Between Cruikshank and Leech there existed little sympathy and less intimacy. The extravagant caricature that pervaded so much of
Cruikshank's work, and from which Leech was entirely free, blinded Leech a
little to the great merit of Cruikshank's serious work; nevertheless it must not
be forgotten that the only lessons in etching Leech ever had he received from
George Cruikshank.

"Another grievance against *Punch* was that *Punch's* figure was stolen from
his book (to which Payne Collier had written the text), and the paper itself
was but an imitation of his own short-lived monthly magazine, *Omnibus*. With
greater reason could he complain that the *Punch* pocket-books were copied from
his *Comic Almanacks*—as they were—and that the imitation killed the originals
after a contest of a dozen years; but the idea of *Punch* being copied from the
Omnibus with which it had hardly a single point in common, save humor and
illustration, has probably as much foundation as Cruikshank's claim against
Harrison Ainsworth and others," which will be mentioned later.

Nevertheless *Punch* rendered ample tribute to his genius in its pages in various ways and when he died announced: "England is the poorer by what she
can ill spare—a man of genius. Good, kind, genial, honest, enthusiastic George
Cruikshank . . . has passed away."

*Illustrations for
German texts*

The supernatural and the melodramatic held a strong attraction for the
"Immortal George," as he was nicknamed, and he indulged this taste to the full
in eight illustrations for a weird German story, *Peter Schlemihl*. "This, together

with *Grimm's Popular Tales*, attained the rare distinction of being republished in Germany with the original text . . . to please Germans by means of illustrations to German text, especially ones so truly national as *Peter Schlemihl* and Grimm's stories, was a distinction of the rarest for a foreigner to obtain."[5]

For Robert Hunt's two-volume collection, *Popular Romances of West England or the Drolls, Traditions and Superstitions of Old Cornwall*, Cruikshank drew the frontispieces. The Giant Bolster making the trip from Beacon to Carn Bred in one six-mile stride is a wonder, while the dizzy Flight of Witches over the sea on broomsticks and the black cats in Volume Two, make a delightful Hallowe'en picture. We might add, however, that the witches are far better than the cats. Cruikshank was rather weak on cats.

In Thomas Keightley's *Fairy Mythology* he has only a frontispiece, a delightful conglomeration of dragons, giants, witches, gnomes, water nixies, dancing fairies, and pixies in a mad whirl around the weathercock. How is it possible to get such expression and animation in such tiny figures! It is one of the most charming, delicate, and imaginative things Cruikshank ever did, and remembering *Grimm's Popular Tales* we wish he might have gone right on making illustrations for this book.

The volume now available under the title of *The Cruikshank Fairy Book* originally appeared serially as *The Fairy Library* and contained the four old tales: "Puss in Boots," "Hop-o'-My-Thumb," "Jack and the Bean Stalk," and "Cinderella." *Cruikshank Fairy Book*

Jack resolutely climbing the bean stalk at so dizzy a height that he can no longer see the ground but only the clouds floating below and the black crag looming overhead—Jack gayly riding off on the Fairy Harp while the irate giant hurls rocks from above; Cinderella watching her Fairy Godmother change the pumpkin and the rat and the mice and the lizards into coach, horses and servants to take her to the ball; and the Giant Ogre and his seven-league boots pursuing Hop and his brother—these pictures are Cruikshank at his happiest. Not so much can be said for his version of the text, however, for by the time this work was done he had entered upon a new phase of his life and had become a reformer almost to a fanatical degree, even attempting to improve the morals of the old fairy tales by rewriting them, much to the wrath of Charles Dickens, who published as a protest, in *Household Words*, a paper called, "Frauds on the Fairies." Cruikshank promptly answered it through a letter from Hop-o'-My-Thumb, "published at 86 Fleet Street, to be had for a penny."

Harrison Ainsworth's *Tower of London* was a lurid tale, very popular in its day. Into it Cruikshank threw himself so heartily, while making its illustrations, that in the end he was convinced that part of the story was his own conception as well. This happened more than once in his illustrating career and, needless to say, led to complications with the author.

GEORGE CRUIKSHANK : *History and Adventures of Don Quixote*

Aunt Judy's Magazine   In May, 1866, *Aunt Judy's Magazine*, edited by Mrs. Alfred Gatty, published its first issue, and from that time on many of Mrs. Ewing's charming stories appeared in its pages. Cruikshank made the pictures for "Timothy's Shoes," "Amelia and the Dwarfs," "Three Christmas Trees," "The Brownies," "Christmas Crackers," "Benjy in Beastland" and "Lob Lie-by-the-Fire." In writing of "Amelia and the Dwarfs," in her life of Mrs. Ewing, her sister, Horatia Gatty, says: "The Dwarfs inspired Mr. Cruikshank to one of his best water-color sketches; who is the happy possessor thereof I do not know, but the woodcut illustration very inadequately represents the beauty and delicacy of the picture."

So, all in all, George Cruikshank's work belongs to children if ever any artist's did, and the fairies may be said to have pictorially come into their own with him who had a genuine understanding and respect for the antics of the "Little People" within their own realm.

In a fascinating essay, "The Genius of George Cruikshank," first published in the *Westminster Review* of June, 1840, Thackeray, who was always his understanding admirer, emphasized his work for children. "We know not," he says, "if Mr. Cruikshank will be very well pleased at finding his name in such company as that of Clown and Harlequin; but he, like them, is certainly the children's friend. . . . In school boys he revels; plum pudding and holidays his needle has engraved over and over again." Thackeray goes on to recollect his own joy in Cruikshank's pictures as a boy.

Thackeray's essay on Cruikshank

Have we not read all the story-books that his wonderful pencil has illustrated? Did we not forego tarts in order to buy his *Breaking Up* or his *Fashionable Monstrosities* of the year eighteen hundred and something? Have we not before us at this very moment a print of one of the admirable *Illustrations of Phrenology*, which entire work was purchased by a joint stock company of boys, each drawing lots afterwards for the separate prints, and taking his choice in rotation?

Knight's, in Sweeting's Alley; Fairburn's, in a court off Ludgate Hill; Hone's, in Fleet Street—bright, enchanted palaces, which George Cruikshank used to people with grinning, fantastical imps, and merry, harmless sprites—where are they? Fairburn's shop knows him no more; not only has Knight disappeared from Sweeting's Alley, but, as we are given to understand, Sweeting's Alley has disappeared from the face of the globe. . . . Mr. Cruikshank may have drawn a thousand better things, since the days when these were; but they are to us a thousand times more pleasing than anything else he has done. How we used to believe in them! to stray miles out of the way on holidays, in order to ponder for an hour before that delightful window in Sweeting's Alley! in walks through Fleet Street, to vanish abruptly down Fairburn's passage, and there make one at his charming "gratis" exhibition. There used to be a crowd round the window in those days of grinning, good-natured mechanics, who spelt the songs, and spoke them out for the benefit of the company, and who received the points of humour with a general sympathizing roar. . . .

There must be no smiling with Cruikshank. A man who does not laugh outright is a dullard, and has no heart.

IF you are familiar with the cover of London *Punch*, then you know the most famous and well-loved picture ever drawn by Richard Doyle.

Richard Doyle

He was no such clever, prolific artist as Cruikshank; he had no great strength of technique; indeed, his drawing is often faulty; but there is a charm and sweetness about his work typical of the man himself, and the children have every right to claim him as one of their own artists if for nothing else than the pictures he made for Ruskin's *King of the Golden River*.

His father, John Doyle, better known as HB, established his reputation on *Punch* with a series of " Political Sketches " (he objected to the term caricature) and Dick followed in his footsteps, being appointed on the paper when he was only nineteen and signing his early work with the name, " Dick Kitcat." These

RICHARD DOYLE : *King of the Golden River*

first sketches were principally clever comic borders and fanciful initial letters of which he was very fond. Later he was appointed cartoonist and worked side by side with John Leech, and people began to know Dicky Doyle's work by his monogram signature with a " dicky " either perched upon the top or pecking on the ground nearby, according to the artist's fancy.

The " dicky " appeared not only on cartoons but on several amusing series of sketches: " Mr. Pips Hys Diary," " Bird's Eye View of English Society," " Ye Manners and Customs of Ye Englyshe " and best of all " Brown, Jones and Robinson," a hit on his own countrymen abroad.

He and Gilbert Abbott À Beckett were responsible for the popular little monthly *Almanacks* issued by *Punch*. À Beckett was the editor of this " review of everything and everybody," and Doyle illustrated it with small cuts, head- and tail-pieces and fanciful initial letters.

It was in 1849 that he made the famous cover for *Punch*. Various artists had already tried their hands at it, among them, Hablot Knight Brown (" Phiz "), Sir John Gilbert and Kenny Meadows, but Doyle's design was so full of the very spirit of Mr. Punch himself that his cover was adopted at once and has never been changed from that day to this. In M. H. Spielmann's *History of Punch* is a very interesting illustrated account of the making of these various cover designs.

who should I meet on the Third Terrace from this but the identical little valuable trotting slowly towards home.

I am in a very critical state, working away at The History of Belgium which I must either have done by tomorrow morning or give Papa a shilling, so therefore I am working desperately, resolved not to go to bed till I have finished the illustrations. Humphreys Clock was read out this evening and really I dont know what to make of it. SUNDAY. Well now this is all very pleasant. I have won half a crown. Papa liked the illustrations which was also pleasant. I walked in the park till dinner. Mr Selous came to tea "glorious" he took away half a dozen Tournaments to dispose of. Hurra Papa says that Mr O'Fanal showed it to lord Seymour.

MONDAY. James took one to Mr O'Connor and I went to see the people coming from the levee and after seeing the Queen and Prince Albert coming home to Buckingham Palace I went to the opera house to bring Annette home from

RICHARD DOYLE : *A Journal Kept by Richard Doyle in the Year 1840*

One of the most amusing and delightful things Doyle ever did was a pictorial journal which he kept during the year 1840, when he was fifteen. His father had the theory that an artist should learn to draw through accurate observation and memory rather than through academic training, and so the Doyle children (there were five boys and two girls, all artistic in some way) were encouraged to keep posted on the events of the day, to go to ceremonies, reviews and processions, of which there were aplenty in London those days, to write accounts of what they saw and illustrate their notes with sketches. Once a week, usually on Sunday, there was an informal family exhibition, when the results of the week's work were shown.

Dicky Doyle's Journal

Going out to see the sights and making sketches of what he saw was no hardship to Dick, but note-making was a different matter, so, to kill several birds with one stone, he heroically determined upon a pictorial diary. It begins with this entry:

" The first of January—Got up late, very bad. Made good resolutions and did not keep them. Went out and got a cold. Did keep it. First thought I would, then thought I would not, was sure I would, was positive I would not, at last determined I *would* keep a journal. Began it. This is it and I began it on the first of January one thousand eight hundred and forty. Hope I may be skinned alive by wild cats if I do not go on with it."

Then follow his daily doings, written in a most naïve, boyish fashion, and illustrated with the liveliest kind of sketches. It is a picture book that one wishes every boy or girl who has an inclination toward sketching or writing might see.

Dick himself always appears as a lanky lad with a mop of hair over his eyes, standing spellbound before a printshop window (where he fondly imagines he sees one of his own masterpieces); skating on the Serpentine; reluctantly going through the motions of taking dancing lessons or working away " like fury " at his easel while Ruff, the dog, keeps him company. He tells of " slipping into Piccadilly for the purpose of seeing the first number of the new historical novel by H. W. Ainsworth called *The Tower of London*, embellished with three steel engravings and woodcuts by George Cruikshank," and there is a delightful description of the opening day of the Royal Academy Exhibition. He and his brother, Henry, wait in the crowd from ten o'clock until twelve for the doors to open, and then make a mad dash with the rest " to see the principal pictures before the crowd got too great to move." Edwin Landseer's two dog pictures he admires greatly and does not understand how anyone can criticize them un-favorably; but apparently he has not so much to say for a " peculiar picture by W. Etty of ten virgins running about in front of a door (which is beautifully painted). The subject is taken from Scripture but the treatment is dreadfully queer."

We catch a glimpse of Queen Victoria's wedding procession as viewed by a boy jammed in the crowd at St. James Park—the various maneuvers of the Life Guards—band concerts in Kensington Gardens and other gala occasions. One day Dick sees Prince Albert in George Street on his way to Regent's Park and remarks: " His legs looked rather long."

The Doyle family are well represented at picnics, concerts, visiting the zoo and the Tower, going to the races or gathered about the table for a Sunday ex-hibition (Dick looks a bit nervous on this occasion).

During the journal year he seems to have been occupied with a *History of Belgium,* illustrating Scott's *Quentin Durward* " on sheets of double elephant mounted on canvas four feet something by two feet something " and making another large picture called "The Tournament." "The Tournament" was actu-ally printed and sold to various friends and relatives. It was his first success and, needless to say, created considerable excitement for Dick, especially the day the copies arrived from the printer. " O my goodness me, fifty hot-pressed copies of the ' Tournament.' I won't believe it." Later he was actually to see it in a print-shop window. "James came home with an alarm that my thing was in the window of Mr. Fores of Piccadilly. I made off without delay and there to my consternation was the identical culprit lying on its back in the bottom shelf of the window. This is certainly something beyond belief."

It is difficult not to quote at length from the *Journal Kept by Richard Doyle in the Year 1840;* still more tantalizing not to show more of the " several hundred sketches " which illustrate its contents written in the neat script of the day, because any one of these early pictures is more spontaneous and vivid than his later work. *The Journal* was published by Smith and Elder of London in 1885, with an introduction by J. Hungerford Pollen.

Together with Leech, Stanfield, and Maclise, Doyle illustrated Dickens' *Cricket on the Hearth, The Battle of Life,* and *The Chimes.* The weird and the fanciful appealed to him as they had to Cruikshank, but his characters were pre-sented in a more gentle, whimsical way. About 1850 he turned almost entirely to illustrating fairy tales for children. This was soon after his resignation from

His Dickens illustrations

Punch. Doyle was a devout Roman Catholic, and *Punch's* attitude toward certain religious matters so offended him that he refused to continue to work for the paper, much to the regret of everybody concerned.

King of the Golden River and other fairy tales

Ruskin's *King of the Golden River* and Hughes' *Scouring of the White Horse* are probably his best-remembered fairy tale pictures. Those of us who first knew *The King of the Golden River*, with Doyle's pictures, instinctively associate the story of Gluck and the Black Brothers with wind and rain and grimness of high mountains and miss the same in more recent illustrations for the book.

Besides illustrating these stories, Doyle made pictures for *The Enchanted Crow, The Feast of Dwarfs, Fortune's Favorite, The Fairy Ring* (a collection of stories translated from the German), *Merry Pictures, Mark Lemon's Enchanted Doll, Juvenile Calendar* and *In Fairyland.*

In Fairyland is without doubt the high spot of this phase of Doyle's work— a series of exquisite fairy fantasies, conceived with charm and vigor and delight-

RICHARD DOYLE : *Scouring of the White Horse*

ful humor, as well as a rare sense of design. The delicacy of the drawing of these pictures and the porcelain-like clearness of their colors have been skillfully preserved in the reproductions engraved and printed by the master-craftsman, Edmund Evans. *In Fairyland* was originally published in 1870, accompanied by a poem of William Allingham's.

In 1886 the pictures were reissued; this time as illustrations for a story written around them by Andrew Lang, which he called *The Princess Nobody*, *A Tale of Fairyland*, and which he prefaced with the following

BALLAD OF DEDICATION

To all you babes at Branxholm Park
    This book I dedicate:
A book for winter evenings dark,
    Too dark to ride or skate.
I made it up out of my pate,
    And wasted midnight oil
Interpreting each cut and plate
    The Works of DICKY DOYLE!

AT Christmas time, 1850, *Punch* lost Richard Doyle and gained John Tenniel, who for the next fifty years contributed such cartoons as no publication had seen before. Cartoons full of pith and humor, yet drawn with a cold simplicity and elegance of line that brought a dignity hitherto unknown in this particular branch of illustration. He and Leech supplemented one another beautifully. It used to be said, "Leech sketched and Tenniel drew."

John Tenniel

But it is for Alice and Alice alone that he holds a unique place in this chapter. Of all the books of the century, Charles Lutwidge Dodgson's *Alice's Adventures in Wonderland*, published in 1866, and *Through the Looking-Glass*, published in 1872, stand out as perfect examples of author and artist being at one. Alice's birthday might almost be said to have been the April day in 1864 when Tenniel agreed to make the pictures for the book.

Alice, and Through the Looking-Glass

If we may judge from their correspondence, Mr. Dodgson (or Lewis Carroll, as we like better to call him) was no easy one to suit. "No detail was too small for his exact criticism. 'Don't give Alice so much crinoline,' he would write, or 'the White Knight must not have whiskers; he must not be made to look old,'" etc. It worried him a bit because Tenniel never used a model—"vows he no more needs one than I should need a multiplication table to work out a mathematical problem."

On the other hand, he omitted a whole chapter from *Through the Looking-Glass* at Tenniel's suggestion. Originally the book was to have thirteen chapters, but the last one was not quite good enough and was finally left out. Besides, it contained a wasp in a wig and at that Tenniel balked: "A wasp in a wig is altogether beyond the appliance of art."

JOHN TENNIEL : *Alice's Adventures in Wonderland*

JOHN TENNIEL : *Through the Looking-Glass*

"These pictures," says Cosmo Monkhouse in the *Art Journal* for 1901, "combine the merits of two kinds of illustrations: they are as faithful as possible to the text, and at the same time are fresh expressions of an individual, artistic genius. They are divided from his other illustrations and from nearly all those of other men by their exquisite, gentle, and ingenious humor." And he goes on to say, "Fortunately there are few who do not love Alice and have not an intimate acquaintance with the White Rabbit, the March Hare, the White Queen and the rest of that delightful but bewildering company met by Alice in her adventures. Tenniel has drawn them for us so that we could not believe in them one little bit if they were redrawn by anyone else. He has drawn for us Wonderland itself, and above all, Alice, that perfect ideal of an English girl; innocent, brave, kind, and full of faith and spirit. Even her face as drawn by Tenniel has a sweet look of wonder and expectation but never of confusion or fear, whether she finds herself swimming with a mouse or playing croquet with a flamingo for a mallet."

Wise man, Sir John Tenniel; for all the success of Alice he resolutely refused to illustrate another book for children, once the spontaneous impulse to draw for them had passed. "It is a curious fact," he wrote to Lewis Carroll some years later, "that with *Through the Looking-Glass* the faculty of drawing for book illustration departed from me, and notwithstanding all sorts of tempting inducements, I have done nothing in that line since."

ONE naturally associates the name of Arthur Hughes with George MacDonald, since it was for so many of the latter's stories that his illustrations were made.

Arthur Hughes, illustrator of George MacDonald's stories

At the Back of the North Wind and *The Princess and the Goblin*, with his pictures, first appeared serially in *Good Words for the Young*, "a most delightful children's magazine which began as a sixpenny monthly in 1869," and later was edited by George MacDonald himself. It is said that the first five volumes contain no less than 231 drawings by Arthur Hughes.

He also made the illustrations for MacDonald's *Dealings with the Fairies*, "a charming, dumpy little book," very scarce now, as well as for *Ranald Bannerman's Boyhood* and *Gutta Percha Willie*, none of which have been very widely known in this country.

Almost our first introduction to Hughes is in the Christmas number of the *Queen*, 1861, when he made lovely designs for the two old carols, "Hark, the Herald Angels Sing," and "Born on Christmas Eve." "The latter delightful thing," says Forrest Reid, "is a genuine Hughes, showing an old man in spectacles playing a violoncello and a little boy, his head on one side, playing the triangle."

Together with others he contributed to the first illustrated edition of *Tom Brown's School Days* by Thomas Hughes, and for Christina Rossetti's book of rhymes, called *Sing Song*, he drew a most charming series of little pictures. Another book of Christina Rossetti's, *Speaking Likenesses*, also contains his work.

William Allingham's *Music Master* was entirely illustrated by Hughes with the exception of two drawings, one by Millais and the other by Rossetti. It is in this book that Allingham's poem which children love, called "The Fairies," first appeared:

> Up the airy mountain,
> Down the rushy glen,
> We daren't go a-hunting
> For fear of little men.

And here are the little men themselves—Hughes has drawn them with wild locks flying, dancing in a ring under the great full moon, their shadows reflected in the waters of the dark mountain lake.

In 1905 a new edition of George MacDonald's first prose book, *Phantastes*, was published with an interesting preface by his son, Dr. Greville MacDonald, telling how he (the son) bought the copyright and remaining copies of the early edition which had been illustrated without his father's sanction; of how he had wanted to publish the book again as a tribute to his father and how happy he had been in having the help of his father's old friend, Arthur Hughes, in the illustrating of it. "I know," he writes, "of no other living artist who is capable of portraying the spirit of *Phantastes:* and every reader of this edition will, I believe, feel that the illustrations are a part of the romance and will gain through them some perception of the brotherhood between George MacDonald and Arthur Hughes."

Greville MacDonald's books

In 1911 and in 1913, when Greville MacDonald published two books of his own, *The Magic Crook* and *Jack and Jill*, Arthur Hughes, although by that time a man over eighty, illustrated them with all his old charm and spirit.

Despite a certain vagueness, there is always rhythm and beauty in his lines. He was a pupil of Alfred Stevens and he belonged to the Pre-Raphaelite School, though not of the Brotherhood, studying at Somerset House and at the Academy Schools, a fellow student of Rossetti and Holman Hunt. His training partly

ARTHUR HUGHES : *Gutta Percha Willie*

ARTHUR HUGHES: *At the Back of the
North Wind*

ARTHUR HUGHES: *Princess and the Goblin*

accounts for the idealistic always present in his pictures and this together with a certain wistful quality, half of this world, half of the world of make-believe, makes his work so perfectly akin to the spirit of many of George MacDonald's stories—on the borderline as they are between dream and reality.

Speaking of *At the Back of the North Wind*, Forrest Reid says: " These drawings have been conceived in a mysterious world out of space, out of time, a world to which the artist *goes back* so that he is not in the ordinary sense drawing for other children at all, but drawing for himself. It is true the past to which he returns is one in which everything is created anew after the dreamer's desire. This particular dreamer happens to love all that is sweet, gentle, innocent; hence it is with these qualities that the humans he meets are endowed. For they somehow are human—his little boys and girls—in spite of their half-angelic sexlessness and strange air of dreamy gravity."

At the Back of the North Wind

Arthur Hughes's work for children was done almost entirely in black and white. Gleeson White calls him " the children's black and white artist of the sixties, even as Walter Crane was their ' limner in colors.' "

THE ARTISTS WHO WORKED IN COLOR

BEAUTIFUL color in children's picture books is so taken for granted today that it is high time once more to pay tribute to a man who, eighty years ago, was doing pioneer work in this field—Edmund Evans, the English color printer.

Edmund Evans, English color printer

Edmund Evans was not only a skillful craftsman, but a shrewd business man, who did a large amount of trade work, as well as finer things, at his Racquet Court Press, off Fleet Street, in London. Moreover, he was a man with a great appreciation of the beautiful, and an artist in his own right.

It was his vision and skill and determined effort that first brought a greater beauty into English picture books, and made possible much of the work of the three artists about whom the second part of this chapter on illustrators of the nineteenth century is written.

Walter Crane was the first of the trio to have been associated with Edmund Evans.

Walter Crane

About 1859, while John Leech and Tenniel were doing their finest for *Punch*, Walter Crane, the son of an artist, was working hard as an apprentice to W. J. Linton, the wood engraver, and learning to draw on the block. During his lunch hours, Crane would roam through the Temple and out on to

Fleet Street to the old *Punch* office at No. 185, and gloat over the cartoons in the window.

Crane's training began before he ever went to Linton's. Naturally, at home with his father he was in the atmosphere of things artistic, and as a child, according to the family, "he was always tinkering with a pencil."

After practical work with Linton he joined evening classes at Heatherley's, a well-known art school in London, in order to study from the life and costume models. His first independent work began with designs for the paper covers of cheap railway novels (mustard plasters, they were called, because of their yellow hue and sensational character). These were executed by Edmund Evans.

At that time, about 1865, Mr. Evans was taking a definite stand against the crude, colored illustrations on the market for children. He had the courage to believe that paper picture books might be made beautiful in color and design and still be sold for a sixpence "if printed in sufficient quantity." Young Crane was interested in the idea and was easily persuaded to try the experiment with him, but the publishers were not so keen. The public, they maintained, must like the "raw colors and vulgar designs" that Evans complained of since they bought them—so why risk losing on something new?

Nursery picture books and the first toy books

Frederick Warne was the pioneer publisher to fall in with the movement for better color, and Crane's first nursery picture books, *The House That Jack Built*, *Dame Trot and Her Comical Cat* and the *History of Cock Robin and Jenny Wren*, were published by his firm. These were designed with solid black or blue backgrounds, the figures being relieved against them in bright colors. About 1865, the publisher, Routledge, followed suit, and the series of sixpenny picture books Crane made for Routledge numbered about thirty-five titles.

The use of flat, almost primitive colors, bold, black outline drawn with a sure stroke, an ever-present sense of design, were all characteristics of Crane's work from beginning to end, and this second group of books shows the influence of his growing interest in Japanese prints. A navy friend brought Crane some prints, more as a novelty than anything else, but he was charmed with them. "Their treatment," he says, "in definite black outline and flat, brilliant as well as delicate colors, their vivid, dramatic and decorative feeling struck me at once and I endeavored to apply these methods to the modern fanciful and humorous subjects of children's toy books and the methods of wood engraving and machine printing."

One, Two, Buckle My Shoe, and *This Little Pig* are perhaps the simplest of these nursery books in treatment. *The Absurd A B C*, *Valentine and Orson* and *Puss in Boots* show a stunning use of black. Puss begging a pair of boots from the miller's son is one of Crane's most delightful early pictures.

In the *Baby's Alphabet* we find a gay lot of little individual drawings charmingly placed on a page without a sense of overcrowding, but *Blue Beard* and *The Sleeping Beauty* both suffer from too much detail. Design cramps and outweighs the drama of the story of *Blue Beard* and the classic setting of *The Sleeping Beauty* seems forced and lacking in charm and humor. The same may be said of the rather disconcerting introduction of contemporary costume into *Cinderella*.

The Fairy Ship and *King Luckieboy's Party*, however, are two entirely satisfying and festive picture books. Father Christmas arriving at Luckieboy's party in a snow storm is enough to put anyone in holiday humor.

Several of these early picture books were done while Walter Crane and his bride were enjoying a leisurely honeymoon in Italy. "Mother Hubbard's dog," he says, "I took the liberty of depicting as a poodle—that type flourishing at the time in Rome." The drawings, he tells us, "were made on cards in black and white and sent by post to Edmund Evans in London, who had them photographed on the wood and engraved, returning me the proofs to color. This method of work was beginning to supersede the old practice of drawing direct on the block for the engraver. It certainly had its advantages, not the least among which was that of being able to retain the original drawing."

While abroad, something else occurred which is startling evidence of the lack of protection and appreciation accorded an illustrator in those days. "While I was in Italy," writes Crane in his autobiography, "the publishers who at first were by no means converts to the effort we were making to get more artistic color treatment in their books, perceiving a growing demand for them, issued a set of my sixpenny books bound together and called it *Walter Crane's Picture Book*, but without my knowledge. This volume, though far from being what I should have approved in its general format, certainly served as a poster for me; and was, I believe, a commercial success; but as I had no rights in it, it was of no benefit to me in that respect. My drawings for these books were done for a very modest sum and sold outright to the publishers. The engraving and printing was costly, and a very large edition had to be sold in order to make them pay; as many as fifty thousand of a single book, I was told, being necessary. However, if they did not bring in much money, I had the

Walter Crane's Picture Book

fun out of them." The fun consisted in working out a number of theories in color, design, etc., for Crane's work was in the experimental stage and he was strongly under the influence of William Morris and his school of craftsmen.

Hence Crane took toy books more seriously than any of his predecessors had done, and drew every picture with a two-fold aim—as a piece of illustration and likewise as a piece of design. He was one of the first to feel that text and page should be planned in harmony, and he often carried this theory to the extent of executing parts of the text himself in bold, distinctive, red and black letters. The end papers and title pages of his picture books are delightfully entertaining, and even his signature (a long-legged bird set within his monogram) has a style of its own.

The second series of toy books

Beginning about 1873, he designed a second series of toy books for Routledge which Edmund Evans again printed. These sold for a shilling each, and a greater and more pleasing variety of colors was used and the plan of the page was more spacious. Occasionally, as in the first series, they lack humor and are too elaborate. One feels at times Crane's interest in design and setting led him to forget the children for whom these books were intended. "I was," he confessed, "in the habit of putting in all sorts of subsidiary detail that interested me and often made them the vehicle for my ideas in furniture and decoration." Nevertheless these books all have real distinction—*The Yellow Dwarf*, *The Frog Prince*, *The Alphabet of Old Friends*, and the *Hind in the Wood* are delightfully fantastic. *Aladdin* and *Beauty and the Beast* both riot in color, and *Goody Two-Shoes* is the most lovable of them all.

With this series the toy books came to an end. Crane offered to continue them if granted a small royalty, but as the publisher "took the line rather of the provincial trader who said, 'We lose on every article we sell; it is only the quantity that makes it pay,' there was nothing further to be hoped for in that direction, and so," says Crane, "I struck."

Mrs. Molesworth's stories

About this time Mrs. Molesworth began a series of children's stories that were destined to become popular on both sides of the ocean. Beginning with *Carrots*, Walter Crane made the illustrations for about sixteen of them. The majority were done in black and white, with his usual heavy pen strokes; a few were tinted. It is a pity that in the apparently necessary reduction in size the clearness of many of these pictures is lost.

Before telling of Crane's drawings for *The First of May*, we must go back to the year he was seventeen and still at Linton's. At that time Mr. J. R. Wise was about to publish a book on the history and scenery of the New Forest, and his publishers, Smith and Elder, suggested that young Walter Crane draw the illustrations for the book. Accordingly he joined Mr. Wise in the Forest in order, under his directions, to make a series of sketches to be engraved by Linton. But the weather was against them, and they were storm-bound most of the time. " When too wet to go out to sketch," Crane says, " we amused ourselves by composing a mock mediæval ballad of the Red Knight—Mr. Wise wrote the ballad and I engrossed the verses and illustrated them." A review of *The New Forest, Its History and Scenery*, was published in the *Cornhill Magazine* at Christmas time, 1862, and the illustrations were praised as " the work of a very young artist only seventeen," which fact Walter Crane at that time failed to appreciate. " I felt quite full grown and had no wish to have my age published at large."

This early visit to the New Forest led to closer associations with Mr. Wise, whose varied interests and mature companionship meant much to the young artist. They made various walking trips together, and Crane says, " To him I was indebted for my first acquaintance with Emerson. I began with the *Conduct of Life* and found the optimist of Concord very stimulating reading."

Mr. Wise was in Sherwood Forest in the spring of 1878, working under its spell on a fairy masque to be called *The First of May*. He sent for Crane to come down and hear the masque read and to plan some illustrations for it. It was to be published as an illustrated gift book and Walter Crane writes, " Together we made out the scheme of arrangement and list of illustrations for the whole book. . . . The work of my friend was steeped in the knowledge and love of the country and was the product . . . of an ardent lover of nature."

The First of May

The following spring they were again there, working on the book, and the Forest about Edwinstowe and Ollerton was so beautiful that Crane returned in the summer with his wife and family " to enjoy it better and see it in its full panoply of leaves and bracken," while he continued to work on *The First of May*. When the drawings were completed they were so in harmony with the text, so at one with the Forest " as Shakespeare must have imagined it for *Midsummer Night's Dream*," that it seems impossible the book is not the conception of a single mind. It is by far the most imaginative, whimsical, and beautiful thing Crane ever did and it is executed with rare delicacy and skill. Fairies, elves and imps, children, lovers, shepherds and shepherdesses, and the Queen of

WALTER CRANE : *First of May, a Fairy Masque*

the May herself roam the borders of the pages, while birds and insects and beasts of many sorts, real and imaginary, play a part in the revel and dance about their own Maypole.

> Hedgehog, hare, mole, fieldmouse play;
> Squirrel leap with all your might,
> 'Till birds envy you your flight;
> Glitter, insects, scale on scale!
> Dance thou knight in armour, snail!
> Come all creatures here today,
> Welcome to our Queen of May!

The drawings were all made in pencil and were afterwards reproduced by photogravure by Messrs. Goupil and Co., the plates being done in Paris. " The reproductions were slightly reduced in scale, were very well done, and gave the silvery, delicate effect of the pencil drawings most successfully." No font of type was delicate enough to harmonize with the designs, so Crane lettered every word of the text by hand, a tremendous task, but the beauty of the finished page must have rewarded him. The book was dedicated to Charles Darwin, from the author and the artist.

As may be imagined, the cost of the reproduction of *The First of May* was great, and it could only be published in a limited edition; hence this book, which shows Walter Crane at his best, is comparatively little known.

Crane's time was by no means entirely given to illustrating for children. He did many murals, principally of classic subjects, and individual paintings both in oil and water color, exhibiting often at both the Dudley and the Grosvenor Galleries in London, in company with Burne-Jones, Legros, Whistler, Holman Hunt and others who had broken away from the traditions of the Royal Academy and were of the new school of that day. He was active in various art organizations, and the Arts and Crafts Movement, which William Morris had done so much to forward, had his keen and active coöperation. He made many designs for friezes and frieze panels, wallpapers, hangings, etc., and collaborated with Morris on the page decorations for the *Story of the Glittering Plain*, which was printed by the Kelmscott Press.

Crane's work not only for children

As a disciple of Morris he likewise was interested in the Labor Movement, especially in its relation to artists and craftsmen, and was an ardent Socialist, belonging to the Fabian and other Socialistic societies and contributing broadsides and printed matter to their various publications.

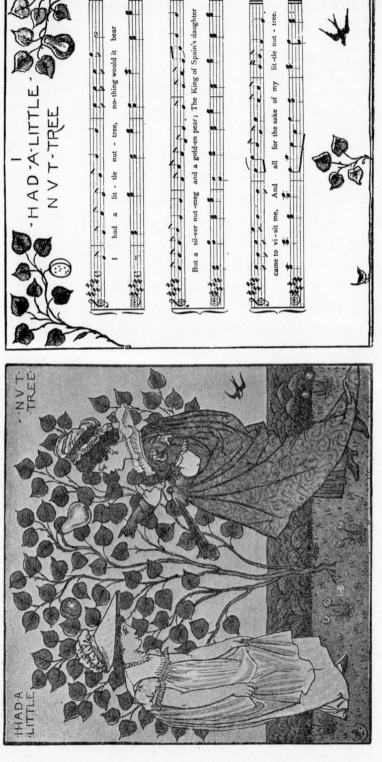

WALTER CRANE : *Baby's Opera*

At the Savile Club he met Robert Louis Stevenson, and out of those chance meetings grew Stevenson's request that he draw the frontispieces for his two books, *Travels with a Donkey* and *An Inland Voyage*, which he did.

Another member of the Savile Club who needed Crane's talent was Professor J. M. D. Meiklejohn of St. Andrew's University. "He had a scheme for a primer embodying a method of teaching to read by associating words with the objects they signify, and without forcing a child to learn the series of misleading and cumbersome sounds which represent the alphabet. He planned a book called the *Golden Primer*, to be issued as a Christmas book full of pictures in color." The scheme interested Crane and he made the pictures. "The professor," he says, "intended to follow this book with others covering the whole field of an educational course, but he did not live to carry out his scheme. . . . The direction in which he was laboring has since been pursued by others and the children of the present age must have a better time of it than their fathers and mothers in acquiring the art of deciphering the English language. I did a large number of the drawings for him for the *Golden Primer* and drew them on a large scale, so that the Professor could use these illustrations when he lectured on the subject, and they were reduced for the book."

The Golden Primer

This was not the only time Crane tried his hand at this type of book, although *Pothooks and Perseverance*, *Slate and Pencilvania*, *The Romance of the Three Rs* and *Little Queen Ann* were all fanciful in tone. These were published by Marcus Ward. Later he did a series of pictures for three practical little linen-bound readers by Nellie Dale, published by Dent.

After completing the toy books, Crane and Edmund Evans planned a book of another order, a book of old rhymes with the music set on one side of the page and the illustration on the other. "*The Baby's Opera* turned out a great success, although at first the trade shook its head, as the sight of a five-shilling book not decently bound in cloth and without any gold on it was an unheard-of thing; and weighing it in their hands and finding it wanting in mere avoirdupois weight, some said, 'This will never do'—but it did. The first edition of ten thousand copies was soon exhausted, and another was called for and another," and we might add that *The Baby's Opera* and its two successors, *The Baby's Bouquet* and *The Baby's Own Æsop*, which were published as companion volumes during the next two Christmas seasons, still remain favorite picture books. There is a distinct charm about the size of these little square books. The tunes for both *The Baby's Opera* and *The Baby's Bouquet* were arranged by Walter

The Baby's Opera and its successors

Crane's sister, Lucy, who was a skillful pianist. The text of *The Baby's Own Æsop* was done by Crane's old master, Linton, who sent it to him from America, where he was living in 1886.

Later, in 1892, "when the babies who were present when *The Baby's Opera* had its first season were all grown up," the three little books were published

WALTER CRANE : *Household Stories*

together in a large de luxe edition for collectors—very fine; but *Triplets*, as the special edition was called, lacks the charm of the individual books.

Grimm's Household Stories   Lucy Crane likewise did the translation of the text of Grimm's *Household Stories*, for which her brother made the illustrations. Some of Crane's most distinctive pen and ink work appears in this book which was engraved by Swain and printed by Clark. The lines are clear-cut and reproduce exceedingly well; the head- and tail-pieces and the initial letters are delightful, and after many years it still holds its place as one of the most pleasing and all-round satisfying editions of the old folk tales, and is perhaps the best known of any of Crane's work.

The same year that *Household Stories* appeared, *Pan Pipes*, another book of old songs with tunes, was finished. " In this," says Crane, " I had the advantage of the coöperation of Mr. Theodore Marzials himself, a most charming song composer. The book was oblong in form, so as to be convenient for the piano, and for each song there was a colored design taking the form of a decorative border. It opened with Malcolm Lawrence's setting for Marlowe's words, ' Come, live with me and be my love.' The rest of the airs were all arranged by Marzials from old traditional ones."

Crane and his family were great travelers, and spent delightful times in Italy, Germany, Hungary and Bohemia. His work was well known and greatly appreciated in both Germany and Hungary, where it was recognized as something new and vital. Special exhibitions of his work were asked for by both countries, and Crane found himself an honored guest when he visited them.

The years 1891 and 1892 were spent in an extended visit to America, where *Crane's visit* his work was exhibited in Boston, Philadelphia, Chicago and St. Louis, and met *to America* with real appreciation, " especially his smaller work and book designs," the favorite being the fanciful designs for *Flora's Feast* (this book was the first of a group of similar fancies, all a trifle self-conscious), *The Flower Wedding, Queen Summer, Floral Fantasy in an Old English Garden, Flowers from Shakespeare's Garden* and *The Masque of Days.*

At the opening of his exhibition at the Arts Club in Philadelphia he met Howard Pyle, whose work he had often admired in American magazines. They must have had much to talk about, those two artists who had so many ideals in common.

Crane made the most amusing collection of family sketches en route. One shows " the Cranes on toast," indicating their reaction to an overheated room in an American hotel.

While in Boston, Winthrop Scudder introduced Walter Crane to the River- *Hawthorne's* side Press and commissioned him to illustrate Hawthorne's *Wonder Book.* It *Wonder Book* was completed in the South the following spring " in a little timber-built cottage at a window looking out on flowering trees of oleander with the red birds of Florida flitting among them." These pictures are done almost entirely in tones of orange, blue and brown, yet so cleverly did Crane vary them that one gets the effect of several colors.

It is fun to think of the Crane family spending the early part of the summer of 1892 on Nantucket, leading the simple life and fending for themselves in a cottage at Wauwinet called The Wreck. The sea breaking all day along the line of shore, the wind catching the crests of the waves and blowing the spray out like the mane of a prancing steed, carried Walter Crane back to the days of his childhood with his brothers at Torquay, watching the " white horses," as they called them, dash themselves against the rocks. Perhaps this made him homesick, for we read of the family's sailing the following month for England.

Crane as teacher

It follows quite naturally that Walter Crane should have taught art as well as practiced it. From 1893 to 1896 he held the Directorship of Design at the Manchester School of Art, and frequently lectured in other places. Later he was appointed Principal in the Royal College of Art in Kensington. Two of his courses of lectures at Manchester were published as books—*The Bases of Design* and *Line and Form*, the latter going further into detail and demonstrating practical methods of work.

The whole history of book-illustration for children owes a big debt to Walter Crane. No one who is interested in his work and the movement that he started should miss reading his autobiography, called *An Artist's Reminiscences*. Another book, *The Art of Walter Crane*, by P. G. Konody, contains many remarkably fine reproductions of his work (the text, however, met with Crane's strong disapproval).

In a special Winter Number of the *Studio* for 1897–98, called "Children's Books and Their Illustrators," Gleeson White gives a full list of Crane's illustrated books up to that date and adds a fine appreciation of him, saying truly, "As a maker of children's books no one ever attempted the task he fulfilled so gayly and no one since has beaten him on his own ground."

Randolph Caldecott

RANDOLPH CALDECOTT was born in the old walled town of Chester on March 22, 1846, and went to King Henry VII School there. The school records tell that he was one of the best boys in the school, but in the present instance we are more interested in hearing that from the time he was six he drew pictures of animals or modeled them in clay or cut them out of wood as his fancy dictated. His father, however, discouraged these artistic tendencies and at the age of fifteen Caldecott was working in a bank at Whitchurch in Shropshire and in his free moments thoroughly enjoying the surrounding country in his own way. He lived in an old farmhouse about two miles out of town and " used to go fishing and shooting, to meets of the hounds, to markets and cattle fairs," absorbing the sights and the sounds and storing up bits in his memory and sketchbook that were to be very useful to him later.

After six years at Whitchurch he was transferred to the Manchester and Salford Bank in the city of Manchester, and there for the next five years he led a very different life. It was characteristic of Caldecott, however, that he made the most of his surroundings, and if he sadly missed the freedom of the Shropshire country and his horse and dogs, he availed himself of all the opportunities the city of Manchester had to offer a bank clerk with a persistent artistic bent. He joined the Brasenose Club; took advantage of the opportunities afforded by the School of Art, and at the homes of "hospitable and artistic friends" saw good work and obtained information regarding various art matters.

"He used to wander about the bustling, murky streets of Manchester, sometimes finding himself in queer out-of-the-way quarters, often coming across an odd character, curious bits of antiquity and the like. Whenever the chance came he made short excursions into the adjacent country and took long walks which were never purposeless."

His first published drawings appeared in a serio-comic paper called the *First published* *Will O' The Wisp* and another called the *Sphinx*. Meanwhile he was making *drawings* hunting sketches and experimenting with his early loves, modeling and woodcarving, as well as carrying on his work in the bank. The latter apparently was never neglected, although his business associates told all manner of amusing stories about finding sketches of horses and dogs and the like on the back of receipt slips, old envelopes, and the blotter on his desk.

By this time his eye was definitely on London and an art career and in 1870 *London Society* he established connections which enabled him to send contributions to the pages of *London Society*. Mr. Henry Blackburn was the editor and he and Caldecott became lifelong friends.

In 1872 he left Manchester for good and settled in London, still drawing for *The Graphic* periodicals and illustrating short stories. The first picture he ever sent to the *Graphic* was "The Quorn Hunt." By April, 1872, he was attending a life class under E. J. Poynter, R.A., and "as this was the turning point in Caldecott's career, it should be recorded that at this time and ever afterwards, Mr. Armstrong, later the Art Director of the South Kensington Museum, was his best friend and counsellor. He had also the advantage of the friendship of George du Maurier, M. Dalou, the sculptor, Charles Keene and others." There was no stopping Caldecott now; with the high spirits and boyish enthusiasm which he never lost he was off at full cry to do the work he most loved.

Realizing his skill in character work, Sampson Low, the publisher, suggested his illustrating a book of summer travel in the Harz Mountains.[6] "Caldecott being then twenty-six " found the idea altogether delightful to him " and here, as in every country he visited in after years, his playful fancy and facility for seizing the grotesque side of things stood him in good stead. In a strange land, amidst unfamiliar scenes and faces, he roamed ' fancy free.' "

Armed with Baedeker's *Guide* and a dialogue book of sentences in German and English, he used to delight to interrogate the wondering natives; the necessary questions difficult to find, and the " ' elaborate and quite unnecessary '

RANDOLPH CALDECOTT : *Harz Mountains, A Tour in the Toy Country*

(as he expressed it) always turning up. Such little incidents gave opportunity to the observant artist to study the faces of the listeners; the interviews conducted slowly and gravely, and ending in a peal of laughter from the natives."[7]

Harz Mountain sketches   The following October some of the Harz Mountain sketches made their appearance in the London *Graphic*, which was the beginning of a long connection with that paper and, when later in the year Mr. Blackburn took others to America with him, Caldecott's name became known on this side of the ocean through the pages of *Harper's Monthly Magazine* for 1873, that magazine which gave so many gifted young artists a start. It was through these sketches that Caldecott had his first contact with Edwin Abbey, the well-known illustrator of old English subjects. Other drawings of Caldecott's were accepted by

the editor of the *Daily Graphic* of New York, and for some time afterwards he *Both artist*
sent contributions to this newspaper. For the majority of Caldecott's offerings *and author*
to the London *Graphic* he was both artist and author. " The ideas were his own
and the letterpress which meanders among the pictures was his own, too."

He experimented with various methods of reproduction. These pictures for
the *Graphic*, for instance, were drawn in pen and ink for direct printing without the help of the wood engraver. No one, however, realized better than
Caldecott himself the added quality that might be given to a drawing through
the work of a careful wood engraver, and all his more serious, permanent work
was put through the regular process, "being photographed on the block and
then passed through the engraver's hands."

There is a sense of freedom in all his drawing—never was an artist who
could tell so much with so few lines; he knew his power in that direction and
delighted in it. But Caldecott's sketches were not dashed off as quickly as one
might imagine. He studied " ' the art of leaving out as a science,' doing nothing
hastily, but thinking long and seriously before putting pen to paper, remembering, as he always said, ' the fewer the lines the less error committed.' "

Generally speaking, the rush and hurry of journalistic work were distasteful to him. His health was never robust and he preferred the type of work
which required quiet and study. Fortunately, commissions of this sort were
beginning to come more frequently, and besides his sketches at this time he was
making a number of studies in oil and water color of water birds—a favorite
subject. Several of these were in the form of decorative panels.

During the summers of 1872, '73 and '74 we find him in a cottage belong- *Old Christmas*
ing to Mr. Blackburn down at Farnham Royal in Buckinghamshire. His studio
was a " loose box " fitted up to suit him and here, in the quiet country looking
out over the woods and fields, he made the sketches for a selection of chapters
out of Washington Irving's *Sketch Book* to be called *Old Christmas*—a piece
of work quite after his own heart, for he loved the same things about old England and old-time English country life that Irving had reveled in so many years
before. These two, who lived a generation apart, had much in common and
came together in rare harmony of spirit in *Old Christmas*. Irving's description
of the stagecoachman, you remember, was almost perfect, but Caldecott's picture of him added the finishing touch, which not only " carried to many a reader
of *Old Christmas* in the New World a living portrait of a past age," but " revealed also the presence of a new illustrator."

Even as he worked on the book Caldecott's style of drawing changed. It became more serious and full in treatment, less sketchy, less inclined toward the ludicrous. It is said the " old man who combined the various offices of gardener, groom and parish clerk at Farnham Royal " stood unconsciously for several drawings in *Old Christmas*, while remembered nooks and corners and byways in Sussex, Kent and Chester played their part in the background of its pictures.

When the book was in preparation Caldecott certainly was fortunate in having the aid of so understanding and sympathetic a wood engraver as J. D. Cooper. In the foreword he shares honors with Mr. Cooper, saying in part: " Before the remembrance of the good old times, so fast passing, should have

RANDOLPH CALDECOTT : *Old Christmas*

entirely passed away, the present artist, R. Caldecott, and engraver, James D. Cooper, planned to illustrate Washington Irving's *Old Christmas*."

Bracebridge Hall Macmillan published *Old Christmas* in 1876 and it met with the fine welcome it deserved. It absolutely established Caldecott's reputation and soon after he was commissioned to do a second book of Irving's, *Bracebridge Hall*, which was equally fine.

At this time, alas, his health began to break and again he went to Northern Italy and the Riviera. One gets no reflection of diminished strength, however, in the humorous sketches in his old vein which he sent back to the *Graphic;*

sketches caught in watering places, health resorts or just by the way. He also did some charming illustrations for a book by Mrs. Comyns Carr called *North Italian Folk*.

It was on his return to England about 1877 or '78 that he began the work that *Caldecott Picture Books* will probably be longest remembered—his picture books; and again Edmund Evans is to be thanked for urging him to do them. Walter Crane's toy books had established a high standard, and before beginning his own work in that field Caldecott went to call on Crane to ask his advice about contacts with publishers, etc. A most congenial friendship resulted and Walter Crane was always generous in his praise of Caldecott's work.

Leslie Brooke, an artist of our own day, who " upholds the fine tradition of English picture-book making established by Walter Crane and Randolph Caldecott," said that " Caldecott is an extreme instance of instinctive drawing," and never is that more truly shown than in his picture books. One feels he let himself go for the children, and all his natural sweetness and gaiety of spirit, all his love of life out-of-doors—and particularly the English out-of-doors— are reflected from the pages of the old nursery jingles, full of children and old folks, huntsmen and country characters. Animals abound in them—horses and dogs and birds—the pages are full of action. Was ever so hurly-burly a chase imagined as that instituted by those " headlong, horn-blowing, cheek-bursting and hopelessly futile Three Jovial Huntsmen? "

A Farmer Went Trotting Upon His Grey Mare, John Gilpin's Ride and *The Fox Jumped Over the Parson's Gate* were subjects after his own heart, while England in the spring comes out of every page of *The House That Jack Built, The Farmer's Boy* and the old May Day ballad, *Come Lasses and Lads*.

The Queen of Hearts, A Frog He Would a'Wooing Go, Hey Diddle Diddle and *Sing a Song of Sixpence* are all treated in a cozy, homey manner with enough jam tarts, blackbird pies, pots of honey and frosted cakes about to make one's mouth water.

Austin Dobson says that in his picture books Caldecott's pencil " played the most engaging variations. Who, for example, ever before conceived of Madam Blaize as a pawnbroker, because—

She freely gave to all the poor,
Who left a pledge behind.

RANDOLPH CALDECOTT :
Queen of Hearts

And where else had the world been shown the authentic, academic presence, the very 'form and pressure' of the 'Great Panjandrum Himself,' with the little round button on top?"

Those who were familiar with the country around Whitchurch were always discovering familiar bits in Caldecott's picture books. He must have loved Malpas Church tower, for it appears in no less than three books: *Baby Bunting, The Fox Jumps Over the Parson's Gate* and *Babes in the Wood*, while you can walk down the main street of Whitchurch just by opening *The Great Panjandrum* at page 6.

He was the despair of a very friendly rival, Kate Greenaway, who was born the same month and year and began designing picture books for children at

RANDOLPH CALDECOTT : *Come Lasses and Lads*

about the same time. When *Hey Diddle Diddle* was about to appear she wrote

Kate Greenaway on Caldecott

to Frederick Locker-Lampson: "I've been to call on the Caldecotts today with Mrs. Evans. My brother showed me some of his (Mr. Caldecott's) new drawings yesterday at Racquet Court. They are so uncommonly clever. The Dish running away with the Spoon—you can't think how much he has made of it. I wish I had such a mind. I'm feeling very low about my own powers just now, for I have been looking at the originals for the new Crane book— some of them are literally dreams of beauty."

There never have been any picture books quite like these of Caldecott's before or since. The spirit of them is so fine and gentle, the fun in them so real that they make a never-ending appeal to children and grown people alike who have a love of beauty and action. Originally they were published singly, in paper covers, for a shilling. Later, an edition was published of several bound together in three books: *Picture Book No. 1*, *Picture Book No. 2* and *The Pan-jandrum Picture Book*. Still later the toy books were all bound together in a large edition entitled *The Complete Collection of Pictures and Songs* with a preface by Austin Dobson.

While stopping in the country at various times Caldecott had the habit of illustrating his letters with amusing sketches. A lively picture of himself was sent to a friend with the following letter from Dodington near Whitchurch in Shropshire where he had been working for some time:

"I feel I owe somebody an apology for staying in the country so long, but don't quite see to whom it is due, so I shall stay two or three days longer, and then I shall indeed hang my harp on a willow tree. It is difficult to screw up the proper amount of courage for leaving the lambkins, the piglets, the foals, the goslings, the calves and the puppies."

"Life in the country with Caldecott was 'worth living' and he chafed much at this period if he had to be with his 'nose to the grindstone,' as he expressed it, in Bloomsbury. Whilst in the country his letters to town were full of sketches, but in letters from London he hardly ever pictured life out of doors."

In the summer of 1878 he and Mr. Blackburn made a trip into Brittany that *The Breton trip* delighted Caldecott's sense of the picturesque. They at first intended to take a gig and drive through the country, making notes and sketches *en route* (nothing pleased Caldecott better than a gig he could drive himself), but their plans had to be changed and to the artist's disgust they must "take a trap instead with a driver"; however, they were on the road and that was always worth a good deal to him. It was the season of fetes and pardons and his pencil was kept busy catching bits here and there. Breton farmers and their cattle, pilgrims at a wayside cross, women at work in the buckwheat fields, a horse fair at Le Folgoet, a cattle fair at Carhaix—everything was food for Caldecott's sketchbook, and Mr. Blackburn anxiously watched him working so feverishly, for he was supposed to be taking this trip mainly for his health.

Mr. Blackburn writes: "Apart from the artistic material so abundant everywhere, Caldecott's love of animals and knowledge of them, his interest in everything connected with farming, markets, country life and surroundings, roused him to exertions at Carhaix which none but the most hardy 'special artist' would have attempted. . . . He made some extraordinarily rapid sketches in colour with the brush direct, without a touch of the pencil or anything to guide him on the paper. Few sketches of this kind exist, excepting rough notes

RANDOLPH CALDECOTT : *Three Jovial Huntsmen*

in books not intended for publication. In the evening the figures in the streets and at the inns had to be noted down."[8]

Caldecott and   Caldecott and Mrs. Ewing met in London in 1879, when "*Jackanapes* was
Mrs. Ewing simmering in her brain." She had greatly admired his work and wanted him to illustrate for her, and he was the ideal person to do it, for they had many tastes and interests in common. He made the pictures for *Jackanapes*, that splendid story of a gallant boy and a gallant horse, also for *Daddy Darwin's Dovecot*, in which he drew birds to his heart's content, and for *Lob Lie-by-the-Fire*, and they might have done many more things together had their lives been spared.

In speaking of Caldecott's love of birds one must not forget a charming little vellum-bound book called *The Owls of Olynn Belfry*. The author bears the initials A.Y.D.; the book bears no date at all, so that it is difficult to know when the drawings were made. It is seldom we find him picturing a fairy, but there is a delightful Fairy Queen in this book, dancing the minuet with a portly old owl.

Caldecott   When Randolph Caldecott crossed the ocean in 1886 bound for America,
in America once more in search of health, he promised the London *Graphic* a series of sketches illustrative of American life—and oh, how he could have caught us! But by the time he reached St. Augustine, Florida, he had little strength left for work, and he died on the 12th of February of that year.

One likes to remember Caldecott at the last, not in a foreign country, but in his garden at Kensington with his family and dogs—or, as on another occasion, in Victoria Street, Westminster, when "to a good old English tune the lasses and lads out of his picture book danced before him, and the fiddler in the costume of the time 'played it wrong.'"

A very real sense of the charm of his personality, the delight of his friendship, is to be found in a memoir of him written by his friend, Henry Blackburn, soon after his death, entitled *Randolph Caldecott, A Personal Memoir of His Early Art Career*. It is to be regretted that a more complete record of Caldecott's life and work was not written later. In his *Memoir*, Blackburn intimates that something of the kind was anticipated, but apparently nothing materialized.

Memoir by Henry Blackburn

Another friend, Frederick Locker-Lampson, summed up Randolph Caldecott's work with these words: "It seems to me that Caldecott's art was of a quality that appears about once in a century. It had delightful characteristics most happily blended. He had a delicate fancy, and his humour was as racy as it was refined. He had a keen sense of beauty and to sum up all, he had *charm*."

"Mine be a cot" for the hours of play,
Of the kind that is built by Miss Greenaway,
Where the walls are low, and the roofs are red
And the birds are gay in the blue o'erhead;
And the dear little figures, in frocks and frills,
Go roaming about at their own sweet wills. . . .
                                        —AUSTIN DOBSON.

Kate Greenaway

IF we turn to Randolph Caldecott for pictures of the English country, we turn to Kate Greenaway, who was born in the same year, for pictures of children and English gardens. Tidy gardens with flower borders, clipped yew hedges, ivy-grown walls and fruit trees abloom—and children in their midst.

She was born at No. 1 Cavendish Street, Hoxton, on St. Patrick's Day, 1846, the daughter of John Greenaway, a prominent wood engraver and draughtsman, whose work may be found in many of the early volumes of the *Illustrated London News* and *Punch*.

Her love of gardens and country scenes began early. The Greenaway children (there were three girls and a boy) spent many delightful days when they were little on the farm of a great-aunt, Mrs. Wise, at Rolleston, a village not far from Nottingham. One of Kate's earliest recollections is of her nurse,

Earliest years

Ann, carrying her to a hayfield. "Ann carried Kate on one arm and on the other a basket of bread and butter and cups, and, somehow, on a third, a can of steaming tea for the thirsty haymakers. . . . Kate was sure that she had now arrived at the age of two, and for the rest of her life she vividly remembered the beauty of the afternoon, the look of the sun, the smell of the tea, the perfume of the hay, and the great feeling of Happiness—the joy and the love of it—from her royal perch on Ann's strong arm "[9] (all of which in later years found its way into her pictures scores of times). It was during these days that she says she "struck up a friendship" with flowers that lasted to her life's end. "There were the snapdragons—these she loved; but the pink moss rose which grew by the dairy window *she revered*. It grew with the gooseberry bushes, plum trees and the laburnum in the little three-cornered garden near the road. . . . But though she loved the garden flowers, they were never to her what those were which grew of their own free will in the fields and hedgerows."

When Kate was between five and six, the family moved to a house near Highbury, and here a new world opened for her—the world of books. Suddenly to her own amazement she found she could read. There were the fascinating two-a-penny fairy tales in colored covers, and larger ones for a penny (but she liked the half-penny ones best). Then there were the verses of Jane and Ann Taylor which she doted on, especially when her mother read them

KATE GREENAWAY:
From an early Christmas card

aloud. Later in her own life she was to pay a tribute to the writers of these verses through the lovely pictures she made for a new edition of the book. Then there were the *Illustrated London News* and *Punch*; the Greenaway children were brought up on both, and during the years of the Indian Mutiny they pored over the cartoons and hair-raising illustrations to their hearts' content. Kate (who by this time was always doing something with her pencil) went further and tried her hand at making pictures of the Mutiny. "I was always drawing people escaping," she says. "I wish I had some of the old drawings, but they were nearly always done on a slate and rubbed off again. We knew all about it from the *Illustrated London News*, and the incident of the Highland woman who heard the bagpipes made a great impression on me. I would sit and think of the Sepoys till I would be wild with terror . . . but I was always drawing the ladies, nurses and children escaping. Mine always escaped and were never taken."

Kate and her sisters were devoted to a large family of dolls. Making clothes for them was one of her delights, and perhaps this was the beginning of her interest in costume which later became so much a part of her art.

At twelve she began to have her first serious art lessons at Miss Springet's *First lessons* school at Canonbury House, which was under the Science and Art Department *in art* (now the Board of Education). Later she attended the Life Classes at Heatherley's, and then the newly opened Slade School in London.

Prizes came early and often to Kate Greenaway, and by the time she was twenty she was exhibiting in the Dudley Gallery a series of small water-color sketches of children and springtime gardens—children dressed in quaint, picturesque costumes of another generation. The dress of her own day seemed ugly to her—so why perpetuate it in pictures? Instead she simply harked back to the end of the eighteenth century and to the type of clothes worn by the country folk about Rolleston when she was a child. This did not mean, however, that " she merely picked up an old book on costumes and adapted them second hand to her use. She began from the very beginning fashioning the dresses with her own hands and dressing up her models and lay figures in order to realize the effect anew."

The first exhibition at the Dudley Gallery proved to be a real success and led to a variety of commissions. Some of the sketches were bought by Mr. Loftie, editor of the *People's Magazine*, and published. Kronheim and Company (color printers in Shoe Lane) asked her to make them some picture books, and Marcus Ward commissioned her to do some Christmas cards and Valentines. Some of these Valentines were later published by Marcus Ward in a book of Valentine verses entitled *The Quiver of Love*. Walter Crane had a Valentine or two in the same book, but neither artist was very proud of them.

Her first work for Kronheim was unsigned. The colors were rather crude *Nursery toy* and the reproduction poor. Another group of nursery toy books done about *books* 1871 and published by Gall and Inglis fared better. Among these are *The Fair One with Golden Locks, Bluebeard, Babes in the Wood, Tom Thumb, Puss in Boots, Hop-o'-My-Thumb, Red Riding Hood, The Blue Bird* and *The White Cat*.

In 1873 she made her first appearance in the magazine, *Little Folks*. The following year she illustrated a book for children by Kathleen Knox called, *Fairy Gifts; or a Wallet of Wonders*, and for the first time saw her name on a title page. Her father did the engraving for this book and so here, as in a number of instances, the initials J. G. and K. G. appear together on a picture.

At thirty-three Kate Greenaway was established with a growing reputation. Her work was appearing regularly in the Royal Academy Exhibitions and at the Dudley Gallery.

But it was Edmund Evans again who saw still greater possibilities in her

KATE GREENAWAY : *Marigold Garden*

work and "so boldly backed his opinion as to print a first edition of twenty thousand copies of a six-shilling book written and illustrated by a young lady who could hardly yet be said to have commanded anything like wide public approval." As usual he was right. *Under the Window*, published at the end of 1878 (the same year as Caldecott's first picture book, *The House That Jack Built*), was by far the finest thing she had done. Its success was immediate and Kate Greenaway's name became a household word not only in Great Britain but on the Continent and in America as well.

Success of Under the Window

Her verses were slight, yet they were sincere and gay, and leading critics of the time thought enough of the book to give it serious consideration. She was "deficient in technique," according to Austin Dobson, "but," he added, "she has the root of the matter in her." Lucky Kate Greenaway, to have had Edmund Evans' skill in interpreting her delicate line and color! In Spielmann and Layard's delightful life of Kate Greenaway, page 64, is a most interesting and detailed description of Edmund Evans' methods of work.

Two years after *Under the Window* was published the original drawings were exhibited at the Fine Arts Society and the art critics were loud in their praises, John Ruskin particularly; and to please John Ruskin was no easy matter. The book was later translated into German and French and hailed by German critics as "a small masterpiece of original stamp, out-and-out English but acceptable to the inhabitants great and small of other civilized nations." It is said that seventy thousand copies were sold in England and thirty thousand in foreign countries.

Meeting with Caldecott

It was about this time that Kate Greenaway and Randolph Caldecott met. They were rivals in the same field, but became delightfully friendly rivals for all the short span of Caldecott's life. A story is told of him that one morning while they were both visiting at the home of the Locker-Lampsons he came downstairs declaring he had lost all the power to work in his own style—everything he attempted came out Kate Greenaway. To prove it he produced a skit so in her style that she was greatly amused and kept it always.

Kate Greenaway's Birthday Book for Children, with verses for every day
of the year by Mrs. Sale Barker, came out in 1880; a chunky little volume which
you remember inspired Stevenson to write *A Child's Garden of Verses*—his own
recollections of childhood with his cousins in the garden of an old Scottish
manse.

The Christmas number of *Punch* for that year made K. G. (as her friends
called her) very happy; and small wonder, for Mr. Linley Sambourne made a
cartoon of "Mr. Punch at Home," invaded by a flight and crowd of artists,
writers and publishers of children's books—"Kate Greenaway, Caldecott, Stacy
Marks, Harrison Weir, Walter Crane and Mrs. Sale Barker; by Macmillan,
Marcus Ward, Bradbury, Edmund Routledge, De la Rue, Hildesheimer,
Duffield and Walker—all caterers for the little ones, for all children," says
Punch in the accompanying text, "are Mr. Punch's pets. Let's see what you've
got, and forthwith he gives the place of honour to Miss Kate Greenaway and
warmly congratulates her on her *Birthday Book for Children*, a most dainty
little work and a really happy thought for Christmas." No wonder Kate Greenaway was pleased. Many times after this she was mentioned in *Punch*, but "no
press notice ever gave her so much pleasure as this first one from the 'little
rascal of Fleet Street.'"

This same year she contributed to *Routledge's Christmas Annual* a delightful frontispiece of a little girl named Fanny. This was a rich number, with
Little Pandora by Walter Crane on one page and Caldecott's calico ponies in a
mad chase to carry their small riders to Banbury Cross on
another, not to mention an illustration by Gustave Doré and
stories by Mrs. Locker and Louisa Alcott—all to be had for
a shilling in those days.

In 1881 appeared *A Day in a Child's Life*, a
book of songs set to music by Myles B. Foster,
organist of the Foundling Hospital, and *Mother
Goose or the Old Nursery Rhymes*. This was one
of the daintiest things she ever did. The title page
with the baby thrown into a basket of roses was
always one of Ruskin's favorites, and Mrs. Allingham said, "No one can draw roses like Kate
Greenaway." The children in her books might
be charming, but the flowers scattered through

KATE GREENAWAY : *Under the Window*

the pages were always sure to be lovely. The critics compared her flower work to that of Van Huysum and Botticelli.

Out of the recollections of her own childish pleasure in the poems of Jane and Ann Taylor she illustrated a new edition and called it *Little Ann*. The book was dedicated to the four children of Frederick Locker.

Greenaway imitators

By this time K. G. was beginning to pay one of the penalties of popularity. She began to have many imitators at home and abroad, some of whom amused her, while others annoyed and disgusted her by plainly copying her badly. In Belgium, where her work was especially admired, not only were her books imitated, but illustrations were copied without permission on plates, handkerchiefs, vases and all sorts of objects which threatened to cheapen her work— the same thing likewise happening in France and Germany. One firm asked if it might name a children's shoe after her. As feet were always one of her weak points in drawing, this was rather amusing.

To her amazement, the style of costume she had adopted in her illustrating, just because it appealed to her as quaint and charming, was beginning to be the rage, and more than a few small boys and girls suffered by being arrayed à la Greenaway when it didn't suit their style.

Illustrating other people's text never appealed to her, and she avoided it as much as possible; nevertheless she was deluged with such requests, and at one time it seemed as if " every amateur who wrote a fairy story or a child's book or a book of verses, and wished to float it on the sea of her popularity, applied to her to illustrate it."

Personal characteristics

In spite of all this she went on quietly and modestly living her own life. Devotion to her work bound her up in a world of her own, which left her little thought or time or strength for the social world outside. Her family, her visits with her few intimate friends, her letters, her garden and her dog made up her entire recreation. In appearance she was the most un-Greenawayish sort of person imaginable. Perhaps it was because she was short and plump that she pictured all her women as tall and slim, while she who thought so much about clothes in her work was entirely indifferent to what she wore herself. Yet she was a domestic person and loved all the homely things about her. "Don't you like the sounds of things in the streets? " she once wrote to a friend. "They want to get up a society to suppress the noises—they asked me to belong and seemed to think it very funny when I said I liked them. I feel so cheerful when I hear an organ playing nice lively tunes. I love a band. I like seeing the Salvation

Army—marching along and singing. I like the sound of the muffin bell, for I seem again a little girl coming home from school in the winter afternoons. . . . I like the flower-sellers and the fruit stalls and the sound of church bells.

"So what could I say? I should not like silence always. It is often when I have had enough silence I go into the cheerful streets and find it a rest."

Her friendship with Frederick Locker (better known as Frederick Locker-Lampson) and his family, which lasted over a period of fifteen years, was most delightful. Through him she grew to know the Brownings and the Tennysons intimately. His letters to her teem with advice, encouragement and warning. "It has occurred to me," he writes in one dated November 28, 1882, "that you are about the only English artist who has ever been the fashion in France"; and when people feared her work might become "mannered" and advised her to change her style, he counter-advised, "Vary it but do not change it."

Frederick Locker, the Brownings and Tennysons

Ruskin took Kate Greenaway's art very seriously from the time he first saw the drawings for *Under the Window*. Later one of his lectures at Oxford

Ruskin's opinion

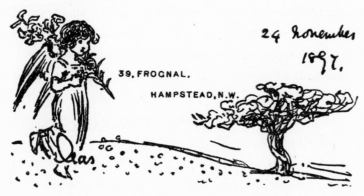

KATE GREENAWAY : *From a letter to Ruskin*

was devoted to "the place occupied by Miss Greenaway in modern art, and bestowed upon her praise without stint. 'Observe,' said he, 'that what this impressionable person *does* draw she draws as like as she can. It is true that the combination or composition of things is not what you see every day. You can't every day, for instance, see a baby thrown into a basket of roses; but when she has once pleasantly invented that arrangement for you, baby is as like baby and rose as like rose as she can possibly draw them. And the beauty of them is in being like, they are blissful just in the degree that they are natural; the fairy-land that she creates for you is not beyond the sky nor beneath the sea, but near you, even at your doors. She does but show you how to see it, and how to cherish.' "

For almost two years they corresponded; then in 1882 they met and from that time on until Ruskin's death in 1900 they were close friends and constant correspondents and Kate Greenaway often visited his home at Brantwood.

Ruskin might be lavish with his praise, but he was also a friend and an honest critic and never hesitated to point out her faults of drawing, which were many. Constantly he urged her to " draw things as they are." " When ARE YOU going to be GOOD and send me a study of anything from nature—the coal scuttle or the dustpan—or a towel on the clothes screen—or the hearthrug on the back of a chair? I'm very cruel, but here's half a year I've been waiting for a bit of Common sense—! "

He was concerned about her occasional lack of the sense of form. " Nobody wants anatomy, but you can't get on without form." " You ought to make notes of groups of children and more full faces than you-face-usually . . . and you should go to some watering place in August with fine sands, and draw no end of bare feet,—and—what else the Graces unveil in the train of the Sea Goddess." He asked with gentle irony for " flowers that won't look as if their leaves had been in curl papers all night "; for children for once without mittens; for " shoes that weren't quite so like mussel shells "; for " sun not like a drop of sealing wax "; for " girls that should be drawn with limbs as well as frocks." " You must give up drawing round hats. It's the hats that always save you from having to do a background—and I'm not going to be put off any more." He sent her lessons in perspective; he told her what pictures to copy at the National Gallery and, as we have seen, ordered her to the seaside to study ankles. " Practice," he said, " from things as they are, and you will find strength and ease and a new fancy and new spirit coming altogether."

Her letters to him were full of her work, of course, and of her love of gardens and flowers and trees—of her dog and her quiet social doings. She wrote daily and illustrated her letters with some of the most charming, spontaneous little sketches that ever slipped off of her broad-nibbed quill pen.

Kate Greenaway's Almanacks are among her best-remembered work. A full set of them today brings a high price. They began in 1883 and

KATE GREENAWAY:
Marigold Garden

with the exception of the year 1896 they appeared annually until 1897—charming, dainty little books which were printed in English, French and German.

In 1884 appeared *The Language of Flowers*. Half of the edition was sent to America, for at that time this country was as enthusiastic over her work as England. It contains some of her most exquisite flower drawing, though Ruskin vowed the flowers looked as if they had been " painted with starch and camomile tea," which remark daunted K. G. not at all. In fact, she seems to have accepted his praise and blame with equal gratitude; but being a person of strong opinions and a firm will, she continued to draw in her own way.

Kate Greenaway's Painting Book was made up of a collection of plates taken from her other books, and lucky were the children who had it to daub with their own brushes in vain imitation of her lovely colors. This was followed by the illustrations for *Mavor's English Spelling Book*. It seems strange to see her pictures without color, but the book contains some of her strongest work beautifully engraved in sepia. The capital letters were afterwards published separately as *Kate Greenaway's Alphabet*—a miniature book.

Perhaps the book that added most to her reputation these years was *Marigold Garden*, like *Under the Window* a picture book with her own verses. The cover alone is enough to make one long to open the gates of *Marigold Garden*. *Marigold Garden*

All this time Edmund Evans continued to be her " middleman between her and the public, that is to say, he was the engraver and responsible man in the enterprise, and it is impossible to estimate even approximately by how much her popularity had been enhanced by his excellent engraving and his usually excellent printing. Some idea of the extent of their partnership may be gathered from the fact that in the twenty years since 1878 there had been issued from the press in book form alone 932,100 copies of their joint productions. How far this enormous number might be increased by Christmas cards and independent designs for magazines it would be useless even to hazard a guess."

She and Ruskin were always planning to do some work together for children; he had all sorts of schemes for her, but the actual instances of their coöperation are slight. In 1885 she drew some cats to go with the extra verses which he made for the old rhyme of *Dame Wiggins of Lee and Her Seven Wonderful Cats*, first printed in 1823. They are just rough sketches because, as Ruskin explained in the preface to this new edition, " My rhymes do not ring like the real ones; and I would not allow Miss Greenaway to subdue the grace of her first sketches to the formality of the earlier work." *Dame Wiggins of Lee*

In the old nursery rhyme, *A Apple Pie*, K. G. let her humor and fancy go, and its pages are more spacious and lively than in many of her books. For once some of her boys and girls cut loose and threw things about.

This same year she made the drawings for Bret Harte's story, *The Queen of the Pirate Isles*. These pictures were treated in quite a realistic manner, were drawn with a stronger line than usual and were less quaint and decorative.

KATE GREENAWAY : *Pied Piper of Hamelin*

Together with Helen Allingham, Caroline Paterson and Harry Furniss, she made the illustrations for William Allingham's *Rhymes for Young Folks*. But

Pied Piper of Hamelin almost the high spot of her work came in 1888, with her pictures for Browning's *Pied Piper of Hamelin*.

Ruskin said it was the " grandest thing " she had ever done and wrote to her: " *The Piper* came by the II post . . . it is all as good and nice as can be, and you have really got through your rats with credit—and the Piper is sublime—and the children lovely. But I am more disappointed in the 'Paradise' than I expected to be—a *real* view of Hampstead ponds in Spring would have been more celestial to me than this customary flat of yours with trees stuck into it at regular distances.—And not a Peacock.—nor a flying horse!! "

The publishers certainly realized the selling worth of her name, for *Kate Greenaway's Book of Games* was brought out in 1889, the same year that she illustrated Beatrice Cresswell's *Royal Progress of King Pepito*, a little unwillingly, we imagine, for the drawings are weak, especially of the grown people. It was in 1889 that Kate Greenaway was elected a member of the Royal Institute of Painters in Water Color.

From 1892 to 1900 no new publication bore her name on its title page with the exception of the *Almanacks*. More and more she was devoting herself to individual pictures, large water colors and some oils, though she never enjoyed working in the later medium. During these years she held several highly successful exhibitions. She was designing bookplates too.

The Aubrey Beardsley school of art (the modern of her day) Kate Greenaway, as might be expected, neither understood nor liked. "When I state *my* likes and dislikes," she said, "they tell me I'm *not* modern, so I suppose I'm not—advanced."

In 1893, for the first time she did some work for an American magazine, *The Ladies' Home Journal*, a series of pen and ink sketches to illustrate some of Laura E. Richards' poems. *Sketches for Laura E. Richards' poems*

John Ruskin died in 1900, and his death brought great sadness to Kate Greenaway. Theirs had been an unusually rich friendship, and she missed him sadly. The last book she ever illustrated was done in this same year, *The April Baby's Book of Tunes* by the Countess von Arnim. These pictures were not engraved by Edmund Evans and show little of her old spirit.

For some time her own health had been steadily failing, although she allowed no hint of this to creep into her daily letters to her friend at Brantwood, which she continued to write long after he was able to reply. Less than a year after Ruskin's death, on November 6, 1901, Kate Greenaway passed away at Frognal, Hampstead.

Many tributes were paid to her memory, not only in England, but in America and France as well. The one we feel might have given her the most pleasure of all was in the Great Ormond Street Children's Hospital—a cot, *Tributes to her memory* endowed by her friends as a fitting memorial to one " who has filled so distinc- tive a place in the world of art, and whose charming treatment of child life endeared her to every home in the Empire."

Life of Kate   The record of her life and work has been beautifully presented by M. H. *Greenaway by*   Spielmann and G. S. Layard in a book called *Kate Greenaway*. It contains her *Spielmann and* *Layard*   childhood recollections of Rolleston, many unpublished pictures privately owned, her correspondence with Ruskin, and other fine bits—a veritable treas- ure trove for the lovers of her art.

In 1921 a collection of Kate Greenaway pictures from originals presented by her to John Ruskin and other personal friends was published in beautiful form by Warne with an appreciation written by H. M. Cundall, I.S., F.S.A. In the front is her portrait taken by a daughter of Edmund Evans in 1895.

No illustrator of children's books of the last generation holds quite the place of Kate Greenaway. The very sight of her little *Almanacks* and picture books brings forth all manner of pleasant recollections from those who pos- sessed them in their own childhood and are eager to have their own children

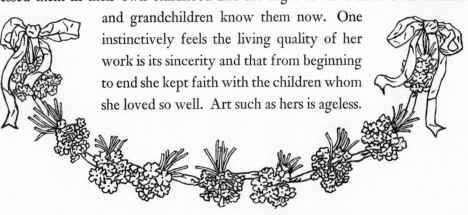

and grandchildren know them now. One instinctively feels the living quality of her work is its sincerity and that from beginning to end she kept faith with the children whom she loved so well. Art such as hers is ageless.

KATE GREENAWAY : *Marigold Garden*

III. Early American Illustration

BERTHA E. MAHONY

ALEXANDER ANDERSON : *Mother Goose's Melodies*

EDWIN A. ABBEY: *The Deserted Village*

Early American Illustration

IN the early days of the American colonies books were largely imported from England. By 1760 Hugh Gaine of New York—printer, publisher, patent medicine seller and employment agent—was importing nearly all of John Newbery's juvenile books then available. But by 1762 he had begun to do his own reprinting of them. Isaiah Thomas of Worcester also imported the Newbery books and copied them. In 1785 Thomas published the first American Mother Goose, and in 1787 an edition of *Little Goody Two-Shoes*, with a frontispiece which looks like the work of Bewick, and has sometimes been credited to him, but probably was done " after " that famous artist. This was not the first edition of *Goody Two-Shoes* to be published in America for that had been brought out in 1775 by Hugh Gaine.

Publishers of the early years, Hugh Gaine, Isaiah Thomas

The last decade of the eighteenth century is important because it was then that Alexander Anderson, called the " father of wood engraving in America," came into note. A New York physician, entirely self-taught in drawing and engraving, he worked first in type-metal. Then he began to experiment in the so-called Bewick white line style. To distinguish it from woodcutting, wood engraving was the term used for the method which employed the end of the wood block and required the use of the graver rather than the knife. Anderson's first book of consequence in this method was *The Looking-Glass for the Mind; or, Intellectual Mirror*, published by W. Durell of New York in 1775, with thirty-seven cuts, " elegantly engraved " after John Bewick.

Alexander Anderson, the American Bewick

Anderson remained the leading wood engraver during the better part of the first half of the nineteenth century, the only other engravers of that time who approached him " in clarity of line or in the integrity of their craftsmanship " being his pupil, John Hall, and Joseph A. Adams, according to Mr. Sinclair Hamilton, the collector of early American illustrated books. Through Anderson and his pupils, the Bewick white line method of wood engraving, " destined to revolutionize book illustration," gradually spread in America.

On December 23, 1823, there appeared anonymously in the Troy (New

A Visit from St. Nicholas

York) *Sentinel* a Christmas ballad entitled "A Visit from St. Nicholas." This had been written a year previously by Clement Clarke Moore for his own family. Here was a gaily imaginative story which brought the Dutch legendary patron of children to American children on Christmas Eve with gifts piled high on his sleigh drawn by " eight tiny reindeer," the whole magic equipage entering homes by way of the chimney. Coming at a time when literature for children was lacking in fun and merriment, but heavy with teaching and moralizing, these verses told their story without a suggestion of either. Proof of children's joy in *A Visit to St. Nicholas* may be had by looking up some of its many illustrators as listed on page 491 in A Bibliography of Authors in this volume.

The Peter Parleys

In 1827 Samuel Goodrich published his *Tales of Peter Parley about America.* This book was followed by many other volumes, often illustrated from the stock woodcuts publishers had on hand. In England, while most of the volumes issued by the " pretenders " were illustrated in the same way, in the best can be found good work by Sir John Gilbert, William Harvey, Sam Williams, Charles Keene and even some drawings signed by George and Robert Cruikshank.

WILLIAM CROOME :
Peter Parley's Christmas Tales

Illustration essentially American in character was slow to develop with us until 1840, but in the thirty years from 1840 to 1870 it advanced to a point of distinction. Mr. F. J. Harvey Darton says that in the '40's between forty and fifty per cent of all books published in America for children were English productions. There was plenty of piracy here, as well as in England, where there were six pseudo " Peter Parleys."

Jacob Abbott's " Rollo " books, beginning in 1834, followers in type of the Peter Parley Books, were illustrated but often with no

The Rollo Books

credit given to the artists. In Abbott's later series, *Rollo's Tour in Europe*, in ten volumes, about half the volumes were signed by Doepler, McLenan and A. Waud. His Franconia Stories, 1850-53, had pictures which give a good idea of interiors and costumes of the day, but who made them we do not know. There were no pictures in Susan Warner's *Wide, Wide World,* 1851, or in its sequel, *Queechy,* 1852. Later editions were illustrated by well-known artists.

However, Hawthorne's *Wonder Book for Girls and Boys,* published by Ticknor, Reed and Fields in Boston, in 1852, had drawings by Hammatt Billings, an architect, and they are credited to him in the book. Christopher P. Cranch's two books—*The Last of the Huggermuggers* and *Kobboltozo*, published by Mayhew and Baker, Boston, 1860 and '61—were illustrated by the author.

In the 1840's America's best-known early illustrator came into note with *F. O. C. Darley* his efforts to interpret American humor of his period. This was Felix Octavius Darley, and his first book illustrations in the medium of wood engraving are probably those which appeared in *Peter Ploddy and Other Oddities* by Joseph C. Neal (Carey & Hart, Philadelphia, 1844). These drawings were engraved by William Croome, a name of some importance in early American illustration. William Croome was born thirty years before Darley and continued to work into the '50's, illustrating many children's books. He engraved a number of Darley's drawings and in John Frost's *History of the United States*, 1843-44, there were drawings by both Darley and Croome.

Darley came into his own with his drawings for Washington Irving's *Sketch Book* and *Rip Van Winkle*, 1848, and for Irving's *Knickerbocker's History of New York* and *Tales of a Traveller*, both 1850. Darley's work showed some influence of Cruikshank. He did a tremendous amount, much of which can be traced through Miss Latimer's bibliographies; the full picture of his adult work can be had from Theodore Bolton's excellent *American Book Illustrators*. It is interesting to know that Darley is collected today by James Daugherty.

In 1846, *Harper's Bible* appeared with many of its drawings by John G. Chapman. In 1853, the *Potiphar Papers* appeared with pictures by Augustus *Augustus* Hoppin. He was a social satirist somewhat like Du Maurier in his style, and he *Hoppin* also illustrated Mrs. A. D. T. Whitney's *Summer in Leslie Goldthwaite's Life*, Dr. Holmes's *Autocrat of the Breakfast Table*, Howells' *Their Wedding Journey*, as well as William Allen Butler's poem of Flora McFlimsey who had absolutely "Nothing to Wear," when that poem appeared in *Harper's Monthly*.

Another name connected with the American school of illustration in the *John McLenan* middle of the nineteenth century is that of John McLenan, who illustrated American editions of Dickens' *Tale of Two Cities* and *Great Expectations* and Wilkie Collins' *Woman in White*.

In 1859 one of the greatest of American illustrators—Winslow Homer— *Winslow* designed the title page of a series of children's books which came out under the *Homer* title, *The Percy Family*, published in Boston by Andrew F. Graves. This was Winslow Homer's first appearance in a book. His first magazine drawing appeared in Ballou's *Pictorial Drawing Room Companion* in 1857, but Mr. Sinclair

THOMAS NAST : *Little Prudy*

AUGUSTUS HOPPIN : *Our Young Folks, December 1866*

Hamilton says, " His finest work came out in *Harper's Weekly* and *Every Saturday*, culminating in 1873 and 1874 in his Gloucester series and cuts such as ' Waiting for a Bite ' and ' Raid on a Sand-Swallow Colony.' " " These drawings," Mr. Hamilton writes, " close to the soil, essentially American in every line, depict the American scene of that day in a way which no other contemporary illustrator approached. Homer's book illustrations never equaled the work he did for these magazines." Mr. Hamilton also calls attention to Frank Jewett Mather, Jr.'s, presentation of the subject of Winslow Homer as

E. B. BENSELL : *St. Nicholas, March 1885*

book illustrator in an article for the November, 1939, *Princeton University Library Chronicle*, which may be consulted in public and college and university libraries, although the edition is exhausted.

Certain magazines for children came into existence from 1865 to 1879 and had great influence upon American illustration, particularly for children. Ticknor and Fields, who published the *Atlantic Monthly*, brought out in January, 1865, the first number of *Our Young Folks*, under the editorship of John T. Trowbridge, Gail Hamilton and Lucy Larcom, all with established reputations in letters. Thomas Bailey Aldrich's *Story of a Bad Boy*, Lucretia Hale's *Peterkin Papers*, Dickens' *Magic Fishbone*, Mrs. Diaz's *William Henry Letters* and Mrs. Whitney's *We Girls*—are just a few of the now famous books which appeared first in *Our Young Folks*. "All that a good modern magazine can offer had been included," wrote Alice M. Jordan in *The Horn Book*. " For their day the illustrations were worthy of the text, representative work of such artists as Winslow Homer, John Gilbert and H. L. Stephens." Just eight years later, in 1873, *Our Young Folks* was sold to Scribner & Company and absorbed by the still more famous *St. Nicholas*, under the editorship of Mary Mapes Dodge, with Frank Stockton as Associate Editor. Later, a new partnership known as The

Our Young Folks

Century Company, having bought out Charles Scribner's interest, became the publisher of *St. Nicholas* from 1881 through 1930.

Riverside Magazine

Another magazine bequeathed a valuable tradition to *St. Nicholas*. Horace Scudder, a member of the publishing house of Hurd and Houghton, predecessors of Houghton, Mifflin Company, started in 1867 and conducted for just four years *The Riverside Magazine for Young People*. Into his magazine he introduced so new a thing as a series of articles on "Books for Young People." At that time criticism of children's books did not exist. Illustrations for *The Riverside Magazine* during 1867 included the names of John La Farge, Thomas Nast, Winslow Homer, E. B. Bensell, H. L. Stephens and F. O. C. Darley. Mr. Scudder said, "I did my best to obtain pictures of child life from painters who were not mere professional book illustrators. It was only now and then that I was able to obtain any simple, unaffected design, showing an understanding of a child's face and figure." Some of the *Riverside's* authors and illustrators went over to *St. Nicholas* and Horace Scudder subscribed to the new magazine for his daughter and followed its development with the greatest interest.

Harper's Young People

Still another magazine of importance was *Harper's Young People*, which was started by Harper and Brothers in 1879 and continued until 1899, changing its name in 1894 to *Harper's Round Table*. The illustrations were considered one of the most important features. Howard Pyle's *Pepper and Salt* and *Wonder Clock* appeared first in *Harper's Young People*. Caldecott's illustrations for *The Queen of Hearts* were published in its pages without color, and work by Edwin Abbey, Sol Eytinge, J. T. McCutcheon, and W. A. Rogers, among others.

St. Nicholas

Only a thorough examination of *St. Nicholas* from its first issue in November, 1873, to the time of Mrs. Dodge's death in 1905 and continuing through William Fayal Clarke's editorship ending in 1927, would reveal all that this magazine meant to the history and development of illustration for children in America.

Horace Scudder did a kind of critical writing about children's books which is much needed from men of letters today. And so did Edmund Lester Pearson. I should hate to confess how many times during the last five years I have read Mr. Pearson's "Wizards and Enchanters" chapter in his now out-of-print volume, *Books in Black and Red*. There he reviews *St. Nicholas* as he read and enjoyed it during his boyhood years, 1880 to 1887.

Some of Frank Stockton's best tales were then appearing—"The Floating

WINSLOW HOMER: *Our Young Folks, June 1867*

Up from broidery frame and book
The Princess lifted a longing look

REGINALD BIRCH : *St. Nicholas, November 1884*

Prince," "How the Aristocrats Sailed Away" and "The Castle of Bim." These stories were illustrated—some by E. B. Bensell and some by Reginald Birch. *Early work of Reginald Birch and E. B. Bensell* This is somewhat earlier work of Reginald Birch than his drawings for *Little Lord Fauntleroy*. Bensell also illustrated Charles Carryl's *Davy and the Goblin* and drew "the immortal picture of the Cockalorum." Reginald Birch illustrated Charles Carryl's second book, *The Admiral's Caravan*, which also appeared first in *St. Nicholas* in 1891–92.

"It was an age of excellent nonsense verse; not so much talk was made about it as at a later date, but more of it was written. The pages of *St. Nicholas* were full of it," Mr. Pearson writes, and sets down some of his favorites, those about "The Carnivoristicous Ounce" and

> There was once an Ichthyosaurus,
> Who lived when the earth was all porous,
>   But he fainted with shame
>   When he first heard his name,
> And departed a long time before us.

J. G. Francis He speaks of J. G. Francis' *Book of Cheerful Cats*, a nonsense classic, and his later *Aztec Fragments*, with its curious old Mexican pictures. He remembered for years a story by S. A. Shields, "Fairy Wishes, Nowadays," in *St. Nicholas*, because of its pictures by A. B. Frost. He was delighted with the nonsense verses by Laura E. Richards, "who does not suffer by comparison with Edward Lear." Mr. Pearson owned as a boy the long-out-of-print *Sketches and Scraps* by Mrs. Richards, containing "The Seven Little Tigers and Their Aged Cook," with pictures by her husband, Henry Richards. "Few works of art," wrote Mr.   *Henry Richards* Pearson, "are so familiar to me as every detail of these, from the heavily dyed beard on the servitor of Bobbily Boo, the king so free,

> He used to drink the Mango Tea
> > Mango Tea and Coffee too,
> He drank them both till his nose turned blue.

to the monocle in the eye of the Fourth Turk, who is coming out to battle with Ponsonby Perks." There was also the Frog, who lived in a bog, on the banks of Lake Okeefinokee, but the *chef-d'œuvre* is probably

> The tale of the little Cossack,
> > Who lived by the river Don.
> He sat on a sea-green hassock,
> > And his grandfather's name was John.

J. G. FRANCIS : *Book of Cheerful Cats*

One would like to know more of E. B. Bensell and J. G. Francis, but information seems to be non-existent. Before leaving the later years of the nineteenth century to Mr. Lawson, there are two more illustrators who should be mentioned. Thomas Nast, who was among the illustrators of *The Riverside Magazine*, made pictures in 1866 for the first edition of Mary Mapes Dodge's *Hans Brinker*. He illustrated a number of children's books, including *Robinson Crusoe* and *A Visit from St. Nicholas*. He was a master of caricature and contributed cartoons now famous to *Harper's Weekly*, cartoons which attacked the Tweed Ring and other corruption with excoriating line. He also made pictures for a number of the *Little Prudy* books and *Dotty Dimple at Home*— a far cry indeed from his cartoons. Thomas Nast was indebted in his early years to another artist whose name will be found in Miss Latimer's bibliographies—Sol Eytinge.

E. W. Kemble, in a delightful article in *The Colophon*, for February 1930, wrote that when Thomas Nast " reigned supreme as the master cartoonist of the country," and the *Daily Graphic* in 1881 was the only illustrated daily in New York, he himself was a budding cartoonist on that paper. Newspapers generally had not begun to publish pictures. Then the old *Life* came along. It was his drawing for *Life* of a small boy being stung by a bee which made Mark Twain want Kemble as the illustrator for *Huckleberry Finn* (1885). Kemble was paid two thousand dollars for his drawings for that book.

In the same article Kemble reported of himself that as a boy he had always liked to draw at night, when his school work was done, soldiers, Indians and long processions of circus parades. These he would cut out with scissors and place on a seam in the carpet, " where they would stretch from wall to wall, and woe betide any one who disarranged this imposing aggregation." After he had finished school and was working at an accounting job in the Western Union Telegraph Company, he took four small comic drawings into Harper and Brothers, at his father's suggestion. Mr. Charles Parsons, the art director, beloved of many famous artists, received them and asked young Kemble to call again in a few days. When Kemble went back to ask timidly for the drawings, Mr. Parsons said, " You don't want to take them all home with you, do you? " At the same time he passed Kemble a slip to present to the cashier. He was paid seventy dollars and that night after work, for fear of being robbed on bus or street car, he walked all the way home from Vesey to Forty-Third Street, and the following week resigned his work with the Western Union to become a staff artist on the *Daily Graphic*.

E. W. KEMBLE: *Adventures of Huckleberry Finn*

Mr. Kemble gives an interesting description of a newspaper art department at that time. "A spacious loft on the top floor of the plant served as the studio. Some ten budding geniuses were seated at tables where their shares in the pictorial features were given them by the art director. Each man was more or less a specialist in his particular line. Gray Parker did horses and social events. Cusaks, a Spaniard, did any old thing and sang snatches from *Carmen* while doing it. Zenope, a Turk, did portraits and delivered monologues of children reciting bits from their Sunday School lessons. C. V. Taylor, long and lanky, with spreading side-whiskers, did cartoons and street scenes. I was cartoonist and character artist. George B. Lucks was a contributor and did wonderful song and dance acts for us whenever he paid a visit to the sanctum. If the West Point cadets were to parade the following day, a full-page spread had to be done the day before. The reviewing stand was put in by one man, the cadets drawn by the military genius, the mayor and his guests inserted by the portrait man, and then the whole masterpiece was pieced together and made ready for the photographer in an adjoining room. The thing that always bothered us was the weather forecast."

Edwin A. Abbey   In *The Colophon* for 1931 (Part VI), W. A. Rogers, the illustrator of *Toby Tyler*, who was working in Harper's art department when Edwin Abbey was there, relates the following: " While Abbey was still occupying a little hutch in the art department at Franklin Square, Fletcher Harper, Jr., used to come up nearly every day to consult with Mr. Parsons about pictures. Mr. Harper was an elderly, fine-looking man who always wore a silk hat and was immaculate in his dress and extremely dignified in manner. We all liked him. Now Abbey's little hutch was the first one inside the wicket gate at the entrance to the department. Somebody once said that ' when Abbey worked he was like a little demon shovelling coal '; then when the tension was at its highest point, something had to give; and up he would jump from his drawing board, stand on his head or turn a half dozen cart-wheels down the art department floor. One day Abbey had rigged up a trapeze from a beam overhead and was busily skinning the cat when Fletcher Harper, Jr., walked in underneath him. A beautiful silk hat forthwith sailed through the air, caromed on Dory Davis's drawing board and collapsed against the farther wall."

Homer's woodblocks   Mr. Rogers has interesting things to say of another great artist. " When Abbey came to Harper's in the early '70's, American illustration was in the doldrums. The slushy school of drawing was in vogue." Most illustrators were

A. B. FROST : *St. Nicholas, January 1885*

C. S. REINHART : *Farm Ballads*

following an easy convention—"with one solitary and glorious exception, a man who only occasionally made a drawing for *Harper's Weekly*—Winslow Homer." Then Mr. Rogers describes one of the very few drawings made by Homer on wood blocks at that time. "It was treated much in the manner of Hiroshigi, although I greatly doubt if Homer had, at that day, ever seen a Hiroshigi print. The picture presented a hillside with two figures and a tree. The color of a boxwood block is beautiful, mellow and warm. White was usually rubbed over it before a drawing was begun, but Homer used the natural color of the wood to produce his highest gray tone. One or two flat washes, exactly the right depth, some bald outlines, a few touches of white and the picture was done. Every vital fact was there and nothing else."

Charles Parsons, Art Director and artists' friend

But, Mr. Rogers continues, while Abbey and others were not slow to learn from Winslow Homer, the slushy school died hard and scathing articles of criticism of Abbey's drawings were written in the newspapers and journals. Mr. Parsons once showed Mr. Rogers a package of hundreds of letters sent in to Henry Mills Alden, protesting against the "new style of drawing." "But Mr. Parsons was always the man of vision—the most practical old dreamer I ever knew. He saw far ahead. He realized that, given men of talent, send them to nature for their inspiration and you are sure to get from each one a distillation of his own. This was Charles Parsons' problem. How he solved it almost to perfection in that stuffy old art department on Franklin Square is answered by five names: Abbey, Reinhart, Smedley, Pyle and Frost."

Except for an occasional chapter, such as Frank Weitenkampf's on "The Illustrators" in his *American Graphic Arts*, there are no books on the subject of early American illustration. It has literally to be dug out of magazines, early books, art columns of newspapers, and exhibition catalogues. Here is a long and wonderfully pleasant and rewarding study for more than one person. Miss Latimer has supplied the names to trace in such a study.

For a considerable amount of the information contained in this survey, I am indebted to Mr. Sinclair Hamilton's article on "Early American Illustration" in the *Princeton University Library Chronicle* for April, 1945. Mr. Hamilton's article is based upon his own collection which he has carried to about the year 1870.

IV. Howard Pyle and His Times

ROBERT LAWSON

HOWARD PYLE : *Pepper and Salt*

HOWARD PYLE : *The Wonder Clock*

Howard Pyle and His Times

Almost seventy years ago, back in 1877, many American children going through their latest copies of *St. Nicholas* discovered some unpretentious little fables with illustrations quite different from those to which they were accustomed. These drawings had a simplicity, a strong, almost heavy line, a quaint, kindly humor quite rare in those days when soft insipidity was considered the only proper fare for children. They were signed with a modest "H. P." *H. P. and St. Nicholas*

None of these children could know then that thirty and more years later, when they had reached middle age, they would still be enjoying fresh illustrations by this same artist, whose initials, by that time, would be one of the most honored signatures in all American illustration. Although they were doubtless pleased by the pictures themselves, they could not realize that they were sharing an historic moment, for these small efforts marked the beginning of a remarkable career and a glorious era.

Howard Pyle was to become more than a great illustrator; he was to become an American institution. He was to stand as a symbol of all that is fine and honest and good in the art of illustration. He was a one-man movement which would exert an incalculable influence on the whole course of illustration in this country. *Pyle's influence on illustration in America*

He has been dead for thirty-five years now, but his spirit shines in much of the best illustration of today, not only in the work of his pupils and their pupils, but in the work of all those who have felt and admired (and who has not?) his high integrity of purpose, his tremendous knowledge and skill. No illustrator worthy of the name can look on the work of Howard Pyle and then do careless or insincere work himself without feeling a sense of personal reproach, a sense of shame that he has failed this good and honest master. His presence is in every decent studio; inspiring, encouraging, helpful, corrective, or justly wrathful.

And in the minds and hearts of innumerable others there are still dreams and visions of color and romance, glimpses of another world of beauty and chivalry, planted there long ago by the incomparable work of this simple, sincere craftsman.

Illustration in the '70s

Illustration in America in 1877 was most uneven and not of a very high standard. Considering that standards and tastes in architecture, decoration, sculpture, painting and much of the literature were, at that time, dreadfully low or nonexistent, illustration does not compare so badly with the other arts. Still, illustration as a profession in itself scarcely existed.

F. O. C. Darley

There was just one exception to this general rule of mediocrity: Felix Octavius Carr Darley. He alone stands out as a truly talented, vigorous, and versatile illustrator. His long and prolific career deserves a chapter of its own, much of his work comparing favorably with that of any of our best illustrators of any period. However, even he at times compromised with the demands of editors and public of the day for slick elegance and sentimentality and some of his illustrations have a Godey-esque quality quite unworthy of his fine talent.

Starting his career about the middle of the century with a brilliant series of illustrations for Washington Irving's Catskill legends, Darley for many years, almost alone, carried the banner of good illustration, to lay it down only when Howard Pyle and the newer generation arrived on the scene in the seventies.

Except for Darley, most of the pictures in our books and magazines were the work of undistinguished hack engravers. True, a few really fine illustrations appeared, but these were done by men who were primarily painters, such artists as Abbey, La Farge, Vedder or Winslow Homer. These men could occasionally be prevailed upon to do a few illustrations for a book or a magazine feature, but their real interest lay in the painting field. The reproductive methods of the day, mostly wood engraving, failed to do true justice to these paintings, skilled though the engravers were, so results were seldom thoroughly satisfying.

Ideals of illustration before Pyle

Moreover, the ideals of illustration, as of painting, were then far different from the era of free and vigorous expressiveness which the advent of Howard Pyle and a few others ushered in. Most of our artists were trained in the studios of Europe where finish and a meticulous copying of the posed model were primary requirements. Editors demanded an exact and photographic rendition of every detail, insisting far more on technical perfection and "elegance" than on character, action or a true understanding of the subject. On the whole, our illustration, like much of our culture, was chiefly a weak imitation of the

European fashion—stilted, lifeless and completely unkeyed to the vigorous life of our young nation.

As for children's illustrators, as we think of them now, there were prac- *Lack of* tically none. The better children's books were largely foreign importations, *children's* principally English. Here we produced a few crudely embellished readers and *illustrators* *Mother Gooses* for the very young, and for those a little older an assortment of sickeningly moral or saccharine tomes designed to uplift and edify. These were mere reflections of the grown-up tastes in a day when a willow weeping over a tombstone was the universal theme of art and literature. A day when children, through books, were exhorted to revere their parents as the godheads of all wisdom and justice; were taught that pain, tribulation, repentance and an early but lingering death from a " wasting disease " were the normal lot of the young. Pets in art, especially birds, were born only *Era of elegance* to die and afford " touching " and " elegant " subjects for the artists' brush. The beauties of nature existed, apparently, merely to illustrate how soon the leaf withers and the brightest flower fades.

Healthy, robust young ones who rebelled at this inevitable cradle-to-sick-bed-to-grave diet often sought refuge in the books of their elders where they found much the same fare, but with at least some variety and change of scene. Here they could gaze at gloomy engravings of the glory that was Greece and *Scenes of gloom* the grandeur that was Rome, at the ivy-draped towers and mossy manor houses of *Picturesque Europe and the British Isles*. " Picturesqueness " and decay seemed synonymous: even the beauty spots of our young, raw country— Niagara Falls, Delaware Water Gap, the Rockies or the Erie Canal—were pictured brooding under leaden skies or a watery moon.

For lighter entertainment children could seek out their mothers' latest copies of *Peterson's Magazine* or *Godey's Lady's Book* and see themselves depicted as smirking little darlings " In a Pout " or " At the Well " or " Playing Doctor." They could wonder why unhappy lovers seemed always parting at stiles or hurling themselves into uninviting bodies of water. Hardier souls might, if allowed, delve into the *Pictorial History of the Great Rebellion* in which, apparently, all battles were fought among moss-grown trees or under that same watery moon, and all battlefields by nightfall had acquired the same fungoid picturesqueness that enwrapped " Heidelberg by Moonlight " or " The Cottage by the Rill."

They might also, if allowed *Harper's Weekly* or *Frank Leslie's Illustrated*

HOWARD PYLE : *Otto of the Silver Hand*

Newspaper, see pictured the bitter intolerance and vicious political controversies that fermented under this cultural veneer of moss-grown and moonlit sentimentality.

It is small wonder that the clean-cut, healthy, joyous work of Howard Pyle came to the children of the late seventies like a fresh breeze flooding a fetid sickroom. *Enter Howard Pyle*

Here was " Picturesque Europe " indeed, but how different! Here were castles, not moss-hung but lived in, spacious, clean; deep-embrasured mullioned windows, massive furniture, rich hangings, moats and drawbridges that worked. Here were towers, not buried in ivy and watery moonlight, but soaring breathlessly into clear and sparkling skies; battered stout balconies and belfries, tiled roofs where pigeons strutted joyfully in the sun.

Here stone-paved courtyards were clean swept, filled with activity. Dogs rollicked, scullions chatted, men-at-arms furbished their weapons. In the surrounding gardens straw beehives stood in orderly rows beneath stout oak shelters. Trees were all about—and such trees! No dreary weeping willows these, nor moss-hung churchyard relics. These trees were vigorous, alive, clad in clean-cut leaves, gay with blossoms or laden with buxom apples or pears.

The villages too were quaint and picturesque, but not with the gloomy picturesqueness of mold and decay. Their crooked tile roofs glittered in the sun. *Gaiety, light and action* Gay curtains and blossoming plants brightened the windows, smoke rose from the chimneys, people bustled in the streets. You could pick out the house you'd like to live in, not die in (at an early age). And always on the hill near the village were the white towers and walls of the great castle, smiling down protectingly.

In this cheery country were no beribboned pug dogs or fat, overstuffed ponies (" Riding the Pony "), nor deceased canaries (" The Dead Bird "). Here were massive, spirited war horses, smart, grinning foxes, mischievous jackdaws. Here gay hares skipped nimbly out of harm's way, birds sang and swirled about the belfries.

And the people! Here were no sanctimonious little prigs with their " wasting diseases "; these were stout, jolly, healthy people. The heroes were handsome muscular princes or clever peasant lads; their heroines golden-haired princesses or well-fed goosegirls. Kings and Queens were human—querulous, futile, or impressively regal. Gorgeously caparisoned knights battled in flower-spangled meadows.

Stiles there were aplenty, but never draped with dreary lovers; on these stiles minstrels sang gay roundelays, gooseherds conversed with rabbits or foxes. Even the Devil appeared frequently, but not as that amorphous threatening menace that blighted the lives and reason of so many Victorian children. *This* Devil was a dapper, handsomely appareled gentleman, clever and unscrupulous yes, but easily outwitted and frustrated by the still cleverer ploughboy hero or his good wife. And the jolly, earthy Men of God; priests, abbots, friars and saints! Stout, jolly, bearded fellows, as handy with staff or cudgel as with the ale mug; ready to drub a villain or perform a miracle with equal good humor. How different from the thin-whiskered, pasty purveyors of gloom, vengeance, repentance and the-wrath-to-come to whom children were accustomed both in real life and in their literature.

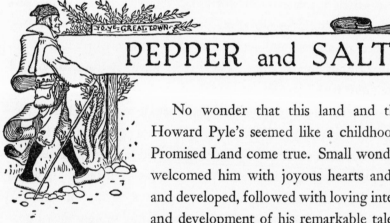

HOWARD PYLE:
Pepper and Salt

No wonder that this land and these people of Howard Pyle's seemed like a childhood vision of the Promised Land come true. Small wonder that children welcomed him with joyous hearts and, as they grew and developed, followed with loving interest the growth and development of his remarkable talent. For young children who discovered these first drawings were privileged to grow up for the next thirty-odd years almost hand in hand with their most beloved illustrator. The maturing of his work kept pace with their broadening horizons.

Pyle's early work
From the jolly young beginnings of *Pepper and Salt* and *The Wonder Clock* he led them into the golden land of Arthurian legend, into the green fastnesses of Sherwood Forest, where Robin Hood and Friar Tuck and Little John hunted the King's deer and baffled the Sheriff of Nottingham. The mysteries and glories of mediæval knighthood he opened to them in *Men of Iron*, the life of the German robber barons in the beautiful *Otto of the Silver Hand*. Soon they had grown up and were reveling in the gloriously colorful pageant that Howard Pyle's now fully-blossomed genius spread before them.

Knights, pirates and Indians, patriots and redcoats, kings, beggars, presidents and tailors, galleons and prairie schooners, farmers and frontiersmen poured from his prodigal easel in a flood tide. All this these now grown-up children were to enjoy until they were well into middle age, and in their old age many of them now turn back to these rich masterpieces for a nostalgic glimpse of a great era in illustration.

Almost simultaneously with the advent of Howard Pyle there came, for some reason, a sudden upsurge in our illustration; a new vigor, a healthy exuberance, truly American. The day of the graveyard, the parting lovers and the withering flower was done. In its stead burst out the new and living art of a more honest generation. In place of the meticulous copying of posed models we had the active, violent, roistering cowboys of Frederick Remington, drawn *Frederick* with complete freedom and vigor; with the raw, glaring sunshine of desert and *Remington* mountain, sweating, sinewy cowponies, blue-clad cavalrymen, paint-daubed Indians. Remington was but the forerunner of a great host of followers, some good, some bad, who were to awaken Americans to the fact that here in the West of our great country was a picturesqueness far more interesting than crumbling Colosseums and rotting lich gates. Though not strictly a " children's illustrator," Remington's work was hailed with joy by every boy who had graduated from lace collars and sailor suits.

The everlastingly ailing pets of former days were now supplanted by the *A. B. Frost* refreshingly active Brer Rabbit and Brer Fox of A. B. Frost. Joel Chandler Harris' *Uncle Remus* as illustrated by Frost is one of those rare cases of a book in which text and illustrations are both so delightful and so perfectly suited one to the other that it is impossible to consider either separately. Not only did Frost—who, by the way, was Howard Pyle's lifelong friend and best man at his wedding—manage to catch all the subtleties of the animals' varied personalities in his magnificently accurate drawings, but every background, no matter how slight, has the flavor of the locality to an amazing degree. I have heard it said by people who knew Joel Chandler Harris and were raised in his countryside that they could almost guarantee to walk to any spot shown in any of the drawings. They have marveled at the skill with which an illustrator, in a few lines, by the drawing of but one bush or a few feet of roadside, could depict a locality so clearly that it could never be mistaken for any other section of the country. But that was the way Frost did things.

One odd, though perfectly understandable thing, about this close and long

The humor of Pyle and Frost

friendship of A. B. Frost and Howard Pyle, is their complete difference, as far as work was concerned, on the point of humor. Pyle's work never gives any indication that he possessed a vestige of a sense of humor; Frost's work simply drips with it. This admiration and appreciation of opposites, of course, often makes for great friendships and doubtless had a part in this one, aided by the fact that they were both sincere and honest workers. Nevertheless, the difference is still there and it seems surprising that Howard Pyle, lacking in the important element of humor, could have achieved the great triumphs of understanding that his work always exhibits. It is not inconceivable that his friendship with Frost helped to supply him with some of this most necessary ingredient to all thorough understanding.

This is not to imply that Howard Pyle was not a jolly and cordial person; he was that and more, beloved by all who came in contact with him. In his work, especially his earlier work for children, there is a delightful atmosphere of good-natured fun and whimsicality, of pleasantly paternal benevolence and good will. But the humor is always conscious. Even in his personal letters his humor is heavy-handed and conscientiously worked at; well-meant, kindly, pleasant—but ponderous.

Frost's humor, on the other hand, was completely natural and pervaded every line and brush-stroke of his drawings; moreover it was a humor typically American, containing a large percentage of satire and keen observation. The very hang of Brer Rabbit's trousers, the messy look of Brer Bear's vest are magnificent caricatures of the usual clothing of the Southern rustic of that day.

There is, of course, the question of whether, strictly speaking, A. B. Frost was a "children's illustrator" and this must be decided by those more interested in strictly speaking. Certainly in his illustrations for *Uncle Remus* he produced one of the most beloved of our children's books, and certainly whole generations of children and adults have writhed with joy over "Our Cat Ate Rat Poison" and his delightful drawings of rustic life which were not done for children at all. Certainly he, Kemble and Remington, all adult illustrators, did a tremendous amount to broaden the horizons of young Americans. Their drawings were more looked-at and more admired by more children than the work of many who worked exclusively for children, so their exact labeling really does not matter.

Abbey's influence

Another friend whose influence seems to appear briefly in Howard Pyle's work was Abbey. In *Pepper and Salt* there appear two or three drawings which have always puzzled me, they are so completely unlike Pyle's usual work. They are weak, thin, scratchy, scattered—in short, terrible. Then I read in some of H. P.'s letters to his mother of his great admiration, almost envy, of his friend Abbey's delicate and refined draughtsmanship.

This, of course, is pure and unimportant speculation, but it seems extremely possible that these two or three unexplainably bad drawings were an unfortunately enthusiastic impulse on Pyle's part to emulate the " delicacy and refinement " of Abbey's work. If so, it was a most unhappy impulse and one which never appears again.

In addition to Pyle, Kemble, Remington and Frost, a whole flood of vigorous and talented new illustrators now appeared; the reproductive processes improved by leaps and bounds and the leading magazines, *Scribner's*, *Harper's*, *Century* and others in the nineties and early nineteen hundreds reached a standard of beauty that has never been equaled since. Children's magazines also flourished, *St. Nicholas, Harper's Young People* and *The Youth's Companion* reaching their zenith during this period.

The illustrated magazines

There was Reginald Birch, whose *Little Lord Fauntleroy* drawings condemned many thousands of unfortunate young Americans to the humiliation of long curls, velvet suits and broad lace collars. Being one of those sufferers has probably unjustly prejudiced me against Birch's work, for while one must admire extravagantly the spirit and skill of his drawings, they always seem completely English; the characters, no matter whom they represent, are always aristocratic little English children and all, unfortunately, reminiscent of the little Lord.

Reginald Birch and Fauntleroy

And there was Palmer Cox and his Brownies. Cox seems now quite forgotten; he is little mentioned in reference books, yet during his heyday the *Brownie Books* were tremendously popular with children. I cannot venture to say how good or bad they were artistically, but they had one quality which children love in their pictures and which no one else has quite approached. Each character of this large band was unmistakably drawn, was easily recognizable in every drawing, and was always consistent in behavior. Thus children could, and invariably did, identify each of the characters with someone they knew in real life and follow each one through all the various adventures. I can remember well with what joy we endowed the Dutchman, the Frenchman, the Dude and all the others with the identities of each other, our uncles, cousins, friends and playmates, and how eagerly we followed them throughout the book.

Palmer Cox and his Brownies

HOWARD PYLE : *Merry Adventures of Robin Hood*

Many splendid illustrators were then at work: Abbey, F. C. Yohn, Walter Appleton Clark, Jules Guerin, A. I. Keller, Edward Penfield, Franklin Booth, and a host of others.

Howard Pyle's pupils now began to make their appearance and soon maga- *Pupils of* zines and books were filled with the colorful work of Maxfield Parrish, Eliza- *Howard Pyle* beth Shippen Green, Jessie Willcox Smith, Harvey Dunn, N. C. Wyeth, Frank Schoonover and many more who had studied under the master.

Some of these perhaps were not children's illustrators, but their influence on children was vast, and far more enduring than that of most illustrators who worked exclusively for children. Maxfield Parrish, for example, did little work actually intended for children. Although much of his illustration was for stories about children, the stories and illustrations were for grownups. Yet who, that was a child during Parrish's best days, can forget the thrill of his singing color, the exquisite accuracy of his draughtsmanship? It is the fashion nowa-days to decry " Maxfield Parrish Prints " and class them with cozy-corners and Mission furniture as evidences of our former bad taste, merely, apparently, be-cause they became too popular. Yet much of the present-day appreciation of the value of real color in art, decoration, and commerce stems largely from the child-hood awakenings which Maxfield Parrish's use of color brought about.

This indeed was a Golden Age of American illustration, a time when the arrival, each month, of *Scribner's*, *Harper's* or the *Century* marked a red-letter day for the entire household. Children wanted or needed no specialized illus-tration with such treasure houses as these to pore over. And then almost every Christmas season there was sure to be a new Howard Pyle book, a treasure that would remain fresh and absorbing for years to come.

The decline of the magazines came about the time of Howard Pyle's death, not because of it, of course, but it has always seemed a rather fitting thing that he passed from the scene before the publications to which he had contributed so generously degenerated into mediocrity and oblivion, as far as illustration is concerned.

Who was this *H.P.* who had such a revolutionary influence on the course *Pyle's* of illustration in America? These first modest drawings in *St. Nicholas* were *background* produced by a quiet, rather studious young man, newly come to New York to seek a living in the arts. Twenty-three years before he had been born of old Quaker stock in Wilmington, Delaware, and had spent an idyllic childhood in and around that quaint old town.

Fortunately for the world, both his parents were people of more than usual culture; his mother especially had a great love for all the arts and the boy soon acquired her enthusiasm for books and pictures. Of equal importance to his future development were his surroundings; the mellow charm of his own home, the old town, rich in the atmosphere of its Colonial past, the love and knowledge of which glows so beautifully in much of his work. I have always felt that the lovely painting, "*When All the World Was Young,*" was a reflection of this serene and tranquil childhood.

With his mother he read and absorbed all the best that was available in books and magazines: Dickens, Thackeray, Percy's *Reliques*, Malory's *Morte d'Arthur*, German and Scandinavian folk tales, the drawings of *Punch* and the *Illustrated London News*. His enthusiasm for all these is shown clearly in his earlier work.

Early training   Always, from the earliest years, he drew and wrote, so it was but natural that, schooldays over, he should have chosen a career in the arts, much to his mother's joy. Here again came a piece of great good fortune, not recognized as such at the moment, but fortune nevertheless.

At that time the conventional course for anyone aspiring to the arts was to go at once to Europe and seek instruction in the great ateliers of Paris and Munich. Here, where theory and the latest fashions in art held sway, individuality was apt to be erased, polished off and fitted into the smooth, slick mode of insipidity that ruled at the moment. Had Howard Pyle, young, modest, not at all sure of himself, been thrown into this stultifying atmosphere where everything American was considered gauche and crude, there is no knowing what would have happened to the tender bud of his genius.

Luckily the family finances did not, at the moment, permit of this European venture and the young man was forced to take up his studies in near-by Philadelphia. Here again Fortune sent him not to the Academy of Fine Arts, but to a small class conducted by a Mr. Van der Weilen, a Dutch artist with a Dutchman's devotion to never-ending effort. Nothing could have been more desirable, for the three years' study under the driving of this exacting master gave the young student a thorough grounding in solid drawing, composition and technique, as well as a love and understanding of the glowing color and rich detail of the great Dutch school.

All these he learned and nothing more; there was nothing to unlearn. He acquired none of the false conventions, the sentimental slickness, the fads and fancies that smothered so much promising young talent. With this firm foundation on which to build he could be himself completely, shape his career as he saw fit. His fancy could roam in whatever fields it chose, unhampered by any preconceived rules or taboos. He could be as American as he pleased, without shame or apology.

This ability to draw firmly and solidly stood him in good stead, for he was one of our first illustrators to cast overboard the then almost complete dependence on the posed model. As his ability and confidence grew, he relied less and less on models, using them only where necessary for the exact hang of a garment or a difficult bit of anatomy. But there was no slavish copying, no hampering of character and action by a stiffly-posed figure.

The story goes (I cannot vouch for its truth, but it sounds likely) that eventually he reached the point where he used but one model for everything. This was his elderly man-of-all-work, who was frequently called in from cutting grass or weeding the garden to assume temporarily the rôle of a pirate, a George Washington or perhaps a mediæval Princess.

After the three years of labor under Mr. Van der Weilen there came a short *The period of* period of indecision when the genius of Howard Pyle might easily have been *indecision* lost to the world. The senior Pyle's business, that of leather, was suffering bad times and for some time the son had been assisting. Now with his studies completed he became more involved in trade; life in Wilmington was gay and pleasant, time of no great moment. It is conceivable that but for the quiet insistence of his mother, Howard Pyle might easily have settled down into the tranquil business and social routine of Wilmington. His artistic career might well have been limited to a few wistful sketches in the margins of the ledgers of " H. Pyle— Leather Merchant."

But again a watchful Fortune intervened. In the spring of seventy-six, he had visited Chincoteague, that truly picturesque little island off the Virginia coast. He had set down his impressions of the place in an article which he illustrated with sketches. It was an excellent little article and the drawings were good, but both might have lain about until forgotten had not Mrs. Pyle urged that they be submitted to a magazine. Accordingly they were dutifully wrapped *Scribner's,* up and sent to *Scribner's Monthly.* *St. Nicholas,*

and the
Almost at once came an acceptance from *Scribner's,* followed shortly by a *New York years* communication from one of the owners of the firm. Here was encouragement indeed! Mr. Roswell Smith urged that young Pyle come to New York, where opportunities would not be lacking to use and develop his talents.

HOWARD PYLE : *Book of King Arthur*

Forgotten in a moment were the leather business and the pleasant social evenings of Wilmington. There came the first surge of that unflagging energy that, for the next thirty-five years, was to make Howard Pyle noted as one of the hardest workers in his field. Hastily he packed up and went to New York.

There he was welcomed pleasantly at *Scribner's*. Mary Mapes Dodge, editor of *St. Nicholas*, accepted and published many of his fables and short stories with their accompanying drawings. The prices seem, today, fantastically low, his reward for some of these delightful fables being less than two dollars and a half each! For other, more ambitious drawings he received such magnificent sums as twelve and fifteen dollars. However, he lived quietly, his expenses were not great, his work was being accepted by various magazines; he was progressing.

Incredible as it seems, many of these early drawings were criticized as being technically " coarse," " cheap," and " vulgar "! Even he, young and uncertain, complains in letters that his work lacks the " refinement " and " elegance " of other artists. To such a low point had the taste of editors and public sunk in their preoccupation with finish and sentiment!

Another worry on young Pyle's mind was the question of whether he should concentrate on writing or illustration. Troubled by his lack of " elegance " in drawing, he rather favored a literary career, while his mother wisely urged that he bend his main efforts to art. However, these vague doubts and the quibbling uncertainties of editors were all brushed aside by the vigorous freshness of his work, by the flood of ideas from his fertile imagination, and most of all by the enthusiasm with which both young and old greeted his illustrations. His mind was automatically freed of the decision on which career should be followed; the demand for drawings was so great that little time was left for writing. Although in the years to come he did produce more charming literature than many an author, illustration was thereafter his chief field.

There were three years in New York; busy, fruitful years in which he met *His rapid* and chummed with the best of the rising young artists—Chase, Abbey, Beck- *advance as* with, Shirlaw, Homer. With them he talked, lived, ate and drank art, absorb- *illustrator* ing the high ideals which were to lift his work so far above the usual run of illustration. Although progress and recognition seemed slow to this eager young man whose brain teemed with ideas—so much to say, so much to do— his advance was really extremely rapid. The end of these three years found him well established as an illustrator, a very acceptable author—and tired of New York.

He returned to Wilmington where, amid his family and old friends, he really settled down to his long and productive career.

*Howard Pyle's
books*
Soon came the first of the books that were to endear Howard Pyle to generations of American children. There was *Robin Hood*, still hailed by many as the most perfect of children's books. Then came the series of delightful verses and stories first published, with their beautiful drawings, in *Harper's Young People*, later collected and made into *Pepper and Salt*. Next came the *Wonder Clock*, following the same scheme. Then came the lovely, wistful tale, *Otto of the Silver Hand*, and later *Men of Iron*.

Still later came the splendid series of Arthurian legends, the stories of *King Arthur and His Knights*, the *Champions of the Round Table*, *Sir Launcelot and His Companions*, and *The Grail and the Passing of Arthur*. The creation of these four stout volumes would have been a worthy life's accomplishment for many an author or illustrator, but Howard Pyle produced them in odd hours over a period of seven years when he was at his busiest, turning out the flood of glorious work that was helping make our magazines the envy of all the world.

*Pyle as teacher
at Drexel*
In 1894–95, Howard Pyle began a work which was to influence tremendously the whole future of American illustration. Having long felt a dissatisfaction with the methods of art instruction then in vogue, he hoped to teach students as he felt they should be taught. In 1894 the Drexel Institute of Arts and Sciences in Philadelphia asked him to take a class in illustration. Although at the time he was at his busiest, and the task meant a great personal sacrifice, Pyle gladly accepted the offer.

For two whole days a week, journeying to and from Wilmington and Philadelphia—in the morning holding consultations with individual students, going through the art schools " from the primary department to the life class," giving criticism and encouragement; lecturing in the afternoon—he gave himself unstintedly. But this was not enough. He offered to give two hours' work in the evening to advanced students.

At Chadds Ford
In 1898 he established, with the co-operation of the Drexel Institute, a summer class at Chadds Ford, Pennsylvania, the Institute giving scholarships for promising students. Howard Pyle charged nothing for his work. Here, near his summer home, in an old gristmill on the Brandywine turned into a studio, his thirty or more students worked through long days inspired by his genius and zest for work.

In 1900 he resigned from Drexel, feeling that he was not accomplishing enough to justify giving two days weekly to it. Early in this year he had a dream of a school at Wilmington. To this end he built a studio alongside his own, at first taking six or nine advanced pupils from various cities. To them he gave instruction without charge, they being only required to pay a small rental to cover the interest on the building, for their models, and heating the building. His work became so famous that in 1903 several hundred applications were presented, but he accepted only three. Here he worked daily with his pupils, lectured to them and to other artists drawn to Wilmington by his presence. Finding it desirable to widen his work, he undertook a series of lectures at the Art Students League in New York, but soon discontinued these when it seemed that the results were not worth the effort involved.

The Wilmington school

Many of the students of Chadds Ford and Wilmington were soon to become almost as dear to children and their parents as the revered master. The work of Maxfield Parrish, N. C. Wyeth, Elizabeth Shippen Green, Jessie Willcox Smith, Thornton Oakley, Harvey Dunn, Stanley Arthurs, Frank Schoonover, W. J. Aylward, Violet Oakley and all the others glowed with the spirit of Howard Pyle's genius. By them it was handed on to pupils of their own or communicated by example to all who loved and admired their work.

Thus, in his teaching, Howard Pyle taught not just a few selected students— he taught and inspired whole generations of illustrators. Today the seeds planted there by the Brandywine continue to bloom and flourish in ever-broadening fields of color and beauty.

Here in quiet Wilmington for thirty years he poured forth an uninterrupted flow of drawings, paintings, books and stories, giving without stint of his fertile imagination, his boundless energy and enthusiasm. Strangely enough, although so much of his work dealt with European scenes, and so much of it was founded on the art of the Dutch and German masters, he had never been abroad. Now, in 1910, he decided to visit Italy and there, in November of the following year, he died, at the unnecessarily early age of fifty-eight. He had given too hard and too generously of his robust strength.

Rich output of the Wilmington years

Much of Howard Pyle's work was definitely intended for children, much was for grownups, yet how can any sharp line of separation be drawn between the two? Certainly James Branch Cabell's *Chivalry* and Woodrow Wilson's *History of the American People* were adult books, but children loved and admired the illustrations. What child was ever too young to thrill at the gorgeous pageantry of Pyle's mediæval paintings, the sparkling drama of his drawings for

Oliver Wendell Holmes's *Bunker Hill Battle,* or those colorful pirates who have been the envy and despair of so many illustrators? No child, even one too young to read, can look through *The Salem Wolf* or *The Mysterious Chest* without delighted shivers at their moonlit terror.

What adult has ever reached an age so dull that he fails to derive complete satisfaction from the intricately simple drawings for *Otto of the Silver Hand* or *Robin Hood?* Children's books both, yet of the volumes which Theodore Roosevelt took along on his famous African hunting trip one was Howard Pyle's *Robin Hood.*

Pyle and the Golden Age of American illustration

And, child or adult, what American has not felt his pulse quicken at the vivid and understanding portrayals of the ragged heroes of Valley Forge, of Kaskaskia, or Bunker Hill? It is impossible to conceive how many thousands of Americans have had their patriotism raised a few degrees, how many horizons have been broadened, how many minds have been wakened to new perceptions of color, design, and sheer beauty by the prodigal output of this one man.

The latter years of the past century and the opening years of this were the Golden Age of American illustration, and of all the many who contributed to its glory Howard Pyle towers like a great oak over the fine but lesser trees of a rich forest.

HOWARD PYLE : *Merry Adventures of Robin Hood*

V. Foreign Picture Books in a Children's Library

MARIA CIMINO

EDY LEGRAND : *Voyages & glorieuses découvertes des grands navigateurs & explorateurs français*

DEBOUT SUR SON SOCLE AGRESTE, LE PETIT JEAN COMPREND QU'IL EST BEAU. DROIT, IMMÖBILE, LES YEUX TOUT RONDS, LES LÈVRES SERRÉES, LES BRAS PENDANTS, LES MAINS OUVERTES ET LES DOIGTS ÉCARTÉS COMME LES RAYONS D'UNE ROUE, IL GOUTE UNE JOIE PIEUSE A SE SENTIR DEVENIR UNE IDOLE.

BOUTET DE MONVEL : *Filles et garçons*

EDITOR'S FOREWORD

AT a time when picture books were scarce in America, and those we had came largely from England, foreign picture books with native texts had much that was valuable to suggest to artists and publishers. Each was a unit from cover to cover. The pictures were an integral part of the whole. They were brought to the attention of artists and publishers as well as to the children chiefly through their showing in the children's rooms of large public libraries.

Because of their importance in influencing the development of children's books here, and because of the part children's libraries have played in making the books available in the United States, we have chosen to present a chapter about the foreign picture books from the standpoint of their use in the Central Children's Room of the New York Public Library.

When the Pratt Institute Free Library of Brooklyn moved into a new building in 1896, Mary Wright Plummer, Director of the Library and the Library School, planned the equipment of its Children's Room, the first room of its kind to be included in an architect's plan. Such foreign picture books as were then available – chiefly French and German – were ordered for its reference and circulating collections. The close relation of the Children's Room to the Art Department of Pratt Institute, in which Arthur Dow was then an instructor, and the broad international outlook of Miss Plummer, who was a linguist and a poet as well as a librarian familiar with European libraries, were powerful influences in determining the service of this room to artists and to children during the years it was administered by Anne Carroll Moore, 1896-1906.

The first planned Children's Room at Pratt Institute

In 1911, when the New York Public Library opened its central building, Miss Moore, who had become Superintendent of its Work with Children five years before, gave to a greatly expanded collection of foreign picture books a setting on equal terms with American and English picture books. The spirit and intention of this Children's Room has been informed and invigorated by a succession of librarians who have brought the cultures of Norway, Sweden, Russia, France, Italy and other countries to its daily service to children and adults. Frances Clarke Sayers, who succeeded Miss Moore in 1941, brought to the direction of the room not only first-hand familiarity with its life and tradition, but a vision of her own for a future in which artists and children continue to flourish.

*Foreign
picture books
in bookshops*

The Bookshop for Boys and Girls in Boston, a department of the Women's Educational and Industrial Union from 1916 to 1936, and under my direction until 1934, was greatly influenced by this New York Children's Library and early presented in its stock picture books from other countries, never having any difficulty in their sale. One day, in 1929 I think, a large new stock of picture books from Russia, representative of the effort then being made to encourage everyone to learn to read, disappeared completely in two hours' time.

In the 1920's, book-buyers could find at Brentano's foreign department, at F. A. O. Schwartz's, at Bonnier's, at French and German bookstores, and with Czech and Russian importers, many fine and stimulating volumes. During the latter part of that decade, Esther Averill, in Paris, and Frances MacIntosh Schwandt, in Berlin, bought foreign picture books for the Bookshop for Boys and Girls. These two women contributed to *Contemporary Illustrators of Children's Books*, published in 1930, chapters upon the outstanding current illustrators for children in France and Germany respectively.

*Some American
books printed
in Europe*

After the First World War, color printing done abroad was the despair of printers and engravers here. In Europe time and labor were cheaper so that much more hand work was used. Book taste was more sophisticated, and expensive experiment in book production more welcome. Their best artists and printers had fun with bookmaking before we did. The result was that some American publishers had books printed in Prague, and in France, Germany, Sweden and Italy.

It was at this time, too, that the Bookshop for Boys and Girls took pride in becoming the American agent for *Daniel Boone*, written by Esther Averill, with pictures by Rojankovsky, and published by Miss Averill in Paris under her own imprint, the Domino Press. This was the first work of Rojankovsky's to be seen in America.

B. E. M.

JOB : *À la gloire des bêtes*

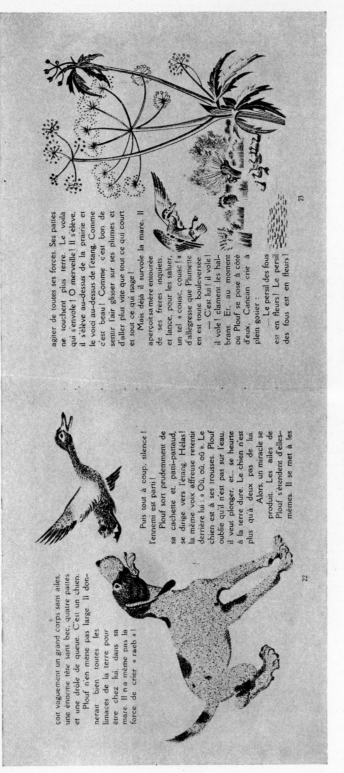

coit vaguement un grand corps sans ailes, une énorme tête sans bec, quatre pattes et une drôle de queue. C'est un chien.

Plouf n'en mène pas large. Il donnerait bien toutes les limaces de la terre pour être chez lui, dans sa mare. Il n'a même pas la force de crier « raeb »!

Puis tout à coup, silence! l'ennemi est parti!

Plouf sort prudemment de sa cachette et, patti-pataud, se dirige vers l'étang. Hélas! la même voix affreuse retentit derrière lui: « Oü, oü, oü ». Le chien est à ses trousses. Plouf oublie qu'il n'est pas sur l'eau, il veut plonger, et... se heurte à la terre dure. Le chien n'est plus qu'à deux pas de lui.

Alors, un miracle se produit. Les ailes de Plouf s'étendent d'elles-mêmes. Il se met à les

22

agiter de toutes ses forces. Ses pattes ne touchent plus terre. Le voilà qui s'envole! O merveille! Il s'élève au-dessus de la prairie et le voici au-dessus de l'étang. Comme c'est beau! Comme c'est bon de sentir l'air glisser sur ses plumes et d'aller plus vite que tout ce qui court et tout ce qui nage!

Mais déjà il survole la mare. Il aperçoit sa mère entourée de ses frères inquiets, et lance, pour les saluer, un tel « couac, couac! » d'allégresse que Plumette en est toute bouleversée.

— C'est lui! il vole! il vole! clament les halbrans. Et, au moment où Plouf se pose à côté d'eux, Cancan crie à plein gosier:

— Le persil des fous est en fleurs! Le persil des fous est en fleurs!

23

FEODOR ROJANKOVSKY : *Plouf canard sauvage*

Foreign Picture Books in a Children's Library

WHEN the Children's Room in the central building of the New York Central Public Library was opened, it became at once a point of international interest. Children's European visitors were delighted to find on its shelves familiar books from their Room at countries so closely associated with those of other countries. They were at- New York tracted by what they called a new idea in education—this bringing before chil- Public Library dren picture books from many lands—and marveled at the resources of this children's library made so immediately accessible to children and adults.

Educators and journalists returning to their own countries wrote about it. A Danish novelist said, " This library work for children is amazing. I was pre- pared for everything else I have seen in America, but this surprises and delights me. It is full of possibilities for future generations. I shall come back again and spend a long time in this beautiful room where all countries are remembered."

To many Americans who had given little or no thought to the idea, it opened new perspectives, awakened a consciousness and appreciation of the culture of countries hitherto unknown to them. Not only did it include the best repre- sentative European picture books for children in its collection, but on its staff, as its first interpreter, was a gifted Norwegian with several languages at her command. The first foreign books were in the French, German, Russian, Swed- First foreign ish and Norwegian languages, with a selection of illustrated books in Czech books borrowed from the large Czech collection in a branch library.

Artists immediately recognized in the collection the value of the work of other artists and returned with suggestions and lists of books to be added. The old Russian picture books illustrated by Ivan Bilibin were acquired in this way. In the summer of 1913 a Norwegian merchant, attracted by what he had read in Norway about the Library, brought a party of friends who had crossed with him on the first ship of the Norwegian Line. He was so interested in what he saw that he was determined to do the same for Bergen, his native city, when he returned. The following Christmas he sent to the Children's Room a

RICHELIEU

...tants et le roi parut, vêtu d'un pourpoint blanc, sa chausse d'écarlate et la botte à la jambe. Les discours échangés furent ceux qui avaient été préparés.

Comme Marie de Médicis essayait de demander une dernière grâce, Louis XIII tourna les talons et s'en alla en appelant : « Albert, Albert!

Luynes! Luynes! »

Elle tomba à moitié évanouie dans un fauteuil. Revenue à elle, elle se prit à sangloter.

23

RICHELIEU

puis descendit à pas précipités les grands escaliers du Louvre, monta dans sa litière et partit, suivie de quelques dames et d'une nombreuse escorte.

Dans le dernier carrosse, mélancolique et résigné, avait pris place l'évêque de Luçon.

Tout le long de la rivière, le cortège s'achemina jusqu'au Pont-Neuf que la reine traversa, saluant, les yeux voilés de larmes, la statue de Henri IV qu'on venait de dresser sur un piédestal construit en marbre de Florence.

MAURICE LELOIR : *Richelieu*

gift of the best Norwegian children's books available at the time. It contained no picture books, as there were none in Norway then, but it gave to the room two of its most prized books, *Snorre Sturlasson kongesgaer* and *Norske folkeeventyr*, illustrated by Erik Werenskiold and other famous Norwegian artists. Later there came a gift of modern Russian picture books from a lecturer and teacher of library science in Russia who had visited the room in 1914.

The exchange of ideas about books and illustration became a usual occurrence in this room. Authors, artists and illustrators, parents, educators, booksellers and publishers came to regard it as an international center of information about children's books. It was soon apparent that the staff should always include one or more librarians with a knowledge and experience of foreign languages. The foreign book collection now numbers twenty-one languages and continues as vital in its appeal, interest and use as it was at its inception.

Professional use of the collection

Picture the shelves, on a wall of the reading room of this children's library, set between two large casement windows with comfortable window seats: here, next to the English and American, the foreign picture books are to be found. As you approach the bookcases you may see, perhaps, the large Mussino *Pinocchio* beckoning to you from a top shelf, or in the next case among the French books, Boutet de Monvel's *Jeanne d'Arc*. As the eye travels down you come upon Vimar's *L'illustre dompteur*, or the magnificent books of scenes from French history illustrated by Job and Leloir; the picture books of André Hellé, Edy Legrand, or the books in the Père Castor series. Among the German books you will find such household favorites as *Der Struwwelpeter* and *Max und Moritz*, and many others from other countries. It is a veritable book fair that meets the eye, telling of the people, heroes and tales of imagination of many lands. These books, with their traditional designs and fine drawings, reflect the folklore, life and character of their people in the most natural and unaffected way. There is a mellowness here and an understanding of the children for whom they are made.

Children accompanied by parents who remember the books from their own childhood in Europe spend long hours with old favorites. Other children drawn to the books by their pictures will follow the thread of the story through the drawings. Time and again, when the English version of *Pinocchio* is in use, they will turn to the Italian one, and completely absorbed will read the story through its remarkable drawings by Attilio Mussino. For through good drawings the imagination may be fired and an unknown place become real. Young

Children's enjoyment of foreign books

men writing home from the wars remark that the French children and country-side bring to mind the picture books of Boutet de Monvel.

Special exhibitions

The foreign picture books are used continually in exhibitions, as they offer rich material to dramatize the subject at hand. The exhibitions, which are an important feature in the regular work of the Children's Room, may be as broad in their scope as is the book collection itself. The work of an artist who has made a definite contribution in the field of book illustration, or the contribution of an entire country, may be the subject. In the planning and arrangement of its exhibitions, the Children's Room draws upon the resources of the other departments in the central building as well as its own. The interest of an exhibit is often extended by material borrowed from the Art and Prints Divisions, Rare Books, the Berg, the Spencer and the Picture Collections as well as from private collectors.

"Children's Books of Yesterday," a notable exhibition, was held in the New York Public Library in 1933. About five hundred books of many countries were included in a joint exhibition arranged by the Metropolitan Museum of Art and the New York Public Library. The books were chosen, not primarily for textual merit, but for their originality, their rarity and historical significance, for qualities of colorful illustration and ingenius design, for their power of evoking lively memories of childhood and youth. Two fascinating items were the first editions of Perrault, 1697, and *Der Struwwelpeter*. Since it was impossible within the space to include in this exhibition many children's books of contemporary interest in various countries, a series of related exhibits of original drawings and books by living artists were shown in the Children's Room throughout the period of the exhibition. France was the first of the continental countries to be presented in this series.

France and the modern picture book

The modern picture book owes much to French genius, and to Boutet de Monvel, whose *Jeanne d'Arc*, published in 1897, started the procession of all the fascinating picture books to come. Before Boutet de Monvel there were not many illustrated books for children in France. There were the early editions of Perrault, later illustrated by Doré and others, and the *Images d'Épinal*, those popular sheets engraved in color that have delighted French children since the end of the eighteenth century. There was also a notable series of illustrated classics with illustrations by Job, Morin, Robida, Vimar and other famous painters. The modern French illustrators are drawn to the *Images d'Épinal* because they are the rich, spontaneous and direct expression of folk art. Boutet de

Monvel, for all his delicacy of line and color, also borrowed from the *Images*, as may be seen in his *Chansons* and *La Fontaine*.

The French exhibition was given its setting by the large canvases of circus clowns of Edy Legrand and his latest illustrations, lithographs for *Les lunettes*

The French Exhibition

BOUTET DE MONVEL : *Chansons de France*

du lion, sent from Paris for the occasion. Edy Legrand's illustration has long interested and influenced young illustrators here and abroad. His pages are remarkable for their felicity of design and the rapport between text and illustration. He draws with a fine critical intelligence that is free of sentimentality and with an imaginative insight which enables him to select the incidents he illustrates and to express so perfectly the child world of *L'île rose,* the mood of the verses in *Petites voix* or to recapture the adventurous spirit of the old French explorers and heroes.

The books of Edy Legrand and the other French illustrators offered a wealth of material to be explored. Here were to be found the picture books of André Hellé, whose *L'arche de Noé* brought new elements into the French picture book when it appeared in 1914; picture books which by their illustrations in simple, bold lines, flat color and good design make pages that are full of fun, ironic and expansive humor, and carry the excitement of a Guignol theatre. Here were also the earlier books from the end of the nineteenth century to the First World War; the large de luxe volumes illustrated with an eye to the storytelling tradition of the period which concerned itself with decorative detail, and the humor or moral of the situation: those splendid volumes with magnificently elaborate pages in which Job recounts the adventures of *Bonaparte*, Leloir the days of *Le Roy Soleil*, Robida, *François I*; or other volumes with the rich humor of Vimar's *L'illustre dompteur* and Hellé's *Fables de la Fontaine*, and the beauty of Boutet de Monvel's *Jeanne d'Arc*, *Nos enfants* and *Chansons de France*.

The French exhibition pointed also to new ideas, with books like Parain's *Mon chat* and Rojankovsky's *Daniel Boone*— Rojankovsky who, by his drawings for *Les petits et les grands*, set the style for the *Père Castor* series, and became its best and most prolific artist. This series, with that of *Le chat perché*, moved the French picture book, in part, from the de luxe into the more popular class.

EDY LEGRAND : *Petites voix*

German picture books   The German picture books presented a direct contrast in the exhibition which followed. Starting with Musaus' *Volksmärchen der Deutschen* and Bechstein's *Märchenbuch*, illustrated by Ludwig Richter, Speckter's *Fabeln für Kinder* and the household volumes of Pletsch, one found the picture books of the German nursery of the middle nineteenth century made by artists whose skill and craftsmanship were steeped in the tradition and style of the period.

Next came *Der Struwwelpeter*—of which it has been said that Dr. Hoffmann first uncorked the comic spirit and mixed enough genuine fun with behavior problems to anticipate the comic strip by half a century—and the *Max und Moritz* of Wilhelm Busch. *Dr. Hoffmann and the comic spirit*

Busch is truly a humorist, who, by his sense of comedy and skill as an artist, portrays the foibles and frailties of human behavior with resourcefulness and

ANDRÉ HELLÉ : *Fables de la Fontaine*

imagination. *Max und Moritz* captures every nuance of spirited small boy pranks. Busch's volumes of drawings are highly appreciated by cartoonists and caricaturists, who turn to him in admiration of his art, the crispness of his wit and humor, and the vitality and conciseness of his statements.

The 1920's yielded a different type of picture book. There is Ernst Kreidolf, Swiss painter, who created beautiful picture books about nature. A sensitive water colorist, he presents imaginatively mountains and snow maidens with a delicacy of line and color-texture that is inspired by the characteristic northern imagination. This style could easily become sentimental in the hands of a less

RUDOLF MATES : *Pohádka lesa*

gifted artist. The books illustrated by Elsa Wenz-Viëtor are bolder in style, color and design. She works more directly, completely absorbed in drawing for children. One feels that Kreidolf draws from an inner poetic urge. The books illustrated by Elsa Eisgruber are also delicate in color, but her work is more modern and stylized. Tom Seidmann-Freud produced the most original books in this group. Eager to recapture the naïve art sense of a child, she worked to create in her books little worlds such as might be imagined by a child.

The French and German picture books are much better known in this country than those of Czechoslovakia. The Czech exhibition, last in this series, was opened by the Czech Consul General. It attracted many new and distinguished artists and other visitors who were interested in the water colors of the Czech countryside by Jan Matulka. It also revealed that the best Czech artists had given time and thought to book illustration for children, preserving

The Czech Exhibition

in their books the folklore, folk art and the imaginative drive and heroism of a people whose culture has survived much adversity. There were the line drawings of Mikulás Alés and Artus Scheiner for the folk tales; Josef Wenig, who drew upon peasant designs, embroideries and wood carvings to give to his illustrations their particular character and flavor; and Fischerová-Kvechová and Rudolf Mates, who also drew upon the peasant work. Mates's picture books, with their rich color and bold design, are lively and vivid, full of folk humor.

The Italian contribution

The books of other European countries represented in the collection have made a definite impression. One of these is Italy. Italy, where the *maschere* are a rich heritage and the most lowly peasant knows and loves the tales, taking pride in his own provincial type among the characters which go back to the

TOM SEIDMANN-FREUD : *Die Fischreise*

ELSA MOESCHLIN-HAMMAR : *Das rote Pferd*

commedia del arte. Where the folk songs and little rhymes for children are repeated all one's life, it is natural that these should furnish the material for the Italian picture books. But the Italian picture books are few. The economy of Italy has never been fully free to establish a sound program of education which would create a demand for good books for children. There is Pinocchio, who himself belongs to the *maschere*. There are many editions of *Pinocchio*. The one illustrated by Attilio Mussino may be regarded for all time as a perfect interpretation. The illustrations are rich in color and design and the pages packed with the activity and vitality of Italian life. There is no confusion. It is like a *commedia del arte* play describing the adventures of this small marionette who in truth represents Italian boyhood and character. This is one of the most popular books in the collection.

ATTILIO MUSSINO:
Le avventure di Pinocchio

Some of the most notable books to come out of Europe after the close of the First World War came from Italy. Two beautiful books appearing at that time were illustrated by Marco Montedoro, a theatrical designer, who later came to America and found his way to the Children's Room. In *Narran le maschere* he presents the *maschere* with a charming formality and décor; for *Cantilene popolari dei bimbi d'Italia* he provides the singing games of each province with gay and decorative settings. Another beautiful book is *L'albero del sogno*, illustrated by Aldo Cosomati. Bruno Angoletta's modern illustrations in bold flat color in the children's monthly, *Giro giro tondo*, were among the first books with this technique to interest illustrators and designers who come to the room.

Schoolbooks of the Fascist regime

One cannot ignore here the schoolbooks published under the Fascist regime, because some of the best-designed and illustrated books for children were published by the State. The Fascist program included compulsory education for every child and toward this end the State produced schoolbooks to set forth its ideology. The

ATTILIO MUSSINO: *Le avventure di Pinocchio*

ABCedario and the first and second grade readers are among the best examples of the modern textbook—for their design, illustration and choice of type—to come from any country. What will come next from Italy, or from any of the war-torn countries, for that matter, we do not know. Let us hope that they will emerge from their confusion with enough economic stability to give their people that ease of spirit which is essential to the artist and his work.

Sweden has the picture books of Carl Larsson, Elsa Beskow and Ottilia *Picture books* Adelborg, which glow with the deep sense of pleasure the Swedish people find *of Sweden* in nature, their countryside, their folklore and family life. These elements give to their books the particular character and charm which endear them to the hearts of small children. In *Ett hem* and *Andras barn*, the beautiful paintings of Carl Larsson show you life at home with his family. Elsa Beskow's picture books have good design and color, and the warmth, simplicity and storytelling qualities which appeal especially to a small child's imagination. In each of her books are

ELSA BESKOW : *Tomtebobarnen*

experiences a child may share—the wonderful adventures of a small boy's ski trip in *Olle's skidfärd*, the making of a new suit for Pelle, or the joys of acquaintance with three old aunts. Naturalness and simplicity give their special charm to Ottilia Adelborg's gay picture books, which interpret the folk customs of her people. *Pelle snygg, och barnen i Snaskeby* is best known to American children as *Clean Peter*.

OTTILIA ADELBORG : *Bilderbok*

From Norway come old sagas and folk tales illustrated by Erik *Norway and* Werenskiold and other leading artists, with drawings that have the strength and *Denmark* vitality of the mediæval imagination which gave form to the tales. Heroic figures, old mediæval motifs and designs interpret magnificently the legendary and early history of Norway in *Snorre Sturlasson*. Werenskiold's drawings for the *Norse folkeeventyr* convey the character of the tales in their fullest sense.

The drawings for Hans Andersen's fairy tales by V. Pedersen, and the picture books of Louis Moe are outstanding in the small collection of Danish books.

Jeg er opdaget, jeg maa løbe, alt hvad jeg kan. — Alle Hundene er efter mig. Øf!

Hjemme igen! — Endelig finder jeg Hvile.

LOUIS MOE: *Brumle-Bumle*

The picture books from Poland were brought out in an exhibition of Polish *Polish Folk Arts* Folk Arts held in 1940, just as Poland fell into the hands of the Nazis. Through *Exhibition* the interest of Irene Piotrovska, who had arranged the art exhibition in the Polish Pavilion at the World's Fair, the Polish Consulate placed a great deal of material at our disposal. The examples of peasant crafts which included the delicate fascinating figures made of paper, eggshells, bits of bread and cheese as Christmas ornaments, paper cut-outs of intricate folk designs, wood carvings, all served to confirm the folk quality in the illustrations in the picture books. On the walls were to be seen the dramatic plates of regional costumes and dances by Zofja Stryjeńska. The entire exhibition moved from the beautiful peasant designs to the bold drawings of Levitt and Him in *Lokomotywa*, with a vivid sense of strength and continuity. The Polish people who visited the room continually throughout the exhibition found in it a reaffirmation of their cultural heritage.

Important
trends in
Russia
From the de luxe books illustrated by Ivan Bilibin, published by the Imperial Government in 1904, to the quantity production of illustrated books by the Soviet Government now, one may view the direction of two important trends of book illustration in that country as well as in Europe. Bilibin's wonderful picture books of the *skazki,* with their drawings of mediæval splendor, are unforgettable, as are the volumes of the peasant animal and folk tales collected by Krylov. In the later books it is impossible to separate demand from publication. The new program of education called for books to be published in large quantities. The most modern and gifted artists have made books for Russian children, to whom the books are often submitted for criticism before publication. Books are being produced to meet every need. Such artists as Lebedev, Radlov, Pakhomov, Charushin, Konashevich and Kuznetzov have illustrated books dealing with the entire scope of industrialized Russia. A five-year plan, life at home in the city and in the country, the building of a dam, a subway, the baking of bread, the story of fishing carry in their design and presentation the freshness of lively imagination and the excitement of the discovery of a new idea. This is realized equally well in the books of folk tales and in the imaginative and

LEVITT I HIM : *Lokomotywa*

Пѣтушокъ угомонился,
Шумъ утихъ и царь забылся.
  Вотъ проходитъ восемь дней,
А отъ войска нѣтъ вѣстей:
Было ль, не было ль сраженья?
Нѣтъ Дадону донесенья.
Пѣтушокъ кричитъ опять —
Кличетъ царь другую рать;
Сына онъ теперь меньшова
Шлетъ на выручку большова.
Пѣтушокъ опять утихъ.
Снова вѣсти нѣтъ отъ нихъ.
Снова восемь дней проходятъ;
Люди въ страхѣ дни проводятъ;

Пѣтушокъ кричитъ опять;
Царь скликаетъ третью рать
И ведетъ ее къ востоку,
Самъ не зная, быть ли проку.
  Войска идутъ день и ночь;
Имъ становится не въ мочь.
Ни побоища, ни стана,
Ни надгробнаго кургана
Не встрѣчаетъ царь Дадонъ.
Что за чудо? мыслитъ онъ.
Вотъ осьмой ужъ день проходитъ,
Войско въ горы царь приводитъ,
И промежъ высокихъ горъ
Видитъ шолковый шатеръ.

Все въ безмолвіи чудесномъ
Вкругъ шатра; въ ущельѣ тѣсномъ
Рать побитая лежитъ.
Царь Дадонъ къ шатру спѣшитъ...
Что за страшная картина!
Передъ нимъ его два сына
Безъ шеломовъ и безъ латъ
Оба мертвые лежатъ,
Мечъ вонзивши другъ во друга.
Бродятъ кони ихъ средь луга
По притоптанной травѣ,
По кровавой муравѣ...
Царь завылъ: „Охъ дѣти, дѣти!
Горе мнѣ! попались въ сѣти

— 7 —

IVAN BILIBIN : *O zolotom pyetushkye*

original stories. These books have a stimulating effect on American artists, who return continually to consult them, for they suggest many possibilities for experiments in techniques of illustration and printing. It has been interesting to note how England has followed this Russian experiment, as may be seen by the excellent work in the " Midgets " and " Puffins " published during the last war.

Russian influence on English and American books

So much for these European picture books in which the adult may see the movements of art, literature and the whole pattern of European life of the last fifty years. Each country's contribution stems from its social and economic philosophy, which in turn stems from the events that shape its thought and history. But the child finds only one thing—how life is in another country. No country can long remain strange to a child who has entered it through its picture books.

A. LAPTEV: *Pyatiletka*

The upheaval and turmoil of Europe at war brought the publication of children's books there to a standstill. Here in the Western Hemisphere, removed from physical contact with war, it continued to flourish and give opportunity to many new ventures. With the removal to Mexico and South America of some Spanish book firms, a few interesting books for children have begun to come from Latin America.

In Mexico, the program is of longest standing. It goes back to the 1920's, when the Ministry of Education first started its program of education for the people. One may recall the schoolbooks illustrated by Diego Rivera, published by the government printing presses. Also the work of René d'Harnoncourt, who made us aware of the richness of the Mexican folk arts. There is also Jean Charlot, who was working for the Ministry of Education at that time, and has illustrated the books of Mexican folk tales for American firms. Charlot's arresting and magnificent paintings have twice been shown in the Children's Room, the last time during the fall of 1945, when they brought to it a sense of the life and atmosphere of Mexican streets and roads with Indian mothers and children at their daily tasks. The paintings of old Mexican toys by Ceferino Palencia, a Spanish painter of entirely different genre, transformed the room into a truly Mexican street fair when they were exhibited in 1944.

From Latin America The first picture book to come from South America was *Lenda da carnaubeira*, published by the Brazilian Ministry of Education in 1939. The following year the Ministry printed an edition in English. At that time the original water colors by Paulo Werneck were sent from Rio de Janeiro to figure in an exhibition of the Brazilian Indian. The interest of Brazilians in this Children's Room is of long standing—thanks to Monteiro Lobato who wrote about it in his book, *America*. Senhor Monteiro Lobato is a pioneer in children's books in Brazil, having translated many of the classics into Portuguese. Recently the Brazilian government presented the Library with a gift of the representative children's books of Brazil. *Brazilian government gift*

Publishers in Argentina are producing some outstanding books, among them collections of folklore and poetry. A splendid example of bookmaking is the beautiful *Geografía Argentina*, illustrated by Horacio Butler. The reprint of the famous Andalusian children's classic *Platero y yo* has fine illustrations by Attilio Rossi.

Latin Americans are finding in the Children's Room possibilities and ideas of education similar to those discovered by its first European visitors of an earlier generation. They, in their turn, are bringing a keenness of perception and an enthusiasm expressed in terms of their own cultures, which seem bound to have a profound effect upon the future of picture books for children. The influence of foreign picture books in an American children's library will never end as long as children and artists continue to come, and as long as the interpretation of its resources is imaginative and strong.

A Selected List of Some Outstanding Foreign Picture Books in the Central Children's Room

---

CZECHOSLOVAKIA

ALEŠ, MIKULÁŠ
  Quis.   *Hloupý Honza.* Topič.

FISCHEROVÁ-KVĚCHOVÁ, MARIE
  Sládek.   *Skřivánčí písně.* Otto.

MATES, RUDOLF
  Kožíšek.   *Pohádka lesa.* Státní Nakladatelství.
  Sedláček.   *Kytka pampelišek.* Ústředniho nák. . . .
  Strnad.   *Byl jeden ptáček.* Černý.

SCHEINER, ARTUŠ
  Němcová.   *Božena Němcová maličkým.* Koči.
  Šimáčková.   *Vyprávěnky šťastného domova pro mládež nejútlejší.* Šimáček.

WENIG, JOSEF
  Hruška.   *Na hyjté.* Černý.
  Sokolova.   *Za slunce a mraszu.* Šimáček.

DENMARK

MOE, LOUIS
                    Brumle-Bumle. Gyldendalske Boghandel.
                    Muntre Billedhistorier for Börn. Gyldendalske Boghandel.

Écoute et guigne si tu veux, mais garde-toi de bondir! Notre petit ami ne chante-rait plus.

NATHALIE PARAIN : *Mon chat*

PIERRE PINSARD : *Petits contes nègres pour les enfants des blancs*

PEDERSEN, V.
 Andersen. *Eventyr i udvalg.* Gyldendalske Boghandel.

SKOVGAARD, NIELS
 Olrik.   *Danske sagn og æventyr fra folkemunde.* Fremtiden.

APPIA, BÉATRICE
     Histoire de Jean Vallade. Editions du Carrefour.

ARNOUX, GUY
 Fauchier-Delavigne. *À propos de chansons.* Berger-Levrault.

BOUTET DE MONVEL, MAURICE
 Eugène. *La civilité puérile et honnête.* Plon-Nourrit.
 France. *Filles et garçons.* Hachette.
 France. *Nos enfants.* Hachette.
     Jeanne d'Arc. Plon-Nourrit.
 La Fontaine. *Fables choisies pour les enfants.* Plon-Nourrit.
     Saint François d'Assise. Plon-Nourrit.
 Weckerlin. *Chansons de France.* Plon-Nourrit.
 Widor. *Vieilles chansons.* Plon-Nourrit.

BRULLER, JEAN
 Dubus. *Pif et Paf.* Nathan.
 Maurois. *Patapoufs & Filifers.* Hartmann.

DE BRUNHOFF, JEAN
     Histoire de Babar, le petit éléphant. Jardin des Modes.

DORÉ, GUSTAVE
 Perrault. *Les contes de Perrault.* Hetzel.

EDY LEGRAND
     Macao et Cosmage. Nouvelle Revue Française.
     Petite histoire de La Fayette. Tolmer.
     Voyages & glorieuses découvertes des grands navigateurs & explorateurs français. Tolmer.
 Ley.   *La nuit de la saint Sylvain.* Calmann-Lévy.
 Ley.   *Petites voix.* Stock.
 Mille. *Line en Nouvelle Calédonie.* Calmann-Lévy.
 Vildrac. *L'île rose.* Tolmer.
 Vildrac. *Les lunettes du lion.* Hartmann.

FRANÇOISE
     La plus vieille histoire du monde. Jardin des Modes.

GUERTIK, HÉLÈNE
     Des poissons. Flammarion. (Collection du Père Castor).
 Lida.   *La ferme du Père Castor.* Flammarion. (Albums du Père Castor).
 Louv'a. *Les bêtes que j'aime.* Flammarion. (Albums du Père Castor).

HALICKA, ALICE
 Murat. *La Fayette.* Bellenand.

FRANCE
(*Continued*)

HELLÉ, ANDRÉ
  Andersen.   *Le petit elfe Ferme l'Oeil.* Tolmer.
  Desbordes-Valmore. *Le livre des enfants.* Garnier.
              L'arche de Noé. Garnier.
              La belle histoire que voilà. Berger-Levrault.
              La boîte à joujoux. Tolmer.
              Histoire de Quillembois soldat. Berger-Levrault.
              Maman. . . les petits bateaux. Ferenczi.
              Le tour du monde en 80 pages. Ferenczi.
  La Fontaine. *Fables.* Berger-Levrault.

IMAGES D'ÉPINAL
              Contes de fées. Imagerie Pellerin.

JOB
  Fabre.   *À la gloire des bêtes.* Mame.
  Lemaître.   *A B C.* Mame.
  Montorgueil. *Bonaparte.* Boivin.
  Montorgueil. *France son histoire.* Boivin.
  Montorgueil. *Louis XI.* Boivin.
  Montorgueil. *Napoléon.* Boivin.

LELOIR, MAURICE
  Cahu.   *Richelieu.* Boivin.
  Toudouze.   *Le Roy Soleil.* Boivin.

MORIN, HENRI
  Cervantes.   *Don Quichotte de la Manche.* Laurens.

OLESIEWICZ, SIGISMOND
  Balzac.   *Napoléon.* Duchartre.
  Brousson.   *Jeanne d'Arc.* Duchartre.

L'ONCLE HANSI
              La merveilleuse histoire du bon S. Florentin d'Alsace. Floury.

PARAIN, NATHALIE
  Aymé.   *Le canard et le panthère.* Gallimard. (Un conte du chat
               perché).
  Aymé.   *Le paon.* Gallimard. (Un conte du chat perché).
  Beucler.   *Mon chat.* Gallimard.
  Celli.   *Allons vite.* Flammarion. (Albums du Père Castor).
  Celli.   *Baba yaga.* Flammarion. (Albums du Père Castor).
  Celli.   *Les jeux en images.* Flammarion. (Albums du Père Castor).
  Tchehkov.   *Chataigne.* Gallimard.

PINCHON, JOSEPH
  Le Cordier. *Aventures de Maître Renard.* Delagrave.

PINSARD, PIERRE
  Cendrars.   *Petits contes nègres pour les enfants des blancs.* Au Sans Pareil.

RABIER, BENJAMIN
              Les méfaits d'Azor. Nilsson.
              Scènes comiques dans la forêt. Garnier.

ROBIDA, ALBERT
              Fabliaux et contes du moyen age. Laurens.
  Robida.   *Le trésor de Carcassonne.* Laurens.
  Toudouze.   *François Ier.* Boivin.

ROJANKOVSKY, FEDOR

	A B C. Flammarion. (Albums du Père Castor).	
Averill.	*Poudre*. Domino Press.	
Celli.	*Les petits et les grands*. Flammarion. (Albums du Père Castor).	
	Daniel Boone. Domino Press.	
Lacôte.	*Calendrier des enfants*. Flammarion. (Albums du Père Castor).	
Lida.	*Froux le lièvre*. Flammarion. (Albums du Père Castor).	
Lida.	*Martin pêcheur*. Flammarion. (Albums du Père Castor).	
Lida.	*Plouf canard sauvage*. Flammarion. (Albums du Père Castor).	
Lida.	*Quipic le hérisson*. Flammarion. (Albums du Père Castor).	
Lida.	*Scaf le phoque*. Flammarion. (Albums du Père Castor).	

TOUCHET, JACQUES
Maeterlinck. *L'oiseau bleu*. Piazza.
Ségur. *Les malheurs de Sophie*. Piazza.

TRANCHANT, MAURICE
Cheronnet. *Algérie*. Duchartre.
Je jongle . . . avec les chiffres. Jardin des Modes.

VIMAR, AUGUSTE
Florian. *Les Fables*. Laurens.
Guigou. *L'arche de Noé*. Plon-Nourrit.
L'illustre dompteur. Plon-Nourrit.
Le roman du Renard. Laurens.

VOGEL, HERMANN
Montorgueil. *Henri IV*. Boivin.

COURBOIN, FRAIPONT, GEOFFROY, GERBAULT, JOB, MORIN, ROBIDA, VIMAR, VOGEL, ZIER
Perrault. *Les contes de Perrault*. Laurens.

BUSCH, WILHELM
Bilderbücher. 3 vol. Braun.
Max und Moritz. Braun.

EISGRUBER, ELSA
Rosmarin und Thymian. Stuffer.
Sause, Kreisel, sause! Stuffer.

HOFFMANN, HEINRICH
Der Struwwelpeter. Insel.

KAULBACH, HERMANN
Güll. *Das Kaulbach-Güll Bilderbuch*. Schnell.

KREIDOLF, ERNST
Alpenblumenmärchen. Rotapfelverlag.
Das Hundefest. Rotapfelverlag.
Ein Wintermärchen. Rotapfelverlag.

LASKE, OSCAR
Die Arche Noah. Schroll.

MEISSEN, CONNY
In die weite Welt. Müller.

MOESCHLIN-HAMMAR, ELSA
Das rote Pferd. Stuffer.

GERMANY   PLETSCH, OSCAR
(*Continued*)   *Allerlei Schnik-Schnak.* Weidmannschen.
                                 Buben und Mädel's. Dürr.
                                 Pletsch-Bilderbuch. Carl.

               RICHTER, LUDWIG
                 Beckstein.   *Märchenbuch.* Wigand.
                 Musäus.   *Volksmärchen der Deutchen.* vonMarger.
                 Siebe.   *Ludwig Richter-Buch für Kinder.* Anton.
                 Sturm.   *Kinderleben in Bild und Wort.* Riehm.

               SCHEEL, MARIANNE
                                 Peters Ferien. Schlüter.

               SEIDMANN-FREUD, TOM
                                 Das Buch der Dinge. Mauritius.
                                 Buch der Hasengeschichten. Peregrin.
                                 Die Fischreise. Peregrin.

               SPECKTER, OTTO
                 Hey.   *Fünfzig Fabeln für Kinder.* Insel.

               TRIER, WALTER
                 Seyffert.   *Spielzeug.* Wasmuth.

ERNST KREIDOLF : *Das Hundefest*

VOGEL, HERMANN
   Grimm.   *Kinder-und Hausmärchen*. Braun.

GERMANY
(*Continued*)

WENZ-VIËTOR, ELSE
   Andersen.   *Daümelinchen*. Stalling.
   Dieck.   *Schweinchen schlachten Würstchen machen Quiek, quiek, quiek!* Stalling.
   Reinheimer.   *Im Blumenhimmel*. Stalling.
   Wenz-Viëtor. *Das grosse Ding*. Stalling.

HOLLAND

BODENHEIM, NELLY
           Handje-Plak. van Looij.
LANGELER, FREDDIE
   van Tienhoven. *Sinterklaas kapoentje*. Kluitman.

ITALY

ANGOLETTA, BRUNO
           Giro giro tondo. Mondadori.
COSOMATI, ALDO
   di Castelbarco. *L'albero del sogno*. Bottega di Poesia.

DELLA TORRE, ANGELO
   Bagagli.   *ABCedario*. Alfieri.

GIGLIUCCI, BONA
           Canzoni popolari per i bambini. Farina.
GIOJA, EDOARDO
           A voi bimbi. Bestetti.

MONTEDORO, MARCO
   Adami.   *Narran le maschere*. Istituto Italiano d'Arti Grafiche.
   Oddone.   *Cantilene popolari dei bimbi d'Italia*. Istituto Italiano d'Arti Grafiche.

MUSSINO, ATTILIO
   Collodi.   *Le avventure di Pinocchio*. Bemporad.

SARRI, CORRADO
   Pagani.   *Grilli canterini*. Pampaloni.

MEXICO AND SOUTH AMERICA

BERNI, ANTONIO
   Rinaldini.   *Historia del General San Martín*. Editorial Sudamericana.

BUTLER, HORACIO
   Oliver.   *Geografía Argentina*. Editorial Sudamericana.

FERNÁNDEZ LEDESMA, GABRIEL
           Album de animales mexicanos. La Secretaría de Educación Pública.
           Juguetes mexicanos. Talleres Gráficos de la Nación.
JARDIM, LUIS
           O Tatu e o Macaco. Ministério da Educação e Saude.
ROSSI, ATTILIO
   Jiménez.   *Platero y yo*. Editorial Losada.

HORACIO BUTLER : *Geografía Argentina*

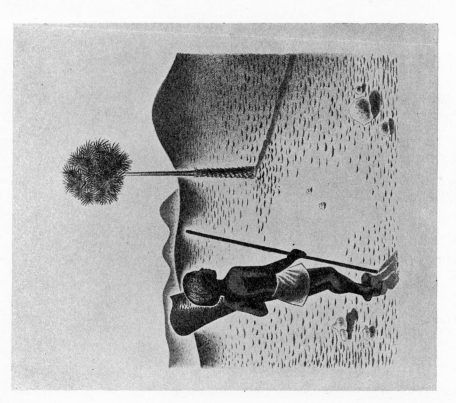

PAULO WERNECK : *Lenda da carnaubeira*

TZAB, MIGUEL
    Mediz Bolio.   *La tierra del faisán y del venado.* Editorial " Mexico."

WERNECK, PAULO
    Bandeira Duarte.   *Lenda da carnaubeira.* Ministério da Educação e Saude.

MEXICO AND
SOUTH AMERICA
(Continued)

NORWAY

NIELSEN, EIVIND
    Holst.   *Norsk billedbog for børn.* Sarheim.

WERENSKIOLD, ERIK
    Asbjørnsen.   *Norske folkeeventyr.* Glydendalske Boghandel.
    Storm.   *Snorre Sturlason kongesagaer.* Stenersen.

POLAND

BCBIŃSKI, STANISLAW
    Porazińska.   *Moja Wólka.* Bibljoteka Polska.

LEVITT I HIM
    Tuwim.   *Lokomotywa.* Przeworski.

POKRZYWNICKA, IRENA
    Makuszyński.   *Moje zabawki.* Bibljoteka Polska.

STRYJEŃSKA, ZOFJA
    Kolędy. Burian.
    Obrzędy polskie. Mortkowicz.
    Pastorałka złozona z 7 kolęd, 1915. Wyd. Warsztatów Krakowskich.
    Rogoszówna.   *Scroczka kaszkę warzyła.* Wyd. Zakladu Narodowego Imienia Ossolinskich.

RUSSIA

BILIBIN, IVAN
    Marya Morevna. Ekspeditziya zagotovleniya gos. bumag.
    Pioryshko Finista. Ekspeditziya zagotovleniya gos. bumag.
    Pushkin.   *Skazka O tzarye Saltanye.* Ekspeditziya zagotovleniya gos. bumag.
    Pushkin.   *Skazka O zolotom pyetushkye.* Ekspeditziya zagotovleniya gos. bumag.
    Skazka Ob Ivanye-tzarevichye. Ekspeditziya zagotovleniya gos. bumag.
    Sestritza Alionushka, bratetz Ivanushka. Ekspeditziya zagotovleniya gos. bumag.
    Tzarevna-lyagushka. Ekspeditziya zagotovleniya gos. bumag.
    Vasilisa Prekrasnaya. Ekspeditziya zagotovleniya gos. bumag.
    Volga Svyatoslavovich. Ekspeditziya zagotovleniya gos. bumag.

CHARUSHIN, YEVGENI IVANOVICH
    Bianchi.   *Pervaya okhota.* Izdat. Detskoi Literatury.
    Marshak.   *Detki v kletke.* Goz. Izdat.
    Sem rasskazov. Det. Izdat.
    Prishvin.   *Zver burunduk.* Izdat. Detskoi Literatury.
    Tzplyachi gorod. Ogiz, Molodaya gvardiya.

ZOFJA STRYJEŃSKA : *Kolędy*

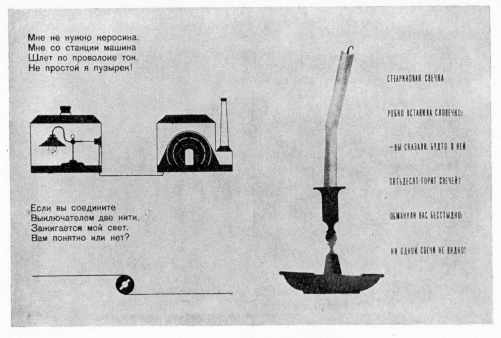

Мне не нужно керосина.
Мне со станции машина
Шлет по проволоке ток.
Не простой я пузырек!

Если вы соедините
Выключателем две нити,
Зажигается мой свет.
Вам понятно или нет?

СТЕАРИНОВАЯ СВЕЧКА

РОБКО ВСТАВИЛА СЛОВЕЧКО:

—ВЫ СКАЗАЛИ, БУДТО В НЕЙ

ПЯТЬДЕСЯТ ГОРИТ СВЕЧЕЙ?

ОБМАНУЛИ ВАС БЕССТЫДНО:

НИ ОДНОЙ СВЕЧИ НЕ ВИДНО!

LEBEDEV : *Vchera i gevodnya*

KONASHEVICH, VLADIMIR MIKHAILOVICH
    Chukovski.   *Skazki.* Academia.
    Marshak.   *Stikhi.* Izdat. Detskoi Literatury.
    Marshak.   *Petrushka Inostranetz.* Gos. Izdat.
    Mirovich.   *Nasha ulitza.* Gos. Izdat.

KUZNETZOV, KONSTANTIN
    Kapitza.   *Pesenki.* Izdat. Detskoi Literatury.
               Kurochka ryaba. Det. Izdat.

LAPTEV, A.
               Pyatiletka. Gos. Izdat.

LEBEDEV, VLADIMIR
               Kto silnei. Izdat. Detskoi Literatury.
               Verkhom. Gos. Izdat.
    Marshak.   *O glupom myshonkye.* Det. Izdat.
    Marshak.   *Pudel.* Ogiz, Molodaya gvardiya.
    Marshak.   *Usaty polosaty.* Detgiz.
    Marshak.   *Vchera i sevodnya.* Ogiz, Molodaya gvardiya.

PAKHOMOV, ALESKSEI
               Leto. Goz. Izdat.
    Marshak.   *Lodyri i kot.* Ogiz. Goz. Izdat. Detskoi Literatury.
    Marshak.   *Master-lomaster.* Ogiz, Molodaya gvardiya.

VASNETZOV, YURY
               Repka. Det. Izdat.
    Tolstoi.   *Tri medvedya.* Ogiz.
    Yershov.   *Koniok-Gorbunok.* Izdat. Detskoi Literatury.

RUSSIA
(Continued)

SWEDEN

ADELBORG, OTTILIA

Ängsblommor. Bonnier.
Bilderbok. Bonnier.
Blomster siffror. Bonnier.
Pelle snygg, och barnen i Snaskeby. Bonnier.
Prinsarnes blomsteralfabet. Bonnier.

BESKOW, ELSA
Andersen. *Tummelisa.* Fritze.
Beskow. *Årets saga.* Åhlén.
Barnen på Solbacka. Wahlström.
Blomsterfesten i täppan. Åhlén.
Lillebrors segelfärd. Ahlén.
Olles skidfärd. Wahlström.
Pelles nya kläder. Åhlén.
Petter och Lotta på äfventyr. Åhlén.
Puttes äfventyr i blåbärsskogen. Wahlström.
Sagan om den lilla lilla gumman. Bonnier.
Tant Gron, Tant Brun och Tant Gredlin. Åhlén.
Tomtebobarnen. Åhlén.

HAMMAR-MOESCHLIN

Blom-Kari. Asherberg.

LARSSON, CARL

Andras barn. Bonnier.
Ett hem. Bonnier.

LEBEDEV : *Kto silnei*

VI. Graphic Processes in Children's Books

HELEN GENTRY

GWEN RAVERAT:
Four Tales from Hans Christian Andersen

RELIEF (*Letterpress*)

a —Impression **cylinder**
a′—Same, enlarged scale
b —Paper
b′—Same, enlarged scale
c —Printing cylinder
c′—Same, enlarged scale
d —Inking roller
e —Inked printing areas; etched, non-printing areas between
f —Printing areas in contact with paper
g —Ink film transferred to paper

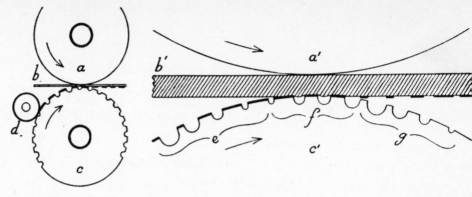

INTAGLIO (*Gravure*)

a —Impression cylinder
a′—Same, enlarged scale
b —Paper
b′—Same, enlarged scale
c —Printing cylinder
c′—Same, enlarged scale
d —Doctor **blade**
d′—Face of Cylinder cleaned by **blade**
e —Ink cleaned off by blade
e′—Ink left in etched cells
f —Ink reservoir
g —Etched cells **after** transfer of ink to paper, as at g′

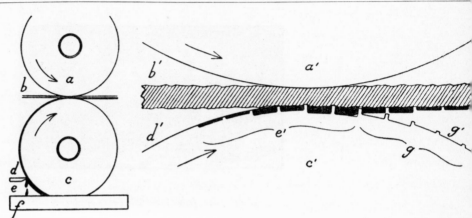

PLANOGRAPHIC (*Offset*)

a —Impression cylinder
a′—Same, enlarged scale
b —Paper
b′—Same, enlarged scale
c —Rubber covered offset cylinder
c′—Same, enlarged scale
d —Printing cylinder
d′—Same, enlarged scale, printing on rubber blanket
e —Inking roller
f —Dampening roller
g —Alternate areas of ink and water
h —Rubber blanket conforming to irregularities in paper
k —Ink, offset from blanket to paper

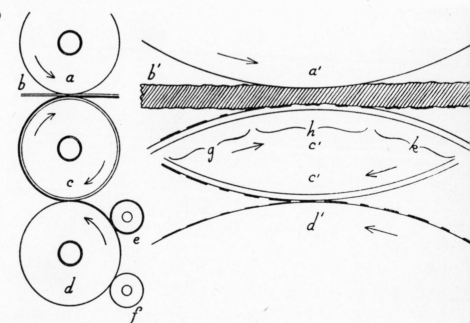

Diagram explaining three methods of printing. Reproduced from The Dolphin.

EDITOR'S FOREWORD

THE more notice we take of the form of a book, and the relation of all the elements involved to each other and to the book's design, the greater will be our pleasure in books and the greater our discrimination. In 1935 one of our outstanding women book designers, Margaret Evans, who has also had much experience in actual printing, presented, in *The Horn Book*, a plea for the same care and taste in making a child's book as would be expended upon an adult text worthy of preservation.

Care and taste in the child's book

"Though the child may notice very little, if at all," she said, "the actual typographical details, though the minutiae of printing niceties be utterly lost so far as conscious appreciation is concerned, still it is not without importance that unconsciously his eye will be trained by good type arrangement and spacing; and the feeling of type well printed on a good paper, encased in decently made covers, will leave its mark." Miss Evans went on to say, "The word 'feeling,' so inevitably called into use in the typographical appreciation of books, is quite as impossible a word to pin into concise definition as the word 'style.' Neither can be taught. They must creep in on one's sensibilities — and the *feeling* of a good book, a well-printed book, will grow within the child's range of appreciation even though he cannot explain his feeling of pleasure in terms of type, margins, paper, the relationship of the illustrations or decorations to the type, etc."

The artist and the machine

In recent years some people who care deeply for art in books have considered that our modern machines were making themselves too strongly felt in our books. The artist who knows his media of reproduction thoroughly and the designer are the answer to this criticism. Lynd Ward, in his introduction to our earlier book, *Contemporary Illustrators of Children's Books*, had this to say: "In the early days of bookmaking, men approached the problems of type and picture with minds free of all considerations save that of making a book. Then gradually the creation of the illustrations was separated from the rest, became involved, complex, a goal in itself. Reproduction entered in, first in the form of human craftsmanship and then, by human ingenuity, in the form of cold machines. Undreamed-of possibilities suddenly leaped upon the scene and after the smoke had to a degree cleared away, we found that what we were offering as illustrations for books were far from being illustrations.

Craftsmanship of bookmaking

"The book artist of today," Mr. Ward said, "is concerned with technique in a far more significant way than were those to whom technique meant, for example, developing the ability to handle a pen so meticulously as to overshadow in complexity the master Aubrey Beardsley. Your contemporary . . . demands of himself, 'What modern processes have been developed that are logically suited to the creation of work that is pure book?' The answering of this question has carried him directly into the craftsmanship of bookmaking, the best possible place for an illustrator to be. . . . Your contemporary is, therefore, in exactly the same relation to his work as were the early bookmakers, whose products have for centuries been held up as most nearly approaching the perfect form. Stimulated by that realization, his illustration has attained a simplicity and an undiluted book quality that has never been achieved in any other way."

An introduction to the graphic processes

Miss Gentry presents, in the chapter which follows, an introduction to the graphic processes which are represented in children's books today, showing from what the current methods have developed. For complete understanding, the layman needs to see the various processes in action. It will help, too, if he considers that while the artist uses tools, paints, and crayons to make his picture, the book designer uses paper, type, pictures and binding to express text fully and harmoniously.

That the book designer regards his tools as expressive for his purposes as the artist's for his, is revealed in the words of one of the foremost designers of our times, W. A. Dwiggins, when he states his belief that a book should be "a reflection of the warm vitality of living things."

B. E. M.

Graphic Processes in Children's Books

A GRAPHIC process, in the sense used here, is a mechanical method of multiplying art work. Basically it is nothing more than printing: inking a surface, then pressing paper against it. The graphic processes in use today are relied upon for all illustrated books, not only those for children.

Long before mechanical methods developed, illustrations were multiplied by *Printing* hand methods. As men worked they used whatever materials they had: Babylo- *by hand* nians stamped clay tablets; ancient Romans wrote on waxed tablets; ancient Greeks scratched in marble; Egyptians drew on a crude paper made from papyrus; American Indians drew on skins. These forms of written communication gave way to better tools for making marks, and better-surfaced substances for taking the marks, as isolated civilizations came into contact with each other. Artisans dropped the old and picked up the new wherever they found it would simplify their work.

As materials and tools work together they naturally influence each other; *New methods* and as the influence deepens, new and ever newer methods grow out of the old. *grow out of* Here are examples of a few such developments: *the old*

The Chinese made paper from tree bark, fish nets, and finally pure rags; and then discovered that the addition of starch would make it smoother. Their method of writing with a brush did not necessarily require smoother paper, but their method of printing undoubtedly did. For they inked a woodblock, laid a sheet upon it, and rubbed the back of the sheet. The smoother and more absorbent the paper, the more ink it would take up and the blacker and sharper the print.

The later Romans evolved the classic letter forms as they wrote in stone with a chisel. When vellum replaced stone, the chisel gave way to the pen. These materials—the smooth point upon the smooth surface—made fast writing possible, and so changed the Roman capitals into forms from which our present lower-case is derived.

The Chinese invented printing from separate characters four hundred years before Gutenberg, but could not make complete use of it for want of suitable ink and a press.

We do not know when the idea of impressing an image first occurred to man, but it was in the seventh century in China that the first pictures were cut into a block of wood and taken off by rubbing. This transfer of the image to paper was a graphic process, the fundamental idea behind the printing press. It took over eight hundred years for it to culminate in Gutenberg's three printing inventions (1445): the type-mold for casting separate letters of the alphabet in metal; the ink viscous enough to stick to the metal; the press itself. Five hundred years have passed since the completion of his inventions, and the graphic processes are still developing.

Today we print from surfaces of copper, brass, zinc, nickel, lead, steel, aluminum, gelatin, rubber, and plastics by electrically-driven presses which send through thousands of sheets an hour. The complex machinery and the great variety of materials hide the fact that the same ancient method is in operation, using the same four elements with which we are all familiar: paper, ink, type, press. An inked roller is passed across the type, then a sheet of paper is pressed against the type. Nothing could be simpler, nor can the largest press do more.

There are three fundamental methods of printing:

The letters of type are in relief—that is, *raised up*. Woodcuts also have their designs in relief, for the artist cuts away everything except the portions which he wishes to print. The ink roller blackens only the high lines or areas, and only the impression of these appears on the paper. *Printing from a raised image is the relief method.*

Scratching in tablets of clay or wax made a design *below* the surface. So does engraving on copper with a sharp tool. When the ink roller passes over an engraving, it not only covers the surface but fills up the scratches or depressions as well. But before the printing takes place, the surface ink is wiped off. Then the pressure of the sheet against the engraving pulls the ink out of the depressions, transferring the design to the paper. The ink is actually deposited upon the paper in minute ridges, which can be felt by the finger tips. *Printing from an image below the surface is the intaglio method.*

A surface can print without being either raised or incised if it is treated with a substance which repels ink. This repellent is placed on the areas which are not to print. The roller deposits ink only upon the untreated portions— the lines or areas which form the design, and only those portions will print.

Printing from an image on the same plane as the non-image portions is the planographic method.

It can readily be seen that the differences in relief, intaglio, and planographic methods are mainly variations in the surfaces which press against the paper. These printing surfaces are called plates. (See Diagram of methods, p. 158.)

Each of the three methods in its development from hand processes has had a long, rich history. We have space to name only the most favored materials and the printing techniques that grew out of them. These techniques, in turn, formed the artists' techniques, and so became responsible for many of the great styles of book illustration.

Materials and techniques

Wood was an early material, both in China and in Europe, for relief printing. It is tough enough to require a strong tool in a strong hand, and yet it does yield to the artist. The woodcut could be placed in the press along with type and printed at the same time. This fact encouraged artists to make the lines of the design about the same thickness as the lines of the type, producing a gratifying harmony in many of the first books.

The use of wood

The early craftsmen who cut pictures and decorations were anonymous. The printers passed the woodcuts around, sometimes from country to country, using them, as often as not, in any book they happened to be printing!

In the first illustrated schoolbook for children, *Orbis Pictus*, the woodcuts were done by one man.

Toward the end of the fifteenth century a painter of renown, E. Reuwich of Mainz, illustrated a book—the first to do so. He cross-hatched woodcuts in order to shade masses, and thereby took relief cuts a step forward. (Compare parallel shadings on p. 13 with the cross-hatchings on pp. 9 and 4.) He was followed, within the next twenty-five years, by some great achievements in illustrating and bookmaking. Among them were such artists as Dürer and Holbein working as book illustrators; the French Books of Hours with their graceful border decorations; the Florentine woodcuts, beautifully harmonized with the type. Neither Dürer nor Holbein cut their own blocks. There were at that time, and until the end of the nineteenth century, woodcutters who executed artists' drawings.

During these centuries that the handpress was used, wood stood up well against the pressure. But in the first quarter of the nineteenth century a steam-driven cylinder press was invented. It printed four thousand sheets an hour, sixteen times more than the best handpress. This meant that plates had to be

Invention of the power press

capable of greater wear. Woodblocks were reinforced by making them of several small blocks fitted together, and so wood continued as the favored material for relief printing, even in newspapers.

*Thomas Bewick
his own
engraver*
The English artist, Thomas Bewick, departed from tradition by cutting his own illustrations on wood. He scooped lines out of the block with a burin, making what was actually an intaglio plate. It was, however, printed as a relief plate: the ink was rolled upon the surface but not allowed to penetrate into the depressions of the design; so when an impression was taken, only the surface printed, leaving the design as white lines in a black background. (Bewick used a combination of black-line and white-line techniques, though his historical importance is based chiefly upon his mastery and popularizing of the latter.) (Compare light and dark portions of trees and foliage, pp. 16 and 17.) Bewick engraved on a cross section of the wood, where the grain did not interfere with the design. This end-grain block could stand more pressure than one in which the grain was side uppermost. Bewick figured that one of his blocks had withstood nine hundred thousand impressions.

Even though Bewick's practice of cutting his own blocks revolutionized woodcutting techniques, few other illustrators followed his example. There were still professional wood engravers. The Dalziel Brothers were among the greatest of the nineteenth century. Two of their masterly jobs were the engravings for Tenniel's *Alice* (p. 50) and Houghton's *Arabian Nights* (p. 179). A comparison of Tenniel's drawings with proofs from the original Dalziel woodblocks reveals that Tenniel owes much of his *Alice* fame to these brothers. They translated his somewhat indecisive and undeveloped pencil sketches into living, glowing characters.

*The use of
copper*
Copper was the first material to be tried for book illustrations by many European printers, and quite naturally: they were printing from type made of metal and knew its lasting qualities. The hardness of metal makes it resist hand tools. A man could gouge great patches out of wood, but the most he could do with copper or steel was to scoop out fine lines. This gave him, of course, an intaglio plate.

This kind of plate needed a press capable of very heavy impression or "squeeze," with equipment for wiping the ink off the surface of the plate before the paper was applied. Type could not be printed in this kind of press. Paper had to be more absorbent than that used for relief printing.

Although copper engraving developed simultaneously with the woodcut, it was not as widely used. Such illustrations had to be printed by a separate press, on a separate sheet, and pasted separately into the book. This required too much labor. Also these plates were short-lived because the edges of the shallow grooves wore down quickly. The method was bound to lose out.

Copper engravings were found to be excellent for maps and music because they were capable of fine, intricate lines, and the lettering could be done directly upon the plate with a tool, doing away with the need for type. As a medium for fine art prints it has attracted great artists of many periods, such as Andrea Mantegna, Peter Breughel, William Blake. Dürer found copper more sympathetic than wood, possibly because he actually tussled with the metal himself instead of leaving the graver to a workman. Eventually there came to copper and steel, as to wood, professionals who engraved the artists' drawings. Hogarth began as one of these professional engravers. *Copper engraving*

During the latter part of the sixteenth century copper engraving received a two-century impetus from the kings and printers of France whose regulations enforced its use. This gave French artists a field day, as one may see in such books as the Ovid of 1767, illustrated by the brilliant talent of the period. It led, however, to the degradation of book design because these illustrations were pasted into the book and, consequently, had no such integration with type as had the woodcut.

Cruikshank engraved his book illustrations. His Grimm was done in copper. The reproduction on page 25 shows the fine lines, but cannot, of course, reveal the intaglio printing method. Some of them, like the *Punch and Judy* of 1827, were colored by stencil.

At the very time the earliest printers were relying upon the human hand to cut their illustration plates, armorers were decorating iron suits by etching with acid. Artists were quick to appropriate the process, and have used acid down to this day to bite lines into steel and copper. Printers were slower, for etching made an intaglio plate which, as we have seen, could not print with type. Not until the middle of the nineteenth century was a method evolved of etching a relief plate. Chemicals ate away the portions *not* to be printed—the blank areas—leaving the lines of the image raised. Acid now became a major factor in revolutionizing plates of all kinds. The hand labor of tooling out the image was eliminated, but someone still had to draw the design upon the plate before it was etched—until the invention of photography, which completed the mechanization of reproduction. *Acid etching eliminates hand labor*

Photography and the photo-engraver

Today the platemaker photographs the drawing, exposes the negative to the printing plate, and then etches the plate. He can use the negative to make either a relief or an intaglio plate. The artist may draw on paper, and draw large or small, for the camera can photograph to any size.

The maker of relief plates is called a photo-engraver. He nails the zinc plate to a block of wood to make it type high, and we get what is called a zinc cut (though zinc is not " cut," as wood once was). The printer locks the cuts into the press with the type and prints them together. We commonly call relief printing letterpress, because it " presses letters (type)."

Gravure

Our modern form of intaglio printing is called gravure, the French for engraving. Not only the illustration is placed on the printing plate, but the type also. A proof of the type is photographed and the negatives of both are exposed to the plate in their respective positions. The necessity for a separate press for each is done away with. Gravure presses are fitted with a scraper, called a " doctor blade," to take off the ink on the surface of the plate.

Relief and intaglio methods of printing are as old as the invention itself, but the planographic method, growing out of the scientific developments of the nineteenth century, is truly modern.

Lithography

Alois Senefelder discovered a planographic method accidentally in 1796 when he wrote his mother's laundry list with a greasy pencil upon a porous stone. Through hundreds of experiments he finally developed by himself a full-fledged printing process—lithography. The artist draws directly upon the stone with the grease pencil and then dampens the stone with water. As the ink roller passes over, the ink (which contains grease) adheres only to the greasy pores, being repelled by the water in the pores of the blank areas. The sheet of paper takes off the ink—and the image—when printed. A scraper moves across the paper to apply pressure, a kind of mechanical version of rubbing. There is also equipment for wetting the plate.

Edmund Evans: his use of lithography and gravure

The color printer, Edmund Evans, gave English-speaking children the benefit of lithographic illustrations when he reproduced by this method the work of Walter Crane, Kate Greenaway, and Randolph Caldecott. He also printed by gravure, bringing out in 1881 Crane's *The First of May: A Fairy Masque* (see p. 60). This book is also historically significant because the text in Crane's handwriting (or, calligraphy) was reproduced upon the plates with the illustrations. Crane worked consistently for unity of type and illustration. His work has become a milestone in book design. Today's interest in calligraphy for picture books is a similar return to one of the fundamentals of book design.

What is believed to be the first British periodical printed by color lithography is *The Little Ones' Own Colored Picture Paper*, London, May, 1885.

Lithography rapidly became a major printing method when a light sheet of grained zinc or aluminum was substituted for the unwieldy stone. The flexible metal could be wrapped around the cylinder of a rotary press. The latest variation is that the plate does not touch the paper. Instead, it prints the design upon a rubber roller which in turn impresses it upon the paper. All contemporary large-quantity lithographic printing is done by this offset method. *Modern lithography*

Designs can be drawn on paper and then transferred to the plate. The artist uses a lithographic (greasy) crayon. The printer dampens between blotters the sheet which bears the drawing, lays it upon the plate, and applies pressure. Much of the crayon transfers to the plate. Then he "fixes" the transferred drawing with a solution of acid and gum arabic, cleans the plate, and has it ready for the press.

Sometimes the artist draws on a small stone or grained zinc plate. A print is taken off and used as a transfer in the method described above. Illustrations in other mediums than lithographic crayon, as well as proofs of type, can be transferred to the plate by photography. In fact, most present-day illustrations are so photographed. Very few are drawn directly upon the plate.

The ways of making paper, and the raw stuffs which go into it, were being modified all during these centuries to suit the different kinds of printing plates and presses. With glue for sizing, and stamping-mills to macerate the old rags, surfaces and weights could be manipulated according to need. Paper was from the beginning the standard printing material. The age and stability of the industry is well illustrated by the Montgolfier family of France, who have been engaged in making paper since 1147. *Changes in paper and ink*

As long as presses were run by man power, sufficient paper could be made of rags, but the steam-power press demanded a wider source of supply. Wood was known to be a possibility, but more than beating was necessary to prepare its fibres. Chemicals eventually solved the problem during the last century. The increasing speed of presses has changed paper. It must absorb ink at an instant's pressure—a " kiss."

Inks, too, have had to fit themselves to speed. Handpress ink is so stiff it almost needs an axe on a cold morning. Ink for modern book presses is about as thick as molasses, and that used on high-speed newspaper presses about like maple syrup.

The graphic processes described so far[10] include all but one of the major developments. This is the method of reproducing tones, such as those in a black-and-white wash or a photograph. A line drawing made with a pen has the same density of blackness everywhere in the line. A stroke of the lithographic crayon has dark and light portions of varying degrees. (When lithographs are drawn directly on the plate or transferred by pressure, the original variation of tones is preserved.) A stroke of a paintbrush likewise has variations in tone. When the crayon or wash stroke is photographed in the usual way, and the negative exposed to the plate, these tonal values do not appear in the metal, for the metal is either etched away, or left to print. There is no halfway point—no way of making the metal stroke print black at one point and gray at another.

Invention of
the halftone

The solution of this problem was so important to the future development of printing that a score of men in England, Europe, and the United States wrestled with it during the latter half of the nineteenth century. The composite invention was completed by Americans, and came to be known as the halftone process.

The toned subject is photographed through a fine screen, the lines of which form tiny areas or "dots." This screen, thus, separates the various tones into microscopic dots varying in size and shape according to the subject. These variations are brought about through the action of light rays in the camera. The photographic negative with its thousands of dots is then exposed in the usual way to letterpress, gravure, or offset plate—as the printer may require—and etched. The dots actually appear on the plate as dots amidst blank areas. The printed effect is one of tones, the lighter areas having smaller dots and shading into the darker areas having larger dots. (See p. 375, etc., under magnifying glass.)

The halftone
in letterpress

Such a plate for letterpress use is called a halftone. It is blocked on wood, as is the zinc cut. Screens of from 120 to 210 lines to the inch are generally used for halftones for book illustration. Newspaper halftones have screens as coarse as 60 lines, and these can be seen by the naked eye. The paper for printing fine-screen halftones by letterpress must be extraordinarily smooth. This is accomplished by coating it with a fine, absorbent clay. Such paper is objectionable in books because it is perishable, and looks and feels unpleasant to most people.

The halftone
in offset

Since the offset halftone plate does not come into direct contact with the paper, but with the rubber roller, its paper does not need a highly coated surface. It must, however, be able to stand moisture without stretching. The offset plate may be made from a combination negative: some portions halftone, some line. And so toned illustrations may be placed on the same plate with the type.

Offset plates are inexpensive and quickly prepared, and capable of running a long time before showing wear.

Gravure is at a disadvantage when it comes to printing type because all subjects for gravure plates must be halftone (screened). Screening breaks up the solid lines of the letters and gives them a ragged appearance. It is so serious a limitation that the process cannot be used for books with much text, but only for picture books and illustrations printed separately from the text. In the gravure plate the halftone dots are etched to varying depths according to the tones—the darker the tone the deeper the dot, or cell; the lighter the tone, the shallower the cells. Consequently, shallow cells carry less ink than deeper ones. This gives to gravure printing wonderful gradations in tone: the sharp white of no ink to the rich black of the deepest cells, which cannot be equaled by any other halftone process. *Advantages and disadvantages in gravure*

As each printing method developed it was used for color. Initials were done in colored inks by early printers, but woodcuts were printed in black and the color added by hand or by stencil. Later, color was added by printing flat tints with solid woodblocks. The intaglio copper plate was also colored by hand in various ways. One way was to rub in several colors on one plate and take them all off by one impression. All of these methods, of course, gave only solid lines or solid areas of flat color. *Printing in solid colors*

Printers could not reproduce the shadings of color in paintings and water colors. The mezzo (half) tint was an effort to do this. It was a copper engraving made upon a surface which had been entirely roughened by a tool. In 1722 the German, Le Blon, made three mezzotints to copy a painting: one plate for each of the primary colors—red, yellow, blue. When printed in these three colors, one upon the other, a good copy of the painting was obtained. Formerly it had taken not only three plates to reproduce a painting, but as many as there were colors, which might be ten or thirty. About this time, also, color was reproduced by printing in black one key mezzotint which contained all the shadings, and then printing over that the solid colors by woodblocks. *The effort to reproduce shadings*

The lithographic stone naturally produced tones because of its porous composition. It was a good color medium for original work, but as a reproduction medium got no further than the mezzotint.

The final major invention in mechanical reproduction of color was the halftone three-color process. This was a photographic development of the halftone. Le Blon had to copy by hand from a painting the yellows on one mezzotint *Invention of the three-color process* plate, the blues on another, the reds on a third. Today, filters are placed in a camera instead. The three primary colors are photographed, one at a time, each through a filter which blots out all light rays except those of the color being photographed. The halftone screen remains in the camera so that each color negative will have the same tones as the original. We get a negative for each primary color, and from these negatives a set of printing plates can be made. The set of negatives may be used to make plates for any method of printing. A fourth plate, printed in black, is added to deepen the darker color values.

Methods and processes in today's printing

Today four-color halftone printing is widely used for children's book illustration. Our three printing methods all use it, some more happily than others. Letterpress is hampered by the coated paper requirements. Such cherished illustrations as Rackham's are reproduced by this method, giving us very poor specimens of bookmaking with type on one kind of paper and pictures on another. Nobody likes books made entirely of coated paper, and there is no other solution. But for printing type no method can equal letterpress. It actually presses the metal letters slightly into the paper, giving a sharp, clean-cut impression. Gravure is forced to spoil the type by etching and is too expensive except for large quantities. Offset lithography is the only one that can print unetched type and halftone illustration together on book paper. This has made it a prolific source of illustrated children's books.

So it has come about that anything an artist draws or paints can be placed upon a suitable plate for printing. For each of the hand operations we have substituted a machine, a chemical, a scientific principle. In command of these processes are artisans as skillful as the old professional engravers of wood and copper. This brief outline cannot give a complete understanding of the reproduction processes, but it may be used as an introduction to further study.

The illustrations in the following outline are examples of the printing and reproduction processes described in this chapter. The letterpress examples are taken from illustrations in this volume, which is itself printed by letterpress. For the offset and gravure examples, however, the actual volumes themselves must be consulted. To appreciate this necessity one has but to compare, for instance, the picture from *Mittens* in this book (p. 299) with the same picture in the original book, *Mittens*. The original is printed by gravure, while here it is printed by letterpress from a halftone cut. The original books must be consulted, also, for colored illustration examples.

Letterpress is better for printing line and flat color illustrations than for shaded *Letterpress*
or toned.

CUT IN WOOD. The cutting action of the tool makes a firm, forceful line. Gill's
horse is the black-on-white technique, while Daglish's mice are the white-on-
black. (cf. Bewick, p. 17.)
Eric Gill, p. 186. Eric Daglish, p. 311.

PEN OR BRUSH LINE DRAWINGS have comparatively free and continuous strokes
because the paper surface offers little resistance. In the Duvoisin, strokes are
made thick or thin by varying pressure on the flexible brush; while in the
Eichenberg, the strokes are of more even weight because the pen is stiffer.
Roger Duvoisin, p. 352. Fritz Eichenberg, p. 304.

FLAT COLOR DRAWINGS (without shading). The raised portions may be areas as
well as lines. One color is printed at a time.
Valenti Angelo, *The Long Christmas* by Ruth Sawyer. Vera Bock, *Arabian Nights*.

SHADED CRAYON DRAWING for letterpress must be coarse in texture. Compare the
Kent with crayons on p. 266, the originals of which were printed by offset.
Rockwell Kent, p. 250.

SHADED DRAWING, FINE CRAYON OR WATER COLOR, must be reproduced by halftone (p. 169), and printed on coated paper. If the illustrations on pp. 218, 242,
269 are examined with a reading glass, the dots can be seen. Dots appear on the
background as well, for the screen in the camera naturally covers it, too. Many
books have water-color illustrations on coated paper. They were printed from
halftones. Compare them with other books having water-color illustrations on
book paper. The latter were undoubtedly printed by offset.

Offset Lithography is better for crayon and wash illustrations than it is for *Offset*
line work.   *lithography*

CRAYON DRAWN ON LITHOGRAPHIC STONE AND TRANSFERRED to the printing plate
is the ideal way of drawing for the process. The fine graining permitted by the
stone is more apparent in black and white than in color illustrations.
Ruth Gannett, *Hipo the Hippo* by Dorothy Thomas, or *Miss Hickory* by Carolyn
Sherwin Bailey. The D'Aulaires, *Leif the Lucky*.

CRAYON DRAWN ON PAPER AND TRANSFERRED to the plate.
Peggy Bacon, *Buttons*, p. 266, and the book.

CRAYON DRAWN ON PAPER AND PHOTOGRAPHED to the plate is the most common
procedure because it is quicker and cheaper. It is less faithful to the original than

transfer. When the drawing is photographed through the halftone screen, the dots break up the crayon strokes. Even an untrained, naked eye can see the difference in such crayon shadings. Also, colors are less clean-cut when printed from halftone plates. Compare the illustrations above (direct reproduction) with those below (photographic reproduction).

Feodor Rojankovsky, *The Tall Book of Mother Goose*. Also compare this book with the Père Castor editions he illustrated in France, some of which were done by direct reproduction. C. H. de Witt, *The Story of Alaska*.

WATER COLOR, OR WASH, DRAWN ON PAPER AND PHOTOGRAPHED to the plate. Here the halftone screen is an advantage because it breaks up the color into shadings. And the printing method is an advantage because it can be done upon regular book paper, instead of coated.

Hardie Gramatky, *Little Toot*, p. 258, and the book. Tasha Tudor, *Tale for Easter*, p. 273, and the book.

Gravure   Gravure, as noted on page 169, cannot be equaled by any other halftone process for illustrations printed separately from the text.

TONED DRAWINGS AND PHOTOGRAPHS reproduce in rich, velvety blacks because the ink is deposited upon the surface of the paper instead of being absorbed by it.

Claire Newberry, *Mittens*, p. 299, and the book. H. B. Kane, *Tale of the Promethea Moth*.

VII. Illustrators of Children's Classics

PHILIP HOFER

ALEXANDER CALDER : *L'Estrange's Æsop*

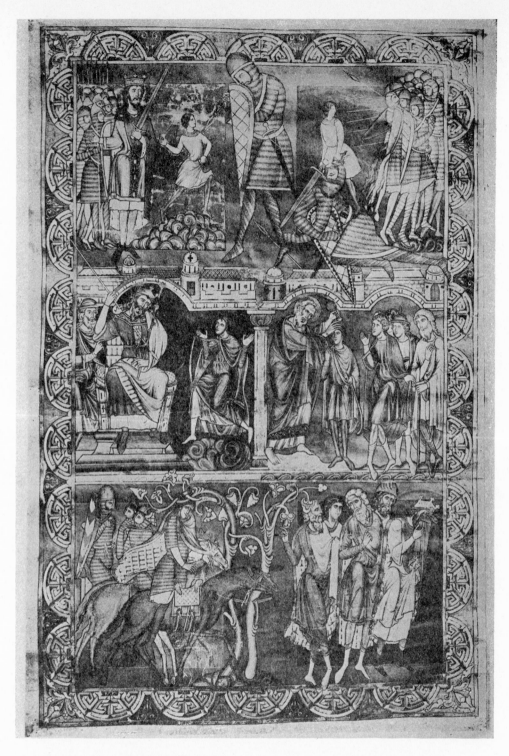

Page from ms. Winchester School "Bible," English, XIIth Century

EDITOR'S FOREWORD

THE editors asked Mr. Hofer to write about the illustrators of those books down through the years which children have adopted for their own. Mr. Hofer might have visited bookstores and asked to see their classics for children. He would doubtless have been shown current editions of Perrault's *Tales*, Grimms' *Fairy Tales*, *Don Quixote*, *Robinson Crusoe*, *Gulliver's Travels*, *Robin Hood*, *King Arthur*, *Water-babies*, *Alice in Wonderland*, and *Treasure Island*. If he had made such a visit, and written his chapter from his findings, he would simply have added a bit more information about certain volumes in our bibliographies.

He has chosen, rather, to take us into the treasure rooms of libraries, *The author's* thereby opening up to many of us new avenues of book adventures and new *personal selection* book knowledge. So that we may not feel uneasy in strange country, he has *of classics* presented us with his personal selection of classics. And thus we have Howard Pyle's *Wonder Clock* and Stevenson's *Treasure Island* hobnobbing with the Malermi Bibles printed in Venice in 1490. That is just the way it should be with books, and children themselves should have more opportunity to see the rare ones, old and new.

The treasure rooms of libraries and museums reveal how long book history *Treasure rooms* is. They show us clay tablets such as were in the library of King Ashurbanipal *of libraries and* of Babylon; the papyrus rolls of King Osymandyas of ancient Egypt; the *museums* scrolls known in India, China and Japan "so many hundreds of years ago that scholars are unable to establish the dates of their first usage," as Lawrence Thompson, of the Princeton University Library, has written; and the scroll libraries of Euripides, Aristotle and Plato. The Persians ransacked the great library of Thebes more than a thousand years before Christ. The Greeks carried away book treasures from Egypt. And Julius Caesar it was who destroyed, though unwittingly, the great library of Ptolemy II at Alexandria.

"The more things change, the more they are the same."

B. E. M.

175

JOHN FLAXMAN : *Iliad of Homer*

Illustrators of Children's Classics

Some very astute opinion maintains that the most important books in literature are those which, although written for adults, have been preëmpted by children. This is, perhaps, only another way of saying that the best is the simplest. But added, in this case, are requirements of group judgment and the lapse of time. Children, like colts, can be led to a stream, but it is impossible, collectively, to make them drink. Nor, in the mass, can they be said to have "adopted" a book until at least several generations have passed. Thus, since children are notably freer of fashion, desire to conform, and prejudice than their elders, their considered judgment should be greatly valued.

One does not have to be adult to appreciate Walt Disney's best movies, the beauty of high mountains, or a thick beefsteak. Such excellences are obvious, and are so taken for granted that they are only truly appreciated when they are no longer to be seen—or tasted. Moreover, children instinctively bring their intelligence to bear at once on the books they read. They are properly wary of their elders' recommendations and gifts (for fear they should be "uplifting" or "instructive"), and they have an intuitive recognition of a good thing. One sometimes wishes we had a few youthful literary critics. We might be spared some very foolish reading!

Of course, some great books, like Newton's *Principia*, Darwin's *Origin of Species*, and Plato's *Dialogues*, are beyond a child's reasoning powers. Children cannot be expected to pick such books out. But these "classics" are not distinguished so much because they are literature as because they are noted milestones in man's expanding knowledge and thought. Even so, they have been adopted by children, to a minor extent, in simplified works like those on the *Wonders of Nature*. And one can hardly conceive any 'teen-age boy reading for the first time the famous account of Socrates' death in Plato's *Phaedo* without the extreme thrill one feels up one's spine when faced with a great verity of life.

In this case, thought, language and style are on the highest level, yet utterly

177

simple. They are ideal for youth and age alike. But children have also proved themselves willing to wade through much irrelevant matter if they sense a basically exciting and alluring story. For example, in *Robinson Crusoe* they are not discouraged by moralizing, nor in Chaucer's *Canterbury Tales* by ancient, difficult language. In both cases they perceive the greatness of the idea and, recognizing the author's ability to unfold it, allow him to do so in his own way.

Classics that stem from folklore and legend

Thus, not all the classics of literature which appeal to children are uncomplicated ones. However, most of them, like Chaucer, stem from simple folk legends: tales of Greek mythology, Æsop's *Fables*, the *Arabian Nights*, *The Song of Roland*, *Arthurian Legends*, *Till Eulenspiegel*, *Reynard the Fox*, the Norse *Sagas*, and the many collections of fairy tales. Indeed, all ages of man are continually attracted by them—if they will permit themselves to be—as in olden times when family and retainers gathered to hear a wandering minstrel or storyteller. These legends are really the accumulated imagination and wisdom of a whole people, and I cannot emphasize too greatly the preëminent place they occupy among the classics which have been annexed by children, nor the intelligence children have shown in so distinguishing them. Even the *Bible*, notwithstanding an overriding spiritual content, falls in the area of folklore. Its *stories*—not, unfortunately, the spiritual lesson—make sacred studies palatable.

Children's appreciation of literary style

Children, on the other hand, have a real appreciation of literary style. The manner of telling is nearly as important to them as the story itself. Otherwise they would not have singled out the great books, which they have, from a host of inferior ones. For example, they seem to have rejected Charles Lamb's *Tales from Shakespeare* despite its author's fame, because of a diffuse style which is quite unlike his clear, concise *Dissertation on Roast Pig*. Moreover, Fox's *Book of Martyrs*, sometimes cited as a classic adopted by children, appeals, if at all, in spite of really gross defects. To be sure, in this case children can smell fire and brimstone at close hand. They can also feast their keen young eyes on woodcuts containing unaccustomed horrors. But I, for one, have never believed that this book was truly liked by children. It has no real plot. The style is heavy, and it simply records a succession of dreary martyrdoms. Surely it must have been picked up mainly in Puritan and Victorian households on Sundays when better stories were forbidden or lacking, and its appeal must have been largely the quite unsabbatical enjoyment of gory details!

But here, at last, is where pictures for the classics which children enjoy come

A. B. HOUGHTON : *Arabian Nights*

in—and better ones than are to be found in any edition of the *Book of Martyrs*. Historically, of course, one should consider first illustrations of the *Bible*, Homer's *Iliad* and *Odyssey*, and Æsop's *Fables*, since they belong to classical antiquity. Some of the earliest "illustrations" still extant are subjects from the *Bible* and the *Iliad*. They are contained in precious illuminated manuscripts, long since locked up in great public collections. Thus they are no longer— if they ever were—illustrations which children knew, and preëmpted, but nearly unrecognizable and very distant ancestors of the ones they know today. Similarly, I doubt if more than one child in a million knows the enchanting woodcuts which illustrate the so-called *Malermi Bibles*, printed at Venice from 1490 to 1494, although they have a directness and charm which any child would comprehend. The few copies of these editions surviving are also in special collections remote from childish hands.

The need for reproductions from Bible manuscripts

It is a pity, but probably it is a fact, that no illustrations, of any book, drawn earlier than the seventeenth century are known generally to children of today except through fragmentary and often inaccurate facsimiles. With the modern reproductive processes, and a progressive attitude among the great libraries, art museums and publishers, there is no reason why this situation cannot be altered. Indeed, there is a wonderful educational and commercial opportunity in the exquisite miniatures which illuminate European *Bible* manuscripts dating from the tenth to the fifteenth centuries. If sufficiently large editions are ordered, and care is taken, modern color reproductions can be well and cheaply done. Russia and Germany have shown the way. The Insel Verlag, of Leipzig, some years before this last war, reproduced a part of the famous German *Manesse Codex* which any child would adore, in gold and colors, to sell for eighty *pfennigs* (twenty cents)! And even before the First World War almost equally fine color work was being done in Russia. I have at my hand an edition of a fairy tale, *Volga*, by no less a writer than Pushkin, which Russian children have adopted. It is illustrated by Ivan Bilibin and happens to have belonged to the Tsarevitch, last of the Romanoffs, when he was eight years old (1912), with an inscription in the Tsarina, his mother's, hand. Soviet children's books have kept up this fine tradition. Our American illustrators and publishers could well afford to seek inspiration in the books of Lebedev, Favorsky and other modern Soviet artists.

But to return to *Bible* illustrations. There are so many editions which children may remember that I cannot begin to name them all. Thus I am forced

IVAN BILIBIN: *The Volga*

to a small choice, and an intensely personal one. I cannot pretend to choose the ones which individual children would enjoy, but can only adopt a policy—as I shall continue to do throughout this chapter—of recommending those which seem to me to have the most lasting merit. It would be fun, also, to write *entirely* about illustrators of whom most children, and even adults, are ignorant in order to spur the reader's curiosity, but this temptation must be resisted.

Bible Illustrators   The artist, Hans Holbein the younger, is certainly well known, but the series of excellent woodcut illustrations of *Old Testament* stories which were published over four hundred years ago are not familiar because of their rarity and the lack of facsimile editions. Perhaps the best *Bible* illustrations of more modern times are William Blake's water-color drawings. If only they were not isolated subjects, never published with the *Bible* text and only known today in reproductions! More available are *The Parables of Our Lord* (1864) and *Bible Gallery* (1880), wood engravings by the Brothers Dalziel, after various artists—notably Sir Frederick Leighton and Sir J. E. Millais. At their best they have directness, simplicity, and conviction. And it is this last quality which seems notably lacking in most *Bible* illustrations since the Reformation! Ludwig Richter and Schnorr von Carolsfeld in Germany, and Gustave Doré in France, drew Bible illustrations a few years earlier which have some merit, although they somehow lack " life." Eric Gill's modern English woodcuts for the *Four Gospels* (1931) are strong, even if they seem an anachronism in the present world. Stephen Gooden's decorations for the *Nonesuch Bible* (London, 1924) have style but do not stir one's imagination. Of more importance seem to me the gorgeous colored aquatints and woodcuts by George Rouault in André Suares' *Passion*, published by Vollard in Paris (1939) and the rather less moving, but able, aquatints of Edy Legrand in *Le Cantique des Cantiques*, Paris, 1930.

The Iliad and the Odyssey   The *Iliad* and the *Odyssey* are equally hard subjects to illustrate, embracing as they do one of the most romantic and yet little known eras of history (or fable). But, fortunately, many children and adults know Flaxman's engravings either, as best seen, in the originals of folio size, or in small reproductions. Cold though they may be, they have beauty, grace and dignity. They derive closely from ancient Greek vase paintings, and thus one imagines one sees in them the classic period. We are too far removed today to know how near the truth they may be, yet to me they are unforgettably linked with these stories as I read them in my childhood.

It is said that the young Keats sat up all night reading Chapman's *Homer*. If

FREDERIC LEIGHTON: *Bible Gallery*

so, the probability is that the copy he read enjoyed little or no illustration. Indeed, despite the wonderful imagery of the text, most editions to this day have been left unillustrated. This was the case in the first printed edition of Florence, 1488. To be sure, John Ogilby, an extraordinarily versatile character, ordered large copper engravings for his metrical translation (London, 1660). They are, however, heavy and dull. Bernard Picart's engravings, in Holland, and Marillier's, in France, during the next century, are but little livelier and seem frivolous.

There were no remotely adequate Victorian illustrations. Max Slevogt illustrated a German edition of the *Iliad* in 1906 with lithographs. Maxfield Parrish attempted a slightly different text in Hawthorne's *Wonder Book and Tanglewood Tales* (1910), which has the merit of his feeling for the far-away and the lighting of a late afternoon sun, but is highly stylized and hence unreal. N. C. Wyeth, a more spirited artist, succeeds little better. Therefore, Bruce Rogers, when he designed the illustrations for T. E. Lawrence's translation which was issued with such fanfare in 1932, returned to Flaxman's idea and copied decorations from Greek vase paintings, which he sensationally rendered with black lines on a gold ground!

Æsop's Fables   In a word, illustrations for Homer, other than Flaxman's, which may be only a personal liking, are not successful. But the designs for Æsop which begin with the first illustrated edition, Ulm, Germany, about 1476, are exactly the reverse. There is a veritable galaxy of good ones from all countries and all periods. I would like to illustrate a dozen in this article: not only the Ulm edition named, but the Verona 1479, the Naples 1485, and a Venetian edition of 1487. None of these are well known to the general public, or to children, but being simple outline woodcuts they could all be successfully redrawn and reproduced at little expense. I am including Francis Barlow's engravings for a London 1665 edition which is still less well known and is one of the finest books of its country and period. Then come the tiny woodcuts for Croxall's 1722 *Fables* which inspired John and Thomas Bewick (1784 and 1818); the beautifully printed Baskerville edition of Æsop's *Select Fables* with rococo engraved decorations by Grignion after Wale; and the dozens of nineteenth-century Æsops all the way down to Arthur Rackham (1912), Agnes Miller Parker (1931) and, almost simpler than the very earliest woodcuts, the line drawings of Alexander Calder in the Harrison of Paris edition (1931). Altogether, Æsop is as perfect a subject for illustration as the Homeric epics are difficult ones. And the contrast could not be greater in the number and variety of successful illustrations. Moreover, as Thomas Fuller, author of the *Worthies of England*, says, " Children cannot read an easier nor men a wiser book."

The *Arabian Nights* are newer to readers of the Western world, but have their roots quite as remotely in the past. There are no illustrated editions earlier than the eighteenth century, and no appropriately illustrated ones till William Harvey's wood engravings for Lane's English translation, London, 1839. If

Arabian Nights

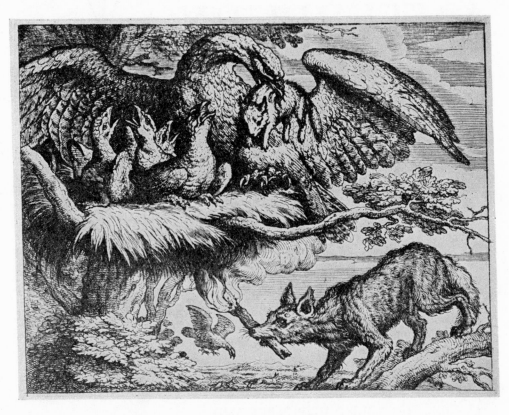

FRANCIS BARLOW : *Æsop*

only Voltaire and Rousseau had not destroyed the fashion for fairy tales in the middle of the eighteenth century! And if only Eugène Delacroix had been invited by an enterprising publisher of the 1830's in France to design woodcuts or lithographs! The best nineteenth-century illustrations are, to my mind, those of A. B. Houghton (London, 1865), and the best modern ones are those of Maxfield Parrish (1909) and Edmund Dulac (1907). But the ideal illustrator for the *Arabian Nights* is yet to be discovered.

The *Arthurian Legends*, which have always been favorites with children,

Arthurian Legends

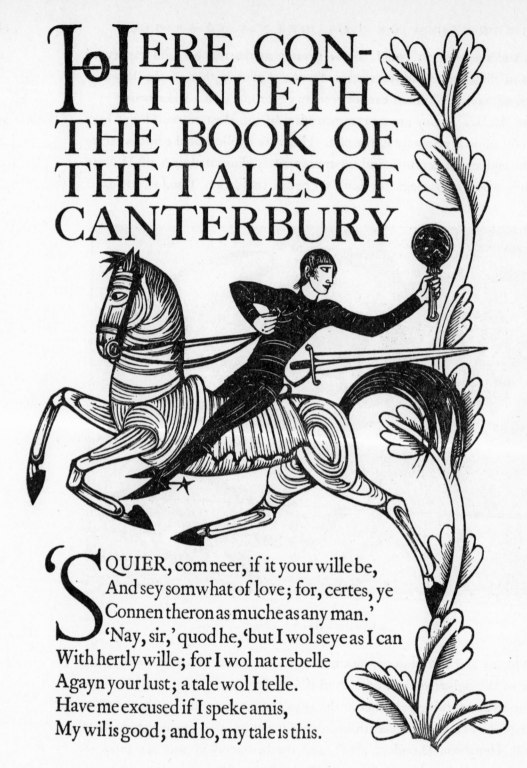

HERE CONTINUETH THE BOOK OF THE TALES OF CANTERBURY

'SQUIER, com neer, if it your wille be,
And sey somwhat of love; for, certes, ye
Connen theron as muche as any man.'
'Nay, sir,' quod he, 'but I wol seye as I can
With hertly wille; for I wol nat rebelle
Agayn your lust; a tale wol I telle.
Have me excused if I speke amis,
My wil is good; and lo, my tale is this.

ERIC GILL : *Canterbury Tales*

although written first for adults, have found sympathetic illustrators, particularly during the last fifty years. Aubrey Beardsley's woodcuts for Malory's *Morte d'Arthur* (London, 1893–4) are his best work even if much too sophisticated for the subject, but Howard Pyle (1903–10) and N. C. Wyeth (1917) in this country have been in many ways better. They are decidedly more vital than near contemporary English efforts by W. Russell Flint (1910–11) and Charles M. Gere (1913).

The *Canterbury Tales* started off bravely, in books, with rough but ready woodcuts in early English editions of Chaucer's work. The Urry edition of 1721 has anonymous small engravings of real directness and worth. But from this date on, till the middle of the nineteenth century, when the Chaucer Society was founded, adults themselves seem to have given up Chaucer because of the difficulty of the language. The "classic" illustrated Chaucer is William Morris' Kelmscott Press edition (Hammersmith, London, 1896), with Burne-Jones' woodcuts. But printed in Gothic type, and ponderous folio in form, not to mention its enormous initial cost, it is scarcely a book which many children will have been given to read. They will be more likely to have seen Hugh Thomson's illustrated edition (London, 1904) or the exceedingly decorative Golden Cockerell Press edition of the *Canterbury Tales*, in four volumes, illustrated with woodcuts by Eric Gill (1929–30). *Canterbury Tales*

Don Quixote is more like Æsop in the number of editions. Over one thousand have been printed since the first appeared (unillustrated) at Madrid in 1605. But far fewer *Don Quixotes* have been satisfactorily interpreted. The Dordrecht (Holland) edition of 1657 first establishes an iconography, but the engravings are really grubby little affairs attributed to Salomon Savry, which can best be flattered by calling them "quaint." There is a wealth of eighteenth-century illustration: in France, Holland, Germany, England and Spain. The best are the French, 1723–4, with engravings after Charles Coypel's famous paintings which used to hang in the Château of Compiègne. They are decorative but too sophisticated and "gallant." Then there is the Spanish Academy edition, printed by Joachim Ibarra at Madrid in 1780, with engravings after Carnicero and others. The latter is the more authentic, as it is the soberer, with a greater sense of the Spanish scene. *Don Quixote*

Once again I must stop to wish for things that never happened: that Hogarth had worked more carefully on a series of eight engravings which he designed for a publisher; that Fragonard had carried further the nineteen crayon and bistre wash drawings he started; that Goya had taken up the theme in any form; or that a far-seeing publisher had commissioned Daumier, who was so entranced with the subject that he repeated it again and again in paintings and drawings! In any one of these cases we might have had great illustrations for Cervantes' masterpiece. But instead we have to content ourselves with Tony Johannot, Célestin Nanteuil, Gustave Doré, and Daniel Vièrge in nineteenth-century France—who are not bad—or with Smirke, Stothard, Alken, Cruikshank, Houghton and Crane at the same period in England—who are less good. More recent artists like William Strang have been unsuccessful, although I personally

DAUMIER: *Painting of Don Quixote and Sancho Panza*

like E. McKnight Kauffer's impressionistic color stencil plates which illustrated the Nonesuch Press (London, 1930) edition, and Hans Alexander Müller's color wood engravings (New York, 1941).

Pilgrim's Progress   Bunyan's *Pilgrim's Progress*, as E. V. Lucas says, in his introduction to the Victoria and Albert Museum Catalogue of 1932, "was written for the simple, not for the immature." Nevertheless, children have certainly adopted it. There is a rousing good story behind the didactic purpose (which children resent, but overlook), and scholars are beginning to feel that the language and style are admirable. Children apparently sensed this long ago; for they have steadily

" demanded " the book. The pity is that they have never received a well-illustrated edition. Like Shakespeare or Milton, it is on such a scale, and means so many different things to different people, that it is exceedingly hard to illustrate. William Harvey failed in England, and Alexander Anderson failed in America, over a century ago. Even William Blake's water colors, which were never published in the artist's lifetime (1757–1827), do not really come off, although the Limited Editions Club (1941) color reproductions are worth examining. Frederick Barnard and William Strang also failed, so we await the day when a serious artist who knows and loves the text will succeed in illustrating it to more than a handful of admirers' satisfaction!

La Fontaine's Fables

La Fontaine's *Fables* are, like Æsop's, a much better subject. From the very first edition in France (1668), with François Chauveau's engraved vignettes, it has been well and frequently illustrated. Indeed, one cannot conceive of an unillustrated edition! Yet Rousseau bitterly attacked the placing of the *Fables* (not just La Fontaine's *Contes!*) in the hands of children. He claimed that only five or six fables were naïve enough. One wonders, therefore, how well Rousseau understood children despite his *Émile* (1762)! But, fortunately, for once, the great French philosopher was not listened to. There were many fine French editions: the great folio edition in four volumes (1775-9), with J. B. Oudry's designs, and a Paris (1796) edition in octavo form, with Simon and Coiny's charming engravings. There were also good German and Dutch illustrations by Meil and Picart

BOUTET DE MONVEL : *Jeanne d'Arc*

and a host of Romantic woodcuts. In our own time are Rudolph Ruzicka's fine, sensitive engravings in the Limited Editions Club issue, printed by Updike (1930), and Stephen Gooden's engravings for a London edition of 1931. Last but not least are: first, the charming French edition, illustrated by Maurice Boutet de Monvel, who was also author of another French classic (which should be in all children's hands, though perhaps not written for them), *Jeanne d'Arc;* and Marc Chagall's etched illustrations for the late Paris publisher, Vollard.

Mother Goose and the Fairy Tales

Mother Goose, which stems from Charles Perrault's *Contes du temps passé*, of 1698, and the folklore of France and England, can be passed over hastily because the best editions are well-known ones: Crane, Caldecott, Kate Greenaway, and Rackham, and the less well-known colored engravings for *Cinderella* (*Cendrillon*) by Jules Pascin, Paris, 1930; so also must the folklore of Germany and Denmark, in the form of Grimm's *Fairy Tales* and Hans Christian Andersen's. In my opinion the best illustrations for Grimm are the head- and tail-piece vignettes by Walter Crane in Macmillan's 1881 edition, and not the better known copper plates of George Cruikshank (1823–26). Similarly, I like Dulac the best of any Andersen illustrator, although I respect the more solid and less colorful work of Speckter, Richter and Pedersen in the nineteenth century.

But best of nearly all fairy-tale compilations I like Howard Pyle's *Wonder Clock* (1888), which I find even better than his more famous *Robin Hood* (1883). In his early outline pen-and-ink style, Pyle reached back towards the best illustrations of the fifteenth and sixteenth centuries—in their directness, their appropriateness, and their consistency. If I think of one book of my childhood most, it is the *Wonder Clock*. Doubtless it was written *for* children, but it is a classic all the same!

Robinson Crusoe

Robinson Crusoe is a much more famous book and one adopted by children because it contains the most appealing situation that an author ever invented. Therefore, it has been universally popular despite long moralizing passages. But it has never been well illustrated—to my taste. The very first editions in England, Holland and France (1719–21) are as good as any. They have a few nice simple engravings—the Dutch and French ones being after designs by Bernard Picart. Yet over a hundred and fifty years later a publisher was using the same illustrations—in the Paris Cazin edition of 1784, in smaller form! Rousseau called *Robinson Crusoe* the only book suitable for Emile. The essential idea of life on a desert island was copied and parodied in a score of different ways. Still, really good illustrations have never appeared, although Bewick,

Stothard, Harvey, Grandville, and—of all people—Gavarni, tried during the last century. The Bewicks were the best because they were the simplest. N. C. Wyeth made a better modern attempt than most in about 1920, and E. A. Wilson in 1930.

Gulliver's Travels shares almost the same popularity and is little finer— so far as illustrations are concerned. Here again the early editions are usually illustrated, and again they are copied throughout the succeeding century. The subject is such an attractive one, for pictorial invention, that it is strange that more, and better, attempts have not been made. Grandville (1838), C. E. Brock (1894), Arthur Rackham (1909), and David Jones (1925) are among the more successful efforts. Hogarth is the artist who could have illustrated the subject best, since he was nearest to the author, not only in country and time, but in the intensity of his political and social satire. But these last are qualities in the book to which children are quite oblivious! *Gulliver's Travels*

Among representative books adopted by children in this very personal choice of mine, there now remain only *Uncle Tom's Cabin*—a great book beloved by children—and Stevenson's *Treasure Island*, which is an even greater story, although it has no significance in social history. There appear to be no good modern illustrations of Mrs. Stowe's classic. One must seemingly fall back on late French romantic illustrations and on the ever-facile George Cruikshank. *Treasure Island* is somewhat better served. Here again we have N. C. Wyeth's dramatic pictures (1911), and E. A. Wilson's illustrations of 1941. In modern France, René Ben-Sussan has done some good lithographic illustrations. *Uncle Tom's Cabin*

One may argue that *Treasure Island* was written for Stevenson's nephew, Lloyd Osbourne, and therefore does not properly fall within the limits of my subject. One may also contend that it is too "young" a book to be given a permanent place. On both these points, opinions differ. The choice I have made has been admitted before to be a personal one. And the purpose of this chapter is not to supply encyclopædic knowledge. Rather it is to offer the reader an introduction to the philosophy and artistic aspects of the subject which may be pursued *much* further, or as *differently* as he pleases with time, interest and the reference collection of a good library. *Treasure Island*

There is only one final point that I would still like to make—and by placing it last, emphasize it strongly. One must realize that the writing of books *for* children is a relatively modern idea. Up till less than two hundred years ago children had to *select for themselves* from among the classics of world literature *Modern idea of books written specially for children* which their parents possessed. I cannot see that children have liked these same texts any better since special simplified editions have been edited and illustrated for them. Indeed, I should say the reverse. For the " simplifying " editors have played havoc with the author's style, the " timing " of his story, and hence with its dramatic sense. The illustrators have done nearly as badly. As a result there is scarcely a children's edition of a world classic which is really equal to the corresponding unsimplified one.

Children's own choice

This is not to say that books in the last two centuries written *directly* for children lack permanent value. On the contrary, there are many great ones and there are many fine illustrations made directly for them. Only these are beyond the scope of this chapter. Comparisons between their merits and the classics here considered would be interesting; for in the latter case no " simplification " was attempted. The illustrations were made freshly, for new texts. But when it comes to classics of *world literature* and children are given a choice, if they are old enough to read easily, they will choose the " grownup " edition nearly every time—for pictures as well as text. And, as so often, they are right!

WALTER CRANE : *Grimm's Household Stories*

VIII. Animated Drawing

HELLMUT LEHMANN-HAUPT

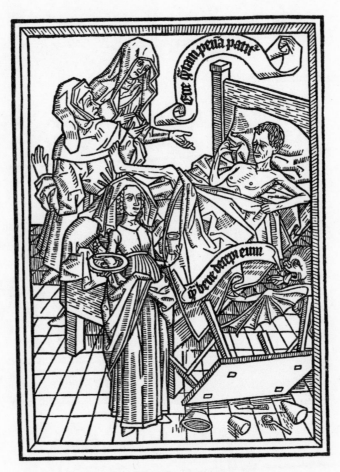

*The sick man's temper tantrums, from a 15th Century
block book, Ars Moriendi*

Temptation of **Adam** *and Expulsion from Paradise* — *9th Century Bamberg Bible*

EDITOR'S FOREWORD

IN 1799, William Blake attempted to illustrate a book for the Reverend Dr. *William Blake on fun, mirth and happiness* Trusler, author of *Hogarth Moralized*, but the point of view of the two men was so far apart that Blake finally gave up the work. In a letter to Dr. Trusler he wrote: "I percieve that your Eye is perverted by Caricature Prints, which ought not to abound as much as they do. Fun I love, but too much Fun is of all things the most loathsom. Mirth is better than Fun, & Happiness is better than Mirth. I feel that a Man may be happy in This World. And I know that This World is a World of Imagination & Vision. I see Every thing I paint In This World, but Everybody does not see alike . . . Some see Nature all Ridicule & Deformity, & by these I shall not regulate my proportions; & some scarce see Nature at all. But to the Eyes of the Man of Imagination, Nature is Imagination Itself."

Blake was writing with the drawings of Hogarth and Rowlandson in mind. What would he say today if he were faced by the 120[11] different comic books which are now published chiefly for children and which sell over 18,000,000 copies each month? This is a sale which has grown up in thirteen years—since 1933, when the first comic book as we know it, today, *Funnies on Parade*, was published. Perhaps he would say, "No Mirth, No Fun." But the sales figures prove that many children and grownups find pleasure in them.

Nor are they a phenomenon without any past. They have an extremely ancient ancestry, as Mr. Lehmann-Haupt shows. "Animated Drawing," a reader *Animated drawing—stories told in pictures* of the manuscript for this book commented, "Is not all drawing animated?" We might have given Mr. Lehmann-Haupt's chapter the title "Narrative Illustration," or "Continuities and Comics" or "Animated Cartoons." Any one of these titles means a story told in pictures. *Pictures only* it was in the beginning. There have been various developments since. Today, as always, the humorous artist and the caricaturist have the skill to drive home unpleasant truths more effectively than words; to delight us all with the amusing way they see things.

There are today plenty of first-rate artists drawing picture-stories full of genuine amusement, fun, and thrills or dramatic interest without vulgarity, brutality or evil suggestion. And children like these fine books. The host of the so-called "comic" books has come into being through the influence of the movies. It is interesting in looking back over this mushroom development to see that artists have gone from earlier and healthier funny books into the movies and then back into books, not always to the benefit of the books.

Possibilities of the future

When the craze for these books has passed — and there are signs today of this reaction — we shall still be living in a picture era, and we shall still have the problem of non-readers, young and old. But we are only at the beginning of visual education. Everyone who examines the comic books of today seems to agree upon one thing — they are not funny. Perhaps, as one of the paradoxes with which life is always presenting us, we shall again have the truly amusing narrative pictures from young illustrators who served in the war. One of the young artists, represented in Part II of this book, who commanded a PT ship in the Pacific area of the War wrote from Mindoro before his release from the Navy:

"I believe that humor is the best possible of all fields for juvenile writing and that the modern world has plenty of it to offer — but doesn't. Why is everyone so serious these days when there are so many delightful mistakes being made all around us? My goal is a comic strip that *is* comic, and my chosen prophet is the late George Herriman who did 'Krazy Kat.' This may not sound like much of a literary project, but I am very tired of un-funny funny papers."

B. E. M.

Scenes from the 10th Century picture scroll of the Book of Joshua

Animated Drawing

I<small>T</small> would be difficult to overestimate the importance of comic books in the life of American youngsters today. They are a class of books which is theirs completely. Even a meager weekly allowance will permit their independent periodical purchase. Moreover, the comic books can easily be borrowed, bartered, or purchased at secondhand. They exist and circulate on a level below the reach of the adult. Censorship is impractical, prohibition unwise. A great deal has been said and written about these comics. Parents and teachers have protested, publishers have apologized and whitewashed. They have caused concern and some violent discussion.

It is the purpose of this volume to develop a picture of the trends and the personalities that have determined the growth of illustration for children and to define its current status. Because of their unorthodox and much-disputed character the comic books present a special problem and they require rather special, careful handling.

Through exhibitions and a certain amount of research in the last few years, the fact has been established that the comics, in spite of their apparent illegitimate and irresponsible character, have behind them a very considerable tradition. As a form of graphic expression they stem from a surprisingly ancient lineage and have roots that reach far back into the beginnings of European art. To explore these traditions is perhaps not without promise, for it may help us to understand more clearly the true character of the comic strip, to recognize its valuable and permanent elements as well as those that are insignificant and incidental.

The question of definition is not quite easy. The current "Comic Book" is neither really a book in the proper sense of the word, nor is it comic. It lacks the coherence and continuity of a book—unless one understands by that term merely the physical unit of a number of pages folded or assembled a certain way and protected with a cover. And while humor is undoubtedly one of the elements that make up the fabric of comic strips today, it is by no means the

197

most important nor even a particularly frequent one. Especially during the war other characteristics have come to the fore and an element of cruelty and brutality is undeniable. Indeed, a very great variety of subjects is treated in the current cartoons, and an analysis of the contents, of the major and minor characters, the social and even political implication, would be a large and interesting undertaking. However, this would not be particularly fruitful here because it will neither throw light on the relationship between the comic strip and the art of illustration for children nor can it answer the question of what the comic strip really is.

Definition of comic strip

The preliminary answer to that question is easily given. The comic strip is an instrument, a graphic medium of expression; the telling of a story by means of a sequence of pictures each of which represents a successive, progressive stage in the development of the story. It is actually a sort of motion picture technique, without photography, using direct drawing on paper. The motion picture film, which we read projected on a screen at an average rate of twenty-four frames per second, is a complete, continuous, realistic, photographic record of the tangible, visible world in motion. The comic strip is a selection, using not a maximum but a minimum of situations recorded in order to convey convincingly and successfully the development of a story in pictures.

Animated cartoons of the motion pictures

The animated cartoon as we see it in the motion picture theater, and which delights us with its perfect synchronization of color, movement, and sound, is perhaps the most highly developed form of the art of storytelling by means of man-made pictures. It is possible to visualize the animated motion picture cartoon as the youngest descendant of a long line of ancestors from whom it has inherited many important features. It is a curious fact that, in some ways, it bears closest resemblance to the earliest antecedents in the realm of book illustration. If you look at the actual Donald Duck film today, you will see a reel of celluloid bearing a continuous sequence of small, brightly colored pictures. Two thousand years ago, stories told by Homer, Virgil, or from the Bible could likewise have been watched unfolding on a long scroll in a continuous procession of scene upon scene. None of such picture scrolls have actually survived to the present day, but there is a good deal of evidence for their existence. The

Ancient prototype— The Joshua Scroll

Joshua Scroll, a thirty-two foot long parchment roll with brief Greek text accompanying the pictures, in the Library of the Vatican, was produced in the tenth century. But the pictures are so classical in general style and in details that it is reasonable to assume that the scroll is a copy of an original produced

much earlier. It is a wonderfully vivid pictorial account which makes the
"reader" feel he is actually witnessing the valiant deeds of Joshua and his men.

Trajan's Column in Rome, erected early in the second century in honor of
the Emperor Trajan, is famous both for the beautiful inscription at its base
which has inspired letter-designers of all ages and countries, and for the pictorial account of the Emperor's victorious Dacian campaign. It is possible to

*Picture story
in stone—
Trajan's Column*

Pictorial account of the Dacian campaign—Trajan's Column in Rome

read the entire story by following the broad band of relief sculpture which
winds around the statue from the base upward. It has been suggested that the
entire column is a gigantic rendering of an illustrated scroll, a monumental
imitation in stone of a current form of pictorial recording. It cannot today be
proved that this was the intention of the ancient sculptor, but Trajan's Column
is an excellent example of the conspicuous use of the continuous narrative technique which one realizes must have been a familiar and popular one in classical
Rome. One can also say that it was even then an ancient and time-honored
device.

To tell a story in pictures is a natural means of communication which we find in all primitive society—among prehistoric European cave dwellers, in ancient China, and more recently among American Indians. But these early pictographs are the ancestor not only of animated drawing, but of writing and illustration, of painting and decoration. When animated drawing is used in preference to other existing and currently practiced techniques, then we

Abraham sends a servant to find his son a wife—early Christian manuscript of the Book of Genesis

can begin to assess its characteristics and the role it plays in the society in which we find it employed.

Bible pictures— The Vienna Genesis

We have seen that towards the end of the Roman Empire, and at the beginning of Mediæval Christian Civilization, animated drawing held a highly honorable place. It served to glorify the deeds of the victorious Emperor Trajan or the biblical warrior Joshua. Other books of the Bible, too, were presented in this fashion to an audience that was perhaps unable to read and must certainly have included children. An animated version of the first book of Moses has come down to us in a famous series of purple-stained parchment leaves which are kept in the Austrian State Library of Vienna. The *Vienna Genesis*, as it is called, probably dates from the fifth century and is so authentic in its description of the Holy Land that it was probably made somewhere nearby. Here the story is developed on a series of strips which are placed below each other on the pages and accompanied by a few lines of text. It is easy to imagine that the pictures were copied from a continuous picture scroll into a codex when the ancient rolls went out of fashion and were replaced by books made of folded pages between wooden boards. As an authentic early pictorialization of the New Testament, the famous *Codex Rossanensis* ranks high. The manuscript is preserved at Rossano in Southern Italy and is of about the same date and regional origin as the *Vienna Genesis*. Here scenes from the life of Christ are developed on a thin strip of ground which one can follow from page to page. Below are shown prophets of the Old Testament, each pointing upward to the fulfillment of his prophecies. The purpose of these illustrations appears thus somewhat broadened. They are not merely narrative, not just a pictorial life of Christ; they also teach a lesson, namely, that Christ and no one else really is the one of whom the old prophets had spoken. This dignified, one might almost say official, use of animated drawing for the popularization of the Bible, and the graphic explanation of theological doctrine, can be traced throughout the entire Middle Ages in countless illuminated manuscripts of widely varying date and origin. These illuminations are often surprisingly direct in their appeal to popular imagination and the simple, naïve taste of children.

Codex Rossanensis

The *Bamberg Bible*, a ninth-century Carolingian manuscript, contains a cartoon sequence of Adam and Eve in the Garden of Eden, the figures drawn with primitive but highly expressive simplicity. The trees are particularly worth noticing. See, for instance, in the reproduction, shown on page 194, how they are not only part of the landscape, and serve to separate one scene from another, but they also are fully animated and take part in the dramatic action. The branches droop sleepily as Adam slumbers and the Lord creates Eve; they are full and round and bear fruit in the temptation scene; they stretch protectingly over Adam and Eve as they discover their nakedness. When the Lord points an accusing finger at Adam, and Adam at Eve, the leaves of the tree also point threateningly, and they become like spearheads as the Archangel drives them out of Paradise. We think immediately of the Disney trees in Snow White's wood, or of Rackham's trees in *Peter Pan in Kensington Gardens*.

The Bamberg Bible

Salome's dance, in a twelfth-century manuscript, is practically a cinematographic experiment in conveying the impression of movement by recording

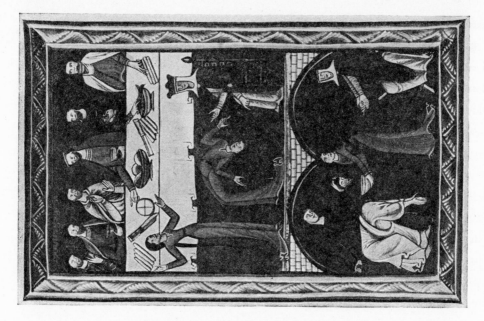

Salome's Dance—from a 12th Century manuscript

Christ entering Jerusalem—from the Codex Rossanensis

closely successive stages of the dance in one single composition. The same merging of a pictorial sequence into a single composition can be observed in another, much later, and much more realistic, illustration of the Garden of Eden, in the famous Book of Hours of the Duc de Berry in Chantilly, an outstanding masterpiece of early fifteenth-century illumination. The Garden of Eden wood-cut in the *Nuremberg Chronicle* is another example of this technique. Like so many other important characteristics of mediæval illumination, animated draw-ing was taken over and utilized in early printed illustration. We find it, for instance, in the block books, where animation served the same basic purpose as in the earlier illuminated manuscripts, namely, to paraphrase the *Bible* stories and to explain the teachings of the Church. But a new element enters in the block book. The artist who drew Adam and Eve in the ninth-century *Bamberg Bible* may have deliberately aimed to please a naïve audience, but quite likely he simply enjoyed giving free rein to his imagination. The fifteenth-century

Book of Hours of the Duc de Berry

block books which, unlike the mediæval manu-scripts, were for sale and intended for a broad, popular audience, were definitely meant to amuse as well as instruct. The artists of the woodcuts in the *Ars Moriendi,* the book that taught how to die at peace with oneself and with God, took great delight in depicting the sick man's tantrums and the alternatingly triumphant and dejected utterances of the devils fighting for the dying man's soul. And why should a fifteenth-century block book printer have chosen such a difficult theological doctrine as that of the Immaculate Conception of the Virgin Mary as the subject for a book of popular religious in-struction? He did it because —under the pretext of defend-ing a major miracle by citing numerous familiar, or smaller

The block books— Ars Moriendi

Temptation and Expulsion from Paradise—Book of Hours of the Duc de Berry

and more plausible ones—it gave him an opportunity to depict not only Danaë and Jupiter's golden embrace, or the miraculous power of the Sirens, but also the farmer carried through the air by a cyclone; the ostrich eggs hatched by the rays of the sun; a she-dog nursing a baby; and similar spectacular scenes. Always within the bounds of its doctrinary intentions, this block book nevertheless approaches a Ripley " odditorium." It definitely caters to the people's appetite for the spectacular and the sensational, much as the morality and miracle plays of the same period offered legitimate excuse for a theater performance in church; for distinctly secular amusement under a thin cloaking of theological respectability.

After the Reformation, and after Humanism and the Renaissance had made themselves felt throughout northern and western Europe, a definite break oc-curred. There is no more attempt to disguise appeals to the ever-present popular taste for primitive sensational pictorialization of " news and features." A new

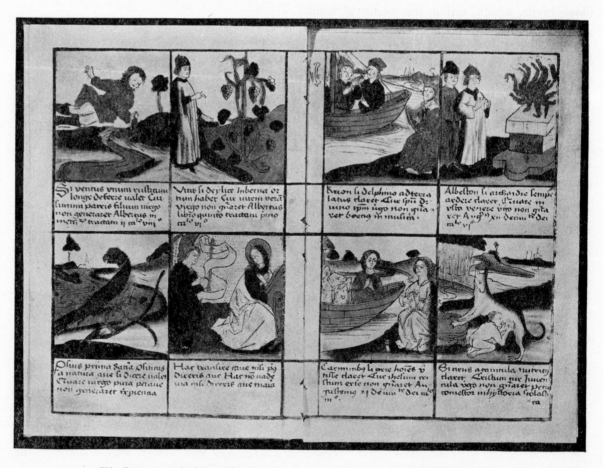

The Defense of the Immaculate Conception—scenes from 15th Century block book

class of illustration develops, the so-called *Imagerie Populaire*, definitely divorced *Advent of the Imagerie Populaire* from the "high-class" graphic art produced by Europe's famous printer-publishers for the civilized taste of aristocracy and wealthy burghers. Copperengraving and etching were the favored techniques of society from the sixteenth to the beginning of the nineteenth century. After Dürer and Holbein, the woodcut loses caste. Holbein's *Dance of Death*, powerful both as religious teaching and social criticism, can be looked upon as the last great woodcut book of universal appeal to rich and poor, to old and young. But soon afterwards the woodcut disappeared from official illustration, to survive in chapbooks and broadsides printed by anonymous, often provincial, printers, sold to the poor by hawkers and peddlers, from door to door, or at the country fairs.

Animated drawing flourished in this realm of the *Imagerie Populaire*. To be *Bilderbogen* sure, it would still be used for an occasional life of a popular saint, such as Saint Nicholas; a clear indication of the children's interest in these picture sheets, the *Bilderbogen*, which sold for a penny plain and twopence colored. But giants and dragons, wars and pestilence, floods and fires, murder and suicide were the favorite topics of these ancestors of the modern tabloid newspaper. Animated drawing had lost the dignified, official position it had enjoyed throughout the Middle Ages.

These brightly colored picture sheets lasted well into the nineteenth cen- *Rodolphe Toepffer* tury, when a significant change took place. Animated drawing once more became legitimate. Credit for this rehabilitation goes to a Geneva artist, Rodolphe Toepffer (1799-1846), the son of a copper-engraver and painter. He is scarcely remembered today, although his *Nouvelles Genevoises* and *Voyages en Zigzag*, illustrated by professional wood-engravers from his free and gracious handsketches, were much admired in the nineteenth century. Early in his life Toepffer came under the influence of Hogarth and Rowlandson, and his work shows his indebtedness to the early masters of English caricature. However, in the use of animated drawing, his development of "pictorial literature"— *Literatur im Bilde* as he called it—Rodolphe Toepffer went far beyond them. In the 1830's and 1840's he produced a series of picture books—*Histoire de M. Jabot*, Geneva, 1833; *Histoire de M. Crepin*, Geneva, 1837; *Histoire de M. Vieux Bois*, 1837; *Le Docteur Festus*, 1840—which can be looked upon as the true beginnings of the modern comic book. He preferred to draw directly on the lithographic stone and he delighted in the speedy and comparatively faithful reproduction of his pen lines.

The Bullfight — popular Spanish woodcut broadside

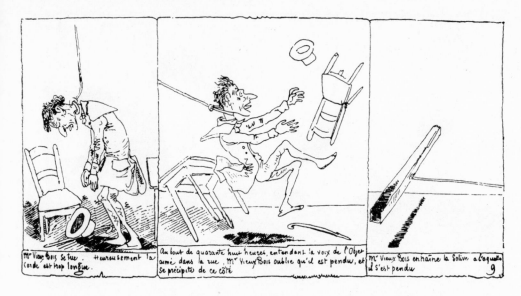

From a 19th Century Comic Book by Rodolphe Toepffer — Histoire de M. Vieux Bois

Gustave Doré, only fifteen years old, followed closely in his footsteps. In 1847 he issued a series of lithographs entitled *Les Travaux d'Hercule*, drawn in a delicate, nervous line greatly reminiscent of Toepffer's work, and a most amusing and original conception of the ancient "Superman." We should not forget that there was no motion picture camera in 1847 to teach the ingenious little draftsman the secret of dissected motion. Seven years later Gustave Doré returned to the comic book, this time with a sophisticated, satirical pen. In his *Histoire pittoresque, dramatique et caricaturale de la Sainte Russie*, published in 1854, he instilled a very personal humor and irony into the time-honored medium of the *Imagerie Populaire*. It is perhaps not without significance that for some time before Gustave's birth his family lived in Épinal, the birthplace of the famous *Images d'Épinal*, of which the observant little boy may well have seen examples in his father's possession.

Gustave Doré

The great German master of the nineteenth-century comic book was Wilhelm Busch (1832–1908). Like Doré he too was very clearly influenced by Rodolphe Toepffer in the quality of his line, in the choice and development of some of his characters and in the whole concept of the story in pictures. Before he attempted the creation of entire comic books, he worked on single sheets as one of a group of artists producing the *Münchner Bilderbogen*, which even then were lifting the old ballad sheet from its humble position and making it a vehicle for much talent, humor and sentiment. "The picture sheets and the picture

Wilhelm Busch

From the Comic Book, Les Travaux d'Hercule, by Gustave Doré

stories originated in such a manner," Wilhelm Busch tells us, " that first the drawings were made. Afterwards the verses were added, just the other way around from regular illustrating." His most famous book is *Max und Moritz,* first published in 1865.

Animated drawing through the 19th century

We might do well to pause a moment from reviewing the procession of animated drawing as it moves through the centuries. What, exactly, has happened to it in the nineteenth century? A form of art that had once, in ancient and mediæval times, been highly honored as a means of historical and religious teaching had then deteriorated, catering to the primitive taste of the poor and the illiterate. Why had it become once more respectable, used by well-known artists who were proud to add their names to the drawings published by well-established firms and sold, not at the street corners, but in regular bookshops and print galleries? I believe the explanation is mainly a sociological one. The French Revolution had torn down the old order of society and brought new classes into positions of power and influence. The people's taste was acknowledged on a new level of legitimacy. It was perhaps no mere coincidence that the first modern comic books to give free play to animated drawing originated in democratic Switzerland and republican France.

The question of legitimacy is an important one, not only as regards the history of animated drawing, but also in its bearing upon children's books as a whole. Before the end of the eighteenth century, children's illustration did not

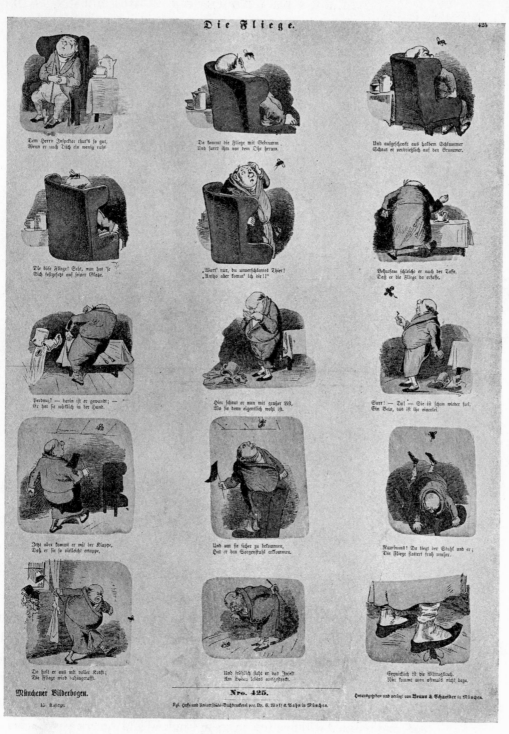

Die Fliege—colored broadside by Wilhelm Busch from the famous Münchner Bilderbogen series

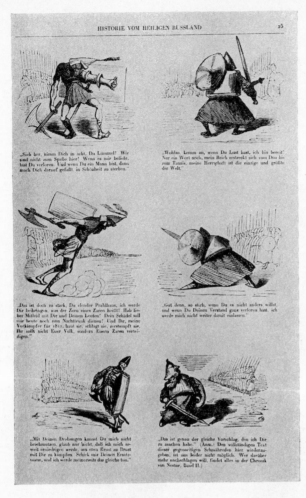

From another Comic Book by Gustave Doré—Histoire
pittoresque, dramatique et caricaturale de la Sainte Russie

From Heinrich Hoffmann's Struwwelpeter—
an illustration from the first edition

exist as a separate, recognized art. Legitimate adult illustration must have been
shared in some small proportion with the children. Much more substantial was
their share in products of the illegitimate *Imagerie Populaire*. It is undoubtedly
no coincidence that *Imagerie Populaire*, and animated drawing with it, became
respectable at about the same time that illustrated children's books came into
their own, in the first half of the nineteenth century.

Struwwelpeter   Dr. Heinrich Hoffmann's *Struwwelpeter*, first published in Frankfurt in
1846, and reissued within a few years in England and America as *Slovenly Peter*,
made excellent use of true animated drawing. The brief case, swimming away
into the distance to the rhythmic accompaniment of a ballet performed by fishes,
is a real " silly symphony," and so is Robert's aeronautical experiment with the

umbrella. From Dr. Hoffmann's *Struwwelpeter*, and the less well-known but very appealing *König Nussknacker* (1879), through the Wilhelm Busch picture books, the tradition of animated drawing reaches into the German children's book of the twentieth century. Arpad Schmidhammer's *Der verlorene Pfennig* (The Lost Penny), published early in the century by Joseph Scholz in Mainz, is a particularly charming and lovable example.

Developments of the 20th century

In her illustrations for *The Pied Piper of Hamelin*, Kate Greenaway interprets the dramatic crescendo of Robert Browning's verse with closely woven sequence of colored drawings which are a masterpiece of cumulative animation. Her contemporary, Randolph Caldecott, too, knew how to play the instrument, and so do Edward Ardizzone, in present-day England, in his *Little Tim* picture books; Jean de Brunhoff, the creator of the immortal " Babar " in France; and Wanda Gág and other contemporary children's illustrators in America.

The technique of animated drawing has found yet another, quite different legitimate application in twentieth-century Europe and America. The modern

Tom Thumb hunting the lost penny in Der verlorene Pfennig, by Schmidhammer

picture novel was created after the First World War by the Flemish artist, Frans Masereel, and adapted to the American scene by Lynd Ward. Like the mediæval block book, the modern picture novel once more searches earnestly for eternal values in human existence,—no more within the framework of theological doctrine, but by bitter social satire and allegorical fantasy. These picture novels, interesting and stimulating as they are, have however remained isolated experiments. They have certainly had no influence on either European or American illustration for children.

It seems to me that genuine animated drawing occurs less frequently in the "legitimate" American children's book than in Europe. If this impression could be substantiated, it would provide further proof of the inescapable fact that in twentieth-century America animated drawing has once more slipped back into the limbo of "illegitimacy." I must confess that, for the moment, I am unable to explain why this should have happened and what it means.

Origin of the comic strip of today   The comic strip of today arose from the comic strip in the American newspaper, where it had flourished since the 1890's. Wilhelm Busch's *Max und Moritz* has been definitely recognized as the model for Rudolph Dirks' "Katzenjammer Kids," which he was asked to develop in 1897 along the lines of the Munich picture book. H. H. Knerr continued this strip when Dirks left the *Journal* in 1914 and started a similar cartoon, "The Captain and the Kids," for the *World*.[12]

That the comic strip, as such, is neither good nor bad, is one obvious conclusion that results from a study of its history. It is not the instrument which is at fault, but the tune that is played on it. That is why any wholesale condemnation of the comics is as unfair as attempts at prohibition are unwise.

Failure of present attempts to raise standards   That all is not well with the comic strip today does not need demonstrating. The worry and concern it causes everybody who is watching over the mental development of children is ample proof. On the other hand, the comic strip could not have developed into an industry of such threatening proportions (twenty-five million comic books each month) if it did not appeal to an enormous number of adults as well. The element of sex appeal in the comic strip is definitely calculated to suit the taste of the adolescent male. Continuous superficial stimulation—the offering of vicarious excitement—is one of the objectionable features. The fascist element (Superman, Wonderwoman) with its acknowledgment of the Fuehrer-Principle is another. A recent discussion of these questions in *Time Magazine* (October 22, 1945) centered on the problem whether the comic strip did not offer the same type of mental "catharsis" which Aristotle had defined as the vital purpose of dramatic art. I agree with those who deny that the comic strip fulfills such a function. On the contrary, the comic strip as practiced today never reaches an artistic climax. The problem of the comic strip is, I believe, very largely an æsthetic one, and its solution can be found in that direction. For this reason it seems to me that the well-meant attempts to raise the standards of the comic book by introducing lofty themes, to restore it to legitimacy by introducing patriotic and religious subjects, are fruitless. Instead of ennobling the comic book these efforts tend to degrade such themes. Of course the Bible stories can be told in animated drawings, as we have seen. The trouble with the current attempts is that they lack true animation. What we see is too often a mere series of stills, animated artificially by inflated speech balloons.[13] The speech balloon in its current elaboration

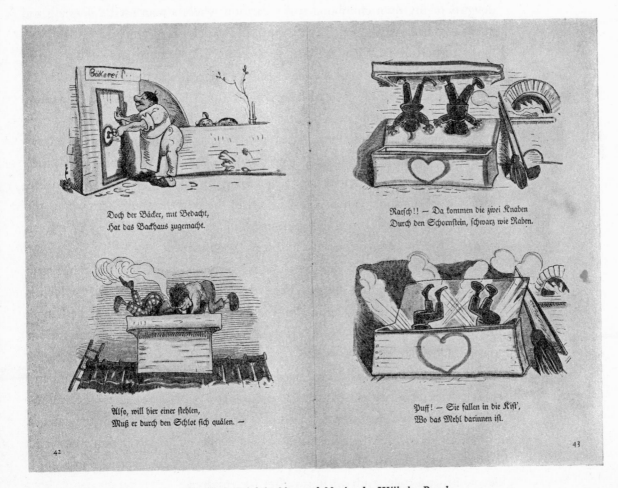

The Sixth Trick in Max und Moritz, by Wilhelm Busch

interferes with the basic simplicity of animated drawing; it sidetracks attention from the pictures which all too often become mere moorings for the balloons— empty stage decoration.

One artist has actually said in print (in *Comics and Their Creators*, by Martin Sheridan) that he cannot afford to draw as he likes, because it would encroach upon the space needed for the speech balloons.

It is amusing how clearly Crockett Johnson, creator of "Barnaby and Mr. O'Malley," senses this. He gets around the problem by animating the very speech balloon itself, when the Invisible Leprechaun speaks, or when Mr. O'Malley loses his voice. The comic strip, as practiced today, is a bastard art, because too often it lacks genuine animation, because it relies on the written word rather than on drawing to make its points.

The misuse of color Color, too, has lost its animating function, its storytelling quality. One of the delights of my own childhood was a cartoon where a man used a divining rod in his own back yard, started excavating, and struck great lumps of shining gold. They turned black when his wife appeared with a lantern and he discovered that he had broken into his own coal cellar. There is also the sixth trick in *Max und Moritz*, where the two bad boys enter the baker's shop by the chimney, from where they drop, coal-black, into the flour box; from there they escape white as ghosts only to fall into the dough, which makes them a creamy-yellow. The baker grabs them and bakes them to a crisp brown. As he turns aside, they eat themselves out of their cocoons and emerge miraculously unharmed in life, limb and coloration. When color is used in the current comic strips, it is too often an automatic routine, dictated not so much by the color needs of a given story, as by the conventions of the three-color process.

Genuine animated drawing has its home today not so much in the comic strip as on the motion picture screen. The only comic strip in print today which is genuine animated drawing appears in the *New Yorker*. Soglow's "Little King" and the Mexican cartoon by de la Torre are the true descendants of the ancient and noble tradition.

The arguments which I have presented in this article are æsthetic ones and in that sense they are one-sided. They do not answer or even discuss all problems that have been raised in the current controversy for and against the comics. I do believe, however, that the chapter approaches the problem from a new and hitherto neglected angle, and one that deserves careful consideration in a book devoted to a serious study of illustration for children.

IX. Developments of the Twentieth Century

MAY MASSEE

C. B. FALLS : *A B C Book*

LYND WARD: *Johnny Tremain*

HENDRIK VAN LOON : *Folk Songs of Many Lands*

EDITOR'S FOREWORD

THE twentieth century in America has seen a unique development of children's books. These books have been of every type and many of them have been genuine expressions of artistic effort in which the arts of writing, illustrating, and bookmaking have united to create a whole capable of giving joy not to childhood alone, but to all ages. At a time of great philosophical and religious confusion, these books have often expressed sound and permanent values.

How have these children's books of sound values and genius happened? They have, first of all, sprung from the particular soil that is America. This is a land of settlers. People from many countries have come here to escape every form of oppression and hardship and to find a better, freer way of life. Their heritage of Old World traditions and cultures, experience of other ways, wide knowledge and abilities have gone into the making of the rich, multi-colored strand which is the atmosphere and life of America. And there has entered into the art process those essential elements of time and space, homesickness, generations of family storytelling, detachment. *The roots of 20th century children's books*

A second reason lies in an essentially American institution, the children's department of public libraries. There one finds respect for, and appreciation of, all races; genuine tolerance of varying points of view; unfailing and deeply imaginative kindness; all the sensitive appreciation of genius, what it means, how it works and how often it grows out of hardship, loneliness and suffering. These children's rooms are now fifty years old. They have themselves created a demand, and have stimulated the school demand, for fine books. They have become, too, more and more articulate in their critical appraisal of books. *Children's departments of public libraries*

The women of fine ability and training who have superintended these children's departments have had a far wider influence in bringing good books into being than is generally realized. Miss Clara Hunt, Director of the Children's

The need for picture books

Work for the Brooklyn Public Library for many years, decided some years ago to bring to the attention of Houghton Mifflin Company in Boston the crying need for picture books. She wrote a letter saying she had a plan to discuss and closed it with the words, "I do not care to speak with a subordinate." Result: Mr. Ferris Greenslet himself called, and there followed somewhat later

E. BOYD SMITH : *Seashore Book*

the publication of Boyd Smith's *Farm Book* and *Seashore Book*. Many instances could be recited.

Publishers appoint special editors of children's books

As a matter of fact, the work of the children's librarians undoubtedly helped to create the third reason for the unique development of children's books in America — the appointment of properly qualified editors of children's books in publishing houses. The first appointment was made in 1919, when Louise Seaman became Editor of Children's Books for the Macmillan Company. In 1922, May Massee was appointed to the same position for Doubleday, Doran, where she remained for ten years, going in 1932 to the Viking Press, where she continues today.

Out of the school and the library into the field of publishing for children these two women came, bringing to their work fine intelligence and sensitive perception; bringing also taste; wide knowledge of books, art and life; and a belief in the importance of books as a source of joy. They brought a new force into the publishing of children's books. Their sympathetic understanding and full appreciation of the creative personality, their enthusiastic succor and protection of their authors and illustrators is the editorial spirit of an earlier and more leisurely time. They knew well the fine examples of bookmaking of other periods — both general and for children — and they called upon the artist to contribute his skill to the whole book. And there came to be such important things to say with pictures, type, paper and cloth that the book-designer grew in importance, too. The first two children's editors were followed by others until now a children's editor is on the staff of almost every publisher.

In spite of the War, many new publishing houses have come into being, thus providing much wider opportunity for many kinds of work to be attempted and appreciated. Now, too, with increased mass production, the artist with popular appeal can earn much more than was possible twenty years ago. In still more cases than previously, the artist now shares half the royalty with the author. The danger lies in the fact that today it is easier and more profitable to turn out picture books than to find good new writers.

The growth of mass production

The artist, on his side, is tempted by work for movies, advertising, comic strips. He must compete with photographs more than ever before. On the other hand, there are signs that a new and excitingly fine type of schoolbook is coming, in the making of which artists will have an important part. And speaking of schools, it was an important day for children when teachers' colleges and college departments of education began to include courses in children's literature, and to build up libraries of the books for teachers in training to examine and enjoy. This important movement will really blossom in far-reaching results for children when teachers read the books for the joy that is in them for themselves.

Miss Massee writes, in the chapter that follows, of English books as well as American. We asked her to write it because of her active part in the developments of the past twenty-five years in America, and her intimate acquaintance with many of the illustrators.

B. E. M.

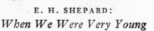

E. H. SHEPARD:
When We Were Very Young

ARTHUR RACKHAM: *Wind in the Willows*

Developments of the Twentieth Century

*Walter Crane
on the
child-like mind*

LATE in the nineteenth and in time for the twentieth century, Walter Crane wrote: " There is a receptive impressionable quality of mind, whether in young or old, which we call child-like. A fresh direct vision, a quickly stimulated imagination, a love of symbolic and typical form, with a touch of poetic suggestion, a delight in frank gay color, and a sensitiveness to the variations of line, and contrasts of form—these are some of the characteristics of the child, whether grown up or not. Happy are they who remain children in these respects through life."

Many artists have a gift of using words as well as pictures. They must have to see so clearly to be able to draw that it is natural they should learn to think as clearly as they see—and from clear thinking to words is an inevitable step. Walter Crane was using his own artist's vision and consequent skill with words when he outlined the child-like characteristics that must be part of every artist's equipment, especially if he is to work for children, and that must be shared in some measure by anyone who tries to appreciate the artist's work.

That bit of wisdom I found and learned by heart when I was young and just beginning my work with books and children. It has helped me all these years and means more to me today than when I first read it because experience has proved its truth. I need it here as a sort of touchstone to help me as I try to remember and put down some of the joy and satisfaction and solid comfort that came with the beautiful books. There weren't so very many in America and most of the best came from England.

*Outstanding
names in the
early years of
the century*

A few names stand out: Hugh Thomson, Arthur Rackham, Leslie Brooke, Beatrix Potter, Cecil Aldin, the Robinson brothers, Francis Bedford, William Nicholson, and later, and for too brief a time, Lovat Fraser. In these United States we had Reginald Birch, the school of Howard Pyle with N. C. Wyeth the leader, Jessie Willcox Smith and Elizabeth Shippen Green, Maxfield Parrish, Willy Pogány, Boutet de Monvel from France, and Willebeek Le Mair from Holland.

Hugh Thomson Hugh Thomson bridged the gap in England, if there was one, from the nineteenth to the twentieth century. Although he had gone to London from Ireland, in 1883, and worked there steadily, his greatest popularity here, the importations of editions of his lovely books, came after 1900. It is characteristic of a good artist that he builds on tradition; and if you find the artists a man admires, you are very apt to find his tradition—the spring that helped him.

HUGH THOMSON : *Cranford*

Hugh Thomson was certainly born with a love of nature in all her variable forms, with a keen eye and a marvelous visual memory, and an inner compulsion to try to transpose to paper the charm, the beauty, and the character of the life about him. Add to this infinite patience and you have the true artist. Apparently Hugh Thomson began to draw at a very early age and never stopped. He worked by himself and had little formal training but a note in his friend's, J. W. Carey's, diary shows the way his mind worked and that he had found his place in the line of tradition.

July 28, 1882. Went to Thomson's with umbrella he had lent me, and had a talk on Caldecott. Hugh was immensely pleased with *The Mad Dog, John Gilpin, The House That Jack Built*, etc. It was a revelation to us all, when we saw what could be done with a simple unshaded outline, provided there was humour and fun in it. Hugh admired Abbey's work in " Harper " and the fine lines took his fancy. He said to me " That is excellent lining for pen and ink. . . ."

Arthur Rackham Arthur Rackham used somewhat the same technique as Hugh Thomson; that is, he made careful and clear pen drawings with everything the pictures needed and then colored the whole in delicate shades to bring out the effect of the drawing and add to its beauty. Rackham, too, admired Edwin A. Abbey.

In a letter published in *The Horn Book* he tells that he had been cutting out the Abbey drawings from old *Harpers'* to make a portfolio—and this was just a year before his death. Artists never stop trying. They are never "finished "— are always seeking some new suggestions, finding pleasure in the perfection of a fellow artist's work.

One day Jimmie Daugherty was talking about artists and he said, " Why, Rackham was the lyric genius of the English people." Of course he was. His drawings are lyric poems in line. They range from the grace of a young birch in springtime to the gnarled strength and eerie root caverns of an age-old beech tree. The earth in its loveliness was his to show, and somehow every drawing was true to the material form of his subject but so imbued with the spirit that his landscapes sing and his people walk the earth in beauty.

ARTHUR RACKHAM : *Rip Van Winkle*

A study of the faces he drew proves him both psychologist and philosopher. No draw-ing is too small to show the character of his model. He knew every line that could be etched on a human face and he drew the lines as carefully and as truly as Nature herself. That is why one can go back to his drawings again and again; every study will reveal more understanding, more kindly and generous humor, and more vivid sense of the things that are unseen. He was equally at home in the best of this world, in the world of faëry and in the world of small animals. He illustrated many books and brought beauty and happy days to thousands of fortunate people who own them.

If the lyric genius of the English glowed in Arthur Rackham, one might say the homely genius of the English made great artists of Leslie Brooke and Beatrix Potter. Leslie Brooke could play with children as children should be played with—he was adept at conjuring up moments of complete gravity that break spontaneously into irresistible chuckles. To know Leslie Brooke one must read his books with children. But to know his friendliness, and see him through grown-up eyes that have watched the children with his books, there is *The Horn Book*, May-June 1941. Here are pictures of Leslie Brooke in his garden, of his young grandson to whom *Johnny Crow's New Garden* is dedicated. Here are

Leslie Brooke

letters he wrote, critical appreciations of other artists' work, a very modest summing up of personal history: "There is really so little to tell. I was born at Birkenhead and received most of my art training at the Schools of the Royal Academy in London. My brother and I were always drawing—like any other children—and I went on drawing; there is my whole story." And then there are delightful tributes from artists, mothers, fathers, librarians, children, grandmothers,—the tributes are rich in interest, variety, warmth, humor,—it is as if Leslie Brooke had given a party and these were his visitors.

> And they danced and they sang, and each visitor's attitude
> Was his very best way of expressing his gratitude
> To Leslie Brooke and his garden.

And the articles are punctuated and illustrated with drawings from *Johnny Crow* and from *Mad Shepherds*, from *Travels Round Our Village* and from *The Jumblies*, from *The Three Bears* and *Ring O' Roses* and *A Roundabout Turn*. It is a joy to read and to look at and makes us realize with Elizabeth MacKinstry

> IN HOMAGE
> Undoubtedly each Leslie Brooke
> Will live, a classic picture book!
> Though other classics may alarm,
> Yours, Mr. Brooke, will always charm.

L. LESLIE BROOKE : *Johnny Crow's Party*

The homely English genius of Beatrix Potter speaks for itself in a letter reprinted in that invaluable anniversary number of *The Horn Book*, May 1944.

The question of " roots " interests me! I am a believer in " breed "; I hold that a strongly marked personality can influence descendants for generations. In the same way that we farmers know that certain sires—bulls, stallions, rams—have been " prepotent " in forming breeds of shorthorns, thoroughbreds, and the numerous varieties of sheep.

I am descended from generations of Lancashire yeomen and weavers; obstinate, hard-headed, *matter-of-fact* folk. (There you find the down-right matter-of-factness which imparts an air of reality.) As far back as I can go, they were Puritans, Nonjurors, Nonconformists, Dissenters. Your *Mayflower* ancestors sailed to America; mine at the same date were sticking it out at home; probably rather enjoying persecution.

The most remarkable old " character " amongst my ancestors—old Abraham Crompton, who sprang from mid-Lancashire, bought land for pleasure in the Lake District, and his descendants seem to have drifted back at intervals ever since—though none of us own any of the land that belonged to old Abraham.

However, it was not the Lake District at all that inspired me to write children's books. I hope this shocking

BEATRIX POTTER : *Little Pig Robinson*

statement will not distress you kind Americans, who see Peter Rabbits under every Westmorland bush. I am inclined to put it down to three things, mainly: (1) The aforesaid matter-of-fact ancestry; (2) The accidental circumstance of having spent a good deal of my childhood in the Highlands of Scotland, with a Highland nurse girl and a firm belief in witches, fairies and the creed of the terrible John Calvin (the creed rubbed off, but the fairies remained); (3) A peculiarly precocious and tenacious memory. I have been laughed at for what I say I can remember; but it is admitted that I can remember quite plainly from one and two years old; not only facts, like learning to walk, but places and sentiments—the way things impressed a very young child. . . .

About 1893 I was interested in a little invalid child, the eldest child of a friend; he had a long illness. I used to write letters with pen and ink scribbles, and one of the letters was Peter Rabbit. . . .

The coloured drawings for Peter Rabbit were done in a garden near Keswick, Cumberland, and several others were painted in the same part of the Lake District. Squirrel Nutkin sailed on Derwentwater; Mrs. Tiggywinkle lived in the Vale of Newlands near Keswick. Later books, such as *Jemima Puddleduck, Ginger and Pickles, The Pie and the Patty Pan,* etc., were done at Sawrey in this southern end of the Lake District. The books relating to Tom Kitten and Samuel Whiskers describe the interior of my old farm house where children are comically impressed by seeing the real chimney and cupboards.

I think I write carefully because I enjoy my writing, and enjoy taking pains over it. I have always disliked writing to order; I write to please myself.

. . . My usual way of writing is to scribble, and cut out, and write it again and again. The shorter and plainer the better. And read the Bible (*unrevised* version and Old Testament) if I feel my style wants chastening. There are many dialect words of the Bible and Shakespeare—and also the forcible direct language—still in use in the rural parts of Lancashire.

So much for herself; and add to this the millions of children of several generations who love her books and call her blessed.

The Robinsons, Ernest Shepard, Francis Bedford

The Robinsons, W. Heath and Charles, made delightful, very simple and completely honest drawings that always blended beautifully with the text they illustrated. They show a man's tenderness for children, and without being sentimental they make you feel that children are the most delightful people in the world. Their edition of Walter de la Mare's *Peacock Pie* and the Andersen *Fairy Tales* were two of their nicest books.

Ernest Shepard has that same charming quality and gaiety and humor in his drawings for *When We Were Very Young* and the other Milne books. It is no wonder that the children love the Shepard drawings, for without being flattering they do show children with their best foot forward. And children like straightforward small drawings that have something to say and say it quietly but with real humor.

Francis Bedford derived right from Arthur Hughes. His drawings haven't the same flowing ease of Hughes' but they have the homely beauty—a genuine peasant quality found more often in the drawings of continental than of English artists.

W. HEATH ROBINSON : *Peacock Pie*

Cecil Aldin carried on the Caldecott tradition of English country life, especially of English dog life. No one has ever equaled or could better his dog
sketches. They are so full of character that to own one of his dog books is
almost as good as to own the dogs themselves.

Lovat Fraser's genius left a blaze of color and unforgettable designs when he died in 1921, really a war
casualty though he was not killed in battle. His stage sets
for *The Beggar's Opera,* his books for the Nonesuch Press
and others are all collectors' items. No one ever made
more gay and rich combinations of pure color held together by strong black round lines made with a reed pen.

In an edition of *Peacock Pie,* published in 1924, Walter
de la Mare wrote: "A few new-old rhymes are included
in this edition of *Peacock Pie!* The embellishments in it
(and it was his own chosen word) were made by Claude
Lovat Fraser in 1912—the rhymes themselves were first
printed in 1913. They are now reproduced in company for the first time, and
a happiness indeed it is to see them together; not only for the sake of the vivid
pictures themselves, and all they give, but because he himself delighted in making

CECIL ALDIN : *Merry Puppy Book*

C. LOVAT FRASER : *Peacock Pie*

them. I can remember, indeed, as vividly as if it were yesterday, talking to him
as he sat at his board with his brush and his bright inks, and watching them
positively leap into life on the paper."

FRANCIS BEDFORD : *Forgotten Tales of Long Ago*

While these outstanding books were coming from England, we in this country had few. There was a group from the Howard Pyle pupils led by N. C. Wyeth. Their paintings made memorable the whole series of the Scribner Classics. Maxfield Parrish made the color drawings for the Eugene Field poems. One of his prints with that marvelous blue sky was standard equipment for every child's bedroom. Jessie Willcox Smith and Elizabeth Shippen Green, with their lovely color pictures for *Mother Goose* and *Child's Garden of Verse*, their page illustrations, and their series of covers for *Good Housekeeping* and *The Ladies' Home Journal*, were very popular. They had high standards of drawing and color work. Their pictures have grace and charm. They are very feminine and tend to idealize and romanticize children, but they give a sense of gracious living before the days of automobiles and apartments and the busyness of life today.

Reginald Birch carried on through all this time the tradition of a good line well used. From the illustrations for *Little Lord Fauntleroy*, which established his popularity, through the 1900's, his drawings for *St. Nicholas* and other magazines stand out and stay in memory for their understanding and illumination of character and scene. Remember John Bennett's *Master Skylark* in the old *St. Nicholas?* The burly tanner, the village children, the geese by the roadside, the big-eyed boy, the great Queen herself, the Drury Lane Theater—they're all vivid pictures. Though they were done so quietly, they had character that only a master can give. Reginald Birch never lowered his standards from *Little Lord Fauntleroy* to the *Gilbert and Sullivan* forty-odd years after. There is the same picture sense, the same careful detail, the same storytelling power, the vivid sense of human values from grave to gay, and integrity of line and design in every drawing that came from his pen.

Joseph Pennell, in his book *Pen Drawing and Pen Draughtsmen*, wrote that Birch scarcely ever used models on his final work but made his drawings from studies, tracing these on Bristol boards, " which he thus keeps thoroughly clean; consequently his work reproduces perfectly well." How engravers and printers must have loved him!

Artists are a hardy folk and the most patient people in the world. Nothing is too much trouble to get a drawing right. First the search for accurate details of some period or event that happens to be needed; then the planning of the sketch, perhaps some work with models for pose or character, then the rough sketch, then the blocking in of the rough sketch on drawing paper. Is that all?

Oh no. Perhaps he puts a tracing paper over this drawing, tries out a few lines more, tries taking out a few lines, very likely transfers just the measuring points to a fresh board and begins all over again. Artists think nothing of throwing away twenty drawings if necessary before the right one is made. This much patience for the main lines of a drawing; but then comes the drudgery process

REGINALD BIRCH : *Last Pirate*

of filling in each little pen stroke or dot placed just so to give the proper shading—hours of just plain labor. No one but an artist would give it cheerfully, but they all do. Yes, artists are the most patient people in the world.

The second quarter of the century

Meanwhile, in those 1900's, things were happening in the book world that were to bring in the great surge—one almost says flood—of children's books that are appearing in the second quarter of this twentieth century. First, of course, was our concept of free and universal education, a concept long established but still to be fully realized. Study of children and their needs developed the idea of more and better books for children and sponsored the children's rooms in public libraries.

Support of beautiful books by the librarians

The more venturesome and imaginative librarians had the wisdom to believe that developing a sense of beauty was a very important part of a child's education. They saw young mothers poring over the delightful interiors in the Carl Larsson books, and making notes for color and arrangements to use in their own homes. They saw designers' eyes grow fairly misty over the lovely blues and grays and reds in the Willebeek Le Mair books. They saw high-school-age children enjoying *Silas Marner* (required reading) when Hugh Thomson showed them how with his pictures of the pitiful old miser and the darling little Eppie. They heard the spontaneous chuckles over " The whale told a *very long tale* " in *Johnny Crow's Garden*. In short, they saw that beautiful books stimulate imagination, rouse human sympathies, bring out the latent sense of humor, help children to be themselves in the best sense of the words, and so to grow into fine livable human beings.

Somewhere about that time the first Russian ballet came to America and brought the marvelous costumes and settings of Bakst. Such a glow of color had never been seen in this country before. And with Nijinsky to dance the color into life, the audiences came away dazzled—to find their surroundings and settings very drab and dreary. Designers caught fire from the glow and very soon we began to see color in textiles, in all the various fabrics for clothes and furnishings. A refreshing note of gaiety crept into the respectable dullness of our "average interior."

Color and the Russian influence

About 1915–1923, George Bellows was showing what a painter could do with lithographs. He liked working on the great stones and his first prints were made by a young lithographer, George C. Miller. The great painter died too young. I have always thought that he would have made some picture books if he had lived. His drawings of children are wonderful; he had so much gusto and humor and he loved to make lithographs. He couldn't have escaped doing children's books.

George Bellows and his lithographs

George Miller is still print-maker-extraordinary for artists who try lithographs for individual drawings or for books. An artist himself, his complete knowledge of the craft—from the choice and preparation of the stone through all the proper strokes of the pencil to the final dramatic pressure and pull of the first proof—has smoothed the way for many artists in the children's book world today.

George Miller, artist and print-maker

But bookmaking was largely a matter of printed pages interspersed at intervals with reproduced paintings which were most apt to be tipped in so that they were easily pulled out and lost. The art of bookmaking—of drawings and text together in inevitable unity—was decidedly not much in evidence and needed to be revived. The audience was here, the libraries and schools were training thousands of children to want more books (to have great bookmakers there must be great audiences, too), the readers were here and the country had become color conscious; the need was for artists to make books and publishers to publish them and booksellers to distribute them.

One best answer to the need was the Bookshop for Boys and Girls in Boston. Established by Bertha E. Mahony under the auspices of the Women's Educational and Industrial Union, the Bookshop was one of the beauty spots of America. Miss Mahony brought the loveliest books and prints and papers from all over the world and displayed them in charming old rooms looking out over the Public Gardens. Here was a place in the new world that John Newbery would have loved. The children brought their parents and the parents brought their children and the uncles and the cousins and the aunts came too as well as any fortunate educator, or author, or artist, or bookseller, or editor or anyone else who had any interest in children's books. They all came away with a growing sense of the realities in the children's book world and, to many, a thrilling sense of the possibilities of the books to come.

The thousands of visitors to the Bookshop for Boys and Girls wanted a catalog of its treasures—so a catalog was made and reprinted and then what more natural than that it should become an annual and semi-annual and finally *The Horn Book* published six times a year with notes of the new books and reminders of the old books. For more than twenty years this unique periodical has been inspiration and satisfaction to all the devoted clan who have anything to do with children's books.

Some time in the early 1900's, Willy Pogány came to add his bit to the growing idea of the necessity for beauty. He was a generous and gifted young Hungarian painter. He brought a suave European technique, a rich sense of color and design, and he made some beautiful books before he drifted to Hollywood. Before he left he had helped several of his young countrymen to make a start in this new world. Most notable of these was Miska Petersham, thoroughly trained and fresh out of art school in Budapest; full of admiration for Italian painting he had enjoyed in his sojourns in Italy, and steeped in the beauty of the ancient peasant art he grew up with in summers on a Hungarian farm. Maud Fuller was his pupil in an art school in New York. They decided after they were married that they would devote their lives to children's books, and so they have. Maud and Miska Petersham: their names are household words wherever children love picture books and undoubtedly they have had more conscientious imitators than any other artists in the field.

The ferment was working. In 1922, Charles Falls decided that he wanted to make an alphabet book for his small daughter. (Small daughters and sons and their needs, both temporal and spiritual, have a tremendous influence on artistic achievement.) Mr. Falls decided to revive the art of wood blocks for books. *C. B. Falls* He would cut an alphabet for his end papers. It is a beautiful alphabet, quiet and *and his* *alphabet book* sure, a sturdy example to add to the thousand years of man's best designing that are inherent in the letters A to Z. Then he would choose an animal for each letter—A is for Antelope, B is for Bear—and he would cut the designs for the animals to be printed in bold black lines. He would cut the blocks for the colors, too, and these should be flat colors for background and for light in the pictures —all good old ideas but used in a modern way that made them brilliantly new. The true vermilion of the book jacket, with the gray elephant picked out with the clear yellow and black, is a familiar sight in every bookshop and in thousands of homes where the book helps train children to love color and to have a feeling for good design. The *Charles Falls' Alphabet Book* encouraged artists and printers and publishers. A new kind of book had found an eager public waiting for it.

The ferment was working. In England, Margery Bianco had written a classic *William* nursery tale, *The Velveteen Rabbit*, and a great portrait painter, William *Nicholson and* Nicholson, had been so charmed by the toy that came alive that he had made *The Velveteen* *Rabbit*

WILLIAM NICHOLSON : *Velveteen Rabbit*

color lithographs for it. The illustrations were real lithographs, drawn on stone, and the first proofs pulled from the stones themselves. Then transfers were made and the book was printed here from zinc plates. Mr. Nicholson railed at the incompetence of our printers and the poor quality of our work and said that our printing was a disgrace to the art. Perhaps today he sees an improvement in our product and perhaps finds work to satisfy even his exacting standards. But *The Velveteen Rabbit* has been on the best-loved list of nursery books for twenty-five years and bids fair to stay there permanently—one of the first modern picture books, a perfect combination of story and pictures.

The Petershams and Poppy Seed Cakes

The next year the Petershams used Miska's understanding of frank gay color in the beautiful old-gold, vermilion, bright blue and black of the pictures for *The Poppy Seed Cakes* by Margery Clark. Before this they had been doing excellent illustration of the more conventional type. This was the first time that they had made a book just the way they wanted to make it. Here was a text that brought the old world into the new and the chance to express the beauty that came with Miska and his knowledge of the traditional peasant art of Europe.

The Petershams have always been innovators. Their *Miki* with its delightful Hungarian pictures ushered in a long line of other artists' children from every quarter of the world. In the school field they illustrated a set of readers that charmed the children so that other publishers scurried around to find artists to create rival sets. They were very much attracted to the Russian educational picture books that showed various phases of Soviet life in revealing and, at the same time, imaginative color lithographs. The best artists have worked on these books —they often have real beauty and humor, they are paperbound, distributed by the millions, and make a unique and thrilling experiment in education.

Picture books of the arts and industries

From the Petershams' interest in these books grew a whole series of picture books of the arts and industries. Here are some of their best drawings and the pictures show their mastery of the lithographer's craft. No one surpasses Miska in his color and in his use of beautiful gray. These books are a monument to their own art and industry and the series would have flowered to more use and beauty if the publishers had not been so insistent on speed and the desire for " one more series this year." Artists do their best work when they can set their own time and pace and do not have to conform too much to a set pattern.

The Christ Child

When they planned *The Christ Child* they had the perfect text in the King James Version. For the pictures they wanted to make the color drawings just

WILLY POGÁNY : *Magyar Fairy Tales*

MAUD AND MISKA PETERSHAM : *Poppy Seed Cakes*

as they would appear in the book. They wanted to forget all the toilsome processes of color separations necessitated by the costs of bookmaking and just make beautiful finished water-color drawings for illustrations. But the book must sell for two dollars and there was no printer here who could undertake such a task of platemaking and printing. So they went to Germany, where they found the three-generations-old firm of Meissner and Buch in Leipzig. These printers were artists as keen as the Petershams to get just the right colors from their plates.

That book was sheer joy in the making from start to finish. A trip to Palestine gave them their inspiration, the costumes, characters and the contours of the country. Add to all these their own great reverence and love for their subject and you have one of the most beautiful books ever made for children. Of course it was an instant and phenomenal success and several years later, under the shadow of Hitlerism and with improvements in our equipment and printing methods, the plates were transferred and the book is now printed here.

William C. D. Glaser and lithographic printing

It was William C. D. Glaser who took over the printing of *The Christ Child*. With Mr. Glaser's untimely death in 1945, the children's book world lost one of its best friends. It was he who invited artists into the printing plant to inspect their proofs and even to work on the plates—this at a time when other printers would not allow artists to enter their doors. He spared no pains to give a book an extra color, a halftone where the budget only allowed a line-cut, a layout that would make an extra print for display; his first idea in planning any book was how much he could give it, not how much he could take out of it. His generous and intelligent coöperation with artists has become the general trade practice, as have numerous other details of manufacture and procedure instigated by him. To his untiring labor and devotion we owe much of the progress in lithographic printing of children's books in the last twenty-five years. He was a true friend to the children.

Ingri and Edgar Parin D'Aulaire

It was W. C. D. Glaser who sponsored the making of the d'Aulaires' first book. Edgar Parin d'Aulaire had appeared from Paris, with a portfolio under his arm, and busied himself with getting a job so that his young wife, Ingri, could pay her passage to this new world. The job and Ingri both materialized, and then began one of the most delightful husband-and-wife careers in the children's book world.

They wanted to make a book about Africa, so they wrote *The Magic Rug*, and Bill Glaser lugged two-hundred-pound stones to their flat in Brooklyn and helped them prop up a table to hold the stones. Now the young artists were ready to work—four drawings on stone for every color picture. They made an elaborate and intricate scale to guide them in using just the right depth of shading for the color they wanted, but I remember the red plate went a little heavy in that book. That taught them that the power press somehow always rolls up the red a little heavier than other colors; so artists draw the red plate a trifle lighter than would seem right.

They learned a hundred other details of their craft and art, and put them all to good use in *Ola*, a beautiful picture book of a small boy's life in Norway and also a tribute to, and a revelation of, a singularly happy childhood that is the foundation of Ingri's personality. This Norwegian childhood and background they now share as they share everything in life. American children's literature is much richer than it ever could have been without Ingri and Edgar, with their wonderful combination of background, imagination, intelligence, skill, and above all, their zest for living.

The D'Aulaires and Ola

Lovat Fraser's use of the reed pen inspired our Elizabeth MacKinstry to experiment with the flexible and sturdy line work that the reed pen makes possible. She designed the book of her own poems, *Puck in Pasture*, chose the type, made the delightful imaginative drawings, plotted each page with loving

Elizabeth MacKinstry

ELIZABETH MACKINSTRY : *Puck in Pasture*

care, and bound it up in gorgeous motley. It was all unconventional but had real beauty and made Bruce Rogers say that this was the first time he'd seen the American spirit expressed in bookmaking. This high praise from the master himself makes that book a pioneer.

Her lovely color drawings for Mme. d'Aulnoy's *The White Cat* show her just as truly a traditional daughter of the eighteenth century, a versatile and delightful artist.

It was Elizabeth MacKinstry who inspired Rachel Field to do her own illustrating for her own poems, *Taxis and Toadstools,* for *Polly Patchwork, A Little Book of Days* and others. She was more author than artist, but still these books make a bright spot in the shelf of the time and have a charm all their own.

Hendrik Van Loon

Hendrik Willem Van Loon had come from Holland. He was a giant of a man with a mind and a heart to correspond. He abominated dullness and he used his pen and colored inks in free, storytelling drawings to add sparkle to all his texts. His books are not only fascinating to the young—they are a challenge to artists and authors. It is impossible to reckon how much dullness we have been spared because Hendrik Willem Van Loon showed how to make books lively. The long shelf beginning with *History with a Match* on to the *Story of Mankind,* the song collections, the biography, history, geography; all were decorated, illustrated, made more truly provocative by his drawings—a great soul; a gifted artist.

James Daugherty

This was a time of beginnings. James Daugherty turned from mural painting to books. He made drawings and paintings to illustrate Stewart Edward White's *Daniel Boone.* It was hard at first, because the mural painter wanted to put a whole wall-full of picture on a page—but it just can't be done and the artist triumphed and recognized the page-limit for illustrations. But he brought a new spirit into book illustration; the American pioneer spirit with the breadth and the strength of it, the beauty of the land and of the people and their gusto. He has the humor and tenderness of a great humanitarian, he can show the rollicking fun of the *Knickerbockers* or of a Kentucky barn dance in his own *Daniel Boone.* He can picture the suavity and the wisdom of the great Benjamin Franklin and the infinite sadness and love for humanity of Abraham Lincoln. And he can be a small boy in the country dreaming a tall tale in *Andy and the Lion.* Whatever he does is fresh and vivid. He is as much a part of the American scene as he is its true portrayer.

Robert Lawson

Robert Lawson was a beginner, too. One of his first jobs of illustrating was done for the *Designer* for the first printing of Carl Sandburg's *Rootabaga Stories.* Even then Robert Lawson was master of his pen and showed that he could take his place in the line of the great tradition from Albert Dürer down to the present. When he was making the drawings for Arthur Mason's *The Wee*

DOROTHY LATHROP : *Little Boy Lost*

Men of Ballywooden, I found that Elizabeth MacKinstry shared my enthusiasm for his work. She had made a portfolio of the " Rootabaga " drawings and she said, " You mark that young man—*he* knows his blacks and whites." So he does, and his colors, too—as time and his maturing have shown. But he was to work for ten years more, illustrating other people's books, before the fortunate collaboration with Munro Leaf made *Ferdinand* and *Wee Gillis*, and started Rob Lawson into writing and illustrating his own books. His backgrounds shine out in *They Were Strong and Good*, while *Ben and Me* and *Rabbit Hill* and the others show him to be witty as well as wise in two of the arts of expression. And he has a rare philosophy—he never takes himself too seriously, and never takes his art too lightly.

Dorothy Lathrop   Dorothy Lathrop was earnestly trying, with the aid of Vassar, to turn herself into a writer, but destiny in the shape of economic insistence decreed otherwise. And her destiny had given her a certain delicate, elusive imagination with a fey quality about it that brought to the young and almost untried artist the joy of illustrating for W. L. Hudson and for Walter de la Mare. And she did not let them down! Of late she has been absorbed by the perfections of small animals; whether Pekingese, or flying squirrel, snail or rabbit—whatever the subject, her drawings have the exquisite precision of a bird's wing, and the quiet integrity of woodland creatures.

Lynd Ward   Lynd Ward was a serious minded young artist who believed wholeheartedly in the work of his hands, and he has trained those square strong hands to bring sure beauty into lines and spaces whether carved on wood or drawn on stone or brushed onto paper. His art is filled with the passionate intensity of his sympathy for the sufferings of humanity and man's striving toward perfection. He can be bitter and ironic as in his *God's Man*, but he can be reverent and imaginative and charming as in Elizabeth Coatsworth's *The Cat Who Went To Heaven*, and whatever book he chooses to illustrate immediately takes on character and style in the best sense of the word.

Valenti Angelo   Valenti Angelo was earning a hard living in San Francisco as a pastry cook's assistant. He decorated the cakes and you may be sure they were works of art. Night school for training and then work for engravers and finally the beautifully illuminated books published by the Grabhorn Press, now collectors' items. But it was to be years later that he produced his own books, his Italian heritage flowering at last, half a world away from its source—but he somehow carries the source within himself, wherever he goes.

HELEN SEWELL: *First Bible*

Helen Sewell   Helen Sewell was earning a living making Christmas cards after a childhood in a Navy family that meant she had been taken all around the world before she was ten. Christmas cards are a seasonal business and between seasons she could squeeze in a book—and we began to look for those books. Her children have more definite quality than most; they live in a world of their own, rather shy though friendly. If Boutet de Monvel were to come to life now, in this country, he might see and draw the children as Helen Sewell does.

Louise Seaman Bechtel wrote a real article about Helen Sewell in *The Horn Book*, March 1946, which should be reprinted in full, but from which we can quote:

The extraordinary number of her books is impressive. Most interesting of all is her range of ability, from the nonsensical, lively comic to the serious and decorative. In every picture, a *story* is always clear. Beyond that, her most thoughtful work gives one a remarkable sense of strength and of peace, of very sure drawing in a firm, daring composition, all held together by a unique magical light, always a light that answers the atmosphere of the story. This is the work of a serious painter. Children who gaze at such pictures are beginning to understand the forms and the integrity of great art.

Lauren Ford,   Lauren Ford was painting children. And it was not until the middle 1930's
Boris   that her foster child and a background of intense personal religious experience
Artzybasheff   inspired *A Little Book About God* and later *The Ageless Story*. In these it is
as if Botticelli's angels found themselves dressed in blue gingham in a Connecticut farmhouse and feeling perfectly at home there. And with it all they have lost none of their beauty though translated into a homely modern setting.

Boris Artzybasheff had come from Russia, a refugee nineteen years old with just two skillful hands to bank on. Life was extremely difficult for him in New York in the 1920's, with precarious jobs for engravers, and tramping the streets looking for more work. But his first book showed that he was to be a designer and that he would make no compromise with his artistic conviction. It was *Verotchka's Tales*, and the illustrations were done in that sort of cranky square-line drawing characteristic of many Russian folk-tale books. So far, so good, but here the young designer stepped in and he wanted designs of birds and whatnot, printed as headings for each page in bright blue—it was like a bluejay perching on a bare branch in the springtime.

LAUREN FORD:
Little Book About God

An extra printing? Nonsense, the publisher would have none of it. But he reckoned without the smiling persuasiveness of the young man. Boris got his blue borders, and from that day to this—from the Greek splendor of his drawings for Padraic Colum's *Orpheus* to the ridiculous absurdity of *Poor Shadullah* or the sensitive realism of his portraits and other illustrations for Anna Hall's *Nansen*—he never has made a book except as he wanted it—and that with a growing sense of design that has become completely satisfying whether in the use of line or shadow, of light or color, or all four.

Ludwig Bemelmans was busily collecting experiences that were to reappear in his own special brand of satiric humor and he was hoarding the memories of his childhood that were to make his first book delightful. But *Hansi* would never have seen the light of day if Kurt Wiese had not come to his rescue. For Ludwig

Ludwig Bemelmans

KURT WIESE : *Saranga, the Pygmy*

Bemelmans is an artist by inspiration and not by craftsmanship. He works hard, will make thirty drawings and throw them all away when he finally gets the right one. But analyze his drawings, the craft of separating his work into four colors and their combinations—that he cannot do and will not try.

Fortunately, Kurt Wiese is a master craftsman and a good friend, so he separated the colors in all those drawings and copied them on zinc plates so deftly that the prints in the book look exactly like Ludwig Bemelmans' original drawings. Kurt Wiese had come to this country from Germany by way of living in

Kurt Wiese

China for nine years. He absorbed so much of Chinese life and spirit that he has been its interpreter not only in his own books, *The Chinese Ink Stick* and others, but also has been called upon to illustrate many more, not the least of which is *The Story About Ping* by Marjorie Flack. Kurt Wiese is so versatile that he is kept busy drawing for other authors. This is partly due to an amazing visual

MARGUERITE DE ANGELI : *Skippack School*

memory—he can draw practically anything he's ever seen—and also he has lived on every continent at some time in his life so has an unusual background of experience to call upon.

Wanda Gág   Wanda Gág was in Minnesota having a difficult girlhood with responsibilities beyond her years. Nevertheless she learned to draw and though she had never been in Europe, her work derived right from the art of her Bohemian ancestors. Her *Millions of Cats* is a perfect nonsense book and has been so adopted by the children. She was the ideal illustrator and translator of Grimm's fairy tales which she did in threes—little books that fit the hand, with black and white lithographs to accompany them.

Feodor Rojankovsky was a Russian refugee in Paris where Esther Averill published his gorgeous *Daniel Boone* and the *Jacques Cartier* with its brilliant black and white drawings. For both of these she wrote the text. Rojankovsky also made the delightful Père Castor books with their softly colored lithograph animal drawings. These are perfect nursery books. Rojankovsky has a genius for the nursery age child and in this country he has enlivened *The Tall Mother Goose* and *Nursery Tales* to the delight of children all over the land.

Marguerite de Angeli, in the last fifteen years, has brought to life in delightful pictures and stories special corners of our land where special people have lived. *Copper-Toed Boots*—upper Michigan in her father's days; *Henner's Lydia* and *The Skippack School*—Pennsylvania Dutch country; *Thee, Hannah!*—the Quakers in Philadelphia. She has found delightful examples of design and crafts and has used them to make her pictures interesting and beautiful. Her work adds much to folk history and puts it in unforgettable form for young children to enjoy.

In the 1920's, Kate Seredy was painting lamp shades in a factory in New York. Later she made Christmas cards, finally illustrated some textbooks, and then found herself truly in the Hungarian farm story, *The Good Master*. This started a shelf of books of which it is hard to say whether the children love pictures or stories best.

THE TORTOISE AND THE HARE

here was once a hare who was always boasting of his speed.

"There is no one in the forest who can run as fast as I can," he told everyone, strutting up and down. "Who wants to race me?"

The other animals were tired of hearing his boasting, but no one ever offered to race him until one day the turtle spoke up.

"I will race with you," he said in his slow way.

105

FEODOR ROJANKOVSKY:
Tall Book of Nursery Tales

Children of today need to see more clearly than ever before in the world, and they demand help to do it. Artists have always taught people to see, and it is natural and right that artists respond to the children's demand with feeling and clarity and vision. They show the

Marjorie Flack

world to the children and stir their imagination to see more for themselves. Marjorie Flack has perhaps more genius as author than as artist, but her unassuming drawings for the *Angus* books with their delightful stories make completely satisfying books for nursery children. And the wise Marjorie persuades other artists to illustrate her stories when she feels they are outside the field of her own experience as picture-maker.

Younger artists carry on the tradition

In the last ten years more artists have added their work. Louis Slobodkin has turned from sculpture to children's books and finds himself equally at home in both. The younger artists who are doing notable work now were just growing up in the first third of the century: Hilda van Stockum in Holland and Ireland, not knowing when she was Dutch and when she was Irish; Elizabeth Jones and Virginia Lee Burton; Leonard Weisgard; Tasha Tudor; Hardie Gramatky; William Pène du Bois; Robert McCloskey;—they were all children when most of the books we have been writing about were being made. We look to them and to many more to carry on the tradition, to add new virtue to a remarkable period in the history of bookmaking.

WANDA GÁG : *Tales from Grimm*

X. The Book Artist: Yesterday and Tomorrow

LYND WARD

WANDA GÁG : *Millions of Cats*

JAMES DAUGHERTY : *Knickerbocker's History of New York*

The Book Artist: Yesterday and Tomorrow

Ours is a world from which the noises of battle have hardly gone. The *The post-war world* shadows of the machines of war still fall across our path, and the faces of war's victims crowd close around us. At a time when we need sober thought, warm understanding, and a clear memory of those glowing concepts for which so many sacrificed so much, we are caught up in a fever of blind activity, a frantic race for the surface trappings of peace-time living. Our minds are assailed with a jumble of charges and countercharges. The international atmosphere is heavy with a fog of fear and suspicion.

This is an hour that calls on all serious and thoughtful citizens for action, action on the political and economic fronts, action that will create the kind of post-war world we dreamed of. In such an hour, fraught with such consequences for the future, it may seem paradoxical to speak of the importance of pictures in books for children.

It is, admittedly, not always easy to see a rational relationship between such *Awareness of permanent values* quiet and insubstantial things as pictures for children and the complicated problems that dominate our horizons. To many they seem completely separate, the gulf between them unbridgeable. For many, basic values and ultimate goals go down too quickly, submerged under the pressing weight of more immediate considerations and the strong compulsions to action. And yet it is only a vigilant awareness of those things that are of permanent importance—liberty, equality, fraternity and the economic and spiritual conditions for cultural growth—that can give meaning to action, and reasonableness to political and social motives.

It is in such perspective that an estimate of our immediate past and present position in the field of illustration in children's books becomes useful.

In the records of the 1930's there will be a great deal written of an upsurge *The 1930's in American art* of interest in mural painting in the United States, of the growth of a new and wider audience for the work of painters who cut loose from the constricting traditions of European prestige and found in American subject matter both excitement and stimulation, and of the popularization of the graphic processes

ROCKWELL KENT: *Saga of Gisli*

whereby it became possible for large numbers of persons to own and enjoy original etchings, lithographs and wood block prints. All this bespeaks a cultural movement of great significance; one whose currents worked changes in both artist and audience, and whose effects will be felt for many years to come.

It was the 1930's, too, that saw book illustration in this country reach maturity. The earlier years, between the great war and the great crash, were years whose dominant characteristic was Exploration, years in which artists were wondering about the potentialities of the book as a medium, when book buyers were becoming aware that productions of singular merit and marked individuality were coming through in book form, when publishers were, thanks to the pioneering faith and the frontier work of a few people of vision, coming to realize that behind the door labeled "juvenile" a very vital and important part of contemporary publishing was being done.

The advance in book illustration

The book artist during the twenties was a somewhat confused fellow. He was able to develop the concept of the book as an integrated production in which his work as a maker of pictures based on the subject matter of the text dovetailed with his function as over-all designer, manipulating details of typography, pictures, layout, end-paper design and binding materials into a single orchestral combination calculated to produce an effect on the reader in tonal harmony with the verbal impact of the text. This concept of the book as a unique physical and emotional phenomenon, as worthy of serious consideration as any other form to which the contemporary artist can dedicate his talents, was a new and imaginatively stimulating idea in the world of graphic art productions. It served to emphasize strongly not only the great gulf separating magazine illustration from illustration for books, but also underlined the difference between making a series of pictures and scattering them indiscriminately among printed signatures of text at the moment of collation in the binder's shop, and, on the other hand, considering in advance and in reference to the development of a story's plot and mood not only the content of each pictorial image in the book, but the precise timing of its impact upon the reader as he turns the page.

The book as an integrated production

But the area in which the book artist was to operate was not very clearly defined. On the one hand we had the sumptuous limited editions in which ostentation usually was an effective obstacle to the functional use of the artist; on the other, the great mass of children's books in which pigeonholing habits surviving from the dark ages of juvenile publishing prescribed the use of one "type" of artist for one category of book, another for another, decreed prosaic

The artist and the book

and pedestrian drawings for informational texts, and in general allowed the original and imaginative craftsman only an occasional "gift" book on which to play with the full tonal range at his command. Between these two extremes lay the great mass of trade publishing, wherein an occasional biography or travel book, and more infrequently a work of poetry or fiction, would be entrusted to an artist for transmutation into an illustrated book. Thus in the twenties there was twisting and turning, attempts in many directions, successful productions in widely separated categories. Kent's *Candide*, Artzybasheff's *Fairy Shoemaker*, Daugherty's *Knickerbocker* and Mahlon Blaine's *Black Majesty* were outstanding books of this decade. Published under the greatest variety of circumstances, aimed at markedly different audiences, displaying the widest range of production cost and retail price, they show similarity only in the medium in which the artists made their originals and in the feeling of a planned and integrated work that is common to all of them.

The artist as explorer   The diversity in these books, diversity not only in subject matter and type, but in audience as well, is indicative of the dominantly exploratory character of the time. It was as though the book artist said, "Look, there are many things that we can do if you will give us the chance—many fields in which we can operate. We have capacities for production that will reward you richly if rightly harnessed. We can take an old classic and infuse it with new life. We can take a biographical study and make its impact on the mind many times more vital, vivid and memorable. We can take a bit of prose or poetry and, using it as a starting point, build around it, and onto it, a sequence of pictures which will make reading that bit of prose an experience entirely different forever thereafter."

Picture books of the 1930's   It was the function of the 1920's, through experimentation in many forms, through exploration of many possibilities, to give the book artist the stature and equipment whereby he was able to make a contribution of value and significance not to one, but to many kinds of books. During the thirties, the technical form in which his talents were to be used most successfully, and with the greatest social value, crystallized in the picture book.

It is true, of course, that during the last decade we have had fine limited editions, particularly reprints of classic works bequeathed to us by earlier generations. Many of these have utilized the work of book artists in a valid and rewarding way. It is true, too, that we have had occasional works of travel or biography that have gained from the contribution made to their final physical

BORIS ARTZYBASHEFF : *Fairy Shoemaker*

appearance by a book artist. And it is equally true that during these years almost all works of fiction for young readers have been produced as illustrated books, and that the experience of reading them would have been a far poorer experience without the work of the artists who made pictures for them. But it is none the less overwhelmingly true that the book work of the thirties that is most significant in itself, and in terms of what it contributes to the world at large, was done in the picture book form.

What picture books can mean to children

This is a highly important fact and it has important implications for all those who are concerned with books, with art, or with children. It means that more and more children are being provided with pictorial experiences that have some permanent value above and beyond the enjoyment of a particular story or the absorption of a special bit of information. In our complicated and mass-produced civilization, the child receives a multitude of visual impressions from earliest infancy. From the newspapers spread on the floor, the magazines scattered over the sofa, from the advertising posters plastered on walls and billboards, from movie screens, electric signs, handbills and comic weeklies, he is attacked with printed and machine-made pictures of an infinite variety. For the most part, the visual effect on the child is incontrovertibly bad, at best factual and banal. There are very few elements in the average pictorial childhood calculated to stimulate an interest in imagery, in understanding through the eye, in penetrating behind superficial appearances, in developing the kind of eye-appetite that leads to a richer and fuller experience in the wide world of pictures to which the adult has access. The growth of the picture book, its wider and fuller use, its establishment as a lively factor in the American Scene, is a development full of promise, a leaven for which many coming generations will be grateful.

Picture books and the artist

To the artist it has meant the maturing of a form in which he can function fully and with a sense of participating in the life of his community in a way that has been increasingly denied to artists by the traditional emphasis on the easel picture, and dominance of the collector, museum and gallery system. This is a form that the artist can take seriously. It calls for the exercise of a wide range of creative powers and provides an added and ultimate satisfaction, that sense of fulfillment that comes to the worker who knows that what he makes meets a human need and that his fellows are the richer for his labors.

The aspect of our children's book production which must of necessity impress itself first upon even the casual observer is the great variety of our contemporary expression. This is a manifestation neither of superficiality nor restlessness, but is the reflection in this area of cultural activity of that great mingling of many diverse currents and traditions that is uniquely American.

By a dozen different methods has our American Scene been enriched by influences from abroad. Book stores and libraries, by the simple device of im- *Influences* porting foreign books to take a place on their shelves beside native stories, have *from abroad* contributed to the flow. Publishers have commissioned artists in England and the continent to produce work for American publication. Artists and writers have gone abroad to live and study, and alien modes and manners have modified, however subtly, the original character of their production. Other creative

LUDWIG BEMELMANS : *Golden Basket*

workers, without leaving the American landscape, have absorbed from foreign-born fathers, mothers, or other relatives, certain of the pictorial tendencies and points of view indigenous to the ancestral homeland.

And beyond all this quiet yet pervasive cultural infiltration there has been *European artists* the direct transfusion of much of the best of living European talent. This is a *in America* process that is, historically, of the essence of American development. Since World War I it has been an increasingly significant factor in the growth of American children's books, and in the last decade, because of the political and economic convulsions that have racked the continent of Europe, the number

ROBERT LAWSON : *They Were Strong and Good*

of book artists who have transferred their lives and their productive abilities to America has been so great as to constitute a major cultural migration. The effects of that influx are widespread and are manifest not only in the quality and character of the works already produced by these new Americans, but in the stimulation, encouragement and broadened perspective they contribute to their fellow craftsmen.

As a result of these many and world-wide influences, we have today unparalleled resources for the making of children's books. We are heir to all the European traditions: the English picture-book tradition of Walter Crane, Randolph Caldecott and Kate Greenaway, of Lovat Fraser and the derivatives of the penny broadside and the white-line engraving; to the French tradition with its double emphasis on the de luxe illustrated edition and the popular pictorial story that emerged when a group of merry iconoclasts sought to recapture the spirit of those earlier days when songs were sung in the streets and market places, and printed images were hawked from door to door throughout the countryside; to the German group, with its curious delicacy and interest in natural phenomena; to the Scandinavian and Central European productions that stem so directly from the peasant art of those countries. We owe, too, something to the wealth of material for children that has been produced in the Soviet Union, with its emphasis on knowing the world as it is and its use of educational psychology reinforced by consultations with groups of children during the process of production. We have drawn, too, on the rich treasures, both of literary and pictorial material, of the Far East, and as a result the accumulation of ideas, interests and influences, which constitute the base upon which creative workers stand, and from which they get spiritual sustenance, is for us in America an international heritage; it provides us with a richness that the world has not known before.

Our resources as heirs to European traditions

From this background of threads of many colors comes the variety of our expression. Among the books published during the past decade you will find works of a dominantly informational character, works whose reason for being is their capacity to amuse, works that combine information and enjoyment in a way that adds up to simple enrichment for the child. In all of these types will be found books that spring from widely different backgrounds, and we would be the poorer for not having all of them. Our collective talent includes the rugged vigor of James Daugherty, the witty cosmopolitanism of Artzybasheff, the decorative simplicity of the d'Aulaires, the engaging humor of Hardie

Variety in character and style

WILLIAM PÈNE DU BOIS : *Three Policemen*

Gramatky and William Pène du Bois, the delicate fun of Robert Lawson, the disarming naïveté of Bemelmans, the brilliant decorative skill of Wanda Gág. From what other soil than our own could there grow, in a single decade, such books as Daugherty's *Daniel Boone* and *Andy and the Lion*, Artzybasheff's *Æsop* and *Seven Simeons*, the d'Aulaires' *Ola*, Gramatky's *Little Toot*, Lawson's *Ferdinand* and *Ben and Me*, and dozens of others. These productions run the gamut of emotion from profound seriousness to hilarious drollery, and utilize a rich, graphic language ranging from the primitive to the most sophisticated. If we need any final testimony to the skill with which our contemporary talent can take the materials of ordinary life and living and give them a highly impressive and lasting pictorial significance, it will be found in the several books of C. H. DeWitt, of which *The Mississippi* and *Alaska* are outstanding.

HARDIE GRAMATKY : *Little Toot*

To this brief indication of the extent of our resources of talent there needs to be added only the notation that the craftsmanship of our book artists has kept pace with their powers of expression. Ours is an age which has, through its emphasis on mass production and specialization, tended to separate the artist from the practical processes whereby his work can be reproduced and made available to the multitudes around him. But the special conditions under which books are produced have proved an exception to the general rule, and the economics of

C. H. DEWITT: *Story of Alaska*

getting lots of color into low-priced books has joined with the graphic artist's natural interest in materials and processes to produce a very healthy relationship between the artist and the practical part of making books. The artist has

The artist and production

to know and understand every detail of production. He has to be familiar with the possibilities and limitations of papers, binding materials, methods of reproduction and the various printing processes. He must understand what is possible and what is impossible in color printing. Increasingly the only way in which several colors can be included is for the artist to make separate drawings for each color. In many instances these drawings will be made directly on stone for subsequent transfer to gigantic offset sheets. Thus the artist is involved up to his neck in the basic process whereby ink is transferred to paper. Of necessity he is close to the roots of his art, and from that closeness to the earth he gains strength and the kind of essential simplicity that promises growth and not decay in the years to come.

Our heritage and its future

The heritage of this fifth decade in the twentieth century in America is a rich one. We have gathered the harvest of those earlier periods of experimentation and exploration. We have assimilated the divers traditions of Western Europe, and welded them into a broad pattern of unparalleled scope and variety. We have had a normal quota of native-born talent lavishly increased by the transplanting to these shores of much of the actively producing talent of the continent. All this adds up to a combination of human and ideological resources without precedent in the field of book production. The possibilities for the future are limitless.

Or, to be blunt, the possibilities for the future are limited only by what barriers to cultural growth may be imposed by the economic and political character of the post-war world that is now taking shape. This is a question that in the past, and particularly to artists, often has seemed remote and abstract. Today it is real and terribly close, and is posed in its ultimate form: are we to live and grow in peace or destroy ourselves with rockets and atomic bombs?

For those who believe in life and human progress there is, of course, but one answer. And we who owe a debt to the cultures of all the peoples of the world know instinctively where that answer lies. We must seek the establishment of the kind of world organization that recognizes the brotherhood of all peoples as the bedrock on which must rest the political and economic structures of the future.

We Americans beyond all others must take the leadership in establishing

INGRI AND EDGAR PARIN D'AULAIRE: *Leif the Lucky*

America's responsibility that kind of world. We have become the carriers, so to speak, of Western culture: through accidents of geography and political currents we have become the stewards of a great trust. If we have learned any one thing from our professional concern with children's books, it is that good is international; that there are values in every nation that must be cherished and preserved. Our children's literature is the symbol and the living proof of that. And if the brutal record of events of recent years has taught us any one thing, it is that evil, too, is international, that what endangers and destroys the lives and culture of one people threatens in equal measure the lives and cultures of their neighbors. Spain, Austria, Czechoslovakia, Poland and France were successive steps along a bloody road of death and destruction that was international in its origins as well as in its effects. And we must never forget that Hitler had to destroy the liberties and free culture of the German people before he could start that dread march that sought to enslave the rest of us.

Requirement for the future: a world completely free We have a world without Hitler, but we need a world without those cancerous ideas that were not his alone and still live, shared by his friends and counterparts in many countries: ideas of enslavement and exploitation, of master races and inferior peoples, of special privilege and individual enrichment at the expense of others. Those ideas, and the complicated social and economic practices that stem from them, stand between us and the future. Only in a world completely free shall we be able to fulfill the promise of our heritage from the past. It is our great responsibility, weighted now with the heavy secret of the atom, to win that world.

LYND WARD : *Woodcut*

PART II. BIOGRAPHIES

VALENTI ANGELO : *Golden Gate*

LEO POLITI : *Stories from the Americas*

Foreword to Part II

HERE living artists who illustrate books for children speak for themselves, and in doing so give their own picture of our times. This presentation of the creative living from which pictures in children's books spring today was wanted as well as the facts of individual lives.

Perhaps there has never been a more difficult time to reach the younger illustrators of this or any other country than during the months May 1, 1945, to May 1, 1946. Many were in the Armed Forces; some had been bombed out more than once and letters were returned marked "Gone Away"; still others were — and still are — among the host of "displaced persons."

It has been our aim to have biographical notes upon every living illustrator whose name appears in the Bibliography of Illustrators on page 385. If names are missing, it is because all efforts to obtain this information have been unsuccessful. In the case of an artist deceased after this material was prepared for printing, the brief biography has been retained.

The space allowed each artist has been governed solely by the character of the material submitted. Unless otherwise noted, the material has come from the artists themselves, members of their families, their publishers, or where no other later material was obtainable, from that submitted for our earlier volume, *Contemporary Illustrators of Children's Books,* published in 1930.

Readers are reminded that books illustrated by the artists are listed not in this section but in Part III. Occasionally, adult books have been mentioned in these notes where the illustrations for them seem important to a presentation of the artist's life and work.

Where dates of birth, or other dates indicative of working time, do not appear in these sketches, the dates of publication for the artists' books as given on pages 385-448 provide information as to period of professional activity.

B. E. M.

PEGGY BACON : *Buttons*

C. W. ANDERSON : *Deep through the Heart*

Brief Biographies of Living Illustrators

Please consult the foreword on page 265 for a description
of the material to be found in this section.

ALAJALOV, CONSTANTIN

*Born November 18, 1900, in Rostov on the Don,
Russia, where his childhood was spent. Attended college in Rostov.*

" LEFT Russia in 1921, spent a year and a half in Constantinople, Turkey, arrived in U. S. A. in 1923, became a
citizen in 1928," — so writes Constantin Alajalov. Alajalov's
parents were in comfortable circumstances and the boy
was given early education including the study of French,
German, English and Italian. He began drawing at five
and in a few years had made up his mind to be an artist.
Beardsley was his first passion and at fifteen he did a
number of drawings in the Beardsley manner, inspired by
Baudelaire's *Fleurs du Mal;* he also illustrated in this period
the lives of Savonarola and Torquemada. His plan to
study at the University of Petrograd was defeated by the
Revolution, but out of this came further training for his
later mural work for he painted the walls of Government
buildings and workingmen's clubs in Baku, Moscow, and
Petrograd. He also made portraits of the leaders including
Lenin and Trotsky. For a while he was secretary to the
Belgian consul in Baku. In 1920 he spent some time in a
northern province of Persia and there the ruler was so
pleased with Alajalov's portrait of his grandfather that he
loaded him with commissions and made him his court
artist. At that time the British were fighting to gain the
province from Russia and bombing planes made the young
artist decide to leave. There followed hard months in
Constantinople when he painted signs in Turkish and
French for bakeries, bars and automobile salesrooms. In
1923 he landed in New York with no money and was
almost immediately recommended by a friend to decorate the restaurant a Russian countess was opening. Other
commissions followed. His first *New Yorker* cover appeared September 25, 1926. Since that time these covers
have become famous. Alajalov has taught at the Phoenix
Art Institute and Alexandre Archipenko's School, both
in New York. He has traveled widely since coming to
America, making annual summer visits during the 1920s
to Paris or the Riviera; Haiti, 1929; Cuba, 1933; Italy, 1938;
Honolulu, 1939. He lives in New York. Most of this
information has been obtained from *Current Biography*.

ANDERSON, CLARENCE WILLIAM

*Born April 12, 1891, in Wahoo, Nebraska. Attended
Wahoo High School and Chicago Art Institute
School.*

AFTER studying at the Art Institute school, C. W. Anderson moved to New York and, early in his career, developed
an interest in horses — an interest which soon absorbed
him completely and eventually dominated his work.
Beginning with drawings and etchings of horses which
the artist made largely for his own instruction and pleasure,
he became a specialist in this field and his work began
to attract national attention. In 1936 he wrote and illustrated his first book about horses and since then has
published a series of similar works, the titles of which
are well known to the American horse-lover — not only
turfmen, but those who ride for pleasure — and especially
among the younger generation. Mr. Anderson is a good
deal of a perfectionist where reproduction of his drawings
is concerned. Seeking the ultimate in reproduction, he
experimented with several mediums and finally began
working in lithography. All the illustrations in his books
are made directly on the stone. While Mr. Anderson is
perhaps most widely known for his illustrations, he has
always painted in color, his special interest being landscape. It is his conviction that the landscape in a horse
subject should not be merely a brushed-in background,
but should have the character and individuality of the
place where the horses are found. Another point the
artist makes is that the horse, from a purely artistic standpoint, possesses such perfect rhythmic proportion that
it is entirely unnecessary to resort to either exaggeration
or distortion in order to achieve good design and composition. In other words, Mr. Anderson believes that if an
artist is capable enough he should, in the same painting,
completely satisfy both the horseman who may know
nothing about art, and the art critic who knows nothing
about horses — and, further, that he should be able to

267

accomplish this without sacrificing any part of his own artistic integrity. C. W. Anderson lives in Mason, New Hampshire.

ANGELO, VALENTI

Born June 23, 1897, in Massarosa, Tuscany, Italy. Childhood was spent in Italy and California.

VALENTI ANGELO — painter, sculptor, illustrator, author — came to America as a small child. He brought with him a warmth of feeling and the sense of decoration which are an Italian heritage, and he received from his new homeland an abiding sense of democracy. Living in California, he worked as a laborer in iron and glass works, in chemical factories, paper mills and other places. Finding that evening art classes could not give him what he wanted, he trained himself, pursuing his own study through libraries and museums. In 1926 an opportunity came for him to work for the Grabhorn Press. There he devoted most of his time to decorating books, among them the folio edition of *Leaves of Grass*. Since then he has illustrated 125 books, thirty-two of them having been included in the American Institute of Graphic Arts' "Fifty Books of the Year" Exhibits. In 1937 he turned his hand to writing and has now published some six books which he has both written and illustrated. These stories of fishermen and laborers are unusual in their expression of the dignity of human life, of the genuine democracy of spirit and of brotherhood. They have humor, adventure and thrills but always they tell a story of everyday living heightened and colored by imagination, and their format expresses their unusual character and quality, as do the author's drawings.

ARDIZZONE, EDWARD

Born October 16, 1900, in Haiphong, Gulf of Tonkin, China. Childhood from the age of five years was spent in England. Attended Clayesmore School.

"I HAVE always loved drawing," Edward Ardizzone writes, "and in childhood ill-spent much of my time scribbling over my lesson books. The first big influence in my life was a present, given to me at school, of a pocket edition of the *Pilgrim's Progress*, with many thumbnail illustrations by an artist unnamed. These illustrations fascinated me and I used to copy them. After leaving school I worked in an office in the City of London and it was not till I was twenty-six, seven years later, that I was able to leave and become, what I had always wanted to be, a full-time professional artist and primarily a painter of pictures. In 1935 I wrote and illustrated the first two of my children's books. These were made up without any thought of publication but just to amuse my two eldest children, then

six and four years old. Since the War, I have been in the army serving first as a gunner and then as an official War Artist in France in 1940; then Libya, Sicily, Italy and Normandy; Italy again, and finally, for the end, in Germany. I now have a third child born in the first year of the War. I hope to be free soon to write and illustrate a new children's book for him."

ARMER, LAURA ADAMS

Born January 12, 1874, in Sacramento, California. Childhood was spent in San Francisco, where California School of Design was attended.

"THE roots out of which my work has grown were nurtured in cosmopolitan San Francisco where artistic adventure lay on the threshold," writes Laura Adams Armer who has always lived in California. "Chinese lacquer boxes held my mother's tea. Japanese paper parasols flaunting the life of the Far East vied with Mexican pottery to create a world of rich fantasy for a little girl of New England ancestry. I reveled in *Harper's Young People* with illustrations of Howard Pyle casting a spell which carried into adult life. Growing up (at the age of seventy-one I am still in the process) it became my good fortune to study art at the California School of Design under the tutelage of Arthur Mathews. It is to him I owe whatever I possess of individual expression, for early in my student life he admonished me: 'Be yourself. Do not touch system with a ten-foot pole.' Aside from his training, I studied Chinese art and language, visited Mexico and the South Seas, and learned the symbolism of Southwest Indians. An ardent novice with little skill, my reverence for all great art has created a world for my later years as full of magic as were the childhood days in San Francisco."

ARMER, SIDNEY

Born April 28, 1871, in San Francisco, where childhood was spent. Attended Mark Hopkins Institute of Art (affiliated with University of California).

SIDNEY ARMER writes that his family, being middle-class conservatives, assumed that all right-minded people go into business. "As I happened to be left-minded, I leaned as far as possible away from that concept. I looked toward the comparative freedom of a career of art. After one year in high school I became an apprentice in a lithograph shop, specializing in designing. However, my love was divided between painting and literature. I dared to entertain a vision of my name on the binding of a best-seller. I never wrote a book but my vision did become a reality. After I became a journeyman designer I aspired to a career of high art, entering the Academy of the San Francisco Art Association as a student. There I met and

EDWARD ARDIZZONE : *Little Tim and the Brave Sea Captain*

VIRGINIA LEE BURTON : *Little House*

later married Laura M. Adams who became a writer of children's books. Coöperation was natural with us and since we had shared the experience of travel it followed that I should share in the illustration of some of my wife's books. So, I have had the experience of seeing my full name, if not on the bindings, at least on the title pages of several volumes."

ARMFIELD, MAXWELL

Born 1862 in England, where he attended the Sidcot and Leighton Park Schools and Birmingham School of Art. Also studied in Paris and in Italy.

MAXWELL ARMFIELD is a writer, lecturer, designer and painter. He has exhibited at the Royal Academy, Paris Salons, Venice International, Berlin, New York and other principal exhibitions. He has lectured on Design and Stage Decoration at the Universities of Columbia, California, New Mexico, and elsewhere. His work is represented in the Luxembourg Museum and the British Museum. Among the books he has written are *An Artist in America*, *An Artist in Italy*, *Stencil Printing*, *A Manual of Tempera Painting*, and *Rhythmic Plays*. His recreations are music and walking. Mr. Armfield's home is in London. This information was obtained from *Who's Who*.

ARTZYBASHEFF, BORIS MIKLAILOVICH

Born 1899 in Kharkov, Central Ukraine, U.S.S.R.

BORIS ARTZYBASHEFF's father was the famous Russian novelist and editor, author of *Sanine*, who died in 1927. His boyhood was spent much in the country, where he observed peasant types and customs, watched the processions at the nearby monastery, and always drew — especially animals. With the coming of the Revolution he entered the Ukrainian Army, suffered in its defeat, but escaped by sea and made his way as a sailor back around the world to fight again. However, he stopped in New York, stirred by the strange skyline, and with a desire to see the city. He was held at Ellis Island, having no friends and only fourteen cents in Turkish money. Finally he was released and made his way alone in New York until he found work in an engraver's shop. This work he disliked so much that he went back to sea but returned to New York, determined to make his way as an artist. A newspaper reporter's write-up of his adventures got him some newspaper work. He began to discover other Russians in New York, and within six years he was making distinguished books. A masterly sense of design, imagination and assured technique bring the meaning of book illustration to fresh life in his work. Before World War II, Artzybasheff returned often to Paris. He lives now in New York.

AULT, NORMAN

Born December 17, 1880, in England. Attended King Edward VI Grammar School, Birmingham, and studied Art and Architecture at West Bromwich and London.

"BORN to a normal English boyhood, but reading perhaps more than the average youngster and preferring games of 'make-believe'— pirates, desert islands, redskins, etc.— rather than football and cricket, I have endeavored to recall some of the reveries of those days in my book, *Dreamland Shores*." Thus Norman Ault wrote of himself in 1930. "Showing an early aptitude for drawing, and persisting later in translating *Cæsar* into pictures instead of English prose, I was allowed to leave the Grammar School for the art school, where, aged about fifteen, I woke up to the beauty of life and nature. With that awakening, poetry took on new meaning and opened the door of imagination, and the next six years were spent studying both art and poetry; so that, at twenty-one, I was knocking on the publishers' doors in London with drawings and poems in my portfolio." In his study of English literature and English lyric poetry, Mr. Ault made a special study of the life and works of Alexander Pope for which the University of Oxford conferred the honorary degree of M.A. in 1941. His recreations are study of prehistoric life and times, and experimental shadow-shows. Among the books he has written or edited, as well as illustrated, are *Life in Ancient Britain* (1920); *The Poet's Life of Christ* (1922); *Elizabethan Lyrics* (1925); and *Seventeenth Century Lyrics* (1928), the last two anthologies not illustrated. Mr. Ault lives in Oxford. Some of this information was obtained from *Who's Who*.

AUSTEN, JOHN

Born 1886.

JOHN AUSTEN is a decorative illustrator. He has exhibited in St. George's and other London Galleries. Among the books he has illustrated for adults are *Tristram Shandy* and *Madame Bovary*. This information was obtained from *Who's Who in Art*.

AVINOFF, ANDREY

Born February 14, 1884, in Tulchin, Russia. Attended the University of Moscow and Prince Nicolas College of Law, Moscow (LL.B. and LL.M., 1905).

DR. AVINOFF writes that he derived stimulation and an interest in art from "boyhood impressions in Russian Turkestan, especially the city of Samarkand and later the mountains of Pamir, the 'roof of the world'; from observations and studies of butterflies (had a collection of about 80,000 specimens, one of the largest on Central Asia);

from an acquaintance with the art of the Russian icon; and from a collection of Renaissance and later paintings in ancestral home in the south of Russia." From 1903 to 1913 he exhibited at St. Petersburg Academy of Art, and in 1904 at the Moscow Society of Painters. He came to this country in 1915. Here he has painted portraits, landscapes, imaginative compositions and murals; designed architectural projects such as an open-air theatre in Florida, and the Russian Room, University of Pittsburgh; made etchings, lithographs, bookplates, and other compositions of graphic art. He has written articles and stories, and has made covers for *Asia, Country Life, Century Magazine, The Carnegie Magazine,* and other periodicals. His book illustrations include an elephant folio of drawings on *The Fall of Atlantis* by Golokhvastoff. He has recently completed a series of about 300 water-color illustrations of the wild flowers of the Upper Ohio Valley (including Pennsylvania) for a book on this subject by Dr. O. E. Jennings, Curator of Botany, Carnegie Museum. He was a member of the Jury of "Scholastic Awards" from the beginning in 1929 and has served every year until 1945 when illness forced his resignation. Each year he purchased examples of the work of high school students and now owns about eighty projects in various media. Dr. Avinoff holds honorary degrees from the University of Pittsburgh and Washington and Jefferson College. He was Assistant and then Advisory Professor of Biology and Fine Arts at the University of Pittsburgh from 1928 to 1945. He is Director Emeritus of the Carnegie Museum. He has exhibited throughout the country and is a member of various organizations having to do with art and archæology. He lectures on Russian Art, the art of Persia, symbolism and design, and nature as reflected in art. His home is in Pittsburgh.

AVISON, GEORGE

Born May 6, 1885, in Norwalk, Connecticut, where childhood was spent. Attended Chase School of Art, New York.

As a boy George Avison wrote adventure stories in his school blankbooks, illustrating them with action pictures. His teachers asked him to decorate the blackboards with murals in colored chalks for holiday programs—"projects," he writes, "executed with much enthusiasm." Upon graduation from high school, he sent a drawing to a Boston engraving house for reproduction "to see how it would look in print." To his surprise he was offered a position on the art staff which he accepted. A few weeks later he decided to lay a better foundation for the work of a professional artist, and gave up his work with the engraving firm to enroll in the Chase School where he studied under Robert Henri, Kenneth Hayes Miller, Edward Penfield, and others. Later he studied under E. M. Ashe and F. C. Yohn and attributes much of his success to these distinguished artists. Visitors to the New York World's Fair, 1939, will remember the quaint "Street of the Nineties," which was recreated from Mr. Avison's scale-drawings and full-color sketches. His home is in Rowayton, Connecticut.

AYLWARD, WILLIAM JAMES

Born September 5, 1875, in Milwaukee, Wisconsin, where childhood was spent and he attended St. John's Cathedral School. Also Chicago Art Institute School; Art Students League, New York; Howard Pyle's School, Wilmington; and studied privately in Europe.

MR. AYLWARD's specialty is marine pictures. "As my father was a ship-builder," he explains, "and vessel-owner in a small way, sailing his own schooner on the Great Lakes, I naturally inclined toward 'sea-stuff' and in my late twenties made a sixteen months' voyage around the world for *Scribner's Magazine,* going out by way of Suez to the Philippines. I returned in the four-masted barque, *Comet* of London, to San Francisco. From material gathered on the trip I wrote and illustrated for *Scribner's* 'Sea Voyage of a Drydock,' May, 1907 — an account of the U. S. Navy's expedition which towed the Drydock *Dewey* from Solomon's Island, Maryland, to Subic Bay, Luzon Base. She was blown up when the war broke out with Japan; and for *Harper's Magazine,* 'Water Life around Singapore,' 'The Harbor of Hong Kong,' etc. The man who influenced me most professionally was Howard Pyle." Mr. Aylward has not specialized in children's illustrations but has done occasional work of this nature, the best known example being his set of illustrations for Jules Verne's *Twenty Thousand Leagues Under the Sea.* He has been Instructor in an Advanced Course on Pictorial Composition at the Newark, New Jersey, Public School of Fine and Industrial Art. Mr. Aylward was one of eight official artists of the A. E. F., with rank of Captain during the First World War. His pictures are in the permanent collections of the Wilmington Museum of Fine Arts; Smithsonian Institute; Library of Congress, National Gallery, Washington; and the Philadelphia Water-Color Club. His home is in Port Washington, New York.

BACON, PEGGY

Born May 2, 1895, in Ridgefield, Connecticut. Attended Kent Place School, Summit, New Jersey; Art Students League and School of Fine and Applied Art, New York.

PEGGY BACON (Margaret Frances Bacon) is the daughter of two well-known artists, Charles Roswell and Elizabeth

(Chase) Bacon. As a child she began to draw pictures before she could talk. She studied under such famous artists as Jonas Lie, John Sloan, George Bellows, George Bridgman, Kenneth Hayes Miller, and Andrew Dasbury. She married Alexander Brook, artist (they were divorced in 1940), and has a son and a daughter now in their twenties. Peggy Bacon taught drawing and composition at the Fieldston Ethical Culture School, 1933-35. She has written poems and made drawings for the *New Yorker* and other magazines. Her pastels, drawings, drypoints and etchings are owned by the Metropolitan and the Whitney Museums, New York City; Brooklyn Museum, Chicago Art Institute, Los Angeles Museum, Carnegie Institute of Pittsburgh, and the San Diego Fine Arts Gallery. She has had many one-man shows in New York and other cities and has exhibited in group exhibitions here and abroad.

BAKER, MARY

Born July 25, 1897, in Runcorn, Cheshire, England, where childhood was spent and she was taught at home. Attended Chester Art School.

"I AM the third of a family of four," writes Mary Baker. "When quite young we all knew what we wanted to be and, happily, were all able to follow our different bents. We had innumerable hobbies, but however trifling or over-ambitious they were, we could always be sure of help and encouragement from our parents. In my late 'teens a few pictures sold to magazines led to my taking a long correspondence course of illustrating with the Press Art School. One of the last lessons showed me the possibilities of silhouette drawing and I decided to use it to illustrate my sister's story *The Black Cats and the Tinker's Wife*. It was quite a traveled manuscript before it found a publisher, but it was successful enough to become the first of a series of which the twenty-second was published last year. When not illustrating, my choice of pursuits is landscape sketching in water colors. I have always been very interested in animals and particularly in watching wild birds. When my father retired we moved to Herefordshire and, after his death, to Sutton Under Brailes, a tiny village in the Cotswolds where there are just enough people and more than enough animals to fill dozens of books."

BALDRIDGE, CYRUS LE ROY

Born May 27, 1889, in Alton, New York. At age of ten and eleven, attended afternoon sessions at Frank Holme's School of Illustration, Chicago — his only formal art education. Chicago University (Ph.B. 1911).

BORN on a farm, Mr. Baldridge has written that he spent his childhood traveling about with his mother who sold cooking utensils from town to town, so that before he was ten, he had lived in nearly every state in the Union. He attended nineteen grammar schools in thirteen different states. His experience — since the University — he has catalogued as follows: Cowpuncher in Texas, 1912. With the First Illinois Cavalry on the Mexican Border, 1916. A Volunteer in the French Army, 1917. A Volunteer with the A. E. F., 1918. Cartoonist, staff of *Stars and Stripes*, 1918-19, and received a Citation. Went on a sketching trip to Japan, Korea, and China, 1919-20. Married Caroline Singer, 1920. Made a sketching trip to the Far East, 1924; to West Africa and Abyssinia in 1927-28; and to India, Palestine, and Persia in 1931-32. He has been a Past President of the National Association of Commercial Arts; The Artists Guild, New York; and the University of Chicago Club of New York; also Past Commander, Willard Straight Post, American Legion. He has taken various prizes for etching, and is the author of *Americanism: What Is It?* (A Definition for School Children). His home is in New York.

BANNERMAN, HELEN

Born in Edinburgh, Scotland, where part of childhood was spent. Studied in Germany. [Died October 13, 1946, in Edinburgh.]

HELEN BANNERMAN was the daughter of an army chaplain. Her father was stationed in many parts of the British Empire and with him his large family always went. At two years of age she was taken to Madeira and spent ten years there. After many years of travel, Helen married an army doctor, spending the thirty years of her married life in India, where her husband strove to stamp out the plague in Madras and Bombay. In 1899, when she was returning to her husband's army post after leaving her two small daughters to be educated in Scotland, she wrote and illustrated *The Story of Little Black Sambo*. The story was mailed home to the children and became a family treasure so loved by the little girls and their friends that it was offered to a publisher. E. V. Lucas "discovered" it, Grant Richards published it in London, and it was issued by Frederick A. Stokes in America the following year. In the years that followed Mrs. Bannerman wrote and illustrated other stories of India published in similar format. She had four children, two girls and two boys. In 1936 Mr. Horace Stokes called upon her in Edinburgh and begged her to write another story of Little Black Sambo, telling her how his own little girls hoped for it. He found Mrs. Bannerman living in a wide, comfortable house, set in a big garden in the southern residential section of Edinburgh, with one of the daughters for whom she had written *Little Black Sambo*. At first she declared another book was impossible — "Little Black Sambo is a middle-aged gentleman now," — but later that

TASHA TUDOR: *Tale for Easter*

summer the manuscript of *Sambo and the Twins* arrived. Since her husband's death some years ago Mrs. Bannerman has lived in Edinburgh. One of her sons is now a doctor in Scotland and the other, an engineer in the Sudan. It was for this younger son that Mrs. Bannerman wrote in 1906 *The Story of the Teasing Monkey*, published in America. When Robert Bannerman's five-year-old son came to America in 1940 as a refugee of the War, he found a dear and familiar welcome in his grandmother's book written for his father.

BANNON, LAURA

Childhood was spent in the country near Traverse City, Michigan. Attended State Normal School, Kalamazoo, Michigan, and Chicago Art Institute School.

LAURA BANNON's background of training and experience has been that of a painter. As a member of the Chicago Society of Artists she has exhibited at the Art Institute in Chicago and at smaller galleries. Painting was supplemented by teaching at the Chicago Art Institute School of Art, as well as supervising the Junior Department of the school, where she pioneered in the field of progressive education for children. Traveling experiences in Mexico, Peru and Japan began to result in an occasional book for children and recently Miss Bannon resigned to devote her time to writing and illustrating books for children. Her home is in Chicago.

BARE, ARNOLD EDWIN

Born 1920 in New York. Childhood was spent on nearby Long Island. Attended New York School of Industrial Art and Yale School of Fine Arts, New Haven.

"NEW YORK CITY has always been my inspiration," Edwin Bare writes. "I was born there but lived in Huntington, Long Island, which was near but oh, so far! I deserted my home-town high school to live alone in New York at seventeen. School started me drawing in a picture-book manner by illustrating the events of history. In high school I studied anatomy and made puppets with Jerome Mayor, the puppeteer. At Yale I majored in scene design under Donald Oenslarger and learned the importance of the setting to any story." To make drawings descriptive of a country and its people came naturally to this artist after he had traveled with his family and had seen other lands and people. He says that he will always want to travel more, but now he is finding out how books are made by working in close connection with a book studio, as he plans new picture books for children. His home is in Huntington, Long Island.

BARNEY, MAGINEL WRIGHT

Born June 19, 1881, in Weymouth, Massachusetts. Childhood was spent in Madison, Wisconsin, where she attended Hillside Home School at Spring Green; also in Oak Park, Illinois. Studied at Chicago Art Institute School.

MAGINEL WRIGHT BARNEY is of pioneer stock—her mother's family coming from Wales and settling in Wisconsin in the early 1840's, her father coming from England. She writes: "My brother is Frank Lloyd Wright, in whose studio and under whose instruction and inspiration I started to learn to draw. After graduating from school I went to the Art Institute in Chicago, leaving to work in an engraving company where commercial art taught me to draw for reproduction, and to work. About this time, an exhibition of Boutet de Monvel's gave me a revelation of how I wanted to work — stemming, as his art did, from the Japanese prints I had been familiar with in my brother's studio. I married Walter Enright, illustrator and cartoonist, and had one child, Elizabeth Enright, who is now an author and illustrator. Later I married Hiram Barney, a lawyer, who died in 1925." Mrs. Barney lives in New York.

BARNHART, NANCY

Born February 17, 1889, in St. Louis, Missouri, where childhood was spent and where she attended Mary Institute. Also Smith College; Art Students League, New York; studied with Maurice Denis, Paris.

"IT was really a testimony to the unity of English and American culture," writes Miss Barnhart, "that I should have illustrated *The Wind in the Willows*, by Kenneth Grahame. One of my earliest and most treasured possessions was a copy of Eugene Field's *Lullaby Land*, which had a heartwarming introduction for English readers by Kenneth Grahame. What a joy in later years to have my drawings accepted for *The Wind in the Willows!* This edition of the book was the first to appear in England with illustrations, though since that time other beautiful editions have been published in England and America." Miss Barnhart lives in Boston.

BATEMAN, HENRY MAYO

Born February 15, 1887, in Mossvale, New South Wales, Australia. Childhood was spent in Essex, England. Attended Forest Hill House School, London.

"FROM my earliest days," writes Henry Bateman, "I intended, if possible, to make humorous drawings for the papers and my schoolbooks were lavishly decorated with comic sketches. My parents encouraged me. Realizing that sound training was essential, I went to art schools where I drew seriously from the age of sixteen to twenty, by which time I was beginning to get little things published. This serious training has stood me in good stead. Soon after my studies ceased, I was busy with work for publication — having some success from the start. I love a country life and foreign travel and am fairly handy at carpentry." Henry Mayo Bateman's home is in Curridge Newbury, Berkshire, England.

BAUMER, LEWIS

Born August 8, 1870, in St. John's Wood, London, where his childhood was spent and where he attended the Royal College of Art, St. John's Wood Art School and the Royal Academy Schools.

" THE only notable fact about my career," the artist writes, " is the fact that nothing notable has ever happened to me. I had no early struggles or privations, as my father always wanted me to be an artist and gave every facility for my education to that end. I lived at home until I was making a sufficient income on which to marry — when I married. I have illustrated many children's books, some of which I also wrote, in the form of nonsense verse. Later on my time was chiefly occupied in drawing for *Punch* and painting and drawing portraits, many of them of children. These I am still doing." Mr. Baumer lives in London.

BEDFORD, FRANCIS DONKIN

Born May 21, 1864, in London where childhood was first spent; then in Surrey and on the south coast. Attended Architectural School, Royal College of Art, and Royal Academy Architectural School, London.

FRANCIS BEDFORD says that he was trained for architecture and that for four years he was a pupil of Sir Arthur Blomfield. " The wish to paint and illustrate gradually prevailed, however, but I have never regretted an architectural training and my work still includes both pictures and illustrations of English and foreign buildings with an occasional return to architectural design. A delight in picture books in my early years led me in the 1880's to try my hand at one for children. It caught the eye of E. V. Lucas, and since then I have enjoyed doing others, as well as paintings in tempera and water color. My work has its roots in nature and the designs of the masters based upon it in architecture, sculpture, painting and book illustration through the ages." Francis Bedford lives in London.

BEMELMANS, LUDWIG

Born April 27, 1898, at Meran, Tirol, Austria. Attended Königliche Realschule at Regensburg and Rothenburg, Bavaria.

LUDWIG BEMELMANS came to this country in 1914 and became a United States citizen in 1918. He has recorded in the Foreword to his book, *My War with the United States* (1937), that on sailing for America at the age of sixteen, from the port of Rotterdam, he bought two pistols and much ammunition to protect himself against the Indians for, from his reading of the books of James Fenimore Cooper and others, he expected to find many Indians on the outskirts of New York City. He enlisted with the United States Army for the First World War but did not go overseas. In the book mentioned above, and in *Life Class* (1938), Bemelmans has told a good deal about his life. In addition to his books, he has contributed articles and pictures to *Vogue, Town and Country, Stage, The New Yorker,* and other magazines. He has traveled widely in the Americas and between the two World Wars also spent considerable time in Europe. In 1935 he married Madeline Freund and has one daughter, Barbara. His home is in New York City. This information was obtained in part from *Who's Who in America.*

BENDA, WLADYSLAW THEODORE

Born January 15, 1873, in Poznan, Poland. There, and in Krakow, childhood was spent. Attended Krakow College of Technology and Art School; also Art School in Vienna.

OF himself, W. T. Benda writes: " I came to America in 1900 to visit my aunt, Helena Modjeska, in California. After two years I moved to New York where I have lived ever since. As I had decided to stay in this country, I became a citizen. In 1905 I began illustrating for magazines and books; in 1914 I began making masks, known to the public as Benda-masks. I continue the same work now. A few years later I married Romola Campfield. Our two daughters, Eleanora and Baria, are both artists."

BENNETT, JOHN

Born May 17, 1865, in Chillicothe, Ohio, where childhood was spent. Attended Art Students League, Cincinnati, and Art Students League, New York.

IT was Thomas Nast's satirical cartoons on the Tweed Ring in *Harper's Weekly* that first interested him in caricature and humorous drawings, Mr. Bennett has written, together with McLenan's humorous drawings in *Harper's Monthly* and Wright's *Caricature History of the Four Georges.* Later influences were Howard Pyle's illustrations and silhouettes, the silhouettes of "Hop" in *St. Nicholas,* the German humorous illustrators and silhouettists in *Fliegende Blaetter* and *Uber Land und Meer.* " Plain necessity," he writes, " turned me to newspaper writing — editorial, reportorial, news correspondence, space-work as a humorous columnist and paragrapher and book-reviewer." He did newspaper cartoons, chalk-plates and sand-papers; contributed text, cartoons and humorous

WARREN CHAPPELL : *Three Hanses*

THOMAS HANDFORTH : *Mei Li*

drawings to *Light,* Chicago, and to *Life,* New York. He became a regular contributor of humorous prose, verse, and silhouette illustrations to *St. Nicholas,* 1891-1901. When Mr. Bennett submitted the unfinished manuscript of *Master Skylark* to Mrs. Mary Mapes Dodge, Editor of *St. Nicholas,* she suggested that he come to New York and finish the book there for her magazine. He lives in Charleston, South Carolina.

BENNETT, RICHARD

Born July 22, 1899, in Ireland. Childhood was spent in Puget Sound Country of the United States. Attended University of Washington, Seattle, and Columbia University.

OF himself the artist has written: " I came from Ireland with my parents when I was four years old and settled in a country place in the Pacific Northwest. At that time the region was so primitive that bears, deer and mountain lions could now and then be seen in the virgin forests surrounding the clearing. After finishing college I taught for twelve years in the Middle West and New York. During this period I made many wood engravings and later, when I began to illustrate books, my technique was more or less influenced by the woodcut manner. In 1931 I illustrated my first book and in 1934 my first original text was published. In the last ten years I have illustrated many books and at present am working on my fifth picture book with my own text and I am making a set of illustrations for a new *Paul Bunyan.*" Richard Bennett lives in Seattle, Washington.

BENTLEY, NICOLAS

Born June 14, 1907, at Highgate, London, where childhood was spent. Attended University College School and Heatherly School of Fine Art, London.

" I HATED school," Nicolas Bentley has written, " and learnt little there, though this was no fault of my teachers. On a roundabout course to becoming a writer, as I hope to do, publicity, gasoline, theatricals of a low sort, and now comic art have all been more or less pleasant interludes. Such talents for illustration as I possess seem partly hereditary. Both my father and grandfather (as well as my godfather, G. K. Chesterton, with whom a good deal of my childhood was spent) drew amusingly and with rather more than amateur skill. Among the influences which helped me to form my childish tastes was my father's collection of illustrated books. These were mostly the works of humorous artists, and those whom I chiefly admired were Caran d'Ache, Steinlen, Doré, Léandre, Gulbransson, William Nicholson, the illustrators of Dickens, and the early *Punch* artists. Among more recent illustrators whose humorous or satirical work I admire are Ralph Barton, George Price, Merwyn Peake and Lewitt-Him." Nicolas Bentley lives in London.

BENTON, THOMAS HART

Born April 15, 1889, in Neosho, Missouri. Attended Western Military Academy; Chicago Art Institute School; Académie Julian, Paris.

THOMAS HART BENTON was named after his great-uncle, Missouri's first Senator. His father, Colonel Benton, was a lawyer, interested in politics. When Colonel Benton was elected to Congress, his son went with him to Washington every fall, returning home in the spring. In summer Benton had to work on the farm. His father wanted him to be a lawyer, but his mother encouraged him in his drawing. His first mural, painted at the age of six, was of a long freight train in charcoal running up the stairway on the new cream-colored wallpaper – the engine puffing heavy black smoke because of the steep grade. He began work as a cartoonist for the Joplin *American* at fourteen dollars a week in 1906. His first work as a professional painter in 1912, after his return from Paris, was strong in the cubist manner of that period. He served in the Navy in the First World War. After his war service, Benton began to express himself objectively and to free himself of European influence. His first public success came when an exhibition of his pictures in Philadelphia attracted the attention of the art collector, Albert Barnes. In 1922 he married Rita Piacenza, and they have two children, Thomas and Jessie. Benton spent a number of summers at Martha's Vineyard, painting landscape and the old native people. A return visit to Missouri in 1924 stimulated his interest in Missouri types and also his interest in America and his desire to know more of it. He began to explore the country, studying life in Texas oil fields, coal mines, ship-building plants, steel mills, and on Mississippi River towboats. He lived among the mountain people of the Ozarks and Tennessee. This exploration is described in his autobiography, *An Artist in America.* He was Director of Painting, Kansas City (Missouri) Art Institute, 1935-41, and when he was asked to take this teaching position, Mr. Benton decided to return to Missouri to live. He helped found, in New York, the Associated American Artists, organized to encourage wider interest in contemporary American Art. His own work has had strong influence on other artists. His murals are in Whitney Museum and New School for Social Research, New York City, and the state capitols of Indiana and Missouri. His home is in Kansas City, Missouri. This information was obtained from *Who's Who in America* and *Current Biography.*

BESKOW, ELSA

Born February 11, 1874, in Stockholm, Sweden, where childhood was spent (with summers in the country), and private schools and the Technical School were attended.

ELSA BESKOW's father was a Norwegian businessman living in Stockholm. Her mother was Swedish. She was the oldest girl in a family of five girls and one boy, who was the first-born child. "In summer time," Mrs. Beskow has written, "we led an extremely happy life in our country home, close to a small, idyllic lake surrounded by birch trees and dark pines. The house was old, with a tile roof under whose eaves the swallows built their nests, and was surrounded by a garden with big apple trees. There we children lived a glorious outdoor life, bathing, rowing, picking berries and wildflowers, and inventing all sorts of games. As far back as I can remember I loved to draw and sketch. I have been told that I also began to make up stories at a very early age which I told to my brother, one year older than I. I was allowed to go to my aunts' small kindergarten at the age of four. My grandmother lived with us, taught me to crochet, and told me many amusing stories. As soon as I learned to read, I spent all my time reading fairy tales, especially those of Hans Christian Andersen. When I was fifteen, my father died, and I went to Technical School in order to be able to earn and help the family as quickly as possible. In spite of economic difficulties we were a very happy family with lots of fun. My first picture book, *The Wee Little Old Woman*, was published in 1892. The same year I was married and went to live in Djursholm, a charming suburb of Stockholm. There my husband, a minister and headmaster of a school, was from the beginning an interested adviser in my work. He himself liked to paint. My five sons, now all grown up, were models and critics for me in their young years. My grandchildren serve me now in the same way." Elsa Beskow still lives in Djursholm, Sweden.

BEST, ALLENA CHAMPLIN
(*pseud.* Erick Berry)

Born January 1, 1892, in New Bedford, Massachusetts. Childhood was spent in Albany, New York, where she attended Albany Academy for Girls. Also attended Eric Pape School, Boston; Pennsylvania Academy of the Fine Arts; and studied in Paris studios.

"MY ancestors built clipper ships in Mystic, Connecticut," Erick Berry writes, "and I was born in the home of the wandering whaler. My father's position as reference librarian in the State Library of Albany gave me my first interest in books. My first art training was with Eric Pape, whose school was run on the then revolutionary lines of the Paris studios. Later at the Pennsylvania Academy, I gained the nickname of Erick, and when I married Carroll

Berry, the artist, I had my present *nom-de-plume.* Just out of art school, I tried my hand at miniatures and murals, at syndicated newspaper advertisements, and the designing of toys, Christmas cards and department store fashions. Eventually the fashions took me to Paris, where I studied for a time, and wandered across Europe making sketches and writing small travel articles. A design for a toy for Volland's led me into illustrating for children, and the desire for more travel took me down the west coast of Africa. The first trip to Nigeria, my marriage to Herbert Best, British Government Officer, and the two long tours which followed, netted me several one-man shows in Paris, Chicago and New York of African tribal types; my first two books, *Black Folk Tales* and *Girls in Africa* and some original research made me a member of the Woman Geographers. About this time Herbert Best and I began our writing collaboration. To date the total of our books is fifty, with about 150 I have illustrated." Erick Berry lives in Fort Ann, New York.

BIANCO, PAMELA

Born December 31, 1906, in London. Her childhood was spent between France, England and Italy, with a brief visit to America.

PAMELA BIANCO is the daughter of the late Francisco Bianco, dealer in rare books and manuscripts, and the well-known author, Margery Bianco, who died in 1943. She was brought to America for a ten months' visit when she was not quite three. Pamela Bianco writes that she began drawing at an early age. When she was eleven years old her drawings were exhibited in Turin and attracted considerable attention. Her first one-man show was at the Leicester Galleries, London, in 1919, and aroused great interest. At this time Walter de la Mare was inspired by some of her drawings to write the exquisite verses for the book entitled *Flora*. She had a second exhibition at the Leicester Galleries in 1920. Her first American exhibition was arranged by Mitchell Kennerley at the Anderson Galleries, New York, in 1922. She then came to America where she has since lived. Pamela Bianco exhibited in San Francisco and Los Angeles in 1922; in Boston and Chicago, 1923; at Knoedler's, New York, in 1924; at the Rehn Galleries, 1928; and at the Ferargil Galleries, 1937. These were all one-man shows held by invitation. In 1930 she was awarded a Guggenheim Fellowship, and spent a year in Florence and Rome, painting and drawing. *The Starlit Journey* was written during this visit. In June, 1930, Pamela Bianco was married to Robert Schlick, a poet from Portland, Oregon. Her son, Lorenzo, was born in 1932. She is entirely self-taught and her work has developed along her own lines of study. Her home is in New York.

BINDER, PEARL

Born June 28, 1904, at Fenley, Staffordshire, England. There and in Lancashire her childhood was spent. Studied at Manchester School of Art and in Paris studios.

OF herself the artist has written as follows: "As a child Pearl Binder was always interested in theatre, costume, caricature and book illustration. In 1925 she left the provinces for London to try her luck. All her early published work shows a strong flair for caricature. In 1926 she spent a year in Paris, drawing for *Le Rire* to augment her income. In 1927 she returned to London and drew for *The Sketch* and various other magazines. In the same year she took up lithography, a medium she has since preferred to all others. Many of her lithographs of the English social scene, including aspects of the mining area in South Wales, were published in *New Masses*. Other lithographs have been of London theatre life and the East End. In 1933, when her first book, *Odd Jobs,* was published, she went to Moscow, returning again in 1934 and 1935, and had a big exhibition there of her lithographs, some of which were purchased for the Moscow Museum of Modern Western Art. In 1936 she married F. Elwyn Jones (now an Army Major), barrister and political writer. From 1936 to now she has written and illustrated several books, had three children, traveled a lot in Europe and done war work. Another aspect of her work is the decorative use of pictures cut from colored papers, bright tinfoils, beads, ribbons, coins, etc. She has also drawn a lot for British television, being one of the first artists to do so, and hopes to continue this work. She acknowledges influences from Phil May, Beardsley, Fish, Steinlen, Daumier, Miguel Covarrubias, El Greco, Holbein and Picasso." Her home is in Cranford, Middlesex, England.

BISCHOFF, ILSE MARTHE

Born November 21, 1903, in New York, where she attended Horace Mann School and Art Students League. Studied also in Paris and Munich.

UNTIL 1938, Miss Bischoff spent all summers in Europe. She owns now a pink brick house in Vermont which is 150 years old, and an ideal place for writing and painting. Painting and wood engraving are her favorite forms of work. The Metropolitan Museum of New York, and the Fine Arts Museums of Baltimore and Boston have bought her prints. Books illustrated by her have twice been selected for the "Fifty Books of the Year" Exhibition. In 1943 she entered Miss Mabel Robinson's Juvenile Workshop at Columbia and in this class wrote *The Painter's Coach.* Her hobbies are collecting eighteenth century porcelain, especially Meissen, and skiing. She lives in New York in winter.

BLAISDELL, ELINORE

Born in Brooklyn, New York, where childhood was first spent, then in Pennsylvania and Baltimore. Attended Art Students League and Naum M. Los School of Art, New York.

"As a child," Miss Blaisdell writes, "I read and reread *Godey's Lady's Book* and loved the pictures. Also all of Howard Pyle — still, in my opinion, the greatest of American illustrators. After that the Italian primitives, and early Renaissance painters. At the moment I've reached the Impressionists, but can't quite approach the moderns." The artist's home is in New York.

BLOCH, LUCIENNE

Born January 5, 1909, in Geneva, Switzerland, where childhood was first spent, then in New York and Cleveland. Studied at Ecole des Beaux Arts, Paris.

AT the age of eleven, Lucienne Bloch was already illustrating books — her own child fantasies such as "The Cat's Weekly Review." After a score of years of hard study — academic training in sculpture and painting in Paris, glass sculpture designing in Holland, assistant to Diego Rivera in Detroit and New York — she returned to her childhood ambition as an illustrator of children's books. As a child, her favorite illustrations were those of Boutet de Monvel in the song book *Chansons de France pour les Petits Français;* now her own three children are her prime inspiration and severest critics. At present, her home is in Flint, Michigan, where she and her husband, Stephen P. Dimitroff, lecture on art and paint murals. She has received many prizes and medals, and her glass sculpture and lithographs are in various museums in the United States and Europe.

BOBRITSKY, VLADIMIR (V. Bobri)

Born in Kharkov, Ukraine. Studied at Kharkov Imperial Arts School.

AT seventeen, Bobritsky was designing sets for the Great Dramatic Theatre at Kharkov. During the Revolution he fought in several armies "with and against." Finally he fled as a refugee to Feodosia, thence to Constantinople. In the Crimea he worked as a wine presser for fruit growers. He made contact with gypsies and joined a band of them as guitar player. He wandered through the Greek islands, and painted ikons. In Istanbul he made decorations and costumes for the *Ballet Russe* of Constantinople to earn his passage money to America. In America he succeeded in setting up a textile printing establishment of his own. He worked for Wanamaker's and became a commercial artist. This information was obtained from an article by Ernest W. Watson in *The American Artist.*

PAUL LANTZ : *Blue Willow*

BOCK, VERA

Born in St. Petersburg, Russia. Childhood was spent in Europe and the United States. Attended schools and art schools in Europe.

VERA BOCK's Russian mother was a concert pianist; her American father was an international banker. During her early childhood in Russia the emphasis of education was on languages. She learned Russian, French, German and English, reading books in all four. She was still a child when, at the outset of the Revolution, her family left Russia and came to the United States. There her education was continued under private instruction. Art has been the constant in her life, for the older she grew the more it attracted her. On subsequent trips to Europe she studied drawing and painting under European artists. Spending a year in England, she devoted herself to the study of wood engraving, illuminating and heraldry, developing at the same time an interest in printing and photoengraving. Vera Bock's career as an illustrator began in 1929 and she now has some twenty-five books to her credit, all of which she has designed as well as illustrated. She lives in New York.

BOSSCHÈRE, JEAN DE

Born 1878 in Belgium.

"IN Russia, Jean de Bosschere is known as the poet and artist of *Beale-Gryne* and *Dolorine et les Ombres,* of which the Russian translation was published in Moscow in 1913. In France, and in his own country, Flanders, he is also distinguished as the author of the *Métiers Divins,* an essay on *La Dialectique du Dessin,* and a study on the Flemish poet and mystic, his friend, Max Elskamp. He has been claimed as a mystic by the mystics, as a Catholic by the Catholics, and Francis Jammes very nearly mistook him for the chief mourner at the *Pompes Funèbres* of departed Symbolism. But he decided that anyhow he is a great poet. That was in March 1913. His earliest work was the illustrations to *Beale-Gryne.* So far the draughtsman's evolution has followed the poet's step by step. He is an artist in whom poet and draughtsman are inseparably and inevitably one. I cannot see him carried away on a surge of patriotism, and chanting the song of Belgium's liberation or celebrating the victories of the Allies once a month with punctual devotion (reference is to World War I). To have achieved, in the teeth of such overwhelming disaster, work of such beauty, of such finish, of such firmness and of such intransigent individuality, is to have kept his soul. Previous to *The Closed Door* there were published by Bosschere in England essays in *King Albert's Book, Westminster* and *Pall Mall Gazettes,* and also a volume, *Twelve Occupations,* with his own drawings in black and white." Extracts from May Sinclair's Introduction to *The Closed Door* (poems) by Jean de Bosschere, illustrated by the author, translated by F. S. Flint, 1917.

BOSTELMANN, ELSE

(Else W. von Roeder-Bostelmann)

Born in Leipzig, Germany, more than fifty years ago. Childhood was spent in Germany and Austria. Attended private schools, University of Leipzig, Academies of Fine Arts in Weimar and Berlin, and Königliche Academy of Graphic Arts in Leipzig. Studied in the United States with Howard Giles.

THE artist has written of herself as follows: "As far as I can think back, I drew and painted. It comforted me as my childhood was lonely without companionship of my own age. My mother fostered my interest, being talented herself. In Weimar, at the Grand Duke Academy of Fine Arts, I had the privilege of studying with the outstanding Russian artist, Sasha Schneider, and with Hans Olde, Ludwig von Hoffman, and others. I received the Gold Medal for drawing at Weimar. Professor Horst Schulze, at the Königliche Academy of Graphic Arts, Leipzig, was a great inspiration. All these studies were leading me to be a portrait painter. But suddenly I turned definitely and completely to nature which had been at all times a great consolation to me. A one-man exhibition followed in Berlin, Dresden, Munich, Leipzig and elsewhere. Coming to America, I stopped painting for ten years during my married life. Then I became a staff artist on four of William Beebe's oceanographic expeditions to Bermuda, where diving with the diving helmet and painting on the ocean ground were the climax of all previous experiences." The artist lives in New York.

BOSWELL, HAZEL

Born September, 1882, in Quebec, Canada. Childhood was spent in Province of Quebec where she was taught at home. Studied in Paris at Ecole de la Grande Chaumière under Mr. Tudor-Hart; also with Richard Miller.

OF herself Miss Boswell writes: "I was born and brought up in Quebec. My summers I spent with my family at Pointe Platon, my grandfather's summer home on his Seigneurie, Lotbinière, forty miles from Quebec, on the St. Lawrence. There as a child I lived intimately among the French Canadians and learned to know them well. When I was eighteen, my grandfather was appointed Lieutenant-Governor of British Columbia, and I went with him and my grandmother for two years to help with their entertaining. After that I traveled and ended by going to Paris to study. When the war broke out in 1914, I became a V.A.D. and worked as Nursing Officer with the St. John's Ambulance Association. Then I took up reconstruction work, finally working with mental cases, the most interesting of all my war work. In 1925, after a visit to England, I organized a committee to carry on voluntary educational work on the Canadian Labrador Coast, a work I am still doing. The first illustrations for *French Canada* did not satisfy me at all; they might have been done for any country. One day I suddenly noticed in a house at Cap-à-l'Aigle two hooked rugs, picturing French Canadian scenes. I was able to borrow the rugs but then had to teach myself to work in a new way, for these rugs and their design were done by people still in the first stage of art, working from what they know, not from what they see or feel; the opposite of my training. With difficulty I gradually taught myself how to combine this new way of work with my own training." Quebec continues to be Miss Boswell's home.

BOURGEOIS, FLORENCE

Born March 16, 1904, in Ventnor City, New Jersey, where her childhood was spent. Smith College, B.A. Columbia University, M.A.

FLORENCE BOURGEOIS, who spent her early years in a lonely spot close to the Atlantic Ocean, says of herself, " As a little girl I passed many hours in exploring the beach, poring over picture books and drawing my own pictures. At seven I had decided to become an illustrator, but gradually became discouraged because I could not draw everything I attempted. By the time I was twelve I regretfully gave up my artistic ambitions and not for many years did I realize that one could learn to draw. Indeed, not until I had been graduated from college and was directing the children's work at the Peoples' Institute in Northampton, Massachusetts, did I again seriously consider illustrating and set about learning to draw. At last, having accumulated a portfolio of drawings made in my spare time, I went to New York to confront the art directors at the various publishing houses. Much to my consternation I was repeatedly asked, 'Have you any texts for these illustrations?' Since it was apparently necessary to write a story in order to illustrate one, I spent several months in trying to write before I succeeded in producing an acceptable manuscript." Miss Bourgeois considers a remodeled Colonial farmhouse near Northampton her home, although she has spent much time in southern New Jersey and at present teaches in a private school near Philadelphia. Her beachcombing childhood, her New England winters, and her knowledge of South Jersey, past and present, have all furnished material for her books.

BRACKER, CHARLES EUGENE

Born October 16, 1895, in Rochester, New York, where childhood was spent. Attended University of Rochester and Syracuse University.

" THE fact that I possessed a male tiger cat started me on my career as animal artist and children's book illustrator," writes Charles Eugene Bracker. " During twenty-five years as a commercial artist in Rochester and New York I created the famous cat, Peake, the husband of Chessie, for the Chesapeake and Ohio Railroad. This cat, I am told, is known throughout the world. This led to several animal books, research for them being done at the American Museum of Natural History and the New York Zoos. The drawing book, *Fun on Paper*, is the application of a short-cut I use in my commercial work. The purpose of the book is purely entertainment but applying the principle will enable anyone to gain facility in drawing."

BRADLEY, WILLIAM H.

Born July 10, 1868, in Boston, Massachusetts.

" WILL BRADLEY " began his career at the age of twelve as a printer's devil on a newspaper in Ishpeming, Michigan. For several decades he was one of the most versatile of our leading artists in graphic arts. In 1895 he founded his own Wayside Press in Springfield, Massachusetts, and there, for a number of years, he printed books and advertising matter. Through his interest in type faces, particularly Caslon, he has left a mark on American typography. Illustration and its relation to typography has been one of his special interests. A children's book, *Peter Poodle: Toy Maker to the King*, 1906, which he wrote and illustrated, is printed in a type of his own design. In addition to illustrations, he has been noted for his posters, especially those done in the 1890's. Their importance was recognized in England, too, where men like William Morris and Aubrey Beardsley had already helped to awaken interest in the new trend in graphic arts. Will Bradley has been one of the best known and most stimulating art directors in New York. He was associated successively between 1907 and 1916 with *Collier's, Good Housekeeping, The Metropolitan Magazine* and *Century Magazine*. His home is in Short Hills, New Jersey. This information was taken from New York Public Library Scrap Books and a biographical notice in *Publishers' Weekly*, May 4, 1940.

BRANSOM, PAUL

Born July 26, 1885, in Washington, D. C., where childhood was spent.

IT is related that on his first day at school, arriving at recess, Paul Bransom, aged six, was so enamoured of the great blackboard spaces, that he began at once to cover them with animals. Of himself Mr. Bransom writes: "When I reached the age of fourteen, I had fully determined to be an artist, left school, and worked for the next four years as a patent, mechanical, and electric draughtsman in turn. At eighteen, I saw I was on the wrong track and took the inevitable flight to New York to seek my fortune. There I found two Zoölogical Parks (one of them bigger and better than anything I had dreamed of), but I couldn't live in the Zoo and worked for a time as free-lance artist illustrating the *New International Encyclopedia*. At length I was engaged to carry on a daily series of comic pictures, whimsical doings of insects, small animals, birds, etc., known as "The News from Bugville" and originated by Gus Dirks. This was great fun and while doing it I had daily contact with many brilliant and unusual men, one of whom, the caricaturist, T. S. Sullivant, was especially interested in animals and a wonderful draughtsman. I owe a great deal to his kind help and advice; also to my friendship with Walt Kuhn, who had just returned from a course of study in Munich with Heinrich Zugel, the noted painter of domestic animals. Kuhn gave me an insight into the principles of construction and organization of form. Meanwhile I spent every spare moment in the Zoölogical Park. When the *Saturday Evening Post* accepted four cover designs and gave me my first animal story to illustrate, I abandoned the comic strip and launched into the field of serious magazine and book illustration. Soon after leaving the *Journal*, my work in the Zoo attracted the generous interest of Dr. William Hornaday, and through him I was accorded the rare privilege and inestimable benefit of having a studio right in the New York Zoölogical Park where I did all my commissions for some years." Paul Bransom lives in New York in winter and in summer at Canada Lake in the Adirondacks.

BRETT, HAROLD M.

Born December, 1882, in Middleboro, Massachusetts. Childhood was spent in Brookline. Attended Museum of Fine Arts School, Boston; Art Students League, New York; and Howard Pyle's School, Wilmington.

HAROLD BRETT is descended from Stephen Hopkins, a passenger on the *Mayflower*. His ancestors have always lived on, or near, Cape Cod. At the Museum School in Boston he studied under Philip Hale and Frank Benson; in New York at the Art Students League under H. Siddons Mowbray, Kenyon Cox and Walter Appleton Clark, and won three scholarships there. He maintained a studio in Wilmington for nine years. His illustrations have appeared in most of the important magazines and in the books of several publishers. In the late 1920's, Mr. Brett began to devote all his time to portrait painting — except

for illustrating the Cape Cod stories of his friend, Joseph Lincoln. He was interested to paint a series of the blue water Cape Cod sea captains still living in that period. He owns an old historical house in Chatham, Cape Cod, called "Old Square Top," where he lives eight months of the year, the rest in a New York studio. He likes to hunt, fish and play golf.

BRICKDALE, ELEANOR FORTESCUE-

Attended Crystal Palace School of Art and Royal Academy Schools, London.

ELEANOR FORTESCUE-BRICKDALE is the daughter of the late M. I. Fortescue-Brickdale, Barrister of Lincoln's Inn. She won a prize of £40 for a design for a public building in 1896. Her first picture was exhibited at the Royal Academy in 1897. Her pictures are in permanent collections at the Walker Art Gallery, London, in Liverpool, Birmingham, Leeds, and other places. She designed the stained-glass windows in the Bristol Cathedral, Brixham. Her home is in London. These facts were obtained from *Who's Who*.

BRIGHTWELL, LEONARD ROBERT

Born May 17, 1889, in London where his childhood was spent in the Clapham and Chiswick districts near Kew. There he attended Alleyn's School, the Latymer Hammersmith, and the Lambeth Art School.

AT the age of six, Leonard Robert Brightwell began to draw animals for fun, and at sixteen for a living. "My first drawing sold for seven shillings and sixpence to the *Boys Own Paper*," he writes, "and from sixteen to forty I worked for all the comic papers, including *Punch*. From the beginning I have been an ardent admirer of Landseer, Briton Riviere, Cecil Aldin, J. A. Shepherd, Harry Rountree, Barei Kano and such Americans as Charles Knight, Bruce Horsfall, Fuertes, Livingston Bull, and Paul Bransom. I now concentrate chiefly on serious work, especially marine life, working for the British Museum, London Zoölogical Society, etc., and I owe much to the privilege of studying animal anatomy in the prosectorium of the London Zoo." Mr. Brightwell served as a soldier in the First World War and as a warden in the Second. He became a Fellow of the London Zoo in 1906 and of the New York Zoo in 1922. This same year he joined the Marine Biological Association and made numerous trips on scientific and commercial deep-sea trawlers, besides much continental travel. His recent work includes museum groups, especially restorations of extinct animals, and animated cartoons both humorous and educational. He makes his home in Surrey, England, and says that he has always received invaluable help from his wife.

RICHARD BENNETT : *It's Perfectly True*

IRENA LORENTOWICZ : *Mr. Bunny Paints the Eggs*

BRITTAN, CHARLES EDWARD

Born June 2, 1870, in Plymouth, England, and educated there.

CHARLES EDWARD BRITTAN studied art under his father who was an artist of the same name. He married Ada Braganza Shilston, and has one son and two daughters. He has exhibited at the Royal Academy, and has had one-man shows at Ackerman Galleries. He is known as a painter of moorland in water colors. Queen Mary purchased his "Loch Ailort." His recreations are fly-fishing, shooting, and golf. Before the war he lived in Lewdon, North Devon. This information was obtained from *Who's Who in Art.*

BROCK, EMMA LILLIAN

Born 1886 in Fort Shaw, Montana. Childhood was spent in Montana, Illinois and Minnesota, and in the cities of New York and Philadelphia. Attended University of Minnesota (M.A.), Minneapolis School of Art, and Art Students League, New York.

EMMA BROCK says that the roots out of which her work has grown are somewhat like those of quack grass, "run a little, root a little, run a little, root a little, and run again." For her first eighteen years she followed a wandering army trail through Minnesota, Colorado, Illinois, Montana, Michigan, New York City, Philadelphia and back to Minnesota, "a life enough like a wonder tale for any child," she writes. "During four years at the University of Minnesota, I specialized in English and writing, and began doing stories about children and odd grownups. Earnings in the Minneapolis Library and in the New York Library made possible study at the Minneapolis School of Art and at the Art Students League of New York under George Bridgman, Boardman Robinson and Joseph Pennell. A wish to write for children, a study in library children's rooms of children and their thinking, an interest in painting pushcart characters in New York and peasants in European markets, and a liking for writing about amusing people—these, combined with a love of travel, resulted in my foreign picture books. Since that time there have been more travelings in Europe and considerable staying at home in St. Paul, Minnesota, with study of the life of middle-west farms and villages and of northern forests along Lake Superior—and books about them."

BROCK, HENRY MATTHEW

Born July 11, 1875, in Cambridge, England. Attended Higher Grade School and Cambridge School of Art.

"H. M." BROCK is the youngest of four artist brothers of whom Charles Edmund Brock was the oldest. He is an illustrator and water-color artist. His first illustrations were published when he was eighteen. His work was first exhibited at the Royal Academy and the Royal Institute of Painters in Water Colours in 1901 and he was made a Member of the Royal Institute in 1906. His drawings have appeared in *Punch, Graphic, Sketch,* and many other magazines. He married Doris Joan Pegram and has one son and two daughters. His home is at Woodstock, Storey's Way, Cambridge. This information was obtained from *Who's Who.*

BROMHALL, WINIFRED

Born in Walsall, England, where childhood was spent. Attended Queen Mary's College, and Walsall Art School, Birmingham; also Birmingham University.

"OF art education, I had very little," writes Winifred Bromhall, "and that little was had at the Walsall Art School. As far back as I can remember I liked drawing better than anything else. I came to America in 1924 and was for some time at the Children's Art Center in Boston. At present I am doing some work in the Art Department of a New York Settlement where the children—mostly Negro, Puerto Rican and Italian—do fascinating pictures."

BRONSON, WILFRID SWANCOURT

Born October 24, 1894, in Morgan Park, Chicago, where childhood was spent and Chicago Art Institute School was attended.

WILFRID BRONSON writes that the town where he was born was small and surrounded by prairies, though it has since been annexed and encompassed by Chicago. "I spent much time in the open," he says of himself, "always fascinated by creatures, drawing them much oftener than other things. It was taken for granted that I should be a painter, so I studied at the Art Institute after finishing high school. I joined the army in the First World War but did not get overseas. After the war I worked in several studios in New York as a mural painter's assistant. Whenever there were animals in the design, I was assigned to draw them. Opportunity came to go on four scientific marine expeditions, one result being the attempt to create good children's books out of the knowledge gained as expeditionary artist. The process has continued along with the addition of articles and illustrations for children's magazines and for adults in *Nature Magazine.*" Mr. Bronson now makes his home in Tallman, New York.

BROWN, PAUL

Born November 27, 1893, in Mapleton, Minnesota. Childhood was spent almost entirely in cities—Milwaukee, Boston, and New York.

PAUL BROWN, whose home now is in Garden City, New York, but whose early childhood saw a good deal of

Milwaukee, Boston, and New York, writes, " My schooling was the usual public school type, but I did not finish high school. When World War I came I entered the service and became a Captain of Infantry, seeing service with the A.E.F. Something of the soil from Blue Earth County, Minnesota, must have been in my blood, for I loved animals and always wanted to draw them. As there is no school where such art is taught, I learned about horses and dogs by getting out in the fields with them. To acquire knowledge I followed polo, horse shows, and Hunt Cup race meetings, going to England for ten consecutive seasons to see the running of the Grand National and other races. As an outlet for my desire to draw horses I started to do children's books in picture form. This led also to limited editions on polo and racing. I am now at work on my twentieth and twenty-first books and have illustrated over seventy-five for other authors. The execution of commissions for portraits, magazine illustration and advertising art has rounded out my career to date with the horse as the chief subject."

BRULLER, JEAN

Born 1902.

JEAN BRULLER is a humorous draughtsman and illustrator. He exhibited in Paris at the Salon des Humoristes in 1923. His illustrated books have been among the most successful. This information was obtained from *Dictionnaire Biographique des Artistes Contemporains*.

BUCKELS, ALEC

ALEC BUCKELS is known to most people in America only by his decorative drawings – his " embellishments " – for Walter de la Mare's *Come Hither*, A Collection of Rhymes and Poems for the Young of All Ages (1923). In *Who's Who in Art* he is listed as etcher and illustrator.

BUFF, CONRAD

Born 1886 in Switzerland where his childhood was spent. Studied in Switzerland and at Art School in Munich.

CONRAD BUFF came to America when he was nineteen years old and he now makes his home in Southern California. He says that he is more truly a Westerner than many a native son. Born the son of an Alpine farmer, and the descendant of a long line of Alpine people, he early left off milking cows when his artistic aptitudes earned him entrance to a government school to learn the designing of lace. The work was arduous, limited, too exacting, and at eighteen, with some hard-earned francs in his pocket, he took off to study art in Munich. Shortly

thereafter an understanding mother supplied the wherewithal and Buff landed in America. He went west directly, stepping off the train at a cow station near the Dakota-Wyoming line, and found there exactly what he had dreamed about. Despite the obstacle of a strange tongue and the economic question of existence, he felt that he was home. He worked as a ranch hand, sheepherder and house painter. Painting in every spare hour, he eventually won the distinguished place in American art that he holds today.

BURBANK, ADDISON BUSHNELL

Born June 1, 1895, in Los Angeles, California, where childhood was first spent, then in Oakland and San Jose. Attended Belmont Military Academy; Santa Clara University; Chicago Art Institute School; Ecole de la Grande Chaumière, Paris; Grand Central Art School, New York.

" MY father being a newspaperman and my mother a poet, I was named Addison as a further inspiration to carry on the literary tradition," writes Addison Burbank. " While still in my crib, however, I began to draw; and at thirteen I won neighborhood fame and a correspondence art course by a drawing of Mrs. A. Mutt in a Directoire gown. In high school I drew for the school publications, but my first job, on leaving, was newspaper reporting. Wanting to study art, I eventually entered the Chicago Art Institute and, while still a student, began selling my work to national magazines. Before long I came to New York. After a year of study and outdoor painting abroad, I was given my first one-man show at Ferargil's on Fifty-Seventh Street in 1927. I won first award for a mural for the Florida Building at the Chicago World's Fair. Going to Guatemala to paint in 1938, I wrote my first book. Since then my time has been split between writing and illustrating. My wife, Covelle Newcomb, also writes and our home, which will always be wherever we park our typewriters and art-kit, is at present in New York City."

BURGESS, GELETT

Born January 30, 1866, in Boston where – with summers in West Falmouth – childhood was spent. Attended Massachusetts Institute of Technology.

GELETT BURGESS says that he has at least ten traceable *Mayflower* ancestors. His education was that of a Civil Engineer and he had no art training whatsoever. After three years with the Southern Pacific Railway, he spent three years as instructor in Mechanical Drawing and Mapping at the University of California. After that, and while he was a designer of furniture in San Francisco, he began the publication of the *Lark*, a small and unique monthly which was the beginning of his literary career, and made him well known as an author and humorist. In the *Lark* he began also his career as a grotesque illustrator, especially with a series of nonsense verses, done all in pure line. At one time he lived in Paris for a period of thirteen years but his home is now in New York City and he is the author of some thirty-five books of short stories, poetry, essays, novels and satire.

BURTON, VIRGINIA LEE

Born August 30, 1909, at Newton Center, Massachusetts. There and in Carmel, California, childhood was spent. Attended California School of Fine Arts and Demetrios School of Drawing and Sculpture, Boston.

VIRGINIA LEE BURTON's father was the first Dean of Massachusetts Institute of Technology. Her husband, George Demetrios, is a well-known sculptor and teacher. She has two sons, Aristides (Aris, for short), aged thirteen, and Michael, aged 10, and it was for them she wrote her books when they were in the " picture book " age. " An illustrator is guided and limited in choice of subject and scene by the author," Virginia Lee Burton writes, " but I have been fortunate in being able to combine the author-illustrator in one, or rather, illustrator-author, because it is the illustration which interests me more. My characters and locale (with one exception, *Calico*) I have chosen from what I found about me. An engine on the Gloucester Branch of the Boston & Maine is the heroine of *Choo Choo*. ' Mary Ann,' Mike Mulligan's steam shovel, I found digging the cellar of the new Gloucester High School. *The Little House* was inspired by the moving of our own house ' into the middle of a field with apple trees growing around,' and *Katy* is the pride and joy of the Gloucester Highway Department. Each new book is an incentive to the artist to spread his roots — to reach out and add to his store of subject material from which he can draw." Virginia Lee Burton Demetrios lives with her family at Folly Cove, Gloucester, Massachusetts.

BUSONI, RAFAELLO

Born February 1, 1900, in Berlin, Germany. Childhood was spent and schools were attended in Germany, Switzerland and the United States.

" ALWAYS I wanted to become a painter," Rafaello Busoni writes. " I remember struggling with the problem of how to draw a nose ' as it looks ' from full face when I was six, and I had my first oil paint set when I was eleven. During the First World War we lived in Switzerland where drawing is considered the very elemental base for any of the fine arts. I tried every technique of the graphic arts: lithography, etching, woodcut, and every means of

direct drawing. Although I spent most of my time painting, I cannot remember any period in which I did not make illustrations for my own pleasure. I chose my topics from among plays and operas and decided to write the text myself to make the books complete. The text — calligraphy plus original drawings — resulted in manuscript books and I have made more than twenty such handwritten books. When my own child was old enough to enjoy books, I got interested in children's books. Quite naturally, out of little talks with my child, grew my first geographical books, which I wrote myself. Subsequently I entered the field of children's books and enjoy it increasingly." Mr. Busoni now lives in New York City.

BUTLER, HORACIO

Born August 28, 1897, in Buenos Aires, Argentina, where his childhood was spent and where he attended Academia de Bellas Artes, Buenos Aires. Later studied in France with Othon Friez.

AFTER finishing his studies in Buenos Aires, Horacio Butler writes, he carried out his wish to live and study in Europe, going to France in 1923, and from then until 1933, spending the summer months each year in Europe, visiting Germany, Italy and Spain. When he returned to Buenos Aires, he devoted himself to designing for the theatre and to making illustrations for books and magazines. His work was shown at the Paris Exposition, 1937, where he won a Gold Medal, and also at the World Fairs of San Francisco and New York. He is represented in the permanent collections of the principal museums of Argentina, the Museum of Modern Art, New York, and the Brooklyn Museum. In 1942 Mr. Butler was invited by the State Department to visit the United States. It was during this visit that he made pictures for Lincoln Kirstein's *Book of the Dance* as well as for other books.

CADY, WALTER HARRISON

Born 1877 in Gardner, Massachusetts, where childhood was spent. In art entirely self-taught.

AT eighteen, Harrison Cady went to New York and sold his first work — a set of decorative initial letters for *Truth Magazine*. This was followed by drawings for a *Mother Goose*. In 1907 he became newspaper artist for the *Brooklyn Eagle*, covering crimes, fires, dog shows and social events, at twenty dollars a week. " No better school for draughtsmanship has ever been devised." In 1907, as the result of a childhood memory of a stone overturned to reveal a tiny black beetle, Mr. Cady began to draw beetles, and sold some of these first pen-and-ink sketches to *Life*. At twenty-four, he joined the staff of *Life* where he was associated with such artists as Charles Dana Gibson, T. S.

PAUL BRANSOM : *Animals of American History*

Sullivant, Wm. H. Walker, Otho Cushing, Angus Mac-Donald and Orson Lowell. His contributions to *Life* were pictorial commentaries upon serious problems of the day as well as amusing drawings of animals and insects. His nonsense drawings have appeared in the children's pages of *Good Housekeeping, Ladies' Home Journal, Country Gentleman* and the *Saturday Evening Post.* He contributed regularly to *St. Nicholas* for a long time. About 1913 he began illustrating Thornton Burgess's *Bedtime Stories* of *Peter Rabbit, Johnny Chuck, Reddy Fox* and the others. In 1915 Harrison Cady married Melina Eldridge of Brooklyn where the Cadys lived until 1939, when they moved to their present home in New York City. In 1920 Mr. Cady bought the old Headland House at Rockport, Massachusetts, which continues to be his summer home. In 1922 he was asked by the New York *Herald Tribune* to contribute a syndicated *Peter Rabbit* series to their Sunday comic section. His etchings are owned by the Metropolitan Museum, Library of Congress, New York Public Library and other noted collections.

CAMERON, KATHARINE
Born in Glasgow, Scotland, where – and in the Scottish Highlands – childhood was spent and the School of Art was attended. Also studied at Académie Colarossi, Paris.

"I was the fourth daughter of Reverend Robert Cameron, minister of the Church of Scotland, and descended from Dr. Archibald Cameron, brother of 'The Gentle Lochiel' of the 'Forty-Five,'" Katharine Cameron Kay writes. "When I returned home from my art study in Paris, I was asked by a publishing firm to do the drawings for two fairy-tale books. This was great fun for me and with ardor I began to reread and illustrate the old tales. My friends and relatives were brought in to sit as models – my brother, Sir D. Y. Cameron, Anna Buchan (O. Douglas), and others. Many books followed after that and many interesting experiences have been mine when illustrating them. I was married to Arthur Kay, art collector and author, and our home is in Edinburgh."

CANZIANI, ESTELLA L. M.
Born 1887 in London where, with travel in Europe, childhood was spent and Sir Arthur Cope's Art School and the Royal Academy Schools were attended.

"My mother, Louisa Starr, was a well-known portrait painter," Miss Canziani writes, "the first woman to receive the gold medal traveling studentship at the Royal Academy Schools and one of the first six women to enter these Schools when opened to women. She was the daughter of Henry Starr of Philadelphia whose family emigrated to America in the ship after the *Mayflower.* My father, Enrico Canziani, was her cousin and also artistic, and was distinguished in Milan at the age of seventeen as a civil engineer. It was natural, therefore, for me to grow up knowing that I would become an artist. My first drawings, at the age of two, were in white chalk on the backs of my mother's canvases. I lived in my parents' surroundings of painting and books, and listened constantly to the talk of distinguished friends from various countries. The old world corner of Kensington with its garden and flowers and birds made me love all nature. I was an only child, but never lonely. I followed my mother by entering the Academy Schools. I was already painting portraits which were exhibited in the Academy and other exhibitions at the age of eighteen or nineteen. I took everything very much for granted and just went on working. Then, while traveling in the mountains of Italy, I became interested in the peasants and their folklore and folkcrafts and that led to my writing and illustrating my first book. Needless to say, other books followed and various publishers asked for illustrations; and it gave me great joy when Walter de la Mare asked me to illustrate his *Songs of Childhood.* I also loved illustrating Mrs. Duncan Jones' *The Lord's Minstrel,* as St. Francis was a saint after my own heart. And thus it was one thing led to another and in spite of two wars and doing war work in hospitals, I also managed to paint, and find and keep my own peace and joy and fun in life." Estella Canziani lives in London in the house where she was born. It is a part of Kensington Palace and was once known as "Queen Anne's Laundry."

CARRICK, VALERY
Born November 7, 1869, in St. Petersburg, Russia.

VALERY CARRICK's father, a Scotsman, had been taken to Russia as a baby in 1828. He died when his son was eight years old, and the boy was brought up by his Russian mother who was a writer and journalist and one of the earliest feminists in Russia. Valery Carrick's vacations were spent among the Russian peasants. The old folktales of Russia he heard from his mother, his nurses, and the peasants on his father's estate from his earliest years, and as a small boy liked to make pictures for them. He became a writer by profession but it was not until 1908, during a visit to England, that he published his caricatures of known British personalities in the *Westminster Gazette, The Manchester Guardian* and the *Liverpool Post.* In 1909 he retold some of the Russian folktales and illustrated them. They were first published in Russia, then in England, in the United States, and in Norway, Holland, and Germany. Since *Picture Tales from the Russian* was published in this country in 1913, five other volumes of Russian tales have appeared with Mr. Carrick's pictures. He has lived in Hvalstad, Norway, since 1918.

CARTER, HELENE

Born in Toronto, Canada, where childhood was spent and she attended Ontario School of Art; also Art Students League and Roerich Academy, New York.

"AFTER training at the Ontario School of Art I worked for a year or more in an advertising agency in Toronto," Helene Carter writes. "In 1914 I came to New York, primarily to study, but ultimately to remain. I went to Italy in 1921 to make the illustrations for two books, one of which was written by the Swiss novelist, Carl Spitteler. In 1930 I returned to Italy, via France, where I gathered the material to illustrate a book on Mont Saint Michel, Carcassonne, and Avignon entitled, *Behind the Battlements.* My work with the late Raymond L. Ditmars brought me into the field of natural history, a collaboration which I have always felt to be a rare privilege. This collaboration has been entirely responsible for the kind of illustration I have done in recent years. These books have, almost without exception, required considerable research but it was through my work with Dr. Ditmars that I found the combination of illustration and research a pleasurable one, albeit exasperating on many occasions."

CHALMERS, AUDREY

Born May 27, 1899, in Montreal, Canada. Childhood was spent in Cobourg, Ontario. Attended Havergal College, Toronto.

AUDREY CHALMERS says that, growing up in the town of Cobourg, she absorbed much from the quaint characters and ways of living, old-fashioned homes and gardens that the town abounded in. "However, it was not until I was living in New York, teaching kindergarten and first grade, that I decided I wanted to write for children. Story-reading periods became my gold mine. I made up my mind I'd find out what children wanted in stories and pictures. Wonderful were those moments when every word of a story went easily home, and equally dreadful when I found myself hurrying over superfluous words with my small audience wriggling in boredom. I've tried ever since to live up to this test. Illustrating my own books began on the advice of my publisher. I enjoy doing either equally well and find they stimulate each other. I like the roots of a story to spring from actual incidents in connection with children. The idea for *Hundreds and Hundreds of Pancakes*, for instance, grew from the fact that when my daughter was small we made rather a ritual of pancakes (with maple syrup) for Sunday morning breakfasts. Then I feel 'at home' with my story even though it is in the fantastic or nonsense class. And unless I feel at home in my writing, and am sure I'm writing what children want to hear, my stories just do not work out." Audrey Chalmers lives in New York.

CHAN, PLATO

Born 1931 in New York City. Attended earlier, and is now once more a student, at Horace Mann-Lincoln School, New York.

PLATO CHAN was born of Chinese parents. His father was in the Chinese diplomatic service. With Mr. Chan the family traveled all over Europe and Asia, living in Germany, France, England, Greece, India and China, and many other places. Plato's parents decided to name him after the planet discovered in the year of his birth, but for a time the new planet had no name and was known as X. So was the Chans' baby. But when Pluto was chosen for the name of the planet, Mr. and Mrs. Chan decided to name their son Plato. Plato began to draw in babyhood. In 1937, when his father was stationed in Paris and Plato was six, the boy designed patterns for several French silk mills. In 1939 he had his first exhibition in Paris, earning several thousand francs for the Chinese Refugee Fund. When China declared war on Germany in December, 1941, Plato, with his mother and sister, Christina (a year older than Plato), were visiting in London. Mr. Chan in Paris was sent to a camp somewhere in Germany and his family have not heard from him since. The Chans stayed on in London where Plato gave several exhibitions, raising over a thousand pounds for war relief. The Duchess of Gloucester bought two of his drawings of horses for her husband. Plato's portrait of the Queen he presented in person to Buckingham Palace. The Chans returned to New York in August, 1945, where Plato and his sister now attend the Horace Mann-Lincoln School.

CHAPPELL, WARREN

Born July 9, 1904, in Richmond, Virginia, where childhood was spent. Attended University of Richmond (B.A. 1926); Art Students League, New York; Offenbacher Werkstatt, Offenbach-am-Main, Germany; and Colorado Springs Fine Arts Center.

WARREN CHAPPELL writes that when he was eleven years old Boardman Robinson's war drawings, made in Russia in 1915, were the earliest influence in bringing him to illustration. "After graduating from the University of Richmond I went back to the Art Students League where I had first begun to study. From 1928 to 1931 I worked as art director of the promotion department of a national magazine, then to Offenbach-am-Main where I learned punch-cutting and type-making in the studio of the late Rudolf Koch and at the Klingspor Type Foundry. When I returned to the United States, in 1932, I began work in my own studio and for the next three years was occupied largely with lettering and typographic design. During this time I was an instructor at the League in the Graphic

Arts Department and published *The Anatomy of Lettering* which was written in memory of Rudolf Koch. In the spring of 1935 I went to Colorado Springs to work as an assistant instructor and to study with Boardman Robinson. Since then I have returned to New York where I have done the body of my illustrated work and the great share of my book typography. During this time I designed the "Lydian" type family for American Typefounders, and "Trajanus" for D. Stemfel in Frankfurt. My work has its roots in the classic approach to drawing as it was developed by the Italian and Dutch painters. I despise technique and search for method only. In this the lucidity of Michelangelo's pen drawings, the shorthand of Rembrandt's sketches and the professional and yet humble attitude of Daumier toward illustration, have served as a constant reminder and as a beacon of what can be and has been done." Mr. Chappell lives in New York.

CHARLOT, JEAN

Born 1898 in Paris where childhood was spent.

An American citizen born in France, Jean Charlot is nevertheless known to critics as "that great Mexican artist" because of his murals at the University of Mexico, frescoes at the Ministry of Education in Mexico City, and various writings on Mexican art and archaeology. He did not, however, go to Mexico until he was twenty-two. At sixteen he was fighting for the life of Paris in World War I, and later commanded troops in North Africa. In World War II he enlisted to serve with the French forces in North Africa and was awaiting call in New York City the day France fell. The life of a mural painter is not an easy one, according to Charlot. He must test his patience waiting for some generous person to "lend" him a wall. In the United States he has depicted the life of St. Bridgid for a church in Peapack, New Jersey; two small frescoes for the University of Iowa; a large mural on the outside façade of the Fine Arts Building of Georgia University. The periods of waiting between murals have been fully filled, he says, with writing, canvas painting, lecturing, archaeological research, teaching, book illustration and the perfecting of a new process of lithograph printing. He has recently been awarded a Guggenheim Fellowship to complete the writing of a history of Mexican mural painting.

CHIANG, YEE

Born May 19, 1903, in Kiu-kiang, China, where his childhood was spent. Attended The Third Middle School of Kiangsi Province and National South-Eastern University, Nanking, China.

Chiang Yee was a member of one of the large families which used to be common in China before the Revolution of 1912 — more than thirty members of the Chiang family being sheltered under one roof. After graduating from the University in Nanking, where he had studied chemistry, he became Local Governor of four Districts in succession in the Provinces of Anhui and Kiangsi. In 1933 he went to England and at different periods lectured on Chinese Language and Literature at the School of Oriental Studies, London University. He took charge, as well, of the Chinese Section at the Wellcome Historical Medical Museum in London. He resigned his work in 1940 to devote himself exclusively to writing and painting. He is married, has two sons and two daughters, and lives in Oxford, England. Mr. Chiang Yee's early life is described in his book, *A Chinese Childhood* (Methuen, London, 1940).

CHILD, CHARLES JESSE

Born January 15, 1901, in Montclair, New Jersey. Childhood was spent in New England where he attended Wilbraham Academy. Also Boston and Harvard Universities.

Travel and residence in Europe and Asia for five years, the artist writes, gave wide background. He has worked in ceramics, textile design, murals, portraits, book illustrations, screens, and in many media. He has musical background and has been a professional cellist. In Washington he has served as assistant to the Director of the National Planning Association; later as Chief of the Art and Music section, in the Division of Cultural Coöperation, Department of State. Mr. Child is now helping to formulate national policy as Adviser in Art and Music to the Office of International Information and Cultural Affairs. This part of the Department of State is engaged in furthering the exchange of knowledge, skills and persons in the arts, sciences, and educational fields between this country and other countries, and the development of policies and programs promoting freedom of information among peoples.

CHRISTY, HOWARD CHANDLER

Born January 10, 1872, in Morgan County, Ohio.

Howard Chandler Christy came to New York in 1893. Since then his work has appeared in the leading magazines of the country. He went to Cuba with the 2nd United States Regulars and "Rough Riders" and saw fighting before Santiago. His letters and illustrations describing this experience were published in *Scribner's Magazine*, *Harper's*, *Collier's Weekly*, and in book form by R. H. Russell. From 1910 on, his illustrations for stories appeared in *The Cosmopolitan* and *Hearst's*. In 1920 he resumed portrait painting and painted portraits of a number of well-known people including President and Mrs.

Coolidge, Charles E. Hughes, Prince Humbert of Italy, Amelia Earhart and Captain Eddie Rickenbacker. His oil, "Signing the Constitution," hangs in the Capitol in Washington. This information was obtained from *Who's Who in American Art*.

COATS, ALICE M.

Born June 15, 1905, in Birmingham, England, where childhood was spent and Birmingham School of Art was attended. Also Slade School of Art, London, and studio of André Lhote, Paris.

ALICE COATS' achievements in art include a number of color wood and lino-cuts (prints of which have been purchased by Queen Mary, by the Victoria and Albert Museum in London, and the State Art Gallery of Poland), landscapes in oil and water color, and mural decorations. *The Story of Horace* was her first attempt at book illustration, and was done in the first place for her own amusement. Though she heard the story from an English source, she believed it to be of American origin. Miss Coats, whose home is in Birmingham, was the founder and secretary of the Birmingham group of artists which has held seven successful exhibitions in London and elsewhere. Her principal hobbies are music and gardening. She is a member of the Women's International Art Club.

COBURN, FREDERICK SIMPSON

Born March 18, 1871, in Upper Melbourne, Province of Quebec, Canada, where childhood was spent. Attended Carl Hecker's School, New York; Berlin Academy; Ecole des Beaux Arts, Paris; Slade School, London; Academy, Antwerp, Belgium.

MR. COBURN writes that he returnd from Paris in 1896 to illustrate Dr. Drummond's *Habitant Poems*. This served to introduce his work to G. P. Putnam's Sons for whom he illustrated Dickens, Irving, Poe, Taylor, Goldsmith and others until 1914, when he abandoned illustration and began to devote all his time to painting. He is now a senior member of the Royal Canadian Academy of Art. His home is in Upper Melbourne, Province of Quebec, Canada.

COLE, WALTER

Born November 26, 1891, in New York, where he attended Art Students League and National Academy of Design.

As a boy, Mr. Cole has written, he had a passion for drawing, but during the summer months, which he always spent in the country, he did not draw at all. In the winter, back in New York, he drew constantly from memory the things he had seen during the summer. Once when he was still very young his teacher asked the boys to draw trains on the blackboard. One boy copied from a sophisticated illustration a complicated head-on view of a train at full speed. This drawing was highly approved, but Walter Cole's, drawn from memory and imagination, a linear picture showing all the train of cars such as a child would naturally draw, the teacher made him erase. He does not think this incident would happen today and is delighted with the progress teachers have made toward understanding art and their encouragement to children to draw instinctively from memory and imagination. Mr. Cole won a scholarship in drawing under George Bridgman at the Art Students League and during the First World War, in which he served as a private with the A.E.F. in France, he painted many water colors of the soldiers and episodes of the war, doing this painting and drawing in the front line trenches with his colonel's authorization. He spent two years touring and sketching in Europe. After returning to New York, Mr. Cole entered the field of commercial art and since that time has specialized in advertising work. His only book for children, *A B C Book of People*, shows the influence of the woodcut, a medium in which he has won recognition. His home is in New York City.

COOK, HOWARD

Born July 16, 1901, in Springfield, Massachusetts, where childhood was first spent, then in Greenfield. Attended Art Students League, New York, and studied independently abroad.

"AFTER studying at the Art Students League," writes Howard Cook, "I spent the next ten years in sketching trips and study of art and native people in Europe, Turkey, Japan and China. I also worked as a quartermaster on a coastal steamer around the banana and mahogany ports of Central America. Crossing the country on the last trip, I passed through Arizona and New Mexico on the train and became so thrilled by the grandeur of the landscape that I returned as soon as possible to live there. Here I met Barbara Latham and we were married in New Mexico where we have lived off and on since, owning a minute 'ranchito.' I illustrated many stories for magazines, had a successful period of work in the graphic arts, followed by a year and a half in Mexico on a Guggenheim Fellowship and its renewal for another year in the Southern United States. All of this time my wife and I lived out of doors and in the blessed mountain and mesa of New Mexico as much as possible, thoroughly in love with all the wonders and beauties of nature, keeping animals and birds, and thus, I suppose, gathering material naturally for the work we like to do. A recent commission of mine has been to serve as artist War Correspondent in the South Pacific area, stationed on the island of New Caledonia and seeing action in the Solomon Islands, on Guadalcanal and in the New Georgias." There are large fresco murals painted by Howard Cook in Springfield, Massachusetts, Pittsburgh, Pennsylvania, and in San Antonio, Texas, the last work taking three years to complete. His home is in Ranchos de Taos, New Mexico.

COONEY, BARBARA

Born August 6, 1917, in Brooklyn, New York. Childhood was spent on Long Island where she attended Great Neck Preparatory School. Also Briarcliff School, and Smith College.

"My father was a stockbroker, my mother painted pictures for fun; so her children did too, and that's how it all began," writes Barbara Cooney. "We lived in a suburb of New York and went to school there. Summers were spent in Maine. After boarding school and college I trudged around New York City with my portfolio. Then I began to write books for myself so I could draw the sort of pictures I wanted. At the Art Students League I learned etching and lithography. In the summer of 1942 I joined the WAAC, and later in that year married Guy Murchie, Jr., war correspondent and author. Honorably discharged the following spring, we lived with our small daughter in Bedford Village, New York, for a year; then in Belchertown, Massachusetts, on a coöperative farming venture. In 1945 we bought a farm in Pepperell, Massachusetts. It is called 'Apple Hill.' There, during the summers, we run a children's camp; during the winters, write and paint pictures."

COSGRAVE, JOHN O'HARA II

Born October 10, 1908, in San Francisco where his childhood was spent. Attended Marin Junior College, University of California, California School of Fine Arts, and studio of André Lhote, Paris.

As a boy he haunted the San Francisco docks where the ships come in. "I had my first boat, a remodeled Navy twenty-eight foot whaleboat, at fourteen," he writes. "At eighteen I re-built another whaleboat and sailed it until I left San Francisco in 1930 to go to Paris. I spent two years in Paris, painting at Lhote's in the morning and in the afternoon, drawing the old houses of Paris. In the summer I went to seaports on the coast of France and painted ships. I also took a tour of France, Switzerland, Germany, Austria, Hungary, Holland and Belgium, drawing ships wherever they were to be found." Upon his return to this country, Mr. Cosgrave began a career which included illustration, book jackets and covers for such magazines as *Motor Boating* and *Fortune.* He served first in the infantry and then in the Office of Strategic Services in World War II. He has now resumed his work as an illustrator. His home is in Brooklyn, New York.

COVARRUBIAS, MIGUEL

Born 1902 in Mexico City.

As a child, Miguel Covarrubias used to draw and make caricatures but he had no formal education of any kind. He learned through observation and hard work. In 1923 he came to New York with a limited scholarship from the Mexican Government. In his first two years here he published two books, designed scenery and costumes for *Androcles and the Lion,* designed three ballets, drew hundreds of caricatures, published a remarkable series of Negro drawings and contributed regularly to *Vanity Fair* (sometimes as many as eight drawings for a single issue); made weekly sketches for the *New Yorker;* went once to France and twice to Mexico. His first exhibition in New York, held at the Whitney Club soon after his arrival, was a tremendous success. His first book was *The Prince of Wales and Other Famous Americans (1925).* In 1932 he went to Bali for the first time, returning there again in 1936. The book which resulted from these two trips — *Island of Bali* — established him as ethnologist and anthropologist. The book is "outstanding for its presentation of Balinese art, culture, and everyday life." It has Mrs. Covarrubias's photographs and Covarrubias's drawings. For Pacific House, at the 1939-40 World's Fair, he made six mural maps of the cultural and economic contribution of the peoples of the Pacific areas. Miguel Covarrubias has done lithographs, oil paintings, murals, book illustrations. In May, 1940, he selected the modern painting section of the exhibition "Twenty Centuries of Mexican Art." In April, 1940, he was awarded a Guggenheim Fellowship to prepare his book on the culture of the Isthmus of Tehuantepec. This information was obtained from *Current Biography.*

COX, E. ALBERT

Born October 16, 1876, in Islington, England. Attended People's Palace E. and Technical School, Bolt Court, Fleet Street, London.

E. Albert Cox worked first as designer for a manufacturing chemist. Afterwards he assisted Frank Brangwyn, R.A., in most of the latter's important works. Mr. Cox executed a panel for the Royal Exchange; eight panels for the board room at Queen's Gate; a decorative panel for the Orient Shipping Company, Cockspur Street Office, and a great many poster designs for shipping and railway companies. In his illustrative work he has liked to portray historic and heroic adventure on land and sea. These facts were obtained from *Who's Who.*

IRENE B. ROBINSON : *Elephants*

CONRAD BUFF : *Kobi*

CREDLE, ELLIS

Born August 18, 1902, in Hyde County, North Carolina, where her childhood was spent. Attended Louisburg College, New York School of Fine and Applied Art, Art Students League, Beaux Arts Institute of Design, and New York School of Interior Decoration.

"I was brought up in the low country of North Carolina," Ellis Credle writes. "Decaying plantation houses and weed-choked gardens made me always conscious of a dead past. In a small rowboat I paddled about the great canals that crisscrossed my father's land, dreaming of the day when I might see the Blue Ridge Country which had been pictured to me as a fabulous land where one could wash one's hands in the clouds. After graduating from college I taught school in the Blue Ridge Mountains, but disliked teaching and four years later went to New York to study art and to learn that North Carolina was not the center of the universe and that people of Anglo-Saxon blood were not always as superior as I had somehow come to believe. The gradual education of my conscience may be easily traced in my books. To help pay my way through art school, I took care of children in the afternoon. On rainy days I made up stories for them, wrote them down and even tried to market them. I read all the books in the Children's Room of the Forty-Second Street Library and analyzed them. At the end of two years I began to write and illustrate *Down Down the Mountain*, a story of the Blue Ridge Mountains. It was accepted and published, and thus the way was opened for other books under my name." Ellis Credle now lives in Alexandria, Virginia. In private life she is Mrs. Charles de Kay Townsend.

CROCKETT, LUCY HERNDON

Born April 4, 1914, in Honolulu, Hawaii. Childhood was spent in Army posts all over the United States, and in South America, Europe, and the Orient. Attended American School, Caracas, Venezuela, and Mayortorne Manor, Buckinghamshire, England.

Lucy Crockett says she likes to get people, action and humor into her drawings, and that she prefers to tackle every illustration as well as every job from a fresh angle to keep herself from getting bored or stale. "I stopped school when I was seventeen," she writes, "to enjoy life as the daughter of an Army colonel in the Philippine Islands. My complete lack of any training in art was a great handicap when I went to New York in 1936 to earn my living, but it also forced me to evoke an individual technique. In April, 1943, I joined the American Red Cross to spend eighteen months in the South Pacific, during which time I designed murals for clubs and conducted art shows. As correspondent for the Red Cross Department of Public Relations, I am about to go overseas on my next assignment and expect to send back illustrations of Red Cross work as well as articles." Her home is at Seven Mile Ford, Virginia.

CROWE, JOCELYN

Born May 22, 1906, in Yelverton, South Devon, England. There and in London and Yorkshire childhood was spent. Attended Wycombe Abbey School, Leeds University and Central School of Arts and Crafts, London.

"My earliest memories are of drawing and painting encouraged and taught by my mother," Jocelyn Crowe writes. "I loved most drawing the Dartmoor ponies which grazed on the Downs around our house. This childish enthusiasm resulted in an early resolve to become an artist. After various diversions I finally became a student in London. Here I encountered among other excellent teachers John Skeaping and Noel Rooke, who introduced me to wood engraving which has become my favorite medium for imaginative work. It was Noel Rooke who fostered my already keen interest in book illustration and under his influence I developed the theories on which my work has been based, that is, that an illustration should be an integral part of book production, enhancing the printed page, not just a pretty picture stuck between leaves. I have also studied modern methods of reproduction and blockmaking, believing that work should be done specifically for the method to be employed in making the book. *The Painted Princess* was an experiment in what could be done with line-blocks alone. In 1938 I was married to a neurologist, Nathaniel Alcock, now in the R.A.F. The war has forced me for the present to give up all work as an artist and to concentrate my time and energy on what has seemed the one essential thing — to bring up my small children (now numbering three) properly fed and healthy." Jocelyn Crowe lives near Henley-on-Thames, England.

CURRY, JOHN STEUART

Born November 14, 1897, at Dunavant, Kansas. Attended Chicago Art Institute School; Geneva College; Russian Academy, Paris; Art Students League, New York. [Died August 29, 1946.]

John Steuart Curry has written, "I was raised on hard work and the Shorter Catechism . . . we were up at four o'clock the year round, feeding the steers, planting and plowing corn, cutting hay and wheat; and in the school months doing half a day's work before we rode to town on horseback to our lessons. But we didn't mind. It was the only life we knew — and I had a good constitution." He has also written, "The struggle of man with nature — this struggle has been a determining factor in my art expression." And later, "It is everyday human material that lends my brush its inspiration." He served in the U. S. Army as private during the First World War. After Geneva College, Mr. Curry went to work in the studio of Harvey Dunn at Tenafly, New Jersey. In 1933 he was awarded the Second Prize at the Carnegie International Exhibition. Early in his career he contributed drawings to various magazines including *St. Nicholas*. He is represented by paintings in permanent collections of the Metropolitan and Whitney Museums, New York; Addison Gallery, Phillips-Andover Academy, Andover, Massachusetts; and the University of Nebraska. He painted frescoes in the Bedford Junior High School, Westport, Connecticut; Decorations for the Department of Justice and Department of Interior Buildings, Washington, D. C.; Murals in Kansas State Capitol, Topeka, Kansas. For a time he was Art Instructor at the Art Students League, New York. From 1936 Mr. Curry was Artist in Residence, College of Agriculture, University of Wisconsin. His home was in Madison, Wisconsin. This information was obtained from *Who's Who in America* and *Current Biography*.

DAGLISH, ERIC FITCH

Born August 29, 1894, in London. There and in the nearby country his childhood was spent. Attended Herford County College, and the Universities of London and of Bonn.

Of himself, Eric Fitch Daglish writes, " My interest in natural history dates back to my earliest days when, as a child, I found a neglected and much overgrown ' grotto ' — relic of the Victorian era — in an unvisited corner of my parents' garden. On turning over the large stones and shells with which the mound was studded, I came upon a curious dank world peopled by such obscure creatures as centipedes, earwigs, wood lice, beetles, slugs, etc. To my childish eyes these were far more fascinating than the elves and fairies on which my imagination had till then been nurtured. Neither my parents nor my nurse could tell me anything about the habits or life histories of these denizens of my newly discovered world. The eager interest engendered did not, however, wane with the years and when old enough to consult books for myself I spent most of my leisure in gathering information on the creatures of the ' grotto ' and on others which had by then become known to me in long periods spent in the garden, fields and woods. My passion for animals caused me while yet in infancy to keep numerous pets, from the familiar rabbit, guinea pig, pigeon and small birds to more unusual subjects, like toads, lizards and snakes. Horses and dogs, too, were my constant companions and, except in war years, I have never since been

without a ' kennel ' and have written a number of books on matters canine. Besides wood engravings, I have used pen-and-ink drawings to illustrate my books. I have also produced a number of water color designs for use on nursery walls and have evolved a method of using color in conjunction with engraved wood blocks which will be used in books which I hope to publish on my return from serving as Squadron Leader in the R.A.F." Eric Daglish's home is in Speen, Aylesbury, England.

DARWIN, ELINOR MAY

Born in County Limerick, Ireland. There and in Kerry childhood was spent and she was taught at home by governesses. Also studied at University College, London.

Elinor Darwin writes that she lived in Ireland until she was seventeen when she went to London to work for the Slade Scholarship of Art at University College. This she succeeded in getting the following year. "All my childhood I made drawings of everything around me — animals working in the fields, old men and women, children — quick drawings of movement and later on more careful sketches," she writes. "My cousin, Charles W. Furse, saw some of these drawings when I was thirteen and began to teach me by correspondence. I filled my sketchbooks and sent them to him in London. Later they returned to me filled with criticisms. He got me to study the work of Charles Keene in the old *Punchs*, and also Randolph Caldecott's children's books. This was a wonderful method of teaching, leaving the pupil free to choose her subjects, to work at them undisturbed. In 1906 I married Bernard Darwin, grandson of the late Charles Darwin. I have worked a good deal at woodcuts, as well as portraits of children and children's book illustrations. The cover of the handbills and publications of the Irish Literary Society was designed by me and is from a woodcut chosen by W. B. Yeats and Lady Gregory. It has been used for years." Elinor Darwin's home is in Downe, Kent, England.

DAUGHERTY, JAMES

Born June 1, 1889, in Asheville, North Carolina. Childhood was spent in Indiana, Ohio, and Washington, D. C. Attended Corcoran School of Art in Washington; Pennsylvania Academy of Fine Arts; and studied with Frank Brangwyn in London.

"My earliest impressions," Mr. Daugherty writes, " are of the life and people on the farms in small towns of the Ohio Valley, so warm and so vivid that I cherish them and relish them increasingly. My grandfather told stories of Daniel Boone and his buckskin men as he had heard them told. My mother, full of fun, sang the Negro songs and told the stories she had learned in Virginia. My father, a graduate of the University of Michigan, read aloud splendidly, and during long hours and even days of my boyhood read me the fine books of England and America from Chaucer to Mark Twain while I drew pictures. My father and I were inseparable companions. It was he who directed me to the Library of Congress and the Art School in the basement of the Corcoran Art Gallery. After my first full year away from home at the Pennsylvania Academy, I spent two wonderful years in London where my father was agent for the Department of Agriculture, and also had some travel in France and Italy. It was in London I first read Walt Whitman and became fired with his vision of America and its possibilities. During the First World War, I worked in shipyards in Baltimore and Newport News camouflaging ships for the Navy and it was while doing this work that I became friends with the distinguished illustrator, Henry Reuterdahl. Later I painted murals for Loew movie houses in New York City. My first book illustrating commission was given me by May Massee, then at Doubleday's. She asked me to make pictures for Stewart Edward White's *Daniel Boone*." Since then James Daugherty has written and illustrated many books and has painted murals, including one large one for the Stamford (Connecticut) High School. He lives with his wife, Sonia Daugherty, author, in Westport, Connecticut, and has one son lately in the Armed Forces of World War II.

D'AULAIRE, EDGAR PARIN

Born September 30, 1898, in Campo Blenio, Ticino, Switzerland. Childhood was spent in Paris, Florence and Munich. Studied at Art Academy and Hoffman School, Munich; in Paris, with André Lhote and Galani.

EDGAR D'AULAIRE comes from an old Huguenot family, his mother being an American, his father an eminent society painter in Italy. His first artistic influence came from his father and from book collectors. After giving up architectural studies in Munich, he began the serious study of art at the Art Academy there, concentrating on the pure study of nature. He then went to study under Matisse at the Hoffman School, Munich, concerning himself with the functioning of space, movement and expression. At Lhote's, in Paris, he studied the principles of abstract composition and later, at Galani's, the graphic arts. In Florence he studied fresco painting, and always maintained a close contact with modern French book illustrators and mural painters. He illustrated fifteen books published in Germany, two published in Paris. In 1925 he married Ingri Mortenson, and in 1929 they came to New York where they continued to live until 1941, making

yearly journeys to France and to Norway. Edgar d'Aulaire now lives on his own farm in Wilton, Connecticut, with his wife, Ingri, and their young son, Ola.

D'AULAIRE, INGRI PARIN

Born December 27, 1904, in Kongsberg, Norway, where childhood was spent and schools through Junior College were attended. Also studied at Institute of Arts and Crafts, Oslo; Hoffman School, Munich; and Académies Lhote, Gauguin, and Scandinave, Paris.

INGRI PARIN D'AULAIRE was the youngest child of Per Mortenson, director of the Royal Norwegian Silvermines. Her early training in literature and history came from her mother, granddaughter of Ole Gabriel Ueland — Norway's Lincoln; her artistic background, from her father's brother, a clergyman and poet, best known through his poems put into music by Grieg and Sinding. Her oldest sister, who had studied art before marrying, had a definite influence upon her. "At sixteen, because my mother insisted on college training before artistic development, I took matters into my own hands and laid my paintings before Harriet Backer, Norway's most eminent woman painter, who gave me her full support," writes Ingri Parin d'Aulaire. "I studied art at Oslo for a year, then spent a year at the Hoffman School in Munich, later going to Paris. In 1925 I married Edgar Parin d'Aulaire, but continued at art school until 1929. After traveling all over Europe and North Africa we came to America to live. There were yearly trips to Norway and France. After our son, Per Ola, was born in 1939, we decided that Connecticut was a better place for a child to grow up in than New York, so we moved to Lia Farm, in Wilton."

DAVIS, MARGUERITE

Born February 10, 1889, in Quincy, Massachusetts, where childhood was spent and where she attended Woodward Institute for Girls. Also Vassar College and Boston Museum of Fine Arts School.

"I BEGAN to illustrate at the age of five," writes Marguerite Davis. "A pencil and paper were more to me during school years than dolls, books or hide-and-seek. And through college I knew that I would take up art as a career. Four years at the Boston Museum School of Fine Arts under the guidance of William Paxton and Philip Hale gave me the foundation that I needed, and to an extra year in the department of design, under Henry Hunt Clark, I owe much of the impetus that followed. It was the happy meeting and friendship with Elizabeth Shippen Green Elliott and several years of her teaching, inspiration and encouragement that determined me to go into illustration. She cleared up the mysteries of its technical and practical sides, revealed its depth and scope, gave it dignity, breathed life, joy and beauty into it. There were, naturally, experimental years at first — advertising, Christmas cards, magazine covers, 'pot-boilers.' But the genial world of children's books, and the congenial contacts with the publishers of children's books, cast its final spell, and an initial contract to 'do' a book sealed my fate." Marguerite Davis's home is in Quincy, Massachusetts.

DAY, MAURICE

> Born July 2, 1892, in Damariscotta, Maine, where childhood was spent. Attended Lincoln Academy, Massachusetts Normal Art School, and Boston Museum of Fine Arts School.

MAURICE DAY engaged in commercial art and illustration until 1930 when he began to do serious painting. Five years later he went to the West Coast, spending most of his time in Hollywood in cartoon studios of Harman-King, Walt Disney and Metro-Goldwyn-Mayer, doing layouts and key color sketches. In Maine he took over five hundred photographs, which were used as reference material in *Bambi*. This was the beginning of a great interest in color photography. In 1942 he returned to Maine to stay and has since been recording his favorite sections in both water color and kodachrome. He is essentially a product of the country and is not happy too long away from woods and fields and streams. To him, "the world is so full of a number of things" and there are little people hiding under every toadstool. He shows his color slides with a lecture — "An Artist's Trail Notes" — which he is constantly editing, striving always toward a more and more interesting record of the cycle of the seasons as seen particularly in small and often commonplace things which have appealed to him for their beauty of color, design or imaginative quality. He married Beatrice Darling of Cambridge in 1917 and has two sons, and one grandson representing the sixth generation to live in the old family home in Damariscotta.

DE ANGELI, MARGUERITE

> Born March 14, 1889, in Lapeer, Michigan. There and in Philadelphia childhood was spent.

MARGUERITE DE ANGELI says that she grew up in a family where the father was a born teller of tales with a gift for drawing and the mother was quiet and efficient, saying to her children, "You can do *anything* you *really want* to do." Drawing, painting, writing and singing were chief interests during her childhood. However, it was not until after her marriage and her children were partly grown that opportunity came for her to study illustration with the help of an artist neighbor, M. L. Bower. "Unlike many people who must have cloistered quiet for creative work," she says, "I work in the center of family activity.

Most of my work has been carried on while rearing five children. Sometimes a room upstairs serves as studio, sometimes a corner of the kitchen, or the dining room near the window where the light is good. When paints, brushes and typewriter are put away, the day may end with eight or nine for dinner, though sometimes now there are only three, and perhaps an evening of music shared by the whole family." Her home is in Philadelphia.

DE MARTELLY, JOHN STOCKTON

> Born September 10, 1903, in Philadelphia. Childhood was spent in Pennsylvania and on the New Jersey coast. Attended Pennsylvania Academy of Fine Arts and Carnegie Institute of Technology; Academy of Fine Arts, Florence; Royal College of Design, London.

IN his early training in Philadelphia, John de Martelly studied under Daniel Garber, Albert Spencer, Hugh Breckenridge, Arthur Corles, Charles Grafly, Henry McCarter and Robert Austin. Under fine masters in Florence and London, he studied etching, engraving on wood and copper, and lithography, working with Malcolm Osburn in London. Upon his return to America he came under the influence of Thomas Hart Benton and through him became Instructor in Graphic Arts and Illustration in the Kansas City Art Institute. John de Martelly has in the past adopted a method used by some of the Renaissance masters: he has developed his subject in clay or wax, "not quite in full relief, but bent and twisted to get the desired light and dark," and then painted it in natural colors to serve as model at nearer distance than in nature. De Martelly has written that the only thing which should be considered in a biographical sketch about himself is "the gradual changing over from the more or less formal aspects of the third dimensional Renaissance background to a concept of a freer nature delighted by the use and shape of the colors as simply as I can express and animate them to suggest the things I see and think about." He often makes a lithograph, too, in the process of working toward his finished painting in oil tempera. Like Benton and Curry, de Martelly is interested in painting the American scene, especially the Middle West. His "Blue Valley Fox Hunt," shown at the American Association of Artists' Tenth Anniversary Exhibition, was reproduced in *The Studio* for June, 1945. Of his "No More Mowing," shown at the 1939 New York World's Fair (the Contemporary Art Exhibition), Donald J. Bear, Director of the Denver Art Museum, wrote in *The Art Digest*, June 1, 1939, "one of the most strikingly original pictures of the entire show." He has won widespread recognition for his paintings and lithographs. His home is Okemos, Michigan. For this note, issues of *The Art Digest, Prints, Studio* and the *American Artist* have been consulted.

CLARE TURLAY NEWBERRY : *Mittens*

BERTA AND ELMER HADER : *Cock-a-doodle-doo*

DENNIS, MORGAN

*Born February 27, 1892, in Boston, Massachusetts,
where childhood was spent in the Dorchester section.
Studied at New School of Design, Boston; with W. H.
W. Bicknell, Provincetown; and with Stanhope
Forbes, R.A., in Cornwall, England.*

OF himself, Morgan Dennis writes, "I worked on Boston
newspapers from 1915 to 1925, doing general illustrating,
while studying etching summers with W. H. W. Bicknell
at Provincetown. Soon after that I started specializing in
etchings of dogs, doing mostly miniatures for children.
I lectured two seasons for the W. Colston Leigh Bureau,
using as a basis a story I did for *Cosmopolitan* called
Autobiography of a Scottie. After my commercial season
is over in New York, I spend the summers in Florida where
I work on my books."

DENNIS, WESLEY

*Born May 16, 1903, in Boston. Childhood was spent
at Falmouth on Cape Cod. Attended New School of
Art, Boston.*

WESLEY DENNIS worked on several Boston newspapers
in their art departments. He did fashions for Jordan
Marsh, then went to Filene's, doing mostly Christmas
cards, and later, portraits. "I didn't like any of these
jobs," he says, "so decided to concentrate on painting
horses, as I liked to be around them. I hung around race
tracks all over the country, camping out in a beach wagon
and selling pictures of horses to their owners. Now I've
settled down on a farm in Montgomery, New York, and
have more art work than I want as well as raising sheep
and pigs on the side."

DERRICK, THOMAS

*Born in Bristol, England, where childhood was spent.
Attended Sidcot School and Royal College of Art,
London.*

THOMAS DERRICK, who lives in Newbury, England, says
of Bristol, where he grew up, that "it is a port as romantic
and older than Boston." He feels that *Alice in Wonderland* with Tenniel's illustrations is the most perfect children's book ever devised. "Randolph Caldecott's and
Walter Crane's picture books also seem to me genuinely
inspired, and classics," he says, "but, generally speaking,
I have noticed that children find the faery-on-toadstool
sort of imaginative picture a bore. Children are intensely
realistic, and for them realism is romance. They used to
like the explicitly informing cuts in Trade Catalogues of
ordinary domestic appliances familiar to them. I do not
think they will care for photographs so much." Mr.
Derrick's home is at Cold Ash, Newbury, England.

DE VEYRAC, ROBERT

*Born October 1, 1901, in France. Attended Aix en
Provence University and Ecole des Beaux Arts, Paris.*

ROBERT DE VEYRAC received his baccalaureate in Greek
Philosophy from Aix en Provence University, and the
French Government Diploma in Architecture from the
National Beaux Arts School. He practiced Architecture
in Paris until 1934, in New York since. His illustration
of children's books, he writes, is only a hobby.

DE WITT, CORNELIUS HUGH

*Born June 6, 1905, in Cassel, Germany. Childhood was
spent in Friesland, Thuringia, the Black Forest, Alsace,
Paris, Venice, Florence, Rome, Naples, and Switzerland. Attended Bremen Gymnasium; Ecole de la
Grande Chaumière and Alliance Française, Paris.*

"MY childhood was spent in Friesland, Thuringia, the
Black Forest, Alsace, Paris, Venice, Florence, Rome,
Naples, and Switzerland," writes Cornelius de Witt. "My
present existence is only a continuation of a life in
fourteenth-century Italy, where I feel most at home. In
the course of wandering through space and time, I met
Brueghel, who appealed to me most for portraying the
earthy human side of life, whereas Giotto, my godfather,
inspired me to follow the spiritual interpretation of all
that is worthy of the human soul. In 1928 I was trans-
planted, in the truest sense of the word, to the new world
and my earlier life and schooling have given me a solid
basis enabling me to express my work in deeper and
broader perspective. Art, like music, appeals to all ages
if expressed from within. This I feel to be essential to
broaden our spiritual existence and culture amidst the
baser side of human strife. To portray our life amidst
contemporary activities and struggles of the past in as
vast a country, filled with natural beauty as is America,
is my chosen task." Cornelius de Witt now lives in New
York City.

D'HARNONCOURT, RENÉ

*Born May 17, 1901, in Vienna, where childhood was
spent. Attended Real Gymnasium, Realschule, and
University at Graz; Technische Hochschule, Vienna.*

RENÉ D'HARNONCOURT traveled extensively in Europe
during his childhood and young manhood, becoming
interested in all forms of folk and primitive art. In 1925
he moved to Mexico where his interest was aroused in
Mexican popular art. "Result," he says, "was Mrs. Morrow's *Painted Pig* in 1930." Following that, he came to
the United States with the Mexican Exhibition, sponsored
by the American Federation of Art. Besides writing and
illustrating several books and directing a series of broad-
casts, his achievements have been: 1934-1936 Instructor of

Art History at Sarah Lawrence College; 1936-1944 General Manager of Indian Arts and Crafts Board for the United States Department of the Interior; 1944 Chairman of Indian Arts and Crafts Board and Vice-President of the Museum of Modern Art in New York where he now lives.

DOANE, PELAGIE

Born 1906 in Palmyra, New Jersey. Childhood was spent in Philadelphia where the School of Design (now Moore Institute) was attended.

PELAGIE DOANE's maternal grandfather, Henry F. Plasschaert, was a sculptor. Her mother is an interior decorator; her father, a newspaperman, editor and writer. "I have always been interested in art," she says. "Coming to New York in 1928 to free-lance, I started in greeting-card work and advanced to illustrating children's books. I am now writing and illustrating children's books entirely."

DOBIAS, FRANK

Born 1902 in the Styria Mountains, Austria. Attended Kunst Gewerke Schule and Kunst Akademie, Vienna.

THE grandparents of Frank Dobias on his mother's side were the De Santis of Rome. His grandfather was an architect. His father and uncle painted as an avocation. He was fortunate enough to study under famous professors in Vienna where the family moved when his schooling began — Cizek for design, Roeler for art in the theatre, and Anton Ritter von Kenner for anatomy. At sixteen, Frank Dobias won a country-wide competition for stage sets to be used in the play *Liliom*, the same sets used when the play opened in America. This brought him cinema work in Berlin and Hamburg where he designed sets and costumes and worked in pictures also. During a period when economic conditions were extremely bad, Dobias and two young friends worked up an acrobatic act with clowning and traveled a year in vaudeville all over Europe. He came to America about 1924 and became an American citizen. In his student days in Vienna he was a champion with the sabre and it has continued to be a hobby. His favorite books as a child were Cooper's *Leather Stocking Tales*, Seton-Thompson's animal stories and *Huckleberry Finn*.

DOBUZHINSKII, MSTISLAV VALERIANOVICH

Born 1875 in Novgorod, Russia. Attended Gymnasium, Vilna; University and Art School for the encouragement of Art, St. Petersburg; Academy of Art, Munich.

DOBUZHINSKII is a Russian painter and illustrator of Polish descent, the son of an army officer of artistic interests. He worked for a short time with the copper engraver,

L. Dimitrieff-Kowkasky. He has played an important part in the development of fine illustrated books in Russia. He also designed and made many pictures for the magazine, *Mir Iskoustva*, edited by Sergei Diaghilev of the Russian Ballet. Later Dobuzhinskii illustrated limited editions of Pushkin, Dostoevsky and many other Russian authors. He has been a subject and portrait painter, an etcher and a theatrical designer. He was a member of a famous pre-Revolutionary group of Russian artists. His pictures and designs are in Moscow Tretiakof Gallery; Russian Museum, Leningrad; British Museum, and Victoria and Albert Museum, London; and Lithuanian Museum, Kaunas. This information was obtained from *International Who's Who*.

DOMBROWSKI, KÄTHE SCHÖNBERGER VON (K. O. S., pseud.)

Born June 11, 1881, near Vienna, Austria.

"As a child I would not play with dolls, but preferred rocking horses, and smuggled rabbits, lizards and donkeys into the nursery," wrote Baroness Dombrowski. "As soon as I was able to hold a piece of chalk, I used to portray the nurse, as well as other interesting people, on the floor of the nursery, and all of them on horseback. This was the beginning of my artistic career. Most of my childhood was spent traveling with my family, and this cosmopolitan life may account for the early development of observation, which is the essential point in my work, and also, perhaps, for those caricatures of humanized animals that gave me such large publicity. My first book of that kind, made when aged twelve to fourteen, was published in Berlin and London. Although interested in every form of nature, I have been labeled as an animal painter. My first marriage, to a German diplomat, took me to Argentine, Brazil and Paraguay and we covered the entire Amazon River from the coast to the Andes, hunting and collecting. Shortly before the outbreak of World War I, I spent six months in Cameroon, West Africa, having a great time with elephants, chameleons and baboons, studying their lives in their native surroundings. There is very little to say about my artistic training, because there was hardly any; in fact I don't believe much in art schools. I never use a model, but I happen to command a kind of camera memory, and besides, what is art without intuition? In 1925 I came to the United States, spending the greater part of the year in New York. My European artist's name proved too awkward in its length for America (Käthe Olshausen-Schönberger) and that is why I adopted the initials, K. O. S." Explorer, painter, etcher, collector of strange animals, author of unique stories.

DOUGLASS, RALPH

Born December 29, 1895, in St. Louis, Missouri. Childhood was spent in Des Moines, Iowa. Attended Monmouth College, A.B., 1920; Chicago Art Institute School; Académie Julian, Paris; Art Students League, New York.

"My interest in drawing," Mr. Douglass writes, "dates from childhood when my brothers and sisters posed for me. I illustrated one high school annual and all the year-books through four years of college, also contributed weekly cartoons to the college paper. During World War I, I drew for the cantonment newspaper at Camp Dodge, Iowa. Later while teaching at the American University at Cairo, Egypt, I drew cartoons for a Cairo sporting magazine, the lines of which had to be translated into Arabic. From 1924 to 1929 I was a staff artist and cartoonist for the *Chicago Daily News*. When a health problem brought our little family to Albuquerque, New Mexico, I became a member of the Art faculty of the University and am now head of that Department. I enjoy painting, particularly in water color, and since 1930 have participated in local and national exhibitions. Several years ago, a colleague, Lloyd Tireman, approached me about illustrating some little stories he was writing about mesa animals. Since then we have published four Mesaland books with eleven more contemplated. While I was with the *Chicago Daily News*, I syndicated a feature cartoon entitled 'Trials of a First Born.' The lively, lovable three-year-old boy who inspired those cartoons was killed a year ago in the battle of the Ardennes, at nineteen. Now this boy's seven-year-old sister is the center of our home and helps me illustrate these children's books." Since 1930 Ralph Douglass has exhibited in the galleries of the Southwest, Washington, Pittsburgh, Kansas City, New York and elsewhere. His work is represented in the School of Oriental Studies, American University, Cairo; the Coronado Library, University of New Mexico; the Museum of New Mexico, Santa Fe; and in private collections.

DU BOIS, WILLIAM PÈNE

Born May 9, 1916, in Nutley, New Jersey. Childhood was spent in the United States and France. Attended Miss Barstow's School, New York; Lycée Hoche, Versailles; Lycée de Nice; and Morristown School.

"At the age of eight, I went to France with my parents and sister," writes Mr. du Bois. "My life there was spent mostly between three places: boarding school in Versailles, weekends in Paris which invariably included a trip to the Cirque d'Hiver, and Villerville, a small resort town in Normandy. I must have gone to the circus more than the average child; I believe thirty times a year was my

usual quota. I liked Music Hall acts, too. Back in the United States at the age of fourteen, I found I knew the complete repertoire of every important vaudeville act. My best friend in school in France was a young Russian whose mother was a lion tamer and whose father walked tightrope above the lion cage. All of this love of the formal excitement of circus life must have somewhat influenced my life and choice of career. But on the other hand, my father is an artist, my mother, a designer of children's clothes. One of my grandfathers wrote extensively on book designing; the other was an appraiser of art objects. I seem to have taken the line of least resistance. In making my own books, I always try to put more in the pictures than in the text. There is very little description in my stories. I try to make them jump from chapter to chapter like a program of vaudeville acts, full of rather unusual action from the far reaches of our globe. I illustrated my first seven books after graduating from prep school, then spent four and one half years in the Army overseas. I married Jane Bouché in 1943, and live usually in New York."

DULAC, EDMUND

Born October 22, 1882, in Toulouse, France. Attended Toulouse University (Litt. Ph.B.); Toulouse Art School, and Académie Julian, Paris.

At the University, Edmund Dulac read law unwillingly. He exhibited portraits at the Paris Salon, 1904-05. He had yearly shows at the Leicester Galleries, London, from 1907 to 1918. In 1912 he became a British citizen. He has painted portraits and caricatures; has designed stage settings and costumes; he painted the decorations for the *Empress of Britain's* smoking room; modeled the King's Poetry Prize Medal; designed the Coronation Stamp (1937) and King George VI's cameo portrait on current stamps; also designed the Free French Colonial stamps and banknotes, the French Metropolitan stamp. His recreations are music, making bamboo flutes, furniture, etc. Edmund Dulac lives in London. Some of this material was obtained from *Who's Who*.

DUNLAP, HOPE

Born February 26, 1880, in Topeka, Kansas. Childhood was spent in Springfield, Ohio, and the Middle West. Attended Chicago Art Institute School and Art Students League, New York.

Hope Dunlap Robinson's father was a Congregational minister, her mother was a musician, and her early years were spent in the Middle West. She attended the Chicago Art Institute where, in addition to the regular staff of teachers, a number of artists of note each year spent some time with the advanced classes, giving instruction and inspiration. After several years of teaching in the children's classes at the Art Institute, she began illustrating for Chicago publishers. Then she went to New York. There she felt that her work was greatly stimulated by a course of lectures with Howard Pyle at the Art Students League. She remained in New York until the time of her marriage to Edward K. Robinson. At present she lives in Watertown, Massachusetts.

DUNN, HARVEY T.

Born March 8, 1884, in Manchester, South Dakota. Childhood was spent on the South Dakota plains. Attended Chicago Art Institute School and Howard Pyle's Wilmington School.

MR. DUNN has summed up a full and active life briefly, as follows: "The first years: the buffalo trails, yokes of oxen, South Dakota shanties, cloud shadows, running before the wind, buttercups in spring, the smell of mint in the hay stacks, Indian scares and the resplendent uniform of Uncle Charleton, captain of cavalry. School: math was tough; got through, though. Art Institute: wonder of wonders, beauty in marble, color, the grand song of opera and the orchestra of Theodore Thomas. Then Howard Pyle, work, romance and war. Teaching. And striving still at it." In addition to his book illustrations, Mr. Dunn has made a steady contribution to the fields of advertising and magazine illustrations. He was an official artist of the A.E.F. during the First World War. Some of his work is in the Smithsonian Institute. He lives in Tenafly, New Jersey.

DUVOISIN, ROGER ANTOINE

Born August 28, 1904, in Geneva, Switzerland. Childhood was spent in Switzerland and France. In Geneva he attended Ecole Professionelle, École des Arts et Métiers, and Ecole des Beaux Arts.

ROGER DUVOISIN's father was an architect. A constant desire to draw led his parents to send him, when he became of age, to the *Ecole des Arts et Métiers* where he specialized in mural painting and stage scenery. "Out of school I began to paint murals and stage scenery, as well as posters and illustrations," he writes. "I did much with ceramics, too, and even became manager of an old French pottery plant. I soon left this, however, to design textiles in Lyons and Paris. It was textile designing which led me to become an American citizen, for, in Paris, an American textile firm offered to bring me to America if I would promise to remain at least four years. A trip to America was an exciting adventure and I made it, looking forward to some interesting experiences. After four or five years, the textile firm went bankrupt; but I was happy here and had no desire to sail back to Europe.

Instead, I published a book which, realizing an old dream to create illustrated stories for children, I had written for my young son. Ever since, I have been writing and illustrating books for children and also drawing illustrations for adult books and for magazines." In 1938 Roger Duvoisin became an American citizen. His home is in Gladstone, New Jersey.

DWIGGINS, WILLIAM ADDISON

Born June 19, 1880, in Martinsville, Ohio. Childhood was spent in Holland, Indiana, and Zanesville, Ohio; attended Frank Holme's School of Illustration, Chicago.

AT the age of nineteen, William A. Dwiggins was sent to Chicago to study art in the Frank Holme School. There through the influence of one of his instructors, Frederic W. Goudy, the well-known designer, he became interested in lettering and printing. For several years he had his own small press in Cambridge, Ohio, but gave it up in 1904 to settle in Hingham, Massachusetts, where he worked as a free lance, supplying "art work" to Boston advertisers. For the past fifteen years or so he has specialized in typographical design for publishers and in the design of type faces. Three distinctive and well-known type faces have been designed by him — Metro in 1929, Electra in 1935 and Caledonia in 1939. In 1929 the American Institute for Graphic Arts awarded him its annual Gold Medal for the previous year. In 1937 the same Institute held an exhibit of over 250 examples of Dwiggins' work and published a catalogue with an appreciation by Paul Hollister. Books designed by Mr. Dwiggins have appeared for years in the Fifty Books exhibits. He has also written and illustrated several books. In his leisure time, Mr. Dwiggins designs, makes, and costumes puppets, and then writes and produces plays in which these delightful figures perform. Mrs. Dwiggins is an enthusiastic partner in these activities. Their home is still in Hingham, Massachusetts.

EDWARDS, GEORGE WHARTON

Born March 14, 1869, in Fairhaven, Connecticut. Studied painting in Antwerp and under Eugène Féyén in Paris and in Brittany.

MR. EDWARDS has been decorated by the French government with the Cross of the Legion of Honor for his life work in art. He is represented in the Luxembourg Museum in Paris and in various museums in the United States. He did the Henry Hudson mural for the United States Military Academy, and is a member of the National Academy of Design and the National Institute of Arts and Letters. His home and studio have been for many years in Greenwich, Connecticut.

FRITZ EICHENBERG: *Padre Porko*

ROBERT MCCLOSKEY: *Make Way for Ducklings*

EDWARDS, LIONEL DALHOUSIE ROBERTSON

Born November 9, 1878, in Clifton, Bristol, England. Childhood was spent in North Wales and London where he was educated privately.

LIONEL EDWARDS says that whatever artistic talent he may possess was probably inherited from his grandmother, an amateur artist and friend of George Romney who painted her portrait. This picture Mr. Edwards believes to be now in the United States. "I started my career," he writes, "while still at art school, as an illustrator of current events in the weekly press. After a while I concentrated entirely on depicting animals and field sports." Mr. Edwards lives in Buckholt, near Salisbury, England.

EICHENBERG, FRITZ

Born October 24, 1901, in Cologne, Germany, where childhood was spent. Attended State Academy of Graphic Arts, Leipzig.

AFTER his period of study in the Academy at Leipzig where he worked under Hugo Steiner-Prag, Fritz Eichenberg obtained a position as a newspaper artist. The need to make rapid sketches at public events of all kinds for newspaper reproduction helped him to develop a summary style of line drawing and composition. In order to illustrate *Tyll Ulenspiegel*, while he was still a student at the Academy, Eichenberg taught himself the technique of wood engraving. He became a successful social and political cartoonist. In the early days of Hitler's rise to power, Eichenberg had caricatured him. It was fortunate that he made up his mind to leave Germany in 1933. He did not like the growing signs of regimentation and he accepted a roving commission from a European publisher to visit Central America. A serious illness in Mexico sent him home by way of New York and he decided he would make America his home. He visited Germany just long enough to settle his affairs and return with his wife and little girl. Arriving in the height of the depression, the Eichenbergs' first two years were hard ones. Finally his work interested Helen Gentry at Holiday House, and he made ten little wood engravings for *Puss in Boots* which was included in the Fifty Books of the Year (1937). Since that time he has not only illustrated a number of children's books but has interpreted some of the most powerful figures in literature — Poe, the Brontës, Dostoevski, Tolstoi, Pushkin, Turgeniev, and Shakespeare. Of himself Fritz Eichenberg writes, "I owe a great debt to the spirits of Dürer, Goya, Doré, Daumier, Menzel and Bewick, whose works I have studied diligently. They have always impressed me with the desire to perfect craftsmanship in even the humblest job. I have also derived benefit from spending much of my childhood and adolescence in the company of animals. This not only means good company but good training for any future illustrator of children's books. Never to be without sketch pad at the zoo or the circus proved more profitable to me than years of study at art school." Mr. Eichenberg lives in Tuckahoe, New York.

EISGRUBER, ELSA

Born in Nuremberg, Germany.

ELSA EISGRUBER'S father was an artist but he died when she was very young. Her stepfather was opposed to an art career for her, so she began to study art very late. She worked two years in Munich and then went to work in Berlin with Mr. Perathoner. She married the sculptor, Mr. Schrott-Fiechtel. Her first book, in silhouette, was published in 1919 by the West Deutsche Publishing Company. The next was a Christmas story; then came *The Elves* by Tieck; followed by *Mousy and the Sausage*, published by Stalling. Other books followed and two of the later ones were published in America. Along with her illustrative work Elsa Eisgruber became interested in making toys and toward the end of the inflation she designed toys for a toy-factory. These were modern interpretations of fairy stories — little wooden figures in charming colors. Many of her toys and pictures she made for her own little boy who died in 1929. She does not like to work in black and white and there is a Chinese quality to the delicacy of her drawing and color.

ELIOT, FRANCES

Born September 2, 1901, on Mt. Desert, Maine. There and in Cambridge, Massachusetts, childhood was spent. Attended Buckingham and Winsor Schools.

"CHILDREN's books have always interested me, and particularly when my three boys were small and eager for pictures and stories," writes Frances Eliot. "People have always interested me; and the feeling that knowledge and understanding lead to good relationships and friendship made me want to draw and write something for the little child that would give him a picture of children beyond his immediate contact. *Pablo's Pipe* sprang from a visit to Mexico, and my sketch book filled with fascinating scenes. *The Traveling Coat* was an attempt to depict the closeness of the world, and to touch on the varied background of the people of the United States. I now have a grandson for whom I feel this understanding is even more important. He may inspire me to further writing and picture making — who knows?" Frances Eliot Fremont-Smith lives in Cambridge, Massachusetts.

ELLIOTT, ELIZABETH SHIPPEN GREEN

Born in Philadelphia. Studied at Pennsylvania Academy of Fine Arts, and with Howard Pyle at Drexel Institute. Also studied six years abroad.

MANY people remember the charming interiors in color which appeared in the *Ladies' Home Journal* in the late nineteenth century. From 1902 to 1911 Elizabeth Shippen Green worked exclusively for *Harper's Magazine.* For four years — 1924, 1928, 1932 and 1936 — she designed the Elizabethan Programmes for the Bryn Mawr May Day Fete. Her illustrations for books, magazine covers and magazine drawings are well known. She has been the recipient of a number of medals and prizes. On June 3, 1911, Elizabeth Shippen Green married Huger Elliott. Her home is in the Mt. Airy section of Philadelphia. This information was obtained in part from *Who's Who in America.*

EMERSON, SYBIL

Born 1895 in Worcester, Massachusetts. Childhood was spent first in Chicago, and then in Columbus where Ohio State University was attended. Also studied at art schools in New York and Paris.

"I STARTED to travel at the age of two when my parents moved from Worcester, first to Chicago and then to Columbus, Ohio," Sybil Emerson says. "It was at Ohio State University that I first became interested in art. After graduating, I went to New York and entered a drawing class at the Art Students League and at an evening school. My family moved to California three years later, so I studied painting in San Francisco and Monterey. From there I went to Paris and continued painting and drawing for ten years. My stories grew out of experiences in France. Mural decorations for kindergarten rooms in the American church, and elsewhere, led me to make the sketches of children in Paris and these suggested the theme of the books. My paintings have been exhibited in the Salon d'Automne and Salon des Tuileries, Paris; the Art Institute, Chicago; the San Francisco Art Association; the Academy, Philadelphia, as well as in New York and other cities. At various times I have taught art and am at present teaching at the Pennsylvania State College." Miss Emerson lives at State College, Pennsylvania.

ENGLEFIELD, CICELY

Born June 29, 1893, in Lee, London, England. Childhood was spent in West Malling, Kent. Attended in London, Maidstone Grammar School, Blackheath High School, St. Martin's School of Art and Central School of Arts and Crafts.

BORN in a suburb of London, Cicely Englefield went, when she was ten years old, to live at West Malling, a village in the Weald of Kent, close to the North Downs. There, with her three brothers and a sister, she grew up in lovely surroundings. The family returned to London in 1916 and some years later she attended as part-time student St. Martin's School of Art and, later, the Central School of Arts and Crafts. "I started illustrating by selling a few drawings to various children's annuals," she writes, "and soon found that I was most interested in natural history subjects. I tried writing my own stories for illustration and now, with only a few exceptions, illustrate nothing but my own books and articles. Wood engraving is my favorite medium for book illustration, but I work also in pen and ink, water color, and lithography." Cicely Englefield lives in London.

ENRIGHT, ELIZABETH

Born September 17, 1910, in Chicago. Childhood was spent in New York and on the island of Nantucket. Attended Edgewood and Miss Barstow's Schools.

ELIZABETH ENRIGHT writes of herself that she was the "only child of two artists: W. J. Enright, the cartoonist, and Marginel Wright Enright, the illustrator; so it was natural that I should brandish a pencil early in life. In 1930, I illustrated my first book and went on from there until 1935, when I began to write a book of my own simply for the luxury of making the kind of illustrations I wanted without any restrictions. During the process, I was snared by the fascination of trying to write and have since turned most of my efforts in that direction. I am married and have two sons, Nicholas and Robin Gillham, both of whom are very good at drawing submarines and dive-bombers. Our home is in New York."

ETS, MARIE HALL

Born December 16, 1895, in Wisconsin where childhood was spent. Attended New York School of Fine and Applied Art; University of Chicago (Ph.B.); Chicago Art Institute School; University of Chicago and Columbia University (graduate work); and studied with Frederick V. Poole.

"OF my early childhood, I remember my brother's teasing and summers in the great northwoods," Marie Hall Ets writes. "I was the fourth of six children in a minister's family. When I was seven years old an art supervisor became interested in my drawing and gave me instruction, so I decided to be an artist. After entering college I left to study art and in one year had a diploma in interior decorating and a job in San Francisco. As my fiancé was going to war, we married. After his death I volunteered for war work. Friends persuaded me to enter social work and while finishing the university I lived at Chicago Commons Settlement House. Much of my social work was with and for children, including a year in Czechoslovakia in Child Health. In child psychology at Columbia I became interested in children's interpretation of drawings and *Mister Penny* followed. My marriage to Harold Ets linked me to the field of medical science from which came *The Story of A Baby*. During his fatal illness, *In The Forest* was made in the woods of Ravinia. The necessity to live only in the present gave us a feeling of oneness with nature which no physical death could destroy, and we delighted in pet creatures of the woods and in the children who wandered in and out leaving fingerprints on my drawings." Marie Hall Ets now lives in New York.

FABRICIUS, JOHAN

Born August 24, 1899, in Bandoeng, Java, Dutch East Indies. Childhood was spent in Java, Holland and France and schools were attended in Surabaya, Batavia, The Hague, and Leyden. Also attended the Academy of Arts in The Hague and Amsterdam.

"AT fourteen I left the East Indies with my parents, to live in Europe," Johan Fabricius writes. "In Paris I was greatly impressed by picture galleries and by personal contact with artists. I decided to become one myself and a year later began the study of art. At twenty-two I left Europe for South America, living in the Gran Chaco of Paraguay and Argentina and doing a lot of painting and drawing. After that I traveled for many years in the countries around the Mediterranean and in the Far East and from there I have just returned. I started to write juveniles and fairy tales, doing the illustrations myself. Also some plays, designing costumes and scenery for them. After that novels, taking my inspiration from Java, and from South America, Italy, Austria and Holland. The War found me in the south of Italy and from there I managed to escape to England. As an author I was on the German blacklist since the spring of 1933 when I protested against the burning of the books at the P.E.N. Congress in Yugoslavia. During the War I broadcast in several languages, mainly to the people of Holland, and after the fall of Japan, the Dutch Government invited me to visit Indonesia. My last publication in England was *Hotel Vesuvius*." Johan Fabricius is living now in London.

FALLS, CHARLES BUCKLES

Born December 10, 1874, in Fort Wayne, Indiana. There and in Grand Rapids, Michigan, childhood was spent.

CHARLES FALLS is entirely self-taught. He started his artistic career on the *Chicago Tribune*. After a period of years in New York, he moved his studio to his home in Falls Village, Connecticut. His posters have won him high rank and he has fared widely in the field of art, illustrating books, designing silks, making lithographs and etchings, designing stage sets and costumes, and painting murals. Some of his murals may be seen in the American Radiator Building and the Players' Club, New York; and the State Office Building, Albany, New York. He believes that an artist's first requisite is an unquenchable love of his work.

FINTA, ALEXANDER

Born June 12, 1881, in Turkeve, Hungary. Childhood was spent in Hungary where Real Gymnasium, Technical School and Commercial Academy were attended; Art Academies in Europe; Columbia University.

ALEXANDER FINTA is as well known as a sculptor in Europe and South America as in the United States. He has won many public monument competitions. Among his marbles and bronzes of noted people are an equestrian statue of General U. S. Grant for the Federal Government; a Civil War Memorial, Los Angeles; a granite statue of Christ, Rio de Janeiro, Brazil. He has written and illustrated several books, as well as short stories and essays in magazines. He has lectured on art and the history of art at museums, clubs and colleges throughout the United States, and has received a number of Awards and Prizes. His work is represented in various museums here and in Europe, including the Numismatic Museum of New York and the National and Fine Arts Museums in Budapest. Mr. Finta came to the United States in 1923, and lives now in Los Angeles, California.

FISCHER, ANTON OTTO

Born February 23, 1882, in Munich. Childhood was spent in Bavaria where Archiepiscopal Seminary was attended at Scheyern; also Académie Julian, Paris.

OF himself, Anton Otto Fischer writes: "At the age of four I lost both parents and a year later was put in an orphan asylum where I stayed for seven years. After grammar school I was sent to a theological seminary to study for the priesthood. Leaving it, at fifteen, I became a printer's devil on a newspaper, but after a short time ran away to sea. The next eight years were spent sailing on German, British, Norwegian and Swedish ships. At twenty-four, I became a model and handyman for the illustrator, A. B. Frost. Leaving him after a year and a half, I went to Paris to study art. I stayed there two years studying at the Académie Julian under Jean Paul Laurens. When my savings were gone I returned to America and started on my career as an illustrator. The roots out of which my work has sprung are the years at sea, sailing before the mast." Anton Fischer's home is in Woodstock, New York.

FLACK, MARJORIE

Born October 23, 1897, in Greenport, Long Island, New York, where childhood was spent. Attended Art Students League, New York.

MARJORIE FLACK writes: "Early in my career, because I could get no books to illustrate, I started writing and illustrating my own. My first book was written at the suggestion of Vilhjalmur Stefansson, the explorer. It was about the Eskimos. In 1919 I married Karl Larsson and had one child, Hilma Charlotte. She is now married to Jay Hyde Barnum, illustrator, and has a son. She has recently illustrated several books of mine for very little children. In 1940 I divorced my first husband and a year later married William Rose Benét."

FLOETHE, RICHARD

Born September 2, 1901, in Essen, Germany. Childhood was spent in Germany. Attended Realschule, Pyrmont; Pedagogium Oberrealschule, Giessen; studied art in Munich, Dortmund, and Weimar.

RICHARD FLOETHE early showed his artistic propensities by drawing caricatures of his teachers in his school books. "I find it difficult to identify the roots out of which my work has grown," he writes. "All I know is that from earliest memory a pencil presented itself as something to draw with and I have been using one ever since. After leaving art school, where I specialized in the graphic arts — learning the techniques of woodcut, lithography, designing of books and typography — I was commissioned to execute a large mural at the International Exposition in Cologne in 1928. Shortly after its completion I sailed for America where I have since resided." Besides many illustrations for both children's and adults' books, Richard Floethe has executed jacket designs, displays, posters, advertising and other forms of commercial art. In the field of fine arts he is known for his watercolors and prints, some of which are in collections of the Metropolitan, St. Louis and Philadelphia Museums, and the Spencer Collection. He is married, has two children, and lives on a farm in Orange County, New York.

FOLKARD, CHARLES JAMES

Born April 6, 1878, in Lewisham, London. Childhood was spent in Ramsgate, Kent, and Rottingdean, Sussex. Attended Colfis School, St. John's Wood Art School and Goldsmiths' Institute Art School, London.

"PRAY forgive delay," wrote Mr. Folkard from Mottingham, under date of July 8, 1945. "This house was one of the badly blasted and it has been difficult to deal with correspondence. My note which appeared in your *Contemporary Illustrators of Children's Books* does so well sum up my youthful feelings and outlook that I feel I can do no better, and shall be glad to have you reprint it."

Charles Folkard became a conjuror because he wanted to illustrate books. It was a long way round, but it led the right way. He didn't know he wanted to draw, he did know he loved books, fantasy and fairy tales for preference. When young he saw Charles Morritt, the conjuror, at the Egyptian Hall, London. Morritt's performance was to him the nearest thing to a fairy tale in real life that he had come across. He determined to become a conjuror, and in time he did. He designed his own programmes, and found he could draw a bit, found he liked designing programmes better than conjuring; oh, so much better! From magicians to fairy tales is no long step. He drew fairy tale pictures, and to such effect that he came to illustrate among other books *Mother Goose, Grimm's Fairy Tales,* and *Aesop's Fables,* yes, and the Italian classic, *Pinocchio.* He is the author of several children's plays and pantomimes, and for seventeen years he contributed the *Teddy Tail* children's feature to the *London Daily Mail.* Mr. Folkard's home is in Mottingham, Kent.

FORD, LAUREN

Born January 23, 1891, in New York. Childhood was spent in Rye, New York, Windham, Connecticut, and Brittany, France. Attended Rye Seminary; Art Students League, New York; and Académie Colarossis, Paris.

THE author-illustrator of the *Little Book about God* and the illustrator of *The Ageless Story* tells us: "I am not an illustrator or a writer. I only illustrated the books that I made for my oldest granddaughter and for my godchild because I wanted these children to have books about the subjects these books are about. The books were taken by the publishers because they thought other children ought to have them. My job is picture painting. My parents had friends who were literary, and also artists. I was not able to pass the examinations to get into college so my parents sent me to the Art Students League, because I was always drawing, and to my uncle in Brittany, as an apprentice, to watch him paint and keep his brushes clean. The village priest at that time gave me my schooling, which was mostly lives of the saints. So I couldn't have very much helped being an artist." Lauren Ford lives now in Bethlehem, Connecticut.

FOSTER, MARCIA LANE

Born August 27, 1897, at Seaton, Devon, England. Attended St. John's Wood Art School, and Central School of Arts and Crafts, London.

MARCIA LANE FOSTER is a wood engraver and illustrator. Her husband is Dudley Jarrett. She has exhibited decorative art at Royal Academy, New English Art Club, the Paris Salon, and the Society of Women Artists. The British Museum owns sixteen of her wood engravings, illustrations for *The Merrie Tales of Jacques Tournebroche*. Her home is in St. John's Wood, London. This information was obtained from *Who's Who in Art*.

FREEDMAN, BARNETT

Born 1901 in London, where childhood was spent. Attended St. Martin's School of Art and the Royal College of Art, London.

BARNETT FREEDMAN was the son of Jewish emigrants from Russia and his early years were spent in London's East End. During his boyhood he was bedridden and had no formal education, but throughout the years in hospital he learned to read voraciously and then to draw. At fifteen he went to work, studying art in the evenings and gaining a scholarship to the Royal College of Art in 1922. After some years of study and work, his paintings began to sell. Lithography, book illustration and industrial design are kindred interests of his. A six-volume edition of *War and Peace* was made memorable with his illustrations, and a lithographic process developed by him was used with success for an edition of Sassoon's *Memoirs of an Infantry Officer* and George Borrow's *Lavengro*. He also made lithographs in color for Shakespeare's *Henry the Fourth*, Part I, a large folio edition. He is now Professor of Art at the Royal College of Art, London.

FREEMAN, MARGARET

Born May 13, 1893, at Cornwall-on-Hudson, New York. Attended Eric Pape School, Boston; Art Students League and National Academy of Design, New York; and studied with Richard Miller in Paris.

MARGARET FREEMAN won a medal while working at the Academy and the final *Concours* in Paris when studying with Mr. Miller. For several years in New York she worked as assistant with Troy and Margaret Kinney and gives credit to them for their splendid criticism of her work. She did some portrait painting but soon gave it up to devote herself entirely to book illustration.

FREUND, RUDOLF

Born April 8, 1915, in Philadelphia, where childhood was spent. Attended Graphic Sketch Club and Philadelphia Museum School of Industrial Art; Art Students League, New York.

"AFTER receiving a scholarship to the Pennsylvania Museum School of Industrial Art and working in a studio doing department store Christmas displays," Rudolf Freund writes, "I burst upon the world only to find, to my surprise and chagrin, that nobody was particularly interested. Then I went to Newfoundland as a designer with the Grenfell Mission, teaching occupational therapy. After fourteen months I returned to this country and secured a position as a preparator in the American Museum of Natural History, New York. Here, through association with the leading scientists and museum men of our time, my artistic meanderings were finally brought to an end and natural history became my sole interest. By virtue of an excellent agent and sympathetic publishers, I have been fortunate and my work has found its way onto the book counters." Rudolf Freund lives in Deep River, Connecticut.

GÁG, FLAVIA

Born May 24, 1907, in New Ulm, Minnesota. There and in Minneapolis childhood was spent. Attended W.P.A. Evening Sketch Class, New York.

" IF arithmetic had been as easy for me as drawing, how much happier my school days would have been! " writes Flavia Gág. "Drawing 'ran in the family,' for both my parents — who died before I was nine — were artistic. Although times were hard, my childhood was a happy one: we were seven children, all drawing together, sewing for our dolls and ourselves, and vacationing at our grandmother's on the Minnesota River. Although I hoped someday to make art my career, I took a high school business course in order to be self-supporting as soon as possible. Soon after graduation I journeyed to New York where I worked as a stenographer for four years. Then, joining my sister Wanda in rural New Jersey, I reveled in drawing, writing, and composing songs to banjo accompaniment. These three became my all-absorbing interests, and before long I wrote my first book. Unable to afford art training, I studied by myself. In 1935 I did my first magazine illustrations. This gave me my start, and ever since then I have been illustrating stories and books, working sometimes in New York, sometimes in New Jersey."

GÁG, WANDA HAZEL

Born March 11, 1893, in New Ulm, Minnesota, where childhood was spent. Attended St. Paul Art School, Minneapolis Art School, and Art Students League, New York. [Died June 27, 1946, in New York.]

" I WAS born in New Ulm, Minnesota, where I grew up amidst Old World customs, songs and folklore," writes Wanda Gág. "Our household teemed with creative ability. My father was an artist and his seven children were always drawing or writing. This happy, carefree life was dimmed first by the death of our father, then of our mother; but although a difficult period followed, we managed to keep the family intact. After graduating from high school, I taught a small country school for a year; later, with the aid of friends and scholarships, I studied art in Minnesota and New York. After trying in vain to sell my children's stories and illustrations, I turned to painting lampshades and commercial art instead. The latter, though profitable, was distasteful to me, so I saved my money and rented a cheap place in the country. Here, painting and drawing exactly as I pleased, I decided, 'Whether anyone else will like what I do is unimportant. I'll draw things the way they look and feel to me.' Soon, then, my work found its way into museums, art galleries and private collections; this in turn leading to the publishing of my rejected juveniles of which *Millions of Cats* was one. I now live on a New Jersey 'farm' most of the year with my husband, Earle Humphreys, my sister Flavia, and Liesl, our cat."

GARNER, ELVIRA

> Born May 24, 1895, in Lebanon, Tennessee, where childhood was spent. Attended Rollins College.

ELVIRA GARNER writes: "I was born in the Tennessee Valley, near Nashville, and for the first fourteen years of my life I was surrounded by a world that seemed to me to be ideal. We lived in a white house shaded by cedars; nearby were a big barn, stables and chicken houses; there was a creek to play in, and always horses and dogs. Then my family moved to Florida. After I attended Rollins College, I was married. My son is now twenty-four. As far back as I can remember I have drawn 'doodles.' If there is a pencil at hand I leave a trail of clues behind me. When I was very young I was sent to a lady to learn art. The business of getting both sides of the vase alike and making the people round and ripe was beyond me. I drew 'doodles' instead. One day in school, when our class was asked to write a paper on Poe's 'Raven,' I did mine and, having time on my hands, discovered that I could draw a raven – a raggedy, rowdy bird, but a raven. So I drew him in various postures up and down the paper. When the papers were collected, I was asked to remain after school and write an unillustrated one. Years later, opening my first little book fresh off the press, I felt almost embarrassed to see my 'doodles' scattered over the pages. I seemed to hear an echo of Miss Amanda's voice saying, 'My dear, we cannot have this. You must remain after classes and rewrite it, and neatly.'" Elvira Garner lives in Sanford, Florida.

GARNETT, EVE

> Born in Worcestershire, England. Attended Chelsea Polytechnic School of Art and Royal Academy Schools, London.

WHILE receiving the first part of her artistic education at the Chelsea Polytechnic, Eve Garnett was awarded a five-year studentship at the Royal Academy Schools. Owing to an illness she was unable to complete more than two years of the studentship but during this time she was awarded the Creswick Prize and Silver Medal for landscape painting. "I had intended specializing in this branch of art and in mural decoration," she writes, "but while still at the Schools I was commissioned by John Lane, Ltd., to illustrate *The London Child* by Evelyn Sharp (Mrs. H. W. Nevinson). While collecting material for this I was so appalled by the conditions prevailing in the poorer quarters of the world's richest city that I determined to devote subsequent work to propaganda in an attempt at showing up some of the evils. The mural decorations, covering forty feet of wall at The Children's House, Bow, London, and my books *The Family From One End Street* and *Is It Well With the Child?* are some of the results of my resolve." Eve Garnett has exhibited at several London galleries. She is at present engaged on illustrations for Penguin Books, Ltd., and a book of short stories dealing with working-class families.

GAY, ZHENYA

OF herself, Zhenya Gay writes: "In common with all children, my interest in art began as soon as I could see, hear, and touch. Like many children, my attempts at expressing myself through the media of pencil, colored crayon, and paintbrush began as soon as I discovered the superiority of these implements to my rattle. Like some children, this early interest developed with the years into a conviction that painting, drawing, and kindred forms of delineation were what I wanted above all to do. I avoided conventional schooling and studied only that which seemed to me to be essential to my chosen work – a thorough knowledge of human and animal anatomy under the tutelage of the sculptor, Solon Borglum, and an absorption of the principles of color, design, and media from observation of, and discussion with, mature and established artists. The years since I have acquired my groundwork have been spent in this and other countries – working and exhibiting." Zhenya Gay lives in New York.

GEISEL, THEODOR SEUSS
(*pseud.* Dr. Seuss)

> Born March 2, 1904, in Springfield, Massachusetts, where childhood was spent. Attended Dartmouth College (1925) and Oxford University; and studied in Europe.

UPON graduating from Dartmouth, Mr. Geisel decided to become a professor of English Literature. He returned to this country after his year at Oxford, followed by a year in Europe, intending to become an instructor in a college but, his publishers write, "he could not break himself of

ERIC FITCH DAGLISH : *Life Story of Beasts*

an old habit of putting on paper the unusual pictures conjured up in dreams – this, despite the fact that he had been warned by experts that he could never learn to be an artist." He has traveled extensively in thirty countries of Europe, the Near East and South America, and has an amateur's interest in archaeology. In recent years he has extended his work to mural painting and sculpture. After three years in the Army, Mr. Geisel is now a screen artist with time out for his own books.

GERE, CHARLES MARCH

Born 1869 in Gloucester, England. Attended schools in Birmingham and the Birmingham School of Art. Also studied in Italy.

CHARLES MARCH GERE was connected for many years, as student and teacher, with the Birmingham School of Art. As book illustrator he worked with William Morris of the Kelmscott Press – later, as illustrator for the Ashendene Press. Now he paints portraits and landscapes. His pictures are in the National Gallery and the Millbank Gallery, London, and in the chief provincial galleries. He lives at Painswick, Gloucestershire, England. These facts were obtained from *Who's Who*.

GERGELY, TIBOR

Born August 3, 1900, in Budapest, Hungary, where childhood was spent.

TIBOR GERGELY, much of whose life has been spent in Austria, Hungary, and Czechoslovakia, says that the roots of his work are in the peasant life which he observed in his early youth and in following years. He never attended any professional schools but is entirely self-taught, his style of painting being determined by the artistic achievement of the "Paris School" of Modern Art. As a painter he has had exhibitions in European and American cities. For many years he worked with Hungarian, Austrian, and German newspapers and magazines doing portraits, cartoons and illustrations, in addition to painting murals, executing stage decorations and illustrating books. He came to the United States in 1939 and now lives permanently in New York, specializing in commercial art and the illustration of children's books.

GERSON, VIRGINIA

Born in New York where childhood and later life have been spent. Taught at home, and then attended Mlle. Lenz' Day School (French), at 33rd Street and Madison Avenue.

"MY 'career' began, I think, when I was about three years old," writes Miss Gerson, "and, sprawling on the floor, drew pictures in colored pencils, like most other little girls – only I went on. When I was about fifteen, Annie Russell, the actress, herself about seventeen at that time, sent me from London a copy of Kate Greenaway's *Under the Window*. I loved it so much, I started making some little pictures. One evening my father brought a gentleman home for dinner, and he saw the little sketches and asked me if I was making a book. I said, 'O no, they are not good enough.' But the next day he sent me a hundred sheets of water-color paper cut just the size of *Under the Window*. So I started off! I made forty-eight little pictures and 'made up' forty-eight jingles to match, and my father put them under his arm and took them down to George Routledge and Sons, London, K. G.'s publishers, and to my joy they bought them. But then came the stumbling block! I was under legal age and they said my father must sign the contract. Oh no! I wanted to sign it myself. At last, getting nowhere with me, the lawyer said the only other way to make it legal was if I would sign a paper promising I would not marry before I was twenty-one. Oh goodness! that was *worse* – I didn't intend to be an old maid, so I wouldn't sign that either! At last, with no alternative, father signed the contract and the book came out. The title was *Little Dignity*. A few years later one of my sisters married William M. Chase, the painter, and it was for 'Cosy,' their first little daughter, that I made up the story of The Happy Heart Family (really the Chase family – father, mother and eight children). It was designed as a tiny book, without any thought of publication. *The Happy Heart Family* was published in 1904. *More Adventures of the Happy Heart Family* in 1905. In 1907 the two books were published as one. The tenth edition appeared in 1939."

GERVIS, RUTH S.

Born 1894 in Frant, Sussex, England, where childhood was spent and private schools in Hastings and Eastbourne were attended.

As the eldest of the six children of the Reverend William C. Streatfeild, late Bishop of Lewes, Ruth Gervis was always fond of using her pencil. She was a delicate child and, often away from school, had plenty of time to draw. "I believe that my interest in children and in movement," she says, "is due to my having been, for part of my childhood, of necessity only a spectator and not a participator in children's games. I learned to enjoy watching the attitudes and movements of others. I obtained what art education was possible in the south of England during the 1914-1918 war and then started teaching and illustrating. In 1928 I married Henry Shorland Gervis, a schoolmaster, giving up most of my teaching to concentrate on the illustrations for a number of children's books. My two children, Nicolette and Paul, have always been most valuable critics and unconscious models." During the recent war, Ruth Gervis has been teaching again, having taken the place of the art master at Sherborne School, Dorset.

GIBBINGS, ROBERT JOHN

Born March 23, 1889, in Cork, Ireland, where childhood was spent. Attended University College, Cork; Slade School, London.

ROBERT GIBBINGS writes: " My father was a Church of Ireland clergyman, so my boyhood was spent in the quiet of the Irish countryside, — in boats along the coast or wandering about the hills and bogs. From the first I wanted to be an artist, but my parents were strangely opposed to the idea. They wanted me to be a doctor. After many failures in the medical school, I was finally allowed to have my way. Then the war of 1914-1918 came and I joined the Royal Munster Fusiliers, served in Gallipoli and had a bullet through my neck. After the war I became a free-lance artist, specializing in wood engraving, until 1924 when I bought the Golden Cockerel Press and set up as a printer of fine editions. Nine years later I sold the Press and some time after that accepted the post of lecturer in Book Production at Reading University. This I held until 1942 when I resigned in order to have more time for wandering. Much of my spare time has been spent in travel and I am now off to the South Seas again." Mr. Gibbings' wandering has resulted in such books as *Sweet Thames Run Softly, Lovely Is the Lee,* and *Coming Down the Wye,* with his pictures and text. Robert Gibbings' home is at Waltham-Saint-Lawrence, Berkshire, England.

GLANCKOFF, SAMUEL

Born October 30, 1894, of Russian parents in New York.

THE fundamentals of Samuel Glanckoff's craftsmanship and style were gathered from an intensive study of the old masters of wood engraving, to whom he turned when, about 1920, he discovered after much experimentation that this was his chosen medium. With the knowledge obtained from his study, and by continued experimentation, he has evolved his own style, one which aims to retain all the rugged qualities of the wood. Samuel Glanckoff is a painter as well as illustrator and has exhibited in New York, Boston and Chicago. Some years ago he painted murals for a public building in Cuba and also spent four years living and sketching in the least inhabited parts of the West Indies. Illustrations of his appeared in *St. Nicholas* and in *Scribner's Magazine.*

GOBLE, WARWICK

Attended City of London Art School.

WARWICK GOBLE is a Londoner by birth and education. After leaving school he spent several years with a printing firm learning chromo-lithography and commercial designing, studying at art school evenings. Working as a free lance, he won a post on the staff of the *Pall Mall Gazette* and later the *Westminster Gazette.* Among his earliest illustrations were drawings for H. G. Wells' *War of the Worlds* which appeared in *Pearson's Magazine* in England and *McClure's* in America. While he has illustrated fairy and adventure stories, he has made pictures for such books as *The Greater Abbeys of England* by Cardinal Gasquet and *The Alhambra* by Washington Irving. He also has a reputation as a water-color painter, and has exhibited at the Royal Academy, Walker Art Gallery, Brighton Fine Art Society, Brook Street Art Gallery. His favorite recreation is travel. He has visited many countries in Europe and the Orient.

GRAMATKY, HARDIE

Born April 12, 1907, in Dallas, Texas. Childhood was spent in Los Angeles, and Stanford University and Chouinard Art School were attended there.

HARDIE GRAMATKY says that California was a wonderful place for an artist to grow up in. " After leaving high school I got a job in a bank, then I 'ghosted' for a comic strip artist and later turned to animating Mickey Mouse. However, I always managed to find time to develop my talent as an artist. Jobs helped me through University and Art School, but I kept time for sketching. Often in those days we would hop in an old jalopy and go off on a sketching trip, staying away for days at a time, stopping anywhere a subject might strike our fancy, and always bringing back a carload of pictures. When I moved to New York I had a studio in a loft overlooking the East River. The boats fascinated me so that I did nothing but make drawings of them all day long. Each one took on a definite personality and soon a story had developed around them." Hardie Gramatky lives in New York City.

GRANT, GORDON

Born June 7, 1875, in San Francisco. Childhood was spent in California and Scotland. Attended Fife Academy, Kirkcaldy; Heatherly and Lambeth Art Schools, London.

GORDON GRANT was born of Scottish parents in San Francisco when the bulk of sea-borne traffic still came and went around Cape Horn. Sailing ships were a familiar sight to him. At thirteen he was bound for school in Scotland on such a ship. Four months at sea made a deep impression on the imaginative boy and ever since ships and sailors have been his main interest in life and art. He has served on the art staff of both East Coast and West Coast newspapers, as well as on magazines in England and America. He painted for the Navy Department the portrait of U.S.S. *Constitution*, prints of which were sold to reconstruct *Old Ironsides*. In the commodore's cabin of the ship hang four of Gordon Grant's paintings of her principal engagements. He is president and one of the founders of the Ship Model Society, and an organizer and trustee of the Marine Museum of the City of New York. He has exhibited in the Paris Salon and the principal cities of the United States. For several years he did general illustrating, but for the last fifteen years he has devoted his entire time to painting and etching. He lives in New York.

GRODIN, ADAMS JOHN

Born 1913 in New York and grew up there.

A. J. GRODIN is of French descent. He has done covers for *Fortune* magazine, designing for special displays by Bonwit-Teller and other exclusive Fifth Avenue stores, some package designing of the finest modern type, and, among advertising art commissions, does all the work for one perfume account of importance. *All the Year Round* was his first book.

GROSE, HELEN MASON

Born 1880 in Providence, Rhode Island, where childhood was spent and Mary C. Wheeler School and Rhode Island School of Design were attended; also Boston Museum of Fine Arts School, and Art Students League, New York.

"MY life has been the usual one of a daughter in a large family in New England with winters in town and summers by the shore," writes Helen Mason Grose. "After my marriage I spent fifteen years in Lancaster, Pennsylvania, and the beautiful surrounding country gave me a glimpse of the many religious groups centered there. Association in my youth with a fine old Rhode Island farmhouse, its mistress and her garden, made me deeply appreciative of old-fashioned days and ways." Mrs. Howard B. Grose lives in Kingston, Rhode Island.

HADER, BERTA

Born in San Pedro, Mexico. Childhood was spent in Mexico, Texas and the city of New York. Attended University of Washington, Seattle, and California School of Design.

THE Haders have written that Berta's parents were Americans living in Mexico (where she was born) because of her father's business interests. When she was a small child her mother spent much time making water-color sketches of Mexican houses and courtyards. The family moved to Texas and then to New York where Berta had most of her schooling. In 1919 she came back to New York from the West Coast and began to specialize in children's feature pages for magazines.

HADER, ELMER STANLEY

Born 1889 in Pajaro, California. Childhood was spent in San Francisco. Attended California School of Design; Académie Julian, Paris.

ELMER HADER's high school studies were interrupted by the earthquake and fire of 1906. He then worked as silversmith's apprentice, surveyor's assistant, and locomotive fireman before taking up the study of painting at the California School of Design. Vaudeville was his steppingstone to the three years in Paris where he worked under the direction of François Flameng, Albert Deschenaud, and others. A summer in Brittany and a sketching trip to England brings us to 1914. He served in the Camouflage Corps of the A.E.F.; opened a studio in New York City and married Berta Hoerner in 1919; moved to Nyack, New Jersey, and shortly after started building their present home on Willow Hill. "And some twenty years later," Elmer Hader writes, "we are still building. It is a lifetime task. *The Little Stone House* gives the pleasanter side of our experiment. The little world about us is beautiful and we take time out to sit on the terrace and look across the wide Tappan Zee to the Tarrytown shore. The birds, squirrels, rabbits and chipmunks are a joy to watch and a tonic as well. Our books have recorded our travels before the war, and now we look forward to further wandering and gathering of new material. Occasionally we drop the pleasant task of writing and making pictures for the very young for the equally pleasant work of sketching and painting outdoors."

HANDFORTH, THOMAS SCOFIELD

Born September 16, 1897, in Tacoma, Washington, where childhood was spent. Attended University of Washington; National Academy of Design and Art Students League, New York; Charles Hawthorne's Summer School, Provincetown; Ecole des Beaux Arts, Académie Delacluse, Académie Colarossis, Académie de la Grande Chaumière, Paris.

THOMAS HANDFORTH writes: "My father, of English parentage, came to the Northwest because it was then the new wonderland of America. My mother came there from North Ireland for the same reason. From an early age I was exposed to Irish lore, English music, Japanese prints. In 1915 I absorbed the arts of foreign countries at the San Francisco Fair. After a university year, I studied

ALDREN A. WATSON : *Little Black Hen*

CYRUS LEROY BALDRIDGE : *Pepperfoot of Thursday Market*

in the art schools of New York, served in the Army, and in 1920 went to Paris where I remained for six years. Then to North Africa. On returning to the Northwest, my pictures were of the timber coast, of the vestiges of Siwash culture, and portraits of children. The year 1930 was spent in Mexico, following the popular festivals for my compositions. A year later a Guggenheim Fellowship took me to the Orient. I lived in Pekin for seven years with sojourns in Mongolia, Japan, Indo-China. Acrobats, strolling players, pilgrims, peasants, were all subjects for lithography, etching and illustration. After the Japanese occupation, I traveled for a year in India, painting Hindu dancers and frontier tribesmen. Back on the West Coast since 1939, my concern now turns more to landscape painting."

HANKEY, WILLIAM LEE

Born March 28, 1869, in Chester, England, where he attended King Edward's Grammar School; also Royal College of Art, London; and studied in Paris.

WILLIAM LEE HANKEY is a painter in oil and water color, an engraver and an aquatint and dry point artist. He has won medals and prizes at exhibitions in England, Spain and America. He has exhibited at the Royal Academy, Royal Society of Painters in Water Colors, Royal Society of Painter-Etchers and Engravers, Royal Institute of Oil Painters, the Paris Salon, and in Continental and Colonial Galleries. His works are owned by the Luxembourg Museum, Paris; the State Museums of Berlin and Prague; the National Gallery of South Africa, Budapest, New Zealand, Melbourne, Ottawa, Bradford, Liverpool, and other places. He has been an instructor of etching at Goldsmiths' College, University of London. During the First World War he was Captain in the 28th London Regiment. This information was obtained from *Who's Who in Art.*

HARDING, CHARLOTTE

Born August 31, 1873, in Newark, New Jersey. Childhood was spent in and near Philadelphia, and attended there Philadelphia School of Design for Women and Pennsylvania Academy of Fine Arts.

CHARLOTTE HARDING BROWN says of herself that she had the usual child's interest in drawing but that a present of a box of oil colors, during a severe illness at the age of twelve, stimulated it. After completing her studies at the Pennsylvania Academy of Fine Arts, she had her own studio and engaged in advertising work and illustrations for children's magazines. Attending Howard Pyle's lecture class at Drexel Institute once a week for a year was a further stimulus to her and she soon began illustrating books, among them Eva March Tappan's *Robin Hood*. She

married James Adams Brown in 1905 and has one daughter. Her home now is on Long Island.

HARGIS, JOHN EDWIN

Born October 10, 1914, in Hughes Springs, Texas. Childhood was spent in Orange and Point Arthur, Texas.

" I BEGAN sketching when I was four years old," writes John Edwin Hargis, " and throughout my childhood drawing was my main pastime. While in high school I made spending money from the sale of cartoons to boys' publications and showcards for stores. Since then I have executed drawings and cartoons for newspapers and worked as a displayman and advertising manager for men's stores. Now I have a boy of my own five years old. I like children very much and get a real satisfaction from doing something to please them." Mr. Hargis lives in Orange, Texas.

HASSELRIIS, ELSE

Born in Skive, Denmark.

ELSE HASSELRIIS was the oldest in a family of nine children. While very small she showed great talent for drawing, and especially for cutting out pictures in black paper. These silhouettes she cut with fine scissors without preliminary drawing and, although she is a successful painter, it is her silhouettes which have won her recognition both in Europe and the United States. She received her art education in Copenhagen and exhibited there and in other European cities. Various European museums have examples of her work. For many years she has also been connected with the Royal Danish Porcelain Factory in Copenhagen. In 1924 she visited New York and exhibited her silhouettes, illustrations for books and for old folk songs, designs for bookplates, and decorative panels. Her home is in Copenhagen.

HAWKINS, SHEILA

Born August 20, 1905, in Kalgoolie, West Australia. Childhood was spent in Perth, Western Australia, Victoria, Australia, and in New Zealand. Attended Toorak College (now Frankston), Victoria.

SHEILA HAWKINS (Mrs. Bowden) has written that she was one of three children whose childhood was free of convention and restrictions. Sand, water, and bush were the children's nursery and their educators. Her father was an artist, an idealist and a dreamer. Their financial position was insecure and their house-moving constant. She has drawn ever since she can remember and it was the natural line to take up on leaving school. As circumstances would not allow her to study serious art, she became a commercial artist. This was always torture to her and she felt she was never very good, though originality got her her own studio and success for a time. She painted on weekends and made children's friezes and toys which she exhibited. She also exhibited her paintings and their weird, imaginative quality caught the public's eye. In 1931 the slump knocked the bottom out of business and she decided to go to Europe. While looking for a job in London, she illustrated *Block Tuppenny*. After this she worked in Shell Mex Advertising, and in 1933-34 as a relaxation from commercial art, wrote and illustrated *Bruzzy Bear*. She has always had the ability to "feel" herself in children and little creatures, and children's stories seem to come naturally. Now she has what she feels is the best of all creations, a "little thing" of her own, a few months old. She hopes to do a lot more books later on.

HEATH, ERNEST DUDLEY
Studied at Royal Academy Schools, London.

ERNEST DUDLEY HEATH is the son of Henry Charles Heath, Miniature Painter to Queen Victoria. He was Lecturer on Art under University of London Extension, 1903-08; Principal of Hampstead Garden Suburb School of Arts and Crafts, 1914-26; taught at Royal College of Art, London, in 1927. He was made a Fellow in the Royal Society of Arts, 1906, and is a Member of the Art Workers' Guild. He is a painter in oil, tempera and water color, as well as an illustrator. He has exhibited at the Royal Academy, London; the Paris Salon, and the Arts and Crafts Exhibit, London. These facts have been obtained from *Who's Who in Art*.

HENDERSON, KEITH
Born 1883 in Scotland. Attended Marlborough School, and studied in Paris.

KEITH HENDERSON married Helen, daughter of Charles Knoxshaw. His pictures are in the public galleries of Manchester, Preston, Birmingham, Worthing, Newport, Leamington, and Dublin. He served with the British Forces in the First World War from 1914 to the end, carrying dispatches for two periods. In the Second World War, he served as War Artist to the Air Force, in 1940. He has been awarded the Order of the British Empire. Was made a member of the London Society of Painters in Water Colors, 1937; he is also a member of the Royal Scottish Water Color Society, and the Royal Institute of Oil Painters. Among the books he has written and illustrated are: *Letters to Helen, Palm-Groves and Humming-birds, Prehistoric Man*, and *Burns by Himself*. Books he has illustrated include *Romaunt of the Rose* and *Green Mansions*. His home is at Spean Bridge, Inverness-shire, Scotland. Some of this information has been obtained from *Who's Who*.

HENDERSON, LE GRAND
Born May 24, 1901, in Torrington, Connecticut, where childhood was spent. Attended Yale University.

LE GRAND HENDERSON writes, "There is little to report about my art work until the night I found myself gazing at the shadowy bulk of a yak in the Central Park Zoo. 'Why is a yak?' I asked myself, and found no available information on the subject. I decided to write an illustrated book about it. A juvenile book seemed the proper medium, as children's minds, being uncluttered with the trivia of years, would approach the subject without strain. I enjoyed doing that book so I wrote and illustrated others. The Mississippi River also seemed a source of material, so I built a shanty boat in which I drifted down to the Gulf of Mexico. My experiences on this trip led to the Augustus books. An old riverman told me how things would be when he heard I was leaving the river. 'You've squshed the mud of the Mississippi a'tween your toes, and you'll come back. You'll be a'settin' up there in New York some day and then all of a sudden you'll see just as clear the river a'shinin' and a'sparklin', an' a shanty boat bobbin' up and down, and you'll smell the river an' the mud—an' you'll come back.' I think he was right." Mr. Henderson now lives in Thomaston, Georgia.

HERRERA, VELINO
Born winter of 1902 in Tsia Pueblo, Bernalillo, New Mexico, where childhood was spent and Tsia Day School was attended; also studied at Santa Fe Indian School.

THE mother of this Pueblo Indian artist named him "Snow-on-the-mountain-boy" because snow covered the Jemez Mountains behind the pueblo when he was born. But he has never told any of his white friends the Indian version of this name because, as he says, "That is my mother's name for me, and it isn't right to let the others use it." He spent his earliest years in the Tsia pueblo, roaming the foothills in search of wild animals, perfecting his knowledge of natural history and going to day school. His mother, whom he admires greatly, was an excellent potter. His father, a fine, aristocratic Indian, taught him all the things a boy of his age should know. But at fourteen, which was the age for his real Indian education to begin, he was sent to the government boarding school at Santa Fe. There "traditional patterns of behavior were done away with without acceptable substitutions." When he was about seventeen he became associated with painters of a group known later as the "Santa Fe School." But a pueblo feud in which his family was involved made it impossible for him to paint with freedom. He gave up painting for a while and tried to adjust himself to life in the pueblo. Eventually he returned to his art and went to live in Santa Fe. "This was a transition period in which Velino found himself as an artist and sought to adjust himself as an individual to whom both Indian and white men's cultures were slightly alien." He is married now and with his Picuris wife and five children lives in Santa Fe and "is busy with all the modern aspects of life, but not neglecting the study and interpretation of that racial heritage in art which has so enriched American life today." His paintings — signed sometimes Mapewi and sometimes Velino Shije — are in many museums including the Santa Fe, the Fogg and the Cleveland Museums. Some of his murals are in the Department of the Interior, Washington, D. C.

HEYNEMAN, ANNE

Born July, 1910, in San Francisco where childhood was spent. Attended University of California; California School of Fine Arts; Le Grand Verger, Lausanne, Switzerland; studios of Lhote and Leger, Paris; Coöperative School for Teachers, New York.

ANNE HEYNEMAN writes that her first drawings of hatchet-faced ladies were much admired by her family, but that she was discouraged early in the pursuit of art by being forced to shade apples at school. "I studied anthropology at the University, but was more interested in caricaturing my professors," she says. "Following college, I studied in Paris for two years and was the despair of all my teachers — since everything seriously intended turned out funny. Then I decided to *start out* funny and had better results. Returning to San Francisco, I worked for a time with puppeteer Percy Dilley and illustrated my first book for designer Helen Gentry. Moving to New York, I found few funny books to illustrate so wrote my own books and illustrated them, also doing some political cartoons for *PM* and the *New Republic*. In 1941 I married Hugh Kappel, the painter, and collaborated with him on *The Happy Hippopotamus*. Studied at the Coöperative School for Teachers to get more firsthand knowledge of children and taught for a year at the City and Country School. Now I am at work on another book of my own." Anne Heyneman lives in New York.

HILDER, ROWLAND

Born June 28, 1905, in Great Neck, Long Island, New York. Childhood was spent in Morristown, New Jersey. Attended Aske's, Hatcham, London and Goldsmiths' College, University of London.

"UP to the age of ten, I spent my life in New Jersey," Rowland Hilder writes. "Then I went to live in London and I have remained in or near London ever since, though I made many trips across the Atlantic in my early youth. These voyages developed a great love of the sea. They

also interfered with any chance of success in my scholastic education. However, they gave me plenty of opportunity for drawing and reading, and my ambition to be a book illustrator was formed very young. This was encouraged into reality by Edmund J. Sullivan, the illustration master at Goldsmiths' College." Mr. Hilder lives in Blackheath, London.

HINTON, CHARLES LOUIS

Born October 18, 1869, in Ithaca, New York. Attended Clapham Parochial School, London; National Academy of Design, New York; Ecole des Beaux Arts and Gérôme Academy, Paris.

THE illustrator of *Emmy Lou, Her Book and Heart* is also a well-known painter and sculptor. Furthermore, as a boy he learned a good deal about stonecutting from assisting his father, Louis J. Hinton, who was an outstanding carver and designer. Some of the elder Hinton's stone carvings are in All Saints' Cathedral in Albany, New York. A traveling scholarship, awarded by the National Academy of Design in New York, took young Charles Hinton to Paris. There he studied painting and sculpture. He is an expert in anatomy and has lectured frequently before medical students. His teaching career has been an active one. He has taught drawing and anatomy at the National Academy of Design since the beginning of the century and is now its Dean. Examples of his painting may be seen in his murals for the Orphans' Court in the City Court House at Wilkesbarre, Pennsylvania, and for the Second National Bank of that city. Mr. Hinton entered the field of illustration shortly after his return from Paris around 1900. His collaboration with *McClure's Magazine* began at that time and led to the first appearance, serially, in the magazine, of *Emmy Lou, Her Book and Heart*. Since then Mr. Hinton has illustrated many textbooks, school readers, holiday books for adults (including some of Hamilton Wright Mabie's) and magazine stories. He has lived for the past thirty years in Bronxville, New York.

HODGES, C. WALTER

Born March 18, 1909, in Beckenham, Kent, England. Attended Dulwich College and Goldsmiths' College School of Art, London.

AFTER studying under Edmund J. Sullivan at Art School, C. Walter Hodges left to design scenery and costumes at the Everyman Theatre in London, 1928-1930. Art theatres, however, do not pay, so he reluctantly abandoned this dream and went into an advertising agency. This work, though lucrative, he found incredibly dull and so abandoned it. He took to free-lance work, illustrating for magazines, newspapers, and books. Now he has about twenty illustrated books to his credit. In 1934 he designed and executed a mural decoration ninety feet long for the Museum of the Chartered Insurance Institute of London, at the opening of which he was presented to King George V and Queen Mary. He has lived in Paris and in the south of Spain, and for a year in New York, which city and its people he says he enjoyed as much as anything he can remember. At present he is living is Sussex, England.

HOGAN, INEZ

Born August 5, 1900, in Washington, D. C., where childhood was spent and she attended Wilson Teachers' College, George Washington University, National Art School and Corcoran Art School; also studied at Berkshire Summer School, Cape Cod Art School, and art schools in Paris.

INEZ HOGAN writes: "Looking back over my life, it seems as if most of my experiences were preparing me to write children's books. Wanting to be an artist, I majored in art when I was in high school. I went to teachers' college so I could teach and earn enough to study art at night and in the summers. My first job was teaching a first grade and the work with young children delighted me so that I refused a promotion to a higher grade with more pay. Later I became a supervisor of art but insisted on work in the primary grades. I took a year off and went to Paris to study, then traveled and painted throughout Europe. Returning to the United States, I wanted to live in New York and *be* an artist, but I found myself supervising art again in public schools. Then opportunity came through a friend to write and illustrate a book for children. As soon as it was published, I resigned my teaching job intending to write and illustrate as a means of furthering my painting career. But, as the years passed, I found my interest in children's books greater than my interest in painting. Now, writing and illustrating books for children is my full-time job. In private life I am Mrs. Randolph T. Bowers. I have no children of my own but I borrow children from my friends just to keep in touch."

HOGNER, NILS

Born July 22, 1893, in Whiteville, Massachusetts. Childhood was spent in Boston where Museum of Fine Arts School and Boston School of Painting were attended; also studied at Rhodes Academy, Copenhagen.

NILS HOGNER started his education in the Boston public schools. His father, a doctor, wanted him to follow a medical career, but Nils showed such an interest in drawing and was so firm about his desire to become a painter that his father sent him abroad to finish his schooling in art. During his time abroad, he studied art under Iver Nyeberg, of the Royal Academy of Arts in Stock-

holm, and in Rhodes Academy in Copenhagen. Returning home, he became a pupil of Arthur M. Hazard at the Boston School of Painting, later continuing his studies at the Museum of Fine Arts School. During World War I he served with the A. E. F. in France. In 1930 he joined the faculty of the University of New Mexico as an art instructor, returning to New York in 1932. Since that time he has devoted himself to book illustration and mural painting. He is at present Treasurer of the National Society of Mural Painters, and a member of the Architectural League of New York and the Salmagundi Club. His home is in New York.

HONORÉ, PAUL

Born May 30, 1885, in Crawford County, Pennsylvania. Childhood was spent in northwestern Pennsylvania, and in Detroit where he attended Art School; also studied art in Philadelphia, and in London under Frank Brangwyn.

BORN of parents of French and Irish blood, in a small Pennsylvania town where his father owned the local mill and the neighbors were all farmers of varying degrees of prosperity, Paul Honoré's first memories are of spring floods, ox teams, and impassable roads, while his earliest dreams were of going to Meadville, fifteen miles away, "a city remote and desirable as the poet's Carcassonne." His first expression of the creative instinct was in mechanical invention; he and a friend spent days building "a new type" of steam engine but it turned out not to be new at all. "My life has been an accumulation of widely varied kaleidoscopic and fortuitous impressions with just the merest thread of premeditation running through it," writes Paul Honoré, "a thread on which at last the variegated facets have fallen into some degree of order, and the rational sequence of a metaphoric as well as a visual spectrum is unfolding. My education, or lack of education, seems to define art as a capacity to project or communicate to others the unique experience which is life's heritage to everyone. The means by which we make the disclosure of the kind of life we have led is unimportant: book illustration, mural painting, and other visual media are all instruments with the same theme." Paul Honoré lives in Port Deposit, Maryland.

HORGAN, PAUL

Born August 1, 1903, in Buffalo, New York, where childhood was spent. Attended New Mexico Military Institute, Eastman School of Music, and University of Rochester.

MR. HORGAN's activities extend beyond the field of illustration. When he was seventeen, he was a reporter and music critic on the *Albuquerque Morning Journal*. In

GARTH WILLIAMS : *Stuart Little*

W. A. DWIGGINS : *Book of Books*

FRITZ KREDEL : *Andersen's Fairy Tales*

Rochester he studied singing at the Eastman School of Music and also worked on the production staff of the Rochester Opera Company. His first published work appeared in *Poetry*, in 1923. His first novel, *The Fault of the Angels,* won the Harper Prize Novel Competition for 1933. In addition to his other novels, Mr. Horgan has contributed stories to the *New Yorker, Harper's Magazine,* and the *North American Review.* He has been Librarian of the New Mexico Military Institute since 1926, and lives in Roswell, New Mexico.

HORSFALL, ROBERT BRUCE

Born October 21, 1868, in Clinton, Iowa, where childhood was spent and J. M. Stich's Art Class was attended. Also studied at Cincinnati Art Academy; and Art Academy in Munich.

ROBERT BRUCE HORSFALL began early to draw. When he was fourteen and had left public school to commence serious study at art school, he was already a fair draftsman of nature subjects. He writes: "I fairly lived the lives of the animals I pictured, often watching for hours on end some insect, or helping some toad or spider get a dinner. After three years in the local art school, I painted pastel portraits for a living and began to have pictures accepted in the Chicago Art Academy and also in Minneapolis and Philadelphia Art Exhibitions. In 1889 I graduated from the Cincinnati Art Academy and in 1891 was awarded the Duveneck Class European Scholarship. Going to New York in 1906, I secured a position with Dr. H. F. Osborn of the American Museum of Natural History to draw fossils. Soon I had entered the field of illustrating, beginning with a story of John Burroughs, then to books by Dallas Lore Sharp and others. It was from here on that Nature's mysteries learned in early childhood — coupled with many Sundays sketching in the Cincinnati Zoo Park and a thorough foundation in anatomy — came into play. All Nature was of interest to me and each subject was analyzed, compared, and its life lived while it was pictured: the spirit of scientific investigation was linked to the field of art." Mr. Horsfall lives in Fairport, New York.

HORVATH, FERDINAND HUSZTI

Born August 28, 1891, in Budapest, Hungary. Childhood was spent in Hungary and Austria. Attended Preparatory School for Engineering eight years. No art training.

FERDINAND HORVATH was about to study art when the First World War broke out. Dutifully he joined his regiment and went to fight the armies of the Czar. He was wounded, captured with a handful of his battered company and taken to the Ural Mountains to be shifted from one prison camp to another. To pass the time, he studied Russian and

started to draw. "After thirty months of boredom," he writes, "I donned a Russian uniform and escaped through Finland and Sweden. In 1921 I arrived in New York and when my forty dollars was spent I went to work — painting window frames on Avenue A, hanging between the eleventh floor and the sidewalk, caulking and painting boat hulls on the Hudson River. After dozens of odd jobs, I went into stage effects, set designing, and finally into animated cartoons. In time I did some work for *Harper's Bazaar* and other New York publications, and finally found my way into book illustration. In 1933 I joined Walt Disney's staff in Hollywood, and worked with Disney as a sketch artist, idea man, and model-creator. After the outbreak of the Second World War I went to North American Aviation and later to Howard Hughes in a technical capacity to work on confidential designs." Mr. Horvath lives now in Hollywood, California.

HOUSER, ALLAN C.

Born June 30, 1914, at Apache, Oklahoma, where childhood was spent. Attended Fort Sill Indian School and Santa Fe Indian School.

ALLAN C. HOUSER writes of himself: "My Indian name is Haozous, which means 'Pulling Roots.' My interest in art began when I was very young and with pencil and ink I would draw pictures of cowboys, horses, buffalo hunts and Indian life; but my art training did not come until 1935 when for two years I attended the Indian Art School at Santa Fe. There I won the school trophy for the most outstanding art work of the year, and there I later opened a studio. My pictures have been exhibited all over the United States, and some of them went to Europe in the Indian Exhibition. In 1938 I painted murals in oils in the Indian Arts and Crafts room in the new Department of the Interior Building in Washington, and I have also done murals for the Indian Schools in Oklahoma and New Mexico. Recently I have studied and worked with frescoes, secco and egg tempera, under Olaf Nordmark, the Swedish muralist. My father, who was with Chief Geronimo continually and served as his interpreter when captured, is my greatest critic. I owe my success to him." Allan Houser now lives in Los Angeles, California.

HOUSMAN, LAURENCE

Born July 18, 1865, in Bromsgrove, Worcestershire, England, where childhood was spent and Bromsgrove School was attended. Also studied at Royal College of Art, London.

LAURENCE HOUSMAN started as an illustrator of books, then he became an author and a writer of fairy tales which he illustrated himself. His main influences were the English

School of Pre-Raphaelites, and A. B. Houghton, illustrator of the Dalziel *Arabian Nights*. His illustrations for *The House of Joy* include portraits of himself and his sister, Clemence Housman, who engraved all the illustrations in his two subsequent books, *The Field of Clover* and *The Blue Moon*. His *New Child's Guide to Knowledge* was written and illustrated to ridicule the "cautionary tales" of Mrs. Elizabeth Turner and others of the pre-Victorian period with whose writings he was afflicted, he says, in the days of his youth. Laurence Housman has also written plays, including *Prunella* (with Granville Barker), *Angels and Ministers*, and *Little Plays of St. Francis*. He lives in Street, Somerset.

HUMMEL, LISL
Born in Vienna, Austria. Studied at Vienna Art School. Later continued art studies in Munich.

LISL HUMMEL's study of drawing was followed by a course in painting. Later in Munich one of her teachers advised her to try her hand at the scissors-cut silhouette because of her unusual skill in draftsmanship. Reproductions of her silhouettes were shown first in Switzerland where they were most enthusiastically received.

HURD, CLEMENT
Born 1908 in New York. There and in Locust, New Jersey, childhood was spent. Attended St. Paul's School, Yale College, and Yale Architectural School. Also studied painting in Paris for two years, chiefly in Leger's studio.

UPON his return to this country, Clement Hurd devoted himself to mural painting and designing. His first illustrating for a child's book was done for Gertrude Stein's *The World Is Round*, published in 1939. William R. Scott, Inc., had asked Miss Stein to write a children's book for them. Upon receipt of this manuscript, they invited several artists to submit drawings which were sent to Paris for Miss Stein's choice. She selected those of Clement Hurd. Since that time, he has worked almost entirely for children's books. Mr. Hurd joined the Army Air Force in 1941 to do camouflage but after the Japs began to be pushed back in the South Pacific there seemed little need for this type of work, and Mr. Hurd switched eventually to Emergency Rescue — that branch of the Air Force which rescues pilots who have been shot down — and from that went into Education and Intelligence work. Now (November, 1945) as he starts his fourth year overseas and waits in a Manila replacement camp for transportation home, he writes of plans for several new books on which he will start work upon his return, and also of his great desire to get back to his farm in Vermont where, Mrs. Hurd says, "We hope to spend most of our time from now on."

HURD, PETER
Born February 22, 1904, in Roswell, New Mexico. Attended New Mexico Military Institute, United States Military Academy, Haverford College, and Pennsylvania Academy of Fine Arts.

MOST of Peter Hurd's life has been spent in the West. His artistic bent was revealed at an early age, and throughout the period of his academic schooling he kept alive his desire to paint. He resigned from the U. S. Military Academy at the end of his second year there and entered Haverford, but his quickening need for creative work induced him to leave college and devote all his time to painting. He was accepted as one of a few pupils by N. C. Wyeth at Chadds Ford, Pennsylvania, working under his distinguished master. His first ideal was to become an illustrator, but very soon he felt the need of freer work in landscape. In 1929 he married N. C. Wyeth's daughter, Henriette Wyeth, the portrait painter. He has two children, Peter Wyeth and Ann Carol. He is represented in permanent collections in the Metropolitan Museum, New York; Rochester, New York; Wilmington, Delaware; Chicago, Illinois; Andover, Massachusetts; Kansas City, Missouri. He has painted murals for the New Mexico Military Institute, the United States Post Offices at Big Spring, Texas, and Almagordo, New Mexico. He was the winner of a competition for three mural panels in the United States Terminal Annex Post Office, Dallas, Texas, 1938. He has won many prizes and has been a member of the National Academy since 1942. In 1942 Mr. Hurd spent three months with United States Army Air Force in England as accredited war correspondent for *Life Magazine*. Some of this information was obtained from *Who's Who*.

HUTTON, CLARKE
Born 1898 in London. There and in Gravesend, Kent, childhood was spent. Attended Central School of Arts and Crafts, London.

CLARKE HUTTON, as he himself has written, became at the age of seventeen assistant to William Pitcher (known by the assumed name, "Carl Wilhelm"), designer of the long line of Ballets before the First World War at the old Empire Theatre, Leicester Square, London. He worked with "Wilhelm" for ten years on various productions including some for Charles Dillingham in New York. In 1926 a visit to Italy completely changed his mind. Painting and the graphic arts became his absorbing interest. Returning to London he studied at the Central School of Arts and Crafts under A. S. Hartwick, R.W.S., who encouraged him to do lithography. Founding his early work in this medium on Daumier and other classic lithographers, he saw the possibilities of it as a medium for book illustration. On the retirement of Hartwick from the Central School in 1930, Clarke Hutton became Instructor in Lithography in his old teacher's place — which post he holds at the present time. His home is at Ightham, Kent, England.

ISHMAEL, WOODI

Born February 1, 1914, in Lewis County, Kentucky. Childhood was spent in Kentucky and in Portsmouth, Ohio. Attended Cleveland School of Art.

WOODI ISHMAEL writes: "The most lasting impressions of my childhood are of Kentucky, its folklore and its history. As a child my imagination was highly stimulated with tales from the land of Simon Kenton and Daniel Boone." His first picture that won any critical acclaim was done at the age of seven on a laundry shirt board while he was convalescing from a long illness. From then on drawing pictures was his "attention getter," and has proved "a very pleasant and satisfactory way of making a living." His education at the Cleveland School of Art was followed by a succession of jobs in an engraving house, an advertising office, and on a newspaper. In 1939 he married Gwen Williams of Cincinnati, and went to New York where he has since been illustrating books and advertising, and acting as art director in an advertising agency. His favorite model is Candace Ishmael, his eight-months-old daughter. His home is in New York City.

IVANOVSKY, ELIZABETH

Born July 25, 1910, in Kichineff, Russian Province of Bessarabia, and was taught at home. Studied later at Kichineff Art School, and at Institut Supérieur des Arts Décoratifs, Brussels.

THE education of Elizabeth Ivanovsky did not follow a conventional pattern. As a little girl, the youngest of five children, she lived what she calls "a wild and free life" with her brothers, her sisters, and many pet animals in a big house in Kichineff where her father was a magistrate. Her father came from Orel, her mother from Moscow. She was taught at home by her mother and began to draw at the age of six. At the age of eight, the Revolution came, the family moved from their large house, her work was slowed down and she began to attend a summer course at the local art school. Soon she was studying human physiognomy and copying Japanese engravings. At eleven, she and her older brother developed an interest in "publishing," and executed various hand-made books at home. The brother wrote the stories and Elizabeth did the illustrations and calligraphy. Their father corrected their spelling. At fourteen, she came under Oscar Wilde's influence and her illustrations grew brighter and deeper. At fifteen her teacher introduced her to Ruskin's books

and she read his complete works. "It was a precious source of learning," she observes. "Ruskin taught me how to treat color with simplicity. He taught me above all that one has to observe and not try to be clever. His influence lasted for some time. Then a book on Dürer's engravings aroused my enthusiasm and I began to etch. As we were very poor, my studies were made possible through various jobs, from lampshade painting to medical drawing." At eighteen, the Roumanian Government invited her to Curtea de Arges in the lower Carpathians, where the Cathedral in Byzantine style is the most famous Roumanian building, in order to study and copy sixteenth century frescoes. Following this summer in the mountains she made a series of black-and-white drawings which, shown in Bucharest, won her a Graphic Arts First Prize. A period of enthusiasm for Byzantine art followed. In 1932 she went to Brussels and studied illustrating, printing, and theatrical costumes at the Institut Supérieur des Arts Décoratifs. In 1937 she decorated the little prince's nursery in the royal palace at Laeken. She is married to a Belgian writer, has a little girl of her own and lives in Brussels.

JAMES, GILBERT

Born in Liverpool.

GILBERT JAMES is an artist who works in black-and-white. After some commercial experience, he went to London and contributed drawings on various subjects to a number of journals. His subjects were chiefly Eastern, such as drawings for *The Song of Solomon*, and the books of *Esther* and *Ruth* from the Old Testament; and the *Rubaiyat* of Omar Khayyám. These facts were obtained from *Who's Who*.

JEMNE, ELSA LAUBACH

Born 1888 in St. Paul, Minnesota, where — with summers in northern Minnesota — childhood was spent. Attended Pennsylvania Academy of Fine Arts.

TWICE while she was at the Pennsylvania Academy, Elsa Jemne writes, she received the Cresson Scholarship for European study. She studied art in Italy and France, and traveled in England and Norway. She married an architect and now has two grown daughters. Her chief work and interest has been mural painting in true fresco and egg tempera on plaster walls in public buildings. She has also painted portraits in oils and water colors which have been exhibited in New York, Chicago, Minneapolis, St. Paul, Philadelphia, Kansas City and other cities. She is now both writing and illustrating children's books which have always interested her. Since her marriage she has lived continuously in St. Paul with frequent trips away — to New York City, summers in Rocky Mountains, Northern Minnesota, etc.

RICHARD FLOETHE : *Theatre Shoes*

JOHNSON, AVERY

Born April 3, 1906, in Wheaton, Illinois. Childhood was spent in that state. Attended Wheaton College (A.B. 1928), and Chicago Art Institute School.

AVERY JOHNSON says that most of his early life was spent in a small Illinois town where his interests included practically everything but art — such as amateur radio, working in a bank, managing a small golf course, and professional singing. "After graduating from college," he writes, "I enrolled in the Art Institute of Chicago. In 1934 I was sent to Key West to paint a series of water colors for the Treasury Department, staying there two years and later spending a year in the Virgin Islands on a similar assignment. Upon returning to the United States, I eventually settled on a hilltop in Denville, New Jersey, to paint water colors, murals, and illustrate children's books. During the last war I designed propaganda leaflets for the Army's psychological warfare in North Africa and Italy."

JOHNSTON, EDITH CONSTANCE FARRINGTON

Born May 2, 1890, in Waucoma, Iowa. Childhood was spent in Blairsburg and Cedar Falls, Iowa, and in Boulder, Colorado. Attended Mount St. Gertrude Academy and University of Colorado (A.B.).

EDITH JOHNSTON writes that her flower painting stems from a long line of English and French ancestors possessed of the gift of being able to record accurately, in line and color, all things that pleased their eyes. Curiosity, wonder, and delight in the life about them spurred them to master the technique needed to set forth its beauty and strangeness on paper or canvas. Among her English ancestors are garden-lovers, science-teachers, and the minor portrait painter, William Robertson. Her French forbears contributed not only a passionate preoccupation with botanical lore, but an appreciation of the achievements of Redoute and other French artists. The hobby of her doctor-father was his garden, and her mother had the ability to teach art to her children. In early years spent in a village on the Iowa prairie, her parents struggled, as only pioneers know how, to familiarize their children with great art, music, literature and science. Occasionally a visiting artist gave them a few lessons. The artist received her first formal art training at Mount St. Gertrude Academy and lessons every summer with private teachers. Afterwards at the University, regular botanical study was begun — the sketching always overshadowing the science. After marriage in 1912, with the bearing and rearing of her children, Mrs. Johnston worked along quietly and meticulously at her flower and insect studies in pencil, ink, and water color. In 1936, after moving to Bronxville, New York, her flower paintings were exhibited and came to the attention of Margaret McKenny, who asked her to collaborate on a wildflower book. Faced with the problem of color reproduction, Mrs. Johnston learned to do her own color separations and to supervise the proving of her plates. Her present lithographic work is considered unique in America. Her home is now in Bronxville, New York.

JONES, ELIZABETH ORTON

Born June 25, 1910, in Highland Park, Illinois, where childhood was spent. Attended House in the Pines, University of Chicago, Chicago Art Institute School, and Ecole des Beaux Arts, Fontainebleau, France.

ELIZABETH JONES writes: "My grandfather Orton had a bookstore in Geneva, New York. He loved books not only for the thoughts they contained, but for their whole make-up. He also loved children, and was always writing stories and plays for them. I never saw him, but I think I inherited much from him. I always drew, and made up stories. When I grew up, I began to draw and write for children. My greatest pleasure has come through making books for them. I have also done etchings, murals and water colors." She speaks also of the deep and lasting effect her early home life had on her mind and imagination. She says, "My parents believed in exposing their children to music, art, literature, and people of various nationalities and walks of life. Two of the people in our home were Bohemian. My first and tenderest roots received much nurture from their joy and boundless imagination." Elizabeth Orton Jones now owns an old-fashioned house with many acres of land in Mason, New Hampshire. She calls her house "Book End."

JONES, HAROLD

Born February 22, 1904, in London where childhood was spent. Attended St. Dunstan's College, and Royal College of Art, London.

"DURING holidays from school," Harold Jones writes, "my brothers and I remained indoors, amusing ourselves by some sort of creative effort. Usually these efforts took the shape of home-produced magazines and the like. We preferred this to the rigors of Rugby football and the monotony of cricket, and we received much encouragement from our Art Master. Years passed, and later, I gained a Scholarship to the Royal College of Art, where Sir William Rothenstein, the Principal, inspired us to draw and compose in the best academic traditions. Following my art training, I taught for a number of years at a boys' school in London, but the urge within me to create was too strong for me to continue full-time teaching for long. I gave up my employment as a teacher and started life as a professional artist. My first illustrations appeared in

1937. Walter de la Mare and I collaborated to produce *This Year, Next Year*, a series of poems and pictures depicting the four seasons. It has been my pleasure to illustrate many children's books since then. Undoubted pleasure it surely is, for to work for children is an inspiration in itself. I have two daughters and I have written and illustrated a book for each. The first, *A Visit to the Farm*, has already made its appearance in the world, but the second is not as yet complete." Harold Jones lives in Putney, London.

JONES, RICHARD C.

Born December 13, 1910, in Chicago. There and in Lancaster, Pennsylvania, his childhood was spent.

RICHARD JONES was always a designer rather than a painter. He says, "My earliest scribbles were purely decorative design. This was not a matter of choice; it was my allotment. Born in an earlier period I could have designed and decorated porcelains." At nineteen he went to New York, with four dollars in his pocket and five complete sets of designs for five books. He was fortunate enough to receive immediate contracts for three of them. Then came the depression, and the books got no further than the first small advance payments. For a time he illustrated book jackets, title pages, and other popular "pot boilers." He writes: "It was not until 1939, when Oxford published my designs for Somerset Maugham's little Siamese fairy tale that I felt any real pleasure for my published work. In 1936 the Spencer Collection of the New York Public Library commissioned me to write and illustrate my diary manuscript, *Islands of the Orient*, but this work is not intended for publication." Mr. Jones lives in New York City.

JONES, WILFRED J.

Born January 20, 1888, in Philadelphia, Pennsylvania, where he spent his childhood and attended the public schools.

OF his life Wilfred Jones writes that during his years at school in Philadelphia he haunted museums and the Public Library, and this opportunity to see pictures and books must be counted as an important part of his schooling. After a year in High School, the urge to concentrate on drawing led him to move on to Art School, but his stay there was short owing to his acute discomfort in the Antique Class to which his extreme youth and inexperience condemned him. He has never been able to think of the period as beneficial to himself or to the school. Nevertheless he does not consider that he can describe himself as "self-trained," for he had the advice and criticism of older artists who had labored in the schools with greater profit. "As to self-discipline, that is something that all of us – in or out of school – must achieve for ourselves. Then, as for everyone who has studied the great work of the past, the artists who created the illuminated manuscripts of Persia, Ireland, Italy and France, and the designers of the woodcut illustrations of the early printed books of Venice, are in a real sense his masters." Design, or the abstract element, seemed as important to him as the imaginative content, and his work, when he first arrived in New York at the age of seventeen, had a decided decorative character. Although that type of work was hardly popular at the time, he nevertheless found editors encouraging, and he even received a few free-lance commissions. But this arrival of his came in the middle of a financial depression, and it was clear that he would have to find a more regular source of income. He was lucky enough to find something in advertising illustration; following this he made newspaper and magazine drawings – book work came much later. Mr. Jones's home is in New York City.

KANE, HENRY B.

Born January 8, 1902, in Cambridge, Massachusetts, where, and in the State of Maine, childhood was spent. Attended Phillips-Exeter Academy, and Massachusetts Institute of Technology.

"I CAN hardly remember the time when I was not drawing," Henry Kane writes. "Photography entered my life in 1912 at the advanced age of ten, and the two have occupied equally important places in my affections. My pursuit of these two forms of art was interrupted, temporarily, by the not-too-assiduous pursuit of knowledge at the two institutions mentioned above. Since then family cares (there are three, including two children, one of each) and the necessity of paying off tradespeople and the national debt, have prompted me to undertake such varied occupations as lighting engineering, kitchen design, advertising, promotion, public relations, and flying for the U. S. Navy. In the meantime I have done advertising, magazine and book illustration for both children and adults, sometimes drawings, sometimes photographs, but mostly in the field of nature in any event. Although my father was a rather accomplished amateur photographer, so far as I know the only other artist in our family is a cousin, Harold Bugbee. I saw him last, when we were ten, as he left New England for Texas to learn to be a cowboy and shoot rattlesnakes. He grew up to illustrate Western books. That hardly seems close enough to have exerted any great influence on me, however. My art training came in drawing cartoons for the alleged humorous magazine at college. It has all been very haphazard." Mr. Kane's home is in Lincoln, Massachusetts.

KATCHAMAKOFF, ATANAS

Born January 31, 1898, at Leskovitz, Bulgaria, where his childhood was spent. Attended University of Sofia, and Sofia National Academy of Fine Arts.

OF the village that was his home, Atanas Katchamakoff writes, "Color . . . color . . . everywhere color. Like fire, like the sun, like copper, like burned copper, like chocolate, and some like nothing ever seen elsewhere. The houses of the village are white with red roofs like red crowns. The background for this dazzling picture is the dark purple Balkan mountains, high up in the sky. These mountains divide Bulgaria in half, the north with severe winters and the south with soft warm winters. Above the village stands the church like a princess, with high towers and a bell; a singing bell which announces many events, good and bad, even the arrival of the gypsy bear in the early spring. Many years ago everyone in the village helped with the making of this bell, giving treasures — ear-rings, silver crosses brought from the Holy Land, golden chains and bracelets — to be cast into the melting pot for the bell, and it was molded by a master smith, the father of Atanas Katchamakoff." Mr. Katchamakoff is a sculptor. He was the first to interpret the American desert in sculpture, in figures which represent the dynamic power of the great wastes. The inspiration for his prize-winning piece of sculpture, "Indian Woman With Papoose," was found on an Indian reservation near Palm Canyon. He has been director of the Palm Springs Art School in California, and head of the El Paséa Art Gallery. His home is in Hollywood, California.

KAUFFER, EDWARD MC KNIGHT

Born 1891 in Great Falls, Montana. Attended Chicago Art Institute School, and studied in Munich and Paris.

EDWARD McKNIGHT KAUFFER was born in America of English parents. He began his artistic career as scene painter in the theatre, studying meanwhile at night schools. Early in 1914 he settled in London and began designing posters for the Underground Railway. Among the books for adults he has illustrated are the Nonesuch Press *Don Quixote* and the Illustrated Modern Library Edition of W. H. Hudson's *Green Mansions*. His work is represented in the permanent collections of the South Kensington Museum, London; Corcoran Art Gallery, Washington, and in Milan. An exhibition of his work was held in the Ashmolean Museum, Oxford, England, in 1926, and a Retrospective Exhibition of his posters was held at the Museum of Modern Art, New York, in 1937. He is a Fellow of the British Institute of Industrial Art and Industry. Edward McKnight Kauffer's home is in London. This information was obtained from *Who's Who.*

KELEN, EMERY

Born December 22, 1896, in Gyor, Hungary. There and on the Hungarian plains his childhood was spent. Attended Art Academies in Budapest, Munich, and Paris.

EMERY KELEN writes: " As a child I spent my summers on the wheat-growing plains of Hungary (the Puszta) and there made my first acquaintance with animals, birds, and wild flowers. I had my first contact with my future juvenile public in 1919 when I was engaged by the government to go with a storyteller from school to school, illustrating the stories on the blackboard while he told them. After three years in Munich, where I contributed to the best-known German humorous magazines, I went to the League of Nations in Geneva as a political cartoonist. Here I was captured by the variety of expressions on the faces of diplomats from all over the world. For fifteen years, in partnership with another artist, I published limited edition albums about every important conference and contributed to newspapers and magazines in every country. In 1938 I came to the United States, and while I continued my political cartooning work through syndicates and in several portfolios for *Fortune Magazine*, I made my first real venture into the children's book field with *Yussuf the Ostrich*. Thus I returned to my first love — animals, birds, and flowers. I prefer to write my own stories and to create my own subjects for illustration. Always on the side of humor, I am chiefly interested in the personality of the animal. I check up carefully on the natural historical background of my models, and my subject, and I seek the advice of as many children as I can lay hold on." Emery Kelen lives in New York.

KENT, ROCKWELL

Born June 21, 1882, at Tarrytown Heights, New York, where childhood was spent. Attended Horace Mann School and Columbia University School of Architecture.

ROCKWELL KENT writes that during his school years he studied art and that he is still studying art. "In the course of many years I worked at practically everything that came along to earn a living for myself and growing family. I have been a lobsterman, a laborer, a carpenter, and a draftsman. I have painted pictures, made wood engravings, lithographs and drawings. I have worked very hard. And feeling entitled, through hard work done, to term myself a working man, I have identified myself with what is called the working class. I have become active in the labor movement, holding it to be the most potent force for good in our Democracy. I am at present a dairy farmer, and I live at Au Sable Forks in that section of New York, the Adirondacks, which its people proudly term 'The North Country.' I have traveled over most of America, in Europe, and in the region of Tierra del Fuego and Cape Horn. I have lived in Newfoundland, Alaska, Ireland, and Greenland. Wherever I have lived or traveled I have painted. And of most of these lives I have written."

KIRMSE, MARGUERITE

Born December 14, 1885, in Bournemouth, England, where childhood was spent and Fontainebleau School for Girls was attended. Also studied in London at Royal Academy School of Music, Frank Calderon's School of Animal Painting, and Polytechnic School of Art.

MARGUERITE KIRMSE was born with a natural love of animals and music and originally studied to become a harpist, but her love of animals and the drawing of them finally took precedence and much of her first work was done in London at the Zoo and at many dog shows. "In 1910 I came to the United States on a visit," she writes, "and was fortunate in securing orders to paint dogs and horses. For a number of years my time was divided between music and art until finally the press of art work forced me virtually to abandon my music. Recognition as an animal painter brought added commissions to paint portraits of dogs and horses as well as to make sketches for various publications. This put an end to music as a career. In 1922 I began making etchings of dogs in dry point and also began illustrating animal stories. My work is done through the media of oil, pastel, crayon, pencil and etching, and I have done a number of works of dogs in bronze." In private life Marguerite Kirmse is Mrs. George W. Cole. She lives on her farm at Bridgewater, Connecticut, where she has kept extensive kennels, the dogs often furnishing living models for her work.

KREDEL, FRITZ

Born February 8, 1900, in Michelstadt, Odenwald, Germany. There and in Darmstadt childhood was spent and schools through the Real Gymnasium were attended. Studied at Art School, Offenbach-am-Main.

FRITZ KREDEL writes of his life as follows: "After the Real Gymnasium I went to war as *Fahnenjunker* to become an army officer. After the war I was first apprenticed in a pharmacy, and later worked with horses on a farm in Pomerania. Always fond of making drawings and water colors, I went finally to the Art School in Offenbach-am-Main and became a student of Professor Rudolf Koch. In 1924 I went to Italy with Professor Victor Hammer from Vienna. Returning to Offenbach in 1925, I taught art under Koch. Left school in 1934 after Koch's death and went to Frankfort-am-Main to continue with other students the *Werkstatt Rudolf Koch*. In 1936 went to Austria to join my friend, Professor Hammer, again.

Came to the United States September 1938. Have become a citizen and feel just fine over here. Professor Hammer is now teaching in Wells College, Aurora, New York."

KUBINYI, KALMAN

Born July 29, 1906, in Cleveland, Ohio, where childhood was spent. Attended Council Educational Alliance, Cleveland School of Art and John Huntington Polytechnic Institute.

KALMAN KUBINYI was born of Magyar parents in that part of Cleveland long known as "Little Italy." He was a pupil of Rolf Stoll and Henry G. Keller and gained much education from his wanderings over the world — New York, Paris, Munich, Budapest, Sarajevo, Ragusa, Korcula, Spalato, and other places. He has received awards and prizes for etchings, landscape paintings and reliefs. One of his murals is in the South High School, Cleveland. He has been an instructor at the John Huntington Polytechnic Institute and the Cleveland School of Art. In addition to being a painter-etcher-teacher, Mr. Kubinyi has done considerable writing.

KUTCHER, BEN

Born August 15, 1895, in Kiev, Russia, where childhood was first spent, then in Philadelphia, where the Pennsylvania Academy of Fine Arts was attended.

BEN KUTCHER came with his family to the United States in 1902 and settled in Philadelphia. He has written, "Much of my early childhood was spent on my grandfather's estate in Russia, where peacocks strolled and fountains played. I had a natural talent for dancing and pantomime, and was at one time tempted to try the stage, but my love for art was too great, and I found dancing as a medium of expression too limited." Upon graduating from high school, Kutcher was awarded a four-year scholarship to the Pennsylvania Academy of Fine Arts. In 1914 he was given the Cresson Traveling Scholarship to Europe. Returning to New York, in 1915, with a series of sketches he had made abroad for Diaghilev's Ballet Russe, he was able to sell these sketches to *Vogue, Town and Country*, and to the *New York Tribune* for a double-page spread in the rotogravure section prior to the arrival of the Russian Ballet with Nijinsky, Bolm, Massine and others. He also became interested at this time in illustrating Oscar Wilde's fairy tales and sold the first four of these to the *Century Magazine* for a Christmas insert. In 1917 he enlisted in the First World War. Advertising, stage production and theatrical work occupied post-war years. In 1927, after settling in California, Kutcher designed his first bookplate, a field to which he has since devoted much time. He was associated, too, with the Vine Street Theatre in Hollywood as art director. His home is now in North Hollywood, California.

ELIZABETH ORTON JONES: *Prayer for a Child*

LACHER, GISELLA LOEFFLER

Born September 24, 1903, in Graz, Austria, where childhood was first spent, then in St. Louis, Missouri.

"WHEN I was a very little girl," writes Gisella Loeffler, "my mother and father went to the 1904 World's Fair in St. Louis — and decided to stay in America. I lived on in Austria with my dear grandfather and grandmother. They had a *Gasthaus* up in the mountains, in the midst of flowering meadows and forests. Among the flowers, friendly cows and sheep grazed. In the forest were tall green pine trees, and ferns and red mushrooms, birds singing all day long, the cuckoo calling, and at night the song of the nightingale. I liked to walk with my grandfather in the forest, in the meadows. I had a little pet goat. And my grandfather's *Gasthaus!* Always there was something going on! In the summertime, the gypsies came in a brightly painted caravan and stayed in the courtyard. They were so merry! They made happy music and danced. Then — puppeteers came from Italy! They talked and gestured and were alive — and funny — but after the show, they used to lie all limp and strange with big heads and features, grinning and staring. Then the Knife Grinder used to come by, wheeling his grindstone and singing. And there were wedding and christening and funeral feasts in my grandfather's *Gasthaus*. One day there came a letter from St. Louis — 'Please will you send Gizi to us.' So Gizi went to St. Louis and grew up in a big city but *never* forgot the good grandfather and grandmother and the *Gasthaus*, the meadows and brooks, the forest and flowers. In St. Louis I lived and went to school, married and had two children and painted pictures. Then one day we went to Taos, New Mexico, where life is in the great open spaces; where the Mexican people sing romantic songs in soft voices; where they pat-pat tortillas and ride on swift pinto horses. And the Indians live in big adobe villages and have corn dances, deer dances and buffalo dances — and the drumbeats go deep into the heart. After some years we went to Hollywood. But now I am back in Taos, working on a little native book. In Los Angeles I decorated a ceiling in the Puppet Show at Bullock's Westwood, and other rooms and houses. I have also written and illustrated articles for *Scripts Magazine*, Bevery Hills.

LANKES, JULIUS J.

Born 1884 in Buffalo, New York, where his childhood was spent and Art Students League there was attended. Also studied at Boston Museum of Fine Arts School.

"I DO not remember a time," J. J. Lankes writes, "when I was not interested in art — certainly long before I knew what the words *art* and *artist* meant, and I was always interested in wood. Our attic was full of odd pieces of fine wood which my father intended to work up. A veiner (or V gouge) was one of my father's tools that especially fascinated me as a boy. It was not far different from tools I use today in making woodcuts. A prayer book with Blake-like illustrations also played a part in my development so that later, when I became acquainted with Blake's work, it was but a continuation of my childhood admiration. My interest in the woodcut medium evolved out of a desire to escape the tedium of drafting rooms — (I was a draftsman in a sporting rifle factory when my first woodcuts were made) — and for a more agreeable and independent means of livelihood. It started with wanting to publish Christmas greetings. The necessity to keep down operating costs prompted investigation into the merits of engraving the designs, and so printing directly from the blocks that I could make in my spare time. Alfred Bartlett inspired this desire. I used to visit his shop in Cornhill as an art student in Boston, where I often paid more for one of his greetings than for a day's meals. The interest in woodcutting was subservient to painting, but economic pressure imposed a greater emphasis on graphic work, and before I realized it I was going full tilt. At present (May, 1945) I am head of the illustrating group at the Langley Memorial Aeronautical Laboratory, Langley Field, Virginia, where the work is of a mechanical nature since it has to do almost entirely with engineers' reports." Mr. Lankes' home is Hilton Village, Virginia.

LANTZ, PAUL

Born February 14, 1908, in Stromberg, Nebraska. Childhood was spent in Montana and Missouri. Attended Kansas City Art Institute and National Academy of Design, New York.

PAUL LANTZ, who spent most of his childhood on a farm, says that he showed an interest in art at the age of five when someone gave him a tablet and some crayons. "I set to work and produced a picture of a man walking down the board walk to the henhouse. Now I concentrate on murals, portraits, illustrations for children's books and depictions of the Western scene. I have never consciously painted in the tradition of any school of aesthetic expression. My purpose has been to master the craft of drawing, design, and painting in order to portray life and nature as I see and feel them, with as much understanding and power as possible. In illustrating, my only roots are in the story itself. I try to depict the character and locale as vividly as possible and that alone, as far as I know, determines the character of the work. I really love children and I like to illustrate the type of story that would inspire in them a love of nature and good music, a respect for the traditions of civilized behavior. I am married and have a baby daughter. Soon we expect to get a ranch in Northern California and raise what I hope will be a large and happy family."

LATHAM, BARBARA

Born June 6, 1896, in Walpole, Massachusetts. Childhood was spent in Norwichtown, Connecticut, and she attended Norwich Academy and Norwich Art School; also Pratt Institute and Art Students League, New York.

OF the roots of her work, Barbara Latham writes that William Closson, wood engraver, was her great-uncle, and he claimed relationship to Benjamin West, early American portrait painter. At the age of eight she received a scholarship to Children's Art Class at Norwich Art School, and from high school another scholarship to the same Art School. From there a scholarship to Pratt Institute. Since then she has traveled and lived in France, Italy, Africa, Canada, Mexico, and in many sections of the United States. Her water colors and prints have been exhibited at the Whitney Museum, the Chicago International, Brooklyn International, National Academy, Metropolitan Museum, Weyhe Gallery, Mortimer Levitt Gallery, and in many other parts of this country as well as Europe. Barbara Latham's home is at Ranchos de Taos, New Mexico. She is the wife of the artist, Howard Cook.

LATHROP, DOROTHY PULIS

Born April 16, 1891, in Albany, New York, where childhood was spent. Also studied at Teachers College, Columbia University; Pennsylvania Academy of Fine Arts; and Art Students League, New York.

I. PULIS LATHROP, Miss Lathrop's mother, was a painter. "It was undoubtedly being in my mother's studio, watching her at work, encouraged by her to experiment with brushes and paints for myself, and receiving from her much training which gave me my first interest in art," Dorothy Lathrop has written. "Talk of art and artists was part of my daily life from earliest childhood. Perhaps my interest in books came to me from my paternal grandfather who had a bookstore in Bridgeport, Connecticut. In fact, during the early years, I wrote more than I drew." Miss Lathrop's father, Cyrus Clark Lathrop, a business man, founded the Boys' Club in Albany and was instrumental in establishing the Juvenile Court there. At Teachers College, Miss Lathrop studied drawing with Arthur Dow. From there she received a diploma in Teaching and taught for two years, beginning to illustrate in 1918 while still teaching. At the Pennsylvania Academy she studied under Henry McCarter, and at the Art Students League with F. Luis Mora. In 1931, encouraged by Louise Seaman, then Editor of Children's Books for the Macmillan Company, she wrote and illustrated her first book,

The Fairy Circus. In 1929, the Newbery Medal was awarded to Rachel Field's *Hitty*, which Dorothy Lathrop illustrated. The first award of the Caldecott Medal was made to her *Animals of the Bible* in 1937. Miss Lathrop still lives in Albany and shares a large two-room, pink tile studio building, set in the midst of apple trees, with her sister, Gertrude Lathrop, the sculptor.

LATTIMORE, ELEANOR FRANCES

Born June 30, 1904, in Shanghai, China. Childhood was spent in China, with a year in Europe, and without formal education. Attended California School of Arts and Crafts; Art Students League and Grand Central Art School, New York.

"I WAS the fourth child of David and Margaret Lattimore," Eleanor Lattimore writes. "When I was a year old, my family moved to North China and it was there — in Paotingfu, Peking, Tientsin — that I grew up. My father was a teacher in Chinese government universities, and in between his classes he taught all five of his own children. When we came to the United States, we lived first in California, then in New Hampshire, where my father was a professor at Dartmouth College for many years. After art school in New York, I free-lanced as an artist. My first book, *Little Pear*, was written in 1930. Since then, I've done little drawing except for making pictures for my own books. In my work, I have drawn on the various backgrounds of my life including South Carolina, where I now live. I am married to Robert Armstrong Andrews, also a writer, and we have two little boys." Eleanor Lattimore's home is Edisto Island, South Carolina.

LAWSON, ROBERT

Born October 4, 1892, in New York. Childhood was spent in Montclair, New Jersey. Attended New York School of Fine and Applied Art.

ROBERT LAWSON as a child showed no special aptitude for drawing or writing. His life was that of the usual child in a usual suburban town. During High School he became somewhat interested in drawing and after graduation attended the above mentioned Art School for three years, studying under Rae Sloan Bredin and Howard Giles. In 1914, he took a studio in Greenwich Village and for three years did magazine illustration, stage settings, and some commercial work. In 1917 Robert Lawson went to France in the Camouflage Section, 40th Engineers. After the war he again took up illustration and commercial work. In 1922, he married Marie Abrams, also an illustrator and author, and in 1923 they settled in Westport, Connecticut, where they still live. Mr. Lawson did commercial work and magazine illustration until 1930. That year he took up etching, and also illustrated his first book — *The Wee*

Men of Ballywooden — by Arthur Mason. In 1931 he was awarded the John Taylor Arms Prize, by the Society of American Etchers. He stopped etching in 1933 and although he continued to do magazine illustration and commercial work for several years, devoted more and more time to books and at present does only books. In 1939 he began to write his own books, the first being *Ben and Me*. In 1941 he was awarded the Caldecott Medal by the American Library Association for his book *They Were Strong and Good*, and in 1945 the Newbery Medal for *Rabbit Hill*.

LEBEDEV, VLADIMIR VASIL'EVICH
Born 1891 in St. Petersburg, Russia.
AT first, Lebedev was an impressionist in his painting; then, in 1918-22, he went over to constructivism and suprematism. His political posters date mainly from this period. He then turned to neo-impressionism. He is noted for his illustrations for children's books. His work may be seen in the Russian Museum, Leningrad (1928), among other places. This information was obtained from the *Allgemeines Lexikon der Bildenden Kunstler von der Antike bis zur Gegenwart* by Thieme and Becker.

LEE, MANNING DE VILLENEUVE
Born March 15, 1894, in Summerville, South Carolina. Childhood was spent in that state and in Georgia. Attended Porter Military Academy and Pennsylvania Academy of Fine Arts.
"ONE of my earliest and most vivid memories," writes Manning Lee, "is of blue-clad soldiers marching past our front gate. The war with Spain was on then and near our place in South Carolina was an army camp. My father being a general in the National Guard, the house was often full of clanking sabres and gold braid. All this made a deep impression on a four-year-old and for years afterward the fly-leaves and margins of school books were embellished with rearing horses, waving flags and all the gory detail of a battlefield. In 1914 I entered the Pennsylvania Academy but left it two years later to go to the Mexican border with the Virginia Field Artillery. Pancho Villa attended to, we were sent back to Virginia only to find ourselves in the First World War. A year and a half in France as an Artillery lieutenant, then back to school. Two years later I was again sent to Europe on an Academy Traveling Scholarship—England, France, Switzerland and Italy. Won the 2nd Toppan Prize on my return. I still like battle scenes, but since there are no glittering sabres and charging steeds in modern warfare, most of these subjects now are drawn from the past. Historical subjects of all kinds interest me. They enable me to hobnob with quaint characters from a bygone era while enjoying at the same time all the modern gadgets and conveniences. A highly satisfactory arrangement." Mr. Lee lives at Ambler, Pennsylvania.

LE MAIR, H. WILLEBEEK
Born April 23, 1889, in Rotterdam, the Netherlands.
WILLEBEEK LE MAIR — for since her marriage she has kept her maiden surname as her pseudonym — was born into one of the oldest Dutch families and grew up in a delightful home, surrounded by beautiful things. Her father was always sketching and in the evenings he told stories to the children and drew pictures for them. Her mother painted and wrote verses. When Willebeek Le Mair was sixteen years old, her mother wrote verses for her to illustrate and they made three books together. She admired the work of Boutet de Monvel, and at her sixteenth year, her parents went with her to Paris to see him and to ask his advice. He made her study anatomy and once every year she had to go to show him her progress, which he would then discuss with her. Also M. Boutet de Monvel gave her useful teaching and advice in painting children's portraits. Her drawing-master in Holland, with whom she took up a deeper study of anatomy, invented for her a special method in order to study the motion of the human body: the model had to move about a circle on the floor, first at a slow rhythm, then at increased speed, so that she walked, ran and danced and was drawn by Willebeek Le Mair from every point of view and at varying speeds, undressed and dressed in all sorts of materials. Toward the end of her girlhood, the artist went with her parents for eighteen months to Arabia and there, in the splendid light, some of her best work was done. When Willebeek Le Mair learned of the religious significance of art in some countries, she began searching for a special philosophy for herself. The Murshid Inayat Khan came to Holland at this time and paid a long visit to her parents. With him was a disciple, the young H. P. Baron van Tuyll van Serooskerken. The Baron became Willebeek Le Mair's husband. Both the Baron and Baroness were deeply interested in the cult of Sufism as taught by Inayat Khan, a religion of universal brotherhood and love, under one Father of all mankind, God. She has illustrated many books, some of which were published in the United States. She decorated a children's playroom on a Dutch ship with panels representing different shops so that the children might play at shopping on the long journey to the Orient. Her decoration of a children's chapel of a certain Catholic church in Holland is well known. She also decorated a children's recreation room in a Hague hospital. Perhaps the work she herself considers best is the book of Christmas Carols published in the fall of 1946. Willebeek Le Mair lives with her husband at The Hague, Netherlands.

LENSKI, LOIS

Born October 14, 1893, in Springfield, Ohio. There and in Anna, Ohio, childhood was spent. Attended Ohio State University (B.S. 1915); Art Students League, New York; Westminster School of Art, London.

"MY paternal grandfather was born in Poland, and my grandmother in Russia," Lois Lenski writes. "It is possible that I may have inherited artistic gifts from them. All my conscious influences, however, have grown out of my American environment. My father was a Lutheran minister. When I was six, we moved to Anna, Ohio, where I learned to know and love small-town and country life. During my four years at the Art Students League in New York, I worked part-time at all kinds of odd jobs to pay my expenses. In 1920, I went to Europe on slender savings, and spent some months in Italy. It was while studying with Walter Bayes at the Westminster School in London that I did my first illustrating of children's books — *The Golden Age* and *Dream Days* by Kenneth Grahame, and Vera Birch's *Green-Faced Frog*. In 1927, I began writing and illustrating my own books. *Skipping Village* and *A Little Girl of 1900* grew directly out of my own childhood in Ohio. My picture books — *The Little Auto* and other early ones — were largely inspired by the interests and needs of my small son. They are all worked out, in advance of publication, with the helpful advice of children themselves. In 1929 we moved to Connecticut and I began to absorb some of the richness of historical background. *Phebe Fairchild Her Book*, 1936, was the first of a group of books for older children growing out of life in a New England environment. More recently, due to an opportunity to travel and explore, I have begun a series of American regional books, in which I hope to present the drama and flavor of life in remote and little known regions of our country, gathering material for pictures and story in each region. The first was *Bayou Suzette*, a story of the Louisiana Cajuns; the second is *Strawberry Girl*, a story of the Florida Crackers; the third is a story of the North Carolina mountains, *Blue Ridge Billy*." Lois Lenski is the wife of Arthur Covey, well-known mural painter. Their home is in Harwinton, Connecticut.

LEWIS, ARTHUR ALLEN

Born April 7, 1873, in Mobile, Alabama. Childhood was spent in Buffalo, New York, where he attended Art Students League, studying under George Bridgman. Also studied at Ecole des Beaux Arts, Paris, under Gérôme.

ALLEN LEWIS exhibited at various salons and at Paris Exposition in 1900 under the name of Arthur Allen Lewis. He returned to the United States in 1902. He was a teacher of wood engraving and color printing, etching,

and illustration, Art Students League, New York City, 1924-32; teacher of wood engraving and etching, New School for Social Research, New York City, 1932-34. The Chicago Society of Etchers awarded Mr. Lewis the Logan Prize in 1916; the Brooklyn Society of Etchers, the Noyes Prize in 1917. He received Bronze Medal, at the St. Louis Exposition, 1904; Gold Medal, San Francisco Exposition, 1915; Silver Medal for Woodcut, Sesquicentennial Exposition, Philadelphia, 1926; the Nathan I. Bizur Prize was awarded him by the Society of American Etchers in 1928; and the John G. Agar Prize by the National Arts Club in 1928. His work is represented in the permanent collections of the Harvard University Library, Metropolitan Museum, New York Public Library, Brooklyn Museum of Arts and Sciences, Chicago Art Institute, Cleveland Museum, Detroit Museum, British Museum, London, and the Bibliothèque Nationale, Paris. He is a National Academician, and a member of the Brooklyn Society of Etchers, also its first president; a member of the American Institute of Graphic Arts, and its vice-president 1928-29; and a member of the Print Makers of California. His home is at Basking Ridge, New Jersey. This material was obtained from *Who's Who in America*.

LEWITT–HIM

LEWITT, JAN
Born April 3, 1907, in Czestochowa, Poland, where childhood was spent.

HIM, GEORGE
Born August 4, 1900, in Lodz, Poland. Childhood was spent in Warsaw and in Moscow. Attended Universities of Moscow, Berlin and Bonn (Ph.D.), and State Academy of Graphic Arts, Leipzig.

JAN LEWITT is self-taught in his work, having picked up art, as he says, while trying to make a living in thirteen different occupations, among them as a worker in machine building, in soap manufacturing, in a distillery, as a brick layer, farm worker, compositor, architect's draftsman and art director. The two artists met for the first time in Warsaw, in 1933, when both had returned to Poland after many years spent abroad. Struck by the similarity of their views in artistic matters, they began to work together. This collaboration has been going on ever since; first in Warsaw, after 1937 in London. Their collaboration is the closest imaginable. "From the first moment when an idea is conceived," they write, "until the moment when the finishing touches are put to a design or story, every phase of the work is carried out jointly." Although Lewitt and Him are both artists in their own right, they feel that the new personality emerging from their work together is different from and superior to either alone. Influences, as far as they are aware of them, stem from

C. WALTER HODGES : *Columbus Sails*

HILDA VAN STOCKUM : *Gerrit and the Organ*

early mediaeval painting, popular art of the early nineteenth century, the work of Picasso, Klee, and the Surrealists. The work of Lewitt-Him is varied and ranges from murals to poster publicity and exhibition design, and books for adults. Their favorite work, however, is the designing of picture books, some of which they write as well as illustrate.

LIDDELL, MARY

Born December 27, 1891, in Lawrenceville, New Jersey. Childhood was spent in Oxford, England; Berlin, Germany; Cambridge, Massachusetts; Austin, Texas; East Orange and Summit, New Jersey; Lexington, Massachusetts; and Louisville, Kentucky.

MARY LIDDELL WEHLE's father was Mark H. Liddell, an English scholar of Scotch and English descent and editor of the Elizabethan Shakspere. In her childhood she lived wherever her father's work took him. Her mother is a Philadelphian, many of whose British, French and Dutch ancestors sought refuge with William Penn. "I married Louis Brandeis Wehle of Louisville and have since lived in Washington and in and around New York," she says. "We have two sons and a daughter and my book, *Little Machinery*, was written and illustrated when the children were very young. We were then living in a pre-Revolutionary stone house in Westchester County, New York, and I noticed that the children's interests revolved about their toys, the small animals on the place, and every sort of machinery that came within their view. With the children running in and out of a big studio behind the house, I evolved a book combining their interests, writing and illustrating it under their constant suggestion and criticism, and taking its title from their own terminology." The Wehles live in New York City.

LOFTING, HUGH

Born January 14, 1886, in Maidenhead, England. Attended a Jesuit School throughout boyhood; Massachusetts Institute of Technology; and London Polytechnic.

BORN of English and Irish stock, Hugh Lofting kept a combination zoo and natural history museum in his mother's linen closet until discovered. He also liked to tell stories to his brothers and sisters. After a short career as an architect, he became a civil engineer and went to Canada, Africa, and the West Indies. In 1912 Mr. Lofting married and settled in the United States. Then came the First World War and in 1916 he enlisted in the British Army. When he was separated from his children, he began letters to them from the trenches. "One thing kept forcing itself more and more upon my attention," he wrote some years ago; "that was the considerable part the animals were playing in the War and that as time

went on they, too, seemed to become fatalists. But their fate was different from the men's. All the resources of a surgery highly developed were brought to men's aid. A seriously wounded horse was put out by a timely bullet. This did not seem quite fair. But to develop a horse surgery as good as that of our Casualty would necessitate a knowledge of horse language. That was the beginning of Dr. Dolittle." It was Mrs. Lofting who first saw the importance of publishing these stories for other children to enjoy and, when the family returned to America, she persuaded her husband to show the manuscript to a publisher. It was immediately accepted and published in 1920. During the next ten years Mr. Lofting wrote and illustrated five other books about the Doctor who "liked animals better even than the best people." In 1923 the Newbery Medal was given to *Dr. Dolittle's Voyages*. Mr. Lofting has lived for some years now in California.

LORENTOWICZ, IRENA

Born 1910 in Warsaw, Poland. Spent childhood in Poland and Paris. Attended Academy of Arts, and International Institute of Theatrical Lyceum in Warsaw; and the Sorbonne, Paris.

IRENA LORENTOWICZ is the daughter of Jan Lorentowicz, author and critic, and founder of the P. E. N. Club of Poland. She was encouraged in her study of art by her mother who was an artist, and came to do much painting for the restoration of mediaeval churches. Then the French Government offered a scholarship at the Sorbonne. She worked for several years in Paris and came to be known for her theatrical designs and ballet scenery. At the Paris Exposition in 1937 she was awarded a Gold Medal for painting and decoration. Her pictures may be seen in Jeu de Paume Musée in Paris, and in other museums of Europe. Escaping from Paris just before the Germans entered in 1940, Miss Lorentowicz lived for two years in Spain and Portugal before reaching New York. Here she began to specialize in children's book illustrations, developing a spirited and colorful style.

LORIOUX, FÉLIX

Born at Angers, France, where he attended Collège Mongazon and Ecole Regionale des Beaux Arts.

FROM his earliest years at the Collège Mongazon in Angers, Felix Lorioux admired the old painter of the frescoes of the chapel. At eighteen, he went to Paris where "the university of hard knocks," not schools or courses, formed him. He went every day to the Louvre, visited other museums constantly and frequented exhibitions "in the fine period when the Impressionists had at last won their place." He worked as a fan-maker, and at many other occupations to gain a living. "A hard period." By chance he met Drayen, the great printer, and worked a great deal for him, acquiring "intellectual and technical flexibility in everything concerning book illustration and publicity." At the same time he received from the house of Hachette a commission to illustrate a series of large albums in a new form. For them he illustrated La Fontaine's *Fables*, two volumes of *Tales* of Perrault, *Malade Imaginaire* by Molière, *Don Quixote* and *Robinson Crusoe*. "After the search for the right composition comes the gaiety of the color, and the search for detail amusing to children and their interests. Children see and retain little things, details, even the most familiar."

LUFKIN, RAYMOND H.

Born January 29, 1897, in Salem, Massachusetts. Childhood was spent in Boston where he attended New School of Design.

DURING his boyhood Raymond Lufkin devoted all his spare time to drawing. His first published work at the age of nine appeared in the *Boston Herald* — a prize-winning pen-and-ink sketch for which he received one dollar. As a free lance artist, with offices in Boston, he did a wide variety of commercial work. While serving in World War I he was given many a ride in Army training planes in Tennessee and Texas in return for drawing postcard sketches of the various pilots. During World War II he designed several war bond posters for the Treasury Department and millions of copies for display were printed for distribution to every classroom and post office in the country. He also produced maps for military purposes. In the early days of the 1930 depression he moved his offices to New York where he worked successfully into the New York field doing a broad range of commercial work. Using his favorite scratchboard medium he has illustrated many children's books for leading publishers. One of his outstanding series of illustrations in color pertains to symbolic happenings on twelve of the principal rivers of the United States — *American Rivers*. The use of unusual color application to his scratchboard technique makes these pictures not only a unique contribution to American art but also a carefully studied addition to illustrated American history. His home is in Tenafly, New Jersey.

MAC BRIDE, MAUD GONNE

Born December 21, 1866, in Tougham, Surrey, England. Childhood was spent in Ireland, in the towns of Donnybrook, Howth and Kildare, where she was educated at home. Studied later in France.

MAUD GONNE MACBRIDE writes: "My excursions into the realms of art and book illustration were so soon interrupted by our war for independence as to be quite insignificant. A few black-and-white decorations, a cover design for poems by Joseph Campbell, black-and-white drawings and some colored illustrations for Ella Young's *Celtic Wonder Tales*, and for her *Coming of Luch* are, as far as I can remember, the only ones I've ever published. Recently a chalk-and-pencil portrait of Iseult Stuart as a young girl, which I had given to W. B. Yeats, was reproduced in a biography of him by Joseph Harce. My whole life has been absorbed in the struggle for Irish freedom, and left me little time for anything else." Her home is in Clonskea, County Dublin.

MC CLOSKEY, ROBERT

Born September 15, 1914, in Hamilton, Ohio, where his childhood was spent. Attended Vesper George School, Boston, and National Academy of Design, New York.

WHEN Robert McCloskey went into the Infantry in August 1943, there was no special classification number for artists. As a child, he drew, painted, and made things, later winning a scholarship to the Vesper George School in Boston where he studied for three years. In 1934 he went to the National Academy in New York for two more years, spending his summers working in Provincetown under Jerry Farnsworth. His first commission was the bas-relief on the City Building of his home town. After an interlude of odd jobs, he returned to New York with the idea for his first book and at the same time got a job assisting Francis Scott Bradford on a mural in Boston. A subsequent stay in Boston germinated the plan of *Make Way for Ducklings*, which was awarded the Caldecott Medal for 1941. Painting and illustrating in New York were interrupted by induction into the Army and eventual assignment to Fort McClellan, Alabama, where he drew diagrams and maps for training. The Infantry belatedly created a classification for artists and as such Robert McCloskey was promoted to Technician Fourth Grade. After his discharge he hopes to experiment with new media developed during the war and to do some sculpture. His home is in Cornwall Bridge, Connecticut, but he has recently bought an island near Hancock Point, Maine, where long summers with his family will probably be spent.

MC CORMICK, ARTHUR DAVID

Born 1860 in Coleraine, Ireland. Studied at Royal College of Art, London.

ARTHUR DAVID McCORMICK has exhibited at the Royal Academy, London, and the Paris Salon. He is a Member of the Royal Institute of Painters in Water Colours. This information has been obtained from *Who's Who in Art*.

MACHETANZ, FREDERICK

Born February 20, 1908, in Kenton, Ohio, in which state his childhood was spent. Attended Ohio State University; Art Institute School and American Academy of Arts, Chicago.

"A six weeks' trip to my uncle's trading post, in the Eskimo village of Unalakleet, Alaska, turned into a wonderful two years' stay," Frederick Machetanz writes. "With it came an intense interest in Eskimos and everything Alaskan, after mingling with these people in all their activities. Returning to the States, a chance to illustrate an Eskimo book came along. After that it was suggested that in order to illustrate more books on my favorite subject, I would have to write them. Thus I did my first writing of Eskimos and sled dogs. During this period I also did some sports illustrating since I have a keen interest in athletics. Then another trip to Alaska, via the Coast Guard Behring Sea and Arctic Patrol, from Ketchikan to Point Barrow. When War was declared, I entered Naval Intelligence. Was on Aleutian duty during the Attu and Kiska Campaigns. At present (May 1945) am a Lieutenant-Commander, USNR, serving under Commander, North Pacific Force in the Aleutians. I have done no illustrating while in the service." Mr. Machetanz's home is in Kenton, Ohio.

MC INTOSH, FRANK

Born 1901 in Portland, Oregon, where his childhood was spent.

When Frank McIntosh finished high school he moved to San Francisco and decided on an art career. He studied in California for five years — drawing, painting and decoration, and developed a special interest in stage design. In 1924 he went to New York and studied with Norman Bel Geddes for a year, and though his interest in the stage was as keen as ever he turned from it abruptly and began a series of cover designs for *Asia Magazine*. Since that time he has worked with designs for covers, advertising art and book illustration. It used to be his plan to spend nine months of each year in New York and three months in California — the time in California being intended for experimental painting.

MAC INTYRE, ELISABETH

Born in Sydney, Australia.

Elisabeth MacIntyre is a young Australian artist. In her own country she is an "idea person" for advertising, has a comic strip, "Ambrose Kangaroo," in the newspapers, and makes many lively books for children. An interested friend sent her work over to New York, where Charles Scribner's Sons published her picture book, *Ambrose Kangaroo*, followed by *Susan Who Lives in Australia*. Her work has a gaiety and freshness, both in text and pictures. Some day she hopes to come to America.

MAC KINSTRY, ELIZABETH

In her teens Elizabeth MacKinstry was a pupil of Ysaye and had a continental reputation as a violinist. A little later, when the violin had to be put away because of ill health, she studied modeling under the aged Rodin and worked in wood for the well-known architect, Ralph Adams Cram. She turned from sculpture to book decoration in 1927, and felt that both sculpture and music influenced her drawing. She reveled in the robust humor and waggery of the eighteenth century. The strongest influence on her work came from that same source from which Lovat Fraser drew so joyously — the gay, flatly colored old woodcuts of Randolph Caldecott's picture books and the prints of the Catnach Press. Another influence was Walter Crane, who "coquetted notoriously," Miss MacKinstry said, "with Japanese prints and blue-willow pattern plates, and set with admirable precision the canon that book decoration should be for a book, fit the shape of its own page and stay flat on it." Indeed, an artist who has a collection of MacKinstry books remarks with discernment that the trinity of her artistic creed is Caldecott, Crane, and Lovat Fraser.

MATES, RUDOLF

Born August 18, 1881, in Pečky, Czechoslovakia.

Rudolf Mates taught for many years before World War II, in Caslov in southeastern Czechoslovakia. He is a landscape painter, a figure painter and above all, a book illustrator for children. His brilliant colors and his humorous conception of animals and insects have made him well known among Americans. His most popular works are *Magic Flutes, The Cock and the Hen,* and *Nursery Rhymes,* all of which have been made available in English translations. This information was supplied by Mrs. Jan Matulka, Webster Branch, New York Public Library.

MATULKA, JAN

Born November 7, 1890, in Vlachovo Brezi, Czechoslovakia. Attended National Academy of Design, New York.

Jan Matulka came to the United States in 1907. A Pulitzer Scholarship from Columbia University gave him an opportunity to travel extensively in the United States, Canada, Mexico, and the Bahamas. In 1919 he went to Paris and worked there until 1926, with an interlude of travel and study in Czechoslovakia. He is above all a painter whose interest lies in color and design. His illustrations for Fillmore's *Czechoslovak Fairy Tales* and *The Shoemaker's Apron* show the influence of the design and forms of peasant ornament. He lives in New York City.

MILHOUS, KATHERINE

Born November 27, 1894, in Philadelphia, and grew up there and in Pitman, New Jersey. Attended the Pennsylvania Museum's School of Industrial Art and the Pennsylvania Academy of Fine Arts.

"I was born in the old part of Philadelphia," Miss Milhous writes, "on the wrong side of Market Street. But my father, a printer, kept shop on both sides of the street — once down by the docks, another time only a block away from where Benjamin Franklin once opened his 'New Printing Office in High Street near the Market,' and again just a stone's throw from Independence Hall. My present studio is in the heart of Philadelphia, and day and night I can hear the rumble of printing presses (not my father's) on the floor below. My background is Quaker and Irish, Methodist and Catholic, with a dash of Pennsylvania Dutch from the Palatinate. That is where the love of design comes in. I began to draw as soon as I could hold a pencil. The family moved to New Jersey and in the camp-meeting town where my school days were spent, I never saw a good painting or piece of sculpture, or heard fine music. Returning to Philadelphia to go to art school, I made up for lost time. I worked for scholarships, did newspaper drawings at night, saved money to travel and to paint in foreign countries. There was more recently a trip by airplane around South America. But it was on camping trips through Pennsylvania in an old Dearborn wagon drawn by a plow horse that I learned to know the folk art of my own people. I have tried my hand at sculpture and murals, water colors and oils. But all that I learned in these media, and all the background gained by traveling at home and abroad, now stands me in good stead in the writing and illustrating of children's books. Nor is this enough."

MOE, LOUIS

Born April 19, 1859, in Arendal, Norway, where his childhood was spent. Studied at Royal Academy, Copenhagen.

"When about eighteen years old," the artist has written, "I was sent to Denmark, where I entered the Royal Academy classes in Copenhagen, and also studied under some of the leading Danish artists of the time. I have produced 120 etchings and lithographs, principally of animals, and am a regular exhibitor at the annual exhibitions of the Danish Royal Academy. At an early age I became familiar with the most interesting life of the animals in the vast forests stretching around my native Arendal, an old shipping town. Almost as early I was engaged in attempts at artistic production, encouraged by the understanding parents who created the happy home of my childhood. My first book for children appeared in 1894. All my books deal with children and animals. Since 1881 I have lived in Copenhagen, married to a Danish lady. Every summer, though, I spend in the land of my childhood on our estate in the midst of the wide-stretching forest regions where the elk and the bear are living, where the beaver builds his dwelling in the lonely streams and where the eagle crosses the clouds."

MOESCHLIN–HAMMAR, ELSA

Born January 7, 1879, in Stockholm, Sweden, where childhood was spent and where she attended Art School. Also studied in Paris, Munich and Rome.

"After study abroad, I went home, married a Swiss author, and had three children," Mrs. Moeschlin-Hammar writes. "It was for my own children I made my first books, only one of which has been translated and published in the United States — *The Red Horse*. The scenes of my books are sometimes Sweden, sometimes Switzerland. I have painted walls and frescoes for children in schools, hospitals and private homes. No work has given me greater pleasure than my books for children. Now I am making a book for my six grandchildren. I have just finished a novel of four hundred pages." Mrs. Moeschlin-Hammar lives in Brissag, Switzerland, and continues to enjoy skiing.

MONSELL, JOHN ROBERT

Born August 15, 1877, at Cahirciveen, County Kerry, Ireland. Childhood was spent at Curragh Chase, Adare, County Limerick. Attended St. Columba's College, Rathfarnham, Dublin.

"My father was Resident Magistrate at Cahirciveen, where the cable starts for America," Mr. Monsell writes. "When he died, we went to live with my mother's uncle, Aubrey de Vere, the poet, at Curragh Chase, and from there I went to school at St. Columba, two of the founders of which had been granduncles of mine, where I generally won the music and drawing prizes. When my sister won the Slade Scholarship for Art, we migrated to London. My first book, *The Pink Knight*, originated in a cluster of children sitting about me while I told them the story, illustrating it meanwhile in a sketch book. It proved a success when published, so I started in earnest. I did a good deal of work for magazines, notably for *London* and *Little Folks*, and later on for Arthur Mee's publications, especially *The Children's Encyclopedia* and *My Magazine*, as well as a number of books, most of which I wrote myself. An early love of heraldry helped

WILFRID BRONSON : *Chisel-tooth Tribe*

LOIS LENSKI : *Phebe Fairchild*

me to design the paper wrappers for the historical books of my wife, Margaret Irwin. My style, such as it is, is founded on childish poring over the picture books of Caldecott, Crane, etc., and, later on, of Caran d'Ache."

MOON, CARL

> Born October 1879 in Wilmington, Ohio, where childhood was spent.

"My work," Carl Moon writes, "dates from a boyhood interest in American Indians, probably the influence of James Fenimore Cooper. I worked in studios in Cincinnati, Ohio, Wheeling, West Virginia, and San Antonio, Texas, then moved to Albuquerque, New Mexico, in 1903, and bought a studio of my own. Began almost immediately to photograph, paint, and write about the Southwest Indians. Wrote for many magazines and a few newspapers mostly descriptive articles, illustrated by my own pictures. In 1906 exhibited my pictures at the White House, at the invitation of President Theodore Roosevelt. Exhibited the same year at National Gallery, by invitation of Dr. Holmes; and at Museum of Natural History in New York, by invitation of Dr. Henry Fairfield Osborn. In 1907 moved to Grand Canyon, Arizona, to begin collection of Indian pictures for Fred Harvey, and spent seven years completing this Collection. In 1914 moved to Pasadena, California, to work independently again, and made collection of about three hundred prints and twenty-four oil paintings of Indians for Mr. Henry E. Huntington for the Huntington Library. In 1924 began publishing a four-volume set of pictorial books, *Indians of the Southwest*, containing twenty-five large prints per volume. These sets are owned by libraries and museums over the country. The Museum of Montclair, New Jersey, owns ten paintings of mine in oil. Recently I made the Florence Rand Lang collection of twenty-six oil paintings of Indians for the Smithsonian Institution at Washington, D. C. My paintings are in many private collections, schools, etc." Carl Moon lives in Pasadena, California.

MORDVINOFF, NICOLAS

> Born September 27, 1911, in Leningrad, Russia. Childhood was spent in Paris, France, where he attended Lycée Jeanson de Sailly and Ecole des Roches.

Nicolas Mordvinoff is the grandson of Admiral Alexandre Mordvinoff. At the age of seven, he left Russia with his parents and went to live in Paris. After study at the schools mentioned above, he worked at his painting with the great French painters, Ozenfaut and Fernand Léger, and made cartoons for the Parisian papers. In 1934 he left Paris for Tahiti in the South Pacific, where he painted in the peace and beauty of tropical nature. There he met William S. Stone, American writer. They became

friends, and from then on collaborated in children's books. Nicolas Mordvinoff's wife is French. He still lives on Tahiti but hopes to come soon to America.

MORTON-SALE, ISOBEL

> Born May 15, 1904, at Chelsea, London. Childhood was spent at Chelsea and Kew. Attended Ramsgate School of Art, Margate, and Central School of Arts, London.

"When I was seven," Mrs. Morton-Sale writes, "the family moved to Kew, where this loveliest of gardens became a place of enchantment through the whole of my childhood. I loved, too, the palace in the garden, where the children of George III had lived, and the paintings and miniatures there. A painting of Princess Charlotte fascinated me. There was a spinet in the room where it hung. It was the one on which Handel had taught the princesses to play. My mother was a Catholic and I went to Mass with her on Sunday mornings, and on Sunday evenings, with my father, to the Scottish Presbyterian Church were John Morton-Sale, a small boy with brilliant red hair, sang solos in the choir. Our acquaintance then was no more than the bows of families leaving church. All through schooldays I scribbled drawings on books when I should have been doing other things. My favorite work is painting children, and designing child covers for periodicals for the Amalgamated Press, and the present series of books created by my husband — *Cherrystones* and *Mulberry Bush*: we asked Eleanor Farjeon to write the verses. During my daughter's first years I did very little published work and devoted all painting time to making studies of her. Later I specialized in paintings of children and illustrated for *Woman's Journal, Good Housekeeping, Leisure*; illustrated a number of books, and have collaborated on some with my husband. Our home is at Edgemoor, Moretonhampstead, Devon."

MORTON-SALE, JOHN

> Born April 29, 1901, in Kensington, London. There and in Putney childhood was spent. Attended Putney School of Art and Central School of Arts and Crafts, London.

"I was born in Kensington, London," Mr. Morton-Sale writes, "the youngest child of conservative Victorian parents, and grew up in the quiet home atmosphere of this period. I was familiar with the art treasures and lovely buildings of a London which seemed to me then so gracious and beautiful. I loved the paintings of Turner and the landscape painters, and, like many town-bred children, I grew to love passionately the greater wonder and beauty of the country. I painted dust covers for my books and illustrated a magazine produced by my brother when we were choir boys of the Scottish Presbyterian Church. It was there I first saw the fair-haired child who eventually became my wife. When we met years later we studied together at the Central School of Arts. We live on Dartmoor, and have one daughter, Cherry-Ann, who writes verse and music and is studying art. I am happiest when painting landscape, out-of-doors." Among the books illustrated by John Morton-Sale is Arnold Bennett's *Old Wives' Tale*, in color, for supplement to the Christmas *Bookman*.

NADEJEN, THEODORE

Born in Russia. Studied under Bakst and other masters. NADEJEN ran away to sea at the age of thirteen or thereabouts and was a sea captain in the Russian Volunteer Fleet until the Revolution. On board ship he spent his leisure time painting and sketching. It was during various intervals on shore that he studied under masters. Upon his arrival in this country he worked first as a stage designer but was more interested in the designing of books. *Skazki* was the first book made here for which he was entirely responsible, and it was chosen by the American Institute for Graphic Arts as one of the "Fifty Books of the Year," 1926-27. It is easy to see in his work the influence of Byzantine art and the painting on Russian ikons.

NAILOR, GERALD A.

Born January 21, 1917, in Crown Point, New Mexico. Childhood was spent in Rehoboth, New Mexico. Attended Albuquerque Indian School and Santa Fe Indian Art School.
"MY parents were Navajo Indians," writes Gerald Nailor, "so I was sent to an Indian Mission School at the age of ten. There I won a scholarship to a public school in Gallup where I had two years of high school, followed by another two years in Albuquerque Indian School. It was at Albuquerque that my interest in art was awakened, and my work there was followed by a further two years' training in Indian Art in Santa Fe. Most of the roots of my work have sprung from experiences among my own tribe of Indians, as I lived the life they led; but my technical training has been derived from my study in Santa Fe." Gerald Nailor lives in Penasco, New Mexico.

NEWBERRY, CLARE TURLAY

Born April 10, 1903, in Enterprise, Oregon. Childhood was spent in Vancouver, Washington. Attended University of Oregon; Art Museum School, Portland, Oregon; California School of Fine Arts; and Académie de la Grande Chaumière, Paris.
CLARE NEWBERRY says she has always loved cats, and that they were the first things she remembers drawing when she started at the age of two. As a child she planned to

write and illustrate children's books. Later she wanted to be a portrait painter, but found New York during the depression a difficult place in which to begin this profession. In 1934 she began to paint cats, and has been painting them and drawing them ever since. She does all her work from live models, and works in water color, charcoal, Conté crayon, pen-and-ink, and pastel. She says, "No, cats don't sit still and pose for me!" Clare Newberry lives in New York.

NICHOLS, DALE

Born July 13, 1904, in David City, Nebraska, where childhood was spent. Attended Chicago Academy of Fine Arts and Chicago Art Institute School.
"FOR twenty years," writes Dale Nichols, "I lived the typical life of a farm boy in Nebraska — milking cows, taking care of sheep, hogs, cattle and work horses. The spaces of the country, and the wonders of Nature fascinated me. Many summer evenings I spent studying the heavens through a battered telescope. From this interest I have formulated my approach to appreciating and producing art. We do not desire pictures of just things, we crave the presence of God whom I have found to be the sum total of the forces which have created me as a part of Nature and now sustain me." After ten years in advertising art work, Dale Nichols began painting in 1934. His first paintings were successful, and his sixteenth oil, "The End of the Hunt," was awarded the William Randolph Hearst Award in an Art Institute Exhibition. There followed in rapid succession twenty-eight Awards for painting and work in the graphic arts. His paintings were shown in the contemporary artists' galleries at the World Fairs of Chicago, New York, Dallas and San Francisco. He is represented in the collections of the Metropolitan Museum; Art Institute of Chicago; Joslyn Memorial, Omaha; University of Illinois; Nebraska Art Association, and many other public and private collections. In 1939-40 he became First Carnegie Visiting Professor and Artist in Residence, University of Illinois. In 1942 he designed the Anti-Tuberculosis Christmas Seal. In 1945 he was appointed Art Editor of the *Encyclopaedia Britannica* Publications. He travels extensively in search of material, living at times in Mexico and Alaska. His home is high on a foothill of the Santa Catalina Mountains, near Tucson, Arizona.

NICHOLS, SPENCER BAIRD

Born February 13, 1875, in Washington, D. C., where childhood was spent and he attended Corcoran School of Art and Art Students League.
"IT is but natural that I became interested in art at an early age," writes Mr. Nichols. "My father was an

eminent wood engraver and my mother was interested in all things related to the arts. In book illustration, whenever I had the choice, I selected stories for children. I have been a student of child life and have found it most fascinating. To my child acquaintances I am known as 'Popy Nick,' to the satisfaction of all concerned." Mr. Nichols has done considerable work in other branches of art. In 1911 he joined the Tiffany Studios in New York and for that firm painted murals and designed mosaics, windows and interiors. Murals by him are in the Central Presbyterian Church (New York City), Kent, Connecticut, High School and Litchfield, Connecticut, High School. Three hundred of his historical portraits are in the National Museum (Washington, D. C.) and a portrait of Andrew Stephenson is in the House of Representatives. Mr. Nichols has taught illustrating at the Art Students League and has been director of art at Marot Junior College at Thompson, Connecticut, since 1934. His winter home is in Alexandria, Virginia; his summer home is in Kent, Connecticut.

NICHOLSON, SIR WILLIAM

Born 1872 at Newark-on-Trent, England, where his childhood was spent and he attended Magnus School. Also studied under Hubert von Herkomer, Bushey, England, and at Académie Julian, Paris.

WILLIAM NICHOLSON's father was William Newzam Nicholson, M.P. At Julian's in Paris he met James Pryde, and collaborated with him under the pseudonym of "The Beggarstaff Brothers," their work having considerable influence on British industrial design before the First World War, notably in posters. When he was twenty, William Nicholson designed and executed a stained glass window for the parish church at Wells. His woodcuts, including that of Queen Victoria, and his portraits are famous. Those of W. E. Henley and Miss Gertrude Jekyll are owned by the Tate Gallery; George Saintsbury, Merton Gallery; Walter Greaves, Manchester. He has exhibited in London, Paris, New York, Venice, the Argentine, and in all the principal cities of England. He has also designed for the theatre. This information was obtained from *Who's Who* and *Who's Who in Art*.

NIELSEN, KAY

Born March 12, 1886, in Copenhagen, Denmark. Studied at Académies Julian and Colarossi, Paris.

"BOTH my father and mother were artists," Kay Nielsen has written. "My father, Martinius Nielsen, was in his youth an actor in the classical repertoire. He became the managing director of the Dagmartheater in Copenhagen. My mother, an actress, who had lived in Paris, and had brought home the great French repertoire of the eighteen eighties, was at the Royal Theater in Copenhagen and later at the Dagmartheater. Since early boyhood I have been drawing. When the sagas were read to me, I drew down the people therein, but I never intended to be an artist. When I was twelve years of age, I was taken out of school and given my own teachers, but at seventeen, I suddenly broke from books and went to Paris to study art. I lived in Paris for seven years and studied under Jean Paul Laurens at the Académie Julian; under Kristian Krog at Académie Colarossis; and under other masters, privately, including Lucien Simon. Always working from nature during school hours, in my free hours I made drawings out of my imagination—*The Book of Death* (unpublished), and illustrations for the works of Heine, Verlaine, and Hans Andersen. In 1911 I left Paris for London and in 1912 had my first show in London. My first show in America was with Scott & Fowles, New York, in 1917. From 1918-1922 I did a series of settings for the Royal Theater in Copenhagen: Shakespeare, *The Tempest;* Oehlenschlaeger, *Aladdin;* Sibelius, *Scaramouche;* Magnussen, *The Dream of a Poet.* I loved the Chinese drawings and carvings in my mother's room, brought home from China by her father. This love for the art of the East has followed me. My artistic wandering started with the early Italians, over Persia to India, to China." Since 1939, Kay Nielsen and Mrs. Nielsen have lived in Los Angeles, California. There he has painted a large mural for the library in the Central Junior High School, "The First Spring," and "The Canticle of the Sun," another mural, for the library of the Emerson Junior High School, Los Angeles.

NISBET, NOEL LAURA

Born December 30, 1887, at Harrow, London, England. Childhood was spent at Clapham, London, where she attended Notre Dame Convent; also at Altrincham and Chester, and in Australia.

"I WAS fortunate in my early days," Noel Nisbet writes, "in being brought up in imaginative surroundings and an atmosphere of books, for my father was a writer of romances, a painter and poet. My early favorites were Grimm's and Hauff's *Fairy Tales* and Lane's *Arabian Nights.* Father soon introduced us to the classic novels, and before I was ten I was familiar with most of Dickens. On my mother's side we were related to Andrew Lang, that great folk and fairy tale writer, so we derived a fondness for folklore and legends from both sides. We went to Australia when I was eight years old but did not settle there. We also had the good fortune to spend some years, from the time I was twelve years old onward, in a romantic old house, dating from the fifteenth century, Beckington Abbey, which provided many a background to future work. The house was reputed haunted, though we never encountered anything to disturb our peace of mind. Later I went to the Art School where I met my husband, Harry Bush, the landscape painter. I soon found illustration was my line. I had two Gold Medals – from National Competition, South Kensington, for black-and-white illustrations and from Royal Academy for a color composition. I was elected to the Royal Institute of Painters in Water Colours after sending for four years, and continue to send annually there and to the Royal Academy. A large, fantastic subject, 'Evil Spirits Who Wander through the World,' was bought for the Newport Art Gallery in 1937."

OAKLEY, THORNTON
Born 1881 in Pittsburgh, Pennsylvania, where his childhood was spent. Attended Shady Side Academy; University of Pennsylvania (M.S. Architecture); and studied with Howard Pyle.

THORNTON OAKLEY spent his boyhood beside the steel mills which engendered in him that love for the immensity of labor that was to influence his industrial pictures in later years. His knowledge of architecture has contributed to the illustration of the travel books which Mrs. Oakley has written. It was Howard Pyle with whom Mr. Oakley studied his finally-chosen profession of illustration, and from whom he received "that inspiring philosophy of art without which no enduring work of beauty ever has been born." From 1914 to 1936, Thornton Oakley was in charge of the Illustration Course at the Philadelphia Museum's School of Industrial Art. He is a Director of the Philadelphia Art Alliance; President of the Alliance Française of Philadelphia; Chairman of Exhibition Committee, American-Swedish Historical Museum, Philadelphia; and President of the Philadelphia Water Color Club. He has received many prizes and medals and his drawings are in many public collections in America and abroad, including the National Gallery and Library of Congress, Washington, D. C., the British Museum, London, and the Luxembourg Museum, Paris. During the first World War, his lithographs of the Hog Island Shipyard were adopted by the United States Government for its Foreign News Service, and reproductions sent throughout the world. For his artistic services to France, the French Government conferred upon him the decoration, "*Officier d'Académie.*" His industrial verse and drawings have had international distribution by the American Federation of Labor. In the mural field, Mr. Oakley has decorated the walls of the Lecture Hall of Franklin Institute, Philadelphia, with six panels. Since the entry of America into the Second World War, he has been engaged in painting, with the permission and coöperation of the Secretary of War and of the Navy, many series of pictures of America's war production, war transportation, and of modern science for the *National Geographic Magazine.*

ORR, MUNRO SCOTT
Born October 7, 1874, at Irvine, Scotland. Attended Glasgow School of Art.

MUNRO ORR, illustrator, painter and etcher, has exhibited at the Royal Scottish Academy, the Royal Glasgow Institute of Fine Arts, the Walker Art Gallery, London, and the Royal Scottish Water Colour Society. These facts have been obtained from *Who's Who in Art.*

OSTMAN, LEMPI
Born July 7, 1899, in Bay Ridge, Brooklyn, New York, where childhood was spent. Attended Pratt Institute; Art League of America (studying with Joseph Pennell); and New York University.

LEMPI OSTMAN taught Fine Arts in New York City High Schools for four years, 1937-41, but found that she preferred illustration and commercial art to teaching. Since 1941 she has been active in those fields. Miss Ostman's father was born in Finland and she herself knows the Finnish language. Her father is an artist also and was associated with the first Finnish newspaper to appear in New York, the *Siirtolainen.* Of the nine Ostman children, six are artists and two teach in art departments of high schools. Lempi Ostman has been a member of the Roehrich Museum, National Women Painters' and Sculptors' Association and exhibits at the American Etchers' Society. Her home is in Brooklyn, New York.

PANESIS, NICHOLAS
Born December 9, 1913, in Middleboro, Massachusetts, where his childhood was spent. Attended Syracuse University.

NICHOLAS PANESIS comes of English and Greek parentage. He majored in painting at Syracuse University, and is a portrait-and-easel painter as well as an illustrator. He has lived in various parts of the United States, including Provincetown, New York and Southern California. His studio and his home are in Middleboro, Massachusetts.

PARRISH, ANNE
Born November 12, 1888, in Colorado Springs, Colorado, where her early childhood was spent and she attended the Misses Ferris' and the San Luis Schools; then in Claymont, Delaware, where she went to the Misses' Hebbs' School, Wilmington. Attended Philadelphia School of Design for Women.

"MY father, Thomas Clarkson Parrish, was an etcher," Anne Parrish writes. "My mother, Anne Lodge Parrish, a portrait painter. My brother Dillwyn and I grew up thinking that of course we would be painters, too. We

both studied at art schools, growing more and more discouraged and finding painting and drawing harder and
harder work, until we realized that what we really wanted
to do was to write. With that, drawing and painting became our great relaxation and pleasure. Most of it was
done for our private amusement, and as part of journals
kept all over the world, but we illustrated together two
books for children that we wrote together, *Knee High to
a Grasshopper* and *The Dream Coach*, and I illustrated my
own *Floating Island*. Later, Dillwyn Parrish turned to
serious painting until his death in 1941. I still paint one
leaf or one butterfly on those rare occasions when I have
enough time, for snails are swift beside me." Anne
Parrish is the widow of Josiah Titzell, and lives at George-
town, Connecticut. She is well known, too, as the author
of a number of novels.

PARRISH, MAXFIELD
*Born July 25, 1870, in Philadelphia, where childhood
was spent. Attended Haverford College, Pennsylvania Academy of Fine Arts, and studied with Howard
Pyle at Drexel Institute.*

THE first work to bring Maxfield Parrish into prominence
as an illustrator was a cover design for *Harper's Weekly*
in 1895. On June 1, 1895, he married Lydia Austin. They
have four children — Dillwyn, Maxfield, Stephen, and
Jean. Mr. Parrish had Honorable Mention at the Paris
Exposition of 1900; Silver Medal, Buffalo Exposition, 1901;
Gold Medal, Architectural League, 1917. In 1914, Haverford College conferred upon him the Honorary Degree
of LL.D. He was made an Associate of the National
Academy, 1905; full Member, 1906. The famous Professor Hubert von Herkomer, who, after being Slade
Professor of Art at Oxford, founded his own school at
Bushey, wrote the publisher of *Dream Days*: "Mr. Parrish has absorbed, yet purified, every modern oddity, and
added to it his own strong, original identity. He has
combined the photographic vision with the pre-Raphaelite feeling. . . . He can give suggestiveness without loss
of unflinching detail. He has a strong sense of romance.
He can be modern, mediaeval, or classic." Maxfield Parrish
lives in a New Hampshire village with Windsor, Vermont, as its Post Office address. Some of this information
was obtained from *Who's Who in America*.

PAULL, GRACE A.
*Born 1898 in Cold Brook, New York. Childhood was
spent in New York State, New Hampshire, and Montreal, Canada. Attended Pratt Institute; Grand Central
Art School and Art Students League, New York.*

GRACE PAULL says it has been her extra-school, out-of-
door activities that have been most influential in determining her choice of a profession. There was mountain

climbing in New Hampshire, skating and skiing and snow-
shoeing in Canada, roaming the fields and woods, following trout streams, sketching the animals and the countryside on the farm in New York State. "A lifelong fondness
for all these things, combined with an equal fondness for
books — what else could she do but make books for boys
and girls who love all these activities, too?" Grace Paull
spends her summers at Cold Brook, New York, and her
winters in New York City.

PEARS, CHARLES
*Born September 9, 1873. Attended East Hardwick
School and Pomfret College, England.*

CHARLES PEARS was official Naval Artist during the First
World War. He painted many pictures of the Navy for
the Imperial War Museum. He has several large pictures
commissioned from the Second World War. Mr. Pears
has painted many posters for the Empire Marketing
Board, the London Underground Railway, and other
Government agencies. His favorite recreation is single-
handed sailing and his sailing interest is reflected in two
of the books he has written and illustrated — *South Coast
Cruising* and *Yachting on the Sunshine Coast*. He is a
Member of the Royal Institute of Oil Painters and President of the Society of Marine Artists. His home is in
London. This information has been obtained from *Who's
Who*.

PEARSE, SUSAN BEATRICE
*Born in London where she studied at Royal College
of Art.*

"MY father, a journalist, died when I was ten years old,"
Susan Pearse writes. "At the age of sixteen, I won a
scholarship for an art training which I finished at the
Royal College. Have illustrated many books."

PECK, ANNE MERRIMAN
*Born July 21, 1884, in Piermont, New York. Child-
hood was spent on Long Island and in Connecticut.
Attended Hartford Art School and New York School
of Fine and Applied Art.*

ANNE MERRIMAN PECK writes: "Drawing and painting
were my chief interest from childhood, so that when it
was a question of choosing between college and art school,
I chose the latter. After studying painting and design
came a period of painting portraits of children, and illustrating fairy tales. Then my interest in people and my
urge to see the world led to vagabond painting and study
trips to Europe. Out of these trips came commissions to
write travel books for young people, illustrated with my
drawings. Illustrative work turned my attention to graphic
arts, particularly woodcuts and lithographs. In recent

years I have been so occupied with travel, especially in Latin America, and with the books which resulted from my journeys, that art work has been mostly confined to illustrations for my own books or those of writer friends. The artist's record of people, customs and beautiful landscapes adds to the writer's record of ways of life and history. The beautiful Arizona desert country is now my inspiration for painting in times of leisure." Her home is in Tucson, Arizona.

PEIRCE, WALDO

Born December 17, 1884, in Bangor, Maine. Attended Phillips-Andover Academy; Harvard College (A.B. 1908); New York Art Students League; and Académie Julian, Paris.

AT Harvard, Waldo Peirce took part in athletics, playing on the football team. For twenty years, from 1912, he lived abroad, studying in various European countries, especially Spain. He served as Ambulance Driver with the French Army, 1915-1917, receiving the *Croix de Guerre;* later served with the American Intelligence Department in Madrid. After the War he lived in Paris, southern France and Tunis. He traveled in Spain with Ernest Hemingway, and secured material in Pamplona for his paintings of bulls. In 1930 he married as his third wife Alzira Boehm, a rising young painter. They have three children, Chamberlain and Michael, twins, and Anna Gabrielle. In 1930, too, he returned to the United States where his paintings have been shown at all the important national and international exhibitions; also at the Wildenstein Galleries, London, and the Museum of Modern Art, Paris. His work is represented in the Metropolitan Museum, Whitney Museum, Pennsylvania Academy of Fine Arts, Addison Gallery of American Art, Andover, Massachusetts, Brooklyn Museum, University of Arizona, and elsewhere. In September 1937, the Midtown Galleries arranged a retrospective exhibition of the previous six years of Peirce's work. In 1939 he made murals for three Post Offices — Westbrook, Maine (lumberjacks stripping bark); Troy, New York (Rip Van Winkle and the Legend of Sleepy Hollow); Peabody, Massachusetts (The Bull Pen). In the winter of 1941, Mr. Peirce made some sketches for the young American Ballet Theatre. He has had a lifelong interest in poetry and collected and illustrated a poetry anthology, *The Children's Hour* (1944). It is interesting to know that Waldo Peirce is himself a prolific writer of long narrative poems or "ballades"; for these he handwrites the text, makes water colors on facing pages, and binds the manuscript books by hand. Mrs. Peirce, a serious artist, exhibits frequently and the Peirce children all paint. This information was obtained from *Current Biography.*

PÉRARD, VICTOR SEMON

Born 1870 in Paris. Childhood was spent in Paris and New York.

"As a child," Mr. Pérard writes, "I played in the Tuileries Gardens adjoining the Louvre Art Galleries in Paris, and when it rained I took refuge in the Museum. The pictures interested me, and on returning home I would often try to draw some of them from memory. After coming to the United States I went to public schools. My love of drawing stayed with me. On leaving school I worked for an artist, George White, an able illustrator and commercial artist, and got practical experience for a few years. Later I worked for the leading publishers. For many years I taught the Life Classes at Cooper Union and later on at the Traphagen School of Fashion. I am now working on a series of books on how to draw figures and animals, etc." Mr. Pérard's home is in New York City.

PETERSHAM, MAUD

Born August 5, 1889, in Kingston, New York. Childhood was spent in New York State, South Dakota and Pennsylvania. Attended Vassar College and New York School of Fine and Applied Art.

MAUD PETERSHAM's father was a Baptist minister. Longing for a son to carry on his work, he had a family of four daughters. Growing up in a parsonage, Maud loved the tales told by visiting missionaries better than the old fairy stories. Living with a Quaker grandfather in the summertime and listening to his stories gave her great awe and respect for what had gone into the making of America. She graduated from Vassar and then studied art in New York. It was not until Maud and Miska Petersham were married and started working together that they found the work they still like best — the making of books for children. Their home and studio is in Woodstock, New York, and with their work, as well as Miska's stamps and Maud's ceramics, they keep very busy. Their son, Miki, was a Navigator on a B24 in the Pacific in World War II.

PETERSHAM, MISKA

Born September 20, 1888, in Törökszentmiklos, Hungary. Childhood was spent in the Alföld, or Puszta, and in Budapest where art school was attended.

MISKA PETERSHAM was born in a small village on the Hungarian plains and was christened Petrezselyem Mikaly by his Catholic parents. When seven years old he managed to save a few pennies and bought a coveted box of paints, changing his idea of being a sea captain to that of becoming an artist. It was not easy for a poor boy at the Art

School in Budapest; but going without meals and walking long distances to save carfare did not seem hard because he was studying what he wanted. He even managed painting trips each summer in Italy. In 1911 he went to England and the next year came to America. Here he found the country he had dreamed of but did not know really existed, and proudly he became an American.

PIPPET, GABRIEL JOSEPH

Born March 19, 1880, in Solihull, Warwickshire, England, where childhood was spent. Attended Ushaw College and Birmingham School of Art.

"MY father was a well-known artist and my earliest remembrances were paint and pictures," Mr. Pippet writes. "I thus received impressions that gave me a bias at an early age towards art. At school I was more interested in drawing and carving than study, though literature has always been a passion. On leaving school I worked with my father till his death. Then I worked with a stained-glass artist and in my spare time illustrated children's books, and on leaving him, owing to illness, I turned my attention mainly at first to pen-and-ink illustrations and wood carving. After the 1914 War I went to Italy to study the mosaics at Ravenna and Venice and on my return I started decorating a church in Droitwich, Worcestershire, entirely in mosaic. I also carved all the statues, reliefs, altars, capitals, Stations of the Cross, etc., in marble, stone, and wood in that church besides many carvings, mosaics, etc., in other churches. And some book work, illustrating by wood engraving. The Droitwich church has become a well-known centre of interest and is known as the 'Church of the Mosaics.' Crowds of people come to see it, including many men and women of the United States Forces during the War just past. When we get back to more ordinary ways of living, I shall have photographs and perhaps a book on everything in the church. I have exhibited in the United States, London, Oxford, Birmingham, Liverpool, and other cities, painting, woodcuts, pen drawings, carvings. For five years I lived on the Gold Coast, West Africa, teaching, painting and carving. In 1942 the King awarded me a Civil List Pension for services to art in England." Gabriel Pippet lives in London.

PISSARRO, LUCIEN

Born February 20, 1863, in Paris. Educated in France.

LUCIEN PISSARRO is the son of Camille Pissarro, painter. He was educated in France but became a British subject in 1916. He is a landscape painter, engraver, and private printer on his own press. He is a Member of the New English Art Club. These facts have been obtained from *Who's Who.*

PITZ, HENRY C.

Born June 16, 1895, in Philadelphia where childhood was spent and where Pennsylvania Museum School of Art and Spring Garden Institute were attended.

SINCE Henry Pitz grew up in an atmosphere of books and music, he developed an early enthusiasm for Howard Pyle, Edwin Abbey and the British book illustrators. He works about equally in the fields of book, magazine and advertising illustration. With a strong bent for history, he even thought of becoming an instructor in that subject, so it is not strange that many of his pictures have a historical background. He has illustrated about 115 books, has written one book, *Early American Costume,* and numerous articles. Mr. Pitz has been instructor at Pennsylvania Academy of Fine Arts and Visiting Lecturer at University of Pennsylvania. He has won fifteen awards, including Dana Gold Medal for Water Color, Pennsylvania Academy; Bronze Medal for Lithography, Paris Exposition; Griscom Prize for Water Color, New York; Bronze Medal for Etching, Los Angeles International Print Exhibition; Silver Medal for Achievement in the Arts, Philadelphia Art Alliance. He has executed murals for government buildings; Chicago Century of Progress Exposition and for Franklin Institute, Philadelphia. His pictures are in the permanent collections of Los Angeles Museum, Congressional Library, Philadelphia Museum, New York Public Library, Denver Museum, and others. At present he is Director of Illustration and Decoration at the Pennsylvania Museum School of Art. His home is at Plymouth Meeting, Pennsylvania.

POGÁNY, WILLY (WILLIAM ANDREW)

Born August 24, 1882, in Szeged, Hungary. There and in Budapest childhood was spent, and in Budapest Technical School and Academy of Art were attended.

OF his life, Mr. Pogány has written that he was born of poor parents; the family moved to Budapest where his father died, leaving the family destitute. He was therefore obliged to do odd jobs for his living at a very early age. When at High School and later at the Technical University, where he studied Engineering, he worked his way through by tutoring other students. His love for painting and drawing drove him finally to leave the University for the Art School. Later he went to Munich and to Paris to continue his studies. In his formative years he was greatly influenced by Chinese and Japanese art, also by illuminated manuscripts and Hungarian Peasant Art. In 1906 he went to London and started illustrating books. He came to the United States in 1915, settled down here permanently and became an American citizen. In England he married Lillian Rose Doris, by whom he had two sons. In America Mr. Pogány married a second time, Elaine

LEONARD WEISGARD : *Little Chicken*

LOUIS SLOBODKIN : *Clear the Track for Michael's Magic Train*

Cox, a writer. He has illustrated over one hundred books, produced a great number of paintings, portraits, and murals, etchings and engravings, water colors, and pen-and-inks. He has designed many theatrical productions, and was for several years Art Director for Hollywood Motion Picture Studios. He is also an architectural designer and sculptor. Among his awards are the following: Gold Medals from Budapest, Leipzig, Panama Pacific Exposition at San Francisco, 1915. Silver Medal of Honor, New York Society of Architects, 1923. Willy Pogány lives in New York City.

POLITI, LEO

Born November 21, 1908, in Fresno, California, where early childhood was spent; later in Milan, Italy. Attended Art Institute, Royal Palace of Monza, near Milan.

"WHEN I was seven," Leo Politi writes, "my family took me to Italy where I lived for seventeen years. I started to draw even before we went to Italy, and before we left America my mother bought me a colorful Indian Chief costume and when I wore it to school in Italy the boys and girls watched me with wonder and followed me to and from school; in fact I became so great a center of attention that my teacher had to ask my mother not to let me wear it to school. One of the books I liked best in Italy was *Pinocchio,* illustrated by Attilio Mussino. At the age of fifteen I was awarded a scholarship to study at the Art Institute at the Royal Palace of Monza near Milan, formerly the residence of King Umberto the First of Italy — a beautiful building surrounded by a great park with lovely old trees and a lake. Here, too, were gardens and a zoo where we drew flowers and animals. It was from this school that I was graduated as a teacher of art. The deepest impressions of my travels in Italy were the works of art in churches and museums, the lovely northern lakes and the beautiful hillside country of central Italy. We also lived in London one year where I went to school. I remember one street where I used to go to watch artists draw on the sidewalk. On my return voyage to America, on the way to California we sailed through the Panama Canal and I was fascinated by the warm beauty of the Central American countries. This, and a later journey to Mexico, made me wish to study and learn more of Latin America and its people, their customs and their great civilization. When I first saw Olvera Street, the colorful Mexican street in Los Angeles, I thought it would be just right for work and for studying. So I settled there where I have sold pictures ever since. More than anything else, I love to draw pictures of small children." Los Angeles, California, is Mr. Politi's home.

PORTINARI, CANDIDO

Born December 29, 1903, at Santa Rosa farm near Brodosqui, Brazil, where his childhood was spent. Studied at National School of Fine Arts, Rio de Janeiro.

CANDIDO PORTINARI was born of parents who were coffee workers, the second in a family of twelve children, and spent his childhood on the coffee plantation. He began at the age of eight to paint. Since he had to work in the fields, he had little schooling. An accident in a soccer game left him with a limp caused by a broken leg, but the enforced quietness made him concentrate upon his drawing. At fifteen, he began to study etching and painting at the National School of Fine Arts in Rio de Janeiro where his work won him prizes and medals and a traveling scholarship which made it possible for him, in 1928, to go to Europe for three years. He is one of the foremost painters in the Americas today. His work stems directly from the soil of his native country. *Maria Rosa,* his only book for children thus far, was done during one of Portinari's visits to the United States when he was painting murals for the Library of Congress in Washington, and because of a New York publisher's interest in having a book about Brazil. In making his illustrations for this book, Portinari tried to find a technique that would appeal to his own small boy, and finally chose the watercolor medium. In addition to those done for the Hispanic Foundation of the Library of Congress, he has painted murals for the Brazilian pavilion at the New York World's Fair, 1939, and an important series for the Ministry of Education, Rio de Janeiro. His home is in Rio de Janeiro. Some of this material was obtained from *Current Biography* and some from the Museum of Modern Art, New York.

PRESTON, ALICE BOLAM

Born March 6, 1889, in Malden, Massachusetts. Childhood was spent at Beverly Farms. Attended Massachusetts School of Art; studied Design with Vesper L. George, and Interior Decoration with Amy L. Sacker, Boston; Painting with Felicie Waldo Howell, New York; Painting with Henry B. Snell in Portugal and Spain, 1928.

ALICE BOLAM PRESTON was gifted as a child with a vivid imagination and love of nature. Coupled with this was a creative turn of mind and the ardent desire to draw and paint. "One of the happiest recollections of my childhood," she writes, "was the joy experienced when, with pencil, crayon or paintbrush, I was creating fanciful pictures — drawing bugs, butterflies, or just decorating the interiors of my storybooks. All through school, the drawing periods were always looked forward to. My chief aim was to prepare for art school. After graduation my first commission was the illustration of a *Baby Book*. I have always been especially interested in illustrating fairy tales. Aside from illustrating, I have exhibited fanciful pictures and flower studies at Boston Art Club, Copley Society, Pen and Brush Club, New York, 'Book-in-Hand Guild' at Society of Odd Volumes, Boston, North Shore Art and Rockport Art Associations." Alice Bolam Preston is Mrs. Frank I. Preston of Beverly Farms, Massachusetts.

PRICE, HATTIE LONGSTREET

Born July 17, 1891, in Germantown, Pennsylvania, where childhood was spent. Attended Pennsylvania Academy of Fine Arts, and Académie Colarossis, Paris.

HATTIE LONGSTREET PRICE was born of Welsh and English parentage. She inherited her artistic ability from her father, who was always a great source of inspiration and encouragement. At an early age she began demonstrating her talents on the blackboards of the schoolrooms. After studying illustration at the Pennsylvania Academy of Fine Arts, under Henry McCarter, she was awarded a European Scholarship, which enabled her to travel and study in the schools of Paris, Munich, Florence, and Rome. Returning home with much inspiration gained from the famous galleries of Europe, she secured her first commission as an illustrator from the Penn Publishing Company of Philadelphia in 1913 to illustrate the *Baby Animal* Series by Captain Kilbourne, U. S. A., which resulted in an association of twenty years. Later she worked for many other publishers. Will Carleton Price is his wife's best critic, and their daughters, Jane and Betty, have been the models for many characters portrayed in her books. Their home is in Germantown, Philadelphia.

PRICE, MARGARET EVANS

Born March 20, 1888, in Chicago. Childhood was spent in Nova Scotia, and in Boston where Massachusetts Normal Art School was attended.

"MY illustrating," Margaret Price writes, "has been a gateway to adventure and to adult education in botany, zoölogy, history, languages, crafts, marine life and many other lines. I went to Trinidad for authentic vegetation for the illustrations for Alice Dalgliesh's *West Indian Play Days;* to North Africa and France for my own *Monkey-Do;* and two separate times to Southern France for material for the Greek-Ligurian background of *The Windy Shore.* I worked in northern bogs drawing moccasin flowers and Indian pipes for Donald Culross Peattie's *Bounty of Earth.* I have studied marine life through glass-bottomed boats and in aquariums, at Monte Carlo,

Bermuda and New York, for my *Legends of the Seven Seas,* and, for *Animals Marooned,* I made the preliminary drawings in Bermuda, where I have a studio in an old farmhouse which my husband and I own. In our garden we have a collection of Bermuda's many indigenous ferns. The house is called 'Fernwall by Saint Anne's.' I collect Gothic wood carving and rare needlework. I garden, swim, enjoy animals and hope to own a monkey or two when my husband relents. I have a son and daughter, now grown, and an adopted son. I have painted many portraits of children and adults, and these hang in homes here and abroad. I have never hesitated to sacrifice professional work to the demands of full living, or to important human values of any sort, and believe that through such sacrifice any vigorous talent will grow, not deteriorate." Mrs. Price lives in East Aurora, New York.

PRICE, NORMAN MILLS

Born April 16, 1877, in Brampton, Ontario, Canada, where childhood was spent. Studied in Toronto at Ontario School of Art; in London, at Goldsmiths' Institute and Westminster School of Art; in Paris, under Jean Paul Laurens at Académie Julian and in studio of Richard Miller.

IN 1902 three young artists, one of whom was Norman Price, worked in an art department in Toronto. Dissatisfied, they longed to spread their wings, decided to quit shop work, go into the country, live close to nature all summer, sketch everything; then go abroad to study. At lilac-time all were busy sketching blossoms and flowers, watching farmers plowing, mooching around field and farmyard, seeing men hoist rafters at barn-raising, thrilling to sunsets and moonlight, watching the blacksmith at his anvil, all sketching everything, or just lying on sunny hillsides dreaming. In the autumn with high hopes and reams of sketches they boarded a cattle-boat for Montreal and worked their way to England. In London they studied, formed a studio, haunted museums and galleries and tramped the English countryside sketching, thrilled by new beauty on every side, saw Edward VII's coronation procession, sat under yew trees, visited castles and cathedrals, heard chimes ringing and skylarks singing. Aiming for better art work, Norman Price made three drawings for *Gulliver's Travels* which led to a commission, twenty color illustrations for a de luxe Lamb's *Tales from Shakespeare.* Other color work followed, in books on poets and musicians and on book jackets. With English wife and child he went to Paris, studied a while, made drawings in Belgium for *Century Magazine* and in 1911 came to U. S. A. Here he painted many covers for *St. Nicholas Magazine.* During the past forty years his signature has appeared on many magazine and book illustrations.

His best known work was for R. W. Chambers' historical romances and A. Kummer's *Leif Erikson the Lucky*. He likes to illustrate interesting things of the past. A United States citizen now, Norman Price lives in New York City.

PRUSZYNSKA, ANIELA

Born about 1888 in Lwow, Poland. Her childhood was spent in Lwow, Krakow and Pustomite, Poland. Educated by private tutors. Later studied in the Biblioteka Zakladu Narodowego im. Ossolinsich, Lwow; the Biblioteka Jagiellonska, Krakow; and Krakow Art Academy.

ANIELA PRUSZYNSKA has lived for a large part of her life in the families of her father and brother, who were overseers in eastern Poland. Most of her pictures have grown out of her work with children in the village of Pustomite where she did an immense number of posters, leaflets, postcards and designs for Christmas plays and festivals. Her pictures have often been medieval in background and design, stemming in inspiration from manuscripts such as the *Codex Balthazar Behema* in the Krakow Library. During the First World War she was a member of the Polish Women's Army, and later engaged in much relief work. She has a decoration from the Polish Government for work done under fire during the Ukrainian seizure of Lwow after the Armistice. No news has been had from Miss Pruszynska since 1939. Her family disappeared during the first Nazi invasion of Poland. The Editors are indebted to Eric P. Kelly for this information.

PYNE, MABLE MANDEVILLE

Born January 15, 1903, in Mount Vernon, New York. Childhood was spent in Brooklyn. Attended Pratt Institute.

MRS. PYNE's father was machinist at the New York Navy Yard. Her mother "painted pansies, roses, and plates — before she had three children." Mrs. Pyne has written that she herself was always drawing through her childhood and growing-up years. She left art school to earn money by fashion drawing. When she grew tired of drawing clothes, she illustrated two children's books and devised a baby book. When she moved to Connecticut with her husband and little girl, Jennifer, they had a brief interval of country pleasures, swimming, skating, etc. She sold *The Little History of the United States* which she had made for Jennifer. Then her husband was commissioned into the Navy and was killed in 1943. She was persuaded to undertake the second "Little" book. The third is now ready for the press. These "Little" books are large-size pictorial history or geography of brief text interspersed with many brightly colored small drawings. Mrs. Pyne lives in Brooklyn, New York.

RAE, JOHN

Born July 4, 1882, in Jersey City, New Jersey. Childhood was spent there and in New England; also in travel in Canada, England, Scotland, France, and elsewhere. Attended Art Students League, New York; and studied with Howard Pyle.

"MY childhood was happy," Mr. Rae writes. "No hardships. I had every advantage and encouragement. My inspiring father, Dr. Walter Rae, was born in Scotland. My mother, Frances Janes Hicks, was born in Vermont. John Hicks, an early American itinerant portrait and sign painter, a friend of Paul Revere, and one of the 'Sons of Liberty,' was my mother's great-grandfather. She was also related to Edward Hicks, the famous Quaker painter. The strongest art influences in my early life were the work of Howard Pyle, A. B. Frost and Frederick Remington, also the paintings in the Metropolitan Museum, New York, to which we often went. I married early, a wonderful wife, Helen Cortelyou, and we have three boys, Walter, Robin and John. Besides writing and illustrating many children's books, I have enjoyed painting portraits of interesting people. I've certainly been lucky." Mr. Rae's home is in North Stonington, Connecticut.

RAVERAT, GWENDOLEN M. (DARWIN)

Born August 26, 1885, in Cambridge, England, where childhood was spent. Attended Slade School of Art and University College, London.

MRS. RAVERAT is the granddaughter of Charles Darwin. In 1911 she married Jacques Raverat, the French designer, and during his life she lived in France. He died in 1925. She has two daughters: Elizabeth, married in 1940 to Edvard Hambro (Norwegian); and Sophie, married in 1940 to Mark Pryor. During World War II, Mrs. Raverat worked as a geographical draughtsman for a branch of the Admiralty. Her home is at Harlton, near Cambridge.

REED, PHILIP G.

Born January 17, 1908, in Park Ridge, Illinois, where his childhood was spent. Attended Chicago Art Institute School.

"HAVING been born into a family which considered good books essential in the education of youngsters," Philip Reed writes, "I was raised on a diet of Howard Pyle, Edwin A. Abbey, Randolph Caldecott, Will Dwiggins, D. B. Updike, Lovat Fraser, William Morris and a host of others. My early interest in drawing, typography and bookmaking springs from such fare. My father operated a small press, as an avocation, in the basement of our house and it was there that I first learned the tools of the trade. Four years' study at the Art Institute of Chicago, under Ernst F. Detterer, rounded out this training and in

1930 I started the Broadside Press at Barrington, Illinois. After three years the shop was moved to Katonah, New York, and after another three years to Park Ridge, Illinois, where my home is. Three years later we became associated with Ernst Hertzberg and Sons in Chicago under the name of The Monastery Hill Press. The purpose of the shop in the past has been the production of decently designed, properly illustrated books and, so far as can be foreseen, that will be its purpose in the future."

REID, STEPHEN

Born May 30, 1873, in Aberdeen, Scotland, where his childhood was spent and he attended Robert Gordon's College and Grey's School of Art; also Royal Scottish Academy, Edinburgh.

BORN of Banffshire farmer stock, Stephen Reid has painted from early childhood. On leaving school he went into an uncle's office but left after four years and had one year of art training while at home. Going to Edinburgh in 1893, he spent three years at the Royal Scottish Academy, then left for London with just over a pound in his pocket and a handful of letters of introduction. In London he has remained. His first years were spent doing black-and-white drawings for various magazines and color illustrations for children's books. During the First World War he started painting large pictures, historical and decorative, and he has continued in this line. He married Kate Cato in 1902 and has a son and a daughter.

REY, HANS AUGUSTO

Born 1898 in Germany. Lived in Brazil from 1923 to 1935 and became a Brazilian citizen.

H. A. REY has published many books for children both in France and England. He was in Paris working on new books when the Germans arrived and he decided it would be wise to leave. He and his wife managed to get out of France by bicycle and to Lisbon where, with hundreds of other refugees, they got a boat for South America. From Brazil the Reys came to New York. Mr. Rey speaks Portuguese, French, German and English. Mrs. Rey collaborates with him in the writing of the books. This information was obtained from *Publishers' Weekly*.

REYNOLDS, FRANK

Born February 13, 1876, in London.

FRANK REYNOLDS joined the *Punch* staff June 25, 1919, and was Art Editor of *Punch*, 1920 to 1930. He has contributed to the *Illustrated London News* and to *Sketch*. He is a Member of the Royal Institute of Painters in Water Colours, having been elected in 1903. His home is at Gigg's Hill Green, Thames Ditton, England. This information was obtained from *Who's Who*.

RICHARDS, GEORGE MATHER

Born September 3, 1880, in Darien, Connecticut. Attended Williams College (1904); New York School of Art; and studied in Europe.

"MY childhood," writes Mr. Richards, "was spent in a Puritan home where art, unless religious, did not exist. Early influences were Ridpath's *World History*, the Library of Congress, the Corcoran Gallery, and Charles Dana Gibson." His teachers included such eminent artists as Douglas John Connah, Robert Henri and Edward Penfield. Mr. Richards married Gertrude Lundborg, an artist. He began his career in New York in the field of advertising and became Art Editor for *Everybody's Magazine*. His magazine and text book illustration led to the illustration of books for children. His home is in New Canaan, Connecticut.

ROBERTS, JACK

Born November 20, 1894.

JACK ROBERTS is a painter of figures, portraits, and landscapes (especially water color). Etcher, wood engraver, illustrator and designer for crafts in Paris. This information was obtained from the *Allgemeines Lexikon der Bildenden Künstler von der Antike bis zur Gegenwart*, by Thieme and Becker.

ROBINSON, BOARDMAN

Born September 6, 1876, in Somerset, Novia Scotia. Childhood was spent in Nova Scotia where he attended Berwick Academy, and in South Wales where he went to private schools in Glamorganshire. Also studied at Massachusetts Normal Art School and at art schools in Paris.

BOARDMAN ROBINSON's father was a sea captain, his mother was the daughter of a farmer. "I remained with my grandfather until I was eight while my parents took my younger brother and sister to sea," he writes. "When my father settled in Cardiff, grandfather took me there and I stayed with my family until 1890, when I returned to Canada. Soon, thereafter, I attended art school in Boston, then went to Paris, traveling and studying for several years. In Paris, in 1903, I married Sally Senter Whitney, a sculptress of San Francisco. We have had three children. Back in New York, I drew for magazines and newspapers until in 1915 I went to the Balkans and Russia as a correspondent. Returning, I became a freelance illustrator and cartoonist. From 1919-30 I taught at the Art Students League, leaving it to join the faculty of the Fountain Valley School for Boys at Colorado Springs and at the same time becoming Director of the Broadmoor Art Academy. This later became the Colorado Springs Fine Arts Center. During fifteen years in Colorado, where I have remained as Director of the Art School, I have

NORA S. UNWIN: *Mountain Born*

ROGER DUVOISIN: *And There Was America*

painted murals and frescoes — notably those in Rockefeller Center, New York, and in the Department of Justice, Washington, D. C. I have done many portraits and easel pictures and illustrated half a dozen books." Boardman Robinson's work is represented in galleries and museums throughout the United States.

ROBINSON, IRENE BOWEN
Born 1891 in South Bend, Washington. Childhood was spent in Indianapolis and Los Angeles. Attended Drury College, Otis Art Institute and Chouinard Art Institute.

"I WAS born in a small village on a hill above the ocean in Washington State, but my family returned to Indiana when I was three years old," Irene Robinson writes. "My interest in animals goes back to my summer holidays on farms in Indiana between the ages of six and twelve. My first attempts to draw were of animals, and I still like to draw them — to watch and study them — better than anything else in art. It was natural that my husband, W. W. Robinson, and I should be interested in the prehistoric animal material of the La Brea Pits, very near our home in Los Angeles. From that first book, *Beasts of the Tar Pits*, developed our series of juveniles. Besides book illustration, I am a painter — both of landscape and still life — and an exhibiting member of California art organizations. I have had a number of one-man shows."

ROBINSON, THOMAS HEATH
Born June 19, 1869, in Islington, London, where childhood was spent and private schools including Islington High School were attended. Also studied at Cook's Art School and Westminster Art School, London.

"AT art school I studied under Solomon J. Solomon, R.A., and Professor Fred Browne," writes Thomas Heath Robinson, "but I can only ascribe my enthusiasm for art to hereditary sources and family surroundings. My grandfather was a wood engraver, my father and uncle were artists well known in their time. It was natural that my two brothers, Charles and W. Heath Robinson, and myself should have had every encouragement and complete understanding of our desires. More information about my two brothers and myself may be had from my brother, W. Heath Robinson's autobiography, *My Line of Life*." (Blackie. London. 1938.)

ROCKWELL, NORMAN
Born February 3, 1894, in New York. Childhood was spent there and in nearby Mamaroneck. Studied at Chase Art School, National Academy of Design and Art Students League.

NORMAN ROCKWELL is the elder son of J. Waring Rockwell, an amateur artist, and grandson on his mother's side of William Hill, an English portrait painter. He showed an early love of drawing and was allowed to begin his study of art at thirteen while continuing his regular schooling. At sixteen, he left High School to study under George Bridgman and Thomas Fogarty at the Art Students League and won two scholarships there. Through Fogarty, he got some assignments to illustrate McBride and Nast publications at seventeen years of age. These led to his shortly becoming Art Editor for the Boy Scout magazine, *Boys' Life*. He also illustrated for *St. Nicholas, American Boy, Everyland* and other magazines during this period. In 1916 he submitted three cover drawings to the Editor of the *Saturday Evening Post*, who bought all at $75 apiece, publishing the first in May 1916. Since then the *Post* has averaged ten Rockwell drawings a year in addition to numerous drawings for inside pages. Norman Rockwell's drawings for The Four Freedoms — now famous everywhere — were first offered in vain to Government departments in 1942, then sold to the *Post* from sketches which took seven months to complete. The First Freedom appeared on a *Post* cover in February 1943. Rockwell enlisted in the Navy for the First World War and while he became First Class Painter and Varnisher, he was held by the Commandant at the Charleston Navy Yard painting naval portraits. In 1922, at the age of twenty-eight, he went abroad and studied in Paris for some months and although the *Post* "gamely" published two of his "abstractionist" covers of that period, he returned to take up his characteristic portrait drawings of American types, taking his material now from the region of his home in Arlington, Vermont. Since 1920 Mr. Rockwell has painted every year, except two, the drawings for the Boy Scout calendar. A mural of his is in Nassau Tavern, Princeton, New Jersey. This information was obtained from *Who's Who in America, Current Biography* and *The New Yorker*.

ROJANKOVSKY, FEODOR STEPANOVICH
Born December 24, 1891, in Mitava, Russia. Childhood was spent in Reval (now Tallinn) and St. Petersburg (now Leningrad). Attended Reval High School and Academy of Fine Arts, Moscow.

"MY father was a school director, my two elder brothers had a talent for painting," says Feodor Rojankovsky, "and my love for art was born in our family. My father had a huge library and I remember many beautiful books in it, among them the Bible with illustrations by Doré: this frightened and fascinated me. Once I visited the circus. A monkey was turning the pages of a book, tigers were jumping, an elephant was playing a street organ. I painted them all. In 1912 I entered the Moscow Fine Art Academy, but two years later I was serving as an officer in the 1914-17 campaign. My regiment traveled through Poland, Prussia, Austria, and Rumania. I drew rarely, but I saw many interesting things. My war sketches were reproduced by art magazines. During the Revolution I started to make children's book illustrations for the young Ukrainian Republic. In 1919 I was mobilized by the 'Voluntary Army' (White Army), and soon my military career was finished behind barbed wire in Poland. Since then I have seen many countries and had many different occupations. In Paris I created books for different publishers, but when the Germans occupied Paris I went to New York where G. Duplaix asked me to work for the books that he created. This year (1945-46) I have the most difficult task — the illustration of the *Bible*." *Daniel Boone* was Rojankovsky's first book published in France and America (Domino Press, 1931). He came to this country in August, 1941.

ROUNDS, GLEN H.

Born 1906 at Near Wall, South Dakota. Childhood was spent in the Powder River country of Montana. Attended Art Institute and Art Students League, Kansas City, Missouri; and New York Art Students League.

"THE horse ranch I grew up on," Glen Rounds writes, "was forty miles from the railroad, but the country was well stocked with horses, cattle, gray wolves, badgers, antelope and the like. Also cowboys, sheepherders, bronco busters, freighters, wolf trappers, and an occasional sheriff, outlaw, or broken-down buffalo hunter — accomplished yarn-spinners, many of them. After high school I started drifting. At first I worked at things that required more muscle than brains — road and lumber camps, sawmills and the like. But wandering from place to place, one picks up skills. I became a right good baker, for one thing. Sign painting proved to be still better, and lightning portraits an improvement on that. Experimented with etching, engraving on copper and wood. Later I began to paint. Covered most of the United States, drawing what pleased me, telling stories and listening to them told, working when I had to. In 1935 I accidentally started writing stories to go with my drawings, and occasionally, if the story pleases me, and I can illustrate it as I please, I illustrate for other writers. From March, 1942, until September, 1945, I was in the Army; Artillery Mechanic for an Anti-Aircraft Battery except for the last nine months, when I was in the Infantry, helping train recruits. No overseas service. Drawing my twenty-two months' old son, his two cats and one dog is somewhat of a change from soldiers." Mr. Rounds' home is at Southern Pines, North Carolina.

ROUNTREE, HARRY

Born 1878 in Auckland, New Zealand, where his childhood was spent. Attended Queen's College.

HARRY ROUNTREE's father was a New Zealand banker. He married Estella Stewart of Auckland. Came to London in 1901, and published drawings in *Punch*, *The Sketch*, and other journals. At one time he was president of the London Sketch Club. He also served as Captain in The Royal Engineers. He lives at Dormers Wells, Southall, Middlesex, England. This information was obtained from *Who's Who*.

RUZICKA, RUDOLPH

Born June 29, 1883, in Bohemia. Attended Chicago Art Institute School and New York School of Art.

RUDOLPH RUZICKA was brought to this country in 1894. In 1914 he married Filomena Srpova, and has two children — Tatiana and Veronica. He is well known as illustrator and designer. His work is represented in print collections of the Metropolitan Museum of Art, New York City; the Congressional Library, Washington, D. C.; the Chicago Art Institute, and the Newark, New Jersey, Museum. He was awarded the Alice McFadden Brinton Prize, Philadelphia Print Club, 1924; Bronze Medal, Sesquicentennial Exposition, Philadelphia, 1926; Gold Medal, American Institute of Graphic Arts, 1935. He is an Associate Elect, National Academy of Design. With Stanley Morrison, Mr. Ruzicka is author of that memorable small volume, *Recollections of Daniel Berkeley Updike*, published by the Odd Volumes Club of Boston. His home is in New York City. This information was obtained from *Who's Who in America*.

SANCHEZ, CARLOS

Born August 23, 1908, in Toluca, Mexico. Attended Mechanic School and National Academy, Mexico City; and Open Air School of Painting, La Villa.

CARLOS SANCHEZ is the son of a bank accountant and a schoolteacher. "I started taking art seriously in 1924 while going to a Mechanic School in Mexico City in the daytime and working evenings in a commercial studio," Mr. Sanchez has written. "I got a position on a weekly magazine, *Revista de Revistas*, in 1926 and published full-page sketches and regular illustrations. At the same time I made illustrations for *Universal Illustrado* and *Gladiador* magazines. Then, having in mind to hold an exhibition of my drawings, I went to the National Academy and to the Open Air School of Painting at La Villa, in order to get materials for painting oil portraits. At La Villa I worked under the late painter, Fermin Revueltos. My exhibition I held in 1927. In 1928 I came to New York unable to speak or read English. But I had a dear friend, Kenneth Jones. He went with me to see the publishers and when I got a manuscript, he read it to me in English for he did not know Spanish. I had to prove I understood it by pantomime. I had to learn English quick! For about a year I worked for King Features Syndicate, and for *Judge* and other magazines. I also did advertising and industrial designing and work for newspapers. Wishing to study more painting and drawing, I am now in Mexico. Some day I expect to have a one-man show of all my work."

SANDERSON, IVAN T.

Born January 30, 1911, in Edinburgh, Scotland. Childhood was spent in England and France. Attended Eton and Cambridge University.

IVAN SANDERSON left Scotland with his family at the age of five and lived in London. His traveling began immediately after the First World War when all his holidays, until he went to Eton, were spent aboard a relative's yacht which made business trips all over the Mediterranean and north European seas, to Sweden, Norway and the north Atlantic islands. These travels gave great opportunity for zoölogical study; learning marine dredging operations; trips on whalers; visits to uninhabited islands where sea birds breed; to Lapp settlements and the exploration of Norwegian fjords. Eton and Cambridge holidays were always spent on the Continent. Between Eton and Cambridge, when Ivan Sanderson was sixteen to eighteen years of age, he made a trip alone to the Orient and around the world to collect animals. In 1932, immediately after leaving Cambridge, he went to West Africa as leader of a small zoölogical expedition for the Linnæan Society of London, the Royal Society, Cambridge University, British Museum and University College, London. A year was spent in the high forest of the British Cameroons during which many valuable zoölogical specimens were collected and a new method of field research tried out. Mr. Sanderson married in 1934. In 1936 he went to the West Indies and Trinidad and spent several months on Mount Aripo studying the Vampire Bat and the famous Diablotin birds that live only in one cave. He began there the study and construction of a permanent and complete set of equipment for zoölogical research and living in tropical jungles. During later travels in the Caribbean area and British Honduras, he developed further the study of animal distribution according to the mapping of vegetation, first dimly seen in the Orient. This has since become the central theme of all his travels and zoölogical work. Mr. Sanderson's books record his travels and studies.

SAUVAGE, SYLVAIN

Born May 8, 1888, at Baume-les-Messieurs, Jura, France.

SYLVAIN SAUVAGE is an illustrator, etcher, wood engraver, book decorator, designer, and publisher in Paris. He has exhibited at the *Artistes Décorateurs*, and won the silver medal in 1930. These facts were obtained from the *Dictionnaire Biographique des Artistes Contemporains* and the *Allgemeines Lexikon der Bildenden Künstler von der Antike bis zur Gegenwart*.

SCHAEFFER, MEAD

Born July 15, 1898, in Freedom Plains, New York.

MEAD SCHAEFFER studied under Dean Cornwell, pupil of Harvey Dunn, and lives now in Arlington, Vermont.

SCHARL, JOSEF

Born December 9, 1896, in Munich, where his childhood was spent and he attended the Academy of Fine Arts and School of Decorators.

AT fourteen, Josef Scharl began to draw and paint. Apprenticed to a firm of decorators in Munich and often asked to do restoration work in old churches and castles, he had ample opportunity to study mediaeval designs. The First World War intervened and it was not until its close that he was able to resume his art studies. In 1921 he began to work on his own, gaining public recognition when the City of Munich purchased one of his oil paintings. Travel followed, exhibitions and one-man shows in various European cities, and many awards and honors came to him. Self-exiled in 1938, he left Germany for the United States and after traveling and living in different parts of the country for a year or two he began to have one-man shows of his work in cities from New York to San Francisco. Illustrations for an edition of Grimm's *Fairy Tales* were done in 1944 and a year later were widely exhibited. He lives in New York.

SCHOONOVER, FRANK EARLE

Born August 19, 1877, in Oxford, New Jersey. Studied at Drexel Institute under Howard Pyle; also at Howard Pyle's Chadds Ford and Wilmington Schools.

FRANK SCHOONOVER studied under Howard Pyle, at Drexel, for four years, and won two scholarships which enabled him to attend a summer school at Chadds Ford. When Howard Pyle established his own school at Wilmington, Mr. Schoonover continued with him for a number of years. His first practical work was undertaken at Chadds Ford — a book illustration in black-and-white, and numbered One. All pictures made for reproduction since then have been numbered. In order to bring the real out-of-doors into the studio many trips have been made. To Hudson's Bay twice — once by snowshoe and again by canoe. This gave the artist a working knowledge of the life of the Canadian Indian and Eskimos. The Western Indian and cowpuncher were added shortly after, and later on Southern tropical colors were noted by wanderings about the Gulf of Mexico, Central American States and the West Indies. The latter gave an opportunity to visualize the life of the pirates and their haunts. In 1907 the great galleries of England and the Continent were visited. And so the material was gathered and brought to the studio. Mr. Schoonover lives in Wilmington, Delaware.

SCHUYLER, REMINGTON

Born July 8, 1884, in Buffalo, New York. Childhood was spent in Missouri, Michigan, and the West. Attended Engineering School and Washington University in St. Louis.

MR. SCHUYLER's artistic inheritance is a strong one. His father was an author, composer, and educator. His mother was an artist and musician, a relative of the painter-illustrator, Frederic Remington. Equally strong is his love of pioneer life. "I spend at least a month each year," he writes, "under canvas with my sons. When I was a boy, my father took us camping during the summers in the 'hill-billy' country of the Ozarks and in Michigan. We floated down the Big and Little Piney Rivers into the Gasconade River and so home. I spent much time exploring Indian caves and gathering a collection of Indian arrowheads and tomahawks. I left St. Louis to work in an Indian trading post at Okreek, Rosebud Indian Reservation, South Dakota. There were few white men and hundreds of Dakota (Sioux) Indians. I had a wonderful time living with the Indians and playing with the boys. Once I sold my long red hair for a pony. The Indian trimmed his scalp shirt with it. One of my ancestors, Phillipe Pieterse Van Schuyler, was a trusted friend of the Mohawk Indians. So also were his descendants. One of them took a group of Mohawk chiefs to London." A great grandfather introduced merino sheep into America and helped found Hobart College; a grandfather assisted in founding Marshall, Michigan. Mr. Schuyler is a former editor of the *Archaelogical Record*, published by the Peabody Museum, New Haven, and has been connected as a volunteer with the Boy Scouts of America since the beginning. His work for the Boy Scouts has included the writing of Merit Badge Pamphlets on art, sculpture and Indian lore and illustrating for *Boys' Life* and many of their *Handbooks*. His illustrations have

also appeared in several books for young people and most of the leading adult magazines. He divides his time between New York City and Buckingham, Bucks County, Pennsylvania.

SCHWABE, RANDOLPH

Born May 6, 1885, at Barton-upon-Irwell, Manchester, England. Childhood was spent mainly at Hemel Hempstead, Hertfordshire, where he attended Grammar School. Studied at Royal College of Art and Slade School, London; and Académie Julian, Paris, under Jean Paul Laurens.

AFTER his study at the Slade School, Randolph Schwabe spent two years in France and Italy. He is married and has one daughter. He was formerly on the teaching staff of the Royal College of Art under Sir William Rothenstein. From 1930 onwards he was Slade Professor, succeeding Professor Henry Tonks. In 1939 the Slade School was evacuated to the Ruskin School of Drawing, Oxford; returned to London, September, 1945.

SEIGNOBOSC, FRANÇOISE
(*pseud.* Françoise)

Born 1900 in Lodève, Hérault, France. Attended Collège Sévigné, Paris.

FRANÇOISE SEIGNOBOSC is a gifted French artist who in normal times has a winter studio in Paris and in summer lives on a farm in southern France where, like Colette, she has "many, many animals." Animals and children love Françoise for she is gay and friendly and knows the things they like. Children follow her and beg her to draw pictures for them and to tell them stories. The naïve style in which she illustrates her books is the result of seeing things as children see them and would draw them if they had her technical ability. Before the war Françoise paid visits to America. She returned to Paris last in 1939. The drawings she has made during World War II have appeared more often in newspapers than in books because of the paper shortage. Under date of December 10, 1945, Françoise wrote from Paris that while she began to draw at the age of eight, she studied art only after college. Some of the little books she did for Tolmer, the Paris publisher, found their way to the United States. "So I myself went over there one day and I did not regret it. I have now only one wish, to return to America. We have suffered too long. In winter I work in Paris without any fire at all and it is hard. I am hoping now to go to New York in September, 1946, for each day is a struggle to exist. Sometimes one's courage fails after six years of endurance. I think often of America. Everything good is there."

SEREBRIAKOFF, ALEXANDRE

Born September 7, 1907, in Kouzsk, Ukraine, U.S.S.R.

"MY father was a civil engineer who died in 1919, at the age of 37," M. Serebriakoff writes. "I was much influenced by my mother, Madame Zenaide Serebriakoff (born Lanceray), a painter well known in Russia, whose work is represented in the principal State Museums. My grandfather, Eugene Lanceray, of French extraction, was a sculptor, well known in Russia. My grandmother, also of French origin, was the sister of M. Alexandre Benois, decorative painter, designer, and author of Ballets Russes. After attending school in Russia, I came to Paris in 1925, where I have lived ever since. I have never followed any special "school" of art. The family environment and my mother's studio formed my taste and developed my artistic inclinations. For some years now, I have worked for the moving picture industry, as decorator, designer of scenery and costumes, and at all points where the applied arts are involved. I have also made decorative maps for the *Musée des Arts Décoratifs, Palais du Louvre,* and for the *Musée des Colonies* in Paris. I have been associated as a painter with many groups of Russian artists in Paris, in Prague and in Brussels. In the field of illustration, I have worked on children's books for the publishers, Desclée, de Brouwer et Cie., for the *N. R. F.* editions and for other magazines and journals."

SEREDY, KATE

Born November 10, 1896, in Budapest, Hungary. Childhood was spent in Hungary where Normal School and Academy of Art were attended.

"I HAD the usual number of grandparents," writes Kate Seredy, "but in my case the combination was unusual because one was French, one German, one Slovakian and one Turkish. They had but one thing in common and that was activity in some kind of rebellion—political, religious or personal. I grew up in an atmosphere charged with highly individual opinions on all subjects. My collective family had in turn decided that I was to be a teacher, a nurse, a dress-designer, a plain wife complete with children, a thorn-in-the-side of any government in power at any given moment, a painter. The first was my father's idea, the fourth was my mother's. I have at one time or another dabbled in each career, adding occasionally a few ideas of my own. In 1922 I came to America. Learning English by the trial and error method, I earned my living painting lampshades and greeting cards, slowly graduating to fashion design and finally to magazine and book illustrating. I had my own ideas about pictures in books, so I started to write my own books. I also acquired a farm and it, too, has its own ideas on what it wants

to grow. Now, I live on the farm in Montgomery, New York, write and illustrate books, while fervently hoping that no remote ancestor of mine will suggest any more careers."

SETON, ERNEST THOMPSON

Born August 14, 1860, at South Shields, Durham, England. Childhood was spent near Lindsay, and then in Toronto, Ontario, Canada, where Collegiate Institute and Ontario Art School were attended. Also studied at Royal Academy Schools, London, and in Paris. [Died October 23, 1946, at Santa Fé, New Mexico.]

WHEN Ernest Thompson Seton was five years old his father lost his fortune and took his family of ten sons to the backwoods of Canada. There Ernest Seton's interest in woodcraft began. In his nineteenth year he won a gold medal at the Ontario Art School and went to London where a scholarship admitted him to the Royal Academy Schools. He spent two and a half years in London, at night and in all his spare time reading books on natural history in the British Museum Library. He lived on very little and became so weakened by lack of food and over-study that he was forced to return to Canada. Four happy years followed in the newly-settled prairie country of Manitoba — hunting, trapping, farming and camping and in daily contact with Indians. Then came a period of hardship in New York until he was commissioned to make a thousand drawings for the Century Dictionary. This work established him as an illustrator of animal and bird life. At thirty he went to Paris and studied painting for four years, exhibiting animal pictures at the Salon. Returning to America, Seton now devoted himself to writing and illustrating animal stories, the first of their kind. Books and drawings grew out of his wilderness trips from the Arctic to Mexico. *Wild Animals I Have Known* was published in 1898 and sold ten editions the first year. Other books followed. He founded the Woodcraft League, an organization of boys and girls to study outdoor life, out of which grew the College of Indian Wisdom at Santa Fe, New Mexico. He was active in founding the Boy Scouts of America, wrote the first Scout Manual and was for five years Chief Scout. In 1928 he was awarded the John Burroughs Medal for his contribution to natural history, and in 1930 the David Girou Medal for his contribution to natural science. His ninety-acre estate in Greenwich, Connecticut, on which he had a zoo and a lake for wild birds, he sold in 1930 and bought a wild tract of 2500 acres of land near Santa Fe, New Mexico, which has now developed into the Seton Institute dedicated to the conservation of Indian lore, religion and craft. This information was obtained from *The Junior Book of Authors* and *Current Biography.*

VERA BOCK : *Oak Tree House*

JEAN CHARLOT : *Story of Chan Yuc*

SEWELL, HELEN MOORE

Born June 27, 1896, at Mare Island Navy Yard, California. Childhood was spent on the island of Guam, and in Brooklyn and Lake George, New York. Attended Packer Institute; Pratt Institute; and Archipenko's Art School, New York.

HELEN SEWELL was the youngest of three sisters. When she was six years old her father, Commander William E. Sewell, U.S.N., was ordered to Guam as Governor. He took his three little girls with him. The years spent in travel and at Guam were important for Helen Sewell, for during them she acquired an indelible impression of tropical beauty which has influenced all her later life and work. At a very early age she knew that she wanted to be an artist and she never wavered from this pursuit. After the death of her father, she returned to the United States to live with her aunt and uncle. There was a large family of cousins, many of whom were much younger than herself. She writes: "I have always occupied myself with them and with all the children I have known. It was natural that I should turn to making pictures for children. Good art for children must be intelligible to them, so I have always gone to children for my cue and inspiration, and I have found them a rewarding and appreciative public." She lives in New York.

SHARP, WILLIAM

Born June 13, 1900, in Lemberg, Austria (later of Poland; now U. S. S. R.), where childhood was spent and schools were attended. Later studied in Cracow, England, France, and Germany, especially in Berlin and Munich.

WILLIAM SHARP writes that he has worked as a newspaper artist for nearly twenty years, since 1934 in "the good USA." In New York he has been Staff Artist for the *New York Post, PM* and *Esquire.* He has published several portfolios of etchings and lithographs on the legal and medical professions; and has illustrated ten volumes for the Limited Editions Club, including the *Diary of Samuel Pepys,* several novels of Dickens, Poe, *The Brothers Karamazov,* and other books for Random House. His home is at Forest Hills, Long Island, New York.

SHENTON, EDWARD

Born November 29, 1895, in Pottstown, Pennsylvania. Childhood was spent mostly in Philadelphia and New Jersey. Attended Philadelphia Museum School of Industrial Art and Pennsylvania Academy of Fine Arts.

EDWARD SHENTON writes: "At the age of fourteen or thereabouts, with a great sheaf of drawings under my arm, I was taken to see Frederick Gruger. Nothing in my childish efforts could possibly have interested him but he took

time from his work to talk to me about the knowledge, the curiosity for life and its wonders that an illustrator should have. Time has not dimmed or altered the truth of what he said, nor its value to me. From Henry McCarter I received the basic concepts of picture-making and, from the work of Vierge and Rockwell Kent, technical inspiration. But beyond such learning, nature is the perpetual source to which I return to refresh myself and my work. For this reason, living in the country as I do in West Chester, Pennsylvania, among the people who work with the earth, is a stimulating existence. Teaching is also an excellent means of keeping from falling into formulas and repetition. As instructor in illustration at the Pennsylvania Academy of Fine Arts, I am constantly jogged out of my habits by succeeding classes of eager young students."

SHEPARD, ERNEST HOWARD

Born December 10, 1879, in London where he attended St. Paul's School, Heatherly's Art School, and Royal Academy Schools.

ERNEST SHEPARD has received medals for drawing and painting from life. He was the Landseer Scholar, 1899. He exhibited his first picture at the Royal Academy in 1901, and started drawing for *Punch* in 1907. In 1915 he was commissioned in the Royal Artillery and served three years in France, Belgium and Italy. In 1921 he was elected to join the *Punch* table.

SHEPHERD, JAMES AFFLECK

Born November 29, 1867, in London, where he attended various small schools and studied with private tutor; also under Alfred Bryan, the caricaturist. [Died May 10, 1946.]

J. A. SHEPHERD invented and illustrated "Zig-Zags at the Zoo" and "The Arcadian Calendar" for the *Strand Magazine.* He was invited to the staff of *Punch* in 1893, and was for some three years on the staff of the *Illustrated London News.* At the International Exhibition of Humorous Art, Rivoli, Italy, in 1911, Mr. Shepherd was awarded the Gold Medal. Hunting and interest in all animal life are his recreations. His home is at Woodmancote Manor, near Cirencester, Gloucestershire, England. This information was obtained from *Who's Who.*

SHINN, EVERETT

Born November 7, 1876, in Woodstown, New Jersey, where childhood was spent and where he attended Reed's private school and Bacon's Academy. Studied also at Spring Garden Institute and Pennsylvania Academy of Fine Arts.

"MY first ambition was to be a mechanical engineer," writes Everett Shinn. "So, through hard and painstaking drafting with practical work in the machine shop, I was instructed as such at the Spring Garden Institute. Later I became an artist on the *Philadelphia Press*, shifting to other papers and eventually moving to New York where I have continued to live. The roots out of which my work has grown are undoubtedly the training I received while working on newspapers. There were no cameras then, and an artist was expected to remember the things he had seen, return to the office and clear the 'dead line' no matter how cramped he was for time. I have written vaudeville acts, illustrated for magazines, been art director for a number of motion pictures, executed several large murals, and my pictures are represented in many museums." Mr. Shinn lives in New York City.

SIEGEL, WILLIAM

> Born 1905 in a small town near Riga, Latvia. Later attended National Academy of Design, New York.

"As a child," William Siegel wrote, "I had a chance to travel practically all over European and Asiatic Russia. A trip to Samarkand, Turkestan, was particularly memorable. I also visited Germany, and soon after World War I broke out, settled in Southern Russia, where I attended the regular Government School. I cannot remember when I first began to draw. In school, however, occurred my first disappointment in 'art.' During drawing periods I was made to draw cubes, pyramids, etc. I always recall these lessons with aversion. The First World War and the revolution added to my store of impressions, but all the art training I had received until then had been uneven and haphazard. In 1923 I went abroad and stayed in Constantinople and Athens on my way to the United States. Upon arrival here I spent a few years in study, attending the National Academy of Design where I won the Composition Prize of 1927. While in the Academy I began illustrating books. I have also made illustrations for several magazines. Owing to previous experiences, Oriental and Semi-Oriental Art particularly interest me. Architecture, pottery, miniatures, armor, etc., are of great importance to every book illustrator. The peculiar blend of Orient and Occident, of barbarism and civilization, always attracted me. Almost any book that can be treated decoratively appeals to me, provided I have a free hand in designing its format—type, title page, binding, size, etc."

SIMON, HOWARD

> Born July 22, 1903, in New York. There and in its suburbs childhood was spent and New York Preparatory School, University of New York, and National Academy of Design were attended; also Académie Julian, Paris.

HOWARD SIMON has lived in Paris, the Ozarks, San Francisco, Connecticut, and New York State. All of these varied backgrounds have at one time or another been the subject matter for illustrations in the forty-odd books he has illustrated. A good part of this material may be seen in his woodcut plates and paintings which are in many private and public collections. During the years 1931-36, when few homesteads remained open, he proved out a sixty-acre tract in Oachita Forest for which he holds a government deed. "Those years," he says, "were filled with observation of the woodlands, the flora and fauna, and the mountain people particularly. The interest I already had in early American life and its pioneers was confirmed and strengthened by this experience, and it remains a source of inspiration to me." Howard Simon lives in New York in the winter. He is married to Mina Lewiton, the author, and they have a daughter, Bettina.

SIMPSON, MAXWELL STEWART

> Born September 11, 1896, in Elizabeth, New Jersey, where childhood was first spent, then in Thousand Islands, New York State, and in Pennsylvania. Attended National Academy of Design and Art Students League, New York.

MAXWELL STEWART SIMPSON is perhaps better known as a painter and etcher than as an illustrator. Since 1920 he has been a regular exhibitor in the leading exhibitions of oil painting, water color painting, and etching. After his years of study, he traveled extensively in France, Italy, Sicily and England, and in 1929 he lived and painted in Paris for a year. Returning to the United States, he opened a studio in the city in which he was born. He has lived there ever since, except for summers spent in Vermont. The *Aucassin and Nicolette* which he illustrated for Holiday House was selected by the American Institute of Graphic Arts for its "Fifty Books of the Year," 1936.

SLOBODKIN, LOUIS

> Born February 19, 1903, in Albany, New York, where childhood was spent. Attended Beaux Arts Institute of Design, New York.

"MY father and mother," Louis Slobodkin writes, "came from the province of Chernigov, Ukraine, and settled in Albany. Having somehow managed to reach my third year of high school at fifteen, and having read of the early development of the masters, I left school in 1918 and went down to New York to study sculpture, drawing, etc., at the Beaux Arts. From my fifteenth to my twentieth year I studied from life some nine to twelve hours a day. Was awarded twenty-two medals during this time and the Tiffany Foundation Scholarship. For the next ten years I worked as assistant sculptor, occasionally a ghost sculptor, and also received some commissions of my own. Early in that period I shipped to the Argentine as deckhand. In the middle of it I married Florence Gersh.

We have two sons, Larry and Michael. Towards the end of the ten years, I spent a few years in Europe working as a ghost. Since my thirtieth year, I have executed many large commissions of my own, won in open competition, exhibited in many museums, and in 1941 did my first drawings for a book. In my youth a strange boy, whose face I never saw, gave me a most important art lesson as I watched him do a chalk drawing on our school fence. He changed my direction completely from viewing life as a series of patterns to a consciousness that the illusion of form can be indicated on a flat surface. Mere dexterity or surface facility has always seemed to me of little consequence in a plastic or graphic expression. Emotional content and universal truths liberated by a personal aesthetic logic are the qualities I hope to attain in my work. In drawing for books, if my drawing does not extend and enhance the significant thought implied in the text, its value is negligible." Mr. Slobodkin's home is in New York City.

SLOCUM, ROSALIE

Born December 17, 1906, in Providence, Rhode Island. Childhood was spent in Boston and on the Providence River Shore. Attended Massachusetts School of Art and Museum of Fine Arts School, Boston.

"My childhood winters were spent in a rambling Victorian Boston house," Rosalie Slocum writes, "and summers on the delightful Providence River, both rich in vivid experience. During high school a physicist's career lured me. For years, however, I had spent practically every Saturday in the Boston Museum of Fine Arts trying to reproduce, in color, examples of early Egyptian and Ancient Greek Art. Art won. At the Massachusetts School of Art I also worked under the supervision of the child psychologist, Dr. E. Stanley Abbott, and learned to analyze my own early impressions. For two years I was supervisor of art and music in Connecticut, but finally gave up the security of teaching for art in New York City. After several struggling years as commercial artist, an indulgent husband and the congenial atmosphere of Greenwich Village helped me to develop a special approach to children through illustration. In 1935 I had a series of one-man shows of pictures for children in New York, Boston, and Atlanta. I have experimented considerably with reproduction techniques, especially new uses for transparent printer's inks. Each book has been a technical experiment, but I write and illustrate only because I want to. For the last four years I have been busy in a quite different field—Public Relations; conducting government and other important drives and propaganda campaigns." Rosalie Slocum is Mrs. Arthur Goldberg, and her home is in Brooklyn, New York.

SMITH, WILLIAM ARTHUR

Born April 19, 1918, in Toledo, Ohio, where childhood was spent, with much travel over the United States and Canada, and where he attended University of City of Toledo, Keane's Art School and Toledo Museum School of Design.

Of himself, William Arthur Smith writes: "I lived in Toledo until I set up my New York studio in 1937. My early experience was on newspapers, but in New York I was able to concentrate more on my paintings which I had already begun showing in exhibitions. Then I began doing work for book publishers and became a regular contributor to the magazines. March 1942 marked the birth of my most important inspiration to do children's books—the arrival of my son, Richard Keane Smith. Perhaps the deep love for books which I have, plus the natural tendency to express myself in drawing and painting, added to my love for children, is the complete explanation for my interest in children's book illustration. In June 1944 I closed my studio to join the army and am, at present, serving in China. My duties have not prevented my making friends with many Chinese children, whom I have followed into their homes and sketched: an opportunity for which I am thankful. Most of my art training was had under Theodore J. Keane, to whom I owe a debt I can never fully repay." William Arthur Smith makes his home in Toledo.

SOPER, EILEEN A.

Born 1905 in Enfield, Middlesex, England. Childhood was spent in Welwyn, Hertfordshire, where she was taught at home.

Eileen Soper has never attended any art schools, but studied entirely under the tuition of her father, the late George Soper, R.E., who is internationally known for his work as an etcher, engraver and illustrator. "Following in his footsteps," she says, "I started to draw at a very early age. My first etching was made when I was thirteen, and at fifteen two of my etchings were accepted and hung at the Royal Academy, Burlington House, London. From then on I became a regular exhibitor at leading art galleries throughout the world. More recently I have turned to book and magazine illustration, often working in the capacity of artist and author. My subjects cover a wide field, though my preference has always been for children and animals." Eileen Soper has always lived in the country and finds deep joy in the study and friendship of the birds and wild life near her home in Welwyn, Hertfordshire. Her garden, which was made by her father, is kept as a bird sanctuary, part of it being left as a woodland where wild flowers may grow at will. In this atmosphere, and among the child population of her own and neighboring villages, she finds willing models for the books she illustrates.

SOWERBY, AMY MILLICENT
Born in Northumberland, England.

"The late John Sowerby, my father, was an artist and, when I was a child, was engaged in writing and illustrating books for children, later turning to landscape painting," Miss Sowerby has written. "I was painting from earliest childhood and was lucky in finding help and encouragement at home. I attended art classes for a few years, but living some distance in the country it meant only two days a week, but I worked hard at home. Being very fond of children, I turned naturally to painting them and for them. It has always been the beautiful in childhood that has attracted me, not the humorous or grotesque. I love flowers and bright colors, and I generally use these in the backgrounds for my paintings of children. My sister Githa (Mrs. John Kendall), author of *Rutherford and Son* and other plays, wrote the stories and verses for a number of books which I have illustrated."

SPERRY, ARMSTRONG
Born November 7, 1897, in New Haven, Connecticut. Childhood was spent in Stamford, Connecticut, where he attended Stamford Preparatory School. Also Yale University Art School; Art Students League, New York; and Académie Colarossis, Paris.

Armstrong Sperry's earliest enthusiasm was for drawing and painting. When he was a small boy his mother used to say that the surest way of keeping him quiet was to give him a pencil and paper. Growing through adolescence, there was never any doubt in his mind as to his ultimate vocation. His first academic training came at the Yale Art School. This was interrupted, however, when he enlisted in the Navy during the First World War. After the Armistice, he went to New York to study at the Art Students League and there George Bellows and Luis Mora strengthened an enthusiasm which has never flagged. "But all this time a desire to make pictures with words as well as paint was lying dormant," he says. "During two years spent roaming through the islands of the South Pacific, I absorbed unwittingly much of the material I was to use in my later work. In 1933, with the appearance of *One Day with Manu*, I combined, for the first time, the double interests of writing and painting. This marked the beginning of some fourteen books to date, and I am still happily planning others to come." A thirty-acre farm in Vermont, where he spends much of his time raising fine crops, claims whatever is left of Armstrong Sperry's time and energy.

STERN, MARIE SIMCHOW
(pseud. Masha)
Born April 20, 1909, in New York. Childhood was spent in Brooklyn. Attended Pratt Institute and Art Students League, New York.

Marie Simchow Stern was born of Jewish-Russian parents and though the circumstances of the family were far from comfortable there was always a wealth of intellectual ideals. The name of Simkhovitch had been slightly Americanized to Simchow and the family were proud of the artists, poets and writers it was producing. "The city is the real cradle of my formative years," Masha writes. "It offered in its libraries, museums, schools, shops and public buildings the best that the world could produce. I have been influenced not by any painter or school, not even by my own personal life, but by children's book illustration itself. This is the true root of my work. After leaving Pratt Institute in 1930, I spent nine years with a novelty firm as a designer, developing my understanding of technique, style, public taste and my own talent. For the past five years I have been concentrating on book illustration." She is married, has one son, and lives in New York.

STEVENS, LUCY BEATRICE
Born September 4, 1876, in New York where — with summers at various resorts — childhood was spent and private schools were attended, supplemented by tutors.

Lucy Stevens' father was a prominent lawyer and she was named after her mother, Lucy Baldwin. She says that she went to no art school but that critics in her own studio did much to forward her instruction. At an early age her work was recognized and she soon became known as an illustrator, landscapist, and mural painter. Exhibitions of her work have been seen in New York, Boston, and Pomfret, Connecticut, which is her permanent home. Here she is known not only as an artist but also as the producer of the Christmas Pantomime, "Holy Night," which has been shown annually in Pomfret since 1912 at the Christmas season. Her drawings appeared in *St. Nicholas* and in leading magazines of the country.

STEWART, ALLAN
Born February 11, 1865, in Edinburgh, Scotland, where — and in its vicinity — childhood was spent and he attended Newington School, Edinburgh Institution and Royal Scottish Academy.

Allan Stewart writes that illustration of children's books began for him when a publishing firm asked permission to reproduce some historical pictures of his in various of their books. This led to his being asked to do a series of pictures in color for a children's book about Edinburgh. This in turn was followed by a series of pictures for *Tales from Scottish Ballads, Tales of Scottish Castles,* and others. Another firm then asked him to do some work for their school histories, and so it went. As the years passed he found the world of children's book illustration both satisfying and stimulating. In the spring of 1946 his original painting of "King Edward VII Inspecting the Royal Company of Archers, the King's Bodyguard for Scotland" (a company made up traditionally of members of the old families of Scotland), was hung permanently in Holyrood Palace. This was accomplished by the Duke of Hamilton, the hereditary Keeper of Holyrood, who was very anxious to obtain it for that purpose. Mr. Stewart lives in Dalry, Kirkendbrightshire, Scotland.

STOLPER, JOEL
Born in Jersey City, New Jersey. Childhood was spent in New York City.
As a child, Joel Stolper showed a marked aptitude for drawing birds and animals, winning a Wanamaker Award while in elementary school, and having some of his earliest sketches commented on by Charles Dana Gibson. Later, he drifted into boxing, won a Golden Glove at Madison Square Garden, then decided overnight to forsake the ring for paints and brushes. "Loving above all to draw birds and animals," he says, "I find the zoo an inexhaustible treasury of subjects. I make use of all media — oils, water color, dry brush, and especially crayons. Never having had any formal instruction in art, I am self-taught and a severe critic of my work. For diversion, I paint landscapes, portraits, and flowers, and I model animals in clay." Mr. Stolper's home is in New York City.

STONE, HELEN
Born October 31, 1904, in Englewood, New Jersey, where childhood was spent. Attended New York School of Fine and Applied Art, and studied in Paris.
HELEN STONE says that her entry into the field of children's books was sudden and unplanned. "I had never dreamed of illustrating books for juveniles. I am a painter and only by chance stumbled into the field of book illustration. It is, however, a rewarding field, giving full scope to the artist's feeling for design and color, enlivening the sense of humor and beauty. When I was a child, seeing my mother at her easel stimulated me to experiment with brushes. So, instead of selecting academic subjects to follow, I chose art. After studying in New York, where my residence has been more or less continually, I went to Paris. There, a great world of wonder opened before me. Young as I was, I felt dazzled by the length and breadth and depth of it. But subsequent visits, and

getting about to odd parts of the world — Europe, the American tropics, isles of the ancient Mediterranean, the pristine West Indies — opened my eyes still further. Perception was aroused: I felt it did not matter if it took the rest of my life to reflect what I had seen. As I progressed, I showed my work. It was viewed and reviewed not unkindly." Mrs. Stone lives in New York City.

SUBA, SUSANNE
Born December 31, 1913, in Budapest, Hungary. Childhood was spent in Europe and the United States. Attended in Brooklyn Friends School and Pratt Institute.
AT the age of three, crouched under a drawing board in her father's office in Budapest, Susanne Suba writes, she started her career as an artist. Her father, Miklos Suba, was an architect and painter; her mother, May Edwards, was a pianist. She was brought to America as a small child, settling in her mother's native Brooklyn. She is as much at home in the field of advertising as she is in that of book illustration: the Medal Award for newspaper advertising given by the Art Directors' Club of Chicago has been presented to her and several of her books have been included in the "Fifty Best Books of the Year." A book of her *New Yorker* drawings, *Spots by Suba,* was published in 1944. Her work has been exhibited in New York and Boston, and in 1942 the Art Institute of Chicago gave a one-man show of her drawings. She is married to Russell McCracken, writer and editor, and her home is in Chicago.

TAWSE, SYBIL
Attended Lambeth School and Royal College of Art, London.
SYBIL TAWSE was a King's Prize Scholar and a Silver and Bronze Medalist. She has exhibited at the Royal Academy and at the Brighton Art Gallery. Her home is in London. These facts were obtained from *Who's Who in Art.*

TEAGUE, DONALD
Born November 27, 1897, in Brooklyn, New York, where childhood was spent. Attended Art Students League, New York.
HORSES, cowboys, frontier life and history, and ships and the sea are Donald Teague's favorite subjects. In the First World War he served in the Navy and afterward made his first trip to Europe. Since 1920, up to the Second World War, he has spent three or four months annually in travel and has sketched, painted and photographed all over the world. He has made fifteen trips to Europe and one around the world. His travels have brought him in touch with two other wars, the Riff War in North Africa in 1925 and the Chinese-Japanese War

KATE SEREDY : *Ear for Uncle Emil*

in 1937-38. His illustrations are invariably done in water color or gouache, in rather small size. These are preceded by many sketches, and sometimes photographs. Donald Teague has a reputation as a painter and is represented in the national shows. His latest award was the Zabriskie Prize for his water color, *Cap'n Rich*, in the 1944 American Water Color Society Show. He likes to give credit for much aid and encouragement in his early years of work to Dean Cornwell, a pupil of Harvey Dunn who had studied with Howard Pyle. In 1938 Mr. Teague married Verna Timmins, and has two daughters. Their home is in Encino, California.

TENGGREN, GUSTAF

Born November 3, 1896, in Magra, Sweden. Childhood was spent in Sweden and in Gothenburg, the Slöjdföreningens School and Valand School of Fine Arts were attended.

GUSTAF TENGGREN illustrated his first fairy tale — *Bland Tomtar o' Troll* — in Stockholm in 1917 and continued the illustrating of this fairy tale annually for nine years. Since then he has illustrated numerous children's books in Scandinavia and in America. Exhibitions of Mr. Tenggren's work have been held in Gothenburg, Stockholm, and Copenhagen. He lived in Copenhagen during 1918-19 and came to the United States in 1920, where he has lived since. He has traveled and painted in Mexico, Yucatan, and Nova Scotia. He enjoys boating, fishing, and chess. His *Lively Little Rabbit* was chosen by the American Institute of Graphic Arts for its "Fifty Books" Exhibit in 1943, and his *Tenggren's Story Book* in 1944. Mr. Tenggren's home is in West Southport, Maine.

THORNE, DIANA

Born October 7, 1894, in Winnipeg, Manitoba, Canada. Childhood was spent in the West where she studied with private tutors and governesses. Also studied in London, and in France, Germany, and Scotland.

DIANA THORNE writes, "I grew up in Canada on a ranch outside of Winnipeg. I was very young when I began to fashion horses, cows, calves, dogs and hens and other animals, some wild, as coyotes, wolves, foxes, etc. Then my father got me some clay. I did not go to art school until I was sent to France and Germany and later to Scotland to study etching. I painted abroad until I was in my 'teens. All my work up to the great Depression belonged to the Fine Arts field. I painted portraits and exhibited paintings, sculpture and etchings all over this country. In 1929 I settled down to do commercial work in New York. I worked for Henry Quinan, one of the grandest and oldest art editors in the country. I did illustrations and covers, lots and lots of them, for *Woman's Home Companion* and *American Magazine* under him. I also worked for Harry Burton, then art editor of *This Week* Magazine, edited by Mrs. Meloney. I did lots for them, wrote and painted and drew. Then came books and more commercial work. I am still active, writing, drawing and painting." Diana Thorne lives in New York.

THORNYCROFT, ROSALIND

Born September 2, 1891, in Frimley Green, Surrey, England. Childhood was spent in London. Attended King Alfred School; London School of Economics; Slade School of Art; and Académie Julian, Paris.

"MY father, Sir Hamo Thornycroft, and my grandfather, Thomas Thornycroft, were both sculptors," Rosalind Thornycroft writes. "My grandmother, also a sculptress, was the daughter of John Francis, himself a sculptor. Drawing and painting were, therefore, natural and encouraged in our home. My parents' sympathies were much with William Morris's ideas and those of the Pre-Raphaelite school. The colored picture books of Walter Crane were my early delight; later, Diaghilev's Russian Ballet became a tremendous influence. During the early childhood of my three children, we lived in Florence and other parts of Italy. On returning to England I illustrated the books written by my relatives, Herbert and Eleanor Farjeon. When my eldest daughter grew up and became a textile designer, I collaborated with her in making hand-printed materials. I am married to A. E. Popham, Keeper of Prints and Drawings in the British Museum. Our home is in London and for the last few years I have been engaged in miniature photography of the old masters' drawings in relation to my husband's work."

TRESILIAN, CECIL STUART

Born July 12, 1891, in Bristol, England. There and in Liverpool and London childhood was spent and various schools were attended. In London Regent Street Polytechnic School and Royal College of Art.

As a child, Cecil Stuart Tresilian was always interested in ships and shipping at Liverpool and used to try to draw what he saw. He says that he has followed no particular school but that his work is the outcome of his interests which are in animal and human life, and of his studies at school and college. "I enjoy what I consider are the best illustrators," he writes, "such men as Charles Keene, Hugh Thomson, Edmund J. Sullivan and your own Rockwell Kent. After studying at the Polytechnic for a few years, I taught as a pupil-teacher, then gained a Royal Exhibition Scholarship to the Royal College of Art. I had an enjoyable time until war broke out in 1914. Serving with the 12th London Territorial Regiment (the 'Rangers'), I was wounded three times, the last time being taken prisoner. I did some drawing and painting and started a class among my fellow prisoners. When I returned to London, I resumed my work as an illustrator, as well as that of a teacher at the Polytechnic where I have been ever since."

TREVELYAN, PAULINE

Born October 9, 1905, in Morpeth, Northumberland, England. Childhood was spent in Northumberland, Somerset and London. Attended Sidcot School; Prince Max of Baden's School, Salem, Germany; Royal College of Art, London; Reading University.

"My family has lived for over two hundred and fifty years in the fine Border country of Northumberland where I was born and brought up," writes Pauline Trevelyan. "Interest in history runs strong in all of us — my great-great-uncle was Lord Macaulay, my grandfather was Sir George Otto Trevelyan, and my grandmother, Lady Trevelyan, was a fine water color artist. It was her interest that early encouraged me. As I grew up, it was natural that I should prefer to illustrate old songs and historic episodes. After six years at a Quaker co-educational school, I went over to Prince Max of Baden's School at Salem, Germany. Extensive traveling in Europe, Egypt, and the Sudan followed. Returning to England I attended the Royal College of Art before taking a diploma in agriculture at Reading University, completed by practical work on the University Research Farm and with a hill-sheep breeder in Scotland. I was preparing to run my father's estate in Northumberland when I married John Dower, an architect and town planner. For ten years we lived in London. Then when he joined the Army in September 1939, I moved to our Yorkshire house with our three children. Recently we have moved back to the family home in Cambo, Morpeth, Northumberland."

TRIER, WALTER

Born 1890 in Prague where in due time he studied at the Art School. Later became a pupil of Stuck in Munich.

As a boy, Walter Trier has written, he wanted to become a football player and left school with an excellent mark in gymnastics but only passing in drawing. When he applied for entrance at the Art School the principal asked if he had not made a mistake and did not want to become an acrobat rather than an artist. He was soon dropped from the Art School but persisted in his desire to become an artist. He went to Munich where he finally became a pupil of Stuck. At nineteen he began to draw for the chief joke magazines. Later he went to Berlin, and began to illustrate books for children. He illustrated also the German translation of Kipling's *Just So Stories*. He is reported now (spring, 1946) to be living in London.

TROY, HUGH

Born April 28, 1906, in Ithaca, New York, where childhood was spent and Cornell University was attended.

HUGH TROY writes: "After leaving college in 1927, I earned my living by painting mural decorations, augmenting this income by writing short articles and fiction. Through a desire to write and illustrate fanciful things, three children's books have been evolved. More are taking shape within me and will find some form when my present occupation of bombing enemy targets has no future left." During World War II, Hugh Troy was a Captain in the 21st Bomber Command, APO 234. His home is in New York City.

TUDOR, TASHA

Born August 28, 1915, in Boston. Childhood was spent in Redding, Connecticut. Attended Spring Hill School and Boston Museum of Fine Arts School.

TASHA TUDOR says that she comes naturally by her love of drawing, as her mother, Rosamond Tudor, is a portrait painter. "Ever since I was a small child, I wanted to draw pictures and illustrate books," she writes. In 1938 she married Thomas Lieghton McCready, Jr., and they have two children, Bethany Wheelock and Seth Tudor. The McCreadys live on an old farm in Webster, New Hampshire, and have several Jersey cows, Alexander the gander, and numerous other two- and four-footed dependents.

ULREICH, NURA WOODSON
(*pseud.* Nura)

Born December 1899 in Kansas City, Missouri, where childhood was spent. Attended Kansas City Art Institute and Art Students League, Chicago.

NURA writes: "I had a very vivid childhood, and this is the fount drawn upon for my work." She was an extremely imaginative child, always making up plays and games of her own, and when she was very young she created paper dolls which were "the envy of the neighborhood." After art school she went to Europe to study, and became an exhibiting painter and sculptress. During the 1930 depression there was no market for pictures so she turned to books, though publishers told her there was no money in them. As a result she wrote, illustrated, designed and published herself four books for distribution among clients and friends. Two were chosen by the American Institute of Graphic Arts for awards, and one by the Oxford University Press in England. In 1942 the Studio Publications published a book of drawings and paintings including some of Nura's. Many were interested in them, with the result that Studio Publications became her publisher. And Nura writes, "They have NOT lost money on them. All my work, painting, sculpture, lithographs, etc., have dealt with childhood as a 'state of being,' for that is what interests me most." Nura lives in New York.

UNDERWOOD, LEON

Born December 25, 1890, in London. Attended Hampton Gurney School; Royal College of Art and Slade School, London. Studied in Holland, Germany and Russia in 1914.

LEON UNDERWOOD is an artist, sculptor, and engraver; a teacher, writer and inventor. During the First World War he served as Captain in the Camouflage Section, Royal Engineers. In the Second World War he was in Civil Defense Camouflage, 1939-1942. He has had many exhibitions in London Galleries and at the Weyhe Gallery, New York City. He has traveled in Iceland, Canada, the United States and Mexico. His home is at Bishops Itchington, near Leamington Spa, England. This information was obtained from *Who's Who*.

UNWIN, NORA SPICER

Born February 22, 1907, in Tolworth, Surrey, England. There and in Surbiton, near the Thames River, childhood was spent and Surbiton High School was attended. Also studied in Leon Underwood's studio; Kingston School of Art; and Royal College of Art, London.

"MY twin sister and I are the youngest of a family of five," writes Nora Unwin, "and our childhood was a very happy one. We both loved art and music and nearly all leisure time was spent in drawing and painting. My family has been closely connected with books, both through printing and publishing, for several generations and I have often watched the whole process of book production in my father's printing works. My sister became a professional cellist but there was never any doubt that I wished to be an artist. I often used to watch the artist-father of a friend at work; many of his excellent tools and materials became mine in later years. After high school I had eight years of specialized training that were a continuing adventure for me — pottery, wood carving, embroidery, bookbinding, mural decoration, engraving, etching, architecture. All were explored and enjoyed to the full, but wood engraving and book illustration became my greatest loves. My war job of the past five years has had part in my illustrating as it placed me in delightful rural surroundings among a charming group of children. I learned much about children; their interest in, appreciation, and criticism of my work were invaluable, as also their pleasure in serving as models at

a penny a sitting — though they seldom *sat*. More than anything that has happened at an earlier period, these years just past are the productive roots of my work." Nora Unwin lives in Milford, Surrey.

VAN DOREN, MARGARET

Born October 21, 1917, in New York where childhood was spent — with summers in West Cornwall, Connecticut — and City and Country School, Lincoln School, and Cooper Union Art School were attended.

"I FIRST started illustrating children's books in collaboration with my younger sister, who wrote them," Margaret Van Doren Bevans writes. "We did three as a team and later I wrote and illustrated one myself, and several adult books. Mostly, however, I did book jackets and color separation work for offset printers. In the last few years I have done very little work aside from taking care of my two children who were born in 1941 and 1943, but I hope to start again as soon as they are both old enough to go to school. Most of the juvenile illustrations are based on my childhood and pets in West Cornwall." Margaret Van Doren Bevans lives, in winter, in New York.

VAN EVEREN, JAY

ALL Jay Van Everen's work has revealed him to be a lover of New York. He is a fine bookmaker, with the right feeling for decoration in relation to cloth and paper and every other minute detail. His work is very much in the modern manner with strong feeling for black-and-white, and includes tiles, screens, mosaics, frescoes, etc.

VAN STOCKUM, HILDA

Born February 9, 1908, in Rotterdam. Childhood was spent first in Holland, then in Ireland where she studied at the Dublin School of Art. Attended also Academy of Art, Amsterdam, and Corcoran School of Art, Washington, D. C.

HILDA VAN STOCKUM writes: "My father was a captain in the Royal Netherlands Navy, my mother the daughter of Charles Boissevain of Huguenot ancestry. He was an author, a director of a Dutch newspaper, and he had married Emily MacDonnell, the granddaughter of the provost of Trinity College, Dublin. Because of my father, we were always traveling from one place to another. At the age of three, I supposedly drew my first masterpiece. I loved drawing. Paper and pencils always headed the list of my birthday wishes. At twelve, I was sent to a 'real artist' for lessons. He showed me many pictures and developed my taste as well as my skill. Later when we went to Ireland, I was sent to a regular art school where I learned as much or more about human nature as about drawing. Back in Holland at nineteen, I gained admission to the academy and there I was given a thorough grounding for four years. Returning to Dublin, I studied lithography and started to get commissions to illustrate primers and paint portraits. This was interrupted by my meeting Ervin Ross Marlin from New York, who was studying history at Trinity College. We married, and in 1934 I set foot in New York for the first time. Since then it has been mostly books and babies and will be, I hope, for some time." Hilda van Stockum lives in Montreal.

VAUGHAN, ANNE

Born October 2, 1913, in Worcester, Massachusetts, where childhood was spent with summers on Monhegan Island, Maine. Attended Boston Museum of Fine Arts School and Ecole des Beaux Arts, Fontainebleau, France.

"LIKE many members of my family," Anne Vaughan says, "I started painting at the age of two, and I hope I will never have to stop. After finishing school, I designed textiles and toys in New York and later started illustrating, which I like the best of all. At the present time, I am teaching design one day a week at the Worcester Art Museum School, working on my own painting the rest of the week."

VOX, MAXIMILIEN

AN article by Charles Saumier in *L'Amour de l'Art*, No. 2, February 1928, says that the years of World War I turned, for Maximilien Vox, into serious illness involving a long convalescence and rest at the Côte d'Azur. There he and his wife practised the use of the burin and the graver and developed themselves in the art of wood engraving. Mme. Vox became a skillful engraver, working under the pseudonym, "Ariel." Vox made ten frontispieces for the *Hundred Frontispieces* published by Schmidt. In 1920 he engraved his *Six Figures for Shakespeare*. Also illustrated *Balzac in Slippers*. "It was with *Micromegas* and *Lucien Leuwen* that he began to free himself from the timidities of his debut." He worked first for Bernard Grasset and then for Plon. The printer, Charles Peignot, asked him to edit the foundry organ, *Divertissements Typographiques*, as Vox himself states in his own article on the type foundry of Deberny and Peignot in *Gebrauchsgraphik* (vol. 9, 1932). In 1933 he illustrated an edition of Jane Austen which is known as the Vox Edition, to which Professor Emile Legouis, a distinguished French authority on English Literature, contributed the general introduction. For this edition Vox not only made pictures in color and in black-and-white, but designed the format and assisted in the whole production.

WALTON, CECILE
Born March 22, 1891, in Glasgow, Scotland. Studied in London, Edinburgh and Paris.

CECILE WALTON ROBERTSON is a painter and sculptor. Her husband is Eric H. M. Robertson of Edinburgh. She has exhibited at the Royal Academy and with the Royal Society of Painters in Water Colour, London; the London International; Berlin International and in Pittsburgh, Pennsylvania. Her work is owned by Galleries in Dunedin, New Zealand, and Liverpool, England. This information was obtained from *Who's Who in Art.*

WARD, LYND KENDALL
Born June 26, 1905, in Chicago. Childhood was spent in Evanston, Illinois; Newton, Massachusetts; and Englewood, New Jersey. Attended Columbia University and State Academy of Graphic Arts, Leipzig, Germany.

"LYND WARD majored in Fine Arts at Columbia University," Mrs. Ward writes, "and then went to Leipzig, Germany, where he studied graphic arts. On his return he published his first woodcut novel, *God's Man*, followed by five others, *Mad Man's Drum, Wild Pilgrimage, Prelude to a Million Years, Song Without Words*, and *Vertigo*. Lynd Ward is probably best known as a wood engraver, for his woodcut novels, without text, were the first published in this country. But he refuses to be typed in any one medium, and frequently works in water color, oil, lithography, in color as well as black-and-white, and mezzotint. His interests are as varied in the books he illustrates as they are in the art media he employs, and he gets as much pleasure from putting a children's book into pictures as he does the interpretation of adult ideas into form and color and visual life. In 1942 he received the Carteret Book Club Award for Book Illustration, and his books have been included often in the "Fifty Books" selections of the American Institute of Graphic Arts. He has had prints purchased for the permanent collections of the Library of Congress and the Newark Museum. He is vice-president of the American League of Artists, and takes an active interest in the organization. Among the outstanding books Lynd Ward has illustrated for the Limited Editions Club and the Heritage Press are *For Whom the Bell Tolls, In Praise of Folly, Les Misérables,* and *The Count of Monte Cristo.* He lives with his wife (May McNeer) and two children in Leonia, New Jersey, where he works in a studio he has remodeled from an old carriage-room in his barn. He believes in long work days, enlivened principally by his young daughters and his dog, and he takes a little time off occasionally for only two hobbies, playing the accordion and building stone fireplaces, walks and walls." A particular environment which has influenced his work to some extent is his summer home in Canada, far back in the woods, where Lynd Ward has spent a part of almost every year since early childhood.

WATSON, ALDREN AULD

Born May 10, 1917, in Brooklyn, New York. Childhood was spent in New York and Massachusetts. Attended Friends School, Brooklyn, and Art Students League, New York.

"I GREW up in a family of artists," Aldren Watson writes, "with time divided between the city and the country. In the latter, I helped with the chores, built fences, did carpentry, stone masonry, cabinet work. My father's skill embraced a variety of work over and above the fine arts. The toys he made for us stimulated in me a love of craftsmanship, not only in art, but in life. Educated in a Quaker school, I have been a field worker for the American Friends Service Committee for the past four years. In line of duty I have earned a living for my wife and two children, Peter and Wendy, by carpentry, timber cutting, farming. I build furniture in my own shop completely fitted with hand tools. I have my own printing press and bookbinding equipment. Out of this background of education and experience come my illustrations: these are the roots." The Watsons live in Ho-Ho-Kus, New Jersey.

WAUGH, DOROTHY

Born in Burlington, Vermont. Childhood was spent there and in Amherst, Massachusetts, with summers on Grand Isle, Lake Champlain. Attended George School, Massachusetts School of Art, Chicago Art Institute School, and Massachusetts State College. Also evening courses at other art institutions in various parts of the country.

DOROTHY WAUGH writes that while studying at the art school in Boston she worked in landscape architects' offices drawing, designing, making models and supervising work in the field. While studying at the Art Institute School, Chicago, she worked in a commercial art studio doing layout, finished art work, lettering and illustration and copywriting for books, magazines and newspapers. Since 1931 Miss Waugh has done all kinds of art work for publishers in New York, including a series of posters and poster-stickers for the National Park Service. She has handled design and production for the National Park Service, William E. Rudge's Sons, the Montclair Public Library (New Jersey), and others. She has taught graphic arts processes at Cooper Union School of Art and at Parsons School of Design. From May 1937 to January 1940, she was children's editor for Alfred A. Knopf. Miss Waugh has also done considerable writing for newspapers and journals as well as for her own books. She lives in New York City.

WEBB, CLIFFORD CYRIL

Born February 14, 1895, in London. Childhood was spent in Essex. Attended Westminster School of Art, London.

CLIFFORD WEBB writes: "I can remember drawing on the stone floor in the kitchen with colored chalks at the age of seven, emulating the pavement artists I so much admired. That, I think, was the beginning and I have had a soft spot for the pavement artist ever since. At school I somehow managed to do a fair amount of drawing, though the school authority showed little interest in art in those days. Later as a soldier serving in Egypt, Iraq and India, the color and movement and excitement of trying to transfer my impressions to canvas or paper decided my career. The children's books I have done, just one part of my art, were created for my own children, illustrated and written with them and their instructions were carried out. The illustrations were completed first, the text being written around the illustrations. Books for children have always given me a great deal of pleasure to do. I hope I have succeeded in keeping a few thousand children quiet and interested and given poor parents like myself the chance to get on with their work." Clifford Webb lives in Abinger Hammer, Surrey.

WEBBER, IRMA ELEANOR SCHMIDT

Born August 16, 1904, in San Diego, California, where childhood was spent until teen age; then in Berkeley. Attended University of California (A.B. 1926), (M.A. 1927), (Ph.D. 1929).

"WHEN I was a small child," Irma Webber writes, "my mother, whose hobby was art, decided that I should grow up to be an artist. All through my early years she kept me well supplied with art materials and during school vacations took me to art classes with her. My high school electives included art and when I enrolled at the University of California I intended to major in art. However, at the end of my freshman year I found myself the top ranking student in elementary botany and decidedly allergic to a certain art professor. In preference to taking sophomore art work with that professor I changed my major to botany. Scholarships and a Teaching Fellowship in Botany were granted me, and later an A.B. with honors in Botany, followed by a Teachers Credential, and M.A. and Ph.D. In 1927 I married my botanical classmate, John Milton Webber. Our children, a boy and a girl, stimulated my dormant interest in books for children. Their interest in nature, and their praise of pictures I drew to amuse them, caused me to digress from botanical research and try my hand as an author and illustrator of children's nature books." Irma Webber lives in Riverside, California.

ARMSTRONG SPERRY: *Call It Courage*

WEBER, WALTER ALOIS

Born May 23, 1906, in Chicago where childhood was spent "mostly at the Zoo," and where he attended Church School of Art, University of Chicago, Chicago Art Institute and American Academy of Art.

"My natural interest in animals and the burning desire to draw them," writes Walter Weber, "was encouraged by my seventh grade teacher, Mrs. Thompson. She was one of those 'unforgettable characters.' She paid my first semester's tuition at the Saturday morning class at the Church School of Art. After that I worked on scholarships. Through her, too, I was introduced to the scientific staff of the Field Museum in Chicago. These contacts all helped in getting the proper education both in natural history and art, so necessary to an animal artist. My training at the University of Chicago was strictly in biology. Later I attended the Art Institute and served as scientific artist on the staffs of the Field Museum (now the Chicago Natural History Museum), the United States National Museum and the National Park Service. In connection with my work I went on several expeditions: to the South Seas, Panama, Bermuda, Southern Mexico, British Columbia, and to every state in the Union except two, always to gather material for paintings of wild life. One of the highlights in my life was six months spent in Canada with the late Major Allen Brooks, famous Canadian bird artist. Since 1943 I have been a free-lance artist working at my home studio near Vienna, Virginia."

WEISGARD, LEONARD

Born December 13, 1916, in New Haven, Connecticut. Childhood was spent in England, and in New York and Brooklyn. Attended Pratt Institute.

Leonard Weisgard's father was English and much of his childhood was spent in Manchester, Liverpool and London. He attended public schools in New York and after two years at Pratt Institute left to earn his living as a commercial artist. He worked for several New York publications — the *New Yorker*, Crowell-Collier Publications, Condé Nast, *Harper's Bazaar*, etc. — all the while trying to write and illustrate children's books. "My first piece of art work was a valentine painted for a school teacher," he says. "All through my childhood I developed a great distaste for traditional book illustration, especially the kind used in the city school systems where all the wonderful world was depicted dismally and usually in ugly orange. Children's books, and all types of books, for me have been affected by most primitive art forms, from the African Congo cave drawings and sculpture, through the fine work done in primitive German Bible illustrations, their excellent sense of design, the imagination and daring of French children's books, the fine

reality and texture and tactile approach of Russian children's books, and the wonderful, unexplored work of the early American primitives, and the more refined Audubon. I now live and work in Danbury, Connecticut, and want to help produce better and better books."

WELLS, PETER

Born January 8, 1912, in Port Clinton, Ohio. Childhood was spent in Ohio and Bronxville, New York. Attended Morristown Academy, and Yale University (A.B. 1935).

"The war was an unpleasant interruption," Peter Wells writes, "just as I seemed to be getting started. I officered PT 220 in operations at New Guinea, Leyte, Mindoro and Brunei Bay, Borneo, and had a wonderful crew aboard. Most of the drawing I've done during the war was for my crew who all seemed to have children or female charmers with a birthday next week. I did manage to write and/or draw two books for my publishers but wartime paper commitments have been keeping these masterpieces from the eager nippers. I believe that humor is the best possible of all fields for juvenile writing and that the modern world has plenty of it to offer — but doesn't. Why is everyone so serious these days when there are so many delightful mistakes being made all around us? My goal is a comic strip that *is* comic, and my chosen prophet is the late George Herriman who did 'Krazy Kat.' This may not sound like much of a literary project, but I am very tired of un-funny funny papers. My children's books have been my recreation while working for King Features Syndicate — and a lot of fun for me. I have a wife, and three small sons who are rather hard to amuse, so they keep me on my toes. We live in the woods back of Stamford, Connecticut." At Yale, Peter Wells majored in Fine Arts Courses, and was Art Editor of the *Yale Record* as Peter Arno had been in earlier years. He married Helen Rollins during his junior year at Yale. In vacations he worked as deck hand and wireless operator and sailed as far as Russia. In 1942 he was art director for a record company, doing designs for victrola record albums. He has done advertising writing, made comic strip advertisements, and has assisted on the comic strip, "Cap Stubbs and Tippie." His *Mr. Tootwhistle's Invention* won the New York *Herald Tribune* Children's Book Award in the spring of 1942.

WELLS, RHEA

Born September 24, 1891, in Jonesboro, Tennessee. Childhood was spent in Tennessee and Alabama. Attended Maryville College, Chicago Art Institute School, and Hochschule für den Bildenden Künst, Berlin.

Born in the mountains of Tennessee, Rhea Wells lived first in his native town and then in Birmingham, Alabama, until, at seventeen, he went to Chicago to study at the Art Institute. His name is a surname, pronounced to rhyme with "gay." After three years of study he returned to Birmingham to work for a newspaper. In 1913 he went to New York but soon after that was in uniform for a period of armed service. After the war he studied for a year in Germany, but it was while spending some time in the Austrian Alps that he got the idea for the children's biographies of animals which resulted first in *Peppi the Duck*. After another European visit, *Coco the Goat* with a Spanish setting was produced and *Beppo the Donkey* with a Sicilian background. Other books have followed which he has both written and illustrated. At present, Rhea Wells is back in the mountains of Tennessee, living at Jonesboro.

WHEELHOUSE, M. V.

Born in Yorkshire, England. Attended Académie Delecture, Paris.

"THE only art school in which I ever worked," Miss Wheelhouse has written, "was the one mentioned above where I spent some three years a long time ago. After that I settled in London and worked hard. My first success as an illustrator was when, together with a friend, Miss Christina Whyte, I won a competition in *The Bookman*. The winning fairy story was *The Adventures of Merrywink* and the pictures were mine. My second book was a great contrast — illustrations for *Les Maîtres Sonneurs* by George Sand, for George Bell & Sons. After that I did many other books for the same publishers, my greatest pleasure being those charming stories by Mrs. Ewing brought out in their Queen's Treasures Series, and Mrs. Molesworth's *Carrots*. I did other books in the same series. Perhaps one of the nicest children's books I ever illustrated was E. V. Lucas's *Slowcoach*." Miss Wheelhouse lives now in Cambridge, England, where she has a little shop.

WIESE, KURT

Born April 22, 1887, in Minden, Germany, where childhood was spent.

KURT WIESE says that in Minden he lived for fifteen years under a remarkable collection of paintings of the Düsseldorf School. "However, to become an artist was something unheard of, so I was sent to Hamburg to learn the export trade to China. After being able to count the threads of a ten-schilling shirting just by feeling it with my hands, I was sent out to China. I arrived there at the time of a revolution, but I spent the next six years traveling and selling merchandise until the war with Japan broke out. Captured by the Japanese and handed over to the British, I was sent to Australia and lived for five years in the Australian bush as a prisoner of war. These years gave me the courage to throw the Chinese trade into the Australian dust and do the thing I wanted to do. Thus I began to draw. When I returned to Germany, via Africa, the work was a big success and I sold my whole production to a publisher. He gave up when the gold mark came back to life, and as I had no coal for the winter and a strong desire to live under a warm sun and a régime of paper money, I left for Brazil. There followed a year of traveling through another revolution, through jungles, meeting Indians. Another year of illustrating schoolbooks and children's books for a Brazilian publisher, then doing newspaper cartoons and a children's page. Wanderlust seized me again. This time I landed in New York. Now I live on a farm in Frenchtown, New Jersey, near the Delaware River." Since his first book was published in the United States in 1928, Mr. Wiese has illustrated more than a hundred books.

WILKIN, ELOISE BURNS

Born March 30, 1904, in Rochester, New York. Childhood was spent in New York and in Rochester. Attended Rochester Institute of Technology.

ELOISE WILKIN was the third child in a family of four artistically inclined children. Her mother was an accomplished pianist, her father was a writer on the *New York Sun*. At eleven, she won a prize in a Wanamaker Drawing Contest for New York school children; this marked the beginning of her career. She writes: "After completing the Illustration Course at the Institute of Technology in Rochester, I commenced free-lancing and after a year went to New York with a portfolio bigger than I was. My first morning there I went into the Century Company, came back with a book to illustrate, and wired home to my family that I was made! After four years of this kind of pleasant experience and some rebuffs, I was married. Now I live with my husband and our four children in an old stone house outside of Canandaigua, New York; a Persian cat, an English setter and a peppy pony all live there too."

WILLIAMS, GARTH

Born April 16, 1912, in New York. Childhood was spent in New Jersey, Ontario, Canada, and England. Attended in England City of London School, Westminster Art School, and Royal College of Art.

THE parents of Garth Williams were both artists. His father worked for *Punch* and New York publications. Brought up in New Jersey on a farm, and in Ontario, Canada, he was taken to Sutton, Surrey, England, at the age of ten for his schooling. In 1929 Garth Williams went to the Westminster Art School. In 1931 he won a special talent scholarship for oil painting to the Royal College of Art, where he studied mural technique and the craft of painting. During the first of four years at the College he started sculpture in the evenings at the Westminster Art School to improve his drawing. He soon became fully absorbed in sculpture. Graduating in 1934, he won a post-graduate scholarship. After finishing his studies at the Royal College of Art, he organized Luton Art School (1935-36), painted murals including those for the Earl Dudley in Belgrave Square, etc. Garth Williams won the British Prix de Rome for Sculpture in 1936. He returned from Rome in 1938, having studied art in Italy, France, Germany, Hungary, Jugoslavia, Albania, Greece, Turkey, Holland, and Czechoslovakia. In 1938 and 1939, Garth Williams made a number of portrait busts, and became art editor on a proposed woman's magazine. When the Second World War came on, he joined the British Red Cross Civilian Defense, resigning in 1941 after his back was injured in the blitz on London. In November 1941 he returned to the United States and offered his services unsuccessfully to the American Civil Defence and as a camofleur. He made lenses in a war plant until 1943 when his health forced him to rest and he began working for the *New Yorker*. Since 1944 he has devoted almost all his time to book illustrating. He has two daughters by his first marriage and lives in New York.

WILSON, EDWARD A.

Born March 4, 1886, in Glasgow, Scotland. Childhood was spent first in Rotterdam, and then in Chicago, where he attended Chicago Art Institute; also Howard Pyle's School, Wilmington.

As a child Edward Wilson lived for a few years in Rotterdam, Holland. Then, in 1893, his family came to the United States and settled in Chicago, but memories of the tall spars along the quays of Rotterdam were not forgotten and led young Edward to making several voyages on lumber schooners of the Great Lakes. In Chicago he attended night school of the Art Institute. After leaving the Pyle School, Mr. Wilson established his own studio, living and working in New York and Truro, Massachusetts. In 1913 he married Dorothy Roe, and has two daughters. Long known as an outstanding illustrator, Mr. Wilson has also produced stage designs, designs for bookplates, silks, posters, and furniture, and has drawn for advertising, magazines and books. His drawings are in the Metropolitan Museum, New York Public Library, Library of Congress, and in private collections. He won the Art Director Medal, 1926 and 1930; Isidor Prize, 1927; Shaw Prize, 1942. He lives in Brooklyn and Truro, Massachusetts.

WILWERDING, WALTER JOSEPH

Born February 13, 1891, in Winona, Minnesota, where childhood was spent. Attended Minneapolis School of Fine Art.

WALTER WILWERDING writes that he began drawing animals at four, covering every smooth space he could find with crayon and chalk drawings of beasts and birds. "At nine, when I was allowed to borrow books from the Library, I read everything they had about nature and animals. Spare hours after school and holidays were spent in the hills and woods that surrounded Winona. I was sure that I wanted to be a naturalist. At fifteen, I was apprenticed to a taxidermist, working for him after high school hours. Three years of this convinced me that I did not want to work with dead animals. I went to art school and spent many years sketching animals in zoos and in the wilds, and I still do this. It was not until 1919 that I was given my first opportunity to illustrate a book about animals. Some years later I went to East Africa to draw and paint the wild life, and soon I had commenced writing and illustrating short stories about animals. My first book followed after I had made a second trip to East Africa. Now I specialize in paintings of big game animals for exhibition." Walter Wilwerding lives in Minneapolis.

WINTER, MILO KENDALL

Born August 7, 1888, in Princeton, Illinois. Childhood was spent first in Grand Rapids, then in Detroit, Michigan. Attended Chicago Art Institute School.

"I HAVE always lived in the Middle West, my home now being in Lake Forest, Illinois," writes Milo Winter. "My art training was started at the Chicago Art Institute and finished abroad. Illustrating for children has always been the most interesting field for me, though I have departed from it at times. The whimsical and imaginative side of juvenile illustration has been the type of work that I feel I do best, for the obvious reason that I like it most. In 1912 I married Mary Adams. We have two sons: Milo, Jr., painter and teacher at the Rhode Island School of Design, and Munroe Adams, who has been abroad with the Army, making and distributing Occupational maps."

WONSETLER, JOHN CHARLES

Born August 25, 1900, in Camden, New Jersey, where childhood was spent. Attended Philadelphia Museum School of Industrial Art.

"I WAS born of a long line of Pennsylvania Dutch with their innate love of color, beauty and order," says John Charles Wonsetler. "My first tangible influence toward

374 ILLUSTRATORS OF CHILDREN'S BOOKS

a career in art was the Doré Bible given me by my mother when I was six. Unconsciously I absorbed the dramatic force of the great French master. Later I discovered Howard Pyle in the city's Libraries. These two did more than anything else to shape my ambitions. When embarked on my career at the Museum School in Philadelphia, I found myself — like many of the present-day illustrators — a 'grand pupil' of Howard Pyle. Through Thornton Oakley I gained the tenets and teachings of the American master of illustration. Graduating from the school in 1925 with the first prize in illustration, I turned to mural painting and executed many commissions. In 1939 I began the work that had always been of greatest interest to me — illustrating magazines and books for children. Two years later my wife and I saw our first book published, *Me and the General*." John Charles Wonsetler lives in New York.

WOOD, HARRIE

Born April 28, 1902, in Rushford, New York, where childhood was spent. Attended Art Students League, New York, and Pratt Institute.

"My life as an artist," Harrie Wood writes, "was a triple one — painting, book illustration and commercial art, until the last named crowded out the first two. In 1928 I married Marni Wood and have two sons, David and John. My hobbies are gardening and collecting Children's Books. In recent years, while drawing largely for magazines, I have illustrated three books for grownups: *Parties on a Shoestring* by Wood. *Friday to Monday Gardening* by Goldsmith and *Right in Your Own Backyard* by Steck." Mr. Wood lives in Bethel, Connecticut.

WOOD, LAWSON

Born August 23, 1878, in London. Childhood was spent in Surrey where he was educated privately. Attended Slade School of Art.

"My father was Pinhorn Wood, landscape painter, and my grandfather L. J. Wood, R.I., famous for architectural work," writes Mr. Lawson Wood. "Consequently I was given full freedom to develop my natural love for art. My childhood spent in the country endeared animals to me, both to paint and to work actively for their welfare all my life. At sixteen I went to art school in London, studying drawing only. In color work I am self-taught. Later I joined the staff of the late Sir Arthur Pearson, publisher, remaining six years and gaining valuable practical experience and appreciation of the value of versatility in commercial work. I have traveled extensively and voyaged in all kinds of craft for 'copy.' I am a keen lover of out-door life and my recreations are sea-fishing and riding. For many years I have kept a number of horses but not for riding to hounds, for I dislike killing anything. I hate untidiness and keep everything connected with my work — studio, materials and business — in strict order. During World War I, I served in France for nearly three years as an officer in the Balloon Wing of the Royal Flying Corps and at GHQ." Mr. Wood was one of the many bombed out of his home in Eastbourne in 1942.

WOODROFFE, PAUL VINCENT

Born January 25, 1875, at Madras Residency, India. Childhood was spent in Bath, England. Attended Stonyhurst College and Slade School of Art.

WHEN studying art in London, Paul Woodroffe won a first prize for life drawing. Starting on his career as an artist, he early went in for stained glass, carrying out the work at his studio in Chipping Camden and later at Bisley, Gloucestershire. Among other work he designed and executed, after competition, the series of "Rosary" windows for the Lady Chapel of St. Patrick's Cathedral in New York. Paul Woodroffe is recognized as a heraldic and typographic designer. He has been a member of the Art Workers Guild since 1902, and sometime member of the Master Glass Painters Guild. He lives at Axminster, Devon.

WOODWARD, ALICE BOLINGBROKE

Born October 3, 1862, in London, where childhood was spent. Taught at home by governesses. Attended Royal College of Art and Westminster Art School, London; Académie Julian, Paris.

"My father was Dr. Henry Woodward, F.R.S., Keeper of Geology at the British Museum. I was the middle one of seven children. At eight, with two older sisters, I used to draw in the Greek and Roman Galleries at the British Museum. Ruskin once gave us a drawing lesson. From our earliest childhood we all wanted to be artists and drew pictures to all our games and the stories we read or invented. We also easily drew diagrams for my father's lectures and made scientific drawings for him and his friends. I earned in this way the large sum of twenty pounds, and on that started my student days at South Kensington, paying with my earnings for my teaching and my clothes, studying when I could afford it. After a time I went to Westminster and worked under Professor Fred Brown. I also spent three months in Paris at Académie Julian, under Amand Jean. Some of my drawings were published in the *Daily Graphic*. While at Westminster, Mr. Joseph Pennell was good enough to be interested in my work and blew my trumpet for me with the

KATHERINE MILHOUS: *Book for Jennifer*

result that Macmillan and Dent each gave me a book and I got some work on the *Daily Chronicle* which was just starting illustrations. I was frightfully proud, all the others on this job being bigwigs like Whistler. The first studio owned by my sisters and me was in Lunerston Street, Chelsea. It had belonged to Bart, the Costumier, and Oliver Maddox Brown had worked there. We afterwards turned a stable at the back of our house in Chelsea into a studio. Then we moved to Notting Hill. During World War I, I worked at map drawing for the Naval Intelligence Bureau and afterwards we came to Bushey at Hertfordshire and I bought an old studio which had belonged to the Herkomer Colony, which I still use. I have also done a lot of restorations of prehistoric animals for the *Illustrated London News*."

WOODWARD, HILDEGARD

Born February 10, 1898, in Worcester, Massachusetts, where childhood was spent. Attended Museum of Fine Arts School, Boston.

" I GREW up and was educated in New England surroundings, with a New England conscience and a substantial practical sense inherited from Dutch and English pioneer antecedents," Hildegard Woodward writes, " and always there was in me a strong inclination to be an artist. My formal art training was freed somewhat from academic bonds by trips to Europe, study in Paris, and an unconquerable desire to work out painting in my own way. Joining a group of young working artists in Boston started my professional career. Through the illustrator, Marguerite Davis, I began to learn something about the technique of book illustration and made my first contact with a publisher. Years of good stiff training followed, both in drawing and bookmaking, relieved by summers of painting on the coast of Maine and a trip or two to Mexico. New York contacts and contracts with Louise Seaman and the Macmillan Company motivated my move from Boston. More illustrating followed and parallel to the struggle to take root in New York ran the underlying desire to be a painter. I started writing my own books after a while and continued teaching in art schools in Boston and later in private schools in New York. Despite living and working in the city, I have acquired a small place in Connecticut where the real living and the real work go on."

YEATS, JACK BUTLER

Born about 1871 in Sligo, Ireland, where childhood was spent. Educated privately.

As a painter of Irish life and landscapes, Jack Butler Yeats is well known and well represented in Irish and English galleries and in some American ones. His childhood was spent among the mountains and little lakes of County Sligo and his early life was a compound of natural beauty and artistic influences. His father was the distinguished artist, John Butler Yeats, a member of the Royal Hibernian Academy. William Butler Yeats, the poet, was his brother. In addition to his painting, Jack Butler Yeats has written and illustrated several books. He says, " When I search for any artistic influences which may have in some way affected my drawings for children, I remember that I was a child when the books of Randolph Caldecott and Walter Crane were first published: and it would be a shabby-souled child who would not be carried off the ground by *The Three Jovial Huntsmen, John Gilpin, The Hind in the Wood* and *The Fairy Ship*." Mr. Yeats's home is in Dublin and he is a Governor and Guardian of the National Gallery of Ireland.

PART III. BIBLIOGRAPHIES

Compiled by

LOUISE PAYSON LATIMER

A. B. FROST : *Uncle Remus; His Songs
and His Sayings*

F. O. C. DARLEY : *Rip Van Winkle*

A Century and a Half of Illustration

ILLUSTRATION is probably the oldest of the arts. Its history divides roughly into three periods: (1) Before the Manuscript; (2) The Manuscript; and (3) The Printed Book. Period one embraced carvings on bones, on stones, on wood, in caves, in temples, in tombs, and all sorts of primitive messages in picture form, including the symbols which became our alphabet. In period two the miniaturist, the decorator, and the scribe united to make books which have never been equalled for sheer beauty but which were available to very few. Period three followed the advent of printing in the Western World. Books became more abundant and a golden age of illustration, particularly in Germany, began.

But it was long, weary years before children in any country had their own books. With the *Orbis Sensualium Pictus* by John Amos Comenius, an Austrian, published in Nürnberg in 1657 and translated into English in 1658 as *Visible World*, came a faint ray of light for children. This book, which has been called "the first picture book for children," was printed in two columns, one in High Dutch, one in Latin, each page having a crude woodcut aimed to please children. Though a textbook, it evidently did please them, as well as their elders, for it was used in translation throughout Europe for a hundred years or more.

Over a century later came the dawning of the child's day and it came for the most part in England. Indeed for generations the child was indebted mainly to England for his books. Some of these were written and illustrated to entertain him and to satisfy his taste, rather than to inform or reform him. It was at last realized that "the use of books for pleasure is the most satisfactory recreation."[1]

Most of the great illustrators in England and America at one time or another illustrated children's books. This was uniquely true in England. It was also true in England that a large proportion of the artists did some illustrating. Thus these bibliographies not only picture illustrators working especially for children but also most of the illustrators and many of the artists, not primarily illustrators, of the last century and a half.

379

Unfortunately, in America in the Nineteenth Century, some of the best illustrators overlooked children entirely. Unfortunately, too, much of their best work appeared only in magazines and thus is practically lost to present-day adults. Furthermore, a school of able artists, influenced perhaps by Charles Dana Gibson, tended to picture a rather circumscribed contemporary society in magazines and books of ephemeral interest. But we had our Darley, our Pyle, our Frost, our Kemble, our Birch, our Bensell, our Herford, our Newell and many another. What a pity that Edwin A. Abbey, from whom some outstanding English illustration derived, never illustrated a book for children!

These bibliographies aim to give a picture of books illustrated especially for children, or joyously adopted by them, from the first identifiable illustrator of such books to the present time. They include illustrated American and English books which seem of sufficient merit to warrant inclusion. Foreign books, available in translation, are also listed. The original date of the illustrated edition is given.

The lists are not exhaustive in titles since this would result in prohibitive length. When a list could not be complete, effort was made to select the most representative examples of the work of the particular artist. This was done by examination of a large proportion of the books.

Bibliographic work is not easy for a number of reasons: Insufficient data in the national libraries; the tendency of publishers in England and America to omit the name or signature of the illustrator; inability of some publishers to identify the illustrators of their older books ("It is a wise father that knows his own child"); lack of full names of authors and illustrators; coy pseudonyms, and birth dates coyly withheld; changing names of illustrators, authors, and publishers in mid-stream; elusiveness of birth and death dates and even the nationalities of some illustrators; lack of dates of publication.

In a collection of about 2500 illustrated books twenty-eight per cent carry no date. Of these, twenty per cent are English publications, or printed in England, but carrying an American imprint. Eight per cent were published in America. A purchaser of one of these books may be buying a first edition or a tenth (and who can inform him?). "Let the punishment fit the crime!"

Something has been done in the last twenty-five years to improve these conditions, but is it too much to hope that all publishers in England and America will some day give full bibliographic information to the national libraries that they may give complete data on their catalog cards? And could these same publishers be persuaded to maintain an index of their own publications? It would be impossible to estimate the yearly cost of such omissions to libraries, bibliographers, collectors, agents and booksellers. Detective work is not only expensive but time-consuming.

In the preparation of these bibliographies the compiler has had able and continuous assistance from her associates, Elsie Sinclair MacDonald, Evelyn Wainwright Turpin and Nancy Lee Bradfield.

Examining many of the listed books has been a revelation, a treat, and an education. Beginning with the lovable little books with woodcuts plain and woodcuts hand-colored and continuing through the fine work being done today, an adult can revel as does the child. For it should be remembered that an infallible test of a child's book is that it appeals to the adult also. This holds for both the content and the illustration.

Bereft is the child and limited is the adult who has not trod the pleasant ways and garnered the lasting memories of books written and illustrated for children and of the inimitable characters in these books which even today thread adult literature.

While children owe a great debt to the illustrator, the illustrator in turn is indebted to the child. Walter Crane's words written in 1896 are even truer today: "Children's books and so-called children's books hold a peculiar position. They are attractive to designers of an imaginative tendency, for in a sober and matter-of-fact age they afford perhaps the only outlet for unrestricted flights of fancy open to the modern illustrator, who likes to revolt against 'the despotism of facts'."[2] Children, too, like to and do revolt against "the despotism of facts." Let us hope that they always will!

LOUISE PAYSON LATIMER

JOHN LEECH : *Comic Latin Grammar*

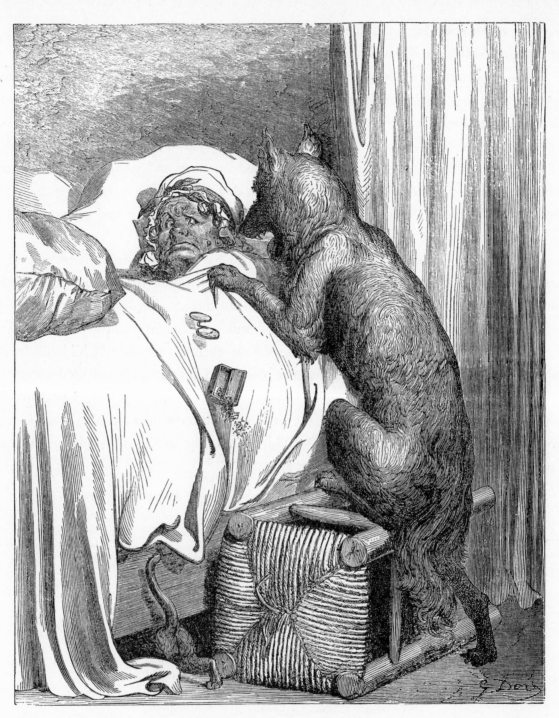

GUSTAV DORÉ: *Popular Fairy Tales*

A BIBLIOGRAPHY OF ILLUSTRATORS
AND THEIR WORKS

HANS TEGNER : *Fairy Tales by Hans Christian Andersen*

BIRKET FOSTER: *Pictures of English Landscape*

THOMAS BEWICK: *British Birds*

A Bibliography of Illustrators and Their Works

" *What is the use of a book,*" thought Alice,
" *without pictures or conversations.*"

—LEWIS CARROLL. *Alice's Adventures in Wonderland*

ABBEY, EDWIN AUSTIN (1852-1911) American
Black. *Judith Shakespeare.* Harper. 1884
Dickens. *Christmas Stories.* Harper. 1875
Goldsmith. *Deserted Village.* Harper. 1902
Goldsmith. *She Stoops to Conquer.* Harper. 1901
Herrick. *Selections from the Hesperides and Noble Numbers of Robert Herrick.* Harper. 1882
Longfellow. *Poetical Works of Henry Wadsworth Longfellow,* 3 v. (with DARLEY and others). Houghton. 1880-83
Old Songs (with A. W. PARSONS). Macmillan. 1889
"*Quiet Life.*" Certain Verses by Various Hands (with A. W. PARSONS). Harper. 1890
Shakespeare. *Comedies of William Shakespeare,* 4 v. Harper. 1896
Sheridan. *Rivals and The School for Scandal* (with others). Chatto. 1885
Stevens. *King Arthur Stories.* Houghton. 1908

ABBOTT, ELENORE PLAISTED (1873-1935) American
Alcott. *Old-fashioned Girl.* Little. 1926
Andersen. *Fairy Tales.* Macrae. 1917
Defoe. *Life of Robinson Crusoe.* Macrae. 1913
Grimm. *Fairy Tales.* Scribner. 1920
Hawthorne. *Wonder Book and Tanglewood Tales.* Macrae. 1926
Stevenson. *Kidnapped.* Macrae. 1915
Wyss. *Swiss Family Robinson.* Macrae. 1914

ABSOLON, JOHN (1815-1895) English
Courtship and Wedding of the Little Man and the Little Maid. Grant and Griffith. 1840
Howitt. *Lillieslea.* Routledge. 1860
Mackarness. *Sunbeam Stories.* Routledge. 1875
Mackarness. *Sunbeam Stories,* Second Series. Routledge. 1875

Mother Goose. *History of Little Bo-Peep.* Addey. 1855
Norton. *Aunt Carry's Ballads for Children.* Cundall. 1847
Songs for the Little Ones at Home (with BIRKET FOSTER). Bickers. 1863
Southey. *Three Bears* (with H. W. WEIR). Addey. 1850
Stoeber. *Curate's Favorite Pupil.* Orr. 1844
Tytler. *Wonder Seeker.* Grant and Griffith. 1846

ADAMS, JOHN WOLCOTT (1874-1925) American
Riley. *Hoosier Romance.* Century. 1910

ADELBORG, EVA OTTILIA (1855-1936) Swedish
Adelborg. *Clean Peter.* Longmans. 1901

ALAJÁLOV, CONSTANTIN (1900-   ) American, b. in Russia
Miller. *Cinderella.* Coward. 1943

ALCOTT, ABBA MAY (1840-1879) American
Alcott. *Little Women.* Part 1. Roberts. 1868

ALDIN, CECIL CHARLES WINDSOR (1870-1935) English
Aldin. *Bunnyborough.* Milford. 1919
Aldin. *Farm Yard Puppies.* Oxford. n.d.
Aldin. *Great Adventure.* Milford. 1921
Aldin. *Just among Friends.* Eyre and Spottiswoode. 1934
Aldin. *Mongrel Puppy Book.* Frowde. 1912
Aldin. *Old Inns.* Heinemann. 1921
Aldin. *Old Manor Houses.* Heinemann. 1923
Aldin. *Us.* Milford. 1922
Aldin. *White Puppy Book.* Frowde. 1917
Barrow. *Hunting Scenes.* Scribner. 1936
Byron. *Happy Family Series,* 6 v. Frowde. 1911

385

Byron. *Jack and Jill*. Frowde. 1914
Byron. *Merry Party Series*, 6 v. Doran. 1914
Cecil Aldin Book. Eyre and Spottiswoode. 1932
De la Ramée. *Moufflou*. Nelson. 1915
Dickens. *Posthumous Papers of the Pickwick Club*,
  2 v. Chapman. 1910
Emanuel. *Dog Day*. Heinemann. 1902
Emanuel. *Dogs of War*. Bradbury, Agnew. 1906
Fleuron. *Wild Horses of Iceland*. Holt. 1933
Irving. *Old Christmas*. Hodder. 1908
Maeterlinck. *My Dog*. Allen. 1913
Masefield. *Right Royal*. Macmillan. 1922
Morton. *Who's Who in the Zoo*. Houghton. 1933
Sewell. *Black Beauty*. Jarrold. 1912
Surtees. *Handley Cross, or Mr. Jorrocks' Hunt*, 2 v.
  Longmans. 1911

ALEXANDER, JOHN WHITE (1856-1915) American
Lowell. *Vision of Sir Launfal* (with B. R. CRANE,
  FREER, GIFFORD, KAPPES, MOWBRAY, SHIRLAW and
  F. H. SMITH). Houghton. 1888

ALKEN, HENRY (1784-1851) English
Surtees. *Jorrocks' Jaunts and Jollities*. Methuen. 1843

ALLINGHAM, HELEN (1848-1926) English
Allingham. *Rhymes for the Young Folk* (with FUR-
  NISS, GREENAWAY and PATERSON). Cassell. 1887
Ewing. *Flat Iron for a Farthing*. Bell. 1903
Ewing. *Six to Sixteen*. Bell. 1899

ANDERSON, ALEXANDER (1775-1870) American
Children's Friend. Munroe & Francis. 1833
Mother Goose. *Only True Mother Goose Melodies*.
  Munroe and Francis. 1833

ANDERSON, CLARENCE WILLIAM (1891-   ) American
Anderson. *Billy and Blaze*. Macmillan. 1936
Anderson. *Black, Bay and Chestnut*. Macmillan. 1939
Anderson. *Blaze and the Forest Fire*. Macmillan. 1938
Anderson. *Blaze and the Gypsies*. Macmillan. 1937
Anderson. *Deep through the Heart*. Macmillan. 1940
Anderson. *Heads Up—Heels Down*. Macmillan. 1944
Anderson. *High Courage*. Macmillan. 1941
Anderson. *Salute*. Macmillan. 1940
Anderson. *Thoroughbreds*. Macmillan. 1942

ANDERSON, VICTOR COLEMAN (1882-1937) American
Page. *Tommy Trot's Visit to Santa Claus*. Scribner.
  1908

ANGELO, VALENTI (1897-   ) American, b. in Italy
Angelo. *Golden Gate*. Viking. 1939
Angelo. *Hill of Little Miracles*. Viking. 1942
Angelo. *Look Out Yonder*. Viking. 1943
Angelo. *Nino*. Viking. 1938
Angelo. *Paradise Valley*. Viking. 1940
Bible. *Psalms of David in the King James Version*.
  Peter Pauper. 1943
Chinese Fairy Tales. Peter Pauper. *n.d.*
Eaton. *Animals' Christmas*. Viking. 1944
Harte. *Luck of Roaring Camp and Other Stories*.
  Peter Pauper. 1943
Longfellow. *Song of Hiawatha*. Peter Pauper. 1942
Moore. *Visit from St. Nicholas*. Hawthorne. 1937

Sawyer. *Long Christmas*. Viking. 1941
Sawyer. *Roller Skates*. Viking. 1936
Vance. *Paula*. Dodd. 1939

ARDIZZONE, EDWARD JEFFREY IRVING (1900-   ) English
Ardizzone. *Little Tim and the Brave Sea Captain*.
  Oxford. 1936
Ardizzone. *Lucy Brown and Mr. Grimes*. Oxford.
  1937
Ardizzone. *Tim and Lucy Go to Sea*. Oxford. 1938
Dickens. *Great Expectations*. Heritage. 1939
Kaeser. *Mimff*. Oxford. 1939

ARMER, LAURA ADAMS (1874-   ) American
Armer. *Forest Pool*. Longmans. 1938
Armer. *Waterless Mountain* (with SIDNEY ARMER).
  Longmans. 1931

ARMER, SIDNEY (1871-   ) American
Armer. *Dark Circle of Branches*. Longmans. 1933
Armer. *Waterless Mountain* (with L. A. ARMER).
  Longmans. 1931

ARMFIELD, MAXWELL (1862-   ) English
Andersen. *Fairy Tales from Hans Andersen*. Dent.
  1910
Andersen. *Mermaid*. Dent. 1913
Andersen. *Ugly Duckling*. Dutton. 1914
Armfield. *Tales from Timbuktu*. Harcourt. 1924
Armfield. *Wonder Tales of the World*. Harcourt.
  1920
Aucassin and Nicolette. Dent. 1910
Shakespeare. *Winter's Tale*. Dent. 1922

ARTZYBASHEFF, BORIS MĪKLAĬLOVĪCH (1899-   ) Ameri-
  can, b. in Russia
Æsop. *Æsop's Fables*. Viking. 1933
Artzybasheff. *Seven Simeons*. Viking. 1937
Bianco. *Apple Tree*. Doran. 1926
Colum. *Forge in the Forest*. Macmillan. 1925
Colum. *Orpheus: Myths of the World*. Macmillan.
  1930
Dorey. *Three and the Moon*. Knopf. 1929
Fairy Shoemaker. Macmillan. 1928
Hall. *Nansen*. Viking. 1940
Herodotus. *Herodotus*. Doubleday. 1929
Mamin. *Verotchka's Tales*. Dutton. 1922
Martineau. *Feats on the Fiord*. Macmillan. 1924
Mirza. *Son of the Sword*. Viking. 1934
Mukerji. *Gay-Neck*. Dutton. 1927
Mukerji. *Ghond, the Hunter*. Dutton. 1928
Young. *Wonder Smith and His Son*. Longmans. 1927

AULAIRE, EDGAR PARIN D' *SEE* D'AULAIRE, EDGAR PARIN

AULAIRE, INGRI MORTENSON D' *SEE* D'AULAIRE, INGRI
  MORTENSON

AULT, NORMAN (1880-   ) English
Darton. *Seven Champions of Christendom*. Stokes.
  1914
Hauff. *Caravan Tales*. Wells Gardner. 1912
Macaulay. *Lays of Ancient Rome*. Dodge. 1912
Tennyson. *Poems*. Wells Gardner. 1913
Whitham. *Shepherd of the Ocean*. Wells Gardner.
  1914

AUSTEN, JOHN (1886-   ) English
Blackmore. *Lorna Doone.* Heritage. 1943
Dickens. *David Copperfield.* Heritage. 1935
Goldsmith. *Vicar of Wakefield.* Heritage. 1939
Perrault. *Tales of Passed Times.* Selwyn. 1922
Shakespeare. *As You Like It.* William Jackson. 1930
Shakespeare. *Comedy of Errors.* Limited Editions. 1939
Shakespeare. *Hamlet.* Selwyn. 1922
Thackeray. *Vanity Fair.* Limited Editions. 1931

AVINOFF, ANDREY (1884-   ) American, b. in Russia
Noel. *Magic Bird of Chomo-Lung-Ma.* Doubleday. 1931

AVISON, GEORGE (1885-   ) American
Thompson. *Gold-seeking on the Dalton Trail.* Little. 1925
Tucker. *Boy Whaleman.* Little. 1924

AYLWARD, WILLIAM JAMES (1875-   ) American
Verne. *Twenty Thousand Leagues under the Sea.* Scribner. 1925

BACON, PEGGY (1895-   ) American
Bacon. *Ballad of Tangle Street.* Macmillan. 1929
Bacon. *Lion-hearted Kitten.* Macmillan. 1927
Bacon. *Mercy and the Mouse.* Macmillan. 1928
Bacon. *Mischief in Mayfield.* Harcourt. 1933
Bacon. *Mystery at East Hatchett.* Viking. 1939
Bacon. *Terrible Nuisance.* Harcourt. 1931
Robinson. *Buttons.* Viking. 1938
Sandburg. *Rootabaga Country.* Harcourt. 1929
Twain. *Adventures of Tom Sawyer.* Peter Pauper. 1943
Untermeyer. *New Songs for New Voices.* Harcourt. 1928

BAKER, MARY (1897-   ) English
Baker. *Black Cats and the Tinker's Wife.* Duffield. 1923
Baker. *Dog, the Brownie and the Bramble Patch.* Duffield. 1924
Baker. *Little Girl Who Curtsied.* Duffield. 1925
Baker. *Lost Merbaby.* Duffield. 1927
Baker. *Mrs. Bobbity's Crust.* Blackwell. 1937
Baker. *Patsy and the Leprechaun.* Duffield. 1933
Baker. *Pedlar's Ware.* Duffield. 1925
Baker. *Pixies and the Silver Crown.* Duffield. 1927
Baker. *Tomson's Hallowe'en.* Duffield. 1929

BALDRIDGE, CYRUS LE ROY (1889-   ) American
Bible. *Parables.* Harper. 1942
Cooper. *Spy.* Minton. 1924
Davis. *Pepperfoot of Thursday Market.* Harper. 1925
Kang. *Happy Grove.* Scribner. 1933
Price. *Middle Country.* World. 1926
Singer. *Ali Lives in Iran.* Holiday. 1937
Singer. *Boomba Lives in Africa.* Holiday. 1935
Singer. *Santa Claus Comes to America.* Knopf. 1942

BALL, ROBERT (1890-   ) American
Akers. *Sleepy Tom.* Putnam. 1939
Brink. *Lad with a Whistle.* Macmillan. 1941.
Orton. *Treasure in the Little Trunk.* Stokes. 1932
Pace. *Clara Barton.* Scribner. 1941
Tennyson. *Idylls of the King.* Heritage. 1939

BANNERMAN, HELEN BRODIE COWAN (1863-1946) English
Bannerman. *Pat and the Spider.* Stokes. 1905
Bannerman. *Sambo and the Twins.* Stokes. 1936
Bannerman. *Story of Little Black Bobtail.* Stokes. 1910
Bannerman. *Story of Little Black Mingo.* Stokes. 1901
Bannerman. *Story of Little Black Quasha.* Stokes. 1908
Bannerman. *Story of Little Black Quibba.* Stokes. 1903
Bannerman. *Story of Little Black Sambo.* Grant and Richards. 1899
Bannerman. *Story of Little Kettle-head.* Stokes. 1904
Bannerman. *Story of the Teasing Monkey.* Stokes. 1907

BANNON, LAURA (*Ac.* 1940) American
Bannon. *Red Mittens.* Houghton. 1946
Bowman. *Pecos Bill.* A. Whitman. 1937
Bowman. *Tales from a Finnish Tupa.* A. Whitman. 1936
Lee. *Chang Chee.* Harper. 1939
Wood. *Pepper Moon.* Longmans. 1940

BARE, ARNOLD EDWIN (1920-   ) American
Kingman. *Ilenka.* Houghton. 1945
Kingman. *Pierre Pidgeon.* Houghton. 1943

BARNARD, FREDERICK D. (1846-1896) English
Bunyan. *Pilgrim's Progress* (with others). Strahan. 1880
Dickens. *Barnaby Rudge.* Chapman. 1870
Dickens. *Bleak House.* Chapman. 1870
Dickens. *Christmas Books.* Chapman. 1870
Dickens. *David Copperfield.* Chapman. 1870
Dickens. *Dombey and Son.* Chapman. 1870
Dickens. *Martin Chuzzlewit.* Chapman. 1870
Dickens. *Nicholas Nickleby.* Chapman. 1870
Dickens. *Sketches by Boz.* Chapman. 1870
Dickens. *Tale of Two Cities.* Chapman. 1870
Hood. *Petsetilla's Posy.* Routledge. 1870
Mitford. *Children of the Village* (with BARNES, M. E. EDWARDS, MURRAY and others). Routledge. 1880

BARNES, ROBERT (1840-1895) English
Gray. *Elegy Written in a Country Churchyard.* Sampson Low. 1868
Mitford. *Children of the Village* (with BARNARD, M. E. EDWARDS, MURRAY and others). Routledge. 1880
Molesworth. *Green Casket and Other Stories.* Chambers. 1890
Molesworth. *Robin Redbreast.* Chambers. 1892
Watts. *Divine and Moral Songs* (with SMALL and others). Sampson Low. 1866

BARNEY, MAGINEL WRIGHT ENRIGHT (1881-   ) American
Dodge. *Hans Brinker*. McKay. 1918
Hunt. *About Harriet*. Houghton. 1916
Mother Goose. *Songs from Mother Goose for Voice and Piano*. Macmillan. 1920
Phillips. *Calico*. Houghton. 1937
Sawyer. *This Way to Christmas*. Harper. 1924
Ségur. *Sophie*. Knopf. 1929
Snedeker. *Downright Dencey*. Doubleday. 1927
Spyri. *Heidi*. Rand. 1921

BARNHART, NANCY (1889-   ) American
Grahame. *Wind in the Willows*. Scribner. 1923
Thacher. *Listening Child*. Macmillan. 1924

BATEMAN, HENRY MAYO (1887-   ) English, b. in Australia
Carroll. *Further Nonsense Verse and Prose*. Appleton. 1926

BATTEN, JOHN DICKSON (1871-1932) English
Arabian Nights Entertainments. *Fairy Tales from the Arabian Nights*. Dent. 1893
Arabian Nights Entertainments. *More Fairy Tales from the Arabian Nights*. Dent. 1895
Jacobs. *Book of Wonder Voyages*. Nutt. 1896
Jacobs. *Celtic Fairy Tales*. Nutt. 1892
Jacobs. *English Fairy Tales*. Nutt. 1890
Jacobs. *Indian Fairy Tales*. Nutt. 1892
Jacobs. *More Celtic Fairy Tales*. Nutt. 1894
Jacobs. *More English Fairy Tales*. Nutt. 1894

BAUMER, LEWIS (1870-   ) English
Baumer. *Jumbles*. Pearson. 1897
Bland. *Story of the Treasure Seekers* (with G. F. BROWNE). Fisher Unwin. 1899
Irving. *Old Christmas and Bracebridge Hall*. Houghton. 1919
Molesworth. *Hermy. The Boys and I. The Three Witches*. Chambers. 1898-1900
Molesworth. *Hoodie*. Chambers. 1897

BAYES, ALFRED WALTER (1832-1909) English
Andersen. *Fairy Tales and Stories*. Warne. 1865
Andersen. *What the Moon Saw*. Routledge. 1866
Ewing. *Old-fashioned Fairy Tales* (with G. F. BROWNE). S.P.C.K. 1882
Round of Days (For other illustrators *see* HOUGHTON, ARTHUR BOYD). Routledge. 1866

BEARD, DANIEL CARTER (1850-1941) American
Twain. *Connecticut Yankee in King Arthur's Court*. Webster. 1889
Twain. *Tom Sawyer Abroad*. Webster. 1894

BEARD, FRANK (1842-1905) American
Eggleston. *Hoosier Schoolmaster*. Orange Judd. 1871

BEARD, WILLIAM HOLBROOK (1824-1900) American
Harris. *Nights with Uncle Remus* (with F. S. CHURCH). Houghton. 1883

BEARDSLEY, AUBREY VINCENT (1872-1898) English
Malory. *Morte Darthur*. Dent. 1893
Malory. *Story of King Arthur*. Penn. 1902

BEDFORD, FRANCIS DONKIN (1864-   ) English
Baring-Gould. *Old English Fairy Tales*. Methuen. 1895
Barrie. *Peter and Wendy*. Scribner. 1911
Battle of the Frogs and Mice. Methuen. 1894
Bedford. *Night of Wonders*. Stokes. 1907
Coatsworth. *Knock at the Door*. Macmillan. 1931
Dickens. *Chimes*. Chapman. n.d.
Dickens. *Christmas Carol*. Macmillan. 1923
Dickens. *Cricket on the Hearth*. Warne. 1927
Dickens. *Magic Fishbone*. Warne. 1922
Goldsmith. *Vicar of Wakefield*. Dent. 1898
Lucas. *Another Book of Verses for Children*. Macmillan. 1907
Lucas. *Book of Shops*. Grant Richards. 1899
Lucas. *Forgotten Tales of Long Ago*. Wells Gardner. 1906
Lucas. *Four and Twenty Toilers*. Grant Richards. 1900
Lucas. *Old Fashioned Tales*. Wells Gardner. 1905
Lucas. *Runaways and Castaways*. Wells Gardner. 1908
MacDonald. *At the Back of the North Wind*. Macmillan. 1924
MacDonald. *Billy Barnicoat*. Dent. 1923
MacDonald. *Count Billy*. Dutton. 1928
MacDonald. *Princess and the Goblin*. Macmillan. 1926
Mother Goose. *Book of Nursery Rhymes*. Methuen. 1897
Roberts. *Under the Tree*. Viking. 1930
Stevens. *Through Merrie England*. Warne. 1928
Taylor. *Original Poems*. Stokes. 1905
Thackeray. *History of Henry Esmond*. Dent. 1898

BEHAM, HANS SEBALD (1500-1550) German
Bible. *Seventy Stories of the Old Testament* (with DÜRER, HOLBEIN THE YOUNGER and SALOMON). Bradford. 1938

BELL, ROBERT ANNING (1863-1933) English
Beauty and the Beast. Dent. 1894
Bunyan. *Pilgrim's Progress*. Methuen. 1898
Grimm. *Fairy Tales*. Dutton. 1901
Jack the Giant Killer. Dent. 1894
Keats. *Poems*. Bell. 1897
Lamb. *Tales from Shakespeare*. Freemantle. 1899
Palgrave. *Golden Treasury*. Dent. 1907
Rhys. *English Fairy Tales* (with HERBERT COLE). Dutton. 1914
Shakespeare. *Midsummer Night's Dream*. Dent. 1895
Shakespeare. *Tempest*. Freemantle. 1901
Sleeping Beauty. Dent. 1894

BEMELMANS, LUDWIG (1898-   ) American, b. in Austria
Bemelmans. *Castle Number Nine*. Viking. 1937
Bemelmans. *Golden Basket*. Viking. 1936
Bemelmans. *Hansi*. Viking. 1934
Bemelmans. *Madeline*. Simon. 1939
Bemelmans. *Quito Express*. Viking. 1938
Leaf. *Noodle*. Stokes. 1937

BENDA, WLADYSLAW THEODORE (1873-   ) American, b. in Poland
Houghton. *Russian Grandmother's Wonder Tales*. Scribner. 1906

J. D. BATTEN : *Fairy Tales from the Arabian Nights*

BENNETT, CHARLES HENRY (1828-1867) English
    Æsop. *Fables of Æsop*. Kent. 1857
    Birds, Beasts and Fishes, an Alphabet for Boys and Girls. Routledge. 1858
    Bunyan. *Pilgrim's Progress*. Longmans. 1859
    Lemon. *Fairy Tales* (with RICHARD DOYLE). Bradbury and Evans. 1868
    Morley. *Fables and Fairy Tales*. Chapman. 1860
    Morley. *Oberon's Horn*. Chapman. 1861
    Musset. *Mr. Wind and Madam Rain*. Sampson Low. 1863
    Nine Lives of a Cat. Griffith, Farran. 1860
    Nursery Fun. Griffith, Farran. 1863
    Thompson. *Nursery Nonsense or Rhymes without Reason*. Griffith, Farran. 1865
    Wills. *Poets' Wit and Humor* (with G. H. THOMAS). Cundall. 1860

BENNETT, JOHN (1865-   ) American
    Bennett. *Pigtail of Ah Lee Ben Loo*. Longmans. 1928

BENNETT, RICHARD (1899-   ) American, b. in Ireland
    Andersen. *It's Perfectly True; and Other Stories*. Harcourt. 1938
    Bennett. *Hannah Marie*. Doubleday. 1939
    Bennett. *Mister Ole*. Doubleday. 1940
    Bennett. *Shawneen and the Gander*. Doubleday. 1937
    Buck. *Harper's Daughter*. Oxford. 1940
    Colum. *Where the Wind Never Blew and the Cocks Never Crew*. Macmillan. 1940
    Davis. *With Cap and Bells*. Harcourt. 1937
    MacManus. *Well o' the World's End*. Macmillan. 1939
    Miller. *Heroes, Outlaws and Funny Fellows*. Doubleday. 1939
    Nolan. *Red Hugh of Ireland*. Harper. 1938

BENSELL, EDMUND BIRCKHEAD (*Ac*. 1892) American
    Carryl. *Davy and the Goblin*. Ticknor. 1886
    Percy. *Boy's Percy*. Scribner. 1892
    Scudder. *Doings of the Bodley Family in Town and Country* (with DARLEY, HERRICK, NAST, M. L. STONE and others). Hurd and Houghton. 1875
    Stockton. *Floating Prince*. Scribner. 1881
    Stockton. *Poor Count's Christmas*. Stokes. 1927
    Stockton. *Ting-a-ling*. Hurd and Houghton. 1870

BENTLEY, NICOLAS (1907-   ) English
    Belloc. *Cautionary Verses* (with LORD BASIL BLACKWOOD). Knopf. 1941

BENTON, THOMAS HART (1889-   ) American
    Parkman. *Oregon Trail*. Doubleday. 1945
    Twain. *Adventures of Huckleberry Finn*. Limited Editions. 1942
    Twain. *Life on the Mississippi*. Heritage. 1944

BERRY, ERICK, *pseud*. SEE BEST, ALLENA CHAMPLIN

BESKOW, ELSA (1874-   ) Swedish
    Beskow. *Adventures of Peter and Lotta*. Harper. 1931
    Beskow. *Aunt Brown's Birthday*. Harper. 1930
    Beskow. *Aunt Green, Aunt Brown, and Aunt Lavender*. Harper. 1928

Beskow. *Buddy's Adventures in the Blueberry Patch*. Harper. *n.d.*
Beskow. *Elf Children of the Woods*. Harper. 1932
Beskow. *Olle's Ski Trip*. Harper. 1928
Beskow. *Pelle's New Suit*. Harper. 1929
Beskow. *Tale of the Wee Little Old Woman*. Harper. 1930
Scherman. *Peter's Voyage*. Knopf. 1931

BEST, ALLENA CHAMPLIN (1892-   ) American (ERICK BERRY, *pseud*.)
    Alcott. *Little Men*. Blue Ribbon. 1933
    Best. *Black Folk Tales*. Harper. 1928
    Best. *Garram the Hunter*. Doubleday. 1930
    Best. *Girls in Africa*. Macmillan. 1928
    Best. *Hearthstone in the Wilderness*. Macmillan. 1944
    Best. *Honey of the Nile*. Oxford. 1938
    Best. *Winged Girl of Knossos*. Appleton. 1933
    Du Chaillu. *Country of the Dwarfs*. Harper. 1928
    Du Chaillu. *Lost in the Jungle*. Harper. 1928
    Du Chaillu. *My Apingi Kingdom*. Harper. 1928
    Du Chaillu. *Stories of the Gorilla Country*. Harper. 1928
    Du Chaillu. *Wild Life under the Equator*. Harper. 1928
    Evans. *Araminta*. Putnam. 1935
    Fyleman. *Princess Comes to Our Town*. Doubleday. 1928
    Gardiner. *Father's Gone A-whaling*. Doubleday. 1926
    Malkus. *Dragon Fly of Zuñi*. Harcourt. 1928

BEST MAUGARD, ADOLFO (1891-   ) American
    Brooks. *To and Again*. Knopf. 1927

BETTS, ETHEL FRANKLIN (*Ac*. 1923) American
    Ingpen. *One Thousand Poems for Children*. Macrae. 1923
    Mother Goose. *Complete Mother Goose*. Stokes. 1909

BEVANS, MARGARET VAN DOREN SEE VAN DOREN, MARGARET

BEWICK, JOHN (1760-1795) English
    Berquin. *Blossoms of Morality*. E. Newbery. 1796
    Berquin. *Looking-glass for the Mind*. E. Newbery. 1792
    Children's Miscellany. John Stockdale. 1787
    Day. *History of Little Jack*. John Stockdale. 1797
    Discreet Princess; or, The Adventures of Finetta. J. Lumsden. 1818. (Attributed to JOHN BEWICK)
    Graciosa and Percinet. H. Mozley. 1806. (Attributed to JOHN BEWICK)
    Harrison's New Nursery Picture Book. J. Harrison, Devizes. *n.d.* about 1792
    History of Sindbad, the Sailor. J. Lumsden. 1819. (Attributed to JOHN BEWICK)
    Kilner. *Memoirs of a Peg Top*. John Marshall. *n.d.*
    Proverbs in Verse; or, Moral Instructions Conveyed in Pictures. I. Souter. *n.d.*
    Riley's Choice Emblems, Natural, Historical, Fabulous, Moral, and Divine; For the Improvement and Pastime of Youth (with others). G. Riley. 1779
    Triumph of Goodnature. J. Harris. *n.d.*

Trusler. *Proverbs Exemplified and Illustrated by Pictures from Real Life. Teaching Morality and a Knowledge of the World.* John Trusler. 1790
Valentine's Gift. J. Lumsden. *n.d.*
Way To Be Happy; or, The History of the Family at Smiledale. J. Lumsden. 1819
Wynne. *Tales for Youth.* E. Newbery. 1794

BEWICK, THOMAS (1753-1828) English
Æsop. *Fables of Æsop and Others.* E. Walker for T. Bewick. 1818
Beilby. *Quadrupeds.* Hodgson, Beilby & Bewick. 1790
Bewick. *British Birds,* 2 v. V. 1 Hodgson for Beilby and T. Bewick. 1797. V. 2 E. Walker for T. Bewick. 1804
Bewick. *Memoir of Thomas Bewick.* Longman, Green, Longman & Roberts. 1862
Bible. *Curious Hieroglyphick Bible.* T. Hodgson. 1776
Bible. *Holy Bible Abridged, Containing the History of the Old Testament.* T. Wilson and R. Spence. 1802
Day, a Pastoral; in Three Parts, viz. Morning, Noon, and Evening. W. Davison. *n.d.*
Death and Burial of Cock Robin with Tragical Death of an Apple Pie. J. Catnach. *n.d.*
Gammer Gurton's Garland of Nursery Songs, and Toby Tickle's Collection of Riddles. J. Lumsden. *n.d.*
Goldsmith. *Vicar of Wakefield.* D. Walker. 1798
Mavor. *English Spelling Book.* T. Wilson and R. Spence. 1806
New Lottery Book of Birds and Beasts for Children to Learn Their Letters as Soon as They Can Speak. T. Saint. 1771
Poetical Fabulator; or, Beauties in Verse. Thomas Wilson. 1810
Present for Little Masters and Misses. J. Catnach. *n.d.*
Pretty Book of Pictures for Little Masters and Misses; or, Tommy Trip's History of Beasts and Birds. T. Saint. 1779
Select Fables in Three Parts. T. Saint. 1784
Trimmer. *Natural History of the Most Remarkable Quadrupeds, Birds, Fishes, Serpents, Reptiles, and Insects,* 2 v. Thomas Tegg. 1826
Winlove. *Pleasing Moralist, or Young Gentlemen and Ladies Preceptor.* T. Wilson and R. Spence. 1803
Young Reader, for Teaching the English Language, and Improving the Mind. J. Mitchell. 1806
Youth's Instructive and Entertaining Storyteller. T. Saint. 1774

BIANCO, PAMELA (1906-   ) American, b. in England
Andersen. *Little Mermaid.* Holiday. 1935
Bianco. *Little Wooden Doll.* Macmillan. 1925
Bianco. *Skin Horse.* Doran. 1927
Blake. *Land of Dreams.* Macmillan. 1928
De La Mare. *Flora.* Lippincott. 1919
Ewing. *Three Christmas Trees.* Macmillan. 1930
Wilde. *Birthday of the Infanta.* Macmillan. 1929

BILIBIN, IVAN A. (1876-   ) Russian
Carpenter. *Tales of a Russian Grandmother.* Doubleday. 1933
Dole. *White Duckling.* Crowell. 1913
Wheeler. *Russian Wonder Tales.* Century. 1912

BILLINGHURST, PERCY J. (*Ac.* 1900) English
Æsop. *Hundred Fables of Æsop.* Lane. 1898
Billinghurst. *Hundred Anecdotes of Animals.* Lane. 1901
La Fontaine. *Hundred Fables of La Fontaine.* Lane. 1900

BILLINGS, HAMMATT (1818-1874) American
Dickens. *Child's Dream of a Star.* Fields, Osgood. 1871
Goldsmith. *Deserted Village.* J. E. Tilton. 1866
Hawthorne. *Wonder Book for Girls and Boys.* Ticknor and Fields. 1852

BINDER, PEARL (1904-   ) English
Austen. *Persuasion.* Gerald Howe. 1928

BIRCH, REGINALD BATHURST (1856-1943) American, b. in England
Alcott. *Little Men.* Little. 1901
Baldwin. *Story of Roland.* Scribner. 1883
Bennett. *Master Skylark.* Century. 1897
Bowen. *Old Tobacco Shop.* Macmillan. 1921
Brown. *Lucky Stone.* Century. 1914
Burnett. *Little Lord Fauntleroy.* Scribner. 1886
Burnett. *Little Lord Fauntleroy.* Scribner. 1911
Burnett. *Little Princess.* Scribner. 1938
Burnett. *Sara Crewe.* Scribner. 1888
Carryl. *Admiral's Caravan.* Century. 1892
Dix. *Soldier Rigdale.* Macmillan. 1899
Jamison. *Lady Jane.* Century. 1891
Jamison. *Toinette's Philip.* Century. 1894
Moore. *Night before Christmas.* Harcourt. 1937
Richards. *Harry in England.* Appleton. 1937
Richards. *I Have a Song to Sing You.* Appleton. 1938
Stockton. *Reformed Pirate.* Scribner. 1936
Stockton. *Story of Viteau.* Scribner. 1884
Untermeyer. *Last Pirate.* Harcourt. 1934
Untermeyer. *Rainbow in the Sky.* Harcourt. 1935

BISCHOFF, ILSE MARTHE (1903-   ) American
Bontemps. *You Can't Pet a Possum.* Morrow. 1934
Foster. *Gigi: the Story of a Merry-go-round Horse.* Houghton. 1943
Hunt. *Little Grey Gown.* Stokes. 1939
Kuebler. *Hansel the Gander.* Morrow. 1930
Moore. *Night before Christmas.* Holiday. 1937

BLACKBURN, JANE (*Ac.* 1855) Scotch
Bible. *Illustrations of Scripture by an Animal Painter with Notes by a Naturalist.* Constable. 1855
Yonge. *Lances of Lynwood.* Parker. 1855

BLACKWOOD, LORD BASIL T. (1870-1917) English
Belloc. *Bad Child's Book of Beasts.* Alden. 1896
Belloc. *Cautionary Tales for Children.* Everleigh Nash. 1908
Belloc. *Cautionary Verses* (with NICOLAS BENTLEY). Knopf. 1941
Belloc. *More Beasts for Worse Children.* Edward Arnold. 1897

BLAINE, MAHLON (*Ac.* 1929) American
Gunterman. *Castles in Spain and Other Enchantments.* Longmans. 1928
Mukerji. *Chief of the Herd.* Dutton. 1929

BLAISDELL, ELINORE (*Ac.* 1942) American
Blaisdell. *Falcon, Fly Back.* Messner. 1939
Goss. *Deep-flowing Brook.* Holt. 1938
Jewett. *God's Troubadour.* Crowell. 1940
Lamb. *Tales from Shakespeare.* Crowell. 1942

BLAKE, WILLIAM (1757-1827) English
Blake. *Gates of Paradise for Children.* Blake. 1793
Blake. *Songs of Experience.* Blake. 1794
Blake. *Songs of Innocence.* Blake. 1789
Bunyan. *Pilgrim's Progress.* Limited Editions. 1941
Gay. *Fables,* 2 v. (with others). John Stockdale. 1793
Little Thumb and the Ogre. R. Dutton. 1788
Salzmann. *Gymnastics for Youth.* J. Johnson. 1800
Wollstonecraft. *Original Stories from Real Life.* J. Johnson. 1791

BLASHFIELD, EDWIN HOWLAND (1848-1936) American
Stockton. *Fanciful Tales.* Scribner. 1894

BLOCH, LUCIENNE (1909-   ) American, b. in Switzerland
Brown. *Willie's Walk to Grandmama.* W. R. Scott. 1944

BOBIŃSKI, STANISLAW (1897-   ) Polish
Porazińska. *In Voytus' Little House.* Roy. 1944
Porazińska. *My Village.* Roy. 1944

BOBRI, V. *SEE* BOBRITSKY, VLADIMIR

BOBRITSKY, VLADIMIR (*Ac.* 1938) American, b. in Russia
Stafford. *Five Proud Riders.* Knopf. 1938

BOCK, VERA (*Ac.* 1944) American, b. in Russia
Bonsels. *Adventures of Maya the Bee.* Boni. 1929
Ershov. *Little Magic Horse.* Macmillan. 1942
Ferris. *Love's Enchantment.* Doubleday. 1944
Gibson. *Jock's Castle.* Longmans. 1940
Gibson. *Oak Tree House.* Longmans. 1936
Kelly. *Girl Who Would Be Queen.* McClurg. 1939
Marshak. *Ring and a Riddle.* Lippincott. 1944
O'Faoláin. *King of the Cats.* Morrow. 1942
Young. *Tangle-coated Horse and Other Tales.* Longmans. 1929

BOOT, WILLIAM HENRY JAMES (-1918) English
Mitford. *Our Village* (with C. O. MURRAY). Sampson Low. 1879

BOSSCHÈRE, JEAN DE (1878-   ) Belgian
Bosschère. *Christmas Tales of Flanders.* Heinemann. 1917
Bosschère. *Folk Tales of Flanders.* Dodd. 1918
Bosschère. *12 Occupations.* Elkin Mathews. 1916
Swift. *Gulliver's Travels.* Heinemann. 1920

BOSTELMANN, ELSE (*Ac.* 1942) American, b. in Germany
Eberle. *Hop, Skip, and Fly.* Holiday. 1937
Gall. *Bushy Tail.* Oxford. 1941
Mellen. *Twenty Little Fishes.* Messner. 1942

BOSWELL, HAZEL (1882-   ) Canadian
Boswell. *French Canada.* Viking. 1938

BOUGHTON, GEORGE HENRY (1834-1905) British-American
Irving. *History of New York,* 2 v. (with DRAKE and H. PYLE). Grolier Club. 1886
IRVING. *Rip Van Winkle and The Legend of Sleepy Hollow.* Macmillan. 1893
King. *To the Front* (with OAKLEY and REMINGTON). Harper. 1908
Longfellow. *Courtship of Miles Standish* (with MERRILL, REINHART and others). Houghton. 1888

BOURGEOIS, FLORENCE (1904-   ) American
Bourgeois. *Beachcomber Bobbie.* Doubleday. 1935
Bourgeois. *Molly and Michael.* Doubleday. 1936
Bourgeois. *Peter, Peter, Pumpkin Grower.* Doubleday. 1937

BOUTET DE MONVEL, LOUIS MAURICE (1850-1913) French
Boutet de Monvel. *Good Children and Bad: A Book for Both.* Cassell. 1890
Boutet de Monvel. *Joan of Arc.* Century. 1907
France. *Girls and Boys.* Duffield. 1913
France. *Our Children.* Duffield. 1917
Green. *Brother of the Birds.* McKay. 1929
La Fontaine. *Select Fables.* S.P.C.K. *n.d.*
Susanna's Auction. Macmillan. 1923
Walter. *Some Nursery Rhymes of Belgium, France and Russia* (with others). Black. 1917
Widor. *Old Songs and Rounds for Little Children.* Duffield. 1912

BOYLE, ELEANOR VERE *SEE* E. V. B., *pseud.*

BRACKER, CHARLES EUGENE (1895-   ) American
Kissin. *Raffy and the Honkebeest.* Messner. 1940
Kissin. *Zic-Zac.* Messner. 1942

BRADLEY, GERTRUDE M. (*Ac.* 1899) English
Agatha F. *Red Hen and Other Fairy Tales.* Wilson. 1893
Hendry. *Just Forty Winks.* Blackie. 1897
Puff-puff. Sands. 1899
Radford. *Songs for Somebody.* Nutt. 1893

BRADLEY, WILLIAM H. (1868-   ) American
Bradley. *Peter Poodle: Toy Maker to the King.* Dodd. 1906
Irving. *Rip Van Winkle.* R. H. Russell. 1897

BRANDLING, HENRY C. (*Ac.* 1860) English
Shakespeare. *Merchant of Venice* (with B. FOSTER and THOMAS). Sampson Low. 1860

BRANGWYN, FRANK (1867-   ) English
Arabian Nights Entertainments. *Arabian Nights.* Gibbings. 1897
Scott. *Cruise of the Midge,* 2 v. Gibbings. 1894
Scott. *Tom Cringle's Log,* 2 v. Gibbings. 1898

BRANSOM, PAUL (1885-   ) American
Æsop. *Argosy of Fables.* Stokes. 1921
Baker. *Dusty Star.* Dodd. 1922
Dodge. *Sandman's Forest.* Scribner. 1918

Fish. *Animals of American History.* Stokes. 1939
Gatti. *Wrath of Moto.* Scribner. 1941
Grahame. *Wind in the Willows.* Scribner. 1913
London. *Call of the Wild.* Macmillan. 1912
McCracken. *Biggest Bear on Earth.* Stokes. 1943
McCracken. *Last of the Sea Otters.* Stokes. 1942
Roberts. *Children of the Wild.* Macmillan. 1913

BREHM, WORTH (1883-1928) American
Tarkington. *Penrod and Sam.* Doubleday. 1916
Twain. *Adventures of Huckleberry Finn.* Harper. 1923
Twain. *Adventures of Tom Sawyer.* Harper. 1920

BRETT, HAROLD M. (1882-   ) American
Aldrich. *Story of a Bad Boy.* Houghton. 1923
Cooper. *Spy.* Houghton. 1924
Hale. *Peterkin Papers.* Houghton. 1924
Schultz. *With the Indians in the Rockies.* Houghton. 1925

BRÉVILLE, JACQUES MARIE GASTON, ONFROY DE   SEE
ONFROY DE BRÉVILLE, JACQUES MARIE GASTON

BRICKDALE, ELEANOR FORTESCUE- (*Ac.* 1925) English
Book of Old English Songs and Ballads. Hodder. *n.d.*
Brickdale. *Carols.* Moring. 1925
Canton. *Story of Saint Elizabeth of Hungary.* Herbert. 1913
Floire and Blancheflor. *Sweet and Touching Tale of Fleur and Blanchefleur.* Daniel O'Connor. 1922
Palgrave. *Golden Treasury of the Best Songs and Lyrical Poetry in the English Language.* Hodder. 1925
Tennyson. *Idylls of the King.* Hodder. 1911

BRIGHTWELL, LEONARD ROBERT (1889-   ) English
Bowen. *Hepzibah Hen Book.* Houghton. 1927
Reynard the Fox. *Reynard the Fox.* Dodd. 1923

BRISSAUD, PIERRE (1885-   ) French
Cormack. *Jacques the Goatherd.* Appleton. 1938
Eaton. *Betsy's Napoleon.* Morrow. 1936

BRITTAN, CHARLES EDWARD (1870-   ) English
Blackmore. *Lorna Doone* (with C. E. BROCK). Sampson Low. 1910

BROCK, CHARLES EDMUND (1870-1938) English
Austen. *Mansfield Park* (in color). Dent. 1908
Austen. *Northanger Abbey* (in color). Dent. 1907
Austen. *Persuasion* (in color). Dent. 1909
Austen. *Pride and Prejudice.* Macmillan. 1896
Austen. *Pride and Prejudice* (in color). Dent. 1907
Austen. *Sense and Sensibility* (in color). Dent. 1908
Blackmore. *Lorna Doone* (with C. E. BRITTAN). Sampson Low. 1910
Bland. *Oswald Bastable and Others* (with H. R. MILLAR). Wells Gardner. 1905
Burnett. *Little Lord Fauntleroy.* Warne. 1925
Chisholm. *Golden Staircase* (with H. M. BROCK). Jack. 1928
Cooper. *Pathfinder.* Macmillan. 1900
Cowper. *Diverting History of John Gilpin.* Dent. 1898

Dickens. *Christmas Carol.* Dent. 1905
Dickens. *Cricket on the Hearth.* Dent. 1905
Dickens. *Holly Tree and Seven Poor Travellers.* Dent. 1900
Dickens. *Martin Chuzzlewit.* Dodd. 1935
Dickens. *Nicholas Nickleby.* Dodd. 1931
Dickens. *Posthumous Papers of the Pickwick Club.* Harrap. 1930
Eliot. *Silas Marner.* Dent. 1905
Farjeon. *Martin Pippin in the Apple Orchard.* Collins. 1928
Gaskell. *Cranford.* Dent. 1904
Gilbert. *Mikado* (with W. R. FLINT). Macmillan. 1928
Gilbert. *Yeomen of the Guard* (with W. R. FLINT). Macmillan. 1929
Goldsmith. *She Stoops to Conquer.* Ginn. 1917
Goldsmith. *Vicar of Wakefield.* Service. 1898
Goldsmith. *Vicar of Wakefield* (in color). Dent. 1904
Hartland. *English Fairy and Folk Tales.* Scott. 1893
Irving. *Keeping of Christmas at Bracebridge Hall.* Dent. 1906
Irving. *Tales from the Alhambra.* Houghton. 1910
Keary. *Heroes of Asgard.* Macmillan. 1930
Kingsley. *Westward Ho!,* 2 v. Macmillan. 1896
Kipling. *All the Puck Stories* (with H. R. MILLAR). Macmillan. 1935
Lamb. *Mrs. Leicester's School.* Wells Gardner. 1904
Mitford. *Our Village.* Dent. 1904
Molesworth. *Cuckoo Clock.* Macmillan. 1931
Scott. *Ivanhoe.* Service. 1897
Scott. *Lady of the Lake.* Service. 1898
Swift. *Travels into Several Remote Nations of the World by Lemuel Gulliver.* Macmillan. 1894
Wiggin. *Penelope's Experiences in Scotland.* Gay and Bird. 1900

BROCK, EMMA LILLIAN (1886-   ) American
Boggs. *Three Golden Oranges.* Macmillan. 1936
Brock. *At Midsummer Time.* Knopf. 1940
Brock. *Greedy Goat.* Knopf. 1931
Brock. *Hen That Kept House.* Knopf. 1933
Brock. *Little Fat Gretchen.* Knopf. 1934
Brock. *Pig with the Front Porch.* Knopf. 1937
Brock. *Runaway Sardine.* Knopf. 1929
Brock. *Till Potatoes Grow on Trees.* Knopf. 1938
Brock. *To Market! To Market!* Knopf. 1930
Browne. *Granny's Wonderful Chair.* Macmillan. 1924
Davis. *Handsome Donkey.* Harcourt. 1933
Horne. *Memoirs of a London Doll.* Macmillan. 1922

BROCK, HENRY MATTHEW (1875-   ) English
Alcott. *Little Women.* Pearson. 1904
Andersen. *Fairy Tales and Stories.* Pearson. 1905
Beauty and the Beast. Warne. 1914
Brock. *Book of Fairy Tales.* Warne. 1914
Brock. *Book of Nursery Tales.* Warne. 1934
Bunyan. *Pilgrim's Progress.* Pearson. 1900
Chisholm. *Golden Staircase* (with C. E. BROCK). Jack. 1928
Cooper. *Deerslayer.* Macmillan. 1900

"At last it flew away"

C. E. BROCK : *Diverting History of John Gilpin*

Cooper. *Last of the Mohicans*. Macmillan. 1900
Cooper. *Pioneers*. Macmillan. 1900
Davidson. *Knight Errant and His Doughty Deeds*. Seeley. 1911
Dickens. *Christmas Carol*. Dodd. 1935
Dickens. *Christmas Tales*. Harrap. 1932
Dickens. *Old Curiosity Shop*. Gresham. 1901
Drinkwater. *All about Me*. Collins. 1928
Drinkwater. *More about Me*. Collins. 1929
Ewing. *Jackanapes and Other Stories*. Bell. 1916
Gaskell. *Cranford*. Service. 1898
Gaskell. *Cranford* (in color). Seeley. 1913
Goldsmith. *Vicar of Wakefield*. Seeley. 1912
Hop o' My Thumb. Warne. 1914
Irving. *Tales of the Alhambra* (with A. A. DIXON). Tuck. 1923
Jack and the Beanstalk. Warne. 1913
Jack the Giant Killer. Newnes. 1906
Kingsley. *Heroes*. Macmillan. 1928
Nichols. *Book of Old Ballads*. Hutchinson. 1934
Puss in Boots. Newnes. 1906
Scott. *Waverley*. Service. 1899
Stevenson. *Treasure Island*. Macmillan. 1928
Thackeray. *Henry Esmond*. Pearson. 1904
Valentine and Orson. Warne. n.d.
Wallace. *Ben Hur*. Pearson. 1901

BROMHALL, WINIFRED (*Ac.* 1945) English
Bromhall. *Belinda's New Shoes*. Knopf. 1945
De La Mare. *Child's Day*. Holt. 1923
Martineau des Chesnez. *Lady Green Satin and Her Maid Rosette*. Macmillan. 1923

BRONSON, WILFRID SWANCOURT (1894-   ) American
Bronson. *Children of the Sea*. Harcourt. 1940
Bronson. *Chisel-tooth Tribe*. Harcourt. 1939
Bronson. *Fingerfins*. Macmillan. 1930
Bronson. *Grasshopper Book*. Harcourt. 1943
Bronson. *Paddlewings*. Macmillan. 1931
Bronson. *Pollwiggle's Progress*. Macmillan. 1932
Coatsworth. *Boy with the Parrot*. Macmillan. 1930
Desmond. *Sea Cats*. Macmillan. 1944

BROOK, PEGGY BACON *SEE* BACON, PEGGY

BROOKE, LEONARD LESLIE (1862-1940) English
Brooke. *Golden Goose*. Warne. 1905
Brooke. *Golden Goose Book*. Warne. 1905
Brooke. *History of Tom Thumb*. Warne. 1904
Brooke. *Johnny Crow's Garden*. Warne. 1903
Brooke. *Johnny Crow's New Garden*. Warne. 1935
Brooke. *Johnny Crow's Party*. Warne. 1907
Brooke. *Little Bo-Peep*. Warne. 1922
Brooke. *Man in the Moon*. Warne. 1913
Brooke. *Oranges and Lemons*. Warne. 1913
Brooke. *Story of the Three Bears*. Warne. 1904
Brooke. *Story of Three Little Pigs*. Warne. 1904
Brooke. *Tailor and the Crow*. Warne. 1911
Brooke. *This Little Pig Went to Market*. Warne. 1922
Browning. *Pippa Passes*. Duckworth. 1898
Charles. *Roundabout Turn*. Warne. 1930
Grimm. *House in the Wood*. Warne. 1910
Hill. *Truth about Old King Cole*. Warne. 1910

Lear. *Jumblies*. Warne. 1900
Lear. *Pelican Chorus*. Warne. 1900
Molesworth. *Carved Lions*. Macmillan. 1895
Molesworth. *Girls and I*. Macmillan. 1892
Molesworth. *Mary*. Macmillan. 1893
Molesworth. *Miss Mouse and Her Boys*. Macmillan. 1897
Molesworth. *My New Home*. Macmillan. 1894
Molesworth. *Sheila's Mystery*. Macmillan. 1895
Mother Goose. *Nursery Rhyme Book*. Warne. 1897
Mother Goose. *Nursery Rhymes*. Warne. 1916
Mother Goose. *Ring o' Roses*. Warne. 1922
Trollope. *Barchester Towers*. Blackie. 1924

BROOKES, WARWICK (1808-1882) English
Brown. *Marjorie Fleming*. David Douglas. 1884
Round of Days (For other illustrators *see* HOUGHTON, ARTHUR BOYD). Routledge. 1866

BROWN, FORD MADOX (1821-1893) English
Bible. *Art Pictures from the Old Testament* (For other illustrators *see* HOUGHTON, ARTHUR BOYD). S.P.C.K. 1894

BROWN, PAUL (1893-   ) American
Aspden. *Mike of Company D*. Scribner. 1939
Brown. *Crazy Quilt*. Scribner. 1934
Brown. *Fire! the Mascot*. Scribner. 1939
Brown. *No Trouble at All*. Scribner. 1940
Brown. *Piper's Pony*. Scribner. 1935
Brown. *Puff Ball*. Scribner. 1942
Brown. *War Paint*. Scribner. 1936
Davis. *Hobby Horse Hill*. Doubleday. 1939
Downey. *War Horse*. Dodd. 1942
Hall. *College on Horseback*. Random. 1933
Harper. *Flying Hoofs*. Houghton. 1939
Harte. *Bret Harte's Stories of the Old West*. Houghton. 1940

BROWN, WALTER FRANCIS (1853-1929) American
Twain. *Tramp Abroad* (with T. W. WILLIAMS). American Publishing Co. 1879

BROWNE, GORDON FREDERICK (1858-1932) English (A. NOBODY, *pseud.*)
A Apple Pie. Evans. 1890
Andersen. *Fairy Tales*. Wells Gardner. 1902
Aulnoy. *Fairy Tales*. Routledge. 1888
Beauty and the Beast. Blackie. 1886
Blackmore. *Lorna Doone*. Chambers. 1911
Bland. *Five Children* (with H. R. MILLAR). Coward. 1930
Bland. *Story of the Treasure Seekers* (with LEWIS BAUMER). Fisher Unwin. 1899
Browne. *Nonsense for Somebody, Anybody and Everybody*. Gardner, Darton. 1895
Browne. *Some More Nonsense*. Gardner, Darton. 1896
Cervantes Saavedra. *History of Don Quixote*. Stokes. 1921
Corkran. *Down the Snow-stairs*. Blackie. 1887
Crockett. *Surprising Adventures of Sir Toady Lion*. Gardner, Darton. 1897
Defoe. *Robinson Crusoe*. Blackie. 1885

Dr. Jollyboy's A B C. Wells Gardner. 1898

Ewing. *Mary's Meadow.* S.P.C.K. 1886

Ewing. *Old-fashioned Fairy Tales* (with A. W. BAYES). S.P.C.K. 1882

Ewing. *Peace Egg and A Christmas Mumming Play.* S.P.C.K. 1887

Ewing. *Story of a Short Life.* S.P.C.K. 1885

Farrar. *Eric, or Little by Little.* Black. 1899

Froissart. *Stories from Froissart.* Wells Gardner. 1899

Grimm. *Fairy Tales from Grimm.* Wells Gardner. 1894

Henty. *Bonnie Prince Charlie.* Blackie. 1888

Henty. *Lion of St. Mark.* Blackie. 1887

Henty. *Under Drake's Flag.* Blackie. 1887

Henty. *With Clive in India.* Blackie. 1884

Henty. *With Lee in Virginia.* Blackie. 1890

Hop o' My Thumb. Blackie. 1886

Irving. *Rip Van Winkle.* Blackie. 1887

Jones. *Prince Boohoo and Little Smuts.* Gardner, Darton. 1896

La Motte-Fouqué. *Sintram and His Companions, and Undine.* Gardner, Darton. 1896

Lang. *Prince Prigio.* Arrowsmith. 1889

Lang. *Prince Ricardo of Pantouflia.* Arrowsmith. 1893

Masefield. *Book of Discoveries.* Stokes. 1910

Molesworth. *Red Grange.* Methuen. 1891

Reade. *Cloister and the Hearth* (with others). Chambers. 1912

Saintsbury. *National Rhymes of the Nursery.* Wells Gardner. 1897

Scott. *Guy Mannering.* Black. *n.d.*

Scott. *Ivanhoe.* Black. *n.d.*

Shakespeare. *Macbeth.* Longmans. 1899

Swift. *Gulliver's Travels.* Blackie. 1886

Thackeray. *Rose and the Ring.* Chatto. 1909

BROWNE, HABLOT KNIGHT (1815-1882) English (PHIZ, *pseud.*)

Bray. *Peep at the Pixies.* Grant and Richards. 1854

Browne. *Phiz's Toy Book.* Routledge. 1883

Dickens. *Barnaby Rudge* (with GEORGE CATTERMOLE). Chapman. 1841

Dickens. *Bleak House.* Bradbury and Evans. 1853

Dickens. *David Copperfield.* Bradbury and Evans. 1850

Dickens. *Dombey & Son.* Bradbury and Evans. 1848

Dickens. *Little Dorrit.* Bradbury and Evans. 1855

Dickens. *Martin Chuzzlewit.* Chapman. 1844

Dickens. *Master Humphrey's Clock,* 3 v. (with GEORGE CATTERMOLE). Chapman. 1840

Dickens. *Nicholas Nickleby.* Chapman. 1839

Dickens. *Old Curiosity Shop* (with GEORGE CATTERMOLE). Chapman. 1841

Dickens. *Posthumous Papers of the Pickwick Club* (with ROBERT SEYMOUR). Chapman. 1837

Dickens. *Tale of Two Cities.* Chapman. 1859

E. C. *Morals from the Churchyard; in a Series of Cheerful Fables.* Chapman. 1838

Edgeworth. *Parent's Assistant.* Routledge. 1866

Edwards. *Snow Flakes.* Low. 1862

Gatty. *Legendary Tales.* Bell. 1858

Lever. *Charles O'Malley,* 2 v. Curry. 1841

Maitland. *Doll and Her Friends or Memoirs of the Lady Seraphina, by the Author of "Cat and Dog."* Griffith and Farran. 1858

Merry Pictures, by the Comic Hands of Leech, Doyle, Phiz, Crowquill, Meadows, etc. Kent. 1857

Myrtle. *Water Lily.* Bosworth. 1854

Surtees. *Jorrocks' Jaunts and Jollities.* Ackermann. 1838

Swift. *Gulliver's Travels.* Blackie. 1879

BRULLER, JEAN (1902-   ) French

Maurois. *Fatapoufs and Thinifers.* Holt. 1940

BRUNHOFF, JEAN DE (1899-1937) French

Brunhoff. *A B C of Babar.* Random. 1936

Brunhoff. *Babar and Father Christmas.* Random. 1940

Brunhoff. *Babar and His Children.* Random. 1938

Brunhoff. *Babar and Zephir.* Random. 1937

Brunhoff. *Babar the King.* Random. 1935

Brunhoff. *Story of Babar.* Random. 1933

Brunhoff. *Travels of Babar.* Random. 1934

BRUSH, GEORGE DE FOREST (1855-1941) American

Eggleston. *Hoosier Schoolboy.* Scribner. 1883

BUCKELS, ALEC (*Ac.* 1936) English

Buckels. *Three Little Ducklings.* Faber. 1936

De La Mare. *Come Hither.* Knopf. 1928

BUFF, CONRAD (1886-   ) American, b. in Switzerland

Buff. *Dancing Cloud.* Viking. 1937

Buff. *Dash and Dart.* Viking. 1942

Buff. *Kobi.* Viking. 1936

BULL, CHARLES LIVINGSTON (1874-1932) American

Altsheler. *Horsemen of the Plains.* Macmillan. 1910

Linderman. *Kootenai Why Stories.* Scribner. 1926

Roberts. *Kindred of the Wild.* Page. 1902

Sass. *Way of the Wild.* Minton. 1925

Scoville. *More Wild Folk.* Appleton. 1924

Scoville. *Wild Folk* (with C. M. PARK). Little. 1922

BULL, JOHAN (1893-1945) American, b. in Norway

Björnson. *Sunny Hill.* Macmillan. 1932

Lagerlöf. *Diary of Selma Lagerlöf.* Doubleday. 1936

BULL, RENÉ (-1942) English, b. in Ireland

Arabian Nights Entertainments. Arabian Nights. Constable. 1912

La Fontaine. *La Fontaine's Fables* (with C. M. PARK). Nelson. 1905

Swift. *Gulliver's Travels.* Ward. 1928

BURBANK, ADDISON BUSHNELL (1895-   ) American

Burbank. *Cedar Deer.* Coward. 1940

Newcomb. *Vagabond in Velvet.* Longmans. 1942

BURGESS, FRANK GELETT (1866-   ) American

Burgess. *Goop Directory of Juvenile Offenders.* Stokes. 1913

Burgess. *Goop Tales Alphabetically Told.* Stokes. 1904

Burgess. *Goops and How to Be Them.* Stokes. 1900

Burgess. *Lively City o' Ligg.* Stokes. 1899

Burgess. *More Goops and How Not to Be Them.* Stokes. 1903

Burgess. *Why Be a Goop?* Stokes. 1924

BURNE-JONES, EDWARD COLEY (1833-1898) English
  Bible. *Art Pictures from the Old Testament* (For other illustrators *see* HOUGHTON, ARTHUR BOYD). S.P.C.K. 1894
  Gatty. *Parables from Nature* (with COPE, M. E. EDWARDS, FROELICH, HUNT, SPECKTER, TENNIEL, THOMAS and WOLF). Bell and Daldy. 1867
  Maclaren. *Fairy Family.* Longman, Brown, Green, Longmans & Roberts. 1857
  Pictures of Romance and Wonder. Russell. 1902

BURTON, VIRGINIA LEE (1909-   ) American
  Bontemps. *Fast Sooner Hound.* Houghton. 1942
  Bontemps. *Sad-faced Boy.* Houghton. 1937
  Burton. *Calico the Wonder Horse.* Houghton. 1941
  Burton. *Choo Choo.* Houghton. 1937
  Burton. *Katy and the Big Snow.* Houghton. 1943
  Burton. *Little House.* Houghton. 1942
  Burton. *Mike Mulligan and His Steam Shovel.* Houghton. 1939
  Peck. *Don Coyote.* Houghton. 1942

BUSCH, WILHELM (1832-1908) German
  Busch. *Buschel of Merry-thoughts.* Sampson Low. 1868
  Busch. *Buzz a Buzz; or The Bees.* Griffith & Farran. 1872
  Busch. *Fool's Paradise, with the Many Wonderful Adventures There as Seen in the Strange, Surpassing, Peep-Show of Professor Wooley Cobble.* Griffith & Farran. 1883
  Busch. *Hurdy Gurdy.* Stroefer. 187-?
  Busch. *Jack Huckabach, the Scapegrace Raven.* Stroefer. 1874
  Busch. *Max and Moritz, a Story in Seven Tricks.* Braun & Schneider. *n.d.*
  Busch. *Naughty Jemima.* Nimmo. 1872
  Busch. *Plish and Plum.* Roberts. 1883

BUSONI, RAFAELLO (1900-   ) American, b. in Germany
  Busoni. *Somi Builds a Church.* Viking. 1943
  Busoni. *Stanley's Africa.* Viking. 1944
  Ives. *Russia.* Holiday. 1943
  Resnick. *Dragon Ship.* Coward. 1942

BUTLER, HORACIO (1897-   ) Argentine
  Hudson. *Green Mansions.* Knopf. 1943

CADY, WALTER HARRISON (1877-   ) American
  Burnett. *Racketty-Packetty House.* Century. 1914
  Burnett. *Troubles of Queen Silver-Bell.* Century. 1906
  Palmer. *American Songs for Children.* Macmillan. 1931

CALDECOTT, RANDOLPH (1846-1886) English
  A. Y. D. *Owls of Olynn Belfry.* Scribner and Welford. 1885
  Æsop. *Some of Æsop's Fables.* Macmillan. 1883
  Caldecott. *Babes in the Wood.* Routledge. 1879
  Caldecott. *Come Lasses and Lads.* Routledge. 1884

Caldecott. *Elegy on the Death of a Mad Dog.* Routledge. 1879
Caldecott. *Farmer's Boy.* Routledge. 1881
Caldecott. *Fox Jumps over the Parson's Gate.* Routledge. 1883
Caldecott. *Frog He Would A-wooing Go.* Routledge. 1883
Caldecott. *Graphic Pictures* (4 v. in one). Routledge. 1891
Caldecott. *Great Panjandrum Himself.* Routledge. 1885
Caldecott. *Hey Diddle Diddle and Baby Bunting.* Routledge. 1882
Caldecott. *Hey Diddle Diddle Picture Book.* Routledge. 1883
Caldecott. *House That Jack Built.* Routledge. 1878
Caldecott. *House That Jack Built* (Facsimile of Original Sketches). Warne. *n.d.*
Caldecott. *Milkmaid.* Routledge. 1882
Caldecott. *Mrs. Mary Blaize.* Routledge. 1885
Caldecott. *Panjandrum Picture Book.* Warne. 1885
Caldecott. *Picture Book, No. 1.* Warne. 1879
Caldecott. *Picture Book, No. 1* (Miniature). Warne. 1906
Caldecott. *Picture Book, No. 2.* Warne. 1879
Caldecott. *Picture Book, No. 2* (Miniature). Warne. 1906
Caldecott. *Picture Book, No. 3* (Miniature). Warne. 1907
Caldecott. *Picture Book, No. 4* (Miniature). Warne. 1907
Caldecott. *Queen of Hearts.* Routledge. 1881
Caldecott. *Ride a Cock-horse to Banbury Cross and A Farmer Went Trotting upon His Grey Mare.* Routledge. 1884
Caldecott. *Sing a Song for Sixpence.* Routledge. 1880
Caldecott. *Sketch-book of R. Caldecott's.* Routledge. 1883
Caldecott. *Three Jovial Huntsmen.* Routledge. 1880
Cowper. *Diverting History of John Gilpin.* Routledge. 1878
Ewing. *Daddy Darwin's Dovecot.* S.P.C.K. 1881
Ewing. *Jackanapes.* S.P.C.K. 1884
Ewing. *Lob Lie-by-the-fire.* S.P.C.K. 1883
Irving. *Bracebridge Hall.* Macmillan. 1876
Irving. *Old Christmas.* Macmillan. 1875
Irving. *Sketch Book.* Macmillan. 1876
Tennyson. *Jack and the Beanstalk. English Hexameters.* Macmillan. 1886

CALDWELL, E. (-1930) English
  Fitzpatrick. *Jock of the Bushveld.* Longmans. 1908

CALVERT, EDITH (*Ac.* 1898) English
  Stow. *Baby Lays.* Elkin Mathews. 1897
  Stow. *More Baby Lays.* Elkin Mathews. 1898

CAMERON, KATHARINE (*Ac.* 1910) Scotch
  Aucassin and Nicolette. Foulis. 1908
  Chisholm. *Celtic Tales.* Dutton. 1910

CANZIANI, ESTELLA L. M. (1887-   ) English
  De La Mare. *Songs of Childhood.* Longmans. 1923

CARRICK, VALÉRY (1869-   ) British, b. in Russia
 Carrick. *Animal Picture Tales from Russia*. Stokes. 1930
 Carrick. *More Russian Picture Tales*. Blackwell. 1914
 Carrick. *Picture Tales from the Russian*. Blackwell. 1913
 Carrick. *Still More Russian Picture Tales*. Blackwell. 1915
 Carrick. *Tales of Wise and Foolish Animals*. Stokes. 1928
 Carrick. *Valéry Carrick's Picture Folk-tales*. Stokes. 1926
 Fyleman. *Picture Rhymes from Foreign Lands*. Stokes. 1935

CARROLL, LEWIS, *pseud.* (1832-1898) English
 (CHARLES LUTWIDGE DODGSON)
 Carroll. *Alice's Adventures Under Ground; Being a Facsimile of the Original Ms*. Macmillan. 1886

CARTER HELENE (*Ac.* 1943) American, b. in Canada
 Ditmars. *Book of Prehistoric Animals*. Lippincott. 1935
 Ditmars. *Book of Zoögraphy*. Lippincott. 1934
 Ditmars. *Twenty Little Pets from Everywhere*. Messner. 1943
 Lucas. *Earth Changes*. Lippincott. 1937
 Lucas. *Fruits of the Earth*. Lippincott. 1942
 Ransome. *Swallowdale*. Lippincott. 1932
 Ransome. *Swallows and Amazons*. Lippincott. 1931
 Ransome. *Winter Holiday*. Lippincott. 1934
 Spitteler. *Two Little Misogynists*. Holt. 1922
 Wordsworth. *Wayside Flowers*. Macmillan. 1931

CARY, WILLIAM DE LA MONTAGUE (1840-1922) American
 Brooks. *Master of the Strong Hearts*. Dutton. 1898

CASTAIGNE, ANDRÉ (*Ac.* 1896) French
 Page. *In Ole Virginia* (with CLINEDINST, FROST, H. PYLE, REINHART and SMEDLEY). Scribner. 1896

CATLIN, GEORGE (1796-1872) American
 Catlin. *Boy's Catlin*. Scribner. 1909

CATTERMOLE, GEORGE (1800-1868) English
 Dickens. *Barnaby Rudge* (with H. K. BROWNE). Chapman. 1841
 Dickens. *Master Humphrey's Clock*, 3 v. (with H. K. BROWNE). Chapman. 1840
 Dickens. *Old Curiosity Shop* (with H. K. BROWNE). Chapman. 1841

CHALMERS, AUDREY (1899-   ) Canadian
 Chalmers. *Birthday of Obash*. Oxford. 1937
 Chalmers. *Fancy Be Good*. Viking. 1941
 Chalmers. *Hundreds and Hundreds of Pancakes*. Viking. 1942
 Chalmers. *I Had a Penny*. Viking. 1944
 Chalmers. *Parade of Obash*. Oxford. 1939

CHAMP, *pseud.* SEE CHAMPNEY, JAMES WELLS

CHAMPNEY, JAMES WELLS (1843-1903) American (CHAMP, *pseud.*)
 Champney. *Three Vassar Girls Abroad*. Estes & Lauriat. 1883
 Champney. *Witch Winnie's Mystery* (with C. D. GIBSON). Dodd. 1891
 Warner. *Being a Boy*. Houghton. 1878

CHAN, PLATO (1931-   ) American
 Chan. *Good-luck Horse*. Whittlesey. 1943
 Chan. *Magic Monkey*. McGraw. 1944

CHAPMAN, FREDERICK AUGUSTUS (1818-1891) American
 Burns. *Cotter's Saturday Night*. Scribner. 1867

CHAPMAN, PAUL (*Ac.* 1937) American
 Wright. *Barefoot Days*. Grosset. 1937

CHAPMAN, WILLIAM ERNEST (1865-1945) New Zealander
 Sterling. *Story of Parzival, the Templar*. Dutton. 1911
 Sterling. *Story of Sir Galahad*. Dutton. 1908

CHAPPELL, WARREN (1904-   ) American
 Cervantes Saavedra. *Don Quixote de la Mancha*. Little. 1939
 David. *Three Hanses*. Little. 1942
 Goodwin. *Pleasant Pirate*. Knopf. 1940
 Grimm. *Hansel and Gretel*. Knopf. 1944
 Lowe. *Knight of the Sea*. Harcourt. 1941
 Peter and the Wolf. Knopf. 1940
 Yates. *Patterns on the Wall*. Knopf. 1943

CHARLOT, JEAN (1898-   ) American, b. in France
 Brenner. *Boy Who Could Do Anything*. W. R. Scott. 1942
 Brown. *Child's Good Night Book*. W. R. Scott. 1943
 Ferrer. *Tito's Hats*. Garden City. 1940
 Morris. *Digging in Yucatan*. Doubleday. 1931
 Rhoads. *Story of Chan Yuc*. Doubleday. 1941

CHIANG, YEE (1903-   ) Chinese
 Chiang. *Chin-pao and the Giant Pandas*. Country Life. 1939
 Chiang. *Chinpao at the Zoo*. Methuen. 1941
 Chiang. *Lo Cheng: The Boy Who Wouldn't Keep Still*. Penguin. 1941

CHILD, CHARLES JESSE (1901-   ) American
 Benét. *Book of Americans*. Farrar. 1933

CHRISTY, HOWARD CHANDLER (1872-   ) American
 Churchill. *Crisis*. Macmillan. 1901
 Longfellow. *Courtship of Miles Standish*. Bobbs. 1903
 Page. *Old Gentleman of the Black Stock*. Scribner. 1900
 Riley. *Old Sweetheart of Mine*. Bowen-Merrill. 1902
 Riley. *Out to Old Aunt Mary's*. Bobbs. 1904
 Scott. *Lady of the Lake*. Bobbs. 1910

CHURCH, FREDERICK STUART (1842-1924) American
 Harris. *Nights with Uncle Remus* (with W. H. BEARD). Houghton. 1883
 Harris. *Uncle Remus; His Songs and His Sayings* (with J. H. MOSER). Appleton. 1881

Hawthorne. *Wonder Book for Girls and Boys.* Houghton. 1884
Irving. *Bracebridge Hall*, 2 v. (with RACKHAM, REINHART, SCHMOLZE and others). Putnam. 1896

CLARK, J. B. (*Ac.* 1896) English
Arabian Nights Entertainments. *Sinbad the Sailor, Ali Baba and the Forty Thieves* (with WILLIAM STRANG). Lawrence and Bullen. 1896
Munchausen. *Surprising Adventures of Baron Munchausen* (with WILLIAM STRANG). Lawrence and Bullen. 1895

CLARKE, HARRY (1890-1931) Irish
Andersen. *Fairy Tales.* Harrap. 1931
Coleridge. *Rime of the Ancient Mariner.* Maunsel. 1913
Perrault. *Fairy Tales.* Harrap. 1922
Poe. *Tales of Mystery and Imagination.* Harrap. 1919

CLARKE, J. CLAYTON (1840-1871) English
(KYD, *pseud.*)
Clarke. *Characters of Charles Dickens.* Tuck. 1898

CLAYTON, MARGARET (*Ac.* 1909) English
Darton. *Wonder Book of Beasts.* Wells Gardner. 1909

CLINEDINST, BENJAMIN WEST (1859-1931) American
Barbour. *Half-back.* Appleton. 1899
Page. *In Ole Virginia* (with CASTAIGNE, FROST, H. PYLE, REINHART and SMEDLEY). Scribner. 1896
Stockton. *Buccaneers and Pirates of Our Coast* (with G. E. VARIAN). Macmillan. 1898

COATS, ALICE M. (1905-) English
Coats. *Story of Horace.* Faber. 1937

COBURN, FREDERICK SIMPSON (1871-) Canadian
Dickens. *Chimes.* Putnam. 1911
Dickens. *Christmas Carol.* Putnam. 1900
Dickens. *Cricket on the Hearth.* Putnam. 1900
Irving. *Legend of Sleepy Hollow.* Putnam. 1899
Irving. *Rip Van Winkle.* Putnam. 1899
Poe. *Tales of Edgar Allan Poe.* Putnam. 1911
Taylor. *Boys of Other Countries* (with others). Putnam. 1912

COLE, HERBERT (1867-1931) English
Andrews. *Story of Bayard.* Dutton. 1913
Canton. *Child's Book of Warriors.* Dutton. 1912
Coleridge. *Rime of the Ancient Mariner.* Gay and Bird. 1900
Froissart. *Chronicles of England, France and Spain.* Dutton. 1908
Hutchinson. *Sunset of the Heroes.* Dutton. 1911
Rhys. *English Fairy Tales* (with R. A. BELL). Dutton. 1914
Rhys. *Fairy-gold.* Dutton. 1906
Swift. *Gulliver's Travels.* Lane. 1900

COLE, WALTER (1891-) American
A B C Book of People. Putnam. 1932

COLEMAN, M. E. (*Ac.* 1863) English
Wood. *Natural History for Young People* (with WEIR, WOLF, T. W. WOOD and ZWECKER). Dutton. 1863

COLMAN, SAMUEL, JR. (1832-1920) American
Tennyson. *Idyls of the King* (with SOL EYTINGE, JR.). Ticknor and Fields. 1865
Whittier. *Ballads of New England* (For other illustrators *see* FENN, HARRY). Fields, Osgood. 1869

CONDÉ, J. M. (*Ac.* 1918) American
Harris. *Told by Uncle Remus* (with FROST and VER BECK). McClure. 1905
Harris. *Uncle Remus and the Little Boy.* Small. 1910
Harris. *Uncle Remus Returns* (with A. B. FROST). Houghton. 1918
Paine. *Hollow Tree.* R. H. Russell. 1898
Paine. *Hollow Tree and Deep Woods Book.* Harper. 1905
Paine. *Hollow Tree Nights and Days.* Harper. 1916
Paine. *Hollow Tree Snowed-in Book.* Harper. 1910

COOK, HOWARD NORTON (1901-) American
Cook. *Sammi's Army.* Doubleday. 1943

COOKE, WILLIAM CUBITT (1866-) English
Arblay. *Evelina.* Dent. 1893
Craik. *John Halifax, Gentleman* (with others). Dent. 1898
Goldsmith. *Vicar of Wakefield.* Dent. 1893

COONEY, BARBARA (1917-) American
Cooney. *Kellyhorns.* Farrar. 1942
Cooney. *King of Wreck Island.* Farrar. 1941
Malmberg. *Åke and His World.* Farrar. 1940
Seidlin. *Green Wagons.* Houghton. 1943

COPE, CHARLES WEST (1811-1890) English
Gatty. *Parables from Nature* (For other illustrators *see* BURNE-JONES, EDWARD COLEY). Bell and Daldy. 1867
Jack and the Bean Stalk. Cundall. *n.d.*
Jack the Giant Killer. Cundall. *n.d.*
Watts. *Divine and Moral Songs for the Use of Children.* Van Voorst. 1847

COPELAND, CHARLES G. (1858-) American
Andrews. *Ten Boys.* Ginn.
Cherubini. *Pinocchio in Africa.* Ginn. 1911
Church. *Stories of the Old World.* Ginn. 1916
Hawkes. *Piebald, King of Broncos.* Jacobs. 1912
Hawkes. *Wood and Water Friends.* Macrae. 1925
Lansing. *Page, Esquire and Knight.* Ginn. 1910
Long. *Little Brother to the Bear.* Ginn. 1903
Lorenzini. *Adventures of Pinocchio.* Ginn. 1904

COPPING, HAROLD (1863-) English
Alcott. *Little Women.* Religious Tract Society. 1912
Bunyan. *Pilgrim's Progress.* Religious Tract Society. 1903
Dickens. *Character Sketches from Dickens.* Tuck. 1924
Dickens. *Christmas Carol.* Tuck. 1920
Kingsley. *Westward Ho!* Crowell. 1911

CORBOULD, HENRY (1787-1844) English
Peacock. *Ballad of Sir Horn-Book*. Cundall. *n.d.*
Wyss. *Family Robinson Crusoe*. M. J. Godwin. 1814

CORBOULD, WALTON (*Ac*. 1909) English
Ivimey. *Complete Version of Ye Three Blind Mice*. Warne. 1909

CORY, FANNY YOUNG (1877-   ) American
Brown. *Book of Saints and Friendly Beasts*. Houghton. 1900
Brown. *Pocketful of Posies*. Houghton. 1902
Tappan. *Old Ballads in Prose*. Houghton. 1901

COSGRAVE, JOHN O'HARA, II (1908-   ) American
Columbus. *Log of Christopher Columbus' First Voyage to America*. W. R. Scott. 1938
Frost. *Come in, and Other Poems*. Holt. 1943
Judson. *Donald McKay, Designer of Clipper Ships*. Scribner. 1943
Saint Exupéry. *Wind, Sand and Stars*. Reynal. 1939

COVARRUBIAS, MIGUEL (1902-   ) Mexican
Hudson. *Green Mansions*. Heritage. 1936
Melville. *Typee*. Limited Editions. 1935
Stowe. *Uncle Tom's Cabin*. Limited Editions. 1938

COX, E. ALBERT (1876-   ) English
Kingsley. *Westward Ho!* Dutton. 1923
Macaulay. *Lays of Ancient Rome*. Oxford. 1926

COX, PALMER (1840-1924) Canadian
Cox. *Another Brownie Book*. Appleton. 1890
Cox. *Brownies Abroad*. Century. 1899
Cox. *Brownies around the World*. Century. 1894
Cox. *Brownies at Home*. Century. 1893
Cox. *Brownies in the Philippines*. Century. 1904
Cox. *Brownies' Latest Adventures*. Century. 1910
Cox. *Brownies' Many More Nights*. Century. 1913
Cox. *Brownies: Their Book*. Century. 1887
Cox. *Brownies through the Union*. Century. 1895
Cox. *Comic Yarns*. Union. 1889
Cox. *Palmer Cox Brownie Primer*. Century. 1906
Veale. *Bonny Birds*. Hubbard. 1897
Veale. *Brownies and Other Stories*. Edgewood. 1900
Veale. *Jack the Giant*. Hubbard. 1897
Veale. *Merry Mice*. Hubbard. 1897

CRANE, BRUCE ROBERT (1857-1937) American
Lowell. *Vision of Sir Launfal* (For other illustrators see ALEXANDER, JOHN WHITE). Houghton. 1888

CRANE, WALTER (1845-1915) English
Æsop. *Baby's Own Æsop*. Routledge. 1886
Beeching. *Book of Christmas Verse*. Methuen. 1895
Cervantes Saavedra. *Don Quixote*. Dodd. 1911
Crane. *Columbia's Courtship. Picture History of the United States, with Accompanying Verses*. Prang. 1892
Crane. *Flora's Feast; a Masque of Flowers*. Cassell. 1888
Crane. *Pan Pipes*. Routledge. 1882

Crane. *Toy-books*. Routledge. 1867-1876
Absurd A B C
Aladdin
Alphabet of Old Friends
Annie and Jackie in Town
Baby's Own Alphabet
Beauty and the Beast
Bluebeard
Chattering Jack
Cinderella
Fairy Ship
Forty Thieves
Frog Prince
Gaping Wide-mouth Waddling Frog
Goody Two Shoes
Grammar in Rhyme
Hind in the Wood
How Jessie Was Lost
Jack and the Beanstalk
King Luckieboy's Party
Little Red Riding Hood
Mother Hubbard
Multiplication Table in Verse
My Mother
Noah's Ark Alphabet
Old Courtier
One, Two, Buckle My Shoe
Princess Belle Etoile
Puss-in-boots
Sleeping Beauty
This Little Pig
Three Bears
Valentine and Orson
Yellow Dwarf
Crane. *Toy-books*. Warne. 1865-1866
Cock Robin
Dame Trot and Her Comical Cat
Farmyard Alphabet
House That Jack Built
Railroad Alphabet
Sing a Song of Sixpence
De Morgan. *Necklace of Princess Fiorimonde*. Macmillan. 1880.
Gilbert. *Robin Hood*. Jack. 1912
Grimm. *Household Stories*. Macmillan. 1882
Harrison. *Bric-a-brac Stories*. Scribner. 1885
Hawthorne. *Wonder Book for Girls and Boys*. Osgood, McIlvaine. 1892
Keary. *At Home Again* (with J. G. SOWERBY). Marcus Ward. 1888
Lamb. *Masque of Days*. Cassell. 1901
Macgregor. *Story of Greece Told to Boys and Girls*. Stokes. 1914
Malory. *King Arthur's Knights*. Jack. 1911
Meiklejohn. *Golden Primer*. Blackie. 1886
Molesworth. *Cuckoo Clock*. Macmillan. 1877
Molesworth. *Four Winds Farm*. Macmillan. 1887
Molesworth. *Little Miss Peggy*. Macmillan. 1887
Molesworth. *Rosy*. Macmillan. 1882
Molesworth. *Tapestry Room*. Macmillan. 1879
Molesworth. *Tell Me a Story*. Macmillan. 1875
Mother Goose. *Baby's Bouquet*. Routledge. 1879
Mother Goose. *Baby's Opera*. Routledge. 1877

Mother Goose. *Mother Goose's Nursery Rhymes and Fairy Tales* (with J. GILBERT, TENNIEL, WEIR, ZWECKER and others). Routledge. 1876

Queen Summer. Cassell. 1891

Quiver of Love, a Collection of Valentines (with KATE GREENAWAY). Marcus Ward. 1876

Reynard the Fox. *History of Reynard the Fox.* Nutt. 1894

Shakespeare. *Flowers from Shakespeare's Garden, a Posy from the Plays.* Cassell. 1906

Shakespeare. *Merry Wives of Windsor.* Dent. 1895

Shakespeare. *Tempest.* Dent. 1893

Shakespeare. *Two Gentlemen of Verona.* Dent. 1894

Spenser. *Faerie Queene,* 3 v. George Allen. 1894-96

Warr. *Echoes of Hellas,* 2 v. Ward. 1887

Wilde. *Happy Prince and Other Tales* (with G. P. J. HOOD). Nutt. 1888

Wise. *First of May, a Fairy Masque.* Sotheran. 1881

CREDLE, ELLIS (1902-) American
Credle. *Across the Cotton Patch.* Nelson. 1935
Credle. *Down, Down the Mountain.* Nelson. 1934
Credle. *Goat That Went to School.* Grosset. 1940
Credle. *Little Jeemes Henry.* Nelson. 1936
Credle. *Pepe and the Parrot.* Nelson. 1937
Credle. *Pig-o-wee.* Rand. 1936
Lindsay. *Posey and the Pedlar.* Lothrop. 1938

CREED, CLARA SEE PYM, T., *pseud.*

CROCKETT, LUCY HERNDON (1914-) American
Courlander. *Uncle Bouqui of Haiti.* Morrow. 1942
Crockett. *Capitán.* Holt. 1940
Crockett. *Lucio and His Nuong.* Holt. 1939
Crockett. *That Mario.* Holt. 1940

CROOME, WILLIAM (1790-1860) American
Arthur. *Uncle Ben's New-Year's Gift, and Other Stories.* Lippincott, Grambo. 1852
Edgeworth. *Bracelets; or, Amiability and Industry Rewarded.* G. S. Appleton. 1847
Sinclair. *Holiday House: A Series of Tales.* Robert Carter. 1853

CROWE, JOCELYN (1906-) English
De La Mare. *Peacock Pie.* Holt. 1936

CROWQUILL, ALFRED, *pseud. SEE* FORRESTER, ALFRED HENRY

CRUIKSHANK, GEORGE (1792-1878) English
Ainsworth. *Tower of London.* Bentley. 1840
Ainsworth. *Windsor Castle* (with DELAMOTTE and JOHANNOT). Parry, Blenkarn. 1847
Barham. *Ingoldsby Legends,* 3 v. (with JOHN LEECH). Bentley. 1840-47
Barham. *Ingoldsby Legends* (with LEECH and TENNIEL). Bentley. 1864
Bunyan. *Pilgrim's Progress.* Frowde. 1903
Cervantes Saavedra. *History and Adventures of Don Quixote.* Effingham Wilson. 1833
Clarke. *Kit Bam's Adventures.* Grant and Griffith. 1849
Cowper. *Diverting History of John Gilpin.* Tilt. 1828
Cruikshank. *Comic Alphabet.* 1836

Defoe. *Life and Surprising Adventures of Robinson Crusoe,* 2 v. John Major. 1831
Dickens. *Oliver Twist,* 2 v. Bentley. 1838
Dickens. *Oliver Twist* (in color). Chapman. 1894
Dickens. *Sketches by Boz.* Chapman. 1839
Ewing. *Brownies and Other Tales.* Bell and Daldy. 1870
Ewing. *Lob Lie-by-the-fire.* Bell. 1874
Fairy Library, 4 v.
 Cinderella and the Glass Slipper. Bogue. 1853
 History of Jack and the Beanstalk. Bogue. 1853
 Hop-o'-my-thumb and the Seven-league Boots. Bogue. 1853
 Puss in Boots. Bogue. 1854
Frankum. *Bee and the Wasp.* Tilt. 1832
Friswell. *Out and About.* Groombridge. 1860
Gallery of Comicalities (with R. I. CRUIKSHANK and SEYMOUR). Reeves & T. 1889
Goldsmith. *Vicar of Wakefield.* Cochrane. 1832
Gore. *Snow Storm.* Fisher. 1846
Grego. *Cruikshank's Water Colours.* Black. 1903
Grimm. *German Popular Stories.*
 v. 1 C. Baldwin. 1823
 v. 2 James Robins. 1826
Irving. *Beauties of Washington Irving.* Tegg. 1835
Irving. *History of New York.* Tegg. 1836
Loving Ballad of Lord Bateman. Tilt. 1839
Mayhew. *Good Genius That Turned Everything into Gold.* Bogue. 1847
Munchausen. *Travels and Surprising Adventures of Baron Munchausen.* Tegg. 1867
Pardoe. *Lady Arabella.* Kirby. 1856
Punch and Judy. *Punch and Judy.* S. Prowett. 1828
Smedley. *Frank Fairlegh.* A. Hall, Virtue. 1850
Stowe. *Uncle Tom's Cabin.* Cassell. 1852

CRUIKSHANK, ROBERT ISAAC (1789-1856) English
Dandies' Ball. John Marshall. 1819
Dandy's Perambulations. John Marshall. 1821
Dandy's Wedding. John Marshall. 1821
Gallery of Comicalities (with G. CRUIKSHANK and SEYMOUR). Reeves & T. 1889
Juvenile Verse and Picture Book (with J. GILBERT, TENNIEL and others). Burns. 1848

CURRY, JOHN STEUART (1897-1946) American
Cooper. *Prairie.* Limited Editions. 1940
Crane. *Red Badge of Courage.* Limited Editions. 1944

CURTIS, JESSIE (*Ac.* 1880) American
Aldrich. *Baby Bell* (with MERRILL, MORAN, A. R. WAUD and others). Osgood. 1877
Tennyson. *Songs from the Published Writings of Alfred Tennyson* (with FREDERICKS, HOMER and REINHART). Harper. 1880

DAGLISH, ERIC FITCH (1894-) English
Daglish. *Animals in Black and White,* 6 v. Dent. 1936
Daglish. *How to See Beasts.* Morrow. 1933
Daglish. *How to See Birds.* Morrow. 1932
Daglish. *How to See Plants.* Dent. 1932
Daglish. *Life Story of Beasts.* Morrow. 1931
Daglish. *Life Story of Birds.* Morrow. 1930
Hudson. *Far Away and Long Ago.* Dutton. 1931

DALZIEL, EDWARD (1817-1905) English
Arabian Nights Entertainments. *Dalziel's Arabian Nights*, 2 v. (For other illustrators *see* HOUGHTON, ARTHUR BOYD). Ward, Lock. 1865
Buchanan. *Ballad Stories of the Affections* (with T. B. G. DALZIEL, HOUGHTON, J. LAWSON, PINWELL, SMALL and J. D. WATSON). Routledge. 1869
Golden Thoughts from Golden Fountains (For other illustrators *see* HOUGHTON, ARTHUR BOYD). Warne. 1867
Ingelow. *Poems* (For other illustrators *see* PINWELL, GEORGE JOHN). Roberts. 1867
Mother Goose. *National Nursery Rhymes* (For other illustrators *see* HOUGHTON, ARTHUR BOYD). Novello, Ewer. 1870
Round of Days (For other illustrators *see* HOUGHTON, ARTHUR BOYD). Routledge. 1866
Spirit of Praise (For other illustrators *see* HOUGHTON, ARTHUR BOYD). Warne. 1866

DALZIEL, EDWARD GURDEN (1849-1888) English
Christmas Carols (with T. B. G. DALZIEL, F. A. FRASER, HUGHES and others). Novello, Ewer. 1871
Dickens. *Uncommercial Traveller*. Chapman. 1871
Mother Goose. *National Nursery Rhymes* (For other illustrators *see* HOUGHTON, ARTHUR BOYD). Novello, Ewer. 1870

DALZIEL, THOMAS BOLTO GILCHRIST (1823-1906) English
Arabian Nights Entertainments. *Arabian Nights* (with A. B. HOUGHTON). Warne. 1866
Arabian Nights Entertainments. *Dalziel's Arabian Nights*, 2 v. (For other illustrators *see* HOUGHTON, ARTHUR BOYD). Ward, Lock. 1865
Bible. *Art Pictures from the Old Testament* (For other illustrators *see* HOUGHTON, ARTHUR BOYD). S.P.C.K. 1894
Buchanan. *Ballad Stories of the Affections* (For other illustrators *see* DALZIEL, EDWARD). Routledge. 1869
Bunyan. *Pilgrim's Progress*. Ward, Lock. 1863
Christmas Carols (with E. G. DALZIEL, F. A. FRASER, HUGHES and others). Novello, Ewer. 1871
Golden Thoughts from Golden Fountains (For other illustrators *see* HOUGHTON, ARTHUR BOYD). Warne. 1867
Ingelow. *Poems* (For other illustrators *see* PINWELL, GEORGE JOHN). Roberts. 1867
Mother Goose. *National Nursery Rhymes* (For other illustrators *see* HOUGHTON, ARTHUR BOYD). Novello, Ewer. 1870
Round of Days (For other illustrators *see* HOUGHTON, ARTHUR BOYD). Routledge. 1866
Spirit of Praise (For other illustrators *see* HOUGHTON, ARTHUR BOYD). Warne. 1866

DARLEY, FELIX OCTAVIUS CARR (1822-1888) American
Cooper. *Novels*, 32 v. W. A. Townsend. 1859-61
Cooper. *Red Rover*. Appleton. 1873
Cooper. *Spy*. Appleton. 1873
Dickens. *Little Folks*, 12 v. John Anderson. 1878
Dickens. *Oliver Twist*. W. A. Townsend. 1861
Dodge. *Hans Brinker* (with THOMAS NAST). James O'Kane. 1866

Dodge. *Irvington Stories*. James O'Kane. 1865
Edgeworth. *Moral Tales*. George S. Appleton. 1846
Gordon. *Boarding School Days* (with THOMAS NAST). Hurd and Houghton. 1873
Gordon. *Old Boy's Stories* (with HOMER and NAST). Hurd and Houghton. n.d.
Hawthorne. *Compositions in Outline from Hawthorne's "Scarlet Letter."* Houghton. 1879
Hawthorne. *Scarlet Letter*. Houghton. 1883
Hood. *Poems of Thomas Hood* (with DORÉ, EYTINGE, B. FOSTER and SECCOMBE). Putnam. 1872
Irving. *Alhambra*. Putnam. 1851
Irving. *History of New York by Diedrich Knickerbocker*. Putnam. 1850
Irving. *Illustrations of Legend of Sleepy Hollow*. American Art-Union. 1849
Irving. *Illustrations of Rip Van Winkle*. American Art-Union. 1848
Irving. *Rip Van Winkle*. Cundall. 1850
Irving. *Sketch Book of Geoffrey Crayon*. Putnam. 1848
Longfellow. *Evangeline*. Ticknor and Fields. 1867
Longfellow. *Poetical Works of Henry Wadsworth Longfellow*, 3 v. (with ABBEY and others). Houghton. 1881-1883
Lovechild. *Grandfather Lovechild's Nursery Stories*, 14 pamphlets. George B. Zieber. 1846-1849
Moore. *Visit from St. Nicholas*. Gregory. 1862
Parkman. *California and Oregon Trail*. Putnam. 1849
Poe. *Bells* (with others). Porter and Coates. 1881
Poe. *Poetical Works of Edgar Allan Poe* (with B. FOSTER, PICKERSGILL, TENNIEL and others). Sampson Low. 1858
Scenes in Indian Life. Sinclair. 1843
Scudder. *Doings of the Bodley Family in Town and Country* (with BENSELL, HERRICK, NAST, M. L. STONE and others). Hurd and Houghton. 1875
Tennyson. *Enoch Arden* (with HENNESSY, LaFARGE and E. VEDDER). Ticknor and Fields. 1865
Trowbridge. *Vagabonds*. Gregory. 1864
Whittier. *Ballads of New England* (For other illustrators *see* FENN, HARRY). Fields, Osgood. 1869
Yankee Doodle. Trent, Filmer. 1865

DARWIN, ELINOR MAY MONSELL (*Ac.* 1926) English, b. in Ireland
Darwin. *Tale of Mr. Tootleoo*. Harper. 1926
Darwin. *Tootleoo Two*. Harper. 1928

DAUGHERTY, JAMES HENRY (1889-) American
Bible. *In the Beginning*. Oxford. 1941
Bible. *Kingdom, and the Power, and the Glory*. Knopf. 1929
Daugherty. *Abraham Lincoln*. Viking. 1943
Daugherty. *Andy and the Lion*. Viking. 1938
Daugherty. *Daniel Boone*. Viking. 1939
Daugherty. *Poor Richard*. Viking. 1941
Daugherty. *Way of an Eagle*. Oxford. 1941
Daugherty. *Wings of Glory*. Oxford. 1940
Dickens. *Barnaby Rudge*. Heritage. 1941
Doyle. *White Company*. Harper. 1928
Horne. *King Penguin*. Macmillan. 1925
Irving. *Bold Dragoon*. Knopf. 1930

Irving. *Knickerbocker's History of New York.* Doubleday. 1928
Parkman. *Oregon Trail.* Farrar. 1931
Quiller-Couch. *Splendid Spur.* Doran. 1927
Sandburg. *Abe Lincoln Grows Up.* Harcourt. 1928
Sandburg. *Early Moon.* Harcourt. 1930
Shakespeare. *Three Comedies.* Harcourt. 1929
White. *Daniel Boone, Wilderness Scout.* Doubleday. 1926

D'AULAIRE, EDGAR PARIN (1898-) American, b. in Switzerland
Burglon. *Children of the Soil.* Doubleday. 1932
Everson. *Coming of the Dragon Ships.* Dutton. 1931
Mukerji. *Rama, the Hero of India.* Dutton. 1930
Scott. *Kari.* Doubleday. 1931

D'AULAIRE, EDGAR PARIN and
D'AULAIRE, INGRI MORTENSON (1904-) American, b. in Norway
Aanrud. *Sidsel Longskirt.* Winston. 1935
Aanrud. *Solve Suntrap.* Winston. 1935
Asbjörnsen. *East of the Sun and West of the Moon.* Viking. 1938
Bible. *Lord's Prayer.* Doubleday. 1934
D'Aulaire. *Abraham Lincoln.* Doubleday. 1939
D'Aulaire. *Animals Everywhere.* Doubleday. 1940
D'Aulaire. *Children of the Northlights.* Viking. 1935
D'Aulaire. *Don't Count Your Chicks.* Doubleday. 1943
D'Aulaire. *George Washington.* Doubleday. 1936
D'Aulaire. *Leif the Lucky.* Doubleday. 1941
D'Aulaire. *Magic Rug.* Doubleday. 1931
D'Aulaire. *Ola.* Doubleday. 1932
D'Aulaire. *Ola and Blakken and Line, Sine, Trine.* Doubleday. 1933
D'Aulaire. *Wings for Per.* Doubleday. 1944
Key. *Star Spangled Banner.* Doubleday. 1942

DAVIS, MARGUERITE (1889-) American
Alcott. *Under the Lilacs.* Little. 1928
Richards. *Tirra Lirra.* Little. 1932
Rossetti. *Sing-song.* Macmillan. 1924
Spyri. *Heidi.* Ginn. 1927
Stevenson. *Child's Garden of Verses.* Macmillan. 1924
Tileston. *Sugar and Spice and All That's Nice.* Little. 1910

DAY, MAURICE E. (1892-) American
Bergengren. *Jane, Joseph and John.* Atlantic Monthly. 1921
Beston. *Firelight Fairy Book.* Atlantic Monthly. 1919
Beston. *Starlight Wonder Book.* Atlantic Monthly. 1923
Curtin. *Hero-tales of Ireland.* Little. 1921
Jewett. *Wonder Tales from Tibet.* Little. 1922
Scudder. *Book of Fables and Folk Stories.* Houghton. 1919

DE ANGELI, MARGUERITE LOFFT (1889-) American
Coatsworth. *Alice-all-by-herself.* Macmillan. 1937
De Angeli. *Elin's Amerika.* Doubleday. 1941
De Angeli. *Henner's Lydia.* Doubleday. 1936
De Angeli. *Petite Suzanne.* Doubleday. 1937
De Angeli. *Skippack School.* Doubleday. 1939
De Angeli. *Yonie Wondernose.* Doubleday. 1944
Gray. *Meggy MacIntosh.* Doubleday. 1930
Hawkins. *Prayers and Graces for Little Children.* Grosset. 1941
Meigs. *Covered Bridge.* Macmillan. 1936
Robinson. *In and Out.* Viking. 1943
Worth. *They Loved to Laugh.* Doubleday. 1942

DELAMOTTE, WILLIAM ALFRED (1775-1863) English
Ainsworth. *Windsor Castle* (with G. CRUIKSHANK and JOHANNOT). Parry, Blenkarn. 1847

DE MARTELLY, JOHN STOCKTON (1903-) American
Edmonds. *Wilderness Clearing.* Dodd. 1944
Hudson. *Green Mansions.* Peter Pauper. 1943

DEMING, EDWIN WILLARD (1860-1942) American
Deming. *American Animal Life.* Stokes. 1916
Deming. *Indian Child Life.* Stokes. 1899
Deming. *Little Eagle.* A. Whitman. 1931
Deming. *Many Snows Ago.* Stokes. 1929
Deming. *Red Folk and Wild Folk.* Stokes. 1902
Eastman. *Wigwam Evenings.* Little. 1909
Grinnell. *Jack among the Indians.* Stokes. 1900
Grinnell. *Jack, the Young Canoeman.* Stokes. 1906
Haines. *Indian Boys and Girls.* Stokes. 1906

DE MORGAN, WILLIAM FREND (1839-1917) English
De Morgan. *On a Pincushion.* Seeley. 1877

DENNIS, MORGAN (1892-) American
Dennis. *Pup Himself.* Viking. 1943
Knight. *Friend in the Dark.* Grosset. 1937
Robinson. *Pete.* Viking. 1941

DENNIS, WESLEY (1903-) American
Dennis. *Flip.* Viking. 1941
Dennis. *Flip and the Cows.* Viking. 1942

DERRICK, THOMAS (*Ac.* 1930) English
Alington. *Cautionary Catches.* Blackwell. 1931
Bible. *Prodigal Son and Other Parables.* Blackwell. 1931

DETMOLD, EDWARD JULIUS (1883-) English
Æsop. *Fables.* Hodder. n.d.
Arabian Nights Entertainments. *Tales from the Thousand and One Nights.* Dodd. 1925
Dugdale. *Book of Baby Birds.* Frowde. 1912
Dugdale. *Book of Baby Pets.* Frowde. 1913
E. B. S. *Pictures from Birdland* (with MAURICE DETMOLD). Dent. 1899
Fabre. *Book of Insects.* Dodd. 1921
Kaberry. *Book of Baby Dogs.* Frowde. 1914
Kaberry. *Our Little Neighbors.* Oxford. 1920
Kipling. *Jungle Book* (with MAURICE DETMOLD). Macmillan. 1908
Lemonnier. *Birds and Beasts.* Allen. 1911
Maeterlinck. *Children's Life of the Bee.* George Allen. 1911

DETMOLD, MAURICE (1883-1908) English
    E. B. S. *Pictures from Birdland* (with E. J. DETMOLD).
        Dent. 1899
    Kipling. *Jungle Book* (with E. J. DETMOLD). Macmillan. 1908

DE VEYRAC, ROBERT (1901-   ) American, b. in France
    Brown. *House of a Hundred Windows.* Harper. 1945
    Brown. *Shhhhhh . . . Bang.* Harper. 1943

DEWITT, CORNELIUS HUGH (1905-   ) American, b. in Germany
    Gilchrist. *Story of the Great Lakes.* Harper. 1942
    Lambert. *Story of Alaska.* Harper. 1940
    McClintock. *Story of New England.* Harper. 1941
    McClintock. *Story of the Mississippi.* Harper. 1941
    McNeer. *Story of the Great Plains.* Harper. 1943

D'HARNONCOURT, RENÉ (1901-   ) American, b. in Austria
    D'Harnoncourt. *Hole in the Wall.* Knopf. 1931
    D'Harnoncourt. *Mexicana.* Knopf. 1931
    Morrow. *Beast, Bird and Fish.* Knopf. 1933
    Morrow. *Painted Pig.* Knopf. 1930

DIELMAN, FREDERICK (1847-1935) American
    Warner. *Wide, Wide World.* Lippincott. 1892

DIXON, ARTHUR A. (*Ac.* 1920) English
    Dickens. *Child Characters from Dickens.* Nister. 1905
    Dickens. *Holly Tree.* Nister. 1899
    Gaskell. *Cranford.* Collins. 1906
    Hauff. *Fairy Tales.* Dutton. 1910
    Irving. *Christmas at Bracebridge Hall.* Nister. *n.d.*
    Irving. *Tales of the Alhambra* (with H. M. BROCK). Tuck. 1923
    Kingsley. *Water-babies.* Nister. 1908
    Laboulaye. *Fairy Tales.* Nister. 1909
    Longfellow. *Courtship of Miles Standish.* Dutton. *n.d.*
    Longfellow. *Evangeline.* Dutton. *n.d.*
    Thackeray. *Henry Esmond.* Collins. 1903

DOANE, PELAGIE (1906-   ) American
    Jacobs. *Molly Whuppie.* Oxford. 1939
    Mother Goose. *Mother Goose.* Random. 1940
    Stevenson. *Child's Garden of Verses.* Garden City. 1942

DOBIAS, FRANK (1902-   ) American, b. in Austria
    Bible. *Junior Bible.* Macmillan. 1936
    Kelsey. *Once the Hodja.* Longmans. 1943
    Morris. *Sons of the Volsungs.* Macmillan. 1932
    Siebe. *Kasperle's Adventures.* Macmillan. 1929

DOBUZHINSKII, MSTISLAV VALERIANOVICH (1875-   ) Russian
    Leskov. *Steel Flea.* Harper. 1943

DODGSON, CHARLES LUTWIDGE *SEE* CARROLL, LEWIS, *pseud.*

DOEPLER, CARL EMIL (1824-1905) German
    Abbott. *Emma; or, The Three Misfortunes of a Belle.* Harper. 1856
    Abbott. *History of Hernando Cortez.* Harper. 1855
    Abbott. *History of Josephine.* Harper. 1851
    Abbott. *Rambles among the Alps.* Harper. 1856
    Abbott. *Rollo in Geneva.* Siegel-Cooper. 1858
    Abbott. *Rollo on the Rhine.* Siegel-Cooper. 1858
    Abbott. *Romulus.* Harper. 1852

DOGGETT, ALLEN B. (-1926) American
    Dodge. *Hans Brinker.* Scribner. 1896

DOMBROWSKI, KÄTHE SCHÖNBERGER VON (1881-   ) American, b. in Austria (K. O. S., *pseud.*)
    Bīdpāī. *Jackal in Persia.* Doubleday. 1928
    Dombrowski. *Abdallah and the Donkey.* Macmillan. 1928
    Dombrowski. *Just Horses.* Macmillan. 1930
    Waldeck. *Little Jungle Village.* Viking. 1940

DORÉ, PAUL GUSTAVE (1832-1883) French
    Cervantes Saavedra. *History of Don Quixote.* Cassell. 1863
    Hood. *Poems of Thomas Hood* (with DARLEY, EYTINGE, B. FOSTER and SECCOMBE). Putnam. 1872
    La Fontaine. *Fables of La Fontaine.* Cassell. 1867
    L'Épine. *Days of Chivalry or The Legend of Croquemitaine.* Cassell. 1866
    Munchausen. *Adventures of Baron Munchausen.* Cassell. 1866
    Perrault. *French Fairy Tales.* Didier. 1945
    Popular Fairy Tales. James Miller. 1871
    Rabelais. *Three Good Giants* (with ALBERT ROBIDA). Ticknor. 1887

DOUGLASS, RALPH (1895-   ) American
    Tireman. *Baby Jack and Jumping Jack Rabbit.* University of New Mexico. 1943

DOYLE, RICHARD (1824-1883) English
    Aytoun. *Book of Ballads* (with A. H. FORRESTER). Orr. 1849
    Dickens. *Chimes* (with LEECH, MACLISE and STANFIELD). Chapman. 1845
    Dickens. *Christmas Books* (with E. H. LANDSEER, LEECH, MACLISE, STANFIELD, F. STONE and TENNIEL). Chapman. 1854
    Dickens. *Cricket on the Hearth* (with E. H. LANDSEER, LEECH and STANFIELD). Bradbury and Evans. 1846
    Doyle. *Journal Kept by Richard Doyle in the Year 1840.* Smith, Elder. 1885
    Doyle. *Scenes from English History.* Pall Mall Gazette Office. 1886
    Grimm. *Fairy Ring.* Murray. 1846
    Hervey. *Juvenile Calendar and Zodiac of Homes.* Sampson Low. 1855
    Hughes. *Scouring of the White Horse.* Macmillan. 1858
    In Fairyland, a Series of Pictures of the Elf-world; with a Poem by William Allingham. Longmans, Green, Reader and Dyer. 1870
    Lang. *Princess Nobody.* Longmans. 1886

Lemon. *Enchanted Doll*. Bradbury and Evans. 1849

Lemon. *Fairy Tales* (with C. H. BENNETT). Bradbury and Evans. 1868

Merry Pictures, by the Comic Hands of Leech, Doyle, Phiz, Crowquill, Meadows, etc. Kent. 1857

Montalba. *Fairy Tales of All Nations*. Chapman. 1849

Planché. *Old Fairy Tale Told Anew*. Routledge. 1865

Ruskin. *King of the Golden River*. Smith, Elder. 1851

Story of Jack and the Giants. Cundall and Addey. 1851

Thackeray. *Newcomes*, 2 v. Bradbury and Evans. 1854-55

Thackeray. *Rebecca and Rowena*. Chapman. 1850

DRAKE, WILLIAM HENRY (1856-1926) American

Irving. *History of New York*, 2 v. (with BOUGHTON and H. PYLE). Grolier Club. 1886

Kipling. *Jungle Book* (with J. L. KIPLING and others). Macmillan. 1894

DU BOIS, WILLIAM PÈNE (1916-   ) American

Du Bois. *Flying Locomotive*. Viking. 1941

Du Bois. *Great Geppy*. Viking. 1940

Du Bois. *Three Policemen*. Viking. 1938

DULAC, EDMUND (1882-   ) English, b. in France

Andersen. *Stories from Hans Andersen*. Hodder. 1912

Arabian Nights Entertainments. *Stories from the Arabian Nights*. Hodder. 1907

Brontë. *Jane Eyre*. Dent. 1905

Brontë. *Wuthering Heights*. Dent. 1905

Dulac. *Edmund Dulac's Fairy Book*. Hodder. 1916

Dulac. *Edmund Dulac's Picture Book*. Hodder. *n.d.*

Fairy Garland. Cassell. 1928

Hawthorne. *Tanglewood Tales*. Hodder. 1918

Lyrics . . . from A-Z. Routledge. 1908

Poe. *Poetical Works of Edgar Allan Poe*. Hodder. 1912

Shakespeare. *Tempest*. Doran. 1908

Sleeping Beauty. Hodder. 1910

Stevenson. *Treasure Island*. Doran. 1927

DU MAURIER, GEORGE LOUIS PALMELLA BUSSON (1834-1896) English, b. in France

Collins. *Moonstone* (with F. A. FRASER). Chatto. 1875

Du Maurier. *Legend of Camelot*. Bradbury, Agnew. 1898

Gaskell. *Cousin Phillis*. Smith, Elder. 1865

Gaskell. *Cranford*. Smith, Elder. 1864

Lytton. *Lucile*. Chapman. 1868

Montgomery. *Misunderstood*. Richard Bentley. 1874

Thackeray. *Ballads and The Rose and the Ring* (with FURNISS, THACKERAY and others). Smith, Elder. 1879

Thackeray. *History of Henry Esmond*. Smith, Elder. 1868

Watts. *Divine and Moral Songs* (with C. GREEN, MORTEN, J. D. WATSON and others). Nisbet. 1867

DUNCAN, EDWARD (1804-1882) English

Songs of the Brave. Soldier's Dream and Other Poems and Odes (with B. FOSTER, HUTTULA, MACQUOID and THOMAS). Sampson Low. 1856

DUNLAP, HOPE (1880-   ) American

Browning. *Pied Piper of Hamelin*. Rand. 1910

Craik. *Little Lame Prince*. Rand. 1909

Garnett. *Muffin Shop*. Rand. 1908

Grimm. *Fairy Tales*. Rand. 1913

DUNN, HARVEY T. (1884-   ) American

Brooks. *Boy Emigrants*. Scribner. 1914

Dickens. *Tale of Two Cities*. Cosmopolitan. 1921

DÜRER, ALBRECHT (1471-1528) German

Bible. *Albrecht Dürer's Bible Events*. Cundall. 1848

Bible. *Seventy Stories of the Old Testament* (with BEHAM, HOLBEIN THE YOUNGER and SALOMON). Bradford. 1938

DUVOISIN, ROGER ANTOINE (1904-   ) American, b. in Switzerland

Browning. *Pied Piper of Hamelin*. Grosset. 1936

Duvoisin. *And There Was America*. Knopf. 1938

Duvoisin. *Christmas Whale*. Knopf. 1945

Duvoisin. *Donkey-donkey*. Grosset. 1940

Duvoisin. *They Put Out to Sea*. Knopf. 1943

Elliot. *Jo-Yo's Idea*. Knopf. 1939

Elliot. *Riema, Little Brown Girl of Java*. Knopf. 1937

Elliot. *Soomoon, Boy of Bali*. Knopf. 1938

Fischer. *Dog Cantbark*. Random. 1940

McCullough. *At Our House*. W. R. Scott. 1943

Mother Goose. *Mother Goose*. Heritage. 1936

Stevenson. *Child's Garden of Verses*. Heritage. 1944

DWIGGINS, WILLIAM ADDISON (1880-   ) American

Bible. *Book of Books*. Knopf. 1944

Poe. *Tales*. Donnelley. 1930

E. V. B., *pseud.* (1825-1916) English
(ELEANOR VERE BOYLE)

Andersen. *Fairy Tales*. Sampson Low. 1882

Beauty and the Beast. Sampson Low. 1875

Carové. *Story without an End*. Sampson Low. 1868

Child's Play. Addey. 1852

Child's Summer. Addey. 1853

New Child's Play. Sampson Low. 1877

Peacock's Pleasaunce. Lane. 1908

Tennyson. *May Queen*. Sampson Low. 1861

EDWARDS, GEORGE WHARTON (1869-   ) American

Book of Christmas. Macmillan. 1913

Dodge. *Hans Brinker*. Scribner. 1915

Hawthorne. *Tanglewood Tales for Girls and Boys*. Houghton. 1887

Holmes. *Last Leaf* (with F. H. SMITH). Houghton. 1886

Lummis. *Pueblo Indian Folk-stories*. Appleton. 1910

Mabie. *Book of Old English Ballads*. Macmillan. 1896

Seaman. *Jacqueline of the Carrier-pigeons*. Macmillan. 1910

Seaman. *When a Cobbler Ruled the King*. Macmillan. 1911

EDWARDS, LIONEL DALHOUSIE ROBERTSON (1878-)
English
Golden Gorse. *Moorland Mousie*. Scribner. 1929
Golden Gorse. *Older Mousie*. Scribner. 1932
Kipling. *Maltese Cat*. Doubleday. 1936
Sprigge. *Pony Tracks*. Scribner. 1936

EDWARDS, MARY ELLEN (1839- ?) English
Family Fairy Tales. Hotten. 1864
Gatty. *Parables from Nature* (For other illustrators
see BURNE-JONES, EDWARD COLEY). Bell and Daldy.
1867
Mitford. *Children of the Village* (with BARNARD,
BARNES, MURRAY and others). Routledge. 1880
Molesworth. *Boys and I*. Routledge. 1883
Molesworth. *Hermy*. Routledge. 1885
Molesworth. *Neighbors*. Hatchards. 1889
Molesworth. *Story of a Spring Morning*. Longmans.
1890
Mother's Last Words (with others). Jarrold. 1866
Weatherly. *Adventures of Two Children*. Hildes-
heimer. 1883

EICHENBERG, FRITZ (1901-) American, b. in Germany
Davis. *Padre Porko*. Holiday. 1939
Dobbs. *No Room*. Coward. 1944
Duncan. *Big Road Walker*. Stokes. 1940
Eberle. *Wide Fields*. Crowell. 1943
Hall. *Animals to Africa*. Holiday. 1939
Hoffmann. *Mischief in Fez*. Holiday. 1943
Hughes. *Don't Blame Me*. Harper. 1940
Hunt. *"Have You Seen Tom Thumb?"* Stokes.
1942
Ibsen. *Story of Peer Gynt*. Crowell. 1941
Jagendorf. *Tyll Ulenspiegel's Merry Pranks*. Van-
guard. 1938
Kalevala. *Heroes of the Kalevala*. Messner. 1940
Puss in Boots. Holiday. 1936
Sewell. *Black Beauty*. Grosset. 1945
Swift. *Gulliver's Travels*. Heritage. 1940

EISGRUBER, ELSA (*Ac.* 1929) German
Eisgruber. *Spin Top Spin*. Macmillan. 1929

ELIOT, FRANCES (1901-) American
Eliot. *Pablo's Pipe*. Dutton. 1936
Eliot. *Traveling Coat*. Dutton. 1937

ELLINGFORD, PRISCILLA M. (*Ac.* 1933) English
Graham. *Happy Holidays*. Dutton. 1933
Graham. *Welcome Christmas!* Dutton. 1932

ELLIOTT, ELIZABETH SHIPPEN GREEN (*Ac.* 1930) American
Lamb. *Tales from Shakespeare*. McKay. 1922
Peabody. *Book of the Little Past*. Houghton. 1908
Waller. *Daughter of the Rich*. Little. 1924
Wiggin. *Mother Carey's Chickens*. Houghton. 1930
Willcox. *Torch*. Harper. 1924

EMERSON, SYBIL (1895-) American
Emerson. *Jacques at the Window*. Crowell. 1936
Emerson. *Pigeon House Inn*. Crowell. 1939

ENGLEFIELD, CICELY (1893-) English
Englefield. *House for a Mouse*. Murray. 1936
Englefield. *Katie Caterpillar*. Oxford. 1937
Englefield. *Tale of a Guinea-pig*. Murray. 1935

ENRIGHT, ELIZABETH (1910-) American
Enright. *Kintu; a Congo Adventure*. Farrar. 1935
Enright. *Saturdays*. Farrar. 1941
Enright. *Sea Is All Around*. Farrar. 1940
Enright. *Thimble Summer*. Farrar. 1938

ETS, MARIE HALL (1895-) American
Ets. *In the Forest*. Viking. 1944
Ets. *Mister Penny*. Viking. 1935
Ets. *Story of a Baby*. Viking. 1939

EXTER, ALEXANDRA (1884-) American, b. in Russia
Colmont. *Along the Coast*. Harper. 1939
Colmont. *Down the River*. Harper. 1940
Colmont. *Up the Mountain*. Harper. 1940

EYTINGE, SOL, JR. (1833-1905) American
Alcott. *Work*. Roberts. 1873
Aldrich. *Story of a Bad Boy*. Houghton. 1869
Dickens. *Child-pictures from Dickens*. Ticknor and
Fields. 1867
Dickens. *Christmas Carol*. Fields, Osgood. 1869
Hood. *Poems of Thomas Hood* (with DARLEY, DORÉ,
B. FOSTER and SECCOMBE). Putnam. 1872
Lowell. *Vision of Sir Launfal*. Ticknor and Fields.
1867
Tennyson. *Idyls of the King* (with S. COLMAN, JR.).
Ticknor and Fields. 1865
Whittier. *Ballads of New England* (For other illus-
trators see FENN, HARRY). Fields, Osgood. 1869
Winter Poems by Favorite American Poets (with
FENN, FREDERICKS, HENNESSY, HOMER and others).
Fields, Osgood. 1871

FABRÈS, OSCAR (*Ac.* 1944)
Andersen. *Thumbelina*. Putnam. 1944
Arabian Nights Entertainments. *Arabian Nights*.
Duell. 1944.
Arabian Nights Entertainments. *Seven Voyages of
Sinbad the Sailor*. Duell. 1945
Henius. *Songs and Games of the Americas*. Scrib-
ner. 1943

FABRICIUS, JOHAN WIGMORE (1899-) Dutch
Fabricius. *Java Ho!* Coward. 1931

FALLS, CHARLES BUCKLES (1874-) American
A B C Book. Doubleday. 1923
Bible. *Story of the Birth of Jesus Christ*. Marchbanks.
1929
Bowie. *When Jesus Was Born*. Harper. 1928
Lucas. *Vast Horizons*. Viking. 1943
Modern A B C Book. Day. 1930
Mother Goose. *Mother Goose*. Doubleday. 1924
Shippen. *New Found World*. Viking. 1945
Stevenson. *Two Mediæval Tales*. Limited Editions.
1929

FARNY, HENRY F. (1847-1916) American
Howells. *Boy's Town.* Harper. 1890

FELL, HERBERT GRANVILLE (1872-   ) English
Arabian Nights Entertainments. *Ali Baba and the Forty Thieves.* Dent. 1895
Bible. *Book of Job.* Dent. 1896
Cinderella. Dent. 1895
Fairy Gifts and Tom Hickathrift. Dent. 1895
Hawthorne. *Wonder Book.* Dent. 1903
Hawthorne. *Wonder Book and Tanglewood Tales.* Dent. 1910
Our Lady's Tumbler. Dent. 1894

FENN, HARRY (1845-1911) American, b. in England
Bryant. *Story of the Fountain* (with FREDERICKS, HOMER and others). Appleton. 1871
Kellogg. *Good Old Times.* Lee and Shepard. 1878
Whittier. *Ballads of New England* (with COLMAN, DARLEY, EYTINGE, FREDERICKS, HENNESSY, HOMER and others). Fields, Osgood. 1869
Whittier. *Snow-bound.* Ticknor and Fields. 1868
Winter Poems by Favorite American Poets (with EYTINGE, FREDERICKS, HENNESSY, HOMER and others). Fields, Osgood. 1871

FIELD, RACHEL (1894-1942) American
Farjeon. *Come Christmas.* Stokes. 1927
Field. *All through the Night.* Macmillan. 1940
Field. *Alphabet for Boys and Girls.* Doubleday. 1926
Field. *Little Book of Days.* Doubleday. 1927
Field. *Little Dog Toby.* Macmillan. 1928
Field. *Pocket-handkerchief Park.* Doubleday. 1929
Field. *Polly Patchwork.* Doubleday. 1928
Field. *Taxis and Toadstools.* Doubleday. 1926
Field. *Yellow Shop.* Doubleday. 1931
Gate. *Punch and Robinetta.* Yale. 1923

FILDES, SAMUEL LUKE (1844-1927) English
Dickens. *Mystery of Edwin Drood.* Chapman. 1870

FINTA, ALEXANDER (1881-   ) American, b. in Hungary
Finta. *Herdboy of Hungary.* Harper. 1932
Finta. *My Brothers and I.* Holiday. 1940

FISCHER, ANTON OTTO (1882-   ) American, b. in Germany
Bullen. *Cruise of the Cachalot* (with HENRY REUTERDAHL). Appleton. 1925
Hawes. *Dark Frigate.* Little. 1934
Hawes. *Mutineers.* Little. 1941
Nordhoff. *Pearl Lagoon.* Little. 1924
Pease. *Foghorns.* Doubleday. 1937

FISHER, HARRISON (1875-1934) American
Longfellow. *Hiawatha.* Bobbs. 1906

FITE, ANNE MERRIMAN PECK *SEE* PECK, ANNE MERRIMAN

FLACK, MARJORIE (1897-   ) American
Flack. *Angus and the Cat.* Doubleday. 1931
Flack. *Angus and the Ducks.* Doubleday. 1930
Flack. *Ask Mr. Bear.* Macmillan. 1932
Flack. *Restless Robin.* Houghton. 1937
Flack. *Tim Tadpole and the Great Bullfrog.* Doubleday. 1934

FLAMENG, LEOPOLD (1831-1911) Belgian
Saintine. *Picciola.* Hurd and Houghton. 1866

FLAXMAN, JOHN (1755-1826) English
Homer. *Iliad of Homer;* Engraved from the Compositions of John Flaxman. Longman, Hurst, Rees, & Orme.
Homer. *Odyssey of Homer;* Engraved from the Compositions of John Flaxman. Longman, Hurst, Rees, & Orme. 1805

FLINT, WILLIAM RUSSELL (1880-1944) Scotch
Chaucer. *Canterbury Tales,* 3 v. Medici. 1913
Chaucer. *Tales from Chaucer.* Medici. 1930
Gilbert. *Mikado* (with C. E. BROCK). Macmillan. 1928
Gilbert. *Yeomen of the Guard* (with C. E. BROCK). Macmillan. 1929
Homer. *Odyssey of Homer.* Medici. 1924
Kingsley. *Heroes.* Medici. 1928
Malory. *Le Morte Darthur.* Medici. 1911

FLOETHE, RICHARD (1901-   ) American, b. in Germany
Coyle. *Brittany Summer.* Harper. 1940
Eulenspiegel. *Glorious Adventures of Tyl Eulenspiegel.* Limited Editions. 1934
Fischer. *Street Fair.* Random. 1935
Goudge. *Smoky House.* Coward. 1940
Lorenzini. *Pinocchio, the Adventures of a Marionette.* Limited Editions. 1937
Streatfeild. *Ballet Shoes.* Random. 1937
Streatfeild. *Circus Shoes.* Random. 1939
Streatfeild. *Stranger in Primrose Lane.* Random. 1941
Treadgold. *Left Till Called For.* Doubleday. 1941

FOGARTY, THOMAS (1873-1938) American
Dickens. *People from Dickens.* Scribner. 1935
Pearson. *Voyage of the Hoppergrass.* Macmillan. 1913
Slocum. *Sailing Alone around the World* (with GEORGE VARIAN). Appleton. 1911
White. *Blazed Trail.* McClure. 1902
White. *Gold.* Doubleday. 1913

FOLKARD, CHARLES JAMES (1878-   ) English
Æsop. *Æsop's Fables.* Black. 1912
Garnett. *Ottoman Wonder Tales.* Black. 1915
Grimm. *Fairy Tales.* Black. 1911
Hoffman. *Children's Shakespeare.* Dutton. 1911
Lamb. *Tales from Shakespeare.* Dent. *n.d.*
Lorenzini. *Pinocchio.* Dutton. 1911
Mother Goose. *Land of Nursery Rhyme.* Dutton. 1932
Mother Goose. *Mother Goose's Nursery Rhymes.* Blackie. 1919
Mother Goose's Nursery Tales. Macmillan. 1923
Nyblom. *Jolly Calle.* Dent. *n.d.*
Phillpotts. *Flint Heart.* Dutton. 1910
Wyss. *Swiss Family Robinson.* Dutton. 1910

FORD, HENRY JUSTICE (1860-1941) English
Æsop. *Æsop's Fables.* Fisher Unwin. 1888
Arabian Nights Entertainments. *Arabian Nights' Entertainments.* Longmans. 1898

Benson. *David Blaize and the Blue Door*. Doran. 1919
Bunyan. *Pilgrim's Progress*. S.P.C.K. *n.d.*
Lang. *Animal Story Book*. Longmans. 1896
Lang. *Blue Fairy Book* (with G. P. J. HOOD). Longmans. 1889
Lang. *Blue Poetry Book* (with LANCELOT SPEED). Longmans. 1891
Lang. *Book of Princes and Princesses*. Longmans. 1908
Lang. *Book of Saints and Heroes*. Longmans. 1912
Lang. *Green Fairy Book*. Longmans. 1892
Lang. *Red Fairy Book* (with LANCELOT SPEED). Longmans. 1890
Lang. *Tales of Romance* (with LANCELOT SPEED). Longmans. 1907
Lang. *Tales of Troy and Greece*. Longmans. 1907
Lang. *Violet Fairy Book*. Longmans. 1901
Lang. *Yellow Fairy Book*. Longmans. 1894
Newbolt. *Book of the Happy Warrior*. Longmans. 1917
Scott. *Kenilworth*. Jack. 1907

FORD, LAUREN (1891-   ) American
Bible. *Ageless Story*. Dodd. 1939
Ford. *Little Book about God*. Doubleday. 1934
Ségur. *Memoirs of a Donkey*. Macmillan. 1924

FORRESTER, ALFRED HENRY (1804-1872) English
    (ALFRED CROWQUILL, *pseud.*)
Aytoun. *Book of Ballads*. Orr. 1845
Aytoun. *Book of Ballads* (with RICHARD DOYLE). Orr. 1849
Bayley. *Blue Beard with Illustrations Humorous and Numerous*. Orr. 1842
Bayley. *Little Red Riding Hood*. Orr. 1842
Beschius. *Strange Surprising Adventures of the Venerable Gooroo Simple*. Trübner. 1861
Comic Nursery Tales. Routledge. 1845
Corner. *Beauty and the Beast*. Dean. 1854
Corner. *Whittington and His Cat*. Dean. 1854
Eulenspiegel. *Marvellous Adventures and Rare Conceits of Master Tyll Owlglass*. Trübner. 1859
Fairy Footsteps; or, Lessons from Legends. Henry Lea. *n.d.*
Fairy Tales, 6 v. Routledge. 1857
Forrester. *Picture Fables*. Griffith and Farran. 1854
Krakemsides. *Careless Chicken*. Griffith and Farran. 1853
Krakemsides. *Funny Leaves for the Younger Branches*. Griffith and Farran. 1852
Merry Pictures, by the Comic Hands of Leech, Doyle, Phiz, Crowquill, Meadows, etc. Kent. 1857
Munchausen. *Travels of Baron Munchausen*. Trübner. 1858
Pictorial English Grammar. Clarke. 1841
Tales from the Court of Oberon. Grant and Griffith. *n.d.*
Tales of Magic and Meaning. Grant and Griffith. 1856
Tutor's Assistant or Comic Figures of Arithmetic. J. and F. Harwood. 1843

FORTESCUE-BRICKDALE, ELEANOR *SEE* BRICKDALE, ELEANOR FORTESCUE-

FOSTER, BIRKET (1825-1899) English
Bloomfield. *Farmer's Boy* (with HICKS and WEIR). Sampson Low. 1857
Burns. *Poems and Songs* (with J. GILBERT, F. WALKER, J. D. WATSON and WEIR). Bell and Daldy. 1857
Charlesworth. *Ministering Children* (with HENRY LE JEUNE). Nisbet. 1856
Christmas with the Poets. Bogue. 1851
Coleridge. *Rime of the Ancient Mariner*. Bogue. 1851
Early English Poems (with J. GILBERT, THOMAS and others). Sampson Low. 1863
Edgeworth. *Early Lessons*. Routledge. 1866
Goldsmith. *Traveller*. Bogue. 1856
Gray. *Elegy Written in a Country Churchyard* (with A LADY and THOMAS). Cundall. 1854
Hood. *Poems of Thomas Hood* (with DARLEY, DORÉ, EYTINGE and SECCOMBE). Putnam. 1872
Longfellow. *Evangeline* (with JOHN GILBERT). Bogue. 1850
Longfellow. *Poetical Works* (with others). Bogue. 1852
Milton. *Comus* (with PICKERSGILL and WEIR). Routledge. 1858
Milton. *L'Allegro and Il Penseroso*. Bogue. 1855
Poe. *Poetical Works of Edgar Allan Poe* (with DARLEY, PICKERSGILL, TENNIEL and others). Sampson Low. 1858
Sabbath Bells Chimed by the Poets. Bell and Daldy. 1856
Scott. *Lay of the Last Minstrel* (with JOHN GILBERT). Black. 1854
Shakespeare. *Merchant of Venice* (with BRANDLING and THOMAS). Sampson Low. 1860
Songs for the Little Ones at Home (with JOHN ABSOLON). Bickers. 1863
Songs of the Brave. Soldier's Dream and Other Poems and Odes (with DUNCAN, HUTTULA, MACQUOID and THOMAS). Sampson Low. 1856
Taylor. *Pictures of English Landscape*. Routledge. 1863
Wordsworth. *Deserted Cottage* (with J. GILBERT and WOLF). Routledge. 1859
Wordsworth. *Poems of William Wordsworth* (with J. GILBERT and WOLF). Routledge. 1859

FOSTER, MARCIA LANE (1897-   ) English
France. *Little Sea Dogs*. Dodd. 1925
Macmillan. *Canadian Fairy Tales*. Lane. 1922

FRANCIS, JOSEPH GREENE (1849- ?) American
Francis. *Book of Cheerful Cats*. Century. 1892
Francis. *Joyous Aztecs*. Century. 1929

FRANÇOISE, *pseud. SEE* SEIGNOBOSC, FRANÇOISE

FRASER, CLAUD LOVAT (1890-1921) English
De La Mare. *Peacock Pie*. Constable. 1924
Fraser. *Pirates*. Simpkin, Marshall. 1915
Mother Goose. *Nurse Lovechild's Legacy*. Poetry Bookshop. 1916
Mother Goose. *Nursery Rhymes with Pictures*. Jack. 1919
Nodier. *Luck of the Bean-rows*. Daniel O'Connor. 1921
Nodier. *Woodcutter's Dog*. Daniel O'Connor. 1921

HARRY FURNISS : *Sylvie and Bruno Concluded*

H. J. FORD : *Violet Fairy Book*

FRASER, FRANCIS A. (*Ac.* 1875) English
    Christmas Carols (with E. G. and T. B. G. DALZIEL, HUGHES and others). Novello, Ewer. 1871
    Collins. *Moonstone* (with G. L. P. B. DU MAURIER). Chatto. 1875
    Dickens. *Great Expectations.* Chapman. 1870
    Martineau. *Peasant and the Prince.* Routledge. 1885
    Mother Goose. *National Nursery Rhymes* (For other illustrators *see* HOUGHTON, ARTHUR BOYD). Novello, Ewer. 1870

FREDERICKS, ALFRED (*Ac.* 1881) American
    Bryant. *Little People of the Snow.* Appleton. 1872
    Bryant. *Story of the Fountain* (with FENN, HOMER and others). Appleton. 1871
    Johnson. *Catskill Fairies.* Harper. 1875
    Mabinogion. *Knightly Legends of Wales.* Sampson Low. 1881
    Taylor. *National Ode* (with MORAN, A. R. WAUD and others). William Gill. 1876
    Tennyson. *Songs from the Published Writings of Alfred Tennyson* (with CURTIS, HOMER and REINHART). Harper. 1880
    Whittier. *Ballads of New England* (For other illustrators *see* FENN, HARRY). Fields, Osgood. 1869
    Winter Poems by Favorite American Poets (with EYTINGE, FENN, HENNESSY, HOMER and others). Fields, Osgood. 1871

FREEDMAN, BARNETT (1901-   ) English
    Brontë. *Jane Eyre.* Heritage. 1942
    Dickens. *Adventures of Oliver Twist.* Heritage. 1939

FREEMAN, MARGARET (1893-   ) American
    Capuana. *Italian Fairy Tales.* Dutton. 1929
    Crew. *Saturday's Children.* Little. 1927
    Field. *American Folk and Fairy Tales.* Scribner. 1929

FREER, FREDERICK WARREN (1849-1908) American
    Lowell. *Vision of Sir Launfal* (For other illustrators *see* ALEXANDER, JOHN WHITE). Houghton. 1888

FREUND, RUDOLF (1915-   ) American
    Freund. *American Garden Flowers.* Random. 1943
    Matschat. *American Butterflies and Moths.* Random. 1942

FROELICH, LORENZ (1820-1908) Danish
    Gatty. *Parables from Nature* (For other illustrators *see* BURNE-JONES, EDWARD COLEY). Bell and Daldy. 1867
    Little Rosy's Travels. Appleton. 1872
    Nine Years Old. Macmillan. 1871
    When I Was a Little Girl. Macmillan. 1871

FROST, ARTHUR BURDETT (1851-1928) American
    Aldrich. *Story of a Bad Boy.* Houghton. 1895
    Brooks. *First across the Continent* (with SETON and YOHN). Scribner. 1901
    Carroll. *Rhyme? and Reason?* (with HENRY HOLIDAY). Macmillan. 1883
    Carroll. *Tangled Tale.* Macmillan. 1885

Dickens. *American Notes.* Chapman. 1870
Dickens. *Pickwick Papers.* Ward, Lock. 1881
Frost. *Book of Drawings.* Collier. 1904
Frost. *Bull Calf and Other Tales.* Scribner. 1892
Frost. *Stuff & Nonsense.* Scribner. 1884
Harris. *Tarbaby and Other Rhymes* (with E. W. KEMBLE). Appleton. 1904
Harris. *Told by Uncle Remus* (with CONDÉ and VER BECK). McClure. 1905
Harris. *Uncle Remus and His Friends.* Houghton. 1892
Harris. *Uncle Remus; His Songs and His Sayings.* Appleton. 1895
Harris. *Uncle Remus; His Songs and His Sayings* (with E. W. KEMBLE). Appleton. 1920
Harris. *Uncle Remus Returns* (with J. M. CONDÉ). Houghton. 1918
Major. *Bears of Blue River* (with others). Doubleday. 1901
Page. *In Ole Virginia* (with CASTAIGNE, CLINEDINST, H. PYLE, REINHART and SMEDLEY). Scribner. 1896
Stockton. *Pomona's Travels.* Scribner. 1894
Stockton. *Rudder Grange.* Scribner. 1885
Stockton. *Squirrel Inn.* Century. 1891
Stuart. *Golden Wedding and Other Tales* (with REINHART and SHEPPARD). Harper. 1893
Stuart. *Solomon Crow's Christmas Pockets and Other Tales* (with KEMBLE and others). Harper. 1896
Twain. *Tom Sawyer Abroad; Tom Sawyer, Detective and Other Stories.* Webster. 1896

FUERTES, LOUIS AGASSIZ (1874-1927) American
    Burgess. *Burgess Animal Book for Children.* Little. 1920
    Burgess. *Burgess Bird Book for Children.* Little. 1919
    Burroughs. *Bird Stories from Burroughs.* Houghton. 1911

FULLEYLOVE, JOHN (1845-1908) English
    Dawes. *Bible Stories for Young People.* Crowell. 1923
    Finnemore. *Holy Land.* Macmillan. 1908
    Scott. *Tales of a Grandfather* (with others). T. W. Laurie. 1925

FURNISS, HARRY (1854-1925) Irish
    Allingham. *Rhymes for the Young Folk* (with ALLINGHAM, GREENAWAY and PATERSON). Cassell. 1887
    Carroll. *Story of Sylvie and Bruno.* Macmillan. 1889
    Carroll. *Sylvie and Bruno Concluded.* Macmillan. 1893
    Dickens. *Uncommercial Traveller* in *Oliver Twist and Uncommercial Traveller.* Oxford. n.d.
    Holiday Romps, 4 parts. Routledge. 1886
    Thackeray. *Ballads and The Rose and the Ring* (with DU MAURIER, THACKERAY and others). Smith, Elder. 1879

GÁG, FLAVIA (1907-   ) American
    Scott. *Story of Kattor.* Coward. 1939
    Turner. *Christmas House, the Story of a Visit from Saint Nicholas.* Scribner. 1943

GÁG, WANDA HAZEL (1893-1946) American
Gág. *A B C Bunny*. Coward. 1933
Gág. *Funny Thing*. Coward. 1929
Gág. *Gone Is Gone*. Coward. 1935
Gág. *Millions of Cats*. Coward. 1928
Gág. *Nothing at All*. Coward. 1941
Gág. *Snippy and Snappy*. Coward. 1931
Grimm. *Snow White*. Coward. 1938
Grimm. *Tales from Grimm*. Coward. 1936
Grimm. *Three Gay Tales from Grimm*. Coward. 1943

GARNER, ELVIRA CARTER (1895-) American
Garner. *Ezekiel*. Holt. 1937
Garner. *Ezekiel Travels*. Holt. 1938
Garner. *Sarah Faith Anderson: Her Book*. Messner. 1939
Garner. *'Way Down in Tennessee*. Messner. 1941

GARNETT, EVE (*Ac*. 1938) English
Garnett. *Family from One End Street*. Vanguard. 1938

GASKIN, ARTHUR JOSEPH (1862-1928) English
Andersen. *Stories and Fairy Tales*, 2 v. George Allen. 1893
Baring-Gould. *Book of Fairy Tales*. Methuen. 1894
Neale. *Good King Wenceslas*. Cornish. 1895

GASKIN, MRS. ARTHUR JOSEPH SEE GASKIN, GEORGIE CAVE FRANCE

GASKIN, GEORGIE CAVE FRANCE (*Ac*. 1896) English
A B C. Elkin Mathews. 1896
Gaskin. *Horn-book Jingles*. Leadenhall Press. 1896-97
Watts. *Divine and Moral Songs for Children*. Elkin Mathews. 1896

GAY, ZHENYA (*Ac*. 1939) American
Gay. *Manuelito of Costa Rica*. Messner. 1940
Gay. *170 Cats*. Random. 1939
Gay. *Pancho and His Burro*. Morrow. 1930
Gay. *Sakimura*. Viking. 1937
Gogol. *Taras Bulba*. Knopf. 1915
Hoffmann. *Cat of Paris*. Stokes. 1940
Jones. *Whistler's Van*. Viking. 1936
Sayers. *Mr. Tidy Paws*. Viking. 1936

GEISEL, THEODOR SEUSS (1904-) American
(DR. SEUSS, *pseud*.)
Geisel. *And to Think That I Saw It on Mulberry Street*. Vanguard. 1937
Geisel. *500 Hats of Bartholomew Cubbins*. Vanguard. 1938
Geisel. *Horton Hatches the Egg*. Random. 1940
Geisel. *King's Stilts*. Random. 1939

GÉRARD, JEAN-IGNACE ISIDORE (1803-1847) French
(J. J. GRANDVILLE, *pseud*.)
Defoe. *Life and Strange Surprising Adventures of Robinson Crusoe*. Appleton. 1853
Florian. *Fables*. Willoughby. 1839
La Fontaine. *Fables of La Fontaine*, 2 v. Tappan and Dennett. 1841
Swift. *Travels into Several Remote Nations of the World by Lemuel Gulliver*, *pseud*. Haywood and Moore. 1840

GERE, CHARLES MARCH (1869-) English
Polevoï. *Russian Fairy Tales*. Lawrence and Bullen. 1893

GERGELY, TIBOR (1900-) American, b. in Hungary
Duplaix. *Merry Shipwreck*. Harper. 1942
Duplaix. *Topsy Turvy Circus*. Harper. 1940
Edmonds. *Two Logs Crossing*. Dodd. 1943
Werner. *Noah's Ark*. Grosset. 1943

GERSON, VIRGINIA (*Ac*. 1907) American
Gerson. *Happy Heart Family*. Fox. 1904
Gerson. *More Adventures of the Happy Heart Family*. Fox. 1905

GERVIS, RUTH S. (1894-) English
Barne. *Family Footlights*. Dent. 1939
Barne. *She Shall Have Music*. Dent. 1938
Barne. *Visitors from London*. Dent. 1941

GHEERAERTS, MARCUS, THE ELDER (1516-1590) Flemish
Æsop. *Twenty-four Fables*. Dutton. 1929

GIACOMELLI, HECTOR (1822-1904) French
Howitt. *Sketches of Natural History; or, Songs of Animal Life*. Nelson. 1873
Trimmer. *History of the Robins*. Nelson. 1875

GIBBINGS, ROBERT JOHN (1889-) Irish
Doorly. *Insect Man*. Appleton. 1937
Doorly. *Microbe Man*. Appleton. 1939
Fabre. *Marvels of the Insect World*. Appleton. 1938
Pushkin. *Tale of the Golden Cockerel*. Golden Cockerel. 1936
Waddell. *Beasts and Saints*. Holt. 1934

GIBSON, CHARLES DANA (1867-1944) American
Champney. *Witch Winnie's Mystery* (with J. W. CHAMPNEY). Dodd. 1891
Davis. *Gallegher and Other Stories*. Scribner. 1891
Davis. *Soldiers of Fortune*. Scribner. 1897
Davis. *Van Bibber and Others*. Harper. 1892
Gibson. *People of Dickens*. Russell. 1897
Hawkins. *Prisoner of Zenda*. Holt. 1898

GIBSON, WILLIAM HAMILTON (1850-1896) American
Gibson. *Blossom Hosts and Insect Guests*. Newson. 1901
Gibson. *Eye Spy*. Harper. 1897
Gibson. *Sharp Eyes*. Harper. 1893

GIFFORD, R. SWAIN (1840-1905) American
Lowell. *Vision of Sir Launfal* (For other illustrators *see* ALEXANDER, JOHN WHITE). Houghton. 1888

GILBERT, JOHN (1817-1897) English
Aulnoy. *Fairy Tales*. Routledge. 1855
Bible. *Book of Job*. Nisbet. 1858
Bible. *Proverbs of Solomon*. Nisbet. 1858
Bowers. *Boy's Book of Ballads*. Bell and Daldy. 1861
Burns. *Poems and Songs* (with B. FOSTER, F. WALKER, J. D. WATSON and WEIR). Bell and Daldy. 1857
Dickens. *Posthumous Papers of the Pickwick Club*. Appleyard. 1847

Early English Poems (with B. FOSTER, THOMAS and others). Sampson Low. 1863
Juvenile Verse and Picture Book (with R. I. CRUIK-SHANK, TENNIEL and others). Burns. 1848
Lamb. *Tales from Shakespeare.* Routledge. 1866
Longfellow. *Courtship of Miles Standish.* Routledge. 1859
Longfellow. *Evangeline* (with BIRKET FOSTER). Bogue. 1854
Longfellow. *Poems.* Routledge. 1856
Mother Goose. *Mother Goose's Nursery Rhymes and Fairy Tales* (with W. CRANE, TENNIEL, WEIR, ZWECKER and others). Routledge. 1876
Myrtle. *Pleasures of the Country.* Cundall and Addey. 1851
Scott. *Lay of the Last Minstrel* (with BIRKET FOSTER). Black. 1854
Taylor. *Rhymes for the Nursery.* Strahan. 1870
Wordsworth. *Deserted Cottage* (with B. FOSTER and WOLF). Routledge. 1859
Wordsworth. *Poems of William Wordsworth* (with B. FOSTER and WOLF). Routledge. 1859
Wyss. *Swiss Family Robinson.* Hurd and Houghton. 1865

GILBERT, WILLIAM SCHWENCK (1836-1911) English
Gilbert. *Bab Ballads.* Routledge. 1869
Gilbert. *Magic Mirror.* Strahan. 1866
Gilbert. *More Bab Ballads.* Routledge. 1873
Gilbert. *Songs of a Savoyard.* Routledge. 1890

GILLHAM, ELIZABETH ENRIGHT *SEE* ENRIGHT, ELIZABETH

GLACKENS, WILLIAM J. (1870-1938) American
Page. *Santa Claus's Partner.* Scribner. 1899

GLANCKOFF, SAMUEL (1894-   ) American
Smith. *Señor Zero.* Harcourt. 1931
Tietjens. *Romance of Antar.* Coward. 1929

GOBLE, WARWICK (*Ac.* 1928) English
Chaucer. *Complete Poetical Works of Geoffrey Chaucer.* Macmillan. 1912
Craik. *Fairy Book.* Macmillan. 1913
Craik. *John Halifax, Gentleman.* Oxford. 1914
Day. *Folk-tales of Bengal.* Macmillan. 1912
Irving. *Alhambra.* Macmillan. 1926
James. *Green Willow and Other Japanese Fairy Tales.* Macmillan. 1910
Kingsley. *Water-babies.* Macmillan. 1910
Owen. *Book of Fairy Poetry.* Longmans. 1920
Stevenson. *Kidnapped.* Macmillan. 1925
Stevenson. *Treasure Island.* Macmillan. 1923
Whitney. *Tod of the Fens.* Macmillan. 1928

GODWIN, JAMES (*Ac.* 1875) English
Mackarness. *Sunbeam Stories, Third Series.* Routledge. 1875

GONNE, MAUD *SEE* MACBRIDE, MAUD GONNE

GRAMATKY, HARDIE (1907-   ) American
Gramatky. *Hercules.* Putnam. 1940
Gramatky. *Little Toot.* Putnam. 1939
Gramatky. *Loopy.* Putnam. 1941
Proudfit. *Treasure Hunter.* Messner. 1939

GRANDVILLE, J. J., *pseud. SEE* GÉRARD, JEAN-IGNACE ISIDORE

GRANT, GORDON (1875-   ) American
Coleridge. *Rime of the Ancient Mariner.* Heritage. 1938
Grant. *Half Deck.* Little. 1933
Grant. *Sail Ho!* Payson. 1931
Grant. *Ships under Sail.* Garden City. 1939
Grant. *Story of the Ship.* McLoughlin. 1919
Morrow. *Ship's Monkey.* Morrow. 1933
Porter. *Ransom of Red Chief.* Doubleday. 1918
Stackpole. *Madagascar Jack.* Morrow. 1935
Tarkington. *Penrod.* Doubleday. 1914
Tarkington. *Penrod Jashber.* Doubleday. 1929

GRAY, PAUL (1848-1868) English
Hood. *Jingles and Jokes for Little Folks* (with MORTEN and others). Cassell. 1865
Longfellow. *Poetical Works* (with HOUGHTON, NORTH and SMALL). Warne. *n.d.*
Round of Days (For other illustrators *see* HOUGHTON, ARTHUR BOYD). Routledge. 1866
Spirit of Praise (For other illustrators *see* HOUGHTON, ARTHUR BOYD). Warne. 1866

GREEN, CHARLES (1840-1898) English
Craik. *Playroom Stories.* Griffith and Farran. 1863
Dickens. *Great Expectations.* Chapman. 1870
Dickens. *Old Curiosity Shop.* Chapman. 1871
Lemon. *Tinykin's Transformations.* Slark. 1865
Scott. *Waverley or 'Tis Sixty Years Since.* Black. 1892
Watts. *Divine and Moral Songs* (with DU MAURIER, MORTEN, J. D. WATSON and others). Nisbet. 1867

GREEN, ELIZABETH SHIPPEN *SEE* ELLIOTT, ELIZABETH SHIPPEN GREEN

GREEN, WINIFRED (*Ac.* 1898) English
Lamb. *Mrs. Leicester's School.* Dent. 1899
Lamb. *Poetry for Children.* Dent. 1898
Lamb. *Stories for Children.* Dent. 1903

GREENAWAY, KATE (1846-1901) English
A Apple Pie. Routledge. 1886
Allingham. *Rhymes for the Young Folk* (with ALLINGHAM, FURNISS and PATERSON). Cassell. 1887
Arnim. *April Baby's Book of Tunes.* Macmillan. 1900
Aulnoy. *Madame d'Aulnoy's Fairy Tales,* 9 v. Gall and Inglis. 1871
Aunt Louisa's London Toy Books: Diamonds and Toads. Warne. 1871
Barker. *Kate Greenaway's Birthday Book for Children.* Routledge. 1880.
Browning. *Pied Piper of Hamelin.* Routledge. 1888
Campbell. *Topo.* Marcus Ward. 1878
Cresswell. *Royal Progress of King Pepito.* S.P.C.K. 1889
Dame Wiggins of Lee and Her Seven Wonderful Cats (with R. STENNET). George Allen. 1885
Foster. *Day in a Child's Life.* Routledge. 1881
Greenaway. *Almanacks.* Routledge. 1883-1897 (except 1896)

Greenaway. *Kate Greenaway Pictures from Originals Presented by Her to Her Friends*. Warne. 1921

Greenaway. *Kate Greenaway's Alphabet*. Routledge. 1885

Greenaway. *Kate Greenaway's Book of Games*. Routledge. 1889

Greenaway. *Marigold Garden*. Routledge. 1885

Greenaway. *Under the Window*. Routledge. 1879

Harte. *Queen of the Pirate Isle*. Chatto. 1886

Knox. *Fairy Gifts; or, A Wallet of Wonders*. Griffith and Farran. 1874

Language of Flowers. Routledge. 1884

Mavor. *English Spelling Book*. Routledge. 1885

Mother Goose. *Mother Goose or the Old Nursery Rhymes*. Routledge. 1881

Quiver of Love, a Collection of Valentines (with WALTER CRANE). Marcus Ward. 1876

Ranking. *Flowers and Fancies; Valentines Ancient and Modern*. Marcus Ward. 1882

Taylor. *Little Ann and Other Poems*. Routledge. 1882

Yonge. *Heartsease*. Macmillan. 1879

Yonge. *Heir of Redclyffe*. Macmillan. 1879

GREIFFENHAGEN, MAURICE WILLIAM (1862-1932) English

Dickens. *American Notes*. Chapman. 1898

Scott. *Ivanhoe*. McKay. 1920

GREY OWL (1888-1938) Canadian

Grey Owl. *Sajo and the Beaver People*. Scribner. 1936

GRIBBLE, VIVIEN (-1932) English

Tennyson. *Songs from "The Princess."* Duckworth. 1924

GRISET, ERNEST HENRY (1844-1907) English, b. in France

Æsop. *Æsop's Fables*. Cassell. 1869

Defoe. *Life of Robinson Crusoe*. Hotten. 1869

Greenwood. *Bear King*. Griffith and Farran. 1868

Greenwood. *Hatchet Throwers*. Hotten. 1866

Greenwood. *Legends of Savage Life*. Hotten. 1866

Greenwood. *Purgatory of Peter the Cruel*. Routledge. 1868

Hood. *Griset's Grotesques*. Routledge. 1866

Mother Goose. *National Nursery Rhymes* (For other illustrators *see* HOUGHTON, ARTHUR BOYD). Novello, Ewer. 1870

Prosser. *Original Fables* (with H. W. WEIR and others). Religious Tract Society. 1870

Reynard the Fox. Reynard the Fox. Low. 1872

GRISHINA-GIVAGO, NADEJDA J. (1884-1936) American, b. in Russia

Grishina-Givago. *Gresha and His Clay Pig*. Stokes. 1930

Grishina-Givago. *Magic Squirrel*. Stokes. 1934

Grishina-Givago. *Peter-Pea*. Stokes. 1926

Grishina-Givago. *Shorty*. Stokes. 1924

Grishina-Givago. *Sparrow House*. Stokes. 1928

GRODIN, ADAMS JOHN (1913-   ) American

Grodin. *All the Year Round*. Knopf. 1937

GROSE, HELEN MASON (1880-   ) American

Blackmore. *Lorna Doone*. Macrae. 1917

Hawthorne. *House of the Seven Gables*. Houghton. 1924

Smith. *Jolly Good Times*. Little. 1927

Smith. *Jolly Good Times at School*. Little. 1928

Wiggin. *Birds' Christmas Carol*. Houghton. 1929

Wiggin. *Rebecca of Sunnybrook Farm*. Houghton. 1925

GUERTIK, HÉLÈNE (*Ac.* 1939) American

Lida. *Little French Farm*. Harper. 1939

Louv'a. *Animals I Like*. Poughkeepsie Artists and Writers Guild. 1935

HADER, BERTA HOERNER (*Ac.* 1941) American *and*
HADER, ELMER STANLEY (1889-   ) American

Feuillet. *Story of Mr. Punch*. Dutton. 1929

Hader. *Cock-a-doodle-doo*. Macmillan. 1939

Hader. *Farmer in the Dell*. Macmillan. 1931

Hader. *Spunky*. Macmillan. 1933

Hader. *Story of Pancho*. Macmillan. 1942

Hader. *Tommy Thatcher Goes to Sea*. Macmillan. 1937

Meigs. *Wonderful Locomotive*. Macmillan. 1928

Whitney. *Timothy and the Blue Cart*. Stokes. 1930

Williamson. *Humpy*. Doubleday. 1937

Williamson. *Monkey Tale*. Doubleday. 1929

Williamson. *Stripey, a Little Zebra*. Doubleday. 1939

HALL, SYDNEY PRIOR (1842- ?) English

Hughes. *Tom Brown at Oxford*. Macmillan. 1869

Hughes. *Tom Brown's School Days* (with ARTHUR HUGHES). Macmillan. 1869

HAMMOND, CHRIS (*Ac.* 1897) English

Edgeworth. *Parent's Assistant*. Macmillan. 1897

Edgeworth. *Popular Tales*. Macmillan. 1895

Thackeray. *Newcomes*. Nisbet. 1897

HAMMOND, GERTRUDE DEMAIN (-1934) English

Bunyan. *Pilgrim's Progress*. Black. 1904

Carter. *Shakespeare's Stories of the English Kings*. Harrap. 1910

Dickens. *David Copperfield*. Dodd. 1921

Kingsley. *Hereward, the Wake*. Crowell. 1910

Lamb. *Tales from Shakespeare*. Crowell. 1918

Molesworth. *Jasper*. Macmillan. 1906

Stedman. *Story of Hereward*. Harrap. 1921

HANDFORTH, THOMAS SCOFIELD (1897-   ) American

Coatsworth. *Toutou in Bondage*. Macmillan. 1929

Handforth. *Faraway Meadow*. Doubleday. 1939

Handforth. *Mei Li*. Doubleday. 1938

Smith. *Tranquilina's Paradise*. Minton. 1930

HANKEY, WILLIAM LEE (1869-   ) English

Goldsmith. *Deserted Village*. Constable. 1909

HANSEN, ERNST (1906-   ) Danish

Hanson. *Eric the Red*. Doubleday. 1933

Rasmussen. *Eagle's Gift*. Doubleday. 1932

HARDING, CHARLOTTE (1873-   ) American
  Tappan. *Robin Hood: His Book*. Little. 1903

HARDY, E. STUART (*Ac.* 1898) English
  Grimm. *Fairy Tales* (with others). Nister. 1898
  Mother Goose. *Old Mother Goose Rhymes*. Nister. *n.d.*

HARDY, PAUL (*Ac.* 1864) English
  Macaulay. *Lays of Ancient Rome*. Nister. 1864

HARGIS, JOHN EDWIN (1914-   ) American
  Wood. *American Mother Goose*. Stokes. 1940

HARNONCOURT, RENÉ D' *SEE* D'HARNONCOURT, RENÉ

HARVEY, WILLIAM (1796-1866) English
  Arabian Nights Entertainments. *Arabian Nights Entertainments*, 3 v. C. Knight. 1839-41
  Blind Beggar of Bethnal Green. Jennings and Chaplin. 1832
  Carové. *Story without an End*. Cundall. 1832
  Children in the Wood. Jennings and Chaplin. 1831
  Day. *Sandford and Merton*. Rivington. 1833
  Gay. *Fables of John Gay*. Routledge. 1854
  Lamb. *Tales from Shakespeare*. Baldwin and Cradock. 1838
  Northcote. *One Hundred Fables* (with T. J. NORTHCOTE). Lawford. 1828
  Reid. *Desert Home*. Ticknor. 1863
  Reid. *Young Voyageurs*. Bogue. 1853
  Shakespeare. *Pictorial Edition of the Works of Shakspere*, 8 v. (with others). Routledge. 1828-43

HASSELRIIS, ELSE (*Ac.* 1930) Danish
  Chrisman. *Shen of the Sea*. Dutton. 1925
  Chrisman. *Wind That Wouldn't Blow*. Dutton. 1927
  Dumas. *Nutcracker of Nuremberg*. McBride. 1930

HATHERELL, WILLIAM (1855-1928) English
  Molesworth. *Next-door House*. Chambers. 1893
  Shakespeare. *Tragedy of Romeo and Juliet*. Hodder. 1912
  Twain. *Prince and the Pauper*. Dent. 1923

HAVERS, ALICE MARY (1850-1890) English
  Andersen. *White Swans*. Hildesheimer. 1885
  Cape Town Dicky. C. W. Faulkner. *n.d.*

HAWKINS, SHEILA (1905-   ) Australian
  Hawkins. *Appleby John*. Harper. 1939
  Hawkins. *Pepito*. Harper. 1940

HEATH, ERNEST DUDLEY (*Ac.* 1913) English
  Macgregor. *Story of Rome* (with RAINEY and WOODROFFE). Stokes. 1913

HEIBERG, ASTRI WELHAVEN (1883-   ) Norwegian
  Lagerlöf. *Further Adventures of Nils*. Doubleday. 1911
  Zwilgmeyer. *Four Cousins*. Lothrop. 1923

HEIGHWAY, RICHARD (*Ac.* 1894?) English
  Æsop. *Fables of Æsop*. Macmillan. 1894
  Bluebeard and Puss in Boots. Dent. 1895

HELLÉ, ANDRÉ (1871-   ) French
  Hellé. *Big Beasts and Little Beasts*. Stokes. 1924
  La Fontaine. *Fables of La Fontaine*. Harper. 1940

HEMING, ARTHUR HENRY HOWARD (1870-1940) American
  Heming. *Living Forest*. Doubleday. 1925

HENDERSON, KEITH (1883-   ) Scotch
  Hudson. *Green Mansions*. Duckworth. 1931
  Hudson. *Purple Land*. Duckworth. 1929
  Prescott. *Conquest of Mexico*, 2 v. Chatto. 1922

HENDERSON, LE GRAND (1901-   ) American
  (LE GRAND, *pseud.*)
  Henderson. *Augustus and the Mountains*. Bobbs. 1941
  Henderson. *Augustus and the River*. Bobbs. 1939
  Henderson. *Augustus Drives a Jeep*. Bobbs. 1944
  Henderson. *Augustus Goes South*. Bobbs. 1940
  Henderson. *Glory Horn*. McBride. 1941
  Henderson. *Saturday for Samuel*. Greystone. 1941

HENNESSY, WILLIAM JOHN (1839-1917) American, b. in Ireland
  Tennyson. *Enoch Arden* (with DARLEY, LaFARGE and E. VEDDER). Ticknor and Fields. 1865
  Whittier. *Ballads of New England* (For other illustrators *see* FENN, HARRY). Fields, Osgood. 1869
  Whittier. *Maud Muller*. Ticknor and Fields. 1867
  Winter Poems by Favorite American Poets (with EYTINGE, FENN, FREDERICKS, HOMER and others). Fields, Osgood. 1871
  Yonge. *Caged Lion*. Macmillan. 1880
  Yonge. *Chaplet of Pearls*. Macmillan. 1882
  Yonge. *Dove in the Eagle's Nest*. Macmillan. 1885
  Yonge. *Unknown to History*. Macmillan. *n.d.*

HERFORD, OLIVER (1863-1935) American, b. in England
  Æsop. *Herford Æsop*. Ginn. 1921
  Carroll. *Alice's Adventures in Wonderland*. Ginn. 1917
  Harris. *Aaron in the Wildwoods*. Houghton. 1897
  Harris. *Little Mr. Thimblefinger and His Queer Country*. Houghton. 1894
  Harris. *Mr. Rabbit at Home*. Houghton. 1895
  Harris. *Story of Aaron*. Houghton. 1896
  Herford. *Alphabet of Celebrities*. Small. 1899
  Herford. *Bashful Earthquake*. Scribner. 1898
  Herford. *Child's Primer of Natural History*. Scribner. 1899
  Herford. *Peter Pan Alphabet*. Scribner. 1907
  Herford. *Rubaiyat of a Persian Kitten*. Scribner. 1904
  Jewett. *Con the Wizard*. Stokes. 1905
  Lathrop. *"Behind Time."* Cassell. 1886
  Reed. *Bird-nest Boarding House*. Dutton. 1922
  Wells. *Phenomenal Fauna*. Russell. 1902
  Wiggin. *Timothy's Quest*. Houghton. 1895

HERRERA, VELINO SHIJE (1902-   ) American
  Clark. *In My Mother's House*. Viking. 1941

HERRICK, HENRY W. (1824-1906) American
Abbott. *John Gay; or Work for Boys.* Hurd and Houghton. 1864
Abbott. *Mary Gay; or Work for Girls.* Hurd and Houghton. 1875
Abbott. *William Gay; or Play for Boys.* Hurd and Houghton. 1869
Æsop. *Fables of Æsop.* Houghton. 1865
La Motte-Fouqué. *Undine.* Hurd and Houghton. 1867
Scudder. *Doings of the Bodley Family in Town and Country* (with BENSELL, DARLEY, NAST, M. L. STONE and others). Hurd and Houghton. 1875

HEYNEMAN, ANNE (1910-   ) American
Butler. *Tom Twist.* Holiday. 1938
Cock Robin. Holiday. 1935
Irving. *Rip Van Winkle.* W. R. Scott. 1936
Nelson. *Pinky Finds a Home.* Holiday. 1940

HICKS, GEORGE ELGAR (1824-1914) English
Bloomfield. *Farmer's Boy* (with B. FOSTER and WEIR). Sampson Low. 1857

HILDEBRAND, FLOYD (*Ac.* 1941)
Grimm. *Fairy Tales.* Peter Pauper. 1941

HILDER, ROWLAND (1905-   ) English, b. in America
Lesterman. *Adventures of a Trafalgar Lad.* Cape. 1926
Lesterman. *Second Mate of the Myradale.* Harcourt. 1929
Masefield. *Midnight Folk.* Heinemann. 1931
Melville. *Moby Dick.* Knopf. 1926
Stevenson. *Treasure Island.* Oxford. 1929

HIM, GEORGE (1900-   ) Polish
Lewitt. *Blue Peter* (with JAN LEWITT). Faber. 1943
Lewitt. *Five Silly Cats* (with JAN LEWITT). Minerva. 1944
Lewitt. *Football's Revolt* (with JAN LEWITT). Country Life. 1939
Ross. *Little Red Engine Gets a Name* (with JAN LEWITT). Faber. 1942
Tuwim. *Locomotive, The Turnip, The Birds' Broadcast* (with JAN LEWITT). Faber. 1939

HINTON, CHARLES LOUIS (1869-   ) American
Martin. *Emmy Lou, Her Book and Heart.* McClure, Phillips. 1902

HODGES, C. WALTER (1909-   ) English
Hodges. *Columbus Sails.* Coward. 1939
Smith. *Ship Aground.* Oxford. 1941

HOFFMANN, HEINRICH *SEE* HOFFMANN-DONNER, HEINRICH

HOFFMANN-DONNER, HEINRICH (1809-1894) German
Hoffmann-Donner. *English Struwwelpeter.* Griffith, Farran, Browne. 1848

HOGAN, INEZ (1900-   ) American
Bryant. *Epaminondas and His Auntie.* Houghton. 1938
Hogan. *Elephant Twins.* Dutton. 1936

Hogan. *Nicodemus Helps Uncle Sam.* Dutton. 1943
Hogan. *Twin Colts.* Dutton. 1944
Hogan. *Twin Kids.* Dutton. 1937

HOGNER, NILS (1893-   ) American
Balch. *Indian Paint.* Crowell. 1942
Bible. *Bible Story.* Oxford. 1943
Hogner. *Animal Book.* Oxford. 1942
Hogner. *Education of a Burro.* Nelson. 1936
Hogner. *Navajo Winter Nights.* Nelson. 1935
Purnell. *Pedro the Potter.* Nelson. 1935

HOLBEIN, HANS, THE YOUNGER (1497-1543) German
Bible. *Holbein's Bible Events.* Cundall. *c.*1850
Bible. *Seventy Stories of the Old Testament* (with BEHAM, DÜRER and SALOMON). Bradford. 1938

HOLBERG, RICHARD A. (1889-1942) American
Carr. *Young Mac of Fort Vancouver.* Crowell. 1940
Holberg. *Bells of Amsterdam.* Crowell. 1940
Holberg. *Mitty on Mr. Syrup's Farm.* Doubleday. 1936
Palmer. *Up the River to Danger.* Scribner. 1940

HOLE, WILLIAM BRASSEY (1846-1917) English
Barrie. *Little Minister.* Cassell. 1893
Bible. *Life of Jesus of Nazareth.* Eyre. 1908
Scott. *Heart of Midlothian.* Black. 1893
Stevenson. *Kidnapped.* Cassell. 1895

HOLIDAY, HENRY (1839-1927) English
Carroll. *Hunting of the Snark.* Macmillan. 1876
Carroll. *Lewis Carroll Book.* (with JOHN TENNIEL). Dial. 1931
Carroll. *Rhyme? and Reason?* (with A. B. FROST). Macmillan. 1883

HOLLING, HOLLING CLANCY (1900-   ) American
Crawford. *Blot: Little City Cat.* Smith. 1930
Holling. *Book of Cowboys* (with L. W. HOLLING). Platt. 1936
Holling. *Book of Indians* (with L. W. HOLLING). Platt. 1935
Holling. *Paddle-to-the-Sea.* Houghton. 1941
Holling. *Tree in the Trail.* Houghton. 1942

HOLLING, LUCILLE WEBSTER (*Ac.* 1935) American
Holling. *Book of Cowboys* (with H. C. HOLLING). Platt. 1936
Holling. *Book of Indians* (with H. C. HOLLING). Platt. 1935

HOMER, WINSLOW (1836-1910) American
Bryant. *Story of the Fountain* (with FENN, FREDERICKS and others). Appleton. 1871
Gordon. *Old Boy's Story* (with DARLEY and NAST). Hurd and Houghton. *n.d.*
Lowell. *Courtin'.* Osgood. 1874
Tennyson. *Songs from the Published Writings of Alfred Tennyson* (with CURTIS, FREDERICKS and REINHART). Harper. 1880
Whittier. *Ballads of New England* (For other illustrators *see* FENN, HARRY). Fields, Osgood. 1869
Winter Poems by Favorite American Poets (with EYTINGE, FENN, FREDERICKS, HENNESSY and others). Fields, Osgood. 1871

HONORÉ, PAUL (1885-) American
Auslander. *Winged Horse*. Doubleday. 1927
Finger. *Highwaymen*. McBride. 1923
Finger. *Tales from Silver Lands*. Doubleday. 1924
Finger. *Tales Worth Telling*. Century. 1925
Hakluyt. *Heroes from Hakluyt*. Holt. 1928

HOOD, GEORGE PERCY JACOMB- (1857-1929) English
Lang. *Blue Fairy Book* (with H. J. Ford). Longmans. 1889
Wilde. *Happy Prince and Other Tales* (with WALTER CRANE). Nutt. 1888

HOOD, THOMAS, THE YOUNGER (1835-1874) English
Hood. *Loves of Tom Tucker and Little Bo-Peep*. Griffith and Farran. 1863

HOPKINS, LIVINGSTON (1846-1927) American
La Bedollière. *Story of a Cat*. Houghton. 1878

HOPPIN, AUGUSTUS (1828-1896) American
Alcott. *Three Proverb Stories*. Loring. 1868
Craik. *John Halifax, Gentleman*. Harper. 1877
Holmes. *Autocrat of the Breakfast Table*. Houghton. 1858
Whitney. *Summer in Leslie Goldthwaite's Life*. Houghton. 1867

HORGAN, PAUL (1903-) American
Men of Arms. McKay. 1931

HORSFALL, ROBERT BRUCE (1868-) American
Sharp. *Fall of the Year*. Houghton. 1911
Sharp. *Spring of the Year*. Houghton. 1912
Sharp. *Summer of the Year*. Houghton. 1914
Sharp. *Watcher in the Woods*. Appleton. 1903
Sharp. *Winter of the Year*. Houghton. 1912

HORSLEY, JOHN CALLCOTT (1817-1903) English
Beauty and the Beast. Cundall. 1850
Slater. *Little Princes*. Cundall. 1843

HORVATH, FERDINAND HUSZTI (1891-) American, b. in Hungary
Dunbar. *Sons o' Cormac*. Dutton. 1929
Morris. *Book of the Three Dragons*. Longmans. 1930
Ruskin. *King of the Golden River*. Studio. 1930

HOUGHTON, ARTHUR BOYD (1836-1875) English
Arabian Nights Entertainments. *Arabian Nights* (with T. B. G. DALZIEL). Warne. 1866
Arabian Nights Entertainments. *Dalziel's Arabian Nights*, 2 v. (with E. and T. B. G. DALZIEL, MILLAIS, MORTEN, PINWELL, TENNIEL and J. D. WATSON). Ward, Lock. 1865
Bible. *Art Pictures from the Old Testament* (with F. M. BROWN, BURNE-JONES, T. B. G. DALZIEL, F. LEIGHTON, PICKERSGILL, POYNTER, SANDYS, SOLOMON and WATTS). S.P.C.K. 1894
Bowman. *Boy Pilgrims*. Routledge. 1866
Buchanan. *Ballad Stories of the Affections* (For other illustrators see DALZIEL, EDWARD). Routledge. 1869
Cervantes Saavedra. *Don Quixote de la Mancha*. Warne. 1866
Dickens. *Hard Times and Pictures from Italy*. Chapman. 1866
Dulcken. *Home Thoughts and Home Scenes*. Routledge. 1865

Eiloart. *Ernie at School*. Routledge. 1866
Eiloart. *Ernie Elton, the Lazy Boy*. Routledge. 1865
Golden Thoughts from Golden Fountains (with E. and T. B. G. DALZIEL, J. LAWSON, PINWELL and SMALL). Warne. 1867
Horn of Plenty (with others). William F. Gill. 1876
Ingelow. *Poems* (For other illustrators see PINWELL, GEORGE JOHN). Roberts. 1867
Krylóv. *Krilof and His Fables* (with J. B. ZWECKER). Strahan. 1869
Longfellow. *Poetical Works* (with GRAY, NORTH and SMALL). Warne. n.d.
Mother Goose. *National Nursery Rhymes* (with E., E. G. and T. B. G. DALZIEL, F. A. FRASER, GRISET, HUGHES, MAHONEY, MARKS, PINWELL, SMALL and ZWECKER). Novello, Ewer. 1870
Patient Henry. Warne. 1865
Round of Days (with BAYES, BROOKES, E. and T. B. G. DALZIEL, GRAY, MORTEN, NORTH, PINWELL, F. WALKER and J. D. WATSON). Routledge. 1866
Spirit of Praise (with E. and T. B. G. DALZIEL, GRAY, NORTH, PINWELL and SMALL). Warne. 1866

HOUSER, ALLAN C. (1914-) American
Abeita. *I Am a Pueblo Indian Girl* (with NAILOR and ToHOMA). Morrow. 1939

HOUSMAN, LAURENCE (1865-) English
Housman. *All-Fellows*. Kegan Paul. 1896
Housman. *Doorway in Fairyland*. Cape. 1922
Housman. *Farm in Fairyland*. Kegan Paul. 1894
Housman. *House of Joy*. Kegan Paul. 1895
Housman. *Moonshine and Clover*. Cape. 1922
Housman. *New Child's Guide to Knowledge*. Sidgwick. 1911
MacDonald. *At the Back of the North Wind*. Blackie. 1900
MacDonald. *Princess and the Goblin*. Blackie. 1900
Rossetti. *Goblin Market*. Macmillan. 1893

HUGHES, ARTHUR (1832-1915) English
Allingham. *Music Master* (with MILLAIS and ROSSETTI). Routledge. 1855
Babies' Classics. Longmans. 1904
Christmas Carols (with E. G. and T. B. G. DALZIEL, F. A. FRASER and others). Novello, Ewer. 1871
Hughes. *Tom Brown's School Days* (with S. P. HALL). Macmillan. 1869
MacDonald. *At the Back of the North Wind*. Strahan. 1871
MacDonald. *Dealings with the Fairies*. Strahan. 1867
MacDonald. *Gutta Percha Willie*. King. 1873
MacDonald. *Jack and Jill*. Dent. 1913
MacDonald. *Magic Crook*. Fifield. 1911
MacDonald. *Princess and the Goblin*. Strahan. 1872
MacDonald. *Ranald Bannerman's Boyhood*. Strahan. 1871
Mother Goose. *National Nursery Rhymes* (For other illustrators see HOUGHTON, ARTHUR BOYD). Novello, Ewer. 1870
Rossetti. *Sing-song*. Routledge. 1872
Rossetti. *Speaking Likenesses*. Macmillan. 1874
Tennyson. *Enoch Arden*. Moxon. 1866

HUMMEL, LISL (*Ac.* 1932) Austrian
Fyleman. *Little Christmas Book.* Doran. 1927
Horne. *Good-natured Bear.* Macmillan. 1927
White. *Four Young Kendalls.* Houghton. 1932
White. *Sally in Her Fur Coat.* Houghton. 1929
White. *When Abigail Was Seven.* Houghton. 1931

HUNT, WILLIAM HOLMAN (1827-1910) English
Gatty. *Parables from Nature* (For other illustrators see BURNE-JONES, EDWARD COLEY). Bell and Daldy. 1867
Tennyson. *Poems* (with MILLAIS, MULREADY, ROSSETTI, STANFIELD and others). Moxon. 1857

HURD, CLEMENT (1908-   ) American
Brown. *Runaway Bunny.* Harper. 1942
Hurd. *Sky High.* Lothrop. 1941
Stein. *World Is Round.* W. R. Scott. 1939

HURD, PETER (1904-   ) American
Baldwin. *Story of Roland.* Scribner. 1930
Baldwin. *Story of Siegfried.* Scribner. 1931
Hamilton. *P-zoo.* Coward. 1945

HUTTON, CLARKE (1898-   ) English
Country A B C. Oxford. 1940
Streatfeild. *Harlequinade.* Chatto. 1943
White. *I, the Autobiography of a Cat.* Houghton. 1941

HUTTULA, A. (*Ac.* 1856) English
Songs of the Brave. Soldier's Dream and Other Poems and Odes (with DUNCAN, B. FOSTER, MACQUOID and THOMAS). Sampson Low. 1856

ISHMAEL, WOODI (1914-   ) American
Eaton. *Narcissa Whitman.* Harcourt. 1941
Robinson. *Sons of Liberty.* Dutton. 1941

IVANOVSKY, ELIZABETH (1910-   ) Russian
Gheon. *Saint Nicholas.* Sheed. 1936

IVES, RUTH (*Ac.* 1939) American
Mother Goose. *Mother Goose.* Holiday. 1939

IVINS, FLORENCE WYMAN (*Ac.* 1937) American
Ewing. *Lob Lie-by-the-fire.* Oxford. 1937
Untermeyer. *This Singing World.* Harcourt. 1923

JACKSON, CHRISTINE (*Ac.* 1930) English
Andersen. *Forty Stories.* Faber. 1930

JACOMB-HOOD, GEORGE PERCY *SEE* HOOD, GEORGE PERCY JACOMB-

JAMES, GILBERT (*Ac.* 1914) English
Aucassin and Nicolette. Routledge. 1905
Bible. *Books of Ruth and Esther.* Routledge. 1905
Petrović. *Hero Tales and Legends of the Serbians* (with others). Stokes. 1914

JAMES, WILL (1892-1942) American
James. *Cowboy in the Making.* Scribner. 1937
James. *Cowboys North and South.* Scribner. 1923
James. *Drifting Cowboy.* Scribner. 1925
James. *In the Saddle with Uncle Bill.* Scribner. 1935
James. *My First Horse.* Scribner. 1940
James. *Smoky.* Scribner. 1926
James. *Sun Up; Tales of the Cow Camps.* Scribner. 1931
James. *Uncle Bill.* Scribner. 1932
James. *Young Cowboy.* Scribner. 1935

JARRETT, MARCIA LANE *SEE* FOSTER, MARCIA LANE

JEMNE, ELSA LAUBACH (1888-   ) American
Hamsun. *Norwegian Family.* Lippincott. 1934
Hamsun. *Norwegian Farm.* Lippincott. 1933
MacKaye. *We of Frabo Stand.* Longmans. 1944

JOB, *pseud. SEE* ONFROY DE BRÉVILLE, JACQUES MARIE GASTON

JOHANNOT, TONY (1803-1852) French
Ainsworth. *Windsor Castle* (with G. CRUIKSHANK and DELAMOTTE). Parry, Blenkarn. 1847
Cervantes Saavedra. *Adventures of Don Quixote de la Mancha,* 3 v. J. J. Dubochet. 1837-39
Nodier. *Bean Flower and Pea Blossom.* Chapman. 1846

JOHNSON, AVERY F. (1906-   ) American
Neilson. *Mocha, the Djuka.* Dutton. 1943
White. *Mouseknees.* Random. 1939

JOHNSON, WILLIAM MARTIN (1862-1942) American
Reade. *Cloister and the Hearth,* 2 v. Harper. 1894
Wallace. *Ben Hur,* 2 v. Harper. 1892

JOHNSTON, EDITH CONSTANCE FARRINGTON (1890-   ) American
McKenny. *Book of Wild Flowers.* Macmillan. 1939

JONES, ELIZABETH ORTON (1910-   ) American
Adshead. *Brownies—Hush!* Oxford. 1938
Bible. *David.* Macmillan. 1937
Field. *Prayer for a Child.* Macmillan. 1944
Jones. *Minnie the Mermaid.* Oxford. 1939
Jones. *Ragman of Paris and His Ragamuffins.* Oxford. 1937
Meigs. *Scarlet Oak.* Macmillan. 1938

JONES, HAROLD (1904-   ) English
De La Mare. *This Year: Next Year.* Holt. 1937
Jones. *Visit to the Farm.* Faber. *n.d.*

JONES, RICHARD C. (1910-   ) American
Alcott. *Little Women.* Blue Ribbon. 1933
Eberle. *Sea-horse Adventure.* Holiday. 1937
Eberle. *Spice on the Wind.* Holiday. 1940
Maugham. *Princess September and the Nightingale.* Oxford. 1939
Peter and the Wolf. Oxford. 1940

JONES, WILFRED J. (1888-   ) American
Colum. *Island of the Mighty*. Macmillan. 1924
Coryell. *Scalp Hunters*. Harcourt. 1936
Firdausi. *Epic of Kings*. Macmillan. 1926
French. *Lance of Kanana*. Lothrop. 1932
Hémon. *Maria Chapdelaine*. Macmillan. 1924
Jones. *How the Derrick Works*. Macmillan. 1930
Twain. *Saint Joan of Arc* (with HOWARD PYLE). Harper. 1919

JOSEF, *pseud. SEE* SULLIVAN, JAMES FRANK

K. O. S., *pseud. SEE* DOMBROWSKI, KÄTHE SCHÖNBERGER VON

KANE, HENRY BUGBEE (1902-   ) American
Carrighar. *One Day on Beetle Rock*. Knopf. 1944

KAPPES, ALFRED (1850-1894) American
Froissart. *Boy's Froissart*. Scribner. 1879
Lowell. *Vision of Sir Launfal* (For other illustrators *see* ALEXANDER, JOHN WHITE). Houghton. 1888

KATCHAMAKOFF, ATANAS (1898-   ) American, b. in Bulgaria
Shannon. *Dobry*. Viking. 1934

KAUFFER, EDWARD MCKNIGHT (1891-   ) English, b. in America
Cervantes Saavedra. *Don Quixote de la Mancha*, 2 v. Nonesuch. 1930
Hudson. *Green Mansions*. Illustrated Modern Library. 1944

KAY, KATHARINE CAMERON *SEE* CAMERON, KATHARINE

KEENE, CHARLES SAMUEL (1823-1891) English
Defoe. *Robinson Crusoe*. Burns. 1847
Green's Nursery Annual. Darton and Clark. 1847
Lemon. *Legends of Number Nip*. Macmillan. 1864
Our People. Bradbury. 1881
Reade. *Good Fight*. Harper. 1859
Reid. *Boy Tar*. Kent. 1860

KEEP, VIRGINIA (1878-   ) American
Page. *Two Prisoners*. Harper. 1903

KELEN, EMERY (1896-   ) American, b. in Hungary
Æsop. *Æsop's Fables*. Duell. 1944
Kelen. *Yussuf the Ostrich*. Hyperion. 1943

KELEN, IMRE *SEE* KELEN, EMERY

KELLER, ARTHUR IGNATIUS (1866-1924) American
Dickens. *Christmas Carol*. McKay. 1914
Irving. *Legend of Sleepy Hollow*. Bobbs. 1906
Longfellow. *Hanging of the Crane*. Routledge. 1874
Smith. *Caleb West, Master Diver*. Houghton. 1898
Wister. *Virginian*. Macmillan. 1902

KEMBLE, EDWARD WINDSOR (1861-1933) American
Harris. *Daddy Jake, the Runaway*. Century. 1889
Harris. *On the Plantation*. Appleton. 1892
Harris. *Tarbaby and Other Rhymes* (with A. B. FROST). Appleton. 1904
Harris. *Uncle Remus; His Songs and His Sayings* (with A. B. FROST). Appleton. 1920

Irving. *Knickerbocker's History of New York*, 2 v. Putnam. 1893
Life's Book of Animals (with NEILSON, F. T. RICHARDS and others). Doubleday and McClure. 1898
Page. *Two Little Confederates* (with A. C. REDWOOD). Scribner. 1888
Pendleton. *King Tom and the Runaways*. Appleton. 1890
Smith. *Colonel Carter of Cartersville* (with F. H. SMITH). Houghton. 1891
Stockton. *Story-teller's Pack* (with NEWELL, SMEDLEY, A. B. STEPHENS and others). Scribner. 1897
Stowe. *Uncle Tom's Cabin*, 2 v. Houghton. 1892
Stuart. *Solomon Crow's Christmas Pockets and Other Tales* (with FROST and others). Harper. 1896
Twain. *Adventures of Huckleberry Finn*. Chatto & Windus. 1884
Twain. *Mark Twain's Library of Humour*. Webster. 1888

KENNEDY, J. W. F. (*Ac.* 1908)
Alcott. *Eight Cousins*. Little. 1908
Alcott. *Morning Glories and Queen Aster*. Little. 1904
Alcott. *Silver Pitchers*. Little. 1908

KENT, ROCKWELL (1882-   ) American
Beowulf. *Beowulf*. Random. 1932
Chaucer. *Canterbury Tales*. Covici Friede. 1934
Kent. *N by E*. Harcourt. 1930
Kent. *Rockwellkentiana*. Harcourt. 1933
Kent. *Wilderness*. Putnam. 1920
Melville. *Moby Dick*. Random. 1930
Saga of Gisli. Harcourt. 1936
Shakespeare. *Complete Works*, 2 v. Doubleday. 1936
Shephard. *Paul Bunyan*. Harcourt. 1941

KINGSLEY, CHARLES (1819-1875) English
Kingsley. *Heroes*. Macmillan. 1856

KIPLING, JOHN LOCKWOOD (1837-1911) English
Kipling. *Jungle Book* (with W. H. DRAKE and others). Macmillan. 1894
Kipling. *Kim*. Macmillan. 1901
Kipling. *Second Jungle Book*. Macmillan. 1895
Steel. *Tales of the Punjab*. Macmillan. 1894

KIPLING, RUDYARD (1865-1936) English
Kipling. *Just So Stories*. Macmillan. 1902

KIRMSE, MARGUERITE (1885-   ) American, b. in England
Atkinson. *Greyfriars Bobby*. Harper. 1912
Hudson. *Disappointed Squirrel*. Doubleday. 1925
Knight. *Lassie Come-home*. Winston. 1940
L'Hommedieu. *Macgregor, the Little Black Scottie*. Lippincott. 1941
L'Hommedieu. *Rusty, the Little Red Dachshund*. Lippincott. 1940
Ollivant. *Bob, Son of Battle*. Doubleday. 1924

KITTELSEN, THEODOR (1857-1914) Norwegian
Asbjörnsen. *Fairy Tales from the Far North* (with SINDING and WERENSKIÖLD). Nutt. 1897
Djurklo. *Fairy Tales from the Swedish* (with LARSSON and WERENSKIÖLD). Stokes. 1901

KONEWKA, PAUL (1840-1871) Danish
Konewka. *Black Peter.* Hurd and Houghton. 1870
My Young Days. Seeley. 1871
Shakespeare. *Midsummer Night's Dream.* Roberts.
1870

KORFF, GEORGE (*Ac.* 1944)
Charushin. *Baby Bears.* Macmillan. 1944

KREDEL, FRITZ (1900-) American, b. in Germany
Andersen. *Andersen's Fairy Tales.* Heritage. 1942
Burnett. *Shoemaker's Son.* Random. 1941
Defoe. *Robinson Crusoe.* Doubleday. 1945
Dickens. *Christmas Carol.* Peter Pauper. 1943
Grimm. *Grimm's Fairy Tales.* Stackpole. 1937
Pauli. *Silent Night, the Story of a Song.* Knopf. 1943
Sondergaard. *My First Geography of the Americas.*
Little. 1942

KUBINYI, KÁLMÁN (1906-) American
Gibson. *Goldsmith of Florence.* Macmillan. 1929
Howard. *Sokar and the Crocodile.* Macmillan. 1928

KUTCHER, BEN (1895-) American, b. in Russia
Janvier. *Aztec Treasure House.* Harper. 1918
Maury. *Old Raven's World.* Little. 1931
Ségur. *Princess Rosette and Other Fairy Tales.*
Macrae. 1930

KYD, *pseud. SEE* CLARKE, J. CLAYTON

LADY, A
Gray. *Elegy Written in a Country Churchyard* (with
B. FOSTER and THOMAS). Cundall. 1854

LACHER, GISELLA LOEFFLER (1903-) American, b. in
Austria
Bianco. *Franzi and Gizi.* Messner. 1941

LAFARGE, JOHN (1836-1910) American
Tennyson. *Enoch Arden* (with DARLEY, HENNESSY
and E. VEDDER). Ticknor and Fields. 1865

LALAUZE, ADOLPHE (1838-1905) French
Arabian Nights Entertainments. *Thousand and One
Nights,* 4 v. Nimmo and Bain. 1883
Goldsmith. *Vicar of Wakefield.* Gay and Bird. 1893
Swift. *Travels into Several Remote Nations of the
World by Lemuel Gulliver.* Nimmo and Bain. 1882

LANDSEER, EDWIN HENRY (1802-1873) English
Dickens. *Christmas Books* (with DOYLE, LEECH,
MACLISE, STANFIELD, F. STONE and TENNIEL).
Chapman. 1854
Dickens. *Cricket on the Hearth* (with DOYLE, LEECH
and STANFIELD). Bradbury and Evans. 1846

LANDSEER, THOMAS (1795-1880) English
Hall. *Midsummer Eve* (with MEADOWS, PATON and
others). Longman. 1847
Stories about Dogs. Bogue. 1850
Taylor. *Boy and the Birds.* Darton and Harvey. 1835

LANKES, JULIUS J. (1884-) American
Lagerlöf. *Mårbacka.* Doubleday. 1924
Potter. *Wag-by-wall.* Horn Book. 1944

LANTZ, PAUL (1908-) American
Clark. *Little Navajo Bluebird.* Viking. 1943
Edmonds. *Matchlock Gun.* Dodd. 1941
Edmonds. *Tom Whipple.* Dodd. 1942
Gates. *Blue Willow.* Viking. 1940
Holdridge. *Island Boy.* Holiday. 1942

LARSSON, CARL OLOF (1853-1919) Swedish
Andersen. *Fairy Tales and Stories.* Estes. 1887
Djurklo. *Fairy Tales from the Swedish* (with KIT-
TELSEN and WERENSKIÖLD). Stokes. 1901

LATHAM, BARBARA (1896-) American
Duplaix. *Pedro, Nina and Perrito.* Harper. 1939
Lowrey. *Silver Dollar.* Harper. 1940

LATHROP, DOROTHY PULIS (1891-) American
Andersen. *Little Mermaid.* Macmillan. 1939
Bible. *Animals of the Bible.* Stokes. 1937
Conkling. *Silverhorn.* Stokes. 1924
De La Mare. *Bells and Grass.* Viking. 1942
De La Mare. *Crossings.* Knopf. 1923
De La Mare. *Down-adown-derry.* Constable. 1922
De La Mare. *Dutch Cheese.* Knopf. 1931
De La Mare. *Mr. Bumps and His Monkey.* Winston.
1942
De La Mare. *Three Mulla-mulgars.* Knopf. 1919
Field. *Hitty.* Macmillan. 1929
Hawthorne. *Snow Image.* Macmillan. 1930
Hudson. *Little Boy Lost.* Knopf. 1920
Ingelow. *Mopsa the Fairy.* Harper. 1927
Lathrop. *Colt from Moon Mountain.* Macmillan. 1941
Lathrop. *Fairy Circus.* Macmillan. 1931
Lathrop. *Hide and Go Seek.* Macmillan. 1938
Lathrop. *Presents for Lupe.* Macmillan. 1940
Lathrop. *Puppies for Keeps.* Macmillan. 1943
Lathrop. *Who Goes There?* Macmillan. 1935
MacDonald. *Light Princess.* Macmillan. 1926
MacDonald. *Princess and Curdie.* Macmillan. 1927
Mandal. *Happy Flute.* Stokes. 1939
Snedeker. *Forgotten Daughter.* Doubleday. 1933
Teasdale. *Stars To-night.* Macmillan. 1930

LATTIMORE, ELEANOR FRANCES (1904-) American
Lattimore. *Clever Cat.* Harcourt. 1936
Lattimore. *Little Pear.* Harcourt. 1931
Lattimore. *Peachblossom.* Harcourt. 1943
Lattimore. *Questions of Lifu.* Harcourt. 1942

LAWSON, JOHN (*Ac.* 1883) English
Buchanan. *Ballad Stories of the Affections* (For other
illustrators *see* DALZIEL, EDWARD). Routledge. 1869
Clever Hans. de la Rue. 1883
Golden Thoughts from Golden Fountains (For other
illustrators *see* HOUGHTON, ARTHUR BOYD). Warne.
1867
Patmore. *Children's Garland from the Best Poets.*
Macmillan. 1873

LAWSON, ROBERT (1892-   ) American
Æsop. *Æsop's Fables.* Heritage. 1941
Atwater. *Mr. Popper's Penguins.* Little. 1938
Brewton. *Under the Tent of the Sky.* Macmillan. 1937
Bunyan. *Pilgrim's Progress.* Stokes. 1939
Fish. *Four and Twenty Blackbirds.* Stokes. 1937
Forester. *Poo-Poo and the Dragons.* Little. 1942
Gray. *Adam of the Road.* Viking. 1942
Lang. *Prince Prigio.* Little. 1942
Lawson. *Ben and Me.* Little. 1939
Lawson. *Rabbit Hill.* Viking. 1944
Lawson. *They Were Strong and Good.* Viking. 1940
Leaf. *Story of Ferdinand.* Viking. 1936
Leaf. *Story of Simpson and Sampson.* Viking. 1941
Leaf. *Wee Gillis.* Viking. 1938
Twain. *Prince and the Pauper.* Winston. 1937
Young. *Unicorn with Silver Shoes.* Longmans. 1932

LAYARD, ARTHUR (*Ac.* 1895) English
Marvellous Adventures of Sir John Mandeville. Constable. 1895

LEAR, EDWARD (1812-1888) English
Lear. *Book of Nonsense.* McLean. 1846
Lear. *Complete Nonsense Book.* Duffield. 1911
Lear. *Laughable Lyrics.* Bush. 1877
Lear. *More Nonsense Pictures, Rhymes, Botany, etc.* Routledge. 1872
Lear. *Nonsense Songs, Stories, Botany and Alphabets.* Routledge. 1871
Lear. *Queery Leary Nonsense.* Mills. 1911

LEBEDEV, VLADĪMĪR VASIL'EVĪCH (1891-   ) Russian
Lion and the Ox. Macmillan. 1932

LEE, DORIS EMRICK (1905-   ) American
Thurber. *Great Quillow.* Harcourt. 1944

LEE, MANNING DE VILLENEUVE (1894-   ) American
Leighton. *Singing Cave.* Houghton. 1945

LEE-HANKEY, WILLIAM *SEE* HANKEY, WILLIAM LEE

LEECH, JOHN (1817-1864) English
A'Beckett. *Comic History of England,* 2 v. Punch Office. 1847-48
A'Beckett. *Comic History of Rome.* Bradbury, Evans. 1852
Barham. *Ingoldsby Legends,* 3 v. (with GEORGE CRUIKSHANK). Bentley. 1840-47
Barham. *Ingoldsby Legends* (with G. CRUIKSHANK and TENNIEL). Bentley. 1864
Chatelain. *Silver Swan.* Grant and Griffith. 1847
Comic Nursery Tales, 3 v. (with others). Orr. 1833
Dickens. *Chimes* (with DOYLE, MACLISE and STANFIELD). Chapman. 1845
Dickens. *Christmas Books* (with DOYLE, E. H. LANDSEER, MACLISE, STANFIELD, F. STONE and TENNIEL). Chapman. 1854
Dickens. *Christmas Carol.* Chapman. 1843
Dickens. *Cricket on the Hearth* (with DOYLE, E. H. LANDSEER and STANFIELD). Bradbury and Evans. 1846
Leigh. *Comic English Grammar.* Bentley. 1840
Leigh. *Comic Latin Grammar.* Bentley. 1840
Leigh. *Jack the Giant Killer.* Orr. 1844

Merry Pictures, by the Comic Hands of Leech, Doyle, Phiz, Crowquill, Meadows, etc. Kent. 1857
Nursery Ditties from the Lips of Mrs. Lullaby. Grant and Griffith. 1844
Smith. *Struggles and Adventures of Christopher Tadpole at Home and Abroad.* Bentley. 1848
Stowe. *Uncle Tom's Cabin.* Bogue. 1852
Surtees. *Handley Cross, or Mr. Jorrocks' Hunt.* Bradbury. 1854
Young Troublesome; or Master Jacky's Holidays. Bradbury. 1849

LE GRAND, *pseud.* SEE HENDERSON, LE GRAND

LEIGHTON, CLARE VERONICA HOPE (1900-   ) English
Brontë. *Wuthering Heights.* Random. 1931
Tomlinson. *Sea and the Jungle.* Harper. 1930

LEIGHTON, FREDERICK LEIGHTON, BARON (1830-1896) English
Bible. *Art Pictures from the Old Testament* (For other illustrators *see* HOUGHTON, ARTHUR BOYD). S.P.C.K. 1894
Eliot. *Romola,* 3 v. Smith, Elder. 1863

LEIGHTON, JOHN (1822-1912) English
Alphabet of Drollery. Ackermann. 1848
Ancient Story of the Old Dame and Her Pig. Bogue. n.d.
Cowper. *Diverting History of John Gilpin.* Cundall. 1845
Our Tom Cat and His Nine Lives. Ackermann. n.d.
Pigot. *Life of Man Symbolised by the Months of the Year.* Longmans, Green, Reader, and Dyer. 1866
Royal Picture Alphabet. Ward, Lock. 1856

LE JEUNE, HENRY (1819-1904) English
Charlesworth. *Ministering Children* (with BIRKET FOSTER). Nisbet. 1856

LELOIR, MAURICE (1853- ?) French
Dumas. *Three Musketeers.* Warne. 1896
Saint-Pierre. *Paul and Virginia.* Altemus. 1891

LE MAIR, HENRIETTE WILLEBEEK (1889-   ) Dutch
Elkin. *Children's Corner.* McKay. 1915
Elkin. *Little People.* McKay. 1916
Elkin. *Old Dutch Nursery Rhymes.* McKay. 1917
Jātakas. *Twenty Jātaka Tales.* McKay. 1939
Milne. *Gallery of Children.* McKay. 1925
Mother Goose. *Auntie's Little Rhyme Book.* McKay. n.d.
Mother Goose. *Baby's Little Rhyme Book.* McKay. n.d.
Mother Goose. *Daddy's Little Rhyme Book.* McKay. n.d.
Mother Goose. *Grannie's Little Rhyme Book.* McKay. n.d.
Mother Goose. *Little Songs of Long Ago.* McKay. 1912
Mother Goose. *Mother's Little Rhyme Book.* McKay. n.d.
Mother Goose. *Nursie's Little Rhyme Book.* McKay. n.d.
Mother Goose. *Our Old Nursery Rhymes.* McKay. n.d.
Schumann. *Album.* Augener. n.d.
Stevenson. *Child's Garden of Verses.* McKay. 1926

LEMAIRE, MADELEINE JEANNE (1845-1928) French
Halévy. *Abbé Constantin.* Dodd. 1893

LENSKI, LOIS (1893-   ) American
Barksdale. *First Thanksgiving.* Knopf. 1942
Drummond. *Monkey That Would Not Kill.* Dodd. 1925
Emerson. *Hat-tub Tale.* Dutton. 1928
Emerson. *Mr. Nip and Mr. Tuck.* Dutton. 1930
Grahame. *Dream Days.* Lane. 1922
Grahame. *Golden Age.* Lane. 1921
Hutchinson. *Chimney Corner Fairy Tales.* Minton. 1926
Hutchinson. *Chimney Corner Stories.* Putnam. 1925
Lenski. *A-going to the Westward.* Stokes. 1937
Lenski. *Bayou Suzette.* Stokes. 1943
Lenski. *Bound Girl of Cobble Hill.* Stokes. 1938
Lenski. *Indian Captive.* Stokes. 1941
Lenski. *Jack Horner's Pie.* Harper. 1927
Lenski. *Little Girl of 1900.* Stokes. 1928
Lenski. *Little Sail Boat.* Oxford. 1937
Lenski. *Little Train.* Oxford. 1940
Lenski. *Phebe Fairchild.* Stokes. 1936
Lenski. *Skipping Village.* Stokes. 1927
Lenski. *Strawberry Girl.* Lippincott. 1945
Lenski. *Sugarplum House.* Harper. 1935

LEROY, ADRIEN (*Ac.* 1921)
Rabelais. *Gargantua, par Sautriax.* Duffield. 1921

LEVETUS, CELIA H. (*Ac.* 1899) English
Bain. *Turkish Fairy Tales.* Laurence and Bullen. 1896
Blake. *Songs of Innocence.* Wells Gardner. 1899

LEWIS, ARTHUR ALLEN (1873-   ) American
Field. *Calico Bush.* Macmillan. 1931
Field. *Hepatica Hawks.* Macmillan. 1932
La Motte-Fouqué. *Undine.* Limited Editions. 1930
Longfellow. *Poems.* Illustrated Modern Library. 1944
Scott. *Ivanhoe,* 2 v. Limited Editions. 1940

LEWITT, JAN (1907-   ) Polish
Lewitt. *Blue Peter* (with GEORGE HIM). Faber. 1943
Lewitt. *Five Silly Cats* (with GEORGE HIM). Minerva. 1944
Lewitt. *Football's Revolt* (with GEORGE HIM). Country Life. 1939
Ross. *Little Red Engine Gets a Name* (with GEORGE HIM). Faber. 1942
Tuwim. *Locomotive, The Turnip, The Birds' Broadcast* (with GEORGE HIM). Faber. 1939

LI CHU-T'ANG (*Ac.* 1919) Chinese
Pitman. *Chinese Wonder Book.* Dent. 1919

LIDDELL, MARY (1891-   ) American
Liddell. *Little Machinery.* Doubleday. 1926
Lorenzini. *Adventures of Pinocchio.* Doubleday. 1930

LINTON, JAMES DROMGOLE (1840-1916) English
Shakespeare. *King Henry VIII.* Cassell. 1892
Shakespeare. *Merchant of Venice.* Doran. 1913

LINTON, WILLIAM JAMES (1812-1898) English
Austin. *Moonfolk.* Putnam. 1874
Bryant. *Thanatopsis.* Putnam. 1878-79
History of a Scuttle of Coals in Rhymes and Pictures. Newman. 1866
Linton. *Flower and the Star.* Ticknor and Fields. 1868

LIST, HERTHA (*Ac.* 1940)
Andersen. *Tumblebug and Other Tales.* Harcourt. 1940

LOEFFLER, GISELLA SEE LACHER, GISELLA LOEFFLER

LOFTING, HUGH (1886-   ) American, b. in England
Lofting. *Doctor Dolittle's Caravan.* Stokes. 1926
Lofting. *Doctor Dolittle's Circus.* Stokes. 1924
Lofting. *Doctor Dolittle's Post Office.* Stokes. 1923
Lofting. *Doctor Dolittle's Zoo.* Stokes. 1925
Lofting. *Noisy Nora.* Stokes. 1929
Lofting. *Porridge Poetry.* Stokes. 1924
Lofting. *Story of Doctor Dolittle.* Stokes. 1920
Lofting. *Story of Mrs. Tubbs.* Stokes. 1923
Lofting. *Tommy, Tilly and Mrs. Tubbs.* Stokes. 1936
Lofting. *Voyages of Doctor Dolittle.* Stokes. 1922

LORENTOWICZ, IRENA (1910-   ) Polish
Bernhard. *Lullaby.* Roy. 1944
Goldszmit. *Matthew, the Young King.* Roy. 1945
Maril. *Mr. Bunny Paints the Eggs.* Roy. 1945
Porazińska. *9 Cry-baby Dolls.* Roy. 1945

LORIOUX, FELIX (*Ac.* 1928) French
Reynard the Fox. *Story of Reynard the Fox.* Macmillan. 1928

LOW, WILL HICOX (1853-1932) American
Shakespeare. *As You Like It.* Dodd. 1900

LUFKIN, RAYMOND H. (1897-   ) American
Davis. *Year Is a Round Thing.* Harper. 1938
Emerson. *Magic Tunnel.* Stokes. 1940
Kelly. *At the Sign of the Golden Compass.* Macmillan. 1938
Kelly. *Treasure Mountain.* Macmillan. 1937
Lide. *Ood-le-uk the Wanderer.* Little. 1930
Roos. *Man of Molokai.* Lippincott. 1943

MACBRIDE, MAUD GONNE (1866-   ) Irish
Young. *Celtic Wonder Tales.* Maunsel. 1910

MCCLOSKEY, JOHN ROBERT (1914-   ) American
Bishop. *Man Who Lost His Head.* Viking. 1942
Davis. *Tree Toad.* Stokes. 1942
McCloskey. *Homer Price.* Viking. 1943
McCloskey. *Lentil.* Viking. 1940
McCloskey. *Make Way for Ducklings.* Viking. 1941
Malcolmson. *Yankee Doodle's Cousins.* Houghton. 1941

MCCORMICK, ARTHUR DAVID (1860-   ) Irish
Arabian Nights Entertainments. *Arabian Nights Entertainments* (with W. H. ROBINSON, STRATTON and others). Newnes. 1899
Hudson. *Little Boy Lost.* Duckworth. 1905
Southey. *Life of Nelson.* Houghton. 1926

McCREADY, TASHA TUDOR *SEE* TUDOR, TASHA

MACDONALD, VIOLET M. (*Ac.* 1930) English
Macdonald. *Nursery Tales.* Cape. 1929

MACGREGOR, ARCHIE (*Ac.* 1895) English
Parry. *Butter-Scotia; or, A Cheap Trip to Fairyland.* Nutt. 1896
Parry. *Katawampus.* Nutt. 1895

MACHETANZ, FREDERICK (1908-   ) American
Machetanz. *On Arctic Ice.* Scribner. 1940
Machetanz. *Panuck.* Scribner. 1939

McINTOSH, FRANK (1901-   ) American
Crichton. *Peep-in-the-world.* Longmans. 1929
Lansing. *Magic Gold.* Little. 1928
Topelius. *Canute Whistlewinks and Other Stories.* Longmans. 1927

MACINTYRE, ELISABETH (*Ac.* 1944) Australian
MacIntyre. *Ambrose Kangaroo.* Scribner. 1942
MacIntyre. *Susan Who Lives in Australia.* Scribner. 1944

McKAY, DONALD (1895-   ) American
Dickens. *Pickwick Papers.* Illustrated Modern Library. 1943
Shapiro. *How Old Stormalong Captured Mocha Dick.* Messner. 1942
Shapiro. *Steamboat Bill and the Captain's Top Hat.* Messner. 1943
Summers. *Conquerors of the River.* Oxford. 1939
Twain. *Adventures of Tom Sawyer.* Random. 1930

MACKINSTRY, ELIZABETH A. (*Ac.* 1935) American
Andersen. *Andersen's Fairy Tales.* Coward. 1933
Arabian Nights Entertainments. *Aladdin and the Wonderful Lamp.* Macmillan. 1935
Aulnoy. *White Cat.* Macmillan. 1928
Colum. *Legend of Saint Columba.* Macmillan. 1935
Field. *Eliza and the Elves.* Macmillan. 1926
Field. *Magic Pawnshop.* Dutton. 1927
Geister. *What Shall We Play?* Harper. 1924
Johnson. *Little Book of Necessary Nonsense.* Harper. 1929
MacDonald. *Princess and the Goblin.* Doubleday. 1928
MacKaye. *Tall Tales of the Kentucky Mountains.* Doran. 1926
MacKinstry. *Fairy Alphabet.* Viking. 1933
MacKinstry. *Puck in Pasture.* Doubleday. 1925
Moore. *Night before Christmas.* Dutton. 1928
Noyes. *Forty Singing Seamen.* Stokes. 1930
White. *Snake Gold.* Macmillan. 1926
Wiggin. *Fairy Ring.* Doubleday. 1910
Wiggin. *Tales of Laughter.* Doubleday. 1926

McLENAN, JOHN (1826-1865) American
Abbott. *History of King Philip.* Harper. 1857
Abbott. *Rollo on the Atlantic.* Reynolds. 1853
Dickens. *Great Expectations.* Peterson. 1861
Dickens. *Tale of Two Cities,* 2 v. Peterson. 1859

MACLISE, DANIEL (1806-1870) English
Dickens. *Chimes* (with DOYLE, LEECH and STANFIELD). Chapman. 1845
Dickens. *Christmas Books* (with DOYLE, E. H. LANDSEER, LEECH, STANFIELD, F. STONE and TENNIEL). Chapman. 1854
Moore. *Irish Melodies.* Longman, Brown, Green and Longmans. 1846
Story of the Norman Conquest. Art Union of London. 1846
Tennyson. *Princess.* Moxon. 1860

McNAB, ALLAN (1901-   ) English
Eliot. *Mill on the Floss.* Harper. 1932
Lamb. *Durandal.* Doubleday. 1931

MACQUOID, THOMAS ROBERT (1820-1912) English
Primrose Pilgrimage. Griffith and Farran. 1865
Songs of the Brave. Soldier's Dream and Other Poems and Odes (with DUNCAN, B. FOSTER, HUTTULA and THOMAS). Sampson Low. 1856
Stowe. *Uncle Tom's Cabin* (with G. H. THOMAS). N. Cooke. 1853

MACWHIRTER, JOHN A. (1839-1911) Scotch
Wordsworth. *Poems for the Young* (with J. A. PETTIE). Strahan. 1863

MAHONEY, J. (*Ac.* 1870) English
Dickens. *Child's History of England* (with MARCUS STONE). Chapman. 1868
Dickens. *Little Dorrit.* Chapman. 1870
Dickens. *Oliver Twist.* Chapman. 1870
Dickens. *Our Mutual Friend.* Chapman. 1871
Ingelow. *Little Wonder Horn.* King. 1872
Mother Goose. *National Nursery Rhymes* (For other illustrators *see* HOUGHTON, ARTHUR BOYD). Novello, Ewer. 1870

MAPEWI *SEE* HERRERA, VELINO SHIJE

MARKS, H. STACY (1829-1898) English
Dickens. *Child's History of England.* Chapman. 1873
Marks. *Ridiculous Rhymes.* Routledge. 1869
Mother Goose. *National Nursery Rhymes* (For other illustrators *see* HOUGHTON, ARTHUR BOYD). Novello, Ewer. 1870

MARSH, REGINALD (1898-   ) American
Gury. *'Round and 'Round Horse.* Holt. 1943

MASHA, *pseud. SEE* STERN, MARIE SIMCHOW

MATES, RUDOLF (1881-   ) Czechoslovakian
Kožišek. *Forest Story.* Macmillan. 1929
Kožišek. *Magic Flutes.* Longmans. 1929
Sedláček. *Nursery Rhymes from Bohemia.* McBride. 1929
Szalatnay. *Cock and the Hen.* Szalatnay. 1925

MATULKA, JAN (1890-   ) American, b. in Czechoslovakia
Fillmore. *Czechoslovak Fairy Tales.* Harcourt. 1919
Fillmore. *Shoemaker's Apron.* Harcourt. 1920

MAY, PHILIP WILLIAM (1864-1903) English
  May. *Phil May's A B C.* Leadenhall. 1897
  May. *Phil May's Gutter-snipes.* Macmillan. 1896

MAZER, SONIA (1902-   ) American, b. in Russia
  Mazer. *Masha, a Little Russian Girl.* Doubleday. 1932
  Mazer. *Yossele's Holiday.* Doubleday. 1934

MEADOWS, JOSEPH KENNY (1790-1874) English
  Browne. *Granny's Wonderful Chair and Its Tales of Fairy Times.* Griffith and Farran. 1857
  Hall. *Midsummer Eve* (with T. LANDSEER, PATON and others). Longman. 1847
  Hall. *Prince of the Fair Family* (with others). Chapman. 1866
  Home for the Holidays. Nelson. 1859
  Merry Pictures, by the Comic Hands of Leech, Doyle, Phiz, Crowquill, Meadows, etc. Kent. 1857
  Milton. *L'Allegro and Il Penseroso* (with others). Art Union of London. 1848
  Sydenham Sinbad. J. and C. Brown. 1850

MERRILL, FRANK THAYER (1848- ?) American
  Alcott. *Little Men.* Roberts. 1885
  Alcott. *Little Women.* Roberts. 1880
  Aldrich. *Baby Bell* (with CURTIS, MORAN, A. R. WAUD and others). Osgood. 1877
  Atkinson. *Johnny Appleseed.* Harper. 1915
  Catherwood. *Rocky Fork.* Lothrop. 1911
  Curtiss. *Richard Peters: or, Could He Forgive Him?* Graves and Ellis. 1872
  Diaz. *William Henry and His Friends.* Osgood. 1871
  Dix. *Merrylips.* Macmillan. 1906
  Eggleston. *Long Knives.* Lothrop. 1907
  Hale. *Man Without a Country.* Roberts. 1888
  Irving. *Rip Van Winkle.* Cassino. 1888
  Longfellow. *Courtship of Miles Standish* (with BOUGHTON, REINHART and others). Houghton. 1888
  Richards. *Captain January.* Estes and Lauriat. 1893
  Twain. *Prince and the Pauper.* Osgood. 1882
  Vaile. *Orcutt Girls.* Wilde. 1896

MICHAEL, ARTHUR C. (*Ac.* 1916) English
  Dickens. *Christmas Carol.* Hodder. 1911
  Marshall. *History of France.* Hodder. 1912
  Marshall. *History of Germany.* Frowde. 1913
  Marshall. *This Country of Ours.* Doran. 1917

MILHOUS, KATHERINE (1894-   ) American
  Dalgliesh. *Book for Jennifer.* Scribner. 1940
  Dalgliesh. *Little Angel.* Scribner. 1943
  Dalgliesh. *Once on a Time.* Scribner. 1938
  Hunt. *Billy Button's Buttered Biscuit.* Stokes. 1941
  Milhous. *First Christmas Crib.* Scribner. 1944
  Milhous. *Herodia, the Lovely Puppet.* Scribner. 1942

MILLAIS, JOHN EVERETT (1829-1896) English
  Allingham. *Music Master* (with HUGHES and ROSSETTI). Routledge. 1855
  Arabian Nights Entertainments. Dalziel's Arabian Nights, 2 v. (For other illustrators *see* HOUGHTON, ARTHUR BOYD). Ward, Lock. 1865
  Bible. *Parables of Our Lord.* Routledge. 1864
  Defoe. *Robinson Crusoe.* Macmillan. 1860
  Little Songs for Me to Sing. Cassell. 1865

  Rands. *Lilliput Levee* (with G. J. PINWELL). Strahan. 1864
  Tennyson. *Poems* (with HUNT, MULREADY, ROSSETTI, STANFIELD and others). Moxon. 1857
  Thackeray. *Barry Lyndon.* Smith, Elder. 1879
  Trollope. *Framley Parsonage,* 3 v. Smith, Elder. 1861
  Trollope. *Orley Farm,* 2 v. Chapman. 1862
  Trollope. *Small House at Allington,* 2 v. Smith, Elder. 1864
  Tytler. *Papers for Thoughtful Girls.* Strahan. 1862

MILLAR, H. R. (*Ac.* 1930) English
  Bland. *Book of Dragons.* Harper. 1900
  Bland. *Enchanted Castle.* Unwin. 1907
  Bland. *Five Children* (with G. F. BROWNE). Coward. 1930
  Bland. *Nine Unlikely Tales for Children.* Unwin. 1901
  Bland. *Oswald Bastable and Others* (with C. E. BROCK). Wells Gardner. 1905
  Bland. *Wonderful Garden.* Macmillan. 1911
  Fairy Tales Far and Near. Cassell. 1895
  Golden Fairy Book. Hutchinson. 1894
  Hakluyt. *Hakluyt's Voyages.* Blackwell. 1929
  Kennedy. *New World Fairy Book.* Dutton. 1904
  Kipling. *All the Puck Stories* (with C. E. BROCK). Macmillan. 1935
  Kipling. *Puck of Pook's Hill.* Macmillan. 1906
  Molesworth. *Wood-pigeons and Mary.* Macmillan. 1901
  Tolstoi. *Ivan the Fool.* Walter Scott. 1895
  Tolstoi. *Where Love Is There God Is Also.* Walter Scott. 1896
  Yonge. *Little Duke.* Bell. n.d.

MĪTROKHĪN, DMĪTRIĪ ĪSIDOROVĪCH (1883-   ) Russian
  Ransome. *Old Peter's Russian Tales.* Jack. 1917

MOE, LOUIS MARIA NIELS PEDER HALLING (1859-   ) Norwegian
  Kalkar. *Adventures of Three Little Pigs.* Longmans. 1929
  Kalkar. *Raggle Taggle Bear.* Longmans. 1929
  Moe. *Forest Party.* Coward. 1930
  Moe. *Little Bear-cub; and The Dressed-up Pig.* Coward. 1930
  Moe. *Vain Pussy Cat.* Coward. 1929

MOESCHLIN-HAMMAR, ELSA (1879-   ) Swedish, Living in Switzerland
  Moeschlin-Hammar. *Little Boy with the Big Apples.* Coward. 1932
  Moeschlin-Hammar. *Red Horse.* Coward. 1929

MONSELL, JOHN ROBERT (1877-   ) Irish
  Housman. *What-o'clock Tales.* Stokes. 1932
  Monsell. *Pink Knight.* Chatto. 1907
  Monsell. *Polichinelle.* Oxford. 1928

MOON, CARL (1879-   ) American
  Moon. *Chi-Weé.* Doubleday. 1925
  Moon. *Chi-Weé and Loki of the Desert.* Doubleday. 1926
  Moon. *Flaming Arrow.* Stokes. 1927
  Moon. *Runaway Papoose.* Doubleday. 1928

F. T. MERRILL : *Rip Van Winkle*

MORA, FRANCIS LUIS (1874-1940) American, b. in Uruguay
Kahmann. *Sinfi and the Little Gypsy Goat*. Random. 1940
Sawyer. *Toño Antonio*. Viking. 1934

MORAN, THOMAS (1837-1926) American, b. in England
Aldrich. *Baby Bell* (with CURTIS, MERRILL, A. R. WAUD and others). Osgood. 1877
Brooks. *Boy Emigrants* (with W. L. SHEPPARD). Scribner. 1877
Taylor. *National Ode* (with FREDERICKS, A. R. WAUD and others). William Gill. 1876

MORDVINOFF, NICOLAS (1911-) Russian
Stone. *Pépé Was the Saddest Bird*. Knopf. 1944

MORGAN, ALICE MARY HAVERS *SEE* HAVERS, ALICE MARY

MORTEN, THOMAS (1836-1866) English
Arabian Nights Entertainments. *Dalziel's Arabian Nights*, 2 v. (For other illustrators *see* HOUGHTON, ARTHUR BOYD). Ward, Lock. 1865
Hood. *Jingles and Jokes for Little Folks* (with PAUL GRAY and others). Cassell. 1865
Round of Days (For other illustrators *see* HOUGHTON, ARTHUR BOYD). Routledge. 1866
Swift. *Gulliver's Travels*. Cassell. 1865
Watts. *Divine and Moral Songs* (with DU MAURIER, C. GREEN, J. D. WATSON and others). Nisbet. 1867

MORTON-SALE, ISOBEL (1904-) English
Farjeon. *Cherrystones* (with JOHN MORTON-SALE). Lippincott. 1944
Farjeon. *Martin Pippin in the Daisy Field* (with JOHN MORTON-SALE). Stokes. 1938
Farjeon. *Sing for Your Supper* (with JOHN MORTON-SALE). Stokes. 1938
Grigs. *Yellow Cat* (with JOHN MORTON-SALE). Oxford. 1936
Lynch. *Fiddler's Quest*. Dutton. 1943

MORTON-SALE, JOHN (1901-) English
Farjeon. *Cherrystones* (with ISOBEL MORTON-SALE). Lippincott. 1944
Farjeon. *Martin Pippin in the Daisy Field* (with ISOBEL MORTON-SALE). Stokes. 1938
FARJEON. *Sing for Your Supper* (with ISOBEL MORTON-SALE). Stokes. 1938
Grigs. *Yellow Cat* (with ISOBEL MORTON-SALE). Oxford. 1936

MOSER, JAMES HENRY (1854-1913) American, b. in Canada
Harris. *Uncle Remus; His Songs and His Sayings* (with F. S. CHURCH). Appleton. 1881

MOWBRAY, HARRY SIDDONS (1858-1928) American
Lowell. *Vision of Sir Launfal* (For other illustrators *see* ALEXANDER, JOHN WHITE). Houghton. 1888

MULREADY, WILLIAM (1786-1863) English, b. in Ireland
Dorset. *Lion's Masquerade*. John Harris. 1807
Dorset. *Peacock at Home*. John Harris. 1807
Elephant's Ball by W. B. John Harris. 1807
Godwin. *Fables Ancient and Modern*, 2 v. William Godwin. 1805

Godwin. *Looking Glass*. Thomas Hodgkins. 1805
Goldsmith. *Vicar of Wakefield*. Van Voerst. 1843
Home Treasury Primer. Cundall. 1850
Lamb. *King and Queen of Hearts*. Field and Tuer. 1809
Lamb. *Tales from Shakespeare*, 2 v. Thomas Hodgkins. 1807
Roscoe. *Butterfly's Ball and The Grasshopper's Feast*. John Harris. 1807
Tennyson. *Poems* (with HUNT, MILLAIS, ROSSETTI, STANFIELD and others). Moxon. 1857

MURRAY, CHARLES OLIVER (1842-1923) English
Mitford. *Children of the Village* (with BARNARD, BARNES, M. E. EDWARDS and others). Routledge. 1880
Mitford. *Our Village* (with W. H. J. BOOT). Sampson Low. 1879

MUSSINO, ATTILIO (1878-) Italian
Lorenzini. *Adventures of Pinocchio*. Macmillan. 1925

NADEJEN, THEODORE (*Ac.* 1930) American, b. in Russia
Adams. *Mountains Are Free*. Dutton. 1930
De La Mare. *Stories from the Bible*. McKay. 1929
Mirza. *Myself When Young*. Doubleday. 1929
Zeitlin. *Gessar Khan*. Doran. 1927
Zeitlin. *Skazki*. Doran. 1926

NAILOR, GERALD A. (1917-) American
Abeita. *I Am a Pueblo Indian Girl* (with HOUSER and ToHOMA). Morrow. 1939

NAST, THOMAS (1840-1902) American, b. in Germany
Clarke. *Little Prudy Books*. Lee and Shepard. 1863-65
Defoe. *Robinson Crusoe*. Hurd. 1868
Dickens. *Dickens' Christmas Story of the Goblins Who Stole a Sexton*. McLoughlin. 1867
Dodge. *Hans Brinker* (with F. O. C. DARLEY). James O'Kane. 1866
Gordon. *Boarding School Days* (with F. O. C. DARLEY). Hurd and Houghton. 1873
Gordon. *Old Boy's Story* (with DARLEY and HOMER). Hurd and Houghton. *n.d.*
Moore. *Visit from St. Nicholas*. McLoughlin. 1869
Scudder. *Doings of the Bodley Family in Town and Country* (with BENSELL, DARLEY, HERRICK, M. L. STONE and others). Hurd and Houghton. 1875

NEILSON, HARRY B. (1861-1941) English
Krakemsides. *Careless Chicken*. Warne. 1924
Life's Book of Animals (with KEMBLE, F. T. RICHARDS and others). Doubleday and McClure. 1898

NEWBERRY, CLARE TURLAY (1903-) American
Newberry. *April's Kittens*. Harper. 1940
Newberry. *Babette*. Harper. 1937
Newberry. *Barkis*. Harper. 1938
Newberry. *Cousin Toby*. Harper. 1939
Newberry. *Herbert the Lion*. Brewer. 1931
Newberry. *Marshmallow*. Harper. 1942
Newberry. *Mittens*. Harper. 1936
Newberry. *Pandora*. Harper. 1944

J. W. NORTH : *Songs of Seven*

NEWELL, PETER SHEAF HERSEY (1862-1924) American
Carroll. *Alice's Adventures in Wonderland*. Harper. 1901
Carroll. *Hunting of the Snark and Other Poems*. Harper. 1903
Carroll. *Through the Looking-glass*. Harper. 1902
Garnett. *Creature Songs*. Ditson. 1912
Lee. *Tommy Toddles*. Harper. 1896
Newell. *Hole Book*. Harper. 1908
Newell. *Peter Newell's Pictures and Rhymes*. Harper. 1899
Newell. *Rocket Book*. Harper. 1912
Newell. *Shadow Show*. Century. 1896
Newell. *Slant Book*. Harper. 1910
Newell. *Topsys & Turveys*. Century. 1893
Newell. *Topsys & Turveys*, Second Series. Century. 1894
Page. *Among the Camps* (with ROGERS and SHEPPARD). Scribner. 1891
Reed. *Book of Clever Beasts*. Putnam. 1904
Stockton. *Story-teller's Pack* (with KEMBLE, SMEDLEY, A. B. STEPHENS and others). Scribner. 1897

NEWILL, MARY J. (*Ac.* 1895) English
Andersen. *Nightingale*. Napier. 1894
Mother Goose. *Book of Nursery Songs and Rhymes*. Methuen. 1895

NICHOLS, DALE (1904-   ) American
Dana. *Two Years before the Mast*. Heritage. 1941

NICHOLS, SPENCER BAIRD (1875-   ) American
Dickens. *Christmas Carol*. Stokes. 1913
Dickens. *Christmas Stories*. Cape. 1922
Wilde. *Happy Prince and Other Stories*. Stokes. 1913

NICHOLSON, WILLIAM (1872-   ) English
Alphabet. Heinemann. 1898
Bianco. *Velveteen Rabbit*. Heinemann. 1922
Kipling. *Almanac of Twelve Sports*. Heinemann. 1897
Nicholson. *Characters of Romance*. Heinemann. 1900
Nicholson. *Clever Bill*. Doubleday. 1927
Nicholson. *Pirate Twins*. Faber. 1929
Sassoon. *Memoirs of a Fox-hunting Man*. Faber. 1929
Waugh. *Square Book of Animals*. Heinemann. 1899

NIELSEN, KAY (1886-   ) Danish
Andersen. *Fairy Tales*. Doran. 1924
Asbjörnsen. *East of the Sun and West of the Moon*. Doran. 1922
Grimm. *Hansel and Gretel*. Doran. *n.d.*
Quiller-Couch. *Twelve Dancing Princesses*. Doran. 1923

NISBET, NOEL LAURA (1887-   ) English
Polevoï. *Russian Fairy Tales*. Harrap. 1915

NOBODY, A., *pseud.* SEE BROWNE, GORDON FREDERICK

NORTH, JOHN WILLIAM (1842-1924) English
Ingelow. *Poems* (For other illustrators *see* PINWELL, GEORGE JOHN). Roberts. 1867
Ingelow. *Songs of Seven* (with others). Roberts. 1866
Longfellow. *Poetical Works* (with GRAY, HOUGHTON and SMALL). Warne. *n.d.*

Round of Days (For other illustrators *see* HOUGHTON, ARTHUR BOYD). Routledge. 1866
Spirit of Praise (For other illustrators *see* HOUGHTON, ARTHUR BOYD). Warne. 1866
Wayside Posies (with PINWELL and F. WALKER). Routledge. 1867

NORTHCOTE, THOMAS JAMES (1746-1831) English
Northcote. *One Hundred Fables* (with WILLIAM HARVEY). Lawford. 1828

NURA, *pseud.* SEE ULREICH, NURA WOODSON

OAKLEY, THORNTON (1881-   ) American
King. *To the Front* (with BOUGHTON and REMINGTON). Harper. 1908
Kingsley. *Westward Ho!* Jacobs. 1920
Masson. *Folk Tales of Brittany*. Macrae. 1929

OGDEN, HENRY ALEXANDER (1856-1936) American
Brooks. *Boy of the First Empire*. Century. 1895

OLFERS, SIBYLLE VON (*Ac.* 1930) German
Fish. *When the Root Children Wake Up*. Stokes. 1930

ONFROY DE BRÉVILLE, JACQUES MARIE GASTON (1858-1931) French (JOB, *pseud.*)
Hill. *Washington, Man of Action*. Appleton. 1914
Marie, Queen of Roumania. *Story of Naughty Kildeen*. Harcourt. 1927

OPPER, FREDERICK BURR (1857-1937) American
Æsop. *Æsop's Fables*. Lippincott. 1916
Nye. *History of the United States*. Lippincott. 1894

ORR, MONRO SCOTT (1874-   ) Scotch
Arabian Nights Entertainments. *Arabian Nights' Entertainments*. Holt. 1913
Brontë. *Jane Eyre*. Dodd. 1921

OSTMAN, LEMPI (1899-   ) American
Adams. *Vaino*. Dutton. 1929
Byrne. *With Mikko through Finland*. McBride. 1932

PAGET, HENRY MARRIETT (1857-1936) English
Goldsmith. *Vicar of Wakefield*. Nister. 1898
Pictures from Dickens (with others). Nister. 1895
Scott. *Kenilworth*. Black. 1893
Scott. *Quentin Durward*. Black. 1894

PAGET, SIDNEY EDWARD (1860-1908) English
Doyle. *Adventures of Sherlock Holmes*. Newnes. 1892
Scott. *Old Mortality*. Service and Paton. 1898

PAGET, WALTER STANLEY (1863-1935) English
Arabian Nights Entertainments. *Arabian Nights*. Nister. 1907
Defoe. *Robinson Crusoe*. Cassell. 1896
Henty. *With Moore at Corunna*. Scribner. 1927
Lamb. *Tales from Shakespeare*. Nister. 1901
Marryat. *Children of the New Forest*. Black. 1922
Scott. *Legend of Montrose*. Ward, Lock. 1895
Scott. *Talisman*. Ward, Lock. 1895
Stevenson. *Treasure Island*. Cassell. 1899

PANESIS, NICHOLAS (1913-   ) American
    McMeekin. *Journey Cake*. Messner. 1942
    McMeekin. *Juba's New Moon*. Messner. 1944

PAPE, ERIC (1870-1938) American
    Andersen. *Fairy Tales and Stories*. Macmillan. 1921
    Arabian Nights Entertainments. *Tales of Wonder and Magnificence*. Macmillan. 1923
    Irving. *Rip Van Winkle and The Legend of Sleepy Hollow*. Macmillan. 1925

PAPÉ, FRANK CHEYNE (1878-   ) American
    Buckley. *Children of the Dawn*. Stokes. 1908
    Bunyan. *Pilgrim's Progress*. Dutton. 1910
    Hodges. *When the King Came*. Houghton. 1923
    Homer. *Toils and Travels of Odysseus*. Stokes. 1917
    Lamb. *Tales from Shakspeare*. Warne. 1923
    Wilson. *Indian Story Book*. Macmillan. 1914
    Wilson. *Russian Story Book*. Macmillan. 1916

PARK, CARTON MOORE (1877-   ) English
    Child's Pictorial Natural History. S.P.C.K. 1901
    La Fontaine. *La Fontaine's Fables* (with RENÉ BULL). Nelson. 1905
    Norman. *Book of Elfin Rhymes*. Gay and Bird. 1900
    Park. *Alphabet of Animals*. Blackie. 1899
    Park. *Book of Birds*. Blackie. 1900
    Scoville. *Wild Folk* (with C. L. BULL). Little. 1922

PARRISH, ANNE (1888-   ) American
    Parrish. *Dream Coach* (with G. D. PARRISH). Macmillan. 1924
    Parrish. *Floating Island*. Harper. 1930
    Parrish. *Knee-high to a Grasshopper* (with G. D. PARRISH). Macmillan. 1923

PARRISH, GEORGE DILLWYN (1894-1941) American
    Parrish. *Dream Coach* (with ANNE PARRISH). Macmillan. 1924
    Parrish. *Knee-high to a Grasshopper* (with ANNE PARRISH). Macmillan. 1923

PARRISH, MAXFIELD (1870-   ) American
    Arabian Nights Entertainments. *Arabian Nights*. Scribner. 1909
    Field. *Poems of Childhood*. Scribner. 1904
    Grahame. *Dream Days*. Lane. 1902
    Grahame. *Golden Age*. Lane. 1900
    Hawthorne. *Wonder Book and Tanglewood Tales*. Duffield. 1910
    Irving. *History of New York*. Russell. 1900
    Palgrave. *Golden Treasury of Songs and Lyrics*. Duffield. 1911

PARSONS, ALFRED WILLIAM (1847-1920) English
    Old Songs (with E. A. ABBEY). Macmillan. 1889
    "Quiet Life." Certain Verses by Various Hands (with E. A. ABBEY). Harper. 1890
    Wordsworth. *Selection from the Sonnets of William Wordsworth*. Osgood. 1891

PARSONS, JACYNTH (*Ac*. 1928) English
    Blake. *Songs of Innocence*. Hale. 1927
    Davies. *Forty-nine Poems*. Medici. 1928

PARTRIDGE, JOHN BERNARD (1861-1945) English
    Harker. *Wee Folk, Good Folk*. Duckworth. 1899

PATERSON, CAROLINE (*Ac*. 1887) English
    Allingham. *Rhymes for the Young Folk* (with ALLINGHAM, FURNISS and GREENAWAY). Cassell. 1887

PATON, JOSEPH NOEL (1821-1901) Scotch
    Aytoun. *Lays of the Scottish Cavaliers*. Blackwood. 1863
    Coleridge. *Rime of the Ancient Mariner*. Art Union of London. 1863
    Hall. *Midsummer Eve* (with T. LANDSEER, MEADOWS and others). Longman. 1847
    Kingsley. *Water-babies*. Macmillan. 1863
    Molesworth. *Silverthorns*. Hatchards. 1886
    Shakespeare. *Compositions from The Tempest*. Nimmo. 1877

PAULL, GRACE A. (1898-   ) American
    Bianco. *Good Friends*. Viking. 1934
    Bianco. *Street of Little Shops*. Doubleday. 1932
    Coatsworth. *Dancing Tom*. Macmillan. 1938
    Hunt. *Little Girl with Seven Names*. Stokes. 1936
    Vance. *Star for Hansi*. Harper. 1936
    White. *Lending Mary*. Houghton. 1934

PAYNE, A. WYNDHAM (*Ac*. 1927) English
    Grahame. *Wind in the Willows*. Methuen. 1927
    Peter Piper's Practical Principles. Lane. 1926
    Taylor. *Meddlesome Matty*. Viking. 1926

PAYNE, HENRY A. (1868-   ) English
    Book of Carols. Allen. 1893

PEARS, CHARLES (1873-   ) English
    Andersen. *Little Klaus and Big Klaus*. Gowans and Gray. 1906
    Baldwin. *Pedlar's Pack*. Stokes. 1925
    Dana. *Two Years before the Mast*. Macmillan. 1916
    Dickens. *Christmas Carol*. Library Press. 1905
    Kingsley. *Heroes*. Gowans and Gray. 1907
    Masefield. *Salt-water Poems and Ballads*. Macmillan. 1916

PEARSE, SUSAN BEATRICE (*Ac*. 1927) English
    Dickens. *Captain Boldheart*. Macmillan. 1927
    Dickens. *Magic Fishbone*. Nisbet. 1912
    Heward. *Ameliar-anne and the Green Umbrella*. Macrae. 1920
    Heward. *Twins and Tabiffa*. Macrae. 1923

PECK, ANNE MERRIMAN (1884-   ) American
    Bazin. *Juniper Farm*. Macmillan. 1928
    Dussauze. *Little Jack Rabbit*. Macmillan. 1927
    Newell. *Steppin and Family*. Oxford. 1942
    Peck. *Manoel and the Morning Star*. Harper. 1943
    Peck. *Roundabout South America*. Harper. 1940
    Peck. *Young Canada*. McBride. 1943
    Yonge. *Little Lucy's Wonderful Globe*. Harper. 1927

PEDERSEN, THOMAS VILHELM (1820-1859) Danish
    Andersen. *It's Perfectly True! and Other Stories*. Macmillan. 1937
    Andersen. *Stories and Tales* (with M. L. STONE). Hurd and Houghton. 1871
    Andersen. *Wonder Stories Told for Children* (with M. L. STONE). Hurd and Houghton. 1871

PEGRAM, FRED (1870-   ) English

Arabian Nights Entertainments. *Arabian Nights Entertainments*. Service and Paton. 1898
Dickens. *Martin Chuzzlewit*. Blackie. *n.d.*
Marryat. *Masterman Ready*. Macmillan. 1897
Marryat. *Mr. Midshipman Easy*. Macmillan. 1896
Warner. *Wide, Wide World*. Pearson. *n.d.*

PEIRCE, WALDO (1884-   ) American

Children's Hour. Duell. 1944
Norton. *Magic Bed-knob or How to Become a Witch in Ten Easy Lessons*. Putnam. 1943

PENNELL, JOSEPH (1860-1926) American

Irving. *Alhambra*. Macmillan. 1896

PÉRARD, VICTOR SEMON (1870-   ) American, b. in France

Du Chaillu. *King Mombo*. Scribner. 1902
Irving. *Rip Van Winkle*. Stokes. 1933
Munroe. *With Crockett and Bowie*. Scribner. 1897

PERKINS, LUCY FITCH (1865-1937) American

Andersen. *Twenty Best Fairy Tales by Hans Andersen*. Stokes. 1907
Perkins. *Dutch Twins*. Houghton. 1911
Perkins. *Other "Twins" books*. Houghton. 1912-1935
Pumphrey. *Stories of the Pilgrims*. Rand. 1912
Robin Hood. *Robin Hood; His Deeds and Adventures as Recounted in the Old English Ballads*. Houghton. 1906
Shakespeare. *Midsummer Night's Dream*. Stokes. 1907
Warren. *Little Pioneers*. Rand. 1916

PERTS, M. C. (*Ac.* 1931)

Ershov. *Humpy*. Harper. 1931

PETERSHAM, MAUD FULLER (1889-   ) American *and*
PETERSHAM, MISKA (1888-   ) American, b. in Hungary

Barringer. *Martin the Goose Boy*. Doubleday. 1932
Bible. *Christ Child*. Doubleday. 1931
Bible. *Jesus' Story*. Macmillan. 1942
Bible. *Stories from the Old Testament*. Winston. 1938
Clark. *Poppy Seed Cakes*. Doubleday. 1924
Lamb. *Tales from Shakespeare*. Macmillan. 1923
Mason. *Susannah, the Pioneer Cow*. Macmillan. 1941
Miller. *Children of the Mountain Eagle*. Doubleday. 1927
Petersham. *American A B C*. Macmillan. 1941
Petersham. *Ark of Father Noah and Mother Noah*. Doubleday. 1930
Petersham. *Auntie*. Doubleday. 1932
Petersham. *Get-a-way and Háry János*. Viking. 1933
Petersham. *Miki*. Doubleday. 1929
Petersham. *Rooster Crows*. Macmillan. 1945
Sandburg. *Rootabaga Pigeons*. Harcourt. 1923
Sandburg. *Rootabaga Stories*. Harcourt. 1922
Wheeler. *Albanian Wonder Tales*. Doubleday. 1936

PETHERICK, HORACE WILLIAM (1839-1919) English

Henty. *Cornet of Horse*. S. Low, Marston, Searle and Rivington. 1888

PETTIE, JOHN A. (1839-1893) Scotch

Wordsworth. *Poems for the Young* (with J. A. MAC-WHIRTER). Strahan. 1863

PHIZ, *pseud. SEE* BROWNE, HABLOT KNIGHT

PICKERSGILL, FREDERICK RICHARD (1820-1900) English

Bible. *Art Pictures from the Old Testament* (For other illustrators *see* HOUGHTON, ARTHUR BOYD). S.P.C.K. 1894
Bible. *Lord's Prayer*. Longmans. 1870
Milton. *Comus* (with B. FOSTER and WEIR). Routledge. 1858
Poe. *Poetical Works of Edgar Allan Poe* (with DARLEY, B. FOSTER, TENNIEL and others). Sampson Low. 1858

PINSARD, PIERRE (*Ac.* 1929) French

Cendrars. *Little Black Stories*. Brewer. 1929

PINWELL, GEORGE JOHN (1842-1875) English

Arabian Nights Entertainments. *Dalziel's Arabian Nights*, 2 v. (For other illustrators *see* HOUGHTON, ARTHUR BOYD). Ward, Lock. 1865
Buchanan. *Ballad Stories of the Affections* (For other illustrators *see* DALZIEL, EDWARD). Routledge. 1869
Dickens. *Uncommercial Traveller*. Chapman. 1868
Golden Thoughts from Golden Fountains (For other illustrators *see* HOUGHTON, ARTHUR BOYD). Warne. 1867
Goldsmith. *Dalziel's Illustrated Goldsmith*. Ward, Lock. 1865
Idyllic Pictures. Cassell. 1867
Ingelow. *Poems* (with E. and T. B. G. DALZIEL, HOUGHTON, NORTH, POYNTER, SMALL and WOLF). Roberts. 1867
Lushington. *Hacco the Dwarf and Other Tales*. Griffith and Farran. 1865
Mother Goose. *National Nursery Rhymes* (For other illustrators *see* HOUGHTON, ARTHUR BOYD). Novello, Ewer. 1870
Rands. *Lilliput Levee* (with J. E. MILLAIS). Strahan. 1864
Round of Days (For other illustrators *see* HOUGHTON, ARTHUR BOYD). Routledge. 1866
Spirit of Praise (For other illustrators *see* HOUGHTON, ARTHUR BOYD). Warne. 1866
Wayside Posies (with NORTH and F. WALKER). Routledge. 1867

PIPPET, GABRIEL JOSEPH (1880-   ) English

Mother Goose. *More Old Rhymes with New Tunes*. Longmans. 1925
Mother Goose. *Old Rhymes with New Tunes*. Longmans. 1912
Mother Goose. *Still More Old Rhymes with New Tunes*. Longmans. 1927

PISSARRO, LUCIEN (1863-   ) English, b. in France

Bible. *Book of Ruth, and The Book of Esther*. Hacon. 1896

PITMAN, ROSIE M. M. (*Ac.* 1897) English

Jersey. *Maurice, or The Red Jar.* Macmillan. 1894
La Motte-Fouqué. *Undine.* Macmillan. 1897
Molesworth. *Magic Nuts.* Macmillan. 1898
Molesworth. *Ruby Ring.* Macmillan. 1904

PITZ, HENRY CLARENCE (1895-   ) American

Buchan. *Prester John.* Houghton. 1928
Bush. *Prairie Rose.* Little. 1925
Coblentz. *Falcon of Eric the Red.* Longmans. 1942
Davis. *Hudson Bay Express.* Holiday. 1942
Doyle. *Micah Clarke.* Harper. 1922
Drake. *Indian History for Young Folks.* Harper. 1927
Fenner. *Giants & Witches and a Dragon or Two.* Knopf. 1943
Finger. *Dog at His Heel.* Winston. 1936
Household. *Spanish Cave.* Little. 1936
Irving. *Voyages of Columbus.* Macmillan. 1931
Jordan. *Shoo-fly Pie.* Knopf. 1944
Leighton. *Olaf, the Glorious.* Macmillan. 1929
Ross. *In Mexico They Say.* Knopf. 1942

POCOCK, NOEL   English

Defoe. *Life and Strange Surprising Adventures of Robinson Crusoe.* Doran. *n.d.*
Grimm. *Fairy Tales.* Doran. *n.d.*

POGÁNY, WILLIAM ANDREW (1882-   ) American, b. in Hungary

Arabian Nights Entertainments. *Adventures of Haroun Er Raschid.* Holt. 1923
Arabian Nights Entertainments. *More Tales from the Arabian Nights.* Holt. 1915
Carroll. *Alice's Adventures in Wonderland.* Dutton. 1929
Coleridge. *Rime of the Ancient Mariner.* Doran. 1910
Colum. *Adventures of Odysseus.* Macmillan. 1918
Colum. *Children of Odin.* Macmillan. 1920
Colum. *Frenzied Prince.* McKay. 1943
Colum. *King of Ireland's Son.* Macmillan. 1921
Kúnos. *Turkish Fairy Tales and Folk Tales.* Burt. 1901
Mother Goose. *Willy Pogány's Mother Goose.* Nelson. 1928
Pogány. *Hungarian Fairy Book.* T. Fisher Unwin. 1913
Pogány. *Magyar Fairy Tales.* Dutton. 1930
Pushkin. *Golden Cockerel.* Nelson. 1938
Swift. *Gulliver's Travels.* Macmillan. 1917
Thomas. *Welsh Fairy-book.* Stokes. 1907
Wagner. *Parsifal.* Harrap. 1912
Wagner. *Tale of Lohengrin.* Harrap. 1913
Wagner. *Tannhäuser.* Harrap. 1911

POLITI, LEO (1908-   ) American

Garrett. *Angelo, the Naughty One.* Viking. 1944
Henius. *Stories from the Americas.* Scribner. 1944
Sawyer. *Least One.* Viking. 1941

PORTINARI, CANDIDO (1903-   ) Brazilian

Kelsey. *Maria Rosa.* Doubleday. 1942

POTTER, BEATRIX (1866-1943) English

Potter. *Appley Dapply's Nursery Rhymes.* Warne. 1917
Potter. *Cecily Parsley's Nursery Rhymes.* Warne. 1922
Potter. *Fairy Caravan.* McKay. 1929
Potter. *Fierce Bad Rabbit.* Warne. 1906
Potter. *Ginger and Pickles.* Warne. 1909
Potter. *Pie and the Patty Pan.* Warne. 1905
Potter. *Roly-poly Pudding.* Warne. 1908
Potter. *Story of Miss Moppet.* Warne. 1906
Potter. *Tailor of Gloucester.* Warne. 1903
Potter. *Tale of Benjamin Bunny.* Warne. 1904
Potter. *Tale of Jemima Puddle-Duck.* Warne. 1908
Potter. *Tale of Johnny Town-Mouse.* Warne. 1908
Potter. *Tale of Little Pig Robinson.* McKay. 1930
Potter. *Tale of Mr. Jeremy Fisher.* Warne. 1906
Potter. *Tale of Mr. Tod.* Warne. 1912
Potter. *Tale of Mrs. Tiggy-Winkle.* Warne. 1905
Potter. *Tale of Mrs. Tittlemouse.* Warne. 1911
Potter. *Tale of Peter Rabbit.* Warne. 1903
Potter. *Tale of Pigling Bland.* Warne. 1913
Potter. *Tale of Squirrel Nutkin.* Warne. 1903
Potter. *Tale of the Flopsy Bunnies.* Warne. 1909
Potter. *Tale of Timmy Tiptoes.* Warne. 1911
Potter. *Tale of Tom Kitten.* Warne. 1907
Potter. *Tale of Two Bad Mice.* Warne. 1904

POYNTER, EDWARD JOHN (1836-1919) English

Bible. *Art Pictures from the Old Testament* (For other illustrators *see* HOUGHTON, ARTHUR BOYD). S.P.C.K. 1894
Ingelow. *Poems* (For other illustrators *see* PINWELL, GEORGE JOHN). Roberts. 1867

PRESTON, ALICE BOLAM (1889-   ) American

Bailey. *Little Man with One Shoe.* Little. 1921
Bailey. *Seven Peas in the Pod.* Little. 1919

PRICE, HATTIE LONGSTREET (1891-   ) American

Alcott. *Eight Cousins.* Little. 1927
Alcott. *Rose in Bloom.* Little. 1927
Nash. *Polly's Secret.* Little. 1926

PRICE, MARGARET EVANS (1888-   ) American

Bates. *Once upon a Time.* Rand. 1921
Price. *Monkey-Do.* Harper. 1934

PRICE, NORMAN MILLS (1877-   ) American, b. in Canada

Cormack. *Last Clash of Claymores.* Appleton. 1940
Lamb. *Tales from Shakespeare.* Scribner. 1905

PRUSZYNSKA, ANIELA (1888?-   ) Polish

Kelly. *Blacksmith of Vilno.* Macmillan. 1930
Kelly. *Golden Star of Halich.* Macmillan. 1931
Kelly. *Trumpeter of Krakow.* Macmillan. 1928

PYLE, HOWARD (1853-1911) American

Baldwin. *Story of Siegfried.* Scribner. 1882
Baldwin. *Story of the Golden Age.* Scribner. 1887
Carleton. *Farm Ballads* (with REINHART, SNYDER and others). Harper. 1882
Deland. *Old Chester Tales.* Harper. 1899
Dowd. *Book of the American Spirit.* Harper. 1923

Holmes. *Autocrat of the Breakfast-table*, 2 v. Houghton. 1893

Holmes. *Dorothy Q. together with A Ballad of the Boston Tea Party & Grandmother's Story of Bunker Hill Battle.* Houghton. 1893

Holmes. *Grandmother's Story of Bunker Hill Battle.* Houghton. *n.d.*

Holmes. *One Hoss Shay, with Its Companion Poems.* Houghton. 1892

Irving. *History of New York*, 2 v. (with BOUGHTON and DRAKE). Grolier Club. 1886

Lodge. *Story of the Revolution.* Scribner. 1898

Mitchell. *Hugh Wynne.* Century. 1896

Page. *In Ole Virginia* (with CASTAIGNE, CLINEDINST, FROST, REINHART and SMEDLEY). Scribner. 1896

Pyle. *Book of Pirates.* Harper. 1921

Pyle. *Garden behind the Moon.* Scribner. 1895

Pyle. *Men of Iron.* Harper. 1891

Pyle. *Merry Adventures of Robin Hood.* Scribner. 1883

Pyle. *Otto of the Silver Hand.* Scribner. 1888

Pyle. *Pepper & Salt.* Harper. 1886

Pyle. *Stolen Treasure.* Harper. 1907

Pyle. *Story of Jack Ballister's Fortunes.* Century. 1895

Pyle. *Story of King Arthur and His Knights.* Scribner. 1903

Pyle. *Story of Sir Launcelot and His Companions.* Scribner. 1907

Pyle. *Story of the Champions of the Round Table.* Scribner. 1905

Pyle. *Story of the Grail and the Passing of Arthur.* Scribner. 1910

Pyle. *Twilight Land.* Harper. 1895

Pyle. *Wonder Clock.* Harper. 1887

Tennyson. *Lady of Shalott.* Dodd. 1881

Twain. *Saint Joan of Arc* (with W. J. JONES). Harper. 1919

Van Dyke. *First Christmas Tree.* Scribner. 1897

Yankee Doodle. Dodd. 1881

PYLE, KATHARINE (1863-1938) American

Pyle. *Careless Jane.* Dutton. 1902

Pyle. *Christmas Angel.* Little. 1900

Pyle. *Counterpane Fairy.* Dutton. 1898

Pyle. *Lazy Matilda and Other Tales.* Dutton. 1921

Sewell. *Black Beauty.* Dodd. 1923

White. *Only Child.* Houghton. 1905

PYM, T., *pseud.* (*Ac.* 1893) English
(CLARA CREED)

A B C. W. W. Gardner. 1884

Andersen. *Snow Queen.* W. W. Gardner. 1883

Children Busy, Children Glad, Children Naughty, Children Sad. W. W. Gardner. 1881

Child's Own Story Book. W. W. Gardner. 1883

Crompton. *Gentle Heritage.* A. D. Innes. 1893

Wordsworth. *We Are Seven.* W. W. Gardner. 1880

PYNE, MABLE MANDEVILLE (1903-   ) American

Pyne. *Little Geography of the United States.* Houghton. 1941

Pyne. *Little History of the United States.* Houghton. 1940

RACKHAM, ARTHUR (1867-1939) English

Æsop. *Fables.* Heinemann. 1912

Andersen. *Fairy Tales.* Harrap. 1932

Arblay. *Evelina.* Newnes. 1898

Barham. *Ingoldsby Legends.* Dutton. 1912

Barrie. *Peter Pan in Kensington Gardens.* Hodder. 1906

Barrie. *Peter Pan in Kensington Gardens* (with added illustrations). Hodder. 1912

Bianco. *Poor Cecco.* Doran. 1925

Brown. *Lonesomest Doll.* Houghton. 1928

Browning. *Pied Piper of Hamelin.* Harrap. 1934

Carroll. *Alice's Adventures in Wonderland.* Heinemann. 1907

Cinderella. Heinemann. 1919

Dickens. *Christmas Carol.* Heinemann. 1915

Goldsmith. *Vicar of Wakefield.* Harrap. 1929

Grahame. *Wind in the Willows.* Limited Editions. 1940

Grimm. *Fairy Tales.* Freemantle. 1900

Grimm. *Fairy Tales* (with added illustrations). Constable. 1909

Grimm. *Hansel and Grethel.* Constable. 1920

Grimm. *Little Brother and Little Sister.* Constable. 1917

Grimm. *Snowdrop and Other Tales.* Constable. 1920

Hawthorne. *Wonder Book.* Hodder. 1922

Ibsen. *Peer Gynt.* Lippincott. 1936

Irving. *Bracebridge Hall*, 2 v. (with CHURCH, REINHART, SCHMOLZE and others). Putnam. 1896

Irving. *Legend of Sleepy Hollow.* Harrap. 1928

Irving. *Rip Van Winkle.* Heinemann. 1905

Irving. *Rip Van Winkle* (with added illustrations). Heinemann. 1916

Kipling. *Puck of Pook's Hill.* Doubleday. 1906

Lamb. *Tales from Shakespeare.* Dent. 1899

Lamb. *Tales from Shakespeare* (with added illustrations). Dent. 1909

La Motte-Fouqué. *Undine.* Heinemann. 1909

Lever. *Charles O'Malley.* Service and Paton. 1897

Malory. *Romance of King Arthur and His Knights of the Round Table.* Macmillan. 1917

Martineau. *Feats on the Fjord.* Dent. 1899

Milton. *Comus.* Heinemann. 1921

Moore. *Night Before Christmas.* Harrap. 1931

Mother Goose. *Old Nursery Rhymes.* Heinemann. 1913

Niebuhr. *Greek Heroes.* Cassell. 1903

Poe. *Tales of Mystery and Imagination.* Harrap. 1935

Rackham. *Arthur Rackham Fairy Book.* Harrap. 1933

Rackham. *Arthur Rackham's Book of Pictures.* Heinemann. 1913

Rossetti. *Goblin Market.* Harrap. 1933

Ruskin. *King of the Golden River.* Harrap. 1932

Shakespeare. *Midsummer Night's Dream.* Heinemann. 1908

Shakespeare. *Tempest.* Heinemann. 1926

Sleeping Beauty. Heinemann. 1920

Some British Ballads. Constable. 1919

Steel. *English Fairy Tales.* Macmillan. 1918

Stephens. *Irish Fairy Tales.* Macmillan. 1920

Swift. *Gulliver's Travels.* Dent. 1900

Swift. *Gulliver's Travels* (with added illustrations). Dent. 1909

Wagner. *Rhinegold and The Valkyrie.* Heinemann. 1911

Wagner. *Siegfried and The Twilight of the Gods.* Heinemann. 1911

RADLOV, NIKOLAÏ ERNESTOVĪCH (1889-1943?) Russian
Radlov. *Cautious Carp, and Other Fables in Pictures.* Coward. 1938

RAE, JOHN (1882-   ) American
Churchill. *Crossing.* Macmillan. 1930
Marryat. *Masterman Ready.* Harper. 1928

RAILTON, HERBERT (1858-1910) English
Tristram. *Coaching Days and Coaching Ways* (with HUGH THOMSON). Macmillan. 1888

RAINEY, WILLIAM H. (1852-1936) English
Dickens. *David Copperfield.* Gresham. 1900
Henty. *Roving Commission.* Blackie. 1900
Macgregor. *Story of France.* Stokes. 1920
Macgregor. *Story of Rome* (with HEATH and WOODROFFE). Stokes. 1913
Molesworth. *Meg Langholme.* Chambers. 1897
Plutarch. *Plutarch's Lives for Boys and Girls.* Nelson. 1914

RALSTON, J. McL. (*Ac.* 1886) English
Craik. *Little Lame Prince.* Macmillan. 1875
Craik. *My Mother and I.* Harper. 1874
Dickens. *Child's History of England.* Chapman. 1870
Ralston. *Tippoo, Tale of a Tiger.* Routledge. 1886

RAVEN-HILL, LEONARD (1867-1942) English
Kipling. *Complete Stalky & Co.* Doubleday. 1930
Lucas. *Slowcoach.* Macmillan. 1910

RAVERAT, GWENDOLEN MARY DARWIN (1885-   ) English
Andersen. *Four Tales from Hans Andersen.* Cambridge University. 1935
Farjeon. *Over the Garden Wall.* Stokes. 1933
Grahame. *Cambridge Book of Poetry for Children.* Cambridge University. 1933
Hart. *Runaway.* Macmillan. 1936
Wedgwood. *Bird Talisman.* Faber. 1939

REDWOOD, ALLAN C. (*Ac.* 1888) American
Page. *Two Little Confederates* (with E. W. KEMBLE). Scribner. 1888

REED, PHILIP G. (1908-   ) American
Arabian Nights Entertainments. *Seven Voyages of Sinbad the Sailor.* Holiday. 1939
Dickens. *Christmas Carol.* Holiday. 1941

REID, STEPHEN (1873-   ) Scotch
Bullen. *Cruise of the Cachalot.* McKay. 1926
Bullen. *Frank Brown, Sea Apprentice.* McKay. 1926
Coleridge. *Rime of the Ancient Mariner.* Gowans and Gray. 1906
Gilbert. *Boys' Book of Pirates.* Crowell. 1916
Hull. *Boys' Cuchulain.* Crowell. 1910
Masefield. *Jim Davis.* McKay. 1924
Seven Champions of Christendom. Gowans and Gray. 1907

REINHART, CHARLES STANLEY (1844-1896) American
Carleton. *Farm Ballads* (with H. PYLE, SNYDER and others). Harper. 1882
Irving. *Bracebridge Hall,* 2 v. (with CHURCH, RACKHAM, SCHMOLZE and others). Putnam. 1896
Longfellow. *Courtship of Miles Standish* (with BOUGHTON, MERRILL and others). Houghton. 1888
Page. *In Ole Virginia* (with CASTAIGNE, CLINEDINST, FROST, H. PYLE and SMEDLEY). Scribner. 1896
Page. *Meh Lady.* Scribner. 1893
Stuart. *Golden Wedding and Other Tales* (with FROST and SHEPPARD). Harper. 1893
Tennyson. *Songs from the Published Writings of Alfred Tennyson* (with CURTIS, FREDERICKS and HOMER). Harper. 1880

REMINGTON, FREDERIC (1861-1909) American
Baylor. *Juan and Juanita* (with J. H. SANDHAM). Ticknor. 1888
Garland. *Book of the American Indian.* Harper. 1923
Janvier. *Aztec Treasure House.* Harper. 1890
King. *To the Front* (with BOUGHTON and OAKLEY). Harper. 1908
Longfellow. *Song of Hiawatha.* Houghton. 1891
Parkman. *Oregon Trail.* Little. 1892
Remington. *Crooked Trails.* Harper. 1898
Remington. *Done in the Open.* Collier. 1902
Remington. *Pony Tracks.* Harper. 1895
Wister. *Virginian* (with C. M. RUSSELL). Macmillan. 1911

REUTERDAHL, HENRY (1871-1925) American, b. in Sweden
Bullen. *Cruise of the Cachalot* (with A. O. FISCHER). Appleton. 1925

REY, HANS AUGUSTO (1898-   ) Brazilian, b. in Germany
Mother Goose. *Humpty Dumpty and Other Mother Goose Songs.* Harper. 1943
Payne. *Katy No-Pocket.* Houghton. 1944
Rey. *Cecily G. and the 9 Monkeys.* Houghton. 1942
Rey. *Curious George.* Houghton. 1941
Rey. *How Do You Get There?* Houghton. 1941
Zolotow. *Park Book.* Harper. 1944

REYNOLDS, FRANK (1876-   ) English
Dickens. *David Copperfield.* Hodder. 1911
Dickens. *Old Curiosity Shop.* Hodder. 1913
Dickens. *Posthumous Papers of the Pickwick Club.* Hodder. 1912
"*Punch*" *Pictures.* Cassell. 1922

RHEAD, FREDERICK ALFRED (1855-   ) English
Bunyan. *Pilgrim's Progress* (with G. W. and L. J. RHEAD). Century. 1898
Defoe. *Robinson Crusoe* (with L. J. RHEAD). R. H. Russell. 1900

RHEAD, GEORGE WOOLLISCROFT (1855-1920) English
Bunyan. *Life and Death of Mr. Badman* (with L. J. RHEAD). R. H. Russell. 1900
Bunyan. *Pilgrim's Progress* (with F. A. and L. J. RHEAD). Century. 1898

RHEAD, LOUIS JOHN (1857-1926) American, b. in England
Æsop. *Æsop's Fables*. Harper. 1927
Andersen. *Fairy Tales and Wonder Stories*. Harper. 1914
Arabian Nights Entertainments. *Arabian Nights' Entertainments*. Harper. 1916
Bunyan. *Life and Death of Mr. Badman* (with G. W. RHEAD). R. H. Russell. 1900
Bunyan. *Pilgrim's Progress* (with F. A. and G. W. RHEAD). Century. 1898
Cooper. *Deerslayer*. Harper. 1926
Craik. *Fairy Book*. Harper. 1922
Defoe. *Robinson Crusoe* (with F. A. RHEAD). R. H. Russell. 1900
Dodge. *Hans Brinker*. Harper. 1924
Grimm. *Fairy Tales*. Harper. 1917
Hughes. *Tom Brown's School Days*. Harper. 1911
Lamb. *Tales from Shakespeare*. Harper. 1918
Stevenson. *Kidnapped*. Harper. 1921
Stevenson. *Treasure Island*. Harper. 1915
Swift. *Gulliver's Travels*. Harper. 1913
Wyss. *Swiss Family Robinson*. Harper. 1909

RICHARDS, FREDERICK THOMPSON (1864-1921) American
Life's Book of Animals (with KEMBLE, NEILSON and others). Doubleday and McClure. 1898

RICHARDS, GEORGE MATHER (1880-   ) American
Bunn. *Circus Boy*. Macmillan. 1936
Lindsay. *Johnny Appleseed*. Macmillan. 1928
Stockton. *Casting Away of Mrs. Lecks and Mrs. Aleshine*. Appleton. 1933

RICHARDSON, FREDERICK (1862-1937) American
Stockton. *Queen's Museum*. Scribner. 1906
Thorne-Thomsen. *East o' the Sun and West o' the Moon*. Row. 1912

RICHTER, LUDWIG (1803-1884) German
Bechstein. *As Pretty as Seven*. J. C. Hotten. 1872
Bible. *Lord's Prayer*. Gaber & Richter. 1857
Goldsmith. *Vicar of Wakefield*. G. Wigand. 1841
Nut-Cracker and Sugar-Dolly. Cundall. 1848
Thirkell. *Grateful Sparrow and Other Tales*. Hamish Hamilton. 1935

RICKETTS, CHARLES (1866-1931) English
Bible. *Parables*. Hacon and Ricketts. 1903
Blake. *Songs of Innocence*. Vale. 1897

ROBERTS, JACK (1894-   ) French
Roberts. *Bumpy Bobs, the Pink Hippo*. Duffield. 1926
Roberts. *Wonderful Adventures of Ludo, the Little Green Duck*. Duffield. 1924

ROBERTSON, CECILE WALTON *SEE* WALTON, CECILE

ROBERTSON, WALFORD GRAHAM (1867-   ) English
Ewing. *Old Fashioned Fairy Tales*. Bell. 1919
French Songs of Old Canada. Heinemann. 1904
Old English Songs and Dances. Longmans. 1902
Taylor. *Joan of Arc, Soldier and Saint*. Kenedy. 1920
Tennyson. *Maud*. Lane. 1906

ROBIDA, ALBERT (1848-1926) French
Rabelais. *Three Good Giants* (with P. G. DORÉ). Ticknor. 1887

ROBINSON, BOARDMAN (1876-   ) American, b. in Canada
Melville. *Moby Dick*, 2 v. Limited Editions. 1943

ROBINSON, CHARLES (1870-1937) English
Æsop. *Æsop's Fables*. Dent. 1895
Andersen. *Fairy Tales from Hans Christian Andersen* (with T. H. and W. H. ROBINSON). Dent. 1899
Blake. *Songs of Innocence* (with others). Dutton. 1912
Burnett. *Secret Garden*. Heinemann. 1911
Carroll. *Alice's Adventures in Wonderland*. Cassell. 1910
Field. *Lullaby Land*. Lane. 1898
France. *Bee*. Dent. 1912
Homer. *Adventures of Odysseus*. Dent. 1900
Irving. *Rip Van Winkle*. Stokes. 1914
Jerrold. *Big Book of Fables*. Caldwell. 1912
Jerrold. *Big Book of Fairy Tales*. Blackie. 1910
Jerrold. *Reign of King Oberon*. Dent. 1902
La Motte-Fouqué. *Sintram and His Companions and Aslauga's Knight*. Dent. 1900
Lowry. *Make-believe*. Lane. 1896
MacGregor. *King Longbeard*. Lane. 1898
Mother Goose. *Big Book of Nursery Rhymes*. Blackie. 1911
Mother Goose. *Nursery Rhymes*. Collins. 1928
Perrault. *Fairy Tales*. Dent. 1913
Rhys. *Children's Garland of Verse*. Dent. 1921
Setoun. *Child World*. Lane. 1896
Stevenson. *Child's Garden of Verses*. Lane. 1896
Wilde. *Happy Prince*. Duckworth. 1913

ROBINSON, IRENE BOWEN (1891-   ) American
Robinson. *Ancient Animals*. Macmillan. 1934
Robinson. *Animals in the Sun*. Harper. 1934
Robinson. *At the Seashore*. Macmillan. 1942
Robinson. *At the Zoo*. Macmillan. 1940
Robinson. *Beasts of the Tar Pits*. Macmillan. 1932
Robinson. *Big Boy*. Macmillan. 1944
Robinson. *Book of Bible Animals*. Harper. 1938
Robinson. *Elephants*. Harper. 1935
Robinson. *Lions*. Harper. 1936
Robinson. *On the Farm*. Macmillan. 1939

ROBINSON, THOMAS HEATH (1869-   ) English
Andersen. *Fairy Tales from Hans Christian Andersen* (with CHARLES and W. H. ROBINSON). Dent. 1899
Canton. *Child's Book of Saints*. Dent. 1898
Gaskell. *Cranford*. Bliss, Sands. 1896
Hawthorne. *Scarlet Letter*. Bliss, Sands. 1897
Minssen. *Book of French Songs for the Young*. Dent. 1899
Porter. *Scottish Chiefs*. Dent. 1900
Spenser. *Una and the Red Cross Knight*. Dutton. 1905
Terry. *Tales from Far and Near*. Row. 1926
Thackeray. *History of Henry Esmond*. Allen. 1896
Wilson. *Story of Cortes*. Nelson. 1933
Wyss. *Swiss Family Robinson*. Doran. 1913

D. G. ROSSETTI : *Goblin Market*

ROBINSON, WILLIAM HEATH (1872-1944) English
Andersen. *Danish Fairy Tales and Legends.* Bliss, Sands. 1897
Andersen. *Fairy Tales.* Doran. 1924
Andersen. *Fairy Tales from Hans Christian Andersen* (with CHARLES and T. H. ROBINSON). Dent. 1899
Arabian Nights Entertainments. *Arabian Nights Entertainments* (with McCORMICK, STRATTON and others). Newnes. 1899
Bunyan. *Pilgrim's Progress.* Bliss, Sands. 1897
Cervantes Saavedra. *Don Quixote.* Bliss, Sands. 1897
De La Mare. *Peacock Pie.* Constable. 1917
Kingsley. *Water-babies.* Houghton. 1915
Kipling. *Collected Poems.* Doubleday. 1910
Kipling. *Song of the English.* Hodder. 1909
Lamb. *Tales from Shakespeare.* Bliss, Sands. 1901
Perrault. *Old-time Stories.* Dodd. 1921
Rouse. *Giant Crab and Other Tales from Old India.* Nutt. 1897
Rouse. *Talking Thrush.* Dent. 1899
Shakespeare. *Midsummer Night's Dream.* Holt. 1914
Shakespeare. *Twelfth Night.* Doran. 1914

ROCKWELL, NORMAN (1894-   ) American
Twain. *Adventures of Huckleberry Finn.* Heritage. 1940
Twain. *Adventures of Tom Sawyer.* Heritage. 1936

ROGERS, WILLIAM ALLEN (1854-1931) American
Brooks. *Boy Settlers.* Scribner. 1891
Kaler. *Jenny Wren's Boarding House.* Estes. 1893
Kaler. *Toby Tyler.* Harper. 1881
Munroe. *Canoemates.* Harper. 1890
Munroe. *Raftmates.* Harper. 1893
Page. *Among the Camps* (with NEWELL and SHEPPARD). Scribner. 1891

ROJANKOVSKY, FEODOR STEPANOVICH (1891-   ) Russian
Andersen. *Old Man Is Always Right.* Harper. 1940
Averill. *Daniel Boone.* Domino. 1931
Averill. *Flash.* Smith. 1934
Averill. *Powder.* Random. 1933
Averill. *Voyages of Jacques Cartier.* Viking. 1937
Duplaix. *Animal Stories.* Simon. 1944
Kipling. *Elephant's Child.* Garden City. 1942
Kipling. *How the Camel Got His Hump.* Garden City. 1942
Kipling. *How the Leopard Got His Spots.* Garden City. 1942
Kipling. *How the Rhinoceros Got His Skin.* Garden City. 1942
Lida. *Cuckoo.* Harper. 1942
Lida. *Fluff, the Little Wild Rabbit.* Harper. 1937
Lida. *Kingfisher.* Harper. 1940
Lida. *Plouf, the Little Wild Duck.* Harper. 1936
Lida. *Pompom, the Little Red Squirrel.* Harper. 1936
Lida. *Spiky, the Hedgehog.* Harper. 1938
Mariotti. *Tales of Poindi.* Domino. 1938
Mother Goose. *Tall Book of Mother Goose.* Harper. 1942
Tall Book of Nursery Tales. Harper. 1944

ROSENBERG, ELINORE BLAISDELL *SEE* BLAISDELL, ELINORE

ROSS, GORDON (*Ac.* 1936) American
Dickens. *Christmas Carol.* Limited Editions. *n.d.*
Dickens. *Posthumous Papers of the Pickwick Club.* Heritage. 1936

ROSSETTI, DANTE GABRIEL (1828-1882) English
Allingham. *Flower Pieces.* Reeves and Turner. 1888
Allingham. *Music Master* (with HUGHES and MILLAIS). Routledge. 1855
Rossetti. *Goblin Market.* Macmillan. 1862
Tennyson. *Poems* (with HUNT, MILLAIS, MULREADY, STANFIELD and others). Moxon. 1857

ROUNDS, GLEN H. (1906-   ) American
Blair. *Tall Tale America.* Coward. 1944
Rounds. *Blind Colt.* Holiday. 1941
Rounds. *Lumber Camp.* Holiday. 1937
Rounds. *Ol' Paul, the Mighty Logger.* Holiday. 1936
Rounds. *Pay Dirt.* Holiday. 1938

ROUNTREE, HARRY (1878-   ) English, b. in New Zealand
Æsop. *Æsop's Fables.* Ward, Lock. 1924
Carroll. *Alice's Adventures in Wonderland and Through the Looking-glass.* Collins. 1928
Crichton. *Peep-in-the-world.* Longmans. 1925
Dumas. *Fairy Tales.* Stokes. 1904
Wyss. *Swiss Family Robinson.* Macmillan. 1907

ROWLANDSON, THOMAS (1756-1827) English
Goldsmith. *Vicar of Wakefield.* Ackermann. 1817

RUDLAND, FLORENCE M. (*Ac.* 1902)
Sherwood. *Fairchild Family.* Wells Gardner. 1902

RUSE, MARGARET (1895-1938) American
Newell. *Little Old Woman Who Used Her Head.* Nelson. 1935
Newell. *More about the Little Old Woman Who Used Her Head.* Nelson. 1938

RUSSELL, CHARLES MARION (1864-1926) American
Hough. *Story of the Cowboy* (with others). Appleton. 1897
Linderman. *Indian Old-man Stories.* Scribner. 1920
Linderman. *Indian Why Stories.* Scribner. 1915
Wister. *Virginian* (with FREDERIC REMINGTON). Macmillan. 1911

RUTHERSTON, ALBERT DANIEL (1881-   ) English
Wolfe. *Cursory Rhymes.* Benn. 1928

RUZICKA, RUDOLPH (1883-   ) American, b. in Bohemia
La Fontaine. *Fables of Jean de La Fontaine,* 2 v. Limited Editions. 1930
Thoreau. *Walden.* Lakeside. 1930
Wilde. *Happy Prince and Other Tales.* Overbrook. 1936

SAINT EXUPÉRY, ANTOINE DE (1900-1944) French
Saint Exupéry. *Little Prince.* Reynal. 1943

SALE, ISOBEL MORTON- *SEE* MORTON-SALE, ISOBEL

SALE, JOHN MORTON- *SEE* MORTON-SALE, JOHN

SALOMON, BERNARD (1520-1580) French
Bible. *Seventy Stories of the Old Testament* (with BEHAM, DÜRER and HOLBEIN, THE YOUNGER). Bradford. 1938

SAMBOURNE, EDWARD LINLEY (1844-1910) English
Andersen. *Three Tales of Hans Andersen.* Macmillan. 1910
Brabourne. *Friends and Foes from Fairyland.* Longmans. 1886
Burnand. *New History of Sandford and Merton.* Bradbury, Evans. 1872
Burnand. *Real Robinson Crusoe.* Bradbury, Evans. 1893
Harcourt. *Royal Umbrella.* Griffith and Farran. 1880
Kingsley. *Water-babies.* Macmillan. 1885

SAMIVEL (*Ac.* 1940) French
Samivel. *Brown the Bear.* Murray. 1940
Samivel. *Rufus the Fox.* Harper. 1937

SANCHEZ, CARLOS (1908-   ) Mexican
Belpré. *Perez and Martina.* Warne. 1932
Björnson. *Happy Boy.* Macmillan. 1931
Poe. *Gold-bug and Other Tales and Poems.* Macmillan. 1930
Sawyer. *Picture Tales from Spain.* Stokes. 1936
Smith. *Swain's Saga.* Macmillan. 1931

SANDERSON, IVAN TERRANCE (1911-   ) English
Sanderson. *Animals Nobody Knows.* Viking. 1940
Waldeck. *Treks across the Veldt.* Viking. 1944

SANDHAM, J. HENRY (1842-1910) English
Baylor. *Juan and Juanita* (with FREDERIC REMINGTON). Ticknor. 1888
Burnett. *Editha's Burglar.* Jordan, Marsh. 1888
Trowbridge. *Fortunes of Toby Trafford.* Century. 1890

SANDYS, FREDERICK (1832-1904) English
Bible. *Art Pictures from the Old Testament* (For other illustrators *see* HOUGHTON, ARTHUR BOYD). S.P.C.K. 1894
Sandys. *Reproductions of Woodcuts by F. Sandys.* Hertschel. 1910

SARG, TONY (1882-1942) American, b. in Guatemala
Lefèvre. *Cock, the Mouse, and the Little Red Hen.* Jacobs. 1907
Lefèvre. *Soldier Boy.* Greenberg. 1926
McIsaac. *Tony Sarg Marionette Book.* Viking. 1921
Moses. *Another Treasury of Plays for Children.* Little. 1926
Moses. *Treasury of Plays for Children.* Little. 1921
Sarg. *Tony Sarg's Book of Tricks.* Greenberg. 1928
Wells. *Jungle Man and His Animals.* Duffield. 1925

SAUVAGE, SYLVAIN (1888-   ) French
Shakespeare. *Tragedy of Romeo and Juliet.* Heritage. 1935

SCHAEFFER, MEAD (1898-   ) American
Blackmore. *Lorna Doone.* Dodd. 1930
Bullen. *Cruise of the Cachalot.* Dodd. 1926
Dumas. *Count of Monte Cristo.* Dodd. 1928
Hugo. *Les Misérables.* Dodd. 1925
Malot. *Adventures of Remi.* Rand. 1923
Masefield. *Jim Davis.* Stokes. 1924
Melville. *Moby Dick.* Dodd. 1922
Melville. *Omoo.* Dodd. 1924
Melville. *Typee.* Dodd. 1923
Russell. *Wreck of the Grosvenor.* Dodd. 1923
Scott. *Tom Cringle's Log.* Dodd. 1927

SCHARL, JOSEF (1896-   ) German
Grimm. *Grimm's Fairy Tales.* Pantheon. 1944

SCHELL, FREDERIC B. (-1905) American
Heber. *From Greenland's Icy Mountains.* Porter and Coates. 1884

SCHMOLZE, CARL HEINRICH (1823-1859) American
Irving. *Bracebridge Hall,* 2 v. (with CHURCH, RACKHAM, REINHART and others). Putnam. 1896

SCHOONOVER, FRANK EARLE (1877-   ) American
Collier. *Roland the Warrior.* Harcourt. 1934
Munroe. *Flamingo Feather.* Harper. 1923
Schultz. *Questers of the Desert.* Houghton. 1925
Smith. *Boy Captive of Old Deerfield.* Little. 1929
Wallace. *Arctic Stowaways.* McClurg. 1917

SCHROTT-FIECHTEL, ELSA EISGRUBER *SEE* EISGRUBER, ELSA

SCHUYLER, REMINGTON (1884-   ) American
Emerson. *Indian Hunting Grounds.* Stokes. 1938
Sienkiewicz. *In Desert and Wilderness.* Little. 1923
Skinner. *White Leader.* Macmillan. 1926
White. *Daniel Boone, Wilderness Scout.* Doubleday. 1922

SCHWABE, RANDOLPH (1885-   ) English
De La Mare. *Crossings.* Beaumont. 1921

SCOTT, HILDA (*Ac.* 1939)
Andersen. *Thumbelina.* Holiday. 1939
Cinderella. Holiday. 1938
History of Tom Thumb. Helen Gentry. 1934

SEAVER, ROBERT (*Ac.* 1908)
Cowper. *Diverting History of John Gilpin.* Houghton. 1906
Hood. *Faithless Nelly Gray.* Houghton. 1907
Seaver. *Ye Butcher, Ye Baker, Ye Candlestick Maker.* Houghton. 1908

SECCOMBE, THOMAS STRONG (1840-1899) English
Comic Sketches from the History of England. Allen. 1884
Hood. *Miss Kilmansegg and Her Precious Leg.* Moxon. 1870
Hood. *Poems of Thomas Hood* (with DARLEY, DORÉ, EYTINGE and B. FOSTER). Putnam. 1872
Seccombe. *Good Old Story of Cinderella.* Warne. 1882

SEIGNOBOSC, FRANÇOISE (1900-) French
(FRANÇOISE, *pseud.*)
Mother Goose. *Gay Mother Goose.* Scribner. 1938
Seignobosc. *Gay A B C.* Scribner. 1938
Seignobosc. *Story of Colette.* Scribner. 1940

SELOUS, HENRY COURTENAY (1803-1890) English
Bunyan. *Pilgrim's Progress.* Holloway. 1844
Hamilton. *Parable of the Prodigal Son.* Nisbet. 1867
La Motte-Fouqué. *Sintram and His Companions.*
Burns. 1870

SEREBRIAKOFF, ALEXANDRE A. (1907-) Russian
Lawrence. *Petrouchka.* Random. 1940
Peck. *Belgium.* Harper. 1940

SEREDY, KATE (1896-) American, b. in Hungary
Bible. *Bible Children.* Dodd. 1937
Brink. *Caddie Woodlawn.* Macmillan. 1935
Daugherty. *Broken Song.* Nelson. 1934
Gaggin. *Ear for Uncle Emil.* Viking. 1939
Harper. *Gunniwolf.* McKay. 1936
Sawyer. *Christmas Anna Angel.* Viking. 1944
Seredy. *Good Master.* Viking. 1935
Seredy. *White Stag.* Viking. 1937
Thompson. *With Harp and Lute.* Macmillan. 1935

SETON, ERNEST THOMPSON (1860-1946) American, b. in
England
Brooks. *First across the Continent* (with FROST and
YOHN). Scribner. 1901
Seton. *Biography of a Grizzly.* Century. 1900
Seton. *Lives of the Hunted.* Scribner. 1901
Seton. *Trail of the Sandhill Stag.* Scribner. 1899
Seton. *Wild Animals I Have Known.* Scribner. 1898

SEUSS, DR., *pseud. SEE* GEISEL, THEODOR SEUSS

SEVIER, MICHEL (1886-)
Tolstoi. *Tolstoi for the Young.* Kegan Paul. 1916

SEWELL, HELEN MOORE (1896-) American
A B C for Everyday. Macmillan. 1930
Austen. *Pride and Prejudice.* Limited Editions. 1940
Bible. *First Bible.* Oxford. 1934
Brink. *Baby Island.* Macmillan. 1937
Brontë. *Jane Eyre.* Oxford. 1938
Bulfinch. *Book of Myths.* Macmillan. 1942
Cinderella. Macmillan. 1934
Coatsworth. *Away Goes Sally.* Macmillan. 1934
Coatsworth. *Five Bushel Farm.* Macmillan. 1939
Falkberget. *Broomstick and Snowflake.* Macmillan.
1933
Farjeon. *Ten Saints.* Oxford. 1936
Jarden. *Young Brontës.* Viking. 1938
Noble. *Round of Carols.* Oxford. 1935
Rhys. *Mr. Hermit Crab.* Macmillan. 1929
Sayers. *Bluebonnets for Lucinda.* Viking. 1934
Sayers. *Tag-along Tooloo.* Viking. 1941
Sewell. *Blue Barns.* Macmillan. 1933
Sewell. *Head for Happy.* Macmillan. 1931
Sewell. *Ming and Mehitable.* Macmillan. 1936
Sewell. *Peggy and the Pony.* Oxford. 1937
Smith. *Christmas Tree in the Woods.* Minton. 1932

White. *Where Is Adelaide?* Houghton. 1933
Wilder. *Farmer Boy.* Harper. 1933
Wilder. *Little House in the Big Woods.* Harper. 1932

SEYMOUR, ROBERT (1798-1836) English
Dickens. *Posthumous Papers of the Pickwick Club*
(with H. K. BROWNE). Chapman. 1837
Gallery of Comicalities (with G. and R. I. CRUIK-
SHANK). Reeves and T. 1889

SHARP, WILLIAM (1900-) American, b. in Austria
Dickens. *Old Curiosity Shop.* Heritage. 1941
Lansing. *Leonardo, Master of the Renaissance.*
Crowell. 1942
Poe. *Tales of Mystery & Imagination.* Limited
Editions. 1941

SHAW, JOHN BYAM LISTER (1872-1919) English
Bunyan. *Pilgrim's Progress.* Jack. 1904
Reade. *Cloister and the Hearth.* Chatto. 1909
Shakespeare. *Hamlet.* Bell. 1914
Shakespeare. *Midsummer Night's Dream.* Bell. 1923
Shakespeare. *Twelfth Night.* Bell. 1924
Steel. *Adventures of Akbar.* Stokes. 1913

SHENTON, EDWARD (1895-) American
Meader. *Long Trains Roll.* Harcourt. 1944
Rawlings. *Yearling.* Scribner. 1938
Sawyer. *Year of Jubilo.* Viking. 1940
Young. *Mayflower Boy.* Farrar. 1944

SHEPARD, ERNEST HOWARD (1879-) English
Agnew. *Let's Pretend.* Saville. 1927
Dickens. *Holly Tree and Other Christmas Stories.*
Scribner. 1926
Fraser-Simson. *Fourteen Songs from "When We
Were Very Young."* Dutton. 1925
Fraser-Simson. *Songs from "Now We Are Six."*
Dutton. 1927
Grahame. *Dream Days.* Lane. 1930
Grahame. *Golden Age.* Lane. 1929
Grahame. *Reluctant Dragon.* Holiday. 1938
Grahame. *Wind in the Willows.* Methuen. 1931
Lucas. *Playtime & Company.* Methuen. 1925
Milne. *House at Pooh Corner.* Methuen. 1928
Milne. *Hums of Pooh.* Dutton. 1930
Milne. *Now We Are Six.* Methuen. 1927
Milne. *When We Were Very Young.* Methuen. 1924
Milne. *Winnie-the-Pooh.* Methuen. 1926
Walpole. *Jeremy.* Doran. 1927

SHEPARD, MARY (*Ac.* 1943) English
Ransome. *Pigeon Post.* Lippincott. 1937
Travers. *Mary Poppins.* Reynal. 1934
Travers. *Mary Poppins Comes Back.* Reynal. 1935
Travers. *Mary Poppins Opens the Door.* Reynal.
1943

SHEPHERD, JAMES AFFLECK. (1867-1946) English
Cuming. *Three Jovial Puppies.* Blackie. 1908
De La Mare. *Three Royal Monkeys.* Selwyn. 1924
Harris. *Nights with Uncle Remus.* De La More. 1906
Harris. *Uncle Remus.* Chatto. 1901

SHEPHERD, JESSIE CURTIS *SEE* CURTIS, JESSIE

SHEPPARD, WILLIAM LUDWELL (1833-1912) American
Brooks. *Boy Emigrants* (with THOMAS MORAN). Scribner. 1877
Page. *Among the Camps* (with NEWELL and ROGERS). Scribner. 1891
Stuart. *Golden Wedding and Other Tales* (with FROST and REINHART). Harper. 1893
Trowbridge. *Doing His Best*. Osgood. 1873
Trowbridge. *Fast Friends*. Osgood. 1873
Trowbridge. *Young Surveyor*. Osgood. 1875

SHEPPERSON, CLAUDE ALLIN (1867-1921) English
Shakespeare. *As You Like It*. Longmans. 1900
Shakespeare. *Merchant of Venice*. Longmans. 1899
Shakespeare. *Midsummer Night's Dream*. Longmans. 1906

SHIELDS, FREDERICK JAMES (1833-1911) English
Bunyan. *Pilgrim's Progress*. Simpkin. 1864

SHINN, EVERETT (1876-   ) American
Hale. *Man without a Country*. Random. 1940
Moore. *Night before Christmas*. Winston. 1942
Wilde. *Happy Prince and Other Tales*. Winston. 1940

SHINN, FLORENCE SCOVEL (-1940) American
Rankin. *Dandelion Cottage*. Holt. 1904
Rice. *Lovey Mary*. Century. 1903
Rice. *Mrs. Wiggs of the Cabbage Patch*. Century. 1903
Zollinger. *Maggie McLanehan*. McClurg. 1901
Zollinger. *Widow O'Callaghan's Boys*. McClurg. 1898

SHIRLAW, WALTER (1838-1909) American, b. in Scotland
Lowell. *Vision of Sir Launfal* (For other illustrators see ALEXANDER, JOHN WHITE). Houghton. 1888

SIEGEL, WILLIAM (1905-   ) American, b. in Russia
Carroll. *Land Spell*. Macmillan. 1930
Krasnov. *Yermak the Conqueror*. Duffield. 1930

SIMON, HOWARD (1903-   ) American
Beim. *Little Igloo*. Harcourt. 1941
Levy. *Bombero, Tales from Latin America*. Knopf. 1943
Levy. *Burro That Learned to Dance*. Knopf. 1942
Simon. *Bright Morning*. Dutton. 1939
Simon. *Robin on the Mountain*. Dutton. 1934
Simon. *Teeny Gay*. Dutton. 1936

SIMPSON, MAXWELL STEWART (1896-   ) American
Aucassin and Nicolete. Holiday. 1936

SINDING, OTTO (1842-1909) Norwegian
Asbjörnsen. *Fairy Tales from the Far North* (with KITTELSEN and WERENSKIÖLD). Nutt. 1897

SLOBODKIN, LOUIS (1903-   ) American
Estes. *Hundred Dresses*. Harcourt. 1944
Estes. *Moffats*. Harcourt. 1941
Estes. *Rufus M*. Harcourt. 1943
Estes. *Sun and the Wind and Mr. Todd*. Harcourt. 1943

Hunt. *Young Man of the House*. Lippincott. 1944
Slobodkin. *Clear the Track for Michael's Magic Train*. Macmillan. 1945
Slobodkin. *Friendly Animals*. Vanguard. 1944
Slobodkin. *Magic Michael*. Macmillan. 1944
Thurber. *Many Moons*. Harcourt. 1943

SLOCUM, ROSALIE (1906-   ) American
Brown. *When the Wind Blew*. Harper. 1937

SLOUS, HENRY COURTENAY SEE SELOUS, HENRY COURTENAY

SMALL, WILLIAM (1843-1929) Scotch
Arthur. *Words for the Wise*. Nelson. 1864
Blackmore. *Lorna Doone*. Sampson Low. 1883
Buchanan. *Ballad Stories of the Affections* (For other illustrators see DALZIEL, EDWARD). Routledge. 1869
Golden Thoughts from Golden Fountains. (For other illustrators see HOUGHTON, ARTHUR BOYD). Warne. 1867
Ingelow. *Poems* (For other illustrators see PINWELL, GEORGE JOHN). Roberts. 1867
Longfellow. *Poetical Works* (with GRAY, HOUGHTON and NORTH). Warne. *n.d.*
Mother Goose. *National Nursery Rhymes* (For other illustrators see HOUGHTON, ARTHUR BOYD). Novello, Ewer. 1870
Picture Book. Routledge. 1879
Spirit of Praise (For other illustrators see HOUGHTON, ARTHUR BOYD). Warne. 1866
Watts. *Divine and Moral Songs* (with BARNES and others). Sampson Low. 1866

SMEDLEY, WILLIAM THOMAS (1858-1920) American
Brooks. *In Leisler's Time*. Lothrop. 1886
Page. *In Ole Virginia* (with CASTAIGNE, CLINEDINST, FROST, H. PYLE and REINHART). Scribner. 1896
Page. *Marse Chan*. Scribner. 1892
Stockton. *Story-teller's Pack* (with KEMBLE, NEWELL, A. B. STEPHENS and others). Scribner. 1897

SMITH, ELMER BOYD (1860-1943) American, b. in Canada
Æsop. *Æsop's Fables*. Century. 1911
Anderson. *Seven O'clock Stories*. Putnam. 1920
Andrews. *Enchanted Forest*. Dutton. 1909
Bidpāī. *Tortoise and the Geese*. Houghton. 1908
Brown. *In the Days of Giants*. Houghton. 1902
Brown. *John of the Woods*. Houghton. 1909
Cary. *French Fairy Tales*. Crowell. 1919
Cooper. *Last of the Mohicans*. Houghton. 1910
Dana. *Two Years before the Mast*. Houghton. 1911
Defoe. *Robinson Crusoe*. Houghton. 1909
Harris. *Plantation Pageants*. Houghton. 1899
Holbrook. *Book of Nature Myths*. Houghton. 1902
Marryat. *Children of the New Forest*. Holt. 1911
Meigs. *Willow Whistle*. Macmillan. 1931
Mother Goose. *Boyd Smith Mother Goose*. Putnam. 1919
Schultz. *Sinopah, the Indian Boy*. Houghton. 1913
Scott. *Ivanhoe*. Houghton. 1913
Smith. *After They Came Out of the Ark*. Putnam. 1918
Smith. *Chicken World*. Putnam. 1910
Smith. *Circus and All About It*. Stokes. 1909

Smith. *Country Book.* Stokes. 1924

Smith. *Early Life of Mr. Man before Noah.* Houghton. 1914

Smith. *Farm Book.* Houghton. 1910

Smith. *Fun in the Radio World.* Stokes. 1923

Smith. *In the Land of Make Believe.* Holt. 1916

Smith. *Railroad Book.* Houghton. 1913

Smith. *Santa Claus and All About Him.* Stokes. 1908

Smith. *Seashore Book.* Houghton. 1912

Smith. *So Long Ago.* Houghton. 1944

Smith. *Story of Noah's Ark.* Houghton. 1909

Smith. *Story of Our Country.* Putnam. 1920

Smith. *Story of Pocahontas and Captain John Smith.* Houghton. 1906

SMITH, FRANCIS HOPKINSON (1838-1915) American

Holmes. *Last Leaf* (with G. W. EDWARDS). Houghton. 1886

Lowell. *Vision of Sir Launfal* (For other illustrators see ALEXANDER, JOHN WHITE). Houghton. 1888

Smith. *Colonel Carter of Cartersville* (with E. W. KEMBLE). Houghton. 1891

Smith. *Gondola Days.* Houghton. 1897

Smith. *White Umbrella in Mexico.* Houghton. 1889

SMITH, JESSIE WILLCOX (1863-1935) American

Alcott. *Little Women.* Little. 1915

Alcott. *Old-fashioned Girl.* Little. 1902

Crothers. *Children of Dickens.* Scribner. 1925

Kingsley. *Water-babies.* Dodd. 1916

MacDonald. *At the Back of the North Wind.* McKay. 1919

MacDonald. *Princess and the Goblin.* McKay. 1920

Moore. *'Twas the Night before Christmas.* Houghton. 1912

Mother Goose. *Little Mother Goose.* Dodd. 1914

Sage. *Rhymes of Real Children.* Duffield. 1903

Smith. *Child's Book of Old Verses.* Duffield. 1910

Spyri. *Heidi.* McKay. 1922

Stevenson. *Child's Garden of Verses.* Scribner. 1905

SMITH, JOHN MOYR (*Ac.* 1896) English

Asbjörnsen. *Tales from the Fjeld.* Gibbings. 1896

SMITH, OWEN (*Ac.* 1941) American

Beling. *Wicked Goldsmith.* Harper. 1941

SMITH, WILLIAM ARTHUR (1918-   ) American

Buck. *Chinese Children next Door.* Day. 1942

Buck. *Water-buffalo Children.* Day. 1943

Lim. *Folk Tales from China.* Day. 1944

SMITH, WINIFRED (*Ac.* 1894) English

Gomme. *Children's Singing Games,* 2 v. Nutt. 1894

SNYDER, WILLARD POINSETTE (1853- ?) American

Carleton. *Farm Ballads* (with H. PYLE, REINHART and others). Harper. 1882

SOLOMON, SIMEON (1840-1905) English

Bible. *Art Pictures from the Old Testament* (For other illustrators see HOUGHTON, ARTHUR BOYD). S.P.C.K. 1894

SOPER, EILEEN A. (1905-   ) English

Gould. *Country Days.* Blackie. 1944

Gould. *Farm Holidays.* Blackie. 1944

Gould. *Happy Days on the Farm.* Blackie. 1944

SOUTHALL, JOSEPH EDWARD (1861-1944) English

Perrault. *Story of Bluebeard.* Lawrence and Bullen. 1895

SOWERBY, AMY MILLICENT (*Ac.* 1909) English

Carroll. *Alice's Adventures in Wonderland.* Chatto. 1907

Sowerby. *Childhood.* Duffield. 1907

Sowerby. *Merry Book.* Oxford. 1908

Sowerby. *Wise Book.* Dent. 1906

Stevenson. *Child's Garden of Verses.* Scribner. 1909

SOWERBY, J. G. (*Ac.* 1888) English

Afternoon Tea (with others). Warne. 1880

At Home (with others). Marcus Ward. 1881

Jimmy. Routledge. 1888

Keary. *At Home Again* (with WALTER CRANE). Marcus Ward. 1888

SPECKTER, OTTO (1807-1871) German

Andersen. *Shoes of Fortune and Other Tales* (with others). Chapman. 1847

Gatty. *Parables from Nature.* (For other illustrators see BURNE-JONES, EDWARD COLEY). Bell and Daldy. 1867

Hey. *Child's Picture and Verse Book, Commonly Called Otto Speckter's Fable Book.* Longmans. 1844

Hey. *One Hundred Picture Fables.* Routledge. 1868

Puss in Boots. Appleton. 1845

SPEED, LANCELOT (1860-1932) English

Grimm. *Fairy Tales.* Pearson. 1904

Knowles. *Legends of King Arthur and His Knights.* Warne. 1913

Lang. *Blue Poetry Book* (with H. J. FORD). Longmans. 1891

Lang. *Red Fairy Book* (with H. J. FORD). Longmans. 1890

Lang. *Tales of Romance* (with H. J. FORD). Longmans. 1907

Swift. *Gulliver's Travels.* Pearson. 1905

SPERRY, ARMSTRONG (1897-   ) American

Heal. *Dogie Boy.* A. Whitman. 1943

Means. *Shuttered Windows.* Houghton. 1938

Sperry. *Call It Courage.* Macmillan. 1940

Sperry. *Little Eagle.* Winston. 1938

Sperry. *Wagons Westward.* Winston. 1936

SPURRIER, STEVEN (1878-   ) English

Barne. *We'll Meet in England.* Dodd. 1943

Dickens. *Nicholas Nickleby.* Heritage. 1940

Spring. *Tumbledown Dick.* Viking. 1940

STACEY, WALTER S. (1846- ?) English

Munroe. *White Conquerors.* Scribner. 1893

STANFIELD, WILLIAM CLARKSON (1793-1867) English
Dickens. *Chimes* (with DOYLE, LEECH and MACLISE). Chapman. 1845
Dickens. *Christmas Books* (with DOYLE, E. H. LANDSEER, LEECH, MACLISE, F. STONE and TENNIEL). Chapman. 1854
Dickens. *Cricket on the Hearth* (with DOYLE, E. H. LANDSEER and LEECH). Bradbury and Evans. 1846
Marryat. *Pirate, and The Three Cutters*. Longman, Rees, Orme, Brown, Green and Longman. 1836
Scott. *Tom Cringle's Log* (with F. WALKER and WEIR). Blackwood. 1861
Tennyson. *Poems* (with HUNT, MILLAIS, MULREADY, ROSSETTI and others). Moxon. 1857

STANILAND, CHARLES JOSEPH (1838- ?) English
Henty. *Dragon and the Raven*. Blackie. 1886
Henty. *Young Carthaginian*. Blackie. 1887
Marryat. *Pirate* in *Children of the New Forest*. Routledge. *n.d.*

STEELE, FREDERIC DORR (1873-1944) American
Johnson. *Eternal Boy*. Dodd. 1909
Stockton. *Casting Away of Mrs. Lecks and Mrs. Aleshine*. Century. 1898

STEEN, ELIZABETH KILGORE (-1938)
Steen. *Red Jungle Boy*. Harcourt. 1937

STENNET, R. (*Ac.* 1823) English
Dame Wiggins of Lee and Her Seven Wonderful Cats. Dean and Munday. 1823
Dame Wiggins of Lee and Her Seven Wonderful Cats. (with KATE GREENAWAY). George Allen. 1885

STEPHENS, ALICE BARBER (1858-1932) American
Alcott. *Little Women*. Little. 1902
Alcott. *Under the Lilacs*. Little. 1905
Craik. *John Halifax, Gentleman*. Crowell. 1897
Craik. *Little Lame Prince*. Walter Scott. 1898
Deland. *Katrina*. Wilde. 1898
Stockton. *Story-teller's Pack* (with KEMBLE, NEWELL, SMEDLEY and others). Scribner. 1897
Stuart. *Story of Babette*. Harper. 1894
Wiggin. *Mother Carey's Chickens*. Houghton. 1911

STEPHENS, HENRY LOUIS (1824-1882) American
Æsop. *Fables of Æsop*. Bouton. 1868
Mother Goose. Nursery Rhymes, 2 v. Hurd & Houghton. 1866
Shanley. *Truant Chicken Series*, 3 v. Hurd and Houghton. *n.d.*
Stoddard. *Children in the Woods*. Hurd and Houghton. 1866

STERN, MARIE SIMCHOW (1909-   ) American (MASHA, *pseud.*)
Raymond. *Child's Story of the Nativity*. Random. 1943
Thorn. *Singing Words*. Scribner. 1941
Three Little Kittens. Simon. 1942

STEVENS, LUCY BEATRICE (1876-   ) American
Alcott. *Aunt Jo's Scrap-bag*. Little. 1929
Alcott. *Jack and Jill*. Little. 1928
Jewett. *Betty Leicester*. Houghton. 1929
Yonge. *Chaplet of Pearls*. Duffield. *n.d.*
Yonge. *Little Duke*. Duffield. 1923

STEWART, ALLAN (1865-   ) Scotch
Grierson. *Book of Celtic Stories*. Macmillan. 1908
Grierson. *Children's Book of Edinburgh*. Black. 1906
Grierson. *Children's Tales from Scottish Ballads*. Black. 1906
Grierson. *Tales of Scottish Keeps and Castles for Young People*. Macmillan. 1928
Scott. *Tales of a Grandfather*. Macmillan. 1934

STOLPER, JOEL (*Ac.* 1942) American
Stolper. *Hippo*. Harcourt. 1942
Stolper. *Patches*. Harcourt. 1942
Stolper. *Whiskers*. Harcourt. 1941

STONE, FRANK (1800-1859) English
Dickens. *Christmas Books* (with DOYLE, E. H. LANDSEER, LEECH, MACLISE, STANFIELD and TENNIEL). Chapman. 1854

STONE, HELEN (1904-   ) American
Burton. *Exciting Adventures of Waldo the Duck*. Whittlesey. 1945
McGinley. *Horse Who Lived Upstairs*. Lippincott. 1944
McGinley. *Plain Princess*. Lippincott. 1945

STONE, M. L. (*Ac.* 1875) American
Andersen. *Stories and Tales* (with T. V. PEDERSEN). Hurd and Houghton. 1871
Andersen. *Wonder Stories Told for Children* (with T. V. PEDERSEN). Hurd and Houghton. 1871
Bradford. *Tales for Little Convalescents*. Hurd and Houghton. 1868
Little Lou's Sayings and Doings. Hurd and Houghton. 1868
Scudder. *Doings of the Bodley Family in Town and Country* (with BENSELL, DARLEY, NAST, HERRICK and others). Hurd and Houghton. 1875

STONE, MARCUS (1840-1921) English
Dickens. *Child's History of England*. Chapman. 1865-66
Dickens. *Child's History of England* (with J. MAHONEY). Chapman. 1868
Dickens. *Great Expectations*. Chapman. 1863
Dickens. *Our Mutual Friend*, 2 v. Chapman. 1865

STOTHARD, THOMAS (1755-1834) English
Alphabet. Pickering. *n.d.*
Bunyan. *Pilgrim's Progress*. Pickering. 1788-89
Defoe. *Robinson Crusoe*. John Stockdale. 1790
Goldsmith. *Vicar of Wakefield*. F. Harding. 1792
Watts. *Songs Divine and Moral for the Use of Children*. Chiswick. 1832

STOTT, W. R. S. (*Ac.* 1913) English
Stevenson. *Kidnapped*. Cassell. 1913

STRANG, WILLIAM (1859-1921) Scotch

Arabian Nights Entertainments. *Sinbad the Sailor, Ali Baba and the Forty Thieves* (with J. B. CLARK). Lawrence and Bullen. 1896
Bunyan. *Pilgrim's Progress.* Nimmo. 1895
Munchausen. *Surprising Adventures of Baron Munchausen* (with J. B. CLARK). Lawrence and Bullen. 1895
Sargant. *Book of Ballads.* Elkin Mathews. 1898
Strang. *Book of Giants.* Unicorn. 1898

STRATTON, HELEN (*Ac.* 1915) English

Andersen. *Fairy Tales of Hans Andersen.* Newnes. 1899
Arabian Nights Entertainments. *Arabian Nights Entertainments* (with McCORMICK, W. H. ROBINSON and others). Newnes. 1899
Campbell. *Beyond the Border.* Constable. 1898
Gale. *Songs for Little People.* Constable. 1896
Grimm. *Fairy Tales.* Blackie. 1903
Herbertson. *Heroic Legends.* Caldwell. 1908
Lang. *Book of Myths.* Putnam. 1915
MacDonald. *Princess and Curdie.* Blackie. 1912
Ruskin. *King of the Golden River.* Blackie. n.d.
Shakespeare. *Macbeth.* Duffield. 1909

SUBA, SUSANNE (1913-) American, b. in Hungary

Eyre. *Lottie's Valentine.* Oxford. 1941
Fox. *Little Cat That Could Not Sleep.* Dutton. 1941
Malvern. *Dancing Star.* Messner. 1942
Morrow. *My Favorite Age.* Macmillan. 1943
Morrow. *Pint of Judgment.* Knopf. 1939
Moses. *Here Comes the Circus.* Houghton. 1941

SULLIVAN, EDMUND JOSEPH (1869-1933) English

Goldsmith. *Vicar of Wakefield.* Constable. 1914
Hughes. *Tom Brown's School Days.* Macmillan. 1896
Irving. *Sketch Book.* Newnes. 1902
Marryat. *Pirate and The Three Cutters.* Macmillan. 1897
Scott. *Pirate.* Service. 1897
Shakespeare. *Complete Works,* 3 v. Dutton. 1911
Sheridan. *School for Scandal and The Rivals.* Macmillan. 1896
Tennyson. *Dream of Fair Women.* Grant Richards. 1900
Tennyson. *Maud.* Macmillan. 1922

SULLIVAN, JAMES FRANK (1853-1936) English (JOSEF, *pseud.*)

Allen. *Glimpses of English History.* Downey. 1901
Sullivan. *Flame-flower and Other Stories.* Dent. 1896
Sullivan. *Here They Are!* Longmans, Green. 1897

SUMNER, HEYWOOD (1853-) English

La Motte-Fouqué. *Sintram and His Companions.* Seeley. 1883
La Motte-Fouqué. *Undine.* Chapman. 1888
Peard. *Jacob and the Raven.* George Allen. 1896

SUSSAN, RENÉ BEN (*Ac.* 1938)

Dickens. *Tale of Two Cities.* Heritage. 1938
Sheridan. *School for Scandal.* Limited Editions. 1934

SYMINGTON, J. AYTON (*Ac.* 1905) English

Defoe. *Robinson Crusoe.* Dent. 1905
Scott. *Tom Cringle's Log.* Macmillan. 1895

TABER, I. W. (-1933?) American

Johnson. *Phaeton Rogers* (with others). Scribner. 1881
Kipling. *Captains Courageous.* Century. 1897

TAWSE, SYBIL (*Ac.* 1933) English

Dumas. *Count of Monte Cristo.* Black. 1920
Gaskell. *Cranford.* Black. 1914
Marryat. *Mr. Midshipman Easy.* Macmillan. 1921
Montgomery. *Anne of Green Gables.* Page. 1933
Mother Goose. *Mother Goose.* Harrap. 1932

TAYLOR, ISAAC (1787-1865) English

Taylor. *Signor Topsy-Turvy's Wonderful Magic Lantern.* Tabart. 1810

TEAGUE, DONALD (1897-) American

Cooper. *Pilot.* Minton. 1925
Dickens. *Oliver Twist.* Putnam. 1926
Dickens. *Tale of Two Cities.* Dodd. 1925
Kendall. *Voyage of the Martin Connor.* Houghton. 1931
Wyss. *Swiss Family Robinson.* Minton. 1927

TEALBY, NORMAN (*Ac.* 1931) English

Farjeon. *Tale of Tom Tiddler.* Stokes. 1930
Tolstoi. *Ivan the Fool.* Oxford. 1931

TEGNER, HANS CHRISTIAN HAROLD (1853-1932) Danish

Andersen. *Fairy Tales.* Heinemann. 1900

TENGGREN, GUSTAF (1896-) American, b. in Sweden

Baylor. *Juan and Juanita.* Houghton. 1926
De La Ramée. *Dog of Flanders.* Macmillan. 1925
Duplaix. *Lively Little Rabbit.* Simon. 1943
Good Dog Book. Houghton. 1924
Hawthorne. *Wonder Book and Tanglewood Tales.* Houghton. 1923
Mother Goose. *Mother Goose.* Little. 1940
Spyri. *Heidi.* Houghton. 1923
Tenggren. *Tenggren Story Book.* Simon. 1944
Wheeler. *Sing for Christmas.* Dutton. 1943

TENNIEL, JOHN (1820-1914) English

Æsop. *Æsop's Fables.* Murray. 1848
Æsop. *Æsop's Fables* (with JOSEPH WOLF). Murray. 1858
Arabian Nights Entertainments. *Dalziel's Arabian Nights,* 2 v. (For other illustrators *see* HOUGHTON, ARTHUR BOYD). Ward, Lock. 1865
Barham. *Ingoldsby Legends* (with G. CRUIKSHANK and LEECH). Bentley. 1864
Carroll. *Alice's Adventures in Wonderland.* Macmillan. 1866
Carroll. *Lewis Carroll Book* (with HENRY HOLIDAY). Dial. 1931
Carroll. *Through the Looking-glass and What Alice Found There.* Macmillan. 1871
Dickens. *Christmas Books* (with DOYLE, E. H. LANDSEER, LEECH, MACLISE, STANFIELD and F. STONE). Chapman. 1854

Gatty. *Parables from Nature* (For other illustrators see BURNE-JONES, EDWARD COLEY). Bell and Daldy. 1867

Juvenile Verse and Picture Book (with R. I. CRUIK-SHANK, J. GILBERT and others). Burns. 1848

La Motte-Fouqué. *Undine.* Lumley. 1845

Mother Goose. *Mother Goose's Nursery Rhymes and Fairy Tales* (with W. CRANE, J. GILBERT, WEIR, ZWECKER and others). Routledge. 1876

Poe. *Poetical Works of Edgar Allan Poe* (with DARLEY, B. FOSTER, PICKERSGILL and others). Sampson Low. 1858

THACKERAY, WILLIAM MAKEPEACE (1811-1863) English

Thackeray. *Adventures of Philip* (with FREDERICK WALKER). Smith, Elder. *n.d.*

Thackeray. *Alphabet.* Murray. 1929

Thackeray. *Ballads and The Rose and the Ring* (with DU MAURIER, FURNISS and others). Smith, Elder. 1879

Thackeray. *Doctor Birch and His Young Friends.* Chapman. 1849

Thackeray. *History of Pendennis*, 2 v. Bradbury and Evans. 1849-50

Thackeray. *Rose and the Ring.* Smith, Elder. 1855

Thackeray. *Virginians*, 2 v. Bradbury and Evans. 1858-59

THOMAS, GEORGE HOUSMAN (1824-1868) English

Bunyan. *Pilgrim's Progress.* Nisbet. 1857

Defoe. *Robinson Crusoe.* Cassell. 1864

Early English Poems (with B. FOSTER, J. GILBERT and others). Sampson Low. 1863

Gatty. *Parables from Nature* (For other illustrators see BURNE-JONES, EDWARD COLEY). Bell and Daldy. 1867

Goldsmith. *Vicar of Wakefield.* Sampson Low. 1855

Gray. *Elegy Written in a Country Churchyard* (with B. FOSTER and A LADY). Cundall. 1854

Longfellow. *Hiawatha.* Kent. 1856

Shakespeare. *Merchant of Venice* (with BRANDLING and B. FOSTER). Sampson Low. 1860

Songs of the Brave. Soldier's Dream and Other Poems and Odes (with DUNCAN, B. FOSTER, HUTTULA and MACQUOID). Sampson Low. 1856

Stowe. *Uncle Tom's Cabin* (with T. R. MACQUOID). N. Cooke. 1853

Trollope. *Last Chronicle of Barset*, 2 v. Smith, Elder. 1867

Wills. *Poets' Wit and Humor* (with C. H. BENNETT). Cundall. 1860

THOMASON, JOHN WILLIAM, JR. (1893-1944) American

Crockett. *Adventures of Davy Crockett.* Scribner. 1934

Page. *Two Little Confederates.* Scribner. 1932

THOMPSON, ERNEST SETON SEE SETON, ERNEST THOMPSON

THOMSON, HUGH (1860-1920) English

Addison. *Days with Sir Roger de Coverley.* Macmillan. 1886

Allen. *Kentucky Cardinal and Aftermath.* Macmillan. 1900

Arblay. *Evelina.* Macmillan. 1903

Austen. *Emma.* Macmillan. 1896

Austen. *Mansfield Park.* Macmillan. 1897

Austen. *Northanger Abbey and Persuasion.* Macmillan. 1897

Austen. *Pride and Prejudice.* Allen. 1894

Austen. *Sense and Sensibility.* Macmillan. 1896

Barrie. *Admirable Crichton.* Hodder. 1914

Barrie. *Quality Street.* Hodder. 1913

Chaucer. *Tales of the Canterbury Pilgrims.* Wells Gardner. 1904

Coridon's Song and Other Verses. Macmillan. 1894

Dickens. *Chimes.* Hodder. 1913

Dickens. *Cricket on the Hearth.* Limited Editions. 1933

Dickens. *Pickwick Papers.* Macmillan. 1886

Dobson. *Ballad of Beau Brocade and Other Poems of the XVIIIth Century.* Kegan Paul. 1892

Edgeworth. *Tales from Maria Edgeworth.* Wells Gardner. 1903

Eliot. *Scenes of Clerical Life.* Macmillan. 1906

Eliot. *Silas Marner.* Macmillan. 1907

Gaskell. *Cranford.* Macmillan. 1891

Gaskell. *Cranford* (in color). Macmillan. 1898

Goldsmith. *She Stoops to Conquer.* Hodder. 1912

Goldsmith. *Vicar of Wakefield.* Macmillan. 1890

Hawthorne. *Scarlet Letter.* Methuen. 1920

Hughes. *Tom Brown's School Days.* Leroy Phillips. 1920

Jack the Giant Killer. Macmillan. 1898

Mitford. *Our Village.* Macmillan. 1893

Molesworth. *This and That.* Macmillan. 1899

Old English Songs. Macmillan. 1894

Scott. *Antiquary.* Black. 1891

Scott. *Bride of Lammermoor.* Black. 1891

Scott. *St. Ronan's Well.* Black. 1894

Shakespeare. *As You Like It.* Hodder. 1909

Shakespeare. *Merry Wives of Windsor.* Heinemann. 1910

Sheridan. *School for Scandal.* Hodder. 1911

Thackeray. *History of Henry Esmond.* Macmillan. 1905

Thackeray. *History of Samuel Titmarsh and The Great Hoggarty Diamond.* Wells Gardner. 1902

Tristram. *Coaching Days and Coaching Ways* (with HERBERT RAILTON). Macmillan. 1888

THORNE, DIANA (1894-) American, b. in Canada

Garner. *Little Cat Lost.* Messner. 1943

Hoke. *Major and the Kitten.* Holt. 1941

Inchfawn. *Who Goes to the Wood.* Winston. 1942

Walden. *Igloo.* Putnam. 1931

THORNYCROFT, ROSALIND (1891-) English

Farjeon. *Heroes and Heroines.* Gollancz. 1933

Farjeon. *Italian Peepshow and Other Tales.* Stokes. 1926

Farjeon. *Kings and Queens.* Gollancz. 1932

THULSTRUP, THUR DE (1848-1930) American, b. in Sweden

Munroe. *Flamingo Feather.* Harper. 1887

TOHOMA (*Ac.* 1939) American

Abeita. *I Am a Pueblo Indian Girl* (with HOUSER and NAILOR). Morrow. 1939

Toh-Yah *SEE* Nailor, Gerald A.

Townsend, Frederick Henry (1868-1920) English
Brontë. *Jane Eyre*. Service and Paton. 1898
Dickens. *Child's History of England* (with others). Chapman. 1898
Dickens. *Tale of Two Cities*. Nisbet. 1902
Hawthorne. *House of the Seven Gables*. Service and Paton. 1898
Kipling. *Brushwood Boy*. Doubleday. 1907
Kipling. *They*. Doubleday. 1906
Scott. *Rob Roy*. Service and Paton. 1897

Tresilian, Cecil Stuart (1891-   ) English
Kipling. *All the Mowgli Stories*. Macmillan. 1933
Kipling. *Animal Stories*. Doubleday. 1937

Trevelyan, Pauline (1905-   ) English
Bell. *Lilliburlero*. Oxford. 1933

Trier, Walter (1890-   ) Czechoslovakian
Kästner. *Eleven Merry Pranks of Till the Jester*. Longmans. 1938
Kästner. *Emil and the Detectives*. Doubleday. 1930
Kästner. *Emil and the Three Twins*. Cape. 1935
Kästner. *Flying Classroom*. Cape. 1934
Trier. *Jolly Picnic*. Sylvan. 1944

Troy, Hugh (1906-   ) American
Troy. *Chippendale Dam.* Oxford. 1941
Troy. *Five Golden Wrens*. Oxford. 1943

Tudor, Tasha (1915-   ) American
Mother Goose. *Mother Goose*. Oxford. 1944
Tudor. *Alexander the Gander*. Oxford. 1939
Tudor. *County Fair*. Oxford. 1940
Tudor. *Dorcas Porcus*. Oxford. 1942
Tudor. *Tale for Easter*. Oxford. 1941

Ulreich, Nura Woodson (1899-   ) American (Nura, *pseud.*)
Ulreich. *All Aboard, We Are Off*. Studio. 1944
Ulreich. *Nura's Children Go Visiting*. Studio. 1943

Underwood, Leon (1890-   ) English
Bianco. *Adventures of Andy*. Doran. 1927

Unwin, Nora Spicer (1907-   ) English
Tregarthen. *Doll Who Came Alive*. Faber. 1944
Yates. *Mountain Born*. Coward. 1943
Yates. *Under the Little Fir*. Coward. 1942

Van Doren, Margaret (1917-   ) American
Gale. *One Summer*. Viking. 1936
Gale. *Pony Named Nubbin*. Viking. 1939
Mussey. *Falla, a President's Dog*. Howell, Soskin. 1941

Van Everdingen, Allart (1621-1675) Dutch
Reynard the Fox. *Most Delectable History of Reynard the Fox*. Cundall. 1846

Van Everen, Jay (*Ac.* 1934) American
Charnley. *Jean Lafitte*. Viking. 1934
Davis. *Truce of the Wolf*. Harcourt. 1931
Fillmore. *Laughing Prince*. Harcourt. 1921
Fillmore. *Mighty Mikko*. Harcourt. 1922
Fillmore. *Wizard of the North*. Harcourt. 1923
Moore. *Nicholas*. Putnam. 1924
Moore. *Nicholas and the Golden Goose*. Putnam. 1932

Van Loon, Hendrik Willem (1882-1944) American, b. in Holland
Castagnetta. *Christmas Carols*. Simon. 1937
Van Loon. *Ancient Man*. Boni. 1920
Van Loon. *Around the World with the Alphabet*. Simon. 1935
Van Loon. *Folk Songs of Many Lands*. Simon. 1938
Van Loon. *Golden Book of the Dutch Navigators*. Appleton. 1938
Van Loon. *History with a Match*. McKay. 1917
Van Loon. *Life and Times of Simon Bolivar*. Dodd. 1943
Van Loon. *Romance of Discovery*. McKay. 1917
Van Loon. *Songs America Sings*. Simon. 1939
Van Loon. *Songs We Sing*. Simon. 1936
Van Loon. *Story of Mankind*. Boni. 1921
Van Loon. *Thomas Jefferson*. Dodd. 1943
Van Loon. *Van Loon's Geography*. Simon. 1932

Van Stockum, Hilda (1908-   ) American, b. in Holland
Coblentz. *Beggars' Penny*. Longmans. 1943
Coblentz. *Bells of Leyden Sing*. Longmans. 1944
Troelstra. *Afke's Ten*. Lippincott. 1936
Van Stockum. *Cottage at Bantry Bay*. Viking. 1938
Van Stockum. *Day on Skates*. Harper. 1934
Van Stockum. *Gerrit and the Organ*. Viking. 1943

Varian, George Edmund (1865-1923) American
Hawes. *Great Quest*. Atlantic Monthly. 1921
Hawes. *Mutineers*. Atlantic Monthly. 1920
Kendall. *Romance of the Martin Connor*. Houghton. 1916
Schultz. *Lone Bull's Mistake*. Houghton. 1918
Schultz. *On the Warpath*. Houghton. 1914
Shaw. *Castle Blair*. Little. 1923
Slocum. *Sailing Alone around the World* (with Thomas Fogarty). Appleton. 1911
Stockton. *Buccaneers and Pirates of Our Coast* (with B. W. Clinedinst). Macmillan. 1898

Vaughan, Anne (1913-   ) American
Singh. *Gift of the Forest*. Longmans. 1942
Smith. *Kodru, the Monkey*. Knopf. 1941
Smith. *Kongo, the Elephant*. Knopf. 1939

Vawter, John William (1871-1941) American
Burdette. *Smiles Yoked with Sighs.* Bowen-Merrill. 1900
Mitchell. *Gray Moon Tales*. Bobbs. 1926
Riley. *Book of Joyous Children*. Bobbs. 1902
Riley. *Child-rhymes*. Bobbs. 1898
Riley. *Old Swimmin' Hole, and Other Poems*. Bobbs. 1912
Riley. *Songs of Home*. Bobbs. 1910

VEDDER, ELIHU (1836-1923) American
 Tennyson. *Enoch Arden* (with DARLEY, HENNESSY and LAFARGE). Ticknor and Fields. 1865

VEDDER, SIMON HARMON (1866-1937) English, b. in America
 Scott. *Talisman*. Lippincott. 1915

VER BECK, WILLIAM FRANCIS (1858-1933) American
 Bay. *Danish Fairy & Folk Tales*. Harper. 1899
 Harris. *Told by Uncle Remus* (with CONDÉ and FROST). McClure. 1905
 Howells. *Christmas Every Day and Other Stories*. Harper. 1893
 MacManus. *Donegal Fairy Stories*. Doubleday. 1900
 Paine. *Arkansaw Bear*. Altemus. 1902

VIMAR, AUGUSTE (1851-1916) French
 Guigou. *Animal Trainer*. Duffield. 1910
 Guigou. *Animals in the Ark*. Duffield. 1909
 Vimar. *Clown: The Circus Horse*. Reilly. 1917
 Vimar. *Curly-haired Hen*. Desmond Fitzgerald. 1914

VOX, MAXIMILIEN (*Ac.* 1933) French
 Austen. *Pride and Prejudice*. Dent. 1933
 Austen. *Sense and Sensibility*. Dent. 1933

VYSE, GEORGE HOWARD (*Ac.* 1914)
 Coloma. *Perez the Mouse*. Dodd. 1914

WAIN, LOUIS (1860-1939) English
 Wain. *Cats*. Sands. 1900
 Wain. *Cats at School*. Routledge. 1911
 Wain. *Claws and Paws*. Collins. 1904
 Wain. *Kitten Book*. Treherne. 1903
 Wain. *Pussies and Puppies*. Partridge. 1899

WALKER, ARTHUR GEORGE (1861-1939) English
 Darton. *Wonder Book of Old Romance*. Wells Gardner. 1907
 MacDonald. *Lost Princess; or, The Wise Woman*. Wells Gardner. 1895
 Macleod. *Book of Ballad Stories*. Wells Gardner. 1906
 Macleod. *Book of King Arthur and His Noble Knights*. Wells Gardner. 1900
 Spenser. *Stories from the Faerie Queene*. Wells Gardner. 1897
 Whitham. *Captive Royal Children*. Wells Gardner. 1911

WALKER, DUGALD STEWART (1883-1937) American
 Andersen. *Fairy Tales*. Doubleday. 1914
 Colum. *Boy Who Knew What the Birds Said*. Macmillan. 1918
 Colum. *Girl Who Sat by the Ashes*. Macmillan. 1919
 Hutchinson. *Golden Porch*. Longmans. 1925
 Hutchinson. *Orpheus with His Lute*. Longmans. 1926
 Ingelow. *Mopsa the Fairy*. Macmillan. 1927

WALKER, FREDERICK (1840-1875) English
 Burns. *Poems and Songs* (with B. FOSTER, J. GILBERT, J. D. WATSON and WEIR). Bell and Daldy. 1857
 Dickens. *Hard Times*. Chapman. 1863

Dickens. *Reprinted Pieces*. Chapman. 1862
 Round of Days (For other illustrators *see* HOUGHTON, ARTHUR BOYD). Routledge. 1866
 Scenes and Narratives from the Early History of the United States of America. S.P.C.K. 1862
 Scott. *Tom Cringle's Log* (with STANFIELD and WEIR). Blackwood. 1861.
 Thackeray. *Adventures of Philip* (with W. M. THACKERAY). Smith, Elder. *n.d.*
 Thackeray. *Denis Duval*. Harper. 1864
 Wayside Posies (with NORTH AND PINWELL). Routledge. 1867

WALLIN, SAMUEL (*Ac.* 1848) American
 Child. *Rainbows for Children*. C. S. Francis. 1847
 Sedgwick. *Facts and Fancies for School-day Reading*. Wiley and Putnam. 1848

WALTON, CECILE (1891-) Scotch
 Andersen. *Fairy Tales*. Jack. 1911
 Glínski. *Polish Fairy Tales*. Lane. 1920

WARD, LYND KENDALL (1905-) American
 Beowulf. *Beowulf*. Heritage. 1939
 Coatsworth. *Cat Who Went to Heaven*. Macmillan. 1930
 Colum. *White Sparrow*. Macmillan. 1933
 Forbes. *Johnny Tremain*. Houghton. 1943
 Hewes. *Spice and the Devil's Cave*. Knopf. 1930
 Howard. *Ching-Li and the Dragons*. Macmillan. 1931
 McNeer. *Prince Bantam*. Macmillan. 1929
 McNeer. *Waif Maid*. Macmillan. 1930
 Marryat. *Children of the New Forest*. Macmillan. 1930
 Medary. *Topgallant; a Herring Gull*. Random. 1935
 Reade. *Cloister and the Hearth*, 2 v. Limited Editions. 1932
 Robinson. *Bright Island*. Random. 1937
 Rowe. *Begging Deer*. Macmillan. 1928
 Swift. *Little Red Lighthouse*. Harcourt. 1942

WATSON, ALDREN AULD (1917-) American
 Frost. *Christmas in the Woods*. Harper. 1942
 Irving. *Rip Van Winkle and The Legend of Sleepy Hollow*. Peter Pauper. 1943
 Martin. *Wonder Cat*. Crowell. 1942
 Moore. *Visit from Saint Nicholas*. Peter Pauper. 1945
 O'Faolain. *Little Black Hen*. Random. 1940

WATSON, JOHN DAWSON (1832-1892) English
 Arabian Nights Entertainments. *Dalziel's Arabian Nights*, 2 v. (For other illustrators *see* HOUGHTON, ARTHUR BOYD). Ward, Lock. 1865
 Buchanan. *Ballad Stories of the Affections* (For other illustrators *see* DALZIEL, EDWARD). Routledge. 1869
 Bunyan. *Pilgrim's Progress*. Routledge. 1861
 Burns. *Poems and Songs* (with B. FOSTER, J. GILBERT, F. WALKER and WEIR). Bell and Daldy. 1857
 Defoe. *Robinson Crusoe*. Routledge. 1864
 Round of Days (For other illustrators *see* HOUGHTON, ARTHUR BOYD). Routledge. 1866
 Warner. *Ellen Montgomery's Bookshelf*. Warne. 1866
 Watts. *Divine and Moral Songs* (with DU MAURIER, C. GREEN, MORTEN and others). Nisbet. 1867

WATTS, GEORGE FREDERICK (1817-1904) English
Bible. *Art Pictures from the Old Testament* (For other illustrators *see* HOUGHTON, ARTHUR BOYD). S.P.C.K. 1894

WAUD, A. WILLIAM (*Ac.* 1867) American
Adams. *Siege of Washington, D. C. Written Expressly for Little People.* Dick and Fitzgerald. 1867

WAUD, ALFRED R. (1828-1891) American, b. in England
Aldrich. *Baby Bell* (with CURTIS, MERRILL, MORAN and others). Osgood. 1877
Taylor. *National Ode* (with FREDERICKS, MORAN and others). William Gill. 1876
Trowbridge. *Bound in Honor; or, A Harvest of Wild Oats.* Lee and Shepard. 1877

WAUGH, DOROTHY (*Ac.* 1943) American
Waugh. *Among the Leaves and Grasses.* Holt. 1931
Waugh. *Warm Earth.* Oxford. 1943

WAUGH, IDA (-1919) American
Blanchard. *Wee Babies.* Griffith and Farran. 1882
Waugh. *Holly Berries.* Griffith and Farran. 1881

WEAVER, ANNIE VAUGHAN (1905-   ) American
Weaver. *Boochy's Wings.* Stokes. 1931
Weaver. *Frawg.* Stokes. 1930
Weaver. *Pappy King.* Stokes. 1932

WEBB, CLIFFORD CYRIL (1895-   ) English
Ransome. *Swallows and Amazons.* Cape. 1931
Webb. *Animals from Everywhere.* Warne. 1938
Webb. *Butterwick Farm.* Warne. 1933
Webb. *Jungle Picnic.* Warne. 1934
Webb. *North Pole before Lunch.* Warne. 1936

WEBBER, IRMA ELEANOR SCHMIDT (1904-   ) American
Webber. *Travelers All.* W. R. Scott. 1944
Webber. *Up Above and Down Below.* W. R. Scott. 1943

WEBER, WALTER ALOIS (1906-   ) American
Boulton. *Traveling with the Birds.* Donohue. 1933
Schmidt. *Homes and Habits of Wild Animals.* Donohue. 1939
Schmidt. *Our Friendly Animals and Whence They Came.* Donohue. 1938

WEBSTER, THOMAS (1800-1886) English
Little Red Riding Hood. Cundall. 1850
Mother Goose. *Mother Hubbard.* Cundall. 1850
Thomas. *Gammer Gurton's Garland* (with others). Cundall. 1846

WEGUELIN, JOHN REINHARD (1849-1927) English
Andersen. *Hans Andersen's Fairy Tales.* Lawrence and Bullen. 1893
Andersen. *Little Mermaid and Other Stories.* Lawrence and Bullen. 1892
Henty. *Cat of Bubastes.* Blackie. 1889
Macaulay. *Lays of Ancient Rome.* Longmans. 1881

WEHNERT, EDWARD HENRY (1813-1868) English
Cinderella. Cundall. 1850
Grimm. *Household Stories,* 2 v. Addey. 1853
Keats. *Eve of St. Agnes.* Sampson Low. 1859
Robin Hood. *History of the Bold Robin Hood.* Cundall and Addey. 1850

WEIR, HARRISON WILLIAM (1824-1906) English
Æsop. *Æsop's Fables.* Routledge. 1867
Æsop. *Children's Picture Fable Book.* Harper. 1860
Alphabet of Animals (with WOLF and ZWECKER). Routledge. 1861
Alphabet of Birds (with WOLF and ZWECKER). Routledge. 1861
Bloomfield. *Farmer's Boy* (with B. FOSTER and HICKS). Sampson Low. 1857
Burns. *Poems and Songs* (with B. FOSTER, J. GILBERT, F. WALKER and J. D. WATSON). Bell and Daldy. 1857
Cat and Dog, or Memoirs of Puss and the Captain. Grant and Griffith. 1854
Child's Companion and Juvenile Instructor (with others). Religious Tract Society. 1875
Cock Robin and Jenny Wren. Grant and Griffith. 1840
Corner. *Puss in Boots; or, Charity Rewarded.* Dean. n.d.
Dole. *Crib and Fly.* Griffith and Farran. 1876
How. *Honey Stew.* Jeremiah How. 1846
Howitt. *Our Four-footed Friends.* Partridge. 1868
Lee. *British Animals.* Grant and Griffith. 1853
Milton. *Comus* (with B. FOSTER and PICKERSGILL). Routledge. 1858
Mother Goose. *Mother Goose's Nursery Rhymes and Fairy Tales* (with W. CRANE, J. GILBERT, TENNIEL, ZWECKER and others). Routledge. 1876
Prosser. *Original Fables* (with E. H. GRISET and others). Religious Tract Society. 1870
Scott. *Tom Cringle's Log* (with STANFIELD and F. WALKER). Blackwood. 1861
Southey. *Three Bears* (with JOHN ABSOLON). Addey. 1850
Trimmer. *History of the Robins.* Griffith and Farran. 1869
Wood. *Natural History for Young People* (with COLEMAN, WOLF, T. W. WOOD and ZWECKER). Routledge. 1882

WEISGARD, LEONARD (1916-   ) American
Brown. *Country Noisy Book.* W. R. Scott. 1940
Brown. *Little Chicken.* Harper. 1943
Brown. *Night and Day.* Harper. 1942
Chambers. *Water-carrier's Secrets.* Oxford. 1942
Howard. *Dorinda.* Lothrop. 1944
MacDonald. *Red Light, Green Light.* Doubleday. 1944
Punch and Judy. *Comical Tragedy of Punch and Judy.* W. R. Scott. 1940
Shakespeare. *Under the Greenwood Tree.* Oxford. 1940
Williams. *Timid Timothy.* W. R. Scott. 1944

WELLS, PETER (1912-   ) American
Wells. *Mr. Tootwhistle's Invention.* Winston. 1942

WELLS, RHEA (1891-　　) American
　　Alcover Sureda. *Once There Was and Was Not.* Doubleday. 1931
　　Wells. *Ali the Camel.* Doubleday. 1931
　　Wells. *American Farm.* Doubleday. 1928

WERENSKIÖLD, ERICK THEODOR (1855-1938) Norwegian
　　Asbjörnsen. *Fairy Tales from the Far North* (with KITTELSEN and SINDING). Nutt. 1897
　　Djurklo. *Fairy Tales from the Swedish* (with KITTELSEN and LARSSON). Stokes. 1901

WERNECK, PAULO (*Ac.* 1939) Brazilian
　　Bandeira Duarte. *Legend of the Palm Tree.* Grosset. 1939

WHEELHOUSE, M. V. (*Ac.* 1920) English
　　Alcott. *Little Women.* Bell. 1909
　　Baldwin. *Holly House and Ridge's Row.* Chambers. *n.d.*
　　Eliot. *Silas Marner.* Bell. 1910
　　Ewing. *Flat Iron for a Farthing.* Bell. 1908
　　Ewing. *Jan of the Windmill.* Bell. 1917
　　Ewing. *Mary's Meadow.* Bell. 1915
　　Ewing. *Mrs. Overtheway's Remembrances.* Bell. 1909
　　Ewing. *Six to Sixteen.* Bell. 1908
　　Gaskell. *Cousin Phillis.* Bell. 1908
　　Gaskell. *Cranford.* Bell. 1909
　　Lucas. *Slowcoach.* Wells Gardner. 1910
　　Molesworth. *Carrots.* Bell. 1920

WHEELWRIGHT, ROWLAND (1870-　　) British, b. in Australia
　　Dickens. *Barnaby Rudge.* Dodd. 1931
　　Dickens. *Old Curiosity Shop.* Dodd. 1930
　　Dickens. *Tale of Two Cities.* Dodd. 1925
　　Scott. *Talisman.* Harrap. 1929

WHISTLER, REX JOHN (1905-1944) English
　　Andersen. *Fairy Tales and Legends.* Oxford. 1936
　　De La Mare. *Lord Fish.* Faber. 1933
　　Godley. *Green Outside.* Chatto. 1931
　　Swift. *Gulliver's Travels.* Cresset. *n.d.*

WIESE, KURT (1887-　　) American, b. in Germany
　　Bishop. *Ferryman.* Coward. 1941
　　Bishop. *Five Chinese Brothers.* Coward. 1938
　　Bonsels. *Adventures of Mario.* Boni. 1930
　　Brooks. *More To and Again.* Knopf. 1930
　　Brooks. *Story of Freginald.* Knopf. 1935
　　Brown. *Alexander, the Tale of a Monkey.* Bobbs. 1934
　　Flack. *Story about Ping.* Viking. 1933
　　Gatti. *Adventure in Black and White.* Scribner. 1943
　　Gatti. *Saranga, the Pygmy.* Scribner. 1939
　　Kipling. *All the Mowgli Stories.* Doubleday. 1936
　　Kipling. *Jungle Book.* Doubleday. 1932
　　Lie. *Ekorn.* A. Whitman. 1931
　　Lorenzini. *Pinocchio.* Nelson. 1928
　　O'Brien. *Silver Chief, Dog of the North.* Winston. 1933
　　Pease. *Gay Pippo.* A. Whitman. 1936
　　Salten. *Bambi.* Simon. 1929
　　Spencer. *Three Sisters.* Day. 1939
　　Stong. *Farm Boy.* Doubleday. 1934

Stong. *High Water.* Dodd. 1937
Stong. *Honk: the Moose.* Dodd. 1935
Stong. *No-Sitch: the Hound.* Dodd. 1936
Stong. *Young Settler.* Dodd. 1938
Waldeck. *White Panther.* Viking. 1942
Wiese. *Joe Buys Nails.* Doubleday. 1931
Wiese. *Liang and Lo.* Doubleday. 1930
Wiese. *Rabbits' Revenge.* Coward. 1940
Wiese. *Wallie the Walrus.* Coward. 1930

WILKIN, ELOISE BURNS (1904-　　) American
　　Bacon. *Kitty Come Down.* Oxford. 1944
　　Burns. *Mrs. Peregrine at the Fair.* Messner. 1939
　　Richardson. *Sheep Wagon Family.* McBride. 1941
　　Stone. *Going-on-nine.* Lothrop. 1939

WILLARD, HOWARD W. (1894-　　) American
　　Hogarth. *Australia: the Island Continent.* Houghton. 1943

WILLIAMS, GARTH (1912-　　) English, b. in America
　　White. *Stuart Little.* Harper. 1945

WILLIAMS, MORRIS MEREDITH (1881-　　) English
　　Grierson. *Scottish Fairy Book.* Unwin. 1910
　　Hull. *Northmen in England.* Crowell. 1913
　　Macdonell. *Italian Fairy Book.* Unwin. 1911
　　Platt. *Stories of the Scottish Border.* Crowell. 1911

WILLIAMS, TRUE W. (*Ac.* 1879) American
　　Twain. *Adventures of Tom Sawyer.* American Publishing Co. 1876
　　Twain. *Innocents Abroad.* American Publishing Co. 1869
　　Twain. *Tramp Abroad* (with W. F. BROWN). American Publishing Co. 1879

WILSON, EDWARD ARTHUR (1886-　　) American, b. in Scotland
　　Brontë. *Jane Eyre.* Illustrated Modern Library. 1944
　　Cooper. *Last of the Mohicans.* Limited Editions. 1932
　　Dana. *Two Years before the Mast.* Donnelley. 1930
　　Defoe. *Life and Strange Surprising Adventures of Robinson Crusoe.* Limited Editions. 1930
　　Hale. *Man without a Country.* Limited Editions. 1936
　　Kingsley. *Westward Ho!* 2 v. Limited Editions. *n.d.*
　　McMurtrie. *Wings for Words.* Rand. 1940
　　Overton. *Long Island's Story.* Doubleday. 1929
　　Stevenson. *Treasure Island.* Heritage. 1941
　　Wilson. *Pirate's Treasure.* Volland. 1926

WILSON, PATTEN (*Ac.* 1914) English
　　Bryant. *Best Stories to Tell to Children.* Houghton. 1912
　　Dickens. *Child's History of England.* Dent. 1902
　　Gask. *True Stories about Horses.* Crowell. 1914
　　Shakespeare. *King John.* Longmans. 1899

WILWERDING, WALTER JOSEPH (1891-　　) American
　　Wilwerding. *Jangwa; the Story of a Jungle Prince.* Macmillan. 1935
　　Wilwerding. *Keema of the Monkey People.* Macmillan. 1936

WINTER, MILO KENDALL (1888-) American
Austin. *Trail Book.* Houghton. 1918
Dodge. *Hans Brinker.* Rand. 1916
Dumas. *Three Musketeers.* Rand. 1923
Hawthorne. *Wonder Book.* Rand. 1913
Stevenson. *Treasure Island.* Rand. 1915
Swift. *Gulliver's Travels.* Rand. 1912
Verne. *Twenty Thousand Leagues under the Sea.* Rand. 1922

WOLF, JOSEPH (1820-1899) German, lived in England
Æsop. *Æsop's Fables* (with JOHN TENNIEL). Murray. 1858
Alphabet of Animals (with WEIR and ZWECKER). Routledge. 1861
Alphabet of Birds (with WEIR and ZWECKER). Routledge. 1861
Gatty. *Parables from Nature* (For other illustrators *see* BURNE-JONES, EDWARD COLEY). Bell and Daldy. 1867
Ingelow. *Poems* (For other illustrators *see* PINWELL, GEORGE JOHN). Roberts. 1867
My Pet's Picture Book. Routledge. 1868
Reynard the Fox. *Reynard the Fox after the German Version of Goethe.* Pickering. 1853
Wood. *Natural History for Young People* (with COLEMAN, WEIR, T. W. WOOD and ZWECKER). Routledge. 1882
Wordsworth. *Deserted Cottage* (with B. FOSTER and J. GILBERT). Routledge. 1859
Wordsworth. *Poems of William Wordsworth* (with B. FOSTER and J. GILBERT). Routledge. 1859

WONSETLER, JOHN CHARLES (1900-) American
Wonsetler. *Me and the General* (with others). Knopf. 1941

WOOD, GRANT (1892-1942) American
Horn. *Farm on the Hill.* Scribner. 1936

WOOD, HARRIE MORGAN (1902-) American
Hallock. *Boy Who Was.* Dutton. 1928
Vaughan. *Lucian Goes A-voyaging.* Knopf. 1930

WOOD, LAWSON (1878-) English
Mother Goose. *Old Nursery Rhymes.* Nelson. 1931

WOOD, T. W. (*Ac.* 1882) English
Wood. *Natural History for Young People* (with COLEMAN, WEIR, WOLF and ZWECKER). Routledge. 1882

WOODROFFE, PAUL VINCENT (1875-) English
Aucassin and Nicolette. Murray. 1902
Herrick. *Country Garland of Ten Songs Gathered from the Hesperides.* George Allen. 1897
Macgregor. *Story of Rome* (with HEATH and RAINEY). Stokes. 1913
Mother Goose. *Nursery Rhymes.* Bell. 1895
Mother Goose. *Second Book of Nursery Rhymes.* George Allen. 1896
Mother Goose. *Thirty Old-time Nursery Songs.* Jack. 1912
Shakespeare. *Songs from Shakespeare's Plays.* Dent. 1898
Steedman. *Nursery Tales.* Dent. 1908

WOODVILLE, RICHARD CATON, JR. (1855-1927) English
Molesworth. *Charge Fulfilled.* S.P.C.K. 1886
Weyman. *Under the Red Robe.* Methuen. 1908

WOODWARD, ALICE BOLINGBROKE (1862-) English
Braine. *Princess of Hearts.* Blackie. 1899
Braine. *To Tell the King the Sky Is Falling.* Blackie. 1896
Carroll. *Alice's Adventures in Wonderland.* Bell. 1913
Cat and the Mouse. Blackie. 1899
Clark. *Lost Legends of the Nursery Songs.* Harcourt. 1921
Ewing. *Brownies and Other Tales.* Bell. 1910
Ewing. *Lob Lie-by-the-fire.* Bell. 1909
Hendry. *Red Apple and Silver Bells.* Blackie. 1897
History of Little Goody Two Shoes. Macmillan. 1924
Howes. *Rainbow Children.* Funk. 1912
King. *Adventures in Toyland.* Blackie. 1897
Molesworth. *House That Grew.* Macmillan. 1900
Morris. *Elephant's Apology.* Blackie. 1899
Morris. *Troubles of Tatters & Other Stories.* Blackie. 1898
Mother Goose. *Banbury Cross and Other Nursery Rhymes.* Dent. 1895
Sargant. *Brownie.* Dent. 1897
Sewell. *Black Beauty.* Bell. n.d.

WOODWARD, HILDEGARD (1898-) American
Dalgliesh. *Relief's Rocker.* Macmillan. 1932
Dalgliesh. *Roundabout.* Macmillan. 1934
Woodward. *Jared's Blessing.* Scribner. 1942
Woodward. *Time Was.* Scribner. 1941

WRIGHT, JOHN MASSEY (1777-1866) English
Goldsmith. *Vicar of Wakefield.* Black. 1903

WYETH, NEWELL CONVERS (1882-1945) American
Bible. *Parables of Jesus.* McKay. 1931
Boyd. *Drums.* Scribner. 1928
Bulfinch. *Legends of Charlemagne.* McKay. 1924
Cooper. *Deerslayer.* Scribner. 1925
Cooper. *Last of the Mohicans.* Scribner. 1919
Creswick. *Robin Hood.* McKay. 1917
Defoe. *Robinson Crusoe.* Cosmopolitan. 1920
Doyle. *White Company.* Cosmopolitan. 1922
Fox. *Little Shepherd of Kingdom Come.* Scribner. 1931
Homer. *Odyssey.* Houghton. 1929
Irving. *Rip Van Winkle.* McKay. 1921
Jackson. *Ramona.* Little. 1939
Kingsley. *Westward Ho!* Scribner. 1920
Longfellow. *Courtship of Miles Standish.* Houghton. 1920
Malory. *Boy's King Arthur.* Scribner. 1917
Parkman. *Oregon Trail.* Little. 1925
Porter. *Scottish Chiefs.* Scribner. 1921
Rawlings. *Yearling.* Scribner. 1939
Rollins. *Jinglebob.* Scribner. 1930
Stevenson. *Black Arrow.* Scribner. 1916
Stevenson. *David Balfour.* Scribner. 1924
Stevenson. *Kidnapped.* Scribner. 1913
Stevenson. *Treasure Island.* Scribner. 1911
Verne. *Michael Strogoff.* Scribner. 1927
Verne. *Mysterious Island.* Scribner. 1918

YEATS, JACK BUTLER (1871?-   ) Irish
  Colum. *Big Tree of Bunlahy*. Macmillan. 1933
  Colum. *Boy in Eirinn*. Dutton. 1913
  Defoe. *Robinson Crusoe*, 3 v. Dent. 1895
  Lynch. *Turf-cutter's Donkey*. Dutton. 1935

YOHN, FREDERICK COFFAY (1875-1933) American
  Brooks. *First across the Continent* (with FROST and
    SETON). Scribner. 1901
  Fox. *Little Shepherd of Kingdom Come*. Scribner. 1903
  Lytton. *Last Days of Pompeii*. Scribner. 1926
  Seawell. *Virginia Cavalier*. Harper. 1896
  Smith. *Colonel Carter's Christmas*. Scribner. 1903
  Wiggin. *New Chronicles of Rebecca*. Houghton. 1907

YOUNG, ELLSWORTH (1866-   ) American
  Jātakas. *Jātaka Tales*. Century. 1912
  Jātakas. *More Jātaka Tales*. Century. 1922
  Stuart. *Adventures of Piang*. Appleton. 1917

ZWECKER, JOHN BAPTIST (*Ac.* 1869) German, lived in
  England
  Alphabet of Animals (with WEIR and WOLF). Rout-
    ledge. 1861
  Alphabet of Birds (with WEIR and WOLF). Rout-
    ledge. 1861
  Andersen. *Ice Maiden*. Richard Bentley. 1863
  Krylóv. *Krilof and His Fables* (with A. B. HOUGH-
    TON). Strahan. 1869
  Mother Goose. *Mother Goose's Nursery Rhymes and
    Fairy Tales* (with W. CRANE, J. GILBERT, TENNIEL,
    WEIR and others). Routledge. 1876
  Mother Goose. *National Nursery Rhymes* (For other
    illustrators *see* HOUGHTON, ARTHUR BOYD). Novello,
    Ewer. 1870
  Wood. *Natural History for Young People* (with
    COLEMAN, WEIR, WOLF and T. W. WOOD). Rout-
    ledge. 1882

J. J. GRANDVILLE : *Travels into Several Remote Nations
of the World by Lemuel Gulliver, pseud.*

A BIBLIOGRAPHY OF AUTHORS

HARRISON WEIR: *Puss in Boots*

THOMAS STOTHARD : *Robinson Crusoe*

OTTO SPECKTER: *Picture Fables*

A Bibliography of Authors

He who gives a child a treat
Makes joy-bells ring in Heaven's Street.

— JOHN MASEFIELD. *The Everlasting Mercy*

A Apple Pie. *G. F. Browne*

A Apple Pie. *Greenaway*

A B C. *G. C. F. Gaskin*

A B C. *Pym*

A B C Book. *Falls*

A B C Book of People. *W. Cole*

A B C for Everyday. *Sewell*

A. Y. D.
Owls of Olynn Belfry. *Caldecott*

AANRUD, HANS
Sidsel Longskirt. *E. P. and I. M. D'Aulaire*
Solve Suntrap. *E. P. and I. M. D'Aulaire*

ABBOTT, JACOB
Emma; or, The Three Misfortunes of a Belle. *Doepler*
John Gay; or, Work for Boys. *Herrick*
Mary Gay; or, Work for Girls. *Herrick*
Rambles among the Alps. *Doepler*
Rollo in Geneva. *Doepler*
Rollo on the Atlantic. *McLenan*
Rollo on the Rhine. *Doepler*

Romulus. *Doepler*
William Gay; or, Play for Boys. *Herrick*

ABBOTT, JOHN STEVENS CABOT
History of Hernando Cortez. *Doepler*
History of Josephine. *Doepler*
History of King Philip. *McLenan*

A'BECKETT, GILBERT ABBOTT
Comic History of England, 2 v. *Leech*
Comic History of Rome. *Leech*

ABEITA, LOUISE
I Am a Pueblo Indian Girl. *Houser, Nailor* and *ToHoma*

ADAMS, FRANCIS COLBURN
Siege of Washington, D. C. Written Expressly for Little People. *A. W. Waud*

ADAMS, JULIA DAVIS
Mountains Are Free. *Nadejen*
Vaino. *Ostman*

ADDISON, JOSEPH
Days with Sir Roger de Coverley. *Thomson*

ADELBORG, EVA OTTILIA
  Clean Peter. *Adelborg*

ADSHEAD, GLADYS L.
  Brownies—Hush! *E. O. Jones*

ÆSOP

  Æsop's Fables. *Artzybasheff*
  Æsop's Fables. *Folkard*
  Æsop's Fables. *H. J. Ford*
  Æsop's Fables. *Griset*
  Æsop's Fables. *Kelen*
  Æsop's Fables. *R. Lawson*
  Æsop's Fables. *Opper*
  Æsop's Fables. *L. J. Rhead*
  Æsop's Fables. *C. Robinson*
  Æsop's Fables. *Rountree*
  Æsop's Fables. *E. B. Smith*
  Æsop's Fables. *Tenniel*
  Æsop's Fables. *Tenniel and Wolf*
  Æsop's Fables. *Weir*
  Argosy of Fables. *Bransom*
  Baby's Own Æsop. *W. Crane*
  Children's Picture Fable Book. *Weir*
  Fables. *E. J. Detmold*
  Fables. *Rackham*
  Fables of Æsop. *C. H. Bennett*
  Fables of Æsop. *Heighway*
  Fables of Æsop. *Herrick*
  Fables of Æsop. *H. L. Stephens*
  Fables of Æsop and Others. *T. Bewick*
  Herford Æsop. *Herford*
  Hundred Fables of Æsop. *Billinghurst*
  Some of Æsop's Fables. *Caldecott*
  Twenty-four Fables. *Gheeraerts*

Afternoon Tea. *J. G. Sowerby* and others

AGATHA F.
  Red Hen and Other Fairy Tales. *G. M. Bradley*

AGNEW, GEORGETTE
  Let's Pretend. *E. H. Shepard*

AINSWORTH, WILLIAM HARRISON
  Tower of London. *G. Cruikshank*
  Windsor Castle. *G. Cruikshank, Delamotte* and
    Johannot

AKERS, DWIGHT
  Sleepy Tom. *Ball*

ALCOTT, LOUISA MAY
  Aunt Jo's Scrap-bag. *Stevens*
  Eight Cousins. *Kennedy*
  Eight Cousins. *H. L. Price*
  Jack and Jill. *Stevens*
  Little Men. *Best*
  Little Men. *Birch*
  Little Men. *Merrill*
  Little Women, Part 1. *Alcott*
  Little Women. *H. M. Brock*
  Little Women. *Copping*

  Little Women. *R. C. Jones*
  Little Women. *Merrill*
  Little Women. *J. W. Smith*
  Little Women. *A. B. Stephens*
  Little Women. *Wheelhouse*
  Morning Glories and Queen Aster. *Kennedy*
  Old-fashioned Girl. *Abbott*
  Old-fashioned Girl. *J. W. Smith*
  Rose in Bloom. *H. L. Price*
  Silver Pitchers. *Kennedy*
  Three Proverb Stories. *Hoppin*
  Under the Lilacs. *Davis*
  Under the Lilacs. *A. B. Stephens*
  Work. *Eytinge*

ALCOVER SUREDA, ANTONIO MARÍA
  Once There Was and Was Not. *R. Wells*

ALDIN, CECIL CHARLES WINDSOR
  Bunnyborough. *Aldin*
  Farm Yard Puppies. *Aldin*
  Great Adventure. *Aldin*
  Just among Friends. *Aldin*
  Mongrel Puppy Book. *Aldin*
  Old Inns. *Aldin*
  Old Manor Houses. *Aldin*
  Us. *Aldin*
  White Puppy Book. *Aldin*

ALDRICH, THOMAS BAILEY
  Baby Bell. *Curtis, Merrill, Moran, A. R. Waud* and
    others
  Story of a Bad Boy. *Brett*
  Story of a Bad Boy. *Eytinge*
  Story of a Bad Boy. *Frost*

ALINGTON, CYRIL ARGENTINE
  Cautionary Catches. *Derrick*

ALLEN, F. N.
  Glimpses of English History. *J. F. Sullivan*

ALLEN, JAMES LANE
  Kentucky Cardinal and Aftermath. *Thomson*

ALLINGHAM, WILLIAM
  Flower Pieces. *Rossetti*
  Music Master. *Hughes, Millais* and *Rossetti*
  Rhymes for the Young Folk. *Allingham, Furniss,*
    Greenaway and *Paterson*

Alphabet. *Nicholson*

Alphabet. *Stothard*

Alphabet of Animals. *Weir, Wolf* and *Zwecker*

Alphabet of Birds. *Weir, Wolf* and *Zwecker*

Alphabet of Drollery. *J. Leighton*

ALTSHELER, JOSEPH ALEXANDER
  Horsemen of the Plains. *C. L. Bull*

Ancient Story of the Old Dame and Her Pig. *J. Leighton*

ANDERSEN, HANS CHRISTIAN
Andersen's Fairy Tales. *Kredel*
Andersen's Fairy Tales. *MacKinstry*
Danish Fairy Tales and Legends. *W. H. Robinson*
Fairy Tales. *Abbott*
Fairy Tales. *G. F. Browne*
Fairy Tales. *H. Clarke*
Fairy Tales. *E. V. B.*
Fairy Tales. *Nielsen*
Fairy Tales. *Rackham*
Fairy Tales. *W. H. Robinson*
Fairy Tales. *Tegner*
Fairy Tales. *D. S. Walker*
Fairy Tales. *Walton*
Fairy Tales and Legends. *Whistler*
Fairy Tales and Stories. *Bayes*
Fairy Tales and Stories. *H. M. Brock*
Fairy Tales and Stories. *Larsson*
Fairy Tales and Stories. *Pape*
Fairy Tales and Wonder Stories. *L. J. Rhead*
Fairy Tales from Hans Andersen. *Armfield*
Fairy Tales from Hans Christian Andersen. *C., T. H.
   and W. H. Robinson*
Fairy Tales of Hans Andersen. *Stratton*
Forty Stories. *C. Jackson*
Four Tales from Hans Andersen. *Raverat*
Hans Andersen's Fairy Tales. *Weguelin*
Ice Maiden. *Zwecker*
It's Perfectly True; and Other Stories. *R. Bennett*
It's Perfectly True! and Other Stories. *Pedersen*
Little Klaus and Big Klaus. *Pears*
Little Mermaid. *Bianco*
Little Mermaid. *Lathrop*
Little Mermaid and Other Stories. *Weguelin*
Mermaid. *Armfield*
Nightingale. *Newill*
Old Man Is Always Right. *Rojankovsky*
Shoes of Fortune and Other Tales. *Speckter* and others
Snow Queen. *Pym*
Stories and Fairy Tales, 2 v. *A. J. Gaskin*
Stories and Tales. *Pedersen* and *M. L. Stone*
Stories from Hans Andersen. *Dulac*
Three Tales of Hans Andersen. *Sambourne*
Thumbelina. *Fabrès*
Thumbelina. *Scott*
Tumblebug and Other Tales. *List*
Twenty Best Fairy Tales by Hans Andersen. *Perkins*
Ugly Duckling. *Armfield*
What the Moon Saw. *Bayes*
White Swans. *Havers*
Wonder Stories Told for Children. *Pedersen* and
   M. L. Stone

ANDERSON, CLARENCE WILLIAM
Billy and Blaze. *C. W. Anderson*
Black, Bay and Chestnut. *C. W. Anderson*
Blaze and the Forest Fire. *C. W. Anderson*
Blaze and the Gypsies. *C. W. Anderson*
Deep through the Heart. *C. W. Anderson*
Heads Up—Heels Down. *C. W. Anderson*
High Courage. *C. W. Anderson*
Salute. *C. W. Anderson*
Thoroughbreds. *C. W. Anderson*

ANDERSON, ROBERT GORDON
Seven O'clock Stories. *E. B. Smith*

ANDREWS, JANE
Ten Boys. *Copeland*

ANDREWS, MARIAN (CHRISTOPHER HARE, *pseud.*)
Story of Bayard. *H. Cole*

ANDREWS, MARY RAYMOND SHIPMAN
Enchanted Forest. *E. B. Smith*

ANGELO, VALENTI
Golden Gate. *Angelo*
Hill of Little Miracles. *Angelo*
Look Out Yonder. *Angelo*
Nino. *Angelo*
Paradise Valley. *Angelo*

ARABIAN NIGHTS ENTERTAINMENTS
Adventures of Haroun Er Raschid. *Pogány*
Aladdin and the Wonderful Lamp. *MacKinstry*
Ali Baba and the Forty Thieves. *Fell*
Arabian Nights. *Brangwyn*
Arabian Nights. *R. Bull*
Arabian Nights. *T. B. G. Dalziel* and *Houghton*
Arabian Nights. *Fabrès*
Arabian Nights. *W. S. Paget*
Arabian Nights. *M. Parrish*
Arabian Nights' Entertainments. *H. J. Ford*
Arabian Nights Entertainments, 3 v. *Harvey*
Arabian Nights Entertainments. *McCormick, W. H.
   Robinson, Stratton* and others
Arabian Nights' Entertainments. *Orr*
Arabian Nights' Entertainments. *Pegram*
Arabian Nights' Entertainments. *L. J. Rhead*
Dalziel's Arabian Nights, 2 v. *E.* and *T. B. G. Dalziel,
   Houghton, Millais, Morten, Pinwell, Tenniel* and
   J. D. Watson
Fairy Tales from the Arabian Nights. *Batten*
More Fairy Tales from the Arabian Nights. *Batten*
More Tales from the Arabian Nights. *Pogány*
Seven Voyages of Sinbad the Sailor. *Fabrès*
Seven Voyages of Sinbad the Sailor. *Reed*
Sinbad the Sailor, Ali Baba and the Forty Thieves.
   Clark and *Strang*
Stories from the Arabian Nights. *Dulac*
Tales from the Thousand and One Nights. *E. J. Det-
   mold*
Tales of Wonder and Magnificence. *Pape*
Thousand and One Nights, 4 v. *Lalauze*

ARBLAY, FRANCES BURNEY D'
Evelina. *Cooke*
Evelina. *Rackham*
Evelina. *Thomson*

ARDIZZONE, EDWARD JEFFREY IRVING
Little Tim and the Brave Sea Captain. *Ardizzone*
Lucy Brown and Mr. Grimes. *Ardizzone*
Tim and Lucy Go to Sea. *Ardizzone*

ARIANE, *pseud. SEE* DUPLAIX, GEORGES

A. W. BAYES : *Fairy Tales and Stories*

ARMER, LAURA ADAMS
    Dark Circle of Branches. *S. Armer*
    Forest Pool. *L. A. Armer*
    Waterless Mountain. *L. A.* and *S. Armer*

ARMFIELD, ANNE CONSTANCE SMEDLEY
    Tales from Timbuktu. *Armfield*
    Wonder Tales of the World. *Armfield*

ARNIM, MARY ANNETTE, GRAFIN VON
    April Baby's Book of Tunes. *Greenaway*

ARTHUR, TIMOTHY SHAY
    Uncle Ben's New-Year's Gift, and Other Stories. *Croome*
    Words for the Wise. *Small*

ARTZYBASHEFF, BORIS MĪKHAĬLOVĪCH
    Seven Simeons. *Artzybasheff*

ASBJÖRNSEN, PETER CHRISTEN
    East of the Sun and West of the Moon. *E. P.* and *I. M. D'Aulaire*
    East of the Sun and West of the Moon. *Nielsen*
    Fairy Tales from the Far North. *Kittelsen, Sinding* and *Werenskiöld*
    Tales from the Fjeld. *J. M. Smith*

ASPDEN, DON
    Mike of Company D. *P. Brown*

At Home. *J. G. Sowerby* and others

ATKINSON, ELEANOR STACKHOUSE
    Greyfriars Bobby. *Kirmse*
    Johnny Appleseed. *Merrill*

ATWATER, RICHARD
    Mr. Popper's Penguins. *R. Lawson*

Aucassin and Nicolete. *Simpson*

Aucassin and Nicolette. *Armfield*

Aucassin and Nicolette. *Cameron*

Aucassin and Nicolette. *G. James*

Aucassin and Nicolette. *Woodroffe*

AULAIRE, EDGAR PARIN D' *SEE* D'AULAIRE, EDGAR PARIN

AULNOY, MARIE CATHERINE JUMELLE DE BERNEVILLE, COMTESSE D'
    Fairy Tales. *G. F. Browne*
    Fairy Tales. *J. Gilbert*
    Madame d'Aulnoy's Fairy Tales, 9 v. *Greenaway*
    White Cat. *MacKinstry*

Aunt Louisa's London Toy Books: Diamonds and Toads. *Greenaway*

AUSLANDER, JOSEPH
    Winged Horse. *Honoré*

AUSTEN, JANE
    Emma. *Thomson*
    Mansfield Park. *C. E. Brock*
    Mansfield Park. *Thomson*
    Northanger Abbey. *C. E. Brock*
    Northanger Abbey and Persuasion. *Thomson*
    Persuasion. *Binder*
    Persuasion. *C. E. Brock*
    Pride and Prejudice. *C. E. Brock*
    Pride and Prejudice. *Sewell*
    Pride and Prejudice. *Thomson*
    Pride and Prejudice. *Vox*
    Sense and Sensibility. *C. E. Brock*
    Sense and Sensibility. *Thomson*
    Sense and Sensibility. *Vox*

AUSTIN, JANE GOODWIN
    Moonfolk. *W. J. Linton*

AUSTIN, MARY HUNTER
    Trail Book. *Winter*

AVERILL, ESTHER
    Daniel Boone. *Rojankovsky*
    Flash. *Rojankovsky*
    Powder. *Rojankovsky*
    Voyages of Jacques Cartier. *Rojankovsky*

AYTOUN, WILLIAM EDMONDSTOUNE (BON GAULTIER, *pseud.*)
    Book of Ballads. *Doyle and Forrester*
    Book of Ballads. *Forrester*
    Lays of the Scottish Cavaliers. *Paton*

Babies' Classics. *Hughes*

BACON, FRANCES ELIZABETH
    Kitty Come Down. *Wilkin*

BACON, PEGGY
    Ballad of Tangle Street. *Bacon*
    Lion-hearted Kitten. *Bacon*
    Mercy and the Mouse. *Bacon*
    Mischief in Mayfield. *Bacon*
    Mystery at East Hatchett. *Bacon*
    Terrible Nuisance. *Bacon*

BAILEY, MARGERY
    Little Man with One Shoe. *Preston*
    Seven Peas in the Pod. *Preston*

BAIN, ROBERT NISBET
    Turkish Fairy Tales. *Levetus*

BAKER, MARGARET
    Black Cats and the Tinker's Wife. *Baker*
    Dog, the Brownie and the Bramble Patch. *Baker*
    Little Girl Who Curtsied. *Baker*
    Lost Merbaby. *Baker*
    Mrs. Bobbity's Crust. *Baker*
    Patsy and the Leprechaun. *Baker*
    Pedlar's Ware. *Baker*
    Pixies and the Silver Crown. *Baker*
    Tomson's Hallowe'en. *Baker*

BAKER, OLAF
Dusty Star. *Bransom*

BALCH, GLENN
Indian Paint. *Hogner*

BALDWIN, MRS. ALFRED
Pedlar's Pack. *Pears*

BALDWIN, EDWARD, *pseud.* SEE GODWIN, WILLIAM

BALDWIN, JAMES
Story of Roland. *Birch*
Story of Roland. *P. Hurd*
Story of Siegfried. *P. Hurd*
Story of Siegfried. *H. Pyle*
Story of the Golden Age. *H. Pyle*

BALDWIN, MAY
Holly House and Ridge's Row. *Wheelhouse*

BANDEIRA DUARTE, MARGARIDA ESTRELA
Legend of the Palm Tree. *Werneck*

BANNERMAN, HELEN BRODIE COWAN
Pat and the Spider. *Bannerman*
Sambo and the Twins. *Bannerman*
Story of Little Black Bobtail. *Bannerman*
Story of Little Black Mingo. *Bannerman*
Story of Little Black Quasha. *Bannerman*
Story of Little Black Quibba. *Bannerman*
Story of Little Black Sambo. *Bannerman*
Story of Little Kettle-head. *Bannerman*
Story of the Teasing Monkey. *Bannerman*

BANNON, LAURA
Red Mittens. *Bannon*

BARBOUR, RALPH HENRY
Half-back. *Clinedinst*

BARHAM, RICHARD HARRIS (THOMAS INGOLDSBY, *pseud.*)
Ingoldsby Legends, 3 v. *G. Cruikshank* and *Leech*
Ingoldsby Legends. *G. Cruikshank, Leech* and *Tenniel*
Ingoldsby Legends. *Rackham*

BARING-GOULD, SABINE
Book of Fairy Tales. *A. J. Gaskin*
Old English Fairy Tales. *Bedford*

BARKER, MRS. SALE
Kate Greenaway's Birthday Book for Children. *Greenaway*

BARKSDALE, LENA
First Thanksgiving. *Lenski*

BARNE, KITTY
Family Footlights. *Gervis*
She Shall Have Music. *Gervis*
Visitors from London. *Gervis*
We'll Meet in England. *Spurrier*

BARRIE, JAMES MATTHEW
Admirable Crichton. *Thomson*
Little Minister. *Hole*
Peter and Wendy. *Bedford*

Peter Pan in Kensington Gardens. *Rackham*
Quality Street. *Thomson*

BARRINGER, MARIE
Martin the Goose Boy. *Petersham*

BARROW, ALBERT STEWART (SABRETACHE, *pseud.*)
Hunting Scenes. *Aldin*

BASKIN, MRS. JAMES NOBLE SEE HAINES, ALICE CALHOUN

BATES, KATHERINE LEE
Once upon a Time. *M. E. Price*

Battle of the Frogs and Mice. *Bedford*

BAUMER, LEWIS
Jumbles. *Baumer*

BAY, JENS CHRISTIAN
Danish Fairy & Folk Tales. *Ver Beck*

BAYLEY, F. W. N.
Bluebeard with Illustrations Humorous and Numerous. *Forrester*
Little Red Riding Hood. *Forrester*

BAYLOR, FRANCES COURTENAY
Juan and Juanita. *Remington* and *Sandham*
Juan and Juanita. *Tenggren*

BAZIN, RENÉ
Juniper Farm. *Peck*

Beauty and the Beast. *Bell*

Beauty and the Beast. *H. M. Brock*

Beauty and the Beast. *G. F. Browne*

Beauty and the Beast. *E. V. B.*

Beauty and the Beast. *Horsley*

BECHSTEIN, LUDWIG
As Pretty as Seven. *Richter*

BEDFORD, FRANCIS DONKIN
Night of Wonders. *Bedford*

BEECHING, H. C.
Book of Christmas Verse. *W. Crane*

BEILBY, RALPH
Quadrupeds. *T. Bewick*

BEIM, LORRAINE LEVEY
Little Igloo. *Simon*

BELING, MABEL ASHE
Wicked Goldsmith. *O. Smith*

BELL, FLORENCE EVALEEN ELENORE, LADY
Lilliburlero. *Trevelyan*

BELLOC, HILAIRE
Bad Child's Book of Beasts. *Blackwood*
Cautionary Tales for Children. *Blackwood*
Cautionary Verses. *Bentley* and *Blackwood*
More Beasts for Worse Children. *Blackwood*

BĪDPĀĪ
Jackal in Persia. *Dombrowski*
Tortoise and the Geese. *E. B. Smith*

BILLINGHURST, PERCY J.
Hundred Anecdotes of Animals. *Billinghurst*

Birds, Beasts and Fishes, an Alphabet for Boys and Girls.
C. H. Bennett

BISHOP, CLAIRE HUCHET
Ferryman. *Wiese*
Five Chinese Brothers. *Wiese*
Man Who Lost His Head. *McCloskey*

BJÖRNSON, BJÖRNSTJERNE
Happy Boy. *Sanchez*
Sunny Hill. *J. Bull*

BLACK, WILLIAM
Judith Shakespeare. *Abbey*

BLACKMORE, RICHARD DODDRIDGE
Lorna Doone. *Austen*
Lorna Doone. *Brittan* and *C. E. Brock*
Lorna Doone. *G. F. Browne*
Lorna Doone. *Grose*
Lorna Doone. *Schaeffer*
Lorna Doone. *Small*

BLAIR, WALTER
Tall Tale America. *Rounds*

BLAISDELL, ELINORE
Falcon, Fly Back. *Blaisdell*

BLAKE, WILLIAM
Gates of Paradise for Children. *Blake*
Land of Dreams. *Bianco*
Songs of Experience. *Blake*
Songs of Innocence. *Blake*
Songs of Innocence. *Levetus*
Songs of Innocence. *J. Parsons*
Songs of Innocence. *Ricketts*
Songs of Innocence. *C. Robinson* and others

BLANCHARD, AMY E.
Wee Babies. *I. Waugh*

BLAND, EDITH NESBIT (E. NESBIT, *pseud.*)
Book of Dragons. *Millar*
Enchanted Castle. *Millar*
Five Children. *G. F. Browne* and *Millar*
Nine Unlikely Tales for Children. *Millar*
Oswald Bastable and Others. *C. E. Brock* and *Millar*
Story of the Treasure Seekers. *Baumer* and *G. F.
Browne*
Wonderful Garden. *Millar*

Blind Beggar of Bethnal Green. *Harvey*

BLOOMFIELD, ROBERT
Farmer's Boy. *B. Foster, Hicks* and *Weir*

Bluebeard and Puss in Boots. *Heighway*

BOGGS, RALPH STEELE
Three Golden Oranges. *E. L. Brock*

BON GAULTIER, *pseud. SEE* AYTOUN, WILLIAM EDMONDSTOUNE

BONSELS, WALDEMAR
Adventures of Mario. *Wiese*
Adventures of Maya the Bee. *Bock*

BONTEMPS, ARNA WENDELL
Fast Sooner Hound. *Burton*
Sad-faced Boy. *Burton*
You Can't Pet a Possum. *Bischoff*

Book of Carols. *H. A. Payne*

Book of Christmas. *G. W. Edwards*

Book of Old English Songs and Ballads. *Brickdale*

BOSSCHÈRE, JEAN DE
Christmas Tales of Flanders. *Bosschère*
Folk Tales of Flanders. *Bosschère*
12 Occupations. *Bosschère*

BOSWELL, HAZEL
French Canada. *Boswell*

BOULTON, RUDYERD
Traveling with the Birds. *Weber*

BOURGEOIS, FLORENCE
Beachcomber Bobbie. *Bourgeois*
Molly and Michael. *Bourgeois*
Peter, Peter, Pumpkin Grower. *Bourgeois*

BOUTET DE MONVEL, LOUIS MAURICE
Good Children and Bad: A Book for Both. *Boutet de
Monvel*
Joan of Arc. *Boutet de Monvel*

BOWEN, OLWEN
Hepzibah Hen Book. *Brightwell*

BOWEN, WILLIAM ALVIN
Old Tobacco Shop. *Birch*

BOWERS, G.
Boy's Book of Ballads. *J. Gilbert*

BOWIE, WALTER RUSSELL
When Jesus Was Born. *Falls*

BOWMAN, ANNE
Boy Pilgrims. *Houghton*

BOWMAN, JAMES CLOYD
Pecos Bill. *Bannon*
Tales from a Finnish Tupa. *Bannon*

BOYD, JAMES
Drums. *Wyeth*

BRABOURNE, LORD
Friends and Foes from Fairyland. *Sambourne*

BRADFORD, MRS. S. H.
   Tales for Little Convalescents. *M. L. Stone*

BRADLEY, WILLIAM H.
   Peter Poodle: Toy Maker to the King. *W. H. Bradley*

BRAINE, SHEILA E.
   Princess of Hearts. *A. B. Woodward*
   To Tell the King the Sky Is Falling. *A. B. Woodward*

BRAY, ANNA ELIZA
   Peep at the Pixies. *H. K. Browne*

BRENNER, ANITA
   Boy Who Could Do Anything. *Charlot*

BREWTON, JOHN EDWARD
   Under the Tent of the Sky. *R. Lawson*

BRICKDALE, ELEANOR FORTESCUE-
   Carols. *Brickdale*

BRINK, CAROL RYRIE
   Baby Island. *Sewell*
   Caddie Woodlawn. *Seredy*
   Lad with a Whistle. *Ball*

BROCK, EMMA LILLIAN
   At Midsummer Time. *E. L. Brock*
   Greedy Goat. *E. L. Brock*
   Hen That Kept House. *E. L. Brock*
   Little Fat Gretchen. *E. L. Brock*
   Pig with the Front Porch. *E. L. Brock*
   Runaway Sardine. *E. L. Brock*
   Till Potatoes Grow on Trees. *E. L. Brock*
   To Market! To Market! *E. L. Brock*

BROCK, HENRY MATTHEW
   Book of Fairy Tales. *H. M. Brock*
   Book of Nursery Tales. *H. M. Brock*

BROMHALL, WINIFRED
   Belinda's New Shoes. *Bromhall*

BRONSON, WILFRID SWANCOURT
   Children of the Sea. *Bronson*
   Chisel-tooth Tribe. *Bronson*
   Fingerfins. *Bronson*
   Grasshopper Book. *Bronson*
   Paddlewings. *Bronson*
   Pollwiggle's Progress. *Bronson*

BRONTË, CHARLOTTE
   Jane Eyre. *Dulac*
   Jane Eyre. *Freedman*
   Jane Eyre. *Orr*
   Jane Eyre. *Sewell*
   Jane Eyre. *Townsend*
   Jane Eyre. *E. A. Wilson*

BRONTË, EMILY JANE
   Wuthering Heights. *Dulac*
   Wuthering Heights. *C. V. H. Leighton*

BROOKE, LEONARD LESLIE
   Golden Goose. *Brooke*
   Golden Goose Book. *Brooke*
   History of Tom Thumb. *Brooke*
   Johnny Crow's Garden. *Brooke*
   Johnny Crow's New Garden. *Brooke*
   Johnny Crow's Party. *Brooke*
   Little Bo-Peep. *Brooke*
   Man in the Moon. *Brooke*
   Oranges and Lemons. *Brooke*
   Story of the Three Bears. *Brooke*
   Story of Three Little Pigs. *Brooke*
   Tailor and the Crow. *Brooke*
   This Little Pig Went to Market. *Brooke*

BROOKS, ELBRIDGE STREETER
   Boy of the First Empire. *Ogden*
   In Leisler's Time. *Smedley*
   Master of the Strong Hearts. *Cary*

BROOKS, NOAH
   Boy Emigrants. *Dunn*
   Boy Emigrants. *Moran and Sheppard*
   Boy Settlers. *Rogers*
   First across the Continent. *Frost, Seton and Yohn*

BROOKS, WALTER ROLLIN
   More To and Again. *Wiese*
   Story of Freginald. *Wiese*
   To and Again. *Best Maugard*

BROWN, ABBIE FARWELL
   Book of Saints and Friendly Beasts. *Cory*
   In the Days of Giants. *E. B. Smith*
   John of the Woods. *E. B. Smith*
   Lonesomest Doll. *Rackham*
   Lucky Stone. *Birch*
   Pocketful of Posies. *Cory*

BROWN, JOHN
   Marjorie Fleming. *Brookes*

BROWN, MARGARET WISE
   Child's Good Night Book. *Charlot*
   Country Noisy Book. *Weisgard*
   House of a Hundred Windows. *De Veyrac*
   Little Chicken. *Weisgard*
   Night and Day. *Weisgard*
   Runaway Bunny. *C. Hurd*
   Shhhhhh . . . Bang. *De Veyrac*
   When the Wind Blew. *Slocum*
   Willie's Walk to Grandmama. *Bloch*

BROWN, MARION
   Alexander, the Tale of a Monkey. *Wiese*

BROWN, PAUL
   Crazy Quilt. *P. Brown*
   Fire! the Mascot. *P. Brown*
   No Trouble at All. *P. Brown*
   Piper's Pony. *P. Brown*
   Puff Ball. *P. Brown*
   War Paint. *P. Brown*

BROWNE, FRANCES
    Granny's Wonderful Chair. *E. L. Brock*
    Granny's Wonderful Chair and Its Tales of Fairy
        Times. *Meadows*

BROWNE, GORDON FREDERICK (A. NOBODY, *pseud.*)
    Nonsense for Somebody, Anybody, and Everybody.
        G. F. Browne
    Some More Nonsense. *G. F. Browne*

BROWNE, HABLOT KNIGHT (PHIZ, *pseud.*)
    Phiz's Toy Book. *H. K. Browne*

BROWNING, ROBERT
    Pied Piper of Hamelin. *Dunlap*
    Pied Piper of Hamelin. *Duvoisin*
    Pied Piper of Hamelin. *Greenaway*
    Pied Piper of Hamelin. *Rackham*
    Pippa Passes. *Brooke*

BRUNEFILLE, G. E., *pseud. SEE* CAMPBELL, LADY COLIN

BRUNHOFF, JEAN DE
    A B C of Babar. *Brunhoff*
    Babar and Father Christmas. *Brunhoff*
    Babar and His Children. *Brunhoff*
    Babar and Zephir. *Brunhoff*
    Babar the King. *Brunhoff*
    Story of Babar. *Brunhoff*
    Travels of Babar. *Brunhoff*

BRYANT, SARA CONE
    Best Stories to Tell to Children. *P. Wilson*
    Epaminondas and His Auntie. *Hogan*

BRYANT, WILLIAM CULLEN
    Little People of the Snow. *Fredericks*
    Story of the Fountain. *Fenn, Fredericks, Homer* and
        others
    Thanatopsis. *W. J. Linton*

BUCHAN, JOHN
    Prester John. *Pitz*

BUCHANAN, ROBERT
    Ballad Stories of the Affections. *E.* and *T. B. G. Dal-
        ziel, Houghton, J. Lawson, Pinwell, Small* and
        J. D. Watson

BUCK, ALAN MICHAEL
    Harper's Daughter. *R. Bennett*

BUCK, PEARL SYDENSTRICKER
    Chinese Children next Door. *W. A. Smith*
    Water-buffalo Children. *W. A. Smith*

BUCKELS, ALEC
    Three Little Ducklings. *Buckels*

BUCKLEY, ELSIE FINNIMORE
    Children of the Dawn. *Papé*

BUFF, MARY MARSH
    Dancing Cloud. *Buff*
    Dash and Dart. *Buff*
    Kobi. *Buff*

BULFINCH, THOMAS
    Book of Myths. *Sewell*
    Legends of Charlemagne. *Wyeth*

BULLEN, FRANK THOMAS
    Cruise of the Cachalot. *Fischer* and *Reuterdahl*
    Cruise of the Cachalot. *Reid*
    Cruise of the Cachalot. *Schaeffer*
    Frank Brown, Sea Apprentice. *Reid*

BUNN, HARRIET F.
    Circus Boy. *G. M. Richards*

BUNYAN, JOHN
    Life and Death of Mr. Badman. *G. W.* and *L. J. Rhead*
    Pilgrim's Progress. *Barnard* and others
    Pilgrim's Progress. *Bell*
    Pilgrim's Progress. *C. H. Bennett*
    Pilgrim's Progress. *Blake*
    Pilgrim's Progress. *H. M. Brock*
    Pilgrim's Progress. *Copping*
    Pilgrim's Progress. *G. Cruikshank*
    Pilgrim's Progress. *T. B. G. Dalziel*
    Pilgrim's Progress. *H. J. Ford*
    Pilgrim's Progress. *G. D. Hammond*
    Pilgrim's Progress. *R. Lawson*
    Pilgrim's Progress. *Papé*
    Pilgrim's Progress. *F. A., G. W.* and *L. J. Rhead*
    Pilgrim's Progress. *W. H. Robinson*
    Pilgrim's Progress. *Selous*
    Pilgrim's Progress. *Shaw*
    Pilgrim's Progress. *Shields*
    Pilgrim's Progress. *Stothard*
    Pilgrim's Progress. *Strang*
    Pilgrim's Progress. *Thomas*
    Pilgrim's Progress. *J. D. Watson*

BURBANK, ADDISON BUSHNELL
    Cedar Deer. *Burbank*

BURDETTE, ROBERT JONES
    Smiles Yoked with Sighs. *Vawter*

BURGESS, FRANK GELETT
    Goop Directory of Juvenile Offenders. *Burgess*
    Goop Tales Alphabetically Told. *Burgess*
    Goops and How to Be Them. *Burgess*
    Lively City o' Ligg. *Burgess*
    More Goops and How Not to Be Them. *Burgess*
    Why Be a Goop? *Burgess*

BURGESS, THORNTON WALDO
    Burgess Animal Book for Children. *Fuertes*
    Burgess Bird Book for Children. *Fuertes*

BURGLON, NORA
    Children of the Soil. *E. P. D'Aulaire*

BURNAND, FRANCIS COWLEY
    New History of Sandford and Merton. *Sambourne*
    Real Robinson Crusoe. *Sambourne*

BURNETT, CONSTANCE BUEL
    Shoemaker's Son. *Kredel*

BURNETT, FRANCES HODGSON
Editha's Burglar. *Sandham*
Little Lord Fauntleroy. *Birch*
Little Lord Fauntleroy. *C. E. Brock*
Little Princess. *Birch*
Racketty-Packetty House. *Cady*
Sara Crewe. *Birch*
Secret Garden. *C. Robinson*
Troubles of Queen Silver-Bell. *Cady*

BURNEY, FANNY *SEE* ARBLAY, FRANCES BURNEY D'

BURNS, ESTHER
Mrs. Peregrine at the Fair. *Wilkin*

BURNS, ROBERT
Cotter's Saturday Night. *F. A. Chapman*
Poems and Songs. *B. Foster, J. Gilbert, F. Walker, J. D. Watson and Weir*

BURROUGHS, JOHN
Bird Stories from Burroughs. *Fuertes*

BURTON, EARL
Exciting Adventures of Waldo the Duck. *H. Stone*

BURTON, VIRGINIA LEE
Calico the Wonder Horse. *Burton*
Choo Choo. *Burton*
Katy and the Big Snow. *Burton*
Little House. *Burton*
Mike Mulligan and His Steam Shovel. *Burton*

BUSCH, WILHELM
Buschel of Merry-thoughts. *Busch*
Buzz a Buzz; or, The Bees. *Busch*
Fool's Paradise, with the Many Wonderful Adventures There as Seen in the Strange, Surpassing, Peep-Show of Professor Wolley Cobble. *Busch*
Hurdy Gurdy. *Busch*
Jack Huckabach, the Scapegrace Raven. *Busch*
Max and Moritz, a Story in Seven Tricks. *Busch*
Naughty Jemima. *Busch*
Plish and Plum. *Busch*

BUSH, BERTHA EVANGELINE
Prairie Rose. *Pitz*

BUSONI, RAFAELLO
Somi Builds a Church. *Busoni*
Stanley's Africa. *Busoni*

BUTLER, WILLIAM ALLEN
Tom Twist. *Heyneman*

BYRNE, BESS S.
With Mikko through Finland. *Ostman*

BYRON, MAY C.
Happy Family Series, 6 v. *Aldin*
Jack and Jill. *Aldin*
Merry Party Series, 6 v. *Aldin*

CALDECOTT, RANDOLPH
Babes in the Wood. *Caldecott*
Come Lasses and Lads. *Caldecott*
Elegy on the Death of a Mad Dog. *Caldecott*
Farmer's Boy. *Caldecott*
Fox Jumps over the Parson's Gate. *Caldecott*
Frog He Would A-wooing Go. *Caldecott*
Graphic Pictures. (4 v. in one). *Caldecott*
Great Panjandrum Himself. *Caldecott*
Hey Diddle Diddle and Baby Bunting. *Caldecott*
Hey Diddle Diddle Picture Book. *Caldecott*
House That Jack Built. *Caldecott*
House That Jack Built (Facsimile of Original Sketches). *Caldecott*
Milkmaid. *Caldecott*
Mrs. Mary Blaize. *Caldecott*
Panjandrum Picture Book. *Caldecott*
Picture Book, No. 1. *Caldecott*
Picture Book, No. 1 (Miniature). *Caldecott*
Picture Book, No. 2. *Caldecott*
Picture Book, No. 2 (Miniature). *Caldecott*
Picture Book, No. 3 (Miniature). *Caldecott*
Picture Book, No. 4 (Miniature). *Caldecott*
Queen of Hearts. *Caldecott*
Ride a Cock-horse to Banbury Cross and A Farmer Went Trotting upon His Grey Mare. *Caldecott*
Sing a Song for Sixpence. *Caldecott*
Sketch-book of R. Caldecott's. *Caldecott*
Three Jovial Huntsmen. *Caldecott*

CAMPBELL, LADY COLIN (G. E. BRUNEFILLE, *pseud.*)
Topo. *Greenaway*

CAMPBELL, WALTER DOUGLAS
Beyond the Border. *Stratton*

CANTON, WILLIAM
Child's Book of Saints. *T. H. Robinson*
Child's Book of Warriors. *H. Cole*
Story of Saint Elizabeth of Hungary. *Brickdale*

Cape Town Dicky. *Havers*

CAPUANA, LUIGI
Italian Fairy Tales. *Freeman*

CARLETON, WILL
Farm Ballads. *H. Pyle, Reinhart, Snyder and others*

CAROVÉ, FRIEDRICH WILHELM
Story without an End. *E. V. B.*
Story without an End. *Harvey*

CARPENTER, FRANCES
Tales of a Russian Grandmother. *Bilibin*

CARR, MARY JANE
Young Mac of Fort Vancouver. *Holberg*

CARRICK, VALÉRY
Animal Picture Tales from Russia. *Carrick*
More Russian Picture Tales. *Carrick*
Picture Tales from the Russian. *Carrick*
Still More Russian Picture Tales. *Carrick*
Tales of Wise and Foolish Animals. *Carrick*
Valéry Carrick's Picture Folk-tales. *Carrick*

Children in the Wood. *Harvey*

Children's Friend. *Anderson*

Children's Hour. *Peirce*

Children's Miscellany. *J. Bewick*

Child's Companion and Juvenile Instructor. *Weir* and others

Child's Own Story Book. *Pym*

Child's Pictorial Natural History. *Park*

Child's Play. *E. V. B.*

Child's Summer. *E. V. B.*

Chinese Fairy Tales. *Angelo*

CHISHOLM, LOUEY
    Celtic Tales. *Cameron*
    Golden Staircase. *C. E.* and *H. M. Brock*

CHRISMAN, ARTHUR BOWIE
    Shen of the Sea. *Hasselriis*
    Wind That Wouldn't Blow. *Hasselriis*

Christmas Carols. *E. G.* and *T. B. G. Dalziel, F. A. Fraser, Hughes* and others

Christmas with the Poets. *B. Foster*

CHURCH, ALFRED JOHN
    Stories of the Old World. *Copeland*

CHURCHILL, WINSTON
    Crisis. *Christy*
    Crossing. *Rae*

Cinderella. *Fell*

Cinderella. *Rackham*

Cinderella. *Scott*

Cinderella. *Sewell*

Cinderella. *Wehnert*

CLARK, ANN NOLAN
    In My Mother's House. *Herrera*
    Little Navajo Bluebird. *Lantz*

CLARK, MARGERY, *pseud.*
    Poppy Seed Cakes. *Petersham*

CLARK, MARY SENIOR
    Lost Legends of the Nursery Songs. *A. B. Woodward*

CLARKE, J. CLAYTON (KYD, *pseud.*)
    Characters of Charles Dickens. *J. C. Clarke*

CLARKE, MARY COWDEN
    Kit Bam's Adventures. *G. Cruikshank*

CLARKE, REBECCA SOPHIA (SOPHIE MAY, *pseud.*)
    Little Prudy Books. *Nast*

CLEMENS, SAMUEL LANGHORNE *SEE* TWAIN, MARK, *pseud.*

Clever Hans. *J. Lawson*

COATS, ALICE M.
    Story of Horace. *Coats*

COATSWORTH, ELIZABETH JANE
    Alice-all-by-herself. *De Angeli*
    Away Goes Sally. *Sewell*
    Boy with the Parrot. *Bronson*
    Cat Who Went to Heaven. *Ward*
    Dancing Tom. *Paull*
    Five Bushel Farm. *Sewell*
    Knock at the Door. *Bedford*
    Toutou in Bondage. *Handforth*

COBLENTZ, CATHERINE CATE
    Beggars' Penny. *Van Stockum*
    Bells of Leyden Sing. *Van Stockum*
    Falcon of Eric the Red. *Pitz*

Cock Robin. *Heyneman*

Cock Robin and Jenny Wren. *Weir*

COLERIDGE, SAMUEL TAYLOR
    Rime of the Ancient Mariner. *H. Clarke*
    Rime of the Ancient Mariner. *H. Cole*
    Rime of the Ancient Mariner. *B. Foster*
    Rime of the Ancient Mariner. *Grant*
    Rime of the Ancient Mariner. *Paton*
    Rime of the Ancient Mariner. *Pogány*
    Rime of the Ancient Mariner. *Reid*

COLLIER, VIRGINIA MACMAKIN
    Roland the Warrior. *Schoonover*

COLLIN DELAVAUD, MARIE *SEE* COLMONT, MARIE, *pseud.*

COLLINS, WILLIAM WILKIE
    Moonstone. *Du Maurier* and *F. A. Fraser*

COLLODI, CARLO, *pseud. SEE* LORENZINI, CARLO

COLMONT, MARIE, *pseud.* (MARIE COLLIN DELAVAUD)
    Along the Coast. *Exter*
    Down the River. *Exter*
    Up the Mountain. *Exter*

COLOMA, LOUIS DE
    Perez the Mouse. *Vyse*

COLUM, PADRAIC
    Adventures of Odysseus. *Pogány*
    Big Tree of Bunlahy. *Yeats*
    Boy in Eirinn. *Yeats*
    Boy Who Knew What the Birds Said. *D. S. Walker*
    Children of Odin. *Pogány*
    Forge in the Forest. *Artzybasheff*
    Frenzied Prince. *Pogány*
    Girl Who Sat by the Ashes. *D. S. Walker*
    Island of the Mighty. *W. J. Jones*
    King of Ireland's Son. *Pogány*
    Legend of Saint Columba. *MacKinstry*
    Orpheus: Myths of the World. *Artzybasheff*
    Where the Wind Never Blew and the Cocks Never Crew. *R. Bennett*
    White Sparrow. *Ward*

COLUMBUS, CHRISTOPHER
Log of Christopher Columbus' First Voyage to America. *Cosgrave*

Comic Alphabet. *G. Cruikshank*

Comic Nursery Tales. *Forrester*

Comic Nursery Tales, 3 v. *Leech* and others

Comic Sketches from the History of England. *Seccombe*

CONKLING, HILDA
Silverhorn. *Lathrop*

COOK, HOWARD NORTON
Sammi's Army. *Cook*

COONEY, BARBARA
Kellyhorns. *Cooney*
King of Wreck Island. *Cooney*

COOPER, JAMES FENIMORE
Deerslayer. *H. M. Brock*
Deerslayer. *L. J. Rhead*
Deerslayer. *Wyeth*
Last of the Mohicans. *H. M. Brock*
Last of the Mohicans. *E. B. Smith*
Last of the Mohicans. *E. A. Wilson*
Last of the Mohicans. *Wyeth*
Novels, 32 v. *Darley*
Pathfinder. *C. E. Brock*
Pilot. *Teague*
Pioneers. *H. M. Brock*
Prairie. *Curry*
Red Rover. *Darley*
Spy. *Baldridge*
Spy. *Brett*
Spy. *Darley*

Coridon's Song and Other Verses. *Thomson*

CORKRAN, ALICE
Down the Snow-stairs. *G. F. Browne*

CORMACK, MARIBELLE
Jacques the Goatherd. *Brissaud*
Last Clash of Claymores. *N. M. Price*

CORNER, JULIA
Beauty and the Beast. *Forrester*
Puss in Boots; or, Charity Rewarded. *Weir*
Whittington and His Cat. *Forrester*

CORYELL, HUBERT VANSANT
Scalp Hunters. *W. J. Jones*

Country A B C. *Hutton*

COURLANDER, HAROLD
Uncle Bouqui of Haiti. *Crockett*

Courtship and Wedding of the Little Man and the Little Maid. *Absolon*

COWPER, WILLIAM
Diverting History of John Gilpin *C. E. Brock*
Diverting History of John Gilpin. *Caldecott*
Diverting History of John Gilpin. *G. Cruikshank*
Diverting History of John Gilpin. *J. Leighton*
Diverting History of John Gilpin. *Seaver*

COX, PALMER
Another Brownie Book. *P. Cox*
Brownies Abroad. *P. Cox*
Brownies around the World. *P. Cox*
Brownies at Home. *P. Cox*
Brownies in the Philippines. *P. Cox*
Brownies' Latest Adventures. *P. Cox*
Brownies' Many More Nights. *P. Cox*
Brownies: Their Book. *P. Cox*
Brownies through the Union. *P. Cox*
Comic Yarns. *P. Cox*
Palmer Cox Brownie Primer. *P. Cox*

COX, MRS. WILLIAM N. *SEE* CURTISS, PERCY, *pseud.*

COYLE, KATHLEEN
Brittany Summer. *Floethe*

CRAIK, DINAH MARIA MULOCK
Fairy Book. *Goble*
Fairy Book. *L. J. Rhead*
John Halifax, Gentleman. *Cooke* and others
John Halifax, Gentleman. *Goble*
John Halifax, Gentleman. *Hoppin*
John Halifax, Gentleman. *A. B. Stephens*
Little Lame Prince. *Dunlap*
Little Lame Prince. *Ralston*
Little Lame Prince. *A. B. Stephens*
My Mother and I. *Ralston*
Playroom Stories. *C. Green*

CRANE, STEPHEN
Red Badge of Courage. *Curry*

CRANE, WALTER
Columbia's Courtship. Picture History of the United States, with Accompanying Verses. *W. Crane*
Flora's Feast; a Masque of Flowers. *W. Crane*
Pan Pipes. *W. Crane*
Toy-books. *W. Crane*
Absurd A B C
Aladdin
Alphabet of Old Friends
Annie and Jackie in Town
Baby's Own Alphabet
Beauty and the Beast
Bluebeard
Chattering Jack
Cinderella
Cock Robin
Dame Trot and Her Comical Cat
Fairy Ship
Farmyard Alphabet
Forty Thieves
Frog Prince
Gaping Wide-mouth Waddling Frog
Goody Two Shoes

Grammar in Rhyme
Hind in the Wood
House That Jack Built
How Jessie Was Lost
Jack and the Beanstalk
King Luckieboy's Party
Little Red Riding Hood
Mother Hubbard
Multiplication Table in Verse
My Mother
Noah's Ark Alphabet
Old Courtier
One, Two, Buckle My Shoe
Princess Belle Etoile
Puss-in-boots
Railroad Alphabet
Sing a Song of Sixpence
Sleeping Beauty
This Little Pig
Three Bears
Valentine and Orson
Yellow Dwarf

CRAWFORD, PHYLLIS
Blot: Little City Cat. *H. C. Holling*

CREDLE, ELLIS
Across the Cotton Patch. *Credle*
Down, Down the Mountain. *Credle*
Goat That Went to School. *Credle*
Little Jeemes Henry. *Credle*
Pepe and the Parrot. *Credle*
Pig-o-wee. *Credle*

CRESSWELL, BEATRICE F.
Royal Progress of King Pepito. *Greenaway*

CRESWICK, PAUL
Robin Hood. *Wyeth*

CREW, HELEN CECILIA COALE
Saturday's Children. *Freeman*

CRICHTON, FRANCES ELIZABETH
Peep-in-the-world. *McIntosh*
Peep-in-the-world. *Rountree*

CROCKETT, DAVID
Adventures of Davy Crockett. *Thomason*

CROCKETT, LUCY HERNDON
Capitán. *Crockett*
Lucio and His Nuong. *Crockett*
That Mario. *Crockett*

CROCKETT, SAMUEL RUTHERFORD
Surprising Adventures of Sir Toady Lion. *G. F. Browne*

CROMPTON, FRANCES E.
Gentle Heritage. *Pym*

CROSS, MARY ANN EVANS *SEE* ELIOT, GEORGE, *pseud.*

CROTHERS, SAMUEL McCHORD
Children of Dickens. *J. W. Smith*

CROWQUILL, ALFRED, *pseud. SEE* FORRESTER, ALFRED HENRY

CUMING, E. D.
Three Jovial Puppies. *Shepherd*

CURTIN, JEREMIAH
Hero-tales of Ireland. *Day*

CURTISS, PERCY, *pseud.* (MRS. WILLIAM N. COX)
Richard Peters: or, Could He Forgive Him? *Merrill*

DAGLISH, ERIC FITCH
Animals in Black and White, 6 v. *Daglish*
How to See Beasts. *Daglish*
How to See Birds. *Daglish*
How to See Plants. *Daglish*
Life Story of Beasts. *Daglish*
Life Story of Birds. *Daglish*

DALGLIESH, ALICE
Book for Jennifer. *Milhous*
Little Angel. *Milhous*
Once on a Time. *Milhous*
Relief's Rocker. *H. Woodward*
Roundabout. *H. Woodward*

Dame Wiggins of Lee and Her Seven Wonderful Cats. *Greenaway* and *Stennet*

Dame Wiggins of Lee and Her Seven Wonderful Cats. *Stennet*

DANA, RICHARD HENRY
Two Years before the Mast. *D. Nichols*
Two Years before the Mast. *Pears*
Two Years before the Mast. *E. B. Smith*
Two Years before the Mast. *E. A. Wilson*

Dandies' Ball. *R. I. Cruikshank*

Dandy's Perambulations. *R. I. Cruikshank*

Dandy's Wedding. *R. I. Cruikshank*

DARTON, FREDERICK JOSEPH HARVEY
Seven Champions of Christendom. *Ault*
Wonder Book of Beasts. *Clayton*
Wonder Book of Old Romance. *A. G. Walker*

DARWIN, BERNARD RICHARD MEIRION
Tale of Mr. Tootleoo. *Darwin*
Tootleoo Two. *Darwin*

DAUGHERTY, JAMES HENRY
Abraham Lincoln. *Daugherty*
Andy and the Lion. *Daugherty*
Daniel Boone. *Daugherty*
Poor Richard. *Daugherty*

DAUGHERTY, SONIA MEDVÏEDEVA
Broken Song. *Seredy*
Way of an Eagle. *Daugherty*
Wings of Glory. *Daugherty*

D'AULAIRE, EDGAR PARIN
Abraham Lincoln. *E. P. and I. M. D'Aulaire*
Animals Everywhere. *E. P. and I. M. D'Aulaire*
Children of the Northlights. *E. P. and I. M. D'Aulaire*
Don't Count Your Chicks. *E. P. and I. M. D'Aulaire*
George Washington. *E. P. and I. M. D'Aulaire*
Leif the Lucky. *E. P. and I. M. D'Aulaire*
Magic Rug. *E. P. and I. M. D'Aulaire*
Ola. *E. P. and I. M. D'Aulaire*
Ola and Blakken and Line, Sine, Trine. *E. P. and I. M. D'Aulaire*
Wings for Per. *E. P. and I. M. D'Aulaire*

DAVID, JULIAN
Three Hanses. *Chappell*

DAVIDSON, NORMAN JAMES
Knight Errant and His Doughty Deeds. *H. M. Brock*

DAVIES, WILLIAM HENRY
Forty-nine Poems. *J. Parsons*

DAVIS, HELENE EBELTOFT
Year Is a Round Thing. *Lufkin*

DAVIS, LAVINIA RIKER
Hobby Horse Hill. *P. Brown*

DAVIS, MARY GOULD
Handsome Donkey. *E. L. Brock*
Truce of the Wolf. *Van Everen*
With Cap and Bells. *R. Bennett*

DAVIS, RICHARD HARDING
Gallegher and Other Stories. *C. D. Gibson*
Soldiers of Fortune. *C. D. Gibson*
Van Bibber and Others. *C. D. Gibson*

DAVIS, ROBERT
Hudson Bay Express. *Pitz*
Padre Porko. *Eichenberg*
Pepperfoot of Thursday Market. *Baldridge*

DAVIS, ROBERT HOBART
Tree Toad. *McCloskey*

DAWES, SARAH ELIZABETH
Bible Stories for Young People. *Fulleylove*

DAY, LAL BEHARI
Folk-tales of Bengal. *Goble*

DAY, THOMAS
History of Little Jack. *J. Bewick*
Sandford and Merton. *Harvey*

Day, a Pastoral; in Three Parts, viz. Morning, Noon, and Evening. *T. Bewick*

DE ANGELI, MARGUERITE LOFFT
Elin's Amerika. *De Angeli*
Henner's Lydia. *De Angeli*
Petite Suzanne. *De Angeli*
Skippack School. *De Angeli*
Yonie Wondernose. *De Angeli*

Death and Burial of Cock Robin with Tragical Death of an Apple Pie. *T. Bewick*

DEFOE, DANIEL
Life and Strange Surprising Adventures of Robinson Crusoe. *Gérard*
Life and Strange Surprising Adventures of Robinson Crusoe. *Pocock*
Life and Strange Surprising Adventures of Robinson Crusoe. *E. A. Wilson*
Life and Surprising Adventures of Robinson Crusoe, 2 v. *G. Cruikshank*
Life of Robinson Crusoe. *Abbott*
Life of Robinson Crusoe. *Griset*
Robinson Crusoe. *G. F. Browne*
Robinson Crusoe. *Keene*
Robinson Crusoe. *Kredel*
Robinson Crusoe. *Millais*
Robinson Crusoe. *Nast*
Robinson Crusoe. *W. S. Paget*
Robinson Crusoe. *F. A. and L. J. Rhead*
Robinson Crusoe. *E. B. Smith*
Robinson Crusoe. *Stothard*
Robinson Crusoe. *Symington*
Robinson Crusoe. *Thomas*
Robinson Crusoe. *J. D. Watson*
Robinson Crusoe. *Wyeth*
Robinson Crusoe, 3 v. *Yeats*

DE LA MARE, WALTER JOHN
Bells and Grass. *Lathrop*
Child's Day. *Bromhall*
Come Hither. *Buckels*
Crossings. *Lathrop*
Crossings. *Schwabe*
Down-adown-derry. *Lathrop*
Dutch Cheese. *Lathrop*
Flora. *Bianco*
Lord Fish. *Whistler*
Mr. Bumps and His Monkey. *Lathrop*
Peacock Pie. *Crowe*
Peacock Pie. *C. L. Fraser*
Peacock Pie. *W. H. Robinson*
Songs of Childhood. *Canziani*
Stories from the Bible. *Nadejen*
This Year: Next Year. *H. Jones*
Three Mulla-mulgars. *Lathrop*
Three Royal Monkeys. *Shepherd*

DELAND, ELLEN DOUGLAS
Katrina. *A. B. Stephens*

DELAND, MARGARET
Old Chester Tales. *H. Pyle*

DE LA RAMÉE, LOUISE
Dog of Flanders. *Tenggren*
Moufflou. *Aldin*

DEMING, THERESE OSTERHELD
American Animal Life. *Deming*
Indian Child Life. *Deming*
Little Eagle. *Deming*
Many Snows Ago. *Deming*
Red Folk and Wild Folk. *Deming*

DE MORGAN, MARY EVELYN
    Necklace of Princess Fiorimonde. *W. Crane*
    On a Pincushion. *De Morgan*

DENNIS, MORGAN
    Pup Himself. *M. Dennis*

DENNIS, WESLEY
    Flip. *W. Dennis*
    Flip and the Cows. *W. Dennis*

DESMOND, ALICE CURTIS
    Sea Cats. *Bronson*

D'HARNONCOURT, RENÉ
    Hole in the Wall. *D'Harnoncourt*
    Mexicana. *D'Harnoncourt*

DIAZ, ABBY MORTON
    William Henry and His Friends. *Merrill*

DICKENS, CHARLES
    Adventures of Oliver Twist. *Freedman*
    American Notes. *Frost*
    American Notes. *Greiffenhagen*
    Barnaby Rudge. *Barnard*
    Barnaby Rudge. *H. K. Browne* and *Cattermole*
    Barnaby Rudge. *Daugherty*
    Barnaby Rudge. *Wheelwright*
    Bleak House. *Barnard*
    Bleak House. *H. K. Browne*
    Captain Boldheart. *Pearse*
    Character Sketches from Dickens. *Copping*
    Child Characters from Dickens. *Dixon*
    Child-pictures from Dickens. *Eytinge*
    Child's Dream of a Star. *Billings*
    Child's History of England. *Mahoney* and *M. Stone*
    Child's History of England. *Marks*
    Child's History of England. *Ralston*
    Child's History of England. *M. Stone*
    Child's History of England. *Townsend* and others
    Child's History of England. *P. Wilson*
    Chimes. *Bedford*
    Chimes. *Coburn*
    Chimes. *Doyle, Leech, Maclise* and *Stanfield*
    Chimes. *Thomson*
    Christmas Books. *Barnard*
    Christmas Books. *Doyle, E. H. Landseer, Leech, Maclise, Stanfield, F. Stone* and *Tenniel*
    Christmas Carol. *Bedford*
    Christmas Carol. *C. E. Brock*
    Christmas Carol. *H. M. Brock*
    Christmas Carol. *Coburn*
    Christmas Carol. *Copping*
    Christmas Carol. *Eytinge*
    Christmas Carol. *Keller*
    Christmas Carol. *Kredel*
    Christmas Carol. *Leech*
    Christmas Carol. *Michael*
    Christmas Carol. *S. B. Nichols*
    Christmas Carol. *Pears*
    Christmas Carol. *Rackham*
    Christmas Carol. *Reed*
    Christmas Carol. *Ross*

    Christmas Stories. *Abbey*
    Christmas Stories. *S. B. Nichols*
    Christmas Tales. *H. M. Brock*
    Cricket on the Hearth. *Bedford*
    Cricket on the Hearth. *C. E. Brock*
    Cricket on the Hearth. *Coburn*
    Cricket on the Hearth. *Doyle, E. H. Landseer, Leech* and *Stanfield*
    Cricket on the Hearth. *Thomson*
    David Copperfield. *Austen*
    David Copperfield. *Barnard*
    David Copperfield. *H. K. Browne*
    David Copperfield. *G. D. Hammond*
    David Copperfield. *Rainey*
    David Copperfield. *Reynolds*
    Dickens' Christmas Story of the Goblins Who Stole a Sexton. *Nast*
    Dombey and Son. *Barnard*
    Dombey & Son. *H. K. Browne*
    Great Expectations. *Ardizzone*
    Great Expectations. *F. A. Fraser*
    Great Expectations. *C. Green*
    Great Expectations. *McLenan*
    Great Expectations. *M. Stone*
    Hard Times. *F. Walker*
    Hard Times and Pictures from Italy. *Houghton*
    Holly Tree. *Dixon*
    Holly Tree and Other Christmas Stories. *E. H. Shepard*
    Holy Tree and Seven Poor Travellers. *C. E. Brock*
    Little Dorrit. *H. K. Browne*
    Little Dorrit. *Mahoney*
    Little Folks, 12 v. *Darley*
    Magic Fishbone. *Bedford*
    Magic Fishbone. *Pearse*
    Martin Chuzzlewit. *Barnard*
    Martin Chuzzlewit. *C. E. Brock*
    Martin Chuzzlewit. *H. K. Browne*
    Martin Chuzzlewit. *Pegram*
    Master Humphrey's Clock, 3 v. *H. K. Browne* and *Cattermole*
    Mystery of Edwin Drood. *Fildes*
    Nicholas Nickleby. *Barnard*
    Nicholas Nickleby. *C. E. Brock*
    Nicholas Nickleby. *H. K. Browne*
    Nicholas Nickleby. *Spurrier*
    Old Curiosity Shop. *H. M. Brock*
    Old Curiosity Shop. *H. K. Browne* and *Cattermole*
    Old Curiosity Shop. *C. Green*
    Old Curiosity Shop. *Reynolds*
    Old Curiosity Shop. *Sharp*
    Old Curiosity Shop. *Wheelwright*
    Oliver Twist. *G. Cruikshank*
    Oliver Twist. *Darley*
    Oliver Twist. *Mahoney*
    Oliver Twist. *Teague*
    Our Mutual Friend. *Mahoney*
    Our Mutual Friend, 2 v. *M. Stone*
    People from Dickens. *Fogarty*
    Pickwick Papers. *Frost*
    Pickwick Papers. *McKay*
    Pickwick Papers. *Thomson*
    Posthumous Papers of the Pickwick Club, 2 v. *Aldin*

Posthumous Papers of the Pickwick Club. *C. E. Brock*
Posthumous Papers of the Pickwick Club. *H. K. Browne* and *Seymour*
Posthumous Papers of the Pickwick Club. *J. Gilbert*
Posthumous Papers of the Pickwick Club. *Reynolds*
Posthumous Papers of the Pickwick Club. *Ross*
Reprinted Pieces. *F. Walker*
Sketches by Boz. *Barnard*
Sketches by Boz. *G. Cruikshank*
Tale of Two Cities. *Barnard*
Tale of Two Cities. *H. K. Browne*
Tale of Two Cities. *Dunn*
Tale of Two Cities, 2 v. *McLenan*
Tale of Two Cities. *Sussan*
Tale of Two Cities. *Teague*
Tale of Two Cities. *Townsend*
Tale of Two Cities. *Wheelwright*
Uncommercial Traveller. *E. G. Dalziel*
Uncommercial Traveller. *Pinwell*
Uncommercial Traveller *in* Oliver Twist and Uncommercial Traveller. *Furniss*

Discreet Princess; or, The Adventures of Finetta. *J. Bewick*

DITMARS, RAYMOND LEE
Book of Prehistoric Animals. *Carter*
Book of Zoögraphy. *Carter*
Twenty Little Pets from Everywhere. *Carter*

DIX, BEULAH MARIE
Merrylips. *Merrill*
Soldier Rigdale. *Birch*

DJURKLO, NILS GABRIEL
Fairy Tales from the Swedish. *Kittelsen, Larsson* and *Werenskiöld*

DOBBS, ROSE
No Room. *Eichenberg*

DOBSON, AUSTIN
Ballad of Beau Brocade and Other Poems of the XVIIIth Century. *Thomson*

Dr. Jollyboy's A B C. *G. F. Browne*

DODGE, LOUIS
Sandman's Forest. *Bransom*

DODGE, MARY MAPES
Hans Brinker. *Barney*
Hans Brinker. *Darley* and *Nast*
Hans Brinker. *Doggett*
Hans Brinker. *G. W. Edwards*
Hans Brinker. *L. J. Rhead*
Hans Brinker. *Winter*
Irvington Stories. *Darley*

DODGSON, CHARLES LUTWIDGE *SEE* CARROLL, LEWIS, *pseud.*

DOLE, CHARLES FLETCHER
Crib and Fly. *Weir*

DOLE, NATHAN HASKELL
White Duckling. *Bilibin*

DOMBROWSKI, KÄTHE SCHÖNBERGER VON (K.O.S., *pseud.*)
Abdallah and the Donkey. *Dombrowski*
Just Horses. *Dombrowski*

DOORLY, ELEANOR
Insect Man. *Gibbings*
Microbe Man. *Gibbings*

DOREY, JACQUES
Three and the Moon. *Artzybasheff*

DORSET, CATHERINE ANN
Lion's Masquerade. *Mulready*
Peacock at Home. *Mulready*

DOWD, FRANCIS J.
Book of the American Spirit. *H. Pyle*

DOWNEY, FAIRFAX DAVIS
War Horse. *P. Brown*

DOYLE, ARTHUR CONAN
Adventures of Sherlock Holmes. *S. E. Paget*
Micah Clarke. *Pitz*
White Company. *Daugherty*
White Company. *Wyeth*

DOYLE, RICHARD
Journal Kept by Richard Doyle in the Year 1840. *Doyle*
Scenes from English History. *Doyle*

DRAKE, FRANCIS SAMUEL
Indian History for Young Folks. *Pitz*

DRINKWATER, JOHN
All about Me. *H. M. Brock*
More about Me. *H. M. Brock*

DRUMMOND, HENRY
Monkey That Would Not Kill. *Lenski*

DU BOIS, WILLIAM PÈNE
Flying Locomotive. *Du Bois*
Great Geppy. *Du Bois*
Three Policemen. *Du Bois*

DU CHAILLU, PAUL BELLONI
Country of the Dwarfs. *Best*
King Mombo. *Pérard*
Lost in the Jungle. *Best*
My Apingi Kingdom. *Best*
Stories of the Gorilla Country. *Best*
Wild Life under the Equator. *Best*

DUGDALE, FLORENCE EMILY
Book of Baby Birds. *E. J. Detmold*
Book of Baby Pets. *E. J. Detmold*

DULAC, EDMUND
Edmund Dulac's Fairy Book. *Dulac*
Edmund Dulac's Picture Book. *Dulac*

DULCKEN, HENRY W.
Home Thoughts and Home Scenes. *Houghton*

DUMAS, ALEXANDRE
Count of Monte Cristo. *Schaeffer*
Count of Monte Cristo. *Tawse*
Fairy Tales. *Rountree*
Nutcracker of Nuremberg. *Hasselriis*
Three Musketeers. *Leloir*
Three Musketeers. *Winter*

DU MAURIER, GEORGE LOUIS PALMELLA BUSSON
Legend of Camelot. *Du Maurier*

DUNBAR, ALDIS
Sons o' Cormac. *Horvath*

DUNCAN, EULA GRIFFIN
Big Road Walker. *Eichenberg*

DUPLAIX, GEORGES
Animal Stories. *Rojankovsky*
Lively Little Rabbit. *Tenggren*
Merry Shipwreck. *Gergely*
Pedro, Nina and Perrito. *Latham*
Topsy Turvy Circus. *Gergely*

DUSSAUZE, ALICE
Little Jack Rabbit. *Peck*

DUVOISIN, ROGER ANTOINE
And There Was America. *Duvoisin*
Christmas Whale. *Duvoisin*
Donkey-donkey. *Duvoisin*
They Put Out to Sea. *Duvoisin*

E. B. S.
Pictures from Birdland. *E. J.* and *M. Detmold*

E. C.
Morals from the Churchyard; in a Series of Cheerful Fables. *H. K. Browne*

Early English Poems. *B. Foster, J. Gilbert, Thomas* and others

EASTMAN, CHARLES ALEXANDER
Wigwam Evenings. *Deming*

EATON, ANNE THAXTER
Animals' Christmas. *Angelo*

EATON, JEANETTE
Betsy's Napoleon. *Brissaud*
Narcissa Whitman. *Ishmael*

EBERLE, IRMENGARDE
Hop, Skip and Fly. *Bostelmann*
Sea-horse Adventure. *R. C. Jones*
Spice on the Wind. *R. C. Jones*
Wide Fields. *Eichenberg*

EDGEWORTH, MARIA
Bracelets; or, Amiability and Industry Rewarded. *Croome*
Early Lessons. *B. Foster*
Moral Tales. *Darley*
Parent's Assistant. *H. K. Browne*
Parent's Assistant. *C. Hammond*
Popular Tales. *C. Hammond*
Tales from Maria Edgeworth. *Thomson*

EDMONDS, WALTER DUMAUX
Matchlock Gun. *Lantz*
Tom Whipple. *Lantz*
Two Logs Crossing. *Gergely*
Wilderness Clearing. *De Martelly*

EDWARDS, MATILDA BARBARA BETHAM-
Snow Flakes. *H. K. Browne*

EGGLESTON, EDWARD
Hoosier Schoolboy. *Brush*
Hoosier Schoolmaster. *F. Beard*

EGGLESTON, GEORGE CARY
Long Knives. *Merrill*

EILOART, MRS.
Ernie at School. *Houghton*
Ernie Elton, the Lazy Boy. *Houghton*

EISGRUBER, ELSA
Spin Top Spin. *Eisgruber*

Elephant's Ball by W. B. *Mulready*

ELIOT, FRANCES
Pablo's Pipe. *Eliot*
Traveling Coat. *Eliot*

ELIOT, GEORGE, *pseud.* (MARY ANN EVANS CROSS)
Mill on the Floss. *McNab*
Romola, 2 v. *F. Leighton*
Scenes of Clerical Life. *Thomson*
Silas Marner. *C. E. Brock*
Silas Marner. *Thomson*
Silas Marner. *Wheelhouse*

ELKIN, ROSIE HELEN
Children's Corner. *Le Mair*
Little People. *Le Mair*
Old Dutch Nursery Rhymes. *Le Mair*

ELLIOT, KATHLEEN MORROW
Jo-Yo's Idea. *Duvoisin*
Riema, Little Brown Girl of Java. *Duvoisin*
Soomoon, Boy of Bali. *Duvoisin*

EMANUEL, WALTER
Dog Day. *Aldin*
Dogs of War. *Aldin*

EMERSON, CAROLINE DWIGHT
Hat-tub Tale. *Lenski*
Indian Hunting Grounds. *Schuyler*
Magic Tunnel. *Lufkin*
Mr. Nip and Mr. Tuck. *Lenski*

FIELD, EUGENE
Lullaby Land. *C. Robinson*
Poems of Childhood. *M. Parrish*

FIELD, RACHEL
All through the Night. *Field*
Alphabet for Boys and Girls. *Field*
American Folk and Fairy Tales. *Freeman*
Calico Bush. *Lewis*
Eliza and the Elves. *MacKinstry*
Hepatica Hawks. *Lewis*
Hitty. *Lathrop*
Little Book of Days. *Field*
Little Dog Toby. *Field*
Magic Pawnshop. *MacKinstry*
Pocket-handkerchief Park. *Field*
Polly Patchwork. *Field*
Prayer for a Child. *E. O. Jones*
Taxis and Toadstools. *Field*
Yellow Shop. *Field*

FILLMORE, PARKER HOYSTED
Czechoslovak Fairy Tales. *Matulka*
Laughing Prince. *Van Everen*
Mighty Mikko. *Van Everen*
Shoemaker's Apron. *Matulka*
Wizard of the North. *Van Everen*

FINGER, CHARLES JOSEPH
Dog at His Heel. *Pitz*
Highwaymen. *Honoré*
Tales from Silver Lands. *Honoré*
Tales Worth Telling. *Honoré*

FINNEMORE, JOHN
Holy Land. *Fulleylove*

FINTA, ALEXANDER
Herdboy of Hungary. *Finta*
My Brothers and I. *Finta*

FIRDAUSI
Epic of Kings. *W. J. Jones*

FISCHER, MARJORIE
Dog Cantbark. *Duvoisin*
Street Fair. *Floethe*

FISH, HELEN DEAN
Animals of American History. *Bransom*
Four and Twenty Blackbirds. *R. Lawson*
When the Root Children Wake Up. *Olfers*

FITZPATRICK, JAMES PERCY
Jock of the Bushveld. *Caldwell*

FLACK, MARJORIE
Angus and the Cat. *Flack*
Angus and the Ducks. *Flack*
Ask Mr. Bear. *Flack*
Restless Robin. *Flack*
Story about Ping. *Wiese*
Tim Tadpole and the Great Bullfrog. *Flack*

FLEURON, SVEND
Wild Horses of Iceland. *Aldin*

FLOIRE and BLANCHEFLOR
Sweet and Touching Tale of Fleur and Blanchefleur. *Brickdale*

FLORIAN, JEAN PIERRE CLARIS DE
Fables. *Gérard*

FORBES, ESTHER
Johnny Tremain. *Ward*

FORD, LAUREN
Little Book about God. *L. Ford*

FORESTER, CECIL SCOTT
Poo-Poo and the Dragons. *R. Lawson*

FORRESTER, ALFRED HENRY (ALFRED CROWQUILL, *pseud.*)
Picture Fables. *Forrester*

FORTESCUE-BRICKDALE, ELEANOR SEE BRICKDALE, ELEANOR FORTESCUE-

FOSTER, ELIZABETH
Gigi; the Story of a Merry-go-round Horse. *Bischoff*

FOSTER, MYLES BIRKET
Day in a Child's Life. *Greenaway*

FOX, FRANCES MARGARET
Little Cat That Could Not Sleep. *Suba*

FOX, JOHN, JR.
Little Shepherd of Kingdom Come. *Wyeth*
Little Shepherd of Kingdom Come. *Yohn*

FRANCE, ANATOLE, *pseud.* (JACQUES ANATOLE THIBAULT)
Bee. *C. Robinson*
Girls and Boys. *Boutet de Monvel*
Little Sea Dogs. *M. L. Foster*
Our Children. *Boutet de Monvel*

FRANCIS, JOSEPH GREENE
Book of Cheerful Cats. *Francis*
Joyous Aztecs. *Francis*

FRANÇOISE, *pseud.* SEE SEIGNOBOSC, FRANÇOISE

FRANKUM, RICHARD
Bee and the Wasp. *G. Cruikshank*

FRASER, CLAUD LOVAT
Pirates. *C. L. Fraser*

FRASER-SIMSON, HAROLD
Fourteen Songs from "When We Were Very Young." *E. H. Shepard*
Songs from "Now We Are Six." *E. H. Shepard*

FRENCH, HENRY WILLARD
Lance of Kanana. *W. J. Jones*

French Songs of Old Canada. *W. G. Robertson*

H. K. BROWNE : *Legendary Tales*

GORDON BROWNE : *National Rhymes of the Nursery*

FREUND, GLADYS LYNWALL PRATT
American Garden Flowers. *Freund*

FRISWELL, JAMES HAIN
Out and About. *G. Cruikshank*

FROISSART, JEAN
Boy's Froissart. *Kappes*
Chronicles of England, France and Spain. *H. Cole*
Stories from Froissart. *G. F. Browne*

FROST, ARTHUR BURDETT
Book of Drawings. *Frost*
Bull Calf and Other Tales. *Frost*
Stuff & Nonsense. *Frost*

FROST, FRANCES MARY
Christmas in the Woods. *A. A. Watson*

FROST, ROBERT
Come in, and Other Poems. *Cosgrave*

FYLEMAN, ROSE
Little Christmas Book. *Hummell*
Picture Rhymes from Foreign Lands. *Carrick*
Princess Comes to Our Town. *Best*

GÁG, WANDA HAZEL
A B C Bunny. *W. H. Gág*
Funny Thing. *W. H. Gág*
Gone Is Gone. *W. H. Gág*
Millions of Cats. *W. H. Gág*
Nothing at All. *W. H. Gág*
Snippy and Snappy. *W. H. Gág*

GAGGIN, EVA ROE
Ear for Uncle Emil. *Seredy*

GALE, MARTIN
One Summer. *Van Doren*
Pony Named Nubbin. *Van Doren*

GALE, NORMAN
Songs for Little People. *Stratton*

GALL, ALICE CREW
Bushy Tail. *Bostelmann*

Gallery of Comicalities. *G.* and *R. I. Cruikshank* and *Seymour*

Gammer Gurton's Garland of Nursery Songs, and Toby Tickle's Collection of Riddles. *T. Bewick*

GARDINER, ALICE CUSHING
Father's Gone A-whaling. *Best*

GARLAND, HAMLIN
Book of the American Indian. *Remington*

GARNER, ELVIRA CARTER
Ezekiel. *Garner*
Ezekiel Travels. *Garner*
Little Cat Lost. *Thorne*
Sarah Faith Anderson: Her Book. *Garner*
'Way Down in Tennessee. *Garner*

GARNETT, EVE
Family from One End Street. *Garnett*

GARNETT, LOUISE AYRES
Creature Songs. *Newell*
Muffin Shop. *Dunlap*

GARNETT, LUCY MARY JANE
Ottoman Wonder Tales. *Folkard*

GARRETT, HELEN
Angelo, the Naughty One. *Politi*

GASK, LILIAN
True Stories about Horses. *P. Wilson*

GASKELL, ELIZABETH CLEGHORN
Cousin Phillis. *Du Maurier*
Cousin Phillis. *Wheelhouse*
Cranford. *C. E. Brock*
Cranford. *H. M. Brock*
Cranford. *Dixon*
Cranford. *Du Maurier*
Cranford. *T. H. Robinson*
Cranford. *Tawse*
Cranford. *Thomson*
Cranford. *Wheelhouse*

GASKIN, GEORGIE CAVE FRANCE
Horn-book Jingles. *G. C. F. Gaskin*

GATE, ETHEL MAY
Punch and Robinetta. *Field*

GATES, DORIS
Blue Willow. *Lantz*

GATTI, ATTILIO
Adventure in Black and White. *Wiese*
Saranga, the Pygmy. *Wiese*
Wrath of Moto. *Bransom*

GATTY, MARGARET SCOTT
Legendary Tales. *H. K. Browne*
Parables from Nature. *Burne-Jones, Cope, M. E. Edwards, Froelich, Hunt, Speckter, Tenniel, Thomas* and *Wolf*

GAY, JOHN
Fables, 2 v. *Blake* and others
Fables of John Gay. *Harvey*

GAY, ZHENYA
Manuelito of Costa Rica. *Gay*
170 Cats. *Gay*
Pancho and His Burro. *Gay*
Sakimura. *Gay*

GEISEL, THEODOR SEUSS (DR. SEUSS, *pseud.*)
And to Think That I Saw It on Mulberry Street. *Geisel*
500 Hats of Bartholomew Cubbins. *Geisel*
Horton Hatches the Egg. *Geisel*
King's Stilts. *Geisel*

GEISTER, EDNA
What Shall We Play? *MacKinstry*

GERSON, VIRGINIA
Happy Heart Family. *Gerson*
More Adventures of the Happy Heart Family. *Gerson*

GHEON, HENRI
Saint Nicholas. *Ivanovsky*

GIBSON, CHARLES DANA
People of Dickens. *C. D. Gibson*

GIBSON, KATHARINE
Goldsmith of Florence. *Kubinyi*
Jock's Castle. *Bock*
Oak Tree House. *Bock*

GIBSON, WILLIAM HAMILTON
Blossom Hosts and Insect Guests. *W. H. Gibson*
Eye Spy. *W. H. Gibson*
Sharp Eyes. *W. H. Gibson*

GILBERT, HENRY
Boys' Book of Pirates. *Reid*
Robin Hood. *W. Crane*

GILBERT, WILLIAM
Magic Mirror. *W. S. Gilbert*

GILBERT, WILLIAM SCHWENCK
Bab Ballads. *W. S. Gilbert*
Mikado. *C. E. Brock* and *Flint*
More Bab Ballads. *W. S. Gilbert*
Songs of a Savoyard. *W. S. Gilbert*
Yeomen of the Guard. *C. E. Brock* and *Flint*

GILCHRIST, MARIE EMILIE
Story of the Great Lakes. *De Witt*

GLÍNSKI, ANTONI JÓZEF
Polish Fairy Tales. *Walton*

GODLEY, ELIZABETH
Green Outside. *Whistler*

GODWIN, MARY WOLLSTONECRAFT SEE WOLLSTONECRAFT, MARY

GODWIN, WILLIAM
Fables Ancient and Modern, 2 v. *Mulready*
Looking Glass. *Mulready*

GOGOL, NIKOLAI VASILIEVICH
Taras Bulba. *Gay*

Golden Fairy Book. *Millar*

GOLDEN GORSE, *pseud.*
Moorland Mousie. *L. D. R. Edwards*
Older Mousie. *L. D. R. Edwards*

Golden Thoughts from Golden Fountains. *E.* and *T. B. G. Dalziel, Houghton, J. Lawson, Pinwell* and *Small*

GOLDSMITH, OLIVER
Dalziel's Illustrated Goldsmith. *Pinwell*
Deserted Village. *Abbey*
Deserted Village. *Billings*
Deserted Village. *Hankey*
She Stoops to Conquer. *Abbey*
She Stoops to Conquer. *C. E. Brock*
She Stoops to Conquer. *Thomson*
Traveller. *B. Foster*
Vicar of Wakefield. *Austen*
Vicar of Wakefield. *Bedford*
Vicar of Wakefield. *T. Bewick*
Vicar of Wakefield. *C. E. Brock*
Vicar of Wakefield. *H. M. Brock*
Vicar of Wakefield. *Cooke*
Vicar of Wakefield. *G. Cruikshank*
Vicar of Wakefield. *Lalauze*
Vicar of Wakefield. *Mulready*
Vicar of Wakefield. *H. M. Paget*
Vicar of Wakefield. *Rackham*
Vicar of Wakefield. *Richter*
Vicar of Wakefield. *Rowlandson*
Vicar of Wakefield. *Stothard*
Vicar of Wakefield. *E. J. Sullivan*
Vicar of Wakefield. *Thomas*
Vicar of Wakefield. *Thomson*
Vicar of Wakefield. *Wright*

GOLDSZMIT, HENRYK (JANUSZ KORCZAK, *pseud.*)
Matthew, the Young King. *Lorentowicz*

GOMME, ALICE BERTHA
Children's Singing Games, 2 v. *Winifred Smith*

Good Dog Book. *Tenggren*

GOODWIN, JOHN B. L.
Pleasant Pirate. *Chappell*

GORDON, CLARENCE (VIEUX MOUSTACHE, *pseud.*)
Boarding School Days. *Darley* and *Nast*
Old Boy's Stories. *Darley, Homer* and *Nast*

GORE, CATHERINE GRACE FRANCES
Snow Storm. *G. Cruikshank*

GOSS, MADELEINE BINKLEY
Deep-flowing Brook. *Blaisdell*

GOUDGE, ELIZABETH
Smoky House. *Floethe*

GOULD, ELIZABETH
Country Days. *Soper*
Farm Holidays. *Soper*
Happy Days on the Farm. *Soper*

Graciosa and Percinet. *J. Bewick*

GRAHAM, ELEANOR
Happy Holidays. *Ellingford*
Welcome Christmas! *Ellingford*

G. J. PINWELL : *Dalziel's Illustrated Goldsmith*

GRAHAME, KENNETH
Cambridge Book of Poetry for Children. *Raverat*
Dream Days. *Lenski*
Dream Days. *M. Parrish*
Dream Days. *E. H. Shepard*
Golden Age. *Lenski*
Golden Age. *M. Parrish*
Golden Age. *E. H. Shepard*
Reluctant Dragon. *E. H. Shepard*
Wind in the Willows. *Barnhart*
Wind in the Willows. *Bransom*
Wind in the Willows. *A. W. Payne*
Wind in the Willows. *Rackham*
Wind in the Willows. *E. H. Shepard*

GRAMATKY, HARDIE
Hercules. *Gramatky*
Little Toot. *Gramatky*
Loopy. *Gramatky*

GRANT, GEORGE HOOK
Half Deck. *Grant*

GRANT, GORDON
Sail Ho! *Grant*
Ships under Sail. *Grant*
Story of the Ship. *Grant*

GRAY, ELIZABETH JANET
Adam of the Road. *R. Lawson*
Meggy MacIntosh. *De Angeli*

GRAY, THOMAS
Elegy Written in a Country Churchyard. *Barnes*
Elegy Written in a Country Churchyard. *B. Foster, A Lady* and *Thomas*

GREEN, LOUISA MEIGS
Brother of the Birds. *Boutet de Monvel*

GREEN, OLIVE, *pseud. SEE* REED, MYRTLE

GREENAWAY, KATE
Almanacks 1883-1897 (except 1896). *Greenaway*
Kate Greenaway Pictures from Originals Presented by Her to Her Friends. *Greenaway*
Kate Greenaway's Alphabet. *Greenaway*
Kate Greenaway's Book of Games. *Greenaway*
Marigold Garden. *Greenaway*
Under the Window. *Greenaway*

Green's Nursery Annual. *Keene*

GREENWOOD, JAMES
Bear King. *Griset*
Hatchet Throwers. *Griset*
Legends of Savage Life. *Griset*
Purgatory of Peter the Cruel. *Griset*

GREGO, JOSEPH
Cruikshank's Water Colours. *G. Cruikshank*

GREY OWL
Sajo and the Beaver People. *Grey Owl*

GRIERSON, ELIZABETH WILSON
Book of Celtic Stories. *Stewart*
Children's Book of Edinburgh. *Stewart*
Children's Tales from Scottish Ballads. *Stewart*
Scottish Fairy Book. *M. M. Williams*
Tales of Scottish Keeps and Castles for Young People. *Stewart*

GRIGS, MARY
Yellow Cat. *Isobel* and *John Morton-Sale*

GRIMM, JAKOB LUDWIG KARL
Fairy Ring. *Doyle*
Fairy Tales. *Abbott*
Fairy Tales. *Bell*
Fairy Tales. *Dunlap*
Fairy Tales. *Folkard*
Fairy Tales. *E. S. Hardy* and others
Fairy Tales. *Hildebrand*
Fairy Tales. *Pocock*
Fairy Tales. *Rackham*
Fairy Tales. *L. J. Rhead*
Fairy Tales. *Speed*
Fairy Tales. *Stratton*
Fairy Tales from Grimm. *G. F. Browne*
German Popular Stories, 2 v. *G. Cruikshank*
Grimm's Fairy Tales. *Kredel*
Grimm's Fairy Tales. *Scharl*
Hansel and Gretel. *Chappell*
Hansel and Gretel. *Nielsen*
Hansel and Grethel. *Rackham*
House in the Wood. *Brooke*
Household Stories. *W. Crane*
Household Stories, 2 v. *Wehnert*
Little Brother and Little Sister. *Rackham*
Snow White. *W. H. Gág*
Snowdrop and Other Tales. *Rackham*
Tales from Grimm. *W. H. Gág*
Three Gay Tales from Grimm. *W. H. Gág*

GRINNELL, GEORGE BIRD
Jack among the Indians. *Deming*
Jack, the Young Canoeman. *Deming*

GRISHINA-GIVAGO, NADEJDA J.
Gresha and His Clay Pig. *Grishina-Givago*
Magic Squirrel. *Grishina-Givago*
Peter-Pea. *Grishina-Givago*
Shorty. *Grishina-Givago*
Sparrow House. *Grishina-Givago*

GRODIN, ADAMS JOHN
All the Year Round. *Grodin*

GUIGOU, PAUL
Animal Trainer. *Vimar*
Animals in the Ark. *Vimar*

GUNTERMAN, BERTHA L.
Castles in Spain and Other Enchantments. *Blaine*

GURY, JEREMY
'Round and 'Round Horse. *Marsh*

H ADER, BERTA HOERNER
Cock-a-doodle-doo. *Hader*
Farmer in the Dell. *Hader*
Spunky. *Hader*
Story of Pancho. *Hader*
Tommy Thatcher Goes to Sea. *Hader*

HAINES, ALICE CALHOUN
Indian Boys and Girls. *Deming*

HAKLUYT, RICHARD
Hakluyt's Voyages. *Millar*
Heroes from Hakluyt. *Honoré*

HALE, EDWARD EVERETT
Man without a Country. *Merrill*
Man without a Country. *E. Shinn*
Man without a Country. *E. A. Wilson*

HALE, LUCRETIA PEABODY
Peterkin Papers. *Brett*

HALÉVY, LUDOVIC
Abbé Constantin. *Lemaire*

HALL, ANN MARIA FIELDING
Midsummer Eve. *T. Landseer, Meadows, Paton* and others
Prince of the Fair Family. *Meadows* and others

HALL, ANNA GERTRUDE
Nansen. *Artzybasheff*

HALL, ESTHER GREENACRE
College on Horseback. *P. Brown*

HALL, ROSALYS
Animals to Africa. *Eichenberg*

HALLOCK, GRACE TABER
Boy Who Was. *H. M. Wood*

HAMILTON, ELIZABETH
P-zoo. *P. Hurd*

HAMILTON, JAMES
Parable of the Prodigal Son. *Selous*

HAMSUN, MARIE ANDERSEN
Norwegian Family. *Jenne*
Norwegian Farm. *Jenne*

HANDFORTH, THOMAS SCOFIELD
Faraway Meadow. *Handforth*
Mei Li. *Handforth*

HANSON, LIDA SIBONI
Eric the Red. *Hansen*

HARCOURT, ALFRED FREDERICK POLLOCK
Royal Umbrella. *Sambourne*

HARE, CHRISTOPHER, *pseud. SEE* ANDREWS, MARIAN

HARKER, L. ALLEN
Wee Folk, Good Folk. *Partridge*

HARNONCOURT, RENÉ D' *SEE* D'HARNONCOURT, RENÉ

HARPER, WILHELMINA
Flying Hoofs. *P. Brown*
Gunniwolf. *Seredy*

HARRIS, JOEL CHANDLER
Aaron in the Wildwoods. *Herford*
Daddy Jake, the Runaway. *Kemble*
Little Mr. Thimblefinger and His Queer Country. *Herford*
Mr. Rabbit at Home. *Herford*
Nights with Uncle Remus. *W. H. Beard* and *Church*
Nights with Uncle Remus. *Shepherd*
On the Plantation. *Kemble*
Plantation Pageants. *E. B. Smith*
Story of Aaron. *Herford*
Tarbaby and Other Rhymes. *Frost* and *Kemble*
Told by Uncle Remus. *Condé, Frost* and *Ver Beck*
Uncle Remus. *Shepherd*
Uncle Remus and His Friends. *Frost*
Uncle Remus and the Little Boy. *Condé*
Uncle Remus; His Songs and His Sayings. *Church* and *Moser*
Uncle Remus; His Songs and His Sayings. *Frost*
Uncle Remus; His Songs and His Sayings. *Frost* and *Kemble*
Uncle Remus Returns. *Condé* and *Frost*

HARRISON, CONSTANCE CARY
Bric-a-brac Stories. *W. Crane*

Harrison's New Nursery Picture Book. *J. Bewick*

HART, ELIZABETH ANNA
Runaway. *Raverat*

HARTE, BRET
Bret Harte's Stories of the Old West. *P. Brown*
Luck of Roaring Camp and Other Stories. *Angelo*
Queen of the Pirate Isle. *Greenaway*

HARTLAND, EDWIN SIDNEY
English Fairy and Folk Tales. *C. E. Brock*

HAUFF, WILHELM
Caravan Tales. *Ault*
Fairy Tales. *Dixon*

HAWES, CHARLES BOARDMAN
Dark Frigate. *Fischer*
Great Quest. *Varian*
Mutineers. *Fischer*
Mutineers. *Varian*

HAWKES, CLARENCE
Piebald, King of Bronchos. *Copeland*
Wood and Water Friends. *Copeland*

HAWKINS, ANTHONY HOPE (ANTHONY HOPE, *pseud.*)
Prisoner of Zenda. *C. D. Gibson*

HAWKINS, QUAIL
Prayers and Graces for Little Children. *De Angeli*

HAWKINS, SHEILA
Appleby John. *Hawkins*
Pepito. *Hawkins*

HAWTHORNE, NATHANIEL
Compositions in Outline from Hawthorne's "Scarlet
Letter." *Darley*
House of the Seven Gables. *Grose*
House of the Seven Gables. *Townsend*
Scarlet Letter. *Darley*
Scarlet Letter. *T. H. Robinson*
Scarlet Letter. *Thomson*
Snow Image. *Lathrop*
Tanglewood Tales. *Dulac*
Tanglewood Tales for Girls and Boys. *G. W.
Edwards*
Wonder Book. *Fell*
Wonder Book. *Rackham*
Wonder Book. *Winter*
Wonder Book and Tanglewood Tales. *Abbott*
Wonder Book and Tanglewood Tales. *Fell*
Wonder Book and Tanglewood Tales. *M. Parrish*
Wonder Book and Tanglewood Tales. *Tenggren*
Wonder Book for Girls and Boys. *Billings*
Wonder Book for Girls and Boys. *Church*
Wonder Book for Girls and Boys. *W. Crane*

HEAL, EDITH
Dogie Boy. *Sperry*

HEBER, REGINALD
From Greenland's Icy Mountains. *Schell*

HELLÉ, ANDRÉ
Big Beasts and Little Beasts. *Hellé*

HEMING, ARTHUR HENRY HOWARD
Living Forest. *Heming*

HÉMON, LOUIS
Maria Chapdelaine. *W. J. Jones*

HENDERSON, LE GRAND (LE GRAND, *pseud.*)
Augustus and the Mountains. *L. Henderson*
Augustus and the River. *L. Henderson*
Augustus Drives a Jeep. *L. Henderson*
Augustus Goes South. *L. Henderson*
Glory Horn. *L. Henderson*
Saturday for Samuel. *L. Henderson*

HENDRY, HAMISH
Just Forty Winks. *G. M. Bradley*
Red Apple and Silver Bells. *A. B. Woodward*

HENIUS, FRANK
Songs and Games of the Americas. *Fabrès*
Stories from the Americas. *Politi*

HENRY, O., *pseud. SEE* PORTER, WILLIAM SYDNEY

HENTY, GEORGE ALFRED
Bonnie Prince Charlie. *G. F. Browne*
Cat of Bubastes. *Weguelin*
Cornet of Horse. *Petherick*
Dragon and the Raven. *Staniland*
Lion of St. Mark. *G. F. Browne*
Roving Commission. *Rainey*
Under Drake's Flag. *G. F. Browne*
With Clive in India. *G. F. Browne*
With Lee in Virginia. *G. F. Browne*
With Moore at Corunna. *W. S. Paget*
Young Carthaginian. *Staniland*

HERBERTSON, AGNES GROZIER
Heroic Legends. *Stratton*

HERFORD, OLIVER
Alphabet of Celebrities. *Herford*
Bashful Earthquake. *Herford*
Child's Primer of Natural History. *Herford*
Peter Pan Alphabet. *Herford*
Rubaiyat of a Persian Kitten. *Herford*

HERODOTUS
Herodotus. *Artzybasheff*

HERRICK, ROBERT
Country Garland of Ten Songs Gathered from the
Hesperides. *Woodroffe*
Selections from the Hesperides and Noble Numbers
of Robert Herrick. *Abbey*

HERVEY, ELEANORA LOUISA MONTAGU
Juvenile Calendar and Zodiac of Homes. *Doyle*

HEWARD, CONSTANCE
Ameliar-anne and the Green Umbrella. *Pearse*
Twins and Tabiffa. *Pearse*

HEWES, AGNES DANFORTH
Spice and the Devil's Cave. *Ward*

HEY, WILHELM
Child's Picture and Verse Book, Commonly Called
Otto Speckter's Fable Book. *Speckter*
One Hundred Picture Fables. *Speckter*

HILL, FREDERICK TREVOR
Washington, Man of Action. *Onfroy de Bréville*

HILL, G. F.
Truth about Old King Cole. *Brooke*

History of a Scuttle of Coals in Rhymes and Pictures.
W. J. Linton

History of Little Goody Two Shoes. *A. B. Woodward*

History of Sindbad, the Sailor. *J. Bewick*

History of Tom Thumb. *Scott*

JOSEPH WOLF : *Poems by Jean Ingelow*

HOWELLS, WILLIAM DEAN
Boy's Town. *Farny*
Christmas Every Day and Other Stories. *Ver Beck*

HOWES, EDITH
Rainbow Children. *A. B. Woodward*

HOWITT, MARY BOTHAM
Lillieslea. *Absolon*
Our Four-footed Friends. *Weir*
Sketches of Natural History; or, Songs of Animal Life. **Giacomelli**

HUDSON, WILLIAM HENRY
Disappointed Squirrel. *Kirmse*
Far Away and Long Ago. *Daglish*
Green Mansions. *Butler*
Green Mansions. *Covarrubias*
Green Mansions. *De Martelly*
Green Mansions. *K. Henderson*
Green Mansions. *Kauffer*
Little Boy Lost. *Lathrop*
Little Boy Lost. *McCormick*
Purple Land. *K. Henderson*

HUGHES, RICHARD ARTHUR WARREN
Don't Blame Me. *Eichenberg*

HUGHES, THOMAS
Scouring of the White Horse. *Doyle*
Tom Brown at Oxford. *Hall*
Tom Brown's School Days. *Hall* and *Hughes*
Tom Brown's School Days. *L. J. Rhead*
Tom Brown's School Days. *E. J. Sullivan*
Tom Brown's School Days. *Thomson*

HUGO, VICTOR MARIE
Les Misérables. *Schaeffer*

HULL, ELEANOR
Boy's Cuchulain. *Reid*
Northmen in England. *M. M. Williams*

HUNT, CLARA WHITEHILL
About Harriet. *Barney*

HUNT, MABEL LEIGH
Billy Button's Buttered Biscuit. *Milhous*
"Have You Seen Tom Thumb?" *Eichenberg*
Little Girl with Seven Names. *Paull*
Little Grey Gown. *Bischoff*
Young Man of the House. *Slobodkin*

HURD, EDITH THACHER
Sky High. *C. Hurd*

HUTCHINSON, VERONICA SOMERVILLE
Chimney Corner Fairy Tales. *Lenski*
Chimney Corner Stories. *Lenski*

HUTCHINSON, WINIFRED MARGARET LAMBERT
Golden Porch. *D. S. Walker*
Orpheus with His Lute. *D. S. Walker*
Sunset of the Heroes. *H. Cole*

IBSEN, HENRIK
Peer Gynt. *Eichenberg*
Peer Gynt. *Rackham*

Idyllic Pictures. *Pinwell*

ILIN, M., *pseud.* SEE MARSHAK, IL'ÍA ÍAKOVLEVÍCH

In Fairyland, a Series of Pictures of the Elf-world; with a Poem by William Allingham. *Doyle*

INCHFAWN, FAY
Who Goes to the Wood. *Thorne*

INGELOW, JEAN
Little Wonder Horn. *Mahoney*
Mopsa the Fairy. *Lathrop*
Mopsa the Fairy. *D. S. Walker*
Poems. *E. and T. B. G. Dalziel, Houghton,* **North,** *Pinwell, Poynter, Small* and *Wolf*
Songs of Seven. *North*

INGOLDSBY, THOMAS, *pseud.* SEE BARHAM, RICHARD HARRIS

INGPEN, ROGER
One Thousand Poems for Children. *Betts*

IRVING, WASHINGTON
Alhambra. *Darley*
Alhambra. *Goble*
Alhambra. *Pennell*
Beauties of Washington Irving. *G. Cruikshank*
Bold Dragoon. *Daugherty*
Bracebridge Hall. *Caldecott*
Bracebridge Hall, 2 v. *Church, Rackham, Reinhart, Schmolze* and others
Christmas at Bracebridge Hall. *Dixon*
History of New York, 2 v. *Boughton, Drake* and *H. Pyle*
History of New York. *G. Cruikshank*
History of New York. *M. Parrish*
History of New York by Diedrich Knickerbocker. *Darley*
Illustrations of Legend of Sleepy Hollow. *Darley*
Illustrations of Rip Van Winkle. *Darley*
Keeping of Christmas at Bracebridge Hall. *C. E. Brock*
Knickerbocker's History of New York. *Daugherty*
Knickerbocker's History of New York, 2 v. *Kemble*
Legend of Sleepy Hollow. **Coburn**
Legend of Sleepy Hollow. *Keller*
Legend of Sleepy Hollow. *Rackham*
Old Christmas. *Aldin*
Old Christmas. *Caldecott*
Old Christmas and Bracebridge Hall. *Baumer*
Rip Van Winkle. *W. H. Bradley*
Rip Van Winkle. *G. F. Browne*
Rip Van Winkle. *Coburn*
Rip Van Winkle. *Darley*
Rip Van Winkle. *Heyneman*
Rip Van Winkle. *Merrill*
Rip Van Winkle. *Pérard*
Rip Van Winkle. *Rackham*
Rip Van Winkle. *C. Robinson*
Rip Van Winkle. *Wyeth*

Rip Van Winkle and The Legend of Sleepy Hollow. *Boughton*
Rip Van Winkle and The Legend of Sleepy Hollow. *Pape*
Rip Van Winkle and The Legend of Sleepy Hollow. *A. A. Watson*
Sketch Book. *Caldecott*
Sketch Book. *E. J. Sullivan*
Sketch Book of Geoffrey Crayon. *Darley*
Tales from the Alhambra. *C. E. Brock*
Tales of the Alhambra. *H. M. Brock* and *Dixon*
Voyages of Columbus. *Pitz*

IVES, VERNON
Russia. *Busoni*

IVIMEY, JOHN WILLIAM
Complete Version of Ye Three Blind Mice. *W. Corbould*

Jack and the Beanstalk. *H. M. Brock*

Jack and the Beanstalk. *Cope*

Jack the Giant Killer. *Bell*

Jack the Giant Killer. *H. M. Brock*

Jack the Giant Killer. *Cope*

Jack the Giant Killer. *Thomson*

JACKSON, HELEN MARIA HUNT
Ramona. *Wyeth*

JACOBS, JOSEPH
Book of Wonder Voyages. *Batten*
Celtic Fairy Tales. *Batten*
English Fairy Tales. *Batten*
Indian Fairy Tales. *Batten*
Molly Whuppie. *Doane*
More Celtic Fairy Tales. *Batten*
More English Fairy Tales. *Batten*

JAGENDORF, MORITZ ADOLF
Tyll Ulenspiegel's Merry Pranks. *Eichenberg*

JAMES, GRACE
Green Willow and Other Japanese Fairy Tales. *Goble*

JAMES, WILL
Cowboy in the Making. *W. James*
Cowboys North and South. *W. James*
Drifting Cowboy. *W. James*
In the Saddle with Uncle Bill. *W. James*
My First Horse. *W. James*
Smoky. *W. James*
Sun Up; Tales of the Cow Camps. *W. James*
Uncle Bill. *W. James*
Young Cowboy. *W. James*

JAMISON, CECILLA VIETS
Lady Jane. *Birch*
Toinette's Philip. *Birch*

JANVIER, THOMAS ALLIBONE
Aztec Treasure House. *Kutcher*
Aztec Treasure House. *Remington*

JARDEN, MARY LOUISE
Young Brontës. *Sewell*

JĀTAKAS
Jataka Tales. *Young*
More Jataka Tales. *Young*
Twenty Jātaka Tales. *Le Mair*

JERROLD, WALTER COPELAND
Big Book of Fables. *C. Robinson*
Big Book of Fairy Tales. *C. Robinson*
Reign of King Oberon. *C. Robinson*

JERSEY, COUNTESS OF
Maurice, or The Red Jar. *Pitman*

JEWETT, ELEANOR MYERS
Wonder Tales from Tibet. *Day*

JEWETT, JOHN HOWARD (HANNAH WARNER, *pseud.*)
Con the Wizard. *Herford*

JEWETT, SARAH ORNE
Betty Leicester. *Stevens*

JEWETT, SOPHIE
God's Troubadour. *Blaisdell*

Jimmy. *J. G. Sowerby*

JOHNSON, BURGES
Little Book of Necessary Nonsense. *MacKinstry*

JOHNSON, OWEN McMAHON
Eternal Boy. *Steele*

JOHNSON, ROSSITER
Phaeton Rogers. *Taber* and others

JOHNSON, VIRGINIA W.
Catskill Fairies. *Fredericks*

JONES, ELIZABETH ORTON
Ragman of Paris and His Ragamuffins. *E. O. Jones*

JONES, HAROLD
Visit to the Farm. *H. Jones*

JONES, HARRY
Prince Boohoo and Little Smuts. *G. F. Browne*

JONES, IDWAL
Whistler's Van. *Gay*

JONES, THOMAS ORTON
Minnie the Mermaid. *E. O. Jones*

JONES, WILFRED J.
How the Derrick Works. *W. J. Jones*

JORDAN, MILDRED
Shoo-fly Pie. *Pitz*

JUDSON, CLARA INGRAM
Donald McKay, Designer of Clipper Ships. *Cosgrave*

Juvenile Verse and Picture Book. *R. 1. Cruikshank, J. Gilbert, Tenniel* and others

ALFRED FREDERICKS : *Catskill Fairies*

K. O. S., *pseud. SEE* Dombrowski, Käthe Schönberger von

KABERRY, CHARLES J.
  Book of Baby Dogs. *E. J. Detmold*
  Our Little Neighbors. *E. J. Detmold*

KAESER, H. J.
  Mimff. *Ardizzone*

KAHMANN, MABLE CHESLEY
  Sinfi and the Little Gypsy Goat. *Mora*

KALER, JAMES OTIS (JAMES OTIS, *pseud.*)
  Jenny Wren's Boarding House. *Rogers*
  Toby Tyler. *Rogers*

KALEVALA
  Heroes of the Kalevala. *Eichenberg*

KALKAR, GEORG
  Adventures of Three Little Pigs. *Moe*
  Raggle Taggle Bear. *Moe*

KANG, YOUNGHILL
  Happy Grove. *Baldridge*

KÄSTNER, ERICH
  Eleven Merry Pranks of Till the Jester. *Trier*
  Emil and the Detectives. *Trier*
  Emil and the Three Twins. *Trier*
  Flying Classroom. *Trier*

KEARY, ANNA MARIA
  Heroes of Asgard. *C. E. Brock*

KEARY, ELIZA
  At Home Again. *W. Crane* and *J. G. Sowerby*

KEATS, JOHN
  Eve of St. Agnes. *Wehnert*
  Poems. *Bell*

KEDDIE, HENRIETTA *SEE* TYTLER, SARAH, *pseud.*

KELEN, EMERY
  Yussuf the Ostrich. *Kelen*

KELLOGG, ELIJAH
  Good Old Times. *Fenn*

KELLY, ERIC PHILBROOK
  At the Sign of the Golden Compass. *Lufkin*
  Blacksmith of Vilno. *Pruszynska*
  Girl Who Would Be Queen. *Bock*
  Golden Star of Halich. *Pruszynska*
  Treasure Mountain. *Lufkin*
  Trumpeter of Krakow. *Pruszynska*

KELSEY, ALICE GEER
  Once the Hodja. *Dobias*

KELSEY, VERA
  Maria Rosa. *Portinari*

KENDALL, OSWALD
  Romance of the Martin Connor. *Varian*
  Voyage of the Martin Connor. *Teague*

KENNEDY, HOWARD ANGUS
  New World Fairy Book. *Millar*

KENT, ROCKWELL
  N by E. *Kent*
  Rockwellkentiana. *Kent*
  Wilderness. *Kent*

KEY, FRANCIS SCOTT
  Star Spangled Banner. *E. P.* and *I. M. D'Aulaire*

KILNER, DOROTHY
  Memoirs of a Peg Top. *J. Bewick*

KING, CHARLES
  To the Front. *Boughton, Oakley* and *Remington*

KING, EDITH HALL
  Adventures in Toyland. *A. B. Woodward*

KINGMAN, MARY LEE
  Ilenka. *Bare*
  Pierre Pidgeon. *Bare*

KINGSLEY, CHARLES
  Hereward the Wake. *G. D. Hammond*
  Heroes. *H. M. Brock*
  Heroes. *Flint*
  Heroes. *Kingsley*
  Heroes. *Pears*
  Water-babies. *Dixon*
  Water-babies. *Goble*
  Water-babies. *Paton*
  Water-babies. *W. H. Robinson*
  Water-babies. *Sambourne*
  Water-babies. *J. W. Smith*
  Westward Ho!, 2 v. *C. E. Brock*
  Westward Ho! *Copping*
  Westward Ho! *E. A. Cox*
  Westward Ho! *Oakley*
  Westward Ho!, 2 v. *E. A. Wilson*
  Westward Ho! *Wyeth*

KIPLING, RUDYARD
  All the Mowgli Stories. *Tresilian*
  All the Mowgli Stories. *Wiese*
  All the Puck Stories. *C. E. Brock* and *Millar*
  Almanac of Twelve Sports. *Nicholson*
  Animal Stories. *Tresilian*
  Brushwood Boy. *Townsend*
  Captains Courageous. *Taber*
  Collected Poems. *W. H. Robinson*
  Complete Stalky & Co. *Raven-Hill*
  Elephant's Child. *Rojankovsky*
  How the Camel Got His Hump. *Rojankovsky*
  How the Leopard Got His Spots. *Rojankovsky*
  How the Rhinoceros Got His Skin. *Rojankovsky*
  Jungle Book. *E. J.* and *M. Detmold*
  Jungle Book. *Drake, J. L. Kipling* and others
  Jungle Book. *Wiese*
  Just So Stories. *R. Kipling*
  Kim. *J. L. Kipling*
  Maltese Cat. *L. D. R. Edwards*
  Puck of Pook's Hill. *Millar*
  Puck of Pook's Hill. *Rackham*
  Second Jungle Book. *J. L. Kipling*
  Song of the English. *W. H. Robinson*
  They. *Townsend*

KISSIN, RITA
Raffy and the Honkebeest. *Bracker*
Zic-Zac. *Bracker*

KNIGHT, ERIC MOWBRAY
Lassie Come-home. *Kirmse*

KNIGHT, RUTH ADAMS
Friend in the Dark. *M. Dennis*

KNOWLES, JAMES THOMAS
Legends of King Arthur and His Knights. *Speed*

KNOX, KATHLEEN
Fairy Gifts; or, A Wallet of Wonders. *Greenaway*

KONEWKA, PAUL
Black Peter. *Konewka*

KORCZAK, JANUSZ, *pseud. SEE* GOLDSZMIT, HENRYK

KOŽÍŠEK, JOSEF
Forest Story. *Mates*
Magic Flutes. *Mates*

KRAKEMSIDES, BARON, *pseud.*
Careless Chicken. *Forrester*
Careless Chicken. *Neilson*
Funny Leaves for the Younger Branches. *Forrester*

KRASNOV, PETR NIKOLAEVICH
Yermak the Conqueror. *Siegel*

KRYLÓV, IVÁN ANDRÉYEVICH
Krilof and His Fables. *Houghton* and *Zwecker*

KUEBLER, KATHERINE
Hansel the Gander. *Bischoff*

KÚNOS, IGNAEZ
Turkish Fairy Tales and Folk Tales. *Pogány*

KYD, *pseud. SEE* CLARKE, J. CLAYTON

LA BEDOLLIÈRE, ÉMILE GIGAULT DE
Story of a Cat. *Hopkins*

LABOULAYE, ÉDOUARD RENÉ LEFEBVRE
Fairy Tales. *Dixon*

LA FONTAINE, JEAN DE
Fables of Jean de La Fontaine, 2 v. *Ruzicka*
Fables of La Fontaine. *Doré*
Fables of La Fontaine, 2 v. *Gérard*
Fables of La Fontaine. *Hellé*
Hundred Fables of La Fontaine. *Billinghurst*
La Fontaine's Fables. *R. Bull* and *Park*
Select Fables. *Boutet de Monvel*

LAGERLÖF, SELMA OTTILIANA LOVISA
Diary of Selma Lagerlöf. *J. Bull*
Further Adventures of Nils. *Heiberg*
Mårbacka. *Lankes*

LAMB, CHARLES
King and Queen of Hearts. *Mulready*
Masque of Days. *W. Crane*
Mrs. Leicester's School. *C. E. Brock*
Mrs. Leicester's School. *W. Green*
Poetry for Children. *W. Green*
Stories for Children. *W. Green*
Tales from Shakespeare. *Bell*
Tales from Shakespeare. *Blaisdell*
Tales from Shakespeare. *Elliott*
Tales from Shakespeare. *Folkard*
Tales from Shakespeare. *J. Gilbert*
Tales from Shakespeare. *G. D. Hammond*
Tales from Shakespeare. *Harvey*
Tales from Shakespeare, 2 v. *Mulready*
Tales from Shakespeare. *W. S. Paget*
Tales from Shakespeare. *Papé*
Tales from Shakespeare. *Petersham*
Tales from Shakespeare. *N. M. Price*
Tales from Shakespeare. *Rackham*
Tales from Shakespeare. *L. J. Rhead*
Tales from Shakespeare. *W. H. Robinson*

LAMB, HAROLD
Durandal. *McNab*

LAMBERT, CLARA BREAKEY
Story of Alaska. *De Witt*

LA MOTTE-FOUQUÉ, FRIEDRICH HEINRICH KARL, BARON DE
Sintram and His Companions. *Selous*
Sintram and His Companions. *Sumner*
Sintram and His Companions and Aslauga's Knight. *C. Robinson*
Sintram and His Companions, and Undine. *G. F. Browne*
Undine. *Herrick*
Undine. *Lewis*
Undine. *Pitman*
Undine. *Rackham*
Undine. *Sumner*
Undine. *Tenniel*

LANG, ANDREW
Animal Story Book. *H. J. Ford*
Blue Fairy Book. *H. J. Ford* and *G. P. J. Hood*
Blue Poetry Book. *H. J. Ford* and *Speed*
Book of Saints and Heroes. *H. J. Ford*
Green Fairy Book. *H. J. Ford*
Prince Prigio. *G. F. Browne*
Prince Prigio. *R. Lawson*
Prince Ricardo of Pantouflia. *G. F. Browne*
Princess Nobody. *Doyle*
Red Fairy Book. *H. J. Ford* and *Speed*
Tales of Romance. *H. J. Ford* and *Speed*
Tales of Troy and Greece. *H. J. Ford*
Violet Fairy Book. *H. J. Ford*
Yellow Fairy Book. *H. J. Ford*

LANG, JEANIE
Book of Myths. *Stratton*

LANG, LEONORA BLANCHE
Book of Princes and Princesses. *H. J. Ford*

Language of Flowers. *Greenaway*

LANSING, ELIZABETH CARLETON HUBBARD
Leonardo, Master of the Renaissance. *Sharp*

LANSING, MARION FLORENCE
Magic Gold. *McIntosh*
Page, Esquire and Knight. *Copeland*

LATHROP, DOROTHY PULIS
Colt from Moon Mountain. *Lathrop*
Fairy Circus. *Lathrop*
Hide and Go Seek. *Lathrop*
Presents for Lupe. *Lathrop*
Puppies for Keeps. *Lathrop*
Who Goes There? *Lathrop*

LATHROP, GEORGE PARSONS
"Behind Time." *Herford*

LATTIMORE, ELEANOR FRANCES
Clever Cat. *Lattimore*
Little Pear. *Lattimore*
Peachblossom. *Lattimore*
Questions of Lifu. *Lattimore*

LAWRENCE, ROBERT
Petrouchka. *Serebriakoff*

LAWSON, ROBERT
Ben and Me. *R. Lawson*
Rabbit Hill. *R. Lawson*
They Were Strong and Good. *R. Lawson*

LEAF, MUNRO
Noodle. *Bemelmans*
Story of Ferdinand. *R. Lawson*
Story of Simpson and Sampson. *R. Lawson*
Wee Gillis. *R. Lawson*

LEAR, EDWARD
Book of Nonsense. *Lear*
Complete Nonsense Book. *Lear*
Jumblies. *Brooke*
Laughable Lyrics. *Lear*
More Nonsense Pictures, Rhymes, Botany, etc. *Lear*
Nonsense Songs, Stories, Botany and Alphabets. *Lear*
Pelican Chorus. *Brooke*
Queery Leary Nonsense. *Lear*

LEE, ALBERT
Tommy Toddles. *Newell*

LEE, MELICENT HUMASON
Chang Chee. *Bannon*

LEE, SARAH BOWDITCH
British Animals. *Weir*

LEFÈVRE, FÉLICITÉ
Cock, the Mouse, and the Little Red Hen. *Sarg*
Soldier Boy. *Sarg*

LE GRAND, *pseud. SEE* HENDERSON, LE GRAND

LEIGH, PERCIVAL
Comic English Grammar. *Leech*
Comic Latin Grammar. *Leech*
Jack the Giant Killer. *Leech*

LEIGHTON, MARGARET
Singing Cave. *M. de V. Lee*

LEIGHTON, ROBERT
Olaf, the Glorious. *Pitz*

LEMON, MARK
Enchanted Doll. *Doyle*
Fairy Tales. *C. H. Bennett* and *Doyle*
Legends of Number Nip. *Keene*
Tinykin's Transformations. *C. Green*

LEMONNIER, CAMILLE B.
Birds and Beasts. *E. J. Detmold*

LENSKI, LOIS
A-going to the Westward. *Lenski*
Bayou Suzette. *Lenski*
Bound Girl of Cobble Hill. *Lenski*
Indian Captive. *Lenski*
Jack Horner's Pie. *Lenski*
Little Girl of Nineteen Hundred. *Lenski*
Little Sail Boat. *Lenski*
Little Train. *Lenski*
Phebe Fairchild. *Lenski*
Skipping Village. *Lenski*
Strawberry Girl. *Lenski*
Sugarplum House. *Lenski*

L'ÉPINE, ERNEST
Days of Chivalry or The Legend of Croquemitaine. *Doré*

LESKOV, NIKOLAĬ SEMENOVICH
Steel Flea. *Dobuzhinskiĭ*

LESTERMAN, JOHN
Adventures of a Trafalgar Lad. *Hilder*
Second Mate of the Myradale. *Hilder*

LEVER, CHARLES
Charles O'Malley, 2 v. *H. K. Browne*
Charles O'Malley. *Rackham*

LEVY, HARRY
Bombero, Tales from Latin America. *Simon*
Burro That Learned to Dance. *Simon*

LEWITT, ALINA
Blue Peter. *Him* and *Lewitt*
Five Silly Cats. *Him* and *Lewitt*

LEWITT, JAN
Football's Revolt. *Him* and *Lewitt*

L'HOMMEDIEU, DOROTHY KEASBEY
Macgregor, the Little Black Scottie. *Kirmse*
Rusty, the Little Red Dachshund. *Kirmse*

LIDA

Cuckoo. *Rojankovsky*
Fluff, the Little Wild Rabbit. *Rojankovsky*
Kingfisher. *Rojankovsky*
Little French Farm. *Guertik*
Plouf, the Little Wild Duck. *Rojankovsky*
Pompom, the Little Red Squirrel. *Rojankovsky*
Spiky, the Hedgehog. *Rojankovsky*

LIDDELL, MARY

Little Machinery. *Liddell*

LIDE, ALICE ALISON

Ood-le-uk the Wanderer. *Lufkin*

LIE, HAAKON

Ekorn. *Wiese*

Life's Book of Animals. *Kemble, Neilson, F. T. Richards and others*

LIM SIAN-TEK

Folk Tales from China. *W. A. Smith*

LINDERMAN, FRANK BIRD

Indian Old-man Stories. *Russell*
Indian Why Stories. *Russell*
Kootenai Why Stories. *C. L. Bull*

LINDSAY, MAUD McKNIGHT

Posey and the Pedlar. *Credle*

LINDSAY, NICHOLAS VACHEL

Johnny Appleseed. *G. M. Richards*

LINTON, WILLIAM JAMES

Flower and the Star. *W. J. Linton*

Lion and the Ox. *Lebedev*

Little Lou's Sayings and Doings. *M. L. Stone*

Little Red Riding Hood. *Webster*

Little Rosy's Travels. *Froelich*

Little Songs for Me to Sing. *Millais*

Little Thumb and the Ogre. *Blake*

LODGE, HENRY CABOT

Story of the Revolution. *H. Pyle*

LOFTING, HUGH

Doctor Dolittle's Caravan. *Lofting*
Doctor Dolittle's Circus. *Lofting*
Doctor Dolittle's Post Office. *Lofting*
Doctor Dolittle's Zoo. *Lofting*
Noisy Nora. *Lofting*
Porridge Poetry. *Lofting*
Story of Doctor Dolittle. *Lofting*
Story of Mrs. Tubbs. *Lofting*
Tommy, Tilly and Mrs. Tubbs. *Lofting*
Voyages of Doctor Dolittle. *Lofting*

LONDON, JACK

Call of the Wild. *Bransom*

LONG, WILLIAM J.

Little Brother to the Bear. *Copeland*

LONGFELLOW, HENRY WADSWORTH

Courtship of Miles Standish. *Boughton, Merrill, Reinhart and others*
Courtship of Miles Standish. *Christy*
Courtship of Miles Standish. *Dixon*
Courtship of Miles Standish. *J. Gilbert*
Courtship of Miles Standish. *Wyeth*
Evangeline. *Darley*
Evangeline. *Dixon*
Evangeline. *B. Foster and J. Gilbert*
Hanging of the Crane. *Keller*
Hiawatha. *Fisher*
Hiawatha. *Thomas*
Poems. *J. Gilbert*
Poems. *Lewis*
Poetical Works. *B. Foster and others*
Poetical Works of Henry Wadsworth Longfellow, 3 v. *Abbey, Darley and others*
Poetical Works of Longfellow. *Gray, Houghton, North and Small*
Song of Hiawatha. *Angelo*
Song of Hiawatha. *Remington*

LORENZINI, CARLO (CARLO COLLODI, *pseud.*)

Adventures of Pinocchio. *Copeland*
Adventures of Pinocchio. *Liddell*
Adventures of Pinocchio. *Mussino*
Pinocchio. *Folkard*
Pinocchio. *Wiese*
Pinocchio, the Adventures of a Marionette. *Floethe*

LOUV'A

Animals I Like. *Guertik*

LOVECHILD, LAURENCE, *pseud.* (ELEANOR F. FENN)

Grandfather Lovechild's Nursery Stories, 14 pamphlets. *Darley*

Loving Ballad of Lord Bateman. *G. Cruikshank*

LOWE, CORINNE B.

Knight of the Sea. *Chappell*

LOWELL, JAMES RUSSELL

Courtin'. *Homer*
Vision of Sir Launfal. *Alexander, B. R. Crane, Freer, Gifford, Kappes, Mowbray, Shirlaw and F. H. Smith*
Vision of Sir Launfal. *Eytinge*

LOWREY, JANETTE SEBRING

Silver Dollar. *Latham*

LOWRY, H. D.

Make-believe. *C. Robinson*

LUCAS, EDWARD VERRALL
Another Book of Verses for Children. *Bedford*
Book of Shops. *Bedford*
Forgotten Tales of Long Ago. *Bedford*
Four and Twenty Toilers. *Bedford*
Old Fashioned Tales. *Bedford*
Playtime & Company. *E. H. Shepard*
Runaways and Castaways. *Bedford*
Slowcoach. *Raven-Hill*
Slowcoach. *Wheelhouse*

LUCAS, JANNETTE MAY
Earth Changes. *Carter*
Fruits of the Earth. *Carter*

LUCAS, MARY SEYMOUR
Vast Horizons. *Falls*

LUMMIS, CHARLES FLETCHER
Pueblo Indian Folk-stories. *G. W. Edwards*

LUSHINGTON, HENRIETTA, LADY
Hacco the Dwarf and Other Tales. *Pinwell*

LYNCH, PATRICIA
Fiddler's Quest. *Isobel Morton-Sale*
Turf-cutter's Donkey. *Yeats*

Lyrics . . . from A–Z. *Dulac*

LYTTON, EDWARD GEORGE EARLE LYTTON BULWER-LYTTON, 1ST BARON
Last Days of Pompeii. *Yohn*

LYTTON, EDWARD ROBERT BULWER-LYTTON, 1ST EARL OF (OWEN MEREDITH, *pseud.*)
Lucile. *Du Maurier*

MABIE, HAMILTON WRIGHT
Book of Old English Ballads. *G. W. Edwards*

MABINOGION
Knightly Legends of Wales. *Fredericks*

MACAULAY, THOMAS BABINGTON MACAULAY, 1ST BARON
Lays of Ancient Rome. *Ault*
Lays of Ancient Rome. *E. A. Cox*
Lays of Ancient Rome. *P. Hardy*
Lays of Ancient Rome. *Weguelin*

McCLINTOCK, MARSHALL
Story of New England. *De Witt*
Story of the Mississippi. *De Witt*

McCLOSKEY, JOHN ROBERT
Homer Price. *McCloskey*
Lentil. *McCloskey*
Make Way for Ducklings. *McCloskey*

McCRACKEN, HAROLD
Biggest Bear on Earth. *Bransom*
Last of the Sea Otters. *Bransom*

McCULLOUGH, JOHN G.
At Our House. *Duvoisin*

MacDONALD, GEORGE
At the Back of the North Wind. *Bedford*
At the Back of the North Wind. *Housman*
At the Back of the North Wind. *Hughes*
At the Back of the North Wind. *J. W. Smith*
Dealings with the Fairies. *Hughes*
Gutta Percha Willie. *Hughes*
Light Princess. *Lathrop*
Lost Princess, or, The Wise Woman. *A. G. Walker*
Princess and Curdie. *Lathrop*
Princess and Curdie. *Stratton*
Princess and the Goblin. *Bedford*
Princess and the Goblin. *Housman*
Princess and the Goblin. *Hughes*
Princess and the Goblin. *MacKinstry*
Princess and the Goblin. *J. W. Smith*
Ranald Bannerman's Boyhood. *Hughes*

MacDONALD, GOLDEN
Red Light, Green Light. *Weisgard*

MacDONALD, GREVILLE
Billy Barnicoat. *Bedford*
Count Billy. *Bedford*
Jack and Jill. *Hughes*
Magic Crook. *Hughes*

MACDONALD, VIOLET M.
Nursery Tales. *Macdonald*

MACDONELL, ANNE
Italian Fairy Book. *M. M. Williams*

McGINLEY, PHYLLIS
Horse Who Lived Upstairs. *H. Stone*
Plain Princess. *H. Stone*

MacGREGOR, BARRINGTON
King Longbeard. *C. Robinson*

MACGREGOR, MARY
Story of France. *Rainey*
Story of Greece Told to Boys and Girls. *W. Crane*
Story of Rome. *Heath, Rainey* and *Woodroffe*

MACHETANZ, FREDERICK
On Arctic Ice. *Machetanz*
Panuck. *Machetanz*

MacINTYRE, ELISABETH
Ambrose Kangaroo. *MacIntyre*
Susan Who Lives in Australia. *MacIntyre*

McISAAC, FREDERIC JOHN
Tony Sarg Marionette Book. *Sarg*

MACKARNESS, MATILDA ANNE PLANCHÉ
Sunbeam Stories. *Absolon*
Sunbeam Stories, Second Series. *Absolon*
Sunbeam Stories, Third Series. *Godwin*

MacKAYE, DAVID LORING
We of Frabo Stand. *Jenne*

MacKAYE, PERCY
Tall Tales of the Kentucky Mountains. *MacKinstry*

McKenny, Margaret
Book of Wild Flowers. *Johnston*

MacKinstry, Elizabeth A.
Fairy Alphabet. *MacKinstry*
Puck in Pasture. *MacKinstry*

MacLaren, Archibald
Fairy Family. *Burne-Jones*

MacLeod, Mary
Book of Ballad Stories. *A. G. Walker*
Book of King Arthur and His Noble Knights. *A. G. Walker*

MacManus, Seumas
Donegal Fairy Stories. *Ver Beck*
Well o' the World's End. *R. Bennett*

McMeekin, Isabel McLennan
Journey Cake. *Panesis*
Juba's New Moon. *Panesis*

Macmillan, Cyrus
Canadian Fairy Tales. *M. L. Foster*

McMurtrie, Douglas Crawford
Wings for Words. *E. A. Wilson*

McNeer, May Yonge
Prince Bantam. *Ward*
Story of the Great Plains. *De Witt*
Waif Maid. *Ward*

Maeterlinck, Maurice
Children's Life of the Bee. *E. J. Detmold*
My Dog. *Aldin*

Maitland, Julia C.
Doll and Her Friends, or, Memoirs of the Lady Seraphina, by the author of "Cat and Dog." *H. K. Browne*

Major, Charles
Bears of Blue River. *Frost* and others

Malcolmson, Anne Burnett
Yankee Doodle's Cousins. *McCloskey*

Malkus, Alida Sims
Dragon Fly of Zuñi. *Best*

Malmberg, Bertil
Åke and His World. *Cooney*

Malory, Thomas
Boy's King Arthur. *Wyeth*
King Arthur's Knights. *W. Crane*
Le Morte Darthur. *Flint*
Morte Darthur. *Beardsley*
Romance of King Arthur and His Knights of the Round Table. *Rackham*
Story of King Arthur. *Beardsley*

Malot, Hector Henri
Adventures of Remi. *Schaeffer*

Malvern, Gladys
Dancing Star. *Suba*

Mamin, Dmitriĭ Narkisovich (Mamin-Siberiak, *pseud.*)
Verotchka's Tales. *Artzybasheff*

Mamin-Siberiak, *pseud.* SEE Mamin, Dmitriĭ Narkisovich

Mandal, Sant Ram
Happy Flute. *Lathrop*

Marcliffe, Theophilus, *pseud.* SEE Godwin, William

Marie, Queen of Roumania
Story of Naughty Kildeen. *Onfroy de Bréville*

Maril, Lee
Mr. Bunny Paints the Eggs. *Lorentowicz*

Mariotti, Jean
Tales of Poindi. *Rojankovsky*

Marks, H. Stacy
Ridiculous Rhymes. *Marks*

Marryat, Frederick
Children of the New Forest. *W. S. Paget*
Children of the New Forest. *E. B. Smith*
Children of the New Forest. *Ward*
Masterman Ready. *Pegram*
Masterman Ready. *Rae*
Mr. Midshipman Easy. *Pegram*
Mr. Midshipman Easy. *Tawse*
Pirate *in* Children of the New Forest. *Staniland*
Pirate, and The Three Cutters. *Stanfield*
Pirate, and The Three Cutters. *E. J. Sullivan*

Marshak, Il'ía Íakovlevich (M. Ilin, *pseud.*)
Ring and a Riddle. *Bock*

Marshall, Henrietta Elizabeth
History of France. *Michael*
History of Germany. *Michael*
This Country of Ours. *Michael*

Martin, Dahris Butterworth
Wonder Cat. *A. A. Watson*

Martin, George Madden
Emmy Lou, Her Book and Heart. *Hinton*

Martineau, Harriet
Feats on the Fiord. *Artzybasheff*
Feats on the Fjord. *Rackham*
Peasant and the Prince. *F. A. Fraser*

Martineau des Chesnez, Elizabeth Lair, baronne
Lady Green Satin and Her Maid Rosette. *Bromhall*

Marvellous Adventures of Sir John Mandeville. *Layard*

MASEFIELD, JOHN
Book of Discoveries. *G. F. Browne*
Jim Davis. *Reid*
Jim Davis. *Schaeffer*
Midnight Folk. *Hilder*
Right Royal. *Aldin*
Salt-water Poems and Ballads. *Pears*

MASON, MIRIAM EVANGELINE
Susannah, the Pioneer Cow. *Petersham*

MASSON, ELSIE
Folk Tales of Brittany. *Oakley*

MATSCHAT, CECILE HULSE
American Butterflies and Moths. *Freund*

MAUGHAM, WILLIAM SOMERSET
Princess September and the Nightingale. *R. C. Jones*

MAUROIS, ANDRÉ
Fatapoufs and Thinifers. *Bruller*

MAURY, JEAN WRIGHT WEST
Old Raven's World. *Kutcher*

MAVOR, WILLIAM
English Spelling Book. *T. Bewick*
English Spelling Book. *Greenaway*

MAY, PHILIP WILLIAM
Phil May's A B C. *May*
Phil May's Gutter-snipes. *May*

MAY, SOPHIE, *pseud. SEE* CLARKE, REBECCA SOPHIA

MAYHEW, HENRY
Good Genius That Turned Everything into Gold.
G. Cruikshank

MAZER, SONIA
Masha, a Little Russian Girl. *Mazer*
Yossele's Holiday. *Mazer*

MEADER, STEPHEN WARREN
Long Trains Roll. *Shenton*

MEANS, FLORENCE CRANNELL
Shuttered Windows. *Sperry*

MEDARY, MARJORIE
Topgallant; a Herring Gull. *Ward*

MEIGS, CORNELIA LYNDE
Covered Bridge. *De Angeli*
Scarlet Oak. *E. O. Jones*
Willow Whistle. *E. B. Smith*
Wonderful Locomotive. *Hader*

MEIKLEJOHN, JOHN MILLER DOW
Golden Primer. *W. Crane*

MELLEN, IDA M.
Twenty Little Fishes. *Bostelmann*

MELVILLE, HERMAN
Moby Dick. *Hilder*
Moby Dick. *Kent*
Moby Dick. *B. Robinson*
Moby Dick. *Schaeffer*
Omoo. *Schaeffer*
Typee. *Covarrubias*
Typee. *Schaeffer*

Men of Arms. *Horgan*

MEREDITH, OWEN, *pseud. SEE* LYTTON, EDWARD ROBERT
BULWER-LYTTON, 1ST EARL OF

Merry Pictures, by the Comic Hands of *Leech, Doyle,*
Phiz, Crowquill, Meadows, etc.

MERTON, AMBROSE, *pseud. SEE* THOMAS, WILLIAM JOHN

MILHOUS, KATHERINE
First Christmas Crib. *Milhous*
Herodia, the Lovely Puppet. *Milhous*

MILLER, ALICE DUER
Cinderella. *Alajálov*

MILLER, ELIZABETH CLEVELAND
Children of the Mountain Eagle. *Petersham*

MILLER, LYDIA *SEE* MYRTLE, HARRIET, *pseud.*

MILLER, OLIVE KENNON
Heroes, Outlaws and Funny Fellows. *R. Bennett*

MILNE, ALAN ALEXANDER
Gallery of Children. *Le Mair*
House at Pooh Corner. *E. H. Shepard*
Hums of Pooh. *E. H. Shepard*
Now We Are Six. *E. H. Shepard*
When We Were Very Young. *E. H. Shepard*
Winnie-the-Pooh. *E. H. Shepard*

MILTON, JOHN
Comus. *B. Foster, Pickersgill* and *Weir*
Comus. *Rackham*
L'Allegro and Il Penseroso. *B. Foster*
L'Allegro and Il Penseroso. *Meadows* and others

MINSSEN, BERNARD
Book of French Songs for the Young. *T. H. Robinson*

MIRZA, YOUEL BENJAMIN
Myself When Young. *Nadejen*
Son of the Sword. *Artzybasheff*

MITCHELL, MINNIE BELLE
Gray Moon Tales. *Vawter*

MITCHELL, SILAS WEIR
Hugh Wynne. *H. Pyle*

MITFORD, MARY RUSSELL
Children of the Village. *Barnard, Barnes, M. E.*
Edwards, Murray and others
Our Village. *Boot* and *Murray*
Our Village. *C. E. Brock*
Our Village. *Thomson*

Modern A B C Book. *Falls*

MOE, LOUIS MARIA NIELS PEDER HALLING
Forest Party. *Moe*
Little Bear-Cub; and The Dressed-Up Pig. *Moe*
Vain Pussy Cat. *Moe*

MOESCHLIN-HAMMAR, ELSA
Little Boy with the Big Apples. *Moeschlin-Hammar*
Red Horse. *Moeschlin-Hammar*

MOLESWORTH, MARY LOUISA STEWART
Boys and I. *M. E. Edwards*
Carrots. *Wheelhouse*
Carved Lions. *Brooke*
Charge Fulfilled. *Woodville*
Cuckoo Clock. *C. E. Brock*
Cuckoo Clock. *W. Crane*
Four Winds Farm. *W. Crane*
Girls and I. *Brooke*
Green Casket and Other Stories. *Barnes*
Hermy. *M. E. Edwards*
Hermy. The Boys and I. The Three Witches. *Baumer*
Hoodie. *Baumer*
House That Grew. *A. B. Woodward*
Jasper. *G. D. Hammond*
Little Miss Peggy. *W. Crane*
Magic Nuts. *Pitman*
Mary. *Brooke*
Meg Langholme. *Rainey*
Miss Mouse and Her Boys. *Brooke*
My New Home. *Brooke*
Neighbors. *M. E. Edwards*
Next-door House. *Hatherell*
Red Grange. *G. F. Browne*
Robin Redbreast. *Barnes*
Rosy. *W. Crane*
Ruby Ring. *Pitman*
Sheila's Mystery. *Brooke*
Silverthorns. *Paton*
Story of a Spring Morning. *M. E. Edwards*
Tapestry Room. *W. Crane*
Tell Me a Story. *W. Crane*
This and That. *Thomson*
Wood-pigeons and Mary. *Millar*

MONSELL, JOHN ROBERT
Pink Knight. *Monsell*
Polichinelle. *Monsell*

MONTALBA, ANTHONY
Fairy Tales of All Nations. *Doyle*

MONTGOMERY, FLORENCE
Misunderstood. *Du Maurier*

MONTGOMERY, LUCY MAUD
Anne of Green Gables. *Tawse*

MOON, CARL
Flaming Arrow. *Moon*

MOON, GRACE PURDIE
Chi-Weé. *Moon*
Chi-Weé and Loki of the Desert. *Moon*
Runaway Papoose. *Moon*

MOORE, ANNE CARROLL
Nicholas. *Van Everen*
Nicholas and the Golden Goose. *Van Everen*

MOORE, CLEMENT CLARKE
Night before Christmas. *Birch*
Night before Christmas. *Bischoff*
Night before Christmas. *MacKinstry*
Night before Christmas. *Rackham*
Night before Christmas. *E. Shinn*
'Twas the Night before Christmas. *J. W. Smith*
Visit from St. Nicholas. *Angelo*
Visit from St. Nicholas. *Darley*
Visit from St. Nicholas. *Nast*
Visit from Saint Nicholas. *A. A. Watson*

MOORE, THOMAS
Irish Melodies. *Maclise*

MORLEY, HENRY
Fables and Fairy Tales. *C. H. Bennett*
Oberon's Horn. *C. H. Bennett*

MORRIS, ALICE TALWIN
Elephant's Apology. *A. B. Woodward*
Troubles of Tatters & Other Stories. *A. B. Woodward*

MORRIS, ANN AXTELL
Digging in Yucatan. *Charlot*

MORRIS, KENNETH
Book of the Three Dragons. *Horvath*

MORRIS, WILLIAM
Sons of the Volsungs. *Dobias*

MORROW, ELIZABETH REEVE CUTTER
Beast, Bird and Fish. *D'Harnoncourt*
My Favorite Age. *Suba*
Painted Pig. *D'Harnoncourt*
Pint of Judgment. *Suba*

MORROW, HONORÉ McCUE WILLSIE
Ship's Monkey. *Grant*

MORTON, JOHN BINGHAM
Who's Who in the Zoo. *Aldin*

MOSES, HORACE S.
Here Comes the Circus. *Suba*

MOSES, MONTROSE JONAS
Another Treasury of Plays for Children. *Sarg*
Treasury of Plays for Children. *Sarg*

MOTHER GOOSE
Auntie's Little Rhyme Book. *Le Mair*
Baby's Bouquet. *W. Crane*
Baby's Little Rhyme Book. *Le Mair*
Baby's Opera. *W. Crane*
Banbury Cross and Other Nursery Rhymes. *A. B. Woodward*
Big Book of Nursery Rhymes. *C. Robinson*

Book of Nursery Rhymes. *Bedford*
Book of Nursery Songs and Rhymes. *Newill*
Boyd Smith Mother Goose. *E. B. Smith*
Complete Mother Goose. *Betts*
Daddy's Little Rhyme Book. *Le Mair*
Gay Mother Goose. *Seignobosc*
Grannie's Little Rhyme Book. *Le Mair*
History of Little Bo-Peep. *Absolon*
Humpty Dumpty and Other Mother Goose Songs. *Rey*
Land of Nursery Rhyme. *Folkard*
Little Mother Goose. *J. W. Smith*
Little Songs of Long Ago. *Le Mair*
More Old Rhymes with New Tunes. *Pippet*
Mother Goose. *Doane*
Mother Goose. *Duvoisin*
Mother Goose. *Falls*
Mother Goose. *Ives*
Mother Goose. *Tawse*
Mother Goose. *Tenggren*
Mother Goose. *Tudor*
Mother Goose or The Old Nursery Rhymes. *Greenaway*
Mother Goose's Nursery Rhymes. *Folkard*
Mother Goose's Nursery Rhymes and Fairy Tales. *W. Crane, J. Gilbert, Tenniel, Weir, Zwecker* and others
Mother Hubbard. *Webster*
Mother's Little Rhyme Book. *Le Mair*
National Nursery Rhymes. *E., E. G.* and *T. B. G. Dalziel, F. A. Fraser, Griset, Houghton, Hughes, Mahoney, Marks, Pinwell, Small* and *Zwecker*
Nurse Lovechild's Legacy. *C. L. Fraser*
Nursery Rhyme Book. *Brooke*
Nursery Rhymes. *Brooke*
Nursery Rhymes. *C. Robinson*
Nursery Rhymes, 2 v. *H. L. Stephens*
Nursery Rhymes. *Woodroffe*
Nursery Rhymes with Pictures. *C. L. Fraser*
Nursie's Little Rhyme Book. *Le Mair*
Old Mother Goose Rhymes. *E. S. Hardy*
Old Nursery Rhymes. *Rackham*
Old Nursery Rhymes. *L. Wood*
Old Rhymes with New Tunes. *Pippet*
Only True Mother Goose Melodies. *A. Anderson*
Our Old Nursery Rhymes. *Le Mair*
Ring o' Roses. *Brooke*
Second Book of Nursery Rhymes. *Woodroffe*
Songs from Mother Goose for Voice and Piano. *Barney*
Still More Old Rhymes with New Tunes. *Pippet*
Tall Book of Mother Goose. *Rojankovsky*
Thirty Old-time Nursery Songs. *Woodroffe*
Willy Pogány's Mother Goose. *Pogány*

Mother Goose's Nursery Tales. *Folkard*

Mother's Last Words. *M. E. Edwards* and others

MUKERJI, DHAN GOPAL
Chief of the Herd. *Blaine*
Gay-Neck. *Artzybasheff*
Ghond, the Hunter. *Artzybasheff*
Rama, the Hero of India. *E. P. D'Aulaire*

MULOCK, DINAH MARIA *SEE* CRAIK, DINAH MARIA MULOCK

MUNCHAUSEN, HIERONYMUS KARL FRIEDRICH, BARON
Adventures of Baron Munchausen. *Doré*
Surprising Adventures of Baron Munchausen. *Clark* and *Strang*
Travels and Surprising Adventures of Baron Munchausen. *G. Cruikshank*
Travels of Baron Munchausen. *Forrester*

MUNROE, KIRK
Canoemates. *Rogers*
Flamingo Feather. *Schoonover*
Flamingo Feather. *Thulstrop*
Raftmates. *Rogers*
White Conquerors. *Stacey*
With Crockett and Bowie. *Pérard*

MUSSET, PAUL EDME DE
Mr. Wind and Madam Rain. *C. H. Bennett*

MUSSEY, VIRGINIA HOWELL
Falla, a President's Dog. *Van Doren*

My Pet's Picture Book. *Wolf*

My Young Days. *Konewka*

MYRTLE, HARRIET, *pseud.* (LYDIA MILLER)
Pleasures of the Country. *J. Gilbert*
Water Lily. *H. K. Browne*

NASH, HARRIET A.
Polly's Secret. *H. L. Price*

NEALE, JOHN MASON
Good King Wenceslas. *A. J. Gaskin*

NEILSON, FRANCES FULLERTON
Mocha, the Djuka. *A. F. Johnson*

NELSON, MARGARET WORTHING
Pinky Finds a Home. *Heyneman*

NESBIT, E., *pseud. SEE* BLAND, EDITH NESBIT

New Child's Play. *E. V. B.*

New Lottery Book of Birds and Beasts for Children to Learn Their Letters as Soon as They Can Speak. *T. Bewick*

NEWBERRY, CLARE TURLAY
April's Kittens. *Newberry*
Babette. *Newberry*
Barkis. *Newberry*
Cousin Toby. *Newberry*
Herbert the Lion. *Newberry*
Marshmallow. *Newberry*
Mittens. *Newberry*
Pandora. *Newberry*

NEWBOLT, HENRY JOHN
Book of the Happy Warrior. *H. J. Ford*

J. B. ZWECKER : *National Nursery Rhymes*

NEWCOMB, COVELLE
Vagabond in Velvet. *Burbank*

NEWELL, HOPE HOCKENBERRY
Little Old Woman Who Used Her Head. *Ruse*
More about the Little Old Woman Who Used Her Head. *Ruse*
Steppin and Family. *Peck*

NEWELL, PETER SHEAF HERSEY
Hole Book. *Newell*
Peter Newell's Pictures and Rhymes. *Newell*
Rocket Book. *Newell*
Shadow Show. *Newell*
Slant Book. *Newell*
Topsys & Turveys. *Newell*
Topsys & Turveys, 2nd series. *Newell*

NICHOLS, BEVERLY
Book of Old Ballads. *H. M. Brock*

NICHOLSON, WILLIAM
Characters of Romance. *Nicholson*
Clever Bill. *Nicholson*
Pirate Twins. *Nicholson*

NIEBUHR, BARTHOLD GEORG
Greek Heroes. *Rackham*

Nine Lives of a Cat. *C. H. Bennett*

Nine Years Old. *Froelich*

NOBLE, THOMAS TERTIUS
Round of Carols. *Sewell*

NOBODY, A., *pseud. SEE* BROWNE, GORDON FREDERICK

NODIER, CHARLES
Bean Flower and Pea Blossom. *Johannot*
Luck of the Bean-rows. *C. L. Fraser*
Woodcutter's Dog. *C. L. Fraser*

NOEL, SYBILLE GRAHAM
Magic Bird of Chomo-Lung-Ma. *Avinoff*

NOLAN, JEANETTE COVERT
Red Hugh of Ireland. *R. Bennett*

NORDHOFF, CHARLES BERNARD
Pearl Lagoon. *Fischer*

NORMAN
Book of Elfin Rhymes. *Park*

NORTHCOTE, THOMAS JAMES
One Hundred Fables. *Harvey* and *Northcote*

NORTON, CAROLINE ELIZABETH SARAH
Aunt Carry's Ballads for Children. *Absolon*

NORTON, MARY
Magic Bed-knob or How to Become a Witch in Ten Easy Lessons. *Peirce*

NOYES, ALFRED
Forty Singing Seamen. *MacKinstry*

NURA, *pseud. SEE* ULREICH, NURA WOODSON

Nursery Ditties from the Lips of Mrs. Lullaby. *Leech*

Nursery Fun. *C. H. Bennett*

Nutcracker and Sugar-Dolly. *Richter*

NYBLOM, HELENA AUGUSTA
Jolly Calle. *Folkard*

NYE, BILL, *pseud. SEE* NYE, EDGAR WILSON

NYE, EDGAR WILSON (BILL NYE, *pseud.*)
History of the United States. *Opper*

O'BRIEN, JOHN SHERMAN
Silver Chief, Dog of the North. *Wiese*

O'FAOLÁIN, EILEEN
King of the Cats. *Bock*
Little Black Hen. *A. A. Watson*

Old English Songs. *Thomson*

Old English Songs and Dances. *W. G. Robertson*

Old Songs. *Abbey* and *A. W. Parsons*

OLLIVANT, ALFRED
Bob, Son of Battle. *Kirmse*

ORTON, HELEN FULLER
Treasure in the Little Trunk. *Ball*

OTIS, JAMES, *pseud. SEE* KALER, JAMES OTIS

Our Lady's Tumbler. *Fell*

Our People. *Keene*

Our Tom Cat and His Nine Lives. *J. Leighton*

OVERTON, JACQUELINE MARION
Long Island's Story. *E. A. Wilson*

OWEN, DORA
Book of Fairy Poetry. *Goble*

PACE, MILDRED MASTIN
Clara Barton. *Ball*

PAGE, THOMAS NELSON
Among the Camps. *Newell, Rogers* and *Sheppard*
In Ole Virginia. *Castaigne, Clinedinst, Frost, H. Pyle, Reinhart* and *Smedley*
Marse Chan. *Smedley*
Meh Lady. *Reinhart*
Old Gentleman of the Black Stock. *Christy*
Santa Claus's Partner. *Glackens*
Tommy Trot's Visit to Santa Claus. *V. C. Anderson*
Two Little Confederates. *Kemble* and *Redwood*
Two Little Confederates. *Thomason*
Two Prisoners. *Keep*

PAINE, ALBERT BIGELOW
Arkansaw Bear. *Ver Beck*
Hollow Tree. *Condé*
Hollow Tree and Deep Woods Book. *Condé*
Hollow Tree Nights and Days. *Condé*
Hollow Tree Snowed-in Book. *Condé*

PALGRAVE, FRANCIS TURNER
Golden Treasury. *Bell*
Golden Treasury of Songs and Lyrics. *M. Parrish*
Golden Treasury of the Best Songs and Lyrical Poetry
in the English Language. *Brickdale*

PALMER, ELIZABETH
Up the River to Danger. *Holberg*

PALMER, WINTHROP BUSHNELL
American Songs for Children. *Cady*

PARDOE, JULIA
Lady Arabella. *G. Cruikshank*

PARK, CARTON MOORE
Alphabet of Animals. *Park*
Book of Birds. *Park*

PARKMAN, FRANCIS
California and Oregon Trail. *Darley*
Oregon Trail. *Benton*
Oregon Trail. *Daugherty*
Oregon Trail. *Remington*
Oregon Trail. *Wyeth*

PARRISH, ANNE
Dream Coach. *A. and G. D. Parrish*
Floating Island. *A. Parrish*
Knee-high to a Grasshopper. *A. and G. D. Parrish*

PARRY, EDWARD ABBOTT (JUDGE PARRY)
Butter-Scotia; or, A Cheap Trip to Fairyland. *Mac-gregor*
Katawampus. *Macgregor*

Patient Henry. *Houghton*

PATMORE, COVENTRY
Children's Garland from the Best Poets. *J. Lawson*

PAULI, HERTHA ERNESTINE
Silent Night, the Story of a Song. *Kredel*

PAYNE, EMMY
Katy No-Pocket. *Rey*

PEABODY, JOSEPHINE PRESTON
Book of the Little Past. *Elliott*

PEACOCK, THOMAS LOVE
Ballad of Sir Horn-Book. *H. Corbould*

Peacock's Pleasaunce. *E. V. B.*

PEARD, FRANCES M.
Jacob and the Raven. *Sumner*

PEARSON, EDMUND LESTER
Voyage of the Hoppergrass. *Fogarty*

PEASE, ELEANOR FAIRCHILD
Gay Pippo. *Wiese*

PEASE, HOWARD
Foghorns. *Fischer*

PECK, ANNE MERRIMAN
Belgium. *Serebriakoff*
Manoel and the Morning Star. *Peck*
Roundabout South America. *Peck*
Young Canada. *Peck*

PECK, LEIGH
Don Coyote. *Burton*

PENDLETON, LOUIS BEAUREGARD
King Tom and the Runaways. *Kemble*

PERCY, THOMAS
Boy's Percy. *Bensell*

PERKINS, LUCY FITCH
Dutch Twins. *Perkins*
(Other "Twins" Books)

PERRAULT, CHARLES
Fairy Tales. *H. Clarke*
Fairy Tales. *C. Robinson*
French Fairy Tales. *Doré*
Old-time Stories. *W. H. Robinson*
Story of Bluebeard. *Southall*
Tales of Passed Times. *Austen*

Peter and the Wolf. *Chappell*

Peter and the Wolf. *R. C. Jones*

Peter Piper's Practical Principles. *A. W. Payne*

PETERSHAM, MAUD FULLER
American A B C. *Petersham*
Ark of Father Noah and Mother Noah. *Petersham*
Auntie. *Petersham*
Get-a-way and Háry János. *Petersham*
Miki. *Petersham*
Rooster Crows. *Petersham*

PETROVIĆ, VOJISLAV M.
Hero Tales and Legends of the Serbians. *G. James*
and others

PHILLIPS, ETHEL CALVERT
Calico. *Barney*

PHILLPOTTS, EDEN
Flint Heart. *Folkard*

PHIZ, *pseud. SEE* BROWNE, HABLOT KNIGHT

Pictorial English Grammar. *Forrester*

Picture Book. *Small*

Pictures from Dickens. *H. M. Paget* and others

Pictures of Romance and Wonder. *Burne-Jones*

PIGOT, RICHARD
Life of Man Symbolised by the Months of the Year. *J. Leighton*

PITMAN, NORMAN HINSDALE
Chinese Wonder Book. *Li Chu-T'ang*

PLANCHÉ, JAMES ROBINSON
Old Fairy Tale Told Anew. *Doyle*

PLANCHÉ, MATILDA ANNE *SEE* MACKARNESS, MATILDA ANNE PLANCHÉ

PLATT, WILLIAM
Stories of the Scottish Border. *M. M. Williams*

PLUTARCH
Plutarch's Lives for Boys and Girls. *Rainey*

POE, EDGAR ALLAN
Bells. *Darley* and others
Gold-bug and Other Tales and Poems. *Sanchez*
Poetical Works of Edgar Allan Poe. *Darley, B. Foster, Pickersgill, Tenniel* and others
Poetical Works of Edgar Allan Poe. *Dulac*
Tales. *Dwiggins*
Tales of Edgar Allan Poe. *Coburn*
Tales of Mystery and Imagination. *H. Clarke*
Tales of Mystery and Imagination. *Rackham*
Tales of Mystery & Imagination. *Sharp*

Poetical Fabulator; or, Beauties in Verse. *T. Bewick*

POGÁNY, NÁNDOR
Hungarian Fairy Book. *Pogány*
Magyar Fairy Tales. *Pogány*

POLEVOĬ, PETER NIKOLAEVICH
Russian Fairy Tales. *Gere*
Russian Fairy Tales. *Nisbet*

Popular Fairy Tales. *Doré*

PORAZIŃSKA, JANINA
In Voytus' Little House. *Bobinski*
My Village. *Bobinski*
9 Cry-baby Dolls. *Lorentowicz*

PORTER, JANE
Scottish Chiefs. *T. H. Robinson*
Scottish Chiefs. *Wyeth*

PORTER, WILLIAM SYDNEY (O. HENRY, *pseud.*)
Ransom of Red Chief. *Grant*

POTTER, BEATRIX
Appley Dapply's Nursery Rhymes. *Potter*
Cecily Parsley's Nursery Rhymes. *Potter*
Fairy Caravan. *Potter*
Fierce Bad Rabbit. *Potter*
Ginger and Pickles. *Potter*
Pie and the Patty Pan. *Potter*
Roly-poly Pudding. *Potter*

Story of Miss Moppet. *Potter*
Tailor of Gloucester. *Potter*
Tale of Benjamin Bunny. *Potter*
Tale of Jemima Puddle-Duck. *Potter*
Tale of Johnny Town-Mouse. *Potter*
Tale of Little Pig Robinson. *Potter*
Tale of Mr. Jeremy Fisher. *Potter*
Tale of Mr. Tod. *Potter*
Tale of Mrs. Tiggy-Winkle. *Potter*
Tale of Mrs. Tittlemouse. *Potter*
Tale of Peter Rabbit. *Potter*
Tale of Pigling Bland. *Potter*
Tale of Squirrel Nutkin. *Potter*
Tale of the Flopsy Bunnies. *Potter*
Tale of Timmy Tiptoes. *Potter*
Tale of Tom Kitten. *Potter*
Tale of Two Bad Mice. *Potter*
Wag-by-wall. *Lankes*

PRESCOTT, WILLIAM HICKLING
Conquest of Mexico, 2 v. *K. Henderson*

Present for Little Masters and Misses. *T. Bewick*

Pretty Book of Pictures for Little Masters and Misses; or, Tommy Trip's History of Beasts and Birds. *T. Bewick*

PRICE, MARGARET EVANS
Monkey-Do. *M. E. Price*

PRICE, OLIVIA
Middle Country. *Baldridge*

Primrose Pilgrimage. *Macquoid*

PROSSER, MRS.
Original Fables. *Griset, Weir* and others

PROUDFIT, ISABEL BOYD
Treasure Hunter. *Gramatky*

Proverbs in Verse; or, Moral Instructions Conveyed in Pictures. *J. Bewick*

Puff-puff. *G. M. Bradley*

PUMPHREY, MARGARET BLANCHE
Stories of the Pilgrims. *Perkins*

PUNCH AND JUDY
Comical Tragedy of Punch and Judy. *Weisgard*
Punch and Judy. *G. Cruikshank*

"Punch" Pictures. *Reynolds*

PURNELL, IDELLA
Pedro the Potter. *Hogner*

PUSHKIN, ALEKSANDR SERGEÍEEVICH
Golden Cockerel. *Pogány*
Tale of the Golden Cockerel. *Gibbings*

Puss in Boots. *H. M. Brock*

Puss in Boots. *Eichenberg*

Puss in Boots. *Speckter*

PYLE, HOWARD
Book of Pirates. *H. Pyle*
Garden behind the Moon. *H. Pyle*
Men of Iron. *H. Pyle*
Merry Adventures of Robin Hood. *H. Pyle*
Otto of the Silver Hand. *H. Pyle*
Pepper & Salt. *H. Pyle*
Stolen Treasure. *H. Pyle*
Story of Jack Ballister's Fortunes. *H. Pyle*
Story of King Arthur and His Knights. *H. Pyle*
Story of Sir Launcelot and His Companions. *H. Pyle*
Story of the Champions of the Round Table. *H. Pyle*
Story of the Grail and the Passing of Arthur. *H. Pyle*
Twilight Land. *H. Pyle*
Wonder Clock. *H. Pyle*

PYLE, KATHARINE
Careless Jane. *K. Pyle*
Christmas Angel. *K. Pyle*
Counterpane Fairy. *K. Pyle*
Lazy Matilda and Other Tales. *K. Pyle*

PYNE, MABLE MANDEVILLE
Little Geography of the United States. *Pyne*
Little History of the United States. *Pyne*

Queen Summer. *W. Crane*

"Quiet Life." Certain Verses by Various Hands. *Abbey* and *A. W. Parsons*

QUILLER-COUCH, ARTHUR THOMAS
Splendid Spur. *Daugherty*
Twelve Dancing Princesses. *Nielsen*

Quiver of Love, a Collection of Valentines. *W. Crane* and *Greenaway*

RABELAIS, FRANÇOIS
Gargantua, par Sautriax. *Le Roy*
Three Good Giants. *Doré* and *Robida*

RACKHAM, ARTHUR
Arthur Rackham Fairy Book. *Rackham*
Arthur Rackham's Book of Pictures. *Rackham*

RADFORD, DOLLIE
Songs for Somebody. *G. M. Bradley*

RADLOV, NIKOLAĬ ERNESTOVĬCH
Cautious Carp, and Other Fables in Pictures. *Radlov*

RALSTON, J. McL.
Tippoo, Tale of a Tiger. *Ralston*

RANDS, WILLIAM BRIGHTY
Lilliput Levee. *Millais* and *Pinwell*

RANKIN, CARROLL WATSON
Dandelion Cottage. *F. S. Shinn*

RANKING, MONTGOMERIE
Flowers and Fancies; Valentines Ancient and Modern. *Greenaway*

RANSOME, ARTHUR
Old Peter's Russian Tales. *Mītrokhīn*
Pigeon Post. *M. Shepard*
Swallowdale. *Carter*
Swallows and Amazons. *Carter*
Swallows and Amazons. *Webb*
Winter Holiday. *Carter*

RASMUSSEN, KNUD JOHAN VICTOR
Eagle's Gift. *Hansen*

RAWLINGS, MARJORIE KINNAN
Yearling. *Shenton*
Yearling. *Wyeth*

RAYMOND, LOUISE
Child's Story of the Nativity. *Stern*

READE, CHARLES
Cloister and the Hearth. *G. F. Browne* and others
Cloister and the Hearth, 2 v. *W. M. Johnson*
Cloister and the Hearth. *Shaw*
Cloister and the Hearth, 2 v. *Ward*
Good Fight. *Keene*

REED, MYRTLE (OLIVE GREEN, *pseud.*)
Book of Clever Beasts. *Newell*

REED, VERBENA
Bird-nest Boarding House. *Herford*

REID, THOMAS MAYNE
Boy Tar. *Keene*
Desert Home. *Harvey*
Young Voyageurs. *Harvey*

REMINGTON, FREDERIC
Crooked Trails. *Remington*
Done in the Open. *Remington*
Pony Tracks. *Remington*

RESNICK, WILLIAM S.
Dragon Ship. *Busoni*

REY, HANS AUGUSTO
Cecily G. and the 9 Monkeys. *Rey*
Curious George. *Rey*
How Do You Get There? *Rey*

REYNARD THE FOX
History of Reynard the Fox. *W. Crane*
Most Delectable History of Reynard the Fox. *Van Everdingen*
Reynard the Fox. *Brightwell*
Reynard the Fox. *Griset*
Reynard the Fox after the German Version of Goethe. *Wolf*
Story of Reynard the Fox. *Lorioux*

RHOADS, DOROTHY M.
Story of Chan Yuc. *Charlot*

RHYS, ERNEST
English Fairy Tales. *Bell* and *H. Cole*
Fairy-gold. *H. Cole*

RHYS, GRACE LITTLE
Children's Garland of Verse. *C. Robinson*

RHYS, MIMPSEY
Mr. Hermit Crab. *Sewell*

RICE, ALICE CALDWELL HEGAN
Lovey Mary. *F. S. Shinn*
Mrs. Wiggs of the Cabbage Patch. *F. S. Shinn*

RICHARDS, LAURA ELIZABETH HOWE
Captain January. *Merrill*
Harry in England. *Birch*
I Have a Song to Sing You. *Birch*
Tirra Lirra. *Davis*

RICHARDSON, MYRA REED
Sheep Wagon Family. *Wilkin*

RILEY, JAMES WHITCOMB
Book of Joyous Children. *Vawter*
Child-rhymes. *Vawter*
Hoosier Romance. *Adams*
Old Sweetheart of Mine. *Christy*
Old Swimmin' Hole and Other Poems. *Vawter*
Out to Old Aunt Mary's. *Christy*
Songs of Home. *Vawter*

Riley's Choice Emblems, Natural, Historical, Fabulous, Moral, and Divine; For the Improvement and Pastime of Youth. *J. Bewick* and others

ROBERTS, CHARLES GEORGE DOUGLAS
Children of the Wild. *Bransom*
Kindred of the Wild. *C. L. Bull*

ROBERTS, ELIZABETH MADOX
Under the Tree. *Bedford*

ROBERTS, JACK
Bumpy Bobs, the Pink Hippo. *Roberts*
Wonderful Adventures of Ludo, the Little Green Duck. *Roberts*

ROBIN HOOD
History of the Bold Robin Hood. *Wehnert*
Robin Hood; His Deeds and Adventures as Recounted in the Old English Ballads. *Perkins*

ROBINSON, GERTRUDE
Sons of Liberty. *Ishmael*

ROBINSON, MABEL LOUISE
Bright Island. *Ward*

ROBINSON, THOMAS PENDLETON
Buttons. *Bacon*
In and Out. *De Angeli*
Pete. *M. Dennis*

ROBINSON, WILLIAM WILCOX
Ancient Animals. *I. B. Robinson*
Animals in the Sun. *I. B. Robinson*
At the Seashore. *I. B. Robinson*
At the Zoo. *I. B. Robinson*
Beasts of the Tar Pits. *I. B. Robinson*
Big Boy. *I. B. Robinson*
Book of Bible Animals. *I. B. Robinson*
Elephants. *I. B. Robinson*
Lions. *I. B. Robinson*
On the Farm. *I. B. Robinson*

ROLLINS, PHILIP ASHTON
Jinglebob. *Wyeth*

ROOS, ANN
Man of Molokai. *Lufkin*

ROSCOE, WILLIAM
Butterfly's Ball and The Grasshopper's Feast. *Mulready*

ROSS, DIANA
Little Red Engine Gets a Name. *Him* and *Lewitt*

ROSS, PATRICIA FENT
In Mexico They Say. *Pitz*

ROSSETTI, CHRISTINA GEORGINA
Goblin Market. *Housman*
Goblin Market. *Rackham*
Goblin Market. *Rossetti*
Sing-song. *Davis*
Sing-song. *Hughes*
Speaking Likenesses. *Hughes*

Round of Days. *Bayes, Brookes, E.* and *T. B. G. Dalziel, Gray, Houghton, Morten, North, Pinwell, F. Walker* and *J. D. Watson*

ROUNDS, GLEN
Blind Colt. *Rounds*
Lumber Camp. *Rounds*
Ol' Paul, the Mighty Logger. *Rounds*
Pay Dirt. *Rounds*

ROUSE, WILLIAM
Giant Crab and Other Tales from Old India. *W. H. Robinson*
Talking Thrush. *W. H. Robinson*

ROWE, DOROTHY
Begging Deer. *Ward*

Royal Picture Alphabet. *J. Leighton*

RUSKIN, JOHN
King of the Golden River. *Doyle*
King of the Golden River. *Horvath*
King of the Golden River. *Rackham*
King of the Golden River. *Stratton*

RUSSELL, WILLIAM CLARK
Wreck of the Grosvenor. *Schaeffer*

Sabbath Bells Chimed by the Poets. *B. Foster*

SABRETACHE, *pseud. SEE* BARROW, ALBERT STEWART

Saga of Gisli. *Kent*

SAGE, BETTY
Rhymes of Real Children. *J. W. Smith*

SAINT EXUPÉRY, ANTOINE DE
Little Prince. *Saint Exupéry*
Wind, Sand and Stars. *Cosgrave*

SAINTINE, JOSEPH XAVIER BONIFACE
Picciola. *Flameng*

SAINT-PIERRE, JACQUES HENRI BERNARDIN DE
Paul and Virginia. *Leloir*

SAINTSBURY, GEORGE EDWARD BATEMAN
National Rhymes of the Nursery. *G. F. Browne*

SALTEN, FELIX
Bambi. *Wiese*

SALZMANN, CHRISTIAN GOTTHILF
Gymnastics for Youth. *Blake*

SAMIVEL
Brown the Bear. *Samivel*
Rufus the Fox. *Samivel*

SANDBURG, CARL
Abe Lincoln Grows Up. *Daugherty*
Early Moon. *Daugherty*
Rootabaga Country. *Bacon*
Rootabaga Pigeons. *Petersham*
Rootabaga Stories. *Petersham*

SANDERSON, IVAN TERRANCE
Animals Nobody Knows. *Sanderson*

SANDYS, FREDERICK
Reproductions of Woodcuts by F. Sandys. *Sandys*

SARG, TONY
Tony Sarg's Book of Tricks. *Sarg*

SARGANT, ALICE
Book of Ballads. *Strang*
Brownie. *A. B. Woodward*

SASS, HERBERT RAVENEL
Way of the Wild. *C. L. Bull*

SASSOON, SIEGFRIED LORRAINE
Memoirs of a Fox-hunting Man. *Nicholson*

SAWYER, RUTH
Christmas Anna Angel. *Seredy*
Least One. *Politi*
Long Christmas. *Angelo*
Picture Tales from Spain. *Sanchez*
Roller Skates. *Angelo*
This Way to Christmas. *Barney*
Toño Antonio. *Mora*
Year of Jubilo. *Shenton*

SAYERS, FRANCES CLARKE
Bluebonnets for Lucinda. *Sewell*
Mr. Tidy Paws. *Gay*
Tag-along Tooloo. *Sewell*

Scenes and Narratives from the Early History of the
United States of America. *F. Walker*

Scenes in Indian Life. *Darley*

SCHERMAN, RITA
Peter's Voyage. *Beskow*

SCHMIDT, KARL PATTERSON
Homes and Habits of Wild Animals. *Weber*
Our Friendly Animals and Whence They Came.
Weber

SCHULTZ, JAMES WILLARD
Lone Bull's Mistake. *Varian*
On the Warpath. *Varian*
Questers of the Desert. *Schoonover*
Sinopah, the Indian Boy. *E. B. Smith*
With the Indians in the Rockies. *Brett*

SCHUMANN, ROBERT ALEXANDER
Album. *Le Mair*

SCOTT, ALMA OLIVIA (GEORGIA TRAVERS, *pseud.*)
Story of Kattor. *F. Gág*

SCOTT, GABRIEL
Kari. *E. P. D'Aulaire*

SCOTT, MICHAEL
Cruise of the Midge, 2 v. *Brangwyn*
Tom Cringle's Log, 2 v. *Brangwyn*
Tom Cringle's Log. *Schaeffer*
Tom Cringle's Log. *Stanfield, F. Walker* and *Weir*
Tom Cringle's Log. *Symington*

SCOTT, WALTER
Antiquary. *Thomson*
Bride of Lammermoor. *Thomson*
Guy Mannering. *G. F. Browne*
Heart of Midlothian. *Hole*
Ivanhoe. *C. E. Brock*
Ivanhoe. *G. F. Browne*
Ivanhoe. *Greiffenhagen*
Ivanhoe, 2 v. *Lewis*
Ivanhoe. *E. B. Smith*
Kenilworth. *H. J. Ford*
Kenilworth. *H. M. Paget*
Lady of the Lake. *C. E. Brock*
Lady of the Lake. *Christy*
Lay of the Last Minstrel. *B. Foster* and *J. Gilbert*
Legend of Montrose. *W. S. Paget*
Old Mortality. *S. E. Paget*
Pirate. *E. J. Sullivan*
Quentin Durward. *H. M. Paget*
Rob Roy. *Townsend*
St. Ronan's Well. *Thomson*
Tales of a Grandfather. *Fulleylove* and others
Tales of a Grandfather. *Stewart*

Talisman. *W. S. Paget*
Talisman. *S. H. Vedder*
Talisman. *Wheelright*
Waverley. *H. M. Brock*
Waverley, or 'Tis Sixty Years Since. *C. Green*

SCOVILLE, SAMUEL
More Wild Folk. *C. L. Bull*
Wild Folk. *C. L. Bull* and *Park*

SCUDDER, HORACE ELISHA
Book of Fables and Folk Stories. *Day*
Doings of the Bodley Family in Town and Country. *Bensell, Darley, Herrick, Nast, M. L. Stone,* and others

SEAMAN, AUGUSTA HUIELL
Jacqueline of the Carrier-pigeons. *G. W. Edwards*
When a Cobbler Ruled the King. *G. W. Edwards*

SEAVER, ROBERT
Ye Butcher, Ye Baker, Ye Candlestick Maker. *Seaver*

SEAWELL, MOLLY ELLIOT
Virginia Cavalier. *Yohn*

SECCOMBE, THOMAS STRONG
Good Old Story of Cinderella. *Seccombe*

SEDGWICK, CATHARINE MARIA
Facts and Fancies for School-day Reading. *Wallin*

SEDLÁČEK, HANŬS
Nursery Rhymes from Bohemia. *Mates*

SÉGUR, SOPHIE, COMTESSE DE
Memoirs of a Donkey. *L. Ford*
Princess Rosette and Other Fairy Tales. *Kutcher*
Sophie. *Barney*

SEIDLIN, OSKAR
Green Wagons. *Cooney*

SEIGNOBOSC, FRANÇOISE (FRANÇOISE, *pseud.*)
Gay A B C. *Seignobosc*
Story of Colette. *Seignobosc*

Select Fables in Three Parts. *T. Bewick*

SEREDY, KATE
Good Master. *Seredy*
White Stag. *Seredy*

SETON, ERNEST THOMPSON
Biography of a Grizzly. *Seton*
Lives of the Hunted. *Seton*
Trail of the Sandhill Stag. *Seton*
Wild Animals I Have Known. *Seton*

SETOUN, GABRIEL
Child World. *C. Robinson*

SEUSS, DR., *pseud. SEE* GEISEL, THEODOR SEUSS

Seven Champions of Christendom. *Reid*

SEWELL, ANNA
Black Beauty. *Aldin*
Black Beauty. *Eichenberg*
Black Beauty. *K. Pyle*
Black Beauty. *A. B. Woodward*

SEWELL, HELEN MOORE
Blue Barns. *Sewell*
Head for Happy. *Sewell*
Ming and Mehitable. *Sewell*
Peggy and the Pony. *Sewell*

SHAKESPEARE, WILLIAM
As You Like It. *Austen*
As You Like It. *Low*
As You Like It. *Shepperson*
As You Like It. *Thomson*
Comedies of William Shakespeare, 4 v. *Abbey*
Comedy of Errors. *Austen*
Complete Works, 2 v. *Kent*
Complete Works, 3 v. *E. J. Sullivan*
Compositions from The Tempest. *Paton*
Flowers from Shakespeare's Garden, a Posy from the Plays. *W. Crane*
Hamlet. *Austen*
Hamlet. *Shaw*
King Henry VIII. *J. D. Linton*
King John. *P. Wilson*
Macbeth. *G. F. Browne*
Macbeth. *Stratton*
Merchant of Venice. *Brandling, B. Foster* and *Thomas*
Merchant of Venice. *J. D. Linton*
Merchant of Venice. *Shepperson*
Merry Wives of Windsor. *W. Crane*
Merry Wives of Windsor. *Thomson*
Midsummer Night's Dream. *Bell*
Midsummer Night's Dream. *Konewka*
Midsummer Night's Dream. *Perkins*
Midsummer Night's Dream. *Rackham*
Midsummer Night's Dream. *W. H. Robinson*
Midsummer Night's Dream. *Shaw*
Midsummer Night's Dream. *Shepperson*
Pictorial Edition of the Works of Shakspere, 8 v. *Harvey* and others
Songs from Shakespeare's Plays. *Woodroffe*
Tempest. *Bell*
Tempest. *W. Crane*
Tempest. *Dulac*
Tempest. *Rackham*
Three Comedies. *Daugherty*
Tragedy of Romeo and Juliet. *Hatherell*
Tragedy of Romeo and Juliet. *Sauvage*
Twelfth Night. *W. H. Robinson*
Twelfth Night. *Shaw*
Two Gentlemen of Verona. *W. Crane*
Under the Greenwood Tree. *Weisgard*
Winter's Tale. *Armfield*

SHANLEY, CHARLES D.
Truant Chicken Series, 3 v. *H. L. Stephens*

SHANNON, MONICA
Dobry. *Katchamakoff*

SNEDEKER, CAROLINE DALE
Downright Dencey. *Barney*
Forgotten Daughter. *Lathrop*

Some British Ballads. *Rackham*

SONDERGAARD, ARENSA
My First Geography of the Americas. *Kredel*

Songs for the Little Ones at Home. *Absolon* and *B. Foster*

Songs of the Brave. Soldier's Dream and Other Poems
and Odes. *Duncan, B. Foster, Huttula, Macquoid*
and *Thomas*

SOUTHEY, ROBERT
Life of Nelson. *McCormick*
Three Bears. *Absolon* and *Weir*

SOWERBY, GITHA
Childhood. *A. M. Sowerby*
Merry Book. *A. M. Sowerby*
Wise Book. *A. M. Sowerby*

SPENCER, CORNELIA
Three Sisters. *Wiese*

SPENSER, EDMUND
Faerie Queene, 3 v. *W. Crane*
Stories from the Faerie Queene. *A. G. Walker*
Una and the Red Cross Knight. *T. H. Robinson*

SPERRY, ARMSTRONG
Call It Courage. *Sperry*
Little Eagle. *Sperry*
Wagons Westward. *Sperry*

Spirit of Praise. *E.* and *T. B. G. Dalziel, Gray, Houghton,
North, Pinwell* and *Small*

SPITTELER, CARL FRIEDRICH GEORG
Two Little Misogynists. *Carter*

SPRIGGE, ELIZABETH
Pony Tracks. *L. D. R. Edwards*

SPRING, HOWARD
Tumbledown Dick. *Spurrier*

SPYRI, JOHANNA HEUSSER
Heidi. *Barney*
Heidi. *Davis*
Heidi. *J. W. Smith*
Heidi. *Tenggren*

STACKPOLE, EDOUARD A.
Madagascar Jack. *Grant*

STAFFORD, ANN
Five Proud Riders. *Bobritsky*

STEDMAN, DOUGLAS C.
Story of Hereward. *G. D. Hammond*

STEEDMAN, AMY
Nursery Tales. *Woodroffe*

STEEL, FLORA ANNIE WEBSTER
Adventures of Akbar. *Shaw*
English Fairy Tales. *Rackham*
Tales of the Punjab. *J. L. Kipling*

STEEN, ELIZABETH KILGORE
Red Jungle Boy. *Steen*

STEIN, GERTRUDE
World Is Round. *C. Hurd*

STEPHENS, JAMES
Irish Fairy Tales. *Rackham*

STERLING, MARY BLACKWELL
Story of Parzival, the Templar. *W. E. Chapman*
Story of Sir Galahad. *W. E. Chapman*

STEVENS, FRANK LEONARD
Through Merrie England. *Bedford*

STEVENS, LILLIAN O.
King Arthur Stories. *Abbey*

STEVENSON, ROBERT LOUIS
Black Arrow. *Wyeth*
Child's Garden of Verses. *Davis*
Child's Garden of Verses. *Doane*
Child's Garden of Verses. *Duvoisin*
Child's Garden of Verses. *Le Mair*
Child's Garden of Verses. *C. Robinson*
Child's Garden of Verses. *J. W. Smith*
Child's Garden of Verses. *A. M. Sowerby*
David Balfour. *Wyeth*
Kidnapped. *Abbott*
Kidnapped. *Goble*
Kidnapped. *Hole*
Kidnapped. *L. J. Rhead*
Kidnapped. *Stott*
Kidnapped. *Wyeth*
Treasure Island. *H. M. Brock*
Treasure Island. *Dulac*
Treasure Island. *Goble*
Treasure Island. *Hilder*
Treasure Island. *W. S. Paget*
Treasure Island. *L. J. Rhead*
Treasure Island. *E. A. Wilson*
Treasure Island. *Winter*
Treasure Island. *Wyeth*
Two Mediaeval Tales. *Falls*

STOCKTON, FRANK RICHARD
Buccaneers and Pirates of Our Coasts. *Clinedinst* and
Varian
Casting Away of Mrs. Lecks and Mrs. Aleshine. *G. M.
Richards*
Casting Away of Mrs. Lecks and Mrs. Aleshine. *Steele*
Fanciful Tales. *Blashfield*
Floating Prince. *Bensell*
Pomona's Travels. *Frost*
Poor Count's Christmas. *Bensell*
Queen's Museum. *Richardson*
Reformed Pirate. *Birch*
Rudder Grange. *Frost*
Squirrel Inn. *Frost*
Story of Viteau. *Birch*
Story-teller's Pack. *Kemble, Newell, Smedley, A. B.
Stephens* and others
Ting-a-ling. *Bensell*

STODDARD, RICHARD HENRY
  Children in the Woods. *H. L. Stephens*

STOEBER, KARL
  Curate's Favorite Pupil. *Absolon*

STOLPER, JOEL
  Hippo. *Stolper*
  Patches. *Stolper*
  Whiskers. *Stolper*

STONE, AMY WENTWORTH
  Going-on-nine. *Wilkin*

STONE, WILLIAM STANDISH
  Pépé Was the Saddest Bird. *Mordvinoff*

STONG, PHILIP DUFFIELD
  Farm Boy. *Wiese*
  High Water. *Wiese*
  Honk: the Moose. *Wiese*
  No-Sitch: the Hound. *Wiese*
  Young Settler. *Wiese*

Stories About Dogs. *T. Landseer*

Story of Jack and the Giants. *Doyle*

Story of the Norman Conquest. *Maclise*

STOW, A.
  Baby Lays. *Calvert*
  More Baby Lays. *Calvert*

STOWE, HARRIET ELIZABETH BEECHER
  Uncle Tom's Cabin. *Covarrubias*
  Uncle Tom's Cabin. *G. Cruikshank*
  Uncle Tom's Cabin, 2 v. *Kemble*
  Uncle Tom's Cabin. *Leech*
  Uncle Tom's Cabin. *Macquoid* and *Thomas*

STRANG, WILLIAM
  Book of Giants. *Strang*

STREATFEILD, NOEL
  Ballet Shoes. *Floethe*
  Circus Shoes. *Floethe*
  Harlequinade. *Hutton*
  Stranger in Primrose Lane. *Floethe*

STUART, FLORENCE PARTELLO
  Adventures of Piang. *Young*

STUART, RUTH MCENERY
  Golden Wedding and Other Tales. *Frost, Reinhart* and *Sheppard*
  Solomon Crow's Christmas Pockets and Other Tales. *Frost, Kemble* and others
  Story of Babette. *A. B. Stephens*

SULLIVAN, JAMES FRANK
  Flame-flower and Other Stories. *J. F. Sullivan*
  Here They Are! *J. F. Sullivan*

SUMMERS, RICHARD ALDRICH
  Conquerors of the River. *McKay*

SURTEES, ROBERT SMITH
  Handley Cross, or Mr. Jorrocks' Hunt, 2 v. *Aldin*
  Handley Cross, or Mr. Jorrocks' Hunt. *Leech*
  Jorrocks' Jaunts and Jollities. *Alken*
  Jorrocks' Jaunts and Jollities. *H. K. Browne*

Susanna's Auction. *Boutet de Monvel*

SWIFT, HILDEGARDE HOYT
  Little Red Lighthouse. *Ward*

SWIFT, JONATHAN
  Gulliver's Travels. *Bosschère*
  Gulliver's Travels. *G. F. Browne*
  Gulliver's Travels. *H. K. Browne*
  Gulliver's Travels. *R. Bull*
  Gulliver's Travels. *H. Cole*
  Gulliver's Travels. *Eichenberg*
  Gulliver's Travels. *Morten*
  Gulliver's Travels. *Pogány*
  Gulliver's Travels. *Rackham*
  Gulliver's Travels. *L. J. Rhead*
  Gulliver's Travels. *Speed*
  Gulliver's Travels. *Whistler*
  Gulliver's Travels. *Winter*
  Travels into Several Remote Nations of the World by Lemuel Gulliver. *C. E. Brock*
  Travels into Several Remote Nations of the World by Lemuel Gulliver, pseud. *Gérard*
  Travels into Several Remote Nations of the World by Lemuel Gulliver. *Lalauze*

Sydenham Sinbad. *Meadows*

SZALATNAY, RAFAEL D.
  Cock and the Hen. *Mates*

Tales from the Court of Oberon. *Forrester*

Tales of Magic and Meaning. *Forrester*

Tall Book of Nursery Tales. *Rojankovsky*

TAPPAN, EVA MARCH
  Old Ballads in Prose. *Cory*
  Robin Hood: His Book. *Harding*

TARKINGTON, BOOTH
  Penrod. *Grant*
  Penrod and Sam. *Brehm*
  Penrod Jashber. *Grant*

TAYLOR, ANN AND JANE
  Little Ann and Other Poems. *Greenaway*
  Meddlesome Matty. *A. W. Payne*
  Original Poems. *Bedford*
  Rhymes for the Nursery. *J. Gilbert*
  Signor Topsy-Turvy's Wonderful Magic Lantern. *Taylor*

TAYLOR, BAYARD
  Boys of Other Countries. *Coburn* and others
  National Ode. *Fredericks, Moran, A. R. Waud* and others

TAYLOR, EMILY
Boy and the Birds. *T. Landseer*

TAYLOR, IDA ASHWORTH
Joan of Arc, Soldier and Saint. *W. G. Robertson*

TAYLOR, TOM
Pictures of English Landscape. *B. Foster*

TEASDALE, SARA
Stars To-night. *Lathrop*

TENGGREN, GUSTAF
Tenggren Story Book. *Tenggren*

TENNYSON, ALFRED, LORD
Dream of Fair Women. *E. J. Sullivan*
Enoch Arden. *Darley, Hennessy, LaFarge* and *E. Vedder*
Enoch Arden. *Hughes*
Idylls of the King. *Ball*
Idylls of the King. *Brickdale*
Idyls of the King. *Colman* and *Eytinge*
Lady of Shalott. *H. Pyle*
Maud. *W. G. Robertson*
Maud. *E. J. Sullivan*
May Queen. *E. V. B.*
Poems. *Ault*
Poems. *Hunt, Millais, Mulready, Rossetti, Stanfield, and others*
Princess. *Maclise*
Songs from "The Princess." *Gribble*
Songs from the Published Writings of Alfred Tennyson. *Curtis, Fredericks, Homer* and *Reinhart*

TENNYSON, HALLAM
Jack and the Beanstalk. English Hexameters. *Caldecott*

TERRY, ARTHUR GUY
Tales from Far and Near. *T. H. Robinson*

THACHER, LUCY W. S.
Listening Child. *Barnhart*

THACKERAY, WILLIAM MAKEPEACE
Adventures of Philip. *Thackeray* and *F. Walker*
Alphabet. *Thackeray*
Ballads and The Rose and the Ring. *Du Maurier, Furniss, Thackeray* and others
Barry Lyndon. *Millais*
Denis Duval. *F. Walker*
Dr. Birch and His Young Friends. *Thackeray*
Henry Esmond. *H. M. Brock*
Henry Esmond. *Dixon*
History of Henry Esmond. *Bedford*
History of Henry Esmond. *Du Maurier*
History of Henry Esmond. *T. H. Robinson*
History of Henry Esmond. *Thomson*
History of Pendennis, 2 v. *Thackeray*
History of Samuel Titmarsh and The Great Hoggarty Diamond. *Thomson*
Newcomes, 2 v. *Doyle*
Newcomes. *C. Hammond*
Rebecca and Rowena. *Doyle*

Rose and the Ring. *G. F. Browne*
Rose and the Ring. *Thackeray*
Vanity Fair. *Austen*
Virginians, 2 v. *Thackeray*

THIBAULT, JACQUES ANATOLE *SEE* FRANCE, ANATOLE, *pseud.*

THIRKELL, ANGELA
Grateful Sparrow and Other Tales. *Richter*

THOMAS, WILLIAM JENKYN
Welsh Fairy-book. *Pogány*

THOMAS, WILLIAM JOHN (AMBROSE MERTON, *pseud.*)
Gammer Gurton's Garland. *Webster* and others

THOMPSON, ARTHUR RIPLEY
Gold-seeking on the Dalton Trail. *Avison*

THOMPSON, BLANCHE JENNINGS
With Harp and Lute. *Seredy*

THOMPSON, D'ARCY W.
Nursery Nonsense or Rhymes Without Reason. *C. H. Bennett*

THOMPSON, ERNEST SETON *SEE* SETON, ERNEST THOMPSON

THOREAU, HENRY DAVID
Walden. *Ruzicka*

THORN, ALICE GREEN
Singing Words. *Stern*

THORNE-THOMSEN, GUDRUN
East o' the Sun and West o' the Moon. *Richardson*

Three Little Kittens. *Stern*

THURBER, JAMES
Great Quillow. *D. Lee*
Many Moons. *Slobodkin*

TIETJENS, EUNICE STRONG HAMMOND
Romance of Antar. *Glanckoff*

TILESTON, MARY WILDER
Sugar and Spice and All That's Nice. *Davis*

TIREMAN, LLOYD SPENCER
Baby Jack and Jumping Jack Rabbit. *Douglass*

TOLSTOI, LEO NIKOLAÏEVICH, COUNT
Ivan the Fool. *Millar*
Ivan the Fool. *Tealby*
Tolstoi for the Young. *Sevier*
Where Love Is There God Is Also. *Millar*

TOMLINSON, HENRY MAJOR
Sea and the Jungle. *C. V. H. Leighton*

TOPELIUS, ZAKARIAS
Canute Whistlewinks and Other Stories. *McIntosh*

TRAVERS, GEORGIA, *pseud. SEE* SCOTT, ALMA OLIVIA

TRAVERS, PAMELA L.
Mary Poppins. *M. Shepard*
Mary Poppins Comes Back. *M. Shepard*
Mary Poppins Opens the Door. *M. Shepard*

TREADGOLD, MARY
Left Till Called For. *Floethe*

TREGARTHEN, ENYS
Doll Who Came Alive. *Unwin*

TRIER, WALTER
Jolly Picnic. *Trier*

TRIMMER, SARAH KIRBY
History of the Robins. *Giacomelli*
History of the Robins. *Weir*
Natural History of the Most Remarkable Quadrupeds, Birds, Fishes, Serpents, Reptiles, and Insects, 2 v. *T. Bewick*

TRISTRAM, WILLIAM OUTRAM
Coaching Days and Coaching Ways. *Railton* and *Thomson*

Triumph of Goodnature. *J. Bewick*

TROELSTRA, SJOUKJE
Afke's Ten. *Van Stockum*

TROLLOPE, ANTHONY
Barchester Towers. *Brooke*
Framley Parsonage. *Millais*
Last Chronicle of Barset, 2 v. *Thomas*
Orley Farm, 2 v. *Millais*
Small House at Allington, 2 v. *Millais*

TROWBRIDGE, JOHN TOWNSEND
Bound in Honor; or, A Harvest of Wild Oats. *A. R. Waud*
Doing His Best. *Sheppard*
Fast Friends. *Sheppard*
Fortunes of Toby Trafford. *Sandham*
Vagabonds. *Darley*
Young Surveyor. *Sheppard*

TROY, HUGH
Chippendale Dam. *Troy*
Five Golden Wrens. *Troy*

TRUSLER, JOHN
Proverbs Exemplified and Illustrated by Pictures from Real Life. Teaching Morality and a Knowledge of the World. *J. Bewick*

TUCKER, GEORGE FOX
Boy Whaleman. *Avison*

TUDOR, TASHA
Alexander the Gander. *Tudor*
County Fair. *Tudor*
Dorcas Porcus. *Tudor*
Tale for Easter. *Tudor*

TURNER, THYRA
Christmas House, the Story of a Visit from Saint Nicholas. *F. Gág*

Tutor's Assistant or Comic Figures of Arithmetic. *Forrester.*

TUWIM, JULIAN
Locomotive, The Turnip, The Birds' Broadcast. *Him* and *Lewitt*

TWAIN, MARK, *pseud.* (SAMUEL LANGHORNE CLEMENS)
Adventures of Huckleberry Finn. *Benton*
Adventures of Huckleberry Finn. *Brehm*
Adventures of Huckleberry Finn. *Kemble*
Adventures of Huckleberry Finn. *Rockwell*
Adventures of Tom Sawyer. *Bacon*
Adventures of Tom Sawyer. *Brehm*
Adventures of Tom Sawyer. *McKay*
Adventures of Tom Sawyer. *Rockwell*
Adventures of Tom Sawyer. *T. W. Williams*
Connecticut Yankee in King Arthur's Court. *D. C. Beard*
Innocents Abroad. *T. W. Williams*
Life on the Mississippi. *Benton*
Mark Twain's Library of Humour. *Kemble*
Prince and the Pauper. *Hatherell*
Prince and the Pauper. *R. Lawson*
Prince and the Pauper. *Merrill*
Saint Joan of Arc. *W. J. Jones* and *H. Pyle*
Tom Sawyer Abroad. *D. C. Beard*
Tom Sawyer Abroad; Tom Sawyer, Detective and Other Stories. *Frost*
Tramp Abroad. *W. F. Brown* and *T. W. Williams*

TYTLER, M. FRASER
Wonder Seeker. *Absolon*

TYTLER, SARAH, *pseud.* (HENRIETTA KEDDIE)
Papers for Thoughtful Girls. *Millais*

ULREICH, NURA WOODSON (NURA, *pseud.*)
All Aboard, We Are Off. *Ulreich*
Nura's Children Go Visiting. *Ulreich*

UNTERMEYER, LOUIS
Last Pirate. *Birch*
New Songs for New Voices. *Bacon*
Rainbow in the Sky. *Birch*
This Singing World. *Ivins*

VAILE, CHARLOTTE MARION
Orcutt Girls. *Merrill*

Valentine and Orson. *H. M. Brock*

Valentine's Gift. *J. Bewick*

VANCE, MARGUERITE
Paula. *Angelo*
Star for Hansi. *Paull*

VAN DYKE, HENRY
First Christmas Tree. *H. Pyle*

VAN LOON, HENDRIK WILLEM
Ancient Man. *Van Loon*
Around the World with the Alphabet. *Van Loon*
Folk Songs of Many Lands. *Van Loon*
Golden Book of the Dutch Navigators. *Van Loon*
History with a Match. *Van Loon*
Life and Times of Simon Bolivar. *Van Loon*
Romance of Discovery. *Van Loon*
Songs America Sings. *Van Loon*
Songs We Sing. *Van Loon*
Story of Mankind. *Van Loon*
Thomas Jefferson. *Van Loon*
Van Loon's Geography. *Van Loon*

VAN STOCKUM, HILDA
Cottage at Bantry Bay. *Van Stockum*
Day on Skates. *Van Stockum*
Gerrit and the Organ. *Van Stockum*

VAUGHAN, AGNES CARR
Lucian Goes A-voyaging. *H. M. Wood*

VEALE, E.
Bonny Birds. *P. Cox*
Brownies and Other Stories. *P. Cox*
Jack the Giant. *P. Cox*
Merry Mice. *P. Cox*

VERNE, JULES
Michael Strogoff. *Wyeth*
Mysterious Island. *Wyeth*
Twenty Thousand Leagues under the Sea. *Aylward*
Twenty Thousand Leagues under the Sea. *Winter*

VIEUX MOUSTACHE, *pseud. SEE* GORDON, CLARENCE

VIMAR, AUGUSTE
Clown: The Circus Horse. *Vimar*
Curly-haired Hen. *Vimar*

WADDELL, HELEN JANE
Beasts and Saints. *Gibbings*

WAGNER, RICHARD
Parisfal. *Pogány*
Rhinegold and The Valkyrie. *Rackham*
Siegfried and The Twilight of the Gods. *Rackham*
Tale of Lohengrin. *Pogány*
Tannhäuser. *Pogány*

WAIN, LOUIS
Cats. *Wain*
Cats at School. *Wain*
Claws and Paws. *Wain*
Kitten Book. *Wain*
Pussies and Puppies. *Wain*

WALDECK, JoBESSE McELVEEN
Little Jungle Village. *Dombrowski*

WALDECK, THEODORE J.
Treks across the Veldt. *Sanderson*
White Panther. *Wiese*

WALDEN, JANE BREVOORT
Igloo. *Thorne*

WALLACE, DILLON
Arctic Stowaways. *Schoonover*

WALLACE, LEWIS
Ben Hur. *H. M. Brock*
Ben Hur, 2 v. *W. M. Johnson*

WALLER, MARY ELLA
Daughter of the Rich. *Elliott*

WALPOLE, HUGH
Jeremy. *E. H. Shepard*

WALTER, LAVINIA EDNA
Some Nursery Rhymes of Belgium, France and Russia. *Boutet de Monvel* and others

WARNER, ANNA BARTLETT
Ellen Montgomery's Bookshelf. *J. D. Watson*

WARNER, CHARLES DUDLEY
Being a Boy. *Champney*

WARNER, HANNAH, *pseud. SEE* JEWETT, JOHN HOWARD

WARNER, SUSAN (ELIZABETH WETHERELL, *pseud.*)
Wide, Wide World. *Dielman*
Wide, Wide World. *Pegram*

WARR, GEORGE C.
Echoes of Hellas, 2 v. *W. Crane*

WARREN, MAUDE LAVINIA RADFORD
Little Pioneers. *Perkins*

WATTS, ISAAC
Divine and Moral Songs. *Barnes, Small* and others
Divine and Moral Songs. *Du Maurier, C. Green, Morten, J. D. Watson* and others
Divine and Moral Songs for Children. *G. C. F. Gaskin*
Divine and Moral Songs for the Use of Children. *Cope*
Songs Divine and Moral for the Use of Children. *Stothard*

WAUGH, ARTHUR
Square Book of Animals. *Nicholson*

WAUGH, DOROTHY
Among the Leaves and Grasses. *D. Waugh*
Warm Earth. *D. Waugh*

WAUGH, IDA
Holly Berries. *I. Waugh*

Way To Be Happy; or, The History of the Family at Smiledale. *J. Bewick*

Wayside Posies. *North, Pinwell* and *F. Walker*

WEATHERLY, F. E.
Adventures of Two Children. *M. E. Edwards*

WEAVER, ANNIE VAUGHAN
Boochy's Wings. *Weaver*
Frawg. *Weaver*
Pappy King. *Weaver*

WEBB, CLIFFORD CYRIL
   Animals from Everywhere. *Webb*
   Butterwick Farm. *Webb*
   Jungle Picnic. *Webb*
   North Pole before Lunch. *Webb*

WEBBER, IRMA ELEANOR SCHMIDT
   Travelers All. *Webber*
   Up Above and Down Below. *Webber*

WEDGWOOD, HENRY ALLEN
   Bird Talisman. *Raverat*

WELLS, CAROLYN
   Phenomenal Fauna. *Herford*

WELLS, CARVETH
   Jungle Man and His Animals. *Sarg*

WELLS, PETER
   Mr. Tootwhistle's Invention. *P. Wells*

WELLS, RHEA
   Ali the Camel. *R. Wells*
   American Farm. *R. Wells*

WERNER, JANE
   Noah's Ark. *Gergely*

WETHERELL, ELIZABETH, *pseud. SEE* WARNER, SUSAN

WEYMAN, STANLEY JOHN
   Under the Red Robe. *Woodville*

WHEELER, OPAL
   Sing for Christmas. *Tenggren*

WHEELER, POST
   Albanian Wonder Tales. *Petersham*
   Russian Wonder Tales. *Bilibin*

When I Was a Little Girl. *Froelich*

WHITE, ELIZA ORNE
   Four Young Kendalls. *Hummel*
   I, the Autobiography of a Cat. *Hutton*
   Lending Mary. *Paull*
   Only Child. *K. Pyle*
   Sally in Her Fur Coat. *Hummel*
   When Abigail Was Seven. *Hummel*
   Where Is Adelaide? *Sewell*

WHITE, ELWYN BROOKS
   Stuart Little. *G. Williams*

WHITE, HERVEY
   Snake Gold. *MacKinstry*

WHITE, STEWART EDWARD
   Blazed Trail. *Fogarty*
   Daniel Boone, Wilderness Scout. *Daugherty*
   Daniel Boone, Wilderness Scout. *Schuyler*
   Gold. *Fogarty*

WHITE, WILLIAM CHAPMAN
   Mouseknees. *A. F. Johnson*

WHITHAM, GRACE I.
   Captive Royal Children. *A. G. Walker*
   Shepherd of the Ocean. *Ault*

WHITNEY, ADELINE DUTTON TRAIN
   Summer in Leslie Goldthwaite's Life. *Hoppin*

WHITNEY, ELINOR
   Timothy and the Blue Cart. *Hader*
   Tod of the Fens. *Goble*

WHITTIER, JOHN GREENLEAF
   Ballads of New England. *Colman, Darley, Eytinge,
      Fenn, Fredericks, Hennessy, Homer* and others
   Maud Muller. *Hennessy*
   Snow-bound. *Fenn*

WIDOR, CHARLES MARIE
   Old Songs and Rounds for Little Children. *Boutet
      de Monvel*

WIESE, KURT
   Joe Buys Nails. *Wiese*
   Liang and Lo. *Wiese*
   Rabbits' Revenge. *Wiese*
   Wallie the Walrus. *Wiese*

WIGGIN, KATE DOUGLAS SMITH
   Birds' Christmas Carol. *Grose*
   Fairy Ring. *MacKinstry*
   Mother Carey's Chickens. *Elliott*
   Mother Carey's Chickens. *A. B. Stephens*
   New Chronicles of Rebecca. *Yohn*
   Penelope's Experiences in Scotland. *C. E. Brock*
   Rebecca of Sunnybrook Farm. *Grose*
   Tales of Laughter. *MacKinstry*
   Timothy's Quest. *Herford*

WILDE, OSCAR
   Birthday of the Infanta. *Bianco*
   Happy Prince. *C. Robinson*
   Happy Prince, and Other Stories. *S. B. Nichols*
   Happy Prince, and Other Tales. *W. Crane* and *G. P. J.
      Hood*
   Happy Prince and Other Tales. *Ruzicka*
   Happy Prince, and Other Tales. *E. Shinn*

WILDER, LAURA INGALLS
   Farmer Boy. *Sewell*
   Little House in the Big Woods. *Sewell*

WILLCOX, LOUISE COLLIER
   Torch. *Elliott*

WILLIAMS, GWENEIRA MAUREEN
   Timid Timothy. *Weisgard*

WILLIAMSON, HAMILTON
   Humpy. *Hader*
   Monkey Tale. *Hader*
   Stripey, a Little Zebra. *Hader*

WILLS, W. H.
   Poets' Wit and Humor. *C. H. Bennett* and *Thomas*

WILSON, EDWARD ARTHUR
Pirate's Treasure. *E. A. Wilson*

WILSON, LAWRENCE
Story of Cortes. *T. H. Robinson*

WILSON, RICHARD
Indian Story Book. *Papé*
Russian Story Book. *Papé*

WILWERDING, WALTER JOSEPH
Jangwa; the Story of a Jungle Prince. *Wilwerding*
Keema of the Monkey People. *Wilwerding*

WINLOVE, SOLOMON
Pleasing Moralist, or Young Gentlemen and Ladies
Preceptor. *T. Bewick*

Winter Poems by Favorite American Poets. *Eytinge,
Fenn, Fredericks, Hennessy, Homer* and others

WISE, JOHN R.
First of May, a Fairy Masque. *W. Crane*

WISTER, OWEN
Virginian. *Keller*
Virginian. *Remington* and *Russell*

WOLFE, HUMBERT
Cursory Rhymes. *Rutherston*

WOLLSTONECRAFT, MARY
Original Stories from Real Life. *Blake*

WONSETLER, ADELAIDE HILL
Me and the General. *Wonsetler* and others

WOOD, ESTHER
Pepper Moon. *Bannon*

WOOD, JOHN GEORGE
Natural History for Young People. *Coleman, Weir,
Wolf, T. W. Wood* and *Zwecker*

WOOD, RAY
American Mother Goose. *Hargis*

WOODWARD, HILDEGARD
Jared's Blessing. *H. Woodward*
Time Was. *H. Woodward*

WORDSWORTH, WILLIAM
Deserted Cottage. *B. Foster, J. Gilbert* and *Wolf*
Poems for the Young. *MacWhirter* and *Pettie*
Poems of William Wordsworth. *B. Foster, J. Gilbert*
and *Wolf*
Selections from the Sonnets of William Wordsworth.
A. W. Parsons
Wayside Flowers. *Carter*
We Are Seven. *Pym*

WORTH, KATHRYN
They Loved to Laugh. *De Angeli*

WRIGHT, ANNA ROSE
Barefoot Days. *P. Chapman*

WYNNE, JOHN HUDDLESTONE
Tales for Youth. *J. Bewick*

WYSS, JOHANN DAVID
Swiss Family Robinson. *Abbott*
Swiss Family Robinson. *H. Corbould*
Swiss Family Robinson. *Folkard*
Swiss Family Robinson. *J. Gilbert*
Swiss Family Robinson. *L. J. Rhead*
Swiss Family Robinson. *T. H. Robinson*
Swiss Family Robinson. *Rountree*
Swiss Family Robinson. *Teague*

Yankee Doodle. *Darley*

Yankee Doodle. *H. Pyle*

YATES, ELIZABETH
Mountain Born. *Unwin*
Patterns on the Wall. *Chappell*
Under the Little Fir. *Unwin*

YERSHOV, PETR PAVLOVICH *SEE* ERSHOV, PETR PAVLOVICH

YONGE, CHARLOTTE MARY
Caged Lion. *Hennessy*
Chaplet of Pearls. *Hennessy*
Chaplet of Pearls. *Stevens*
Dove in the Eagle's Nest. *Hennessy*
Heartsease. *Greenaway*
Heir of Redclyffe. *Greenaway*
Lances of Lynwood. *Blackburn*
Little Duke. *Millar*
Little Duke. *Stevens*
Little Lucy's Wonderful Globe. *Peck*
Unknown to History. *Hennessy*

YOUNG, ELLA
Celtic Wonder Tales. *MacBride*
Tangle-coated Horse and Other Tales. *Bock*
Unicorn with Silver Shoes. *R. Lawson*
Wonder Smith and His Son. *Artzybasheff*

YOUNG, STANLEY
Mayflower Boy. *Shenton*

Young Reader, for Teaching the English Language, and
Improving the Mind. *T. Bewick*

Young Troublesome; or Master Jacky's Holidays. *Leech*

Youth's Instructive and Entertaining Storyteller. *T.
Bewick*

ZEITLIN, IDA
Gessar Khan. *Nadejen*
Skazki. *Nadejen*

ZOLLINGER, GULIELMA
Maggie McLanehan. *F. S. Shinn*
Widow O'Callaghan's Boys. *F. S. Shinn*

ZOLOTOW, CHARLOTTE
Park Book. *Rey*

ZWILGMEYER, DIKKEN
Four Cousins. *Heiberg*

PART IV. APPENDIX

OLIVER HERFORD : *Little Mr. Thimblefinger*

FREDERICK WALKER: *Adventures of Philip*

EDWIN A. ABBEY : *Selections from the Hesperides and*
Noble Numbers of Robert Herrick

Sources

Chapter I. ILLUSTRATED BOOKS FOR CHILDREN BEFORE 1800

BLADES, WILLIAM. *The Life and Typography of William Caxton.* 2 Vols. London: Joseph Lilly, 1861-63.

CARY, ELISABETH LUTHER. *The Art of William Blake.* New York: Moffat, Yard & Co., 1907.

COMENIUS, JOHN AMOS. *Orbis Sensualium Pictus; The Visible World, written by the author in Latin and High Dutch; translated into English by Charles Hoole.* New York: T. & J. Swords, 1810.

DARTON, F. J. HARVEY. *Children's Books in England; Five Centuries of Social Life.* Cambridge (England): University Press, 1932.

DOBSON, AUSTIN. *Thomas Bewick and His Pupils.* London: Chatto & Windus, 1884.

DUFF, E. GORDON. *William Caxton.* Chicago: The Caxton Club, 1905.

FIELD, MRS. E. M. *The Child and His Book.* 2nd Edition. London: Wells, Gardner, Darton & Co., 1895.

FOLMSBEE, BEULAH. *Little History of the Horn-book.* Boston: The Horn Book, Inc., 1942.

FURNIVALL, FREDERICK J., ed. *The Babees Book; Stans Puer ad Mensam,* etc., edited by Dr. Furnivall for the Early English Text Society, Original Series No. 32. London: N. Trübner & Co., 1868.

GILCHRIST, ALEXANDER. *Life of William Blake.* 2 Vols. London: Macmillan, 1880.

GUMUCHIAN ET CIE. *Les Livres de L'Enfance du XV⁰ au XIX⁰ Siècle.* 2 Vols. Paris: Gumuchian et Cie., 1930.

JAMES, PHILIP. *Children's Books of Yesterday.* London: Special Autumn Number of *The Studio,* 1933.

McPHARLIN, PAUL. *Bewick's Birds 1797-1804. Publishers' Weekly,* Issue of January 1, 1944.

MORLEY, HENRY. *English Writers,* Vol. 2. London: Cassell & Co., 1887-95.

POLLARD, ALFRED W. *Early Illustrated Books.* New York: Dutton, 1917.

ROSENBACH, A. S. W. *Early American Children's Books.* Portland, Maine: Southworth-Anthoensen Press, 1933.

STONE, WILBUR MACEY. "The Butterfly's Ball." The *Horn Book Magazine*, January-February, 1942.

THOMSON, GLADYS SCOTT. *Life in a Noble Household, 1641-1700*. London: Jonathan Cape, 1937.

TUER, ANDREW W. *History of the Horn-book*. 2 Vols. London: Leadenhall Press, 1896.

TUER, ANDREW W. *Pages and Pictures from Forgotten Children's Books*. London: Leadenhall Press, 1898-99.

TUER, ANDREW W. *Stories from Old-Fashioned Children's Books*. London: Leadenhall Press, 1899-1900.

WEITENKAMPF, FRANK. *The Illustrated Book*. Cambridge: Harvard University Press, 1938.

WHITE, GLEESON. *Children's Books and Their Illustrators*. London: The Special Winter Number of *The Studio*, 1897-98.

WRIGHT, THOMAS. *The Life of William Blake*. 2 Vols. Olney, Bucks: Thomas Wright, 1929.

Chapter II. ILLUSTRATORS OF THE NINETEENTH CENTURY IN ENGLAND

BLACKBURN, HENRY. *Randolph Caldecott, a Personal Memoir*. London: Sampson Low, 1887.

COLLINGWOOD, STUART D. *Life and Letters of Lewis Carroll*. New York: Century Co., 1899.

CRANE, WALTER. *An Artist's Reminiscences*. London: Macmillan, 1907.

DOYLE, RICHARD. *A Journal Kept by Richard Doyle in the Year 1840*. London: Smith, Elder, 1885.

JAMES, PHILIP. *Children's Books of Yesterday*. London: Special Autumn Number, *The Studio*, 1933.

JERROLD, BLANCHARD. *Life of George Cruikshank*. 2 Vols. London: Chatto, 1882.

MACDONALD, GREVILLE. *George MacDonald and His Wife*. New York: Dial Press, 1924.

SPIELMANN, M. H. *History of "Punch."* London: Cassell, 1895.

SPIELMANN, M. H., and LAYARD, G. S. *Kate Greenaway*. New York: Putnam, 1905.

WHITE, GLEESON. *Children's Books and Their Illustrators*. London: Special Winter Number of *The Studio*, 1897-98.

WHITE, GLEESON. *English Illustrators of the Sixties*. London: Constable, 1906.

Chapter III. EARLY AMERICAN ILLUSTRATION

[Also general and chapter introductions]

ANDERSEN, HANS CHRISTIAN. *Fairy Tales*. Translated by H. L. Braekstad. London: Heinneman, 1900.

BARRY, FLORENCE V. *A Century of Children's Books*. New York: George H. Doran Co., *n.d.*

BLAKE, WILLIAM. *Poetry and Prose of William Blake*. Edited by Geoffrey Keynes. London: The Nonesuch Press, 1927.

COLOPHON. *A Book Collectors' Quarterly*. Part I, 1930; Part VI, 1931.

CRANE, WALTER. *The Bases of Design*. London: George Bell & Sons, 1898.

DARTON, F. J. HARVEY. *Children's Books in England, Five Centuries of Social Life*. London: Cambridge University Press, 1932.

HALSEY, ROSALIE V. *Forgotten Books of the American Nursery; A History of the Development of the American Story-Book*. Boston: C. E. Goodspeed & Co., 1911.

HAMILTON, SINCLAIR. *Early American Book Illustrators and Wood Engravers 1670-1870 being a catalogue of a collection of American books illustrated for the most part with woodcuts and wood engravings presented to Princeton University by Sinclair Hamilton*. (Mimeographed Sheets, 1945) Copies of the catalogue may be consulted at The American Antiquarian Society, Worcester, Massachusetts; The Houghton Library at Harvard University and The New York Public Library.

HAZARD, PAUL. *Books, Children and Men*. Translated by Marguerite MacKellar Mitchell. Boston: The Horn Book, Inc., 1944.

LANG, ANDREW. *The Library. With a chapter on Illustrated Books by Austin Dobson*. London: Macmillan Co., 1881.

MIERS, EARL SCHENCK, and ELLIS, RICHARD. *Bookmaking and Kindred Amenities*. New Brunswick: Rutgers University Press, 1942.

PEARSON, EDMUND LESTER. *Books in Black and Red*. New York: Macmillan Co., 1923.

Princeton University Library Chronicle. November, 1939; April, 1945.

Print, A Quarterly Journal of the Graphic Arts. Vol. III, No. 2, 1942; Vol. III, No. 3, 1943.

ROSENBACH, A. S. W. *Early American Children's Books*. Portland, Maine: Southworth-Anthoensen Press, 1933.

SMITH, ELVA S. *The History of Children's Literature. A Syllabus with Selected Bibliographies*. Chicago: American Library Association, 1937.

WEITENKAMPF, FRANK. *American Graphic Art. New edition, revised and enlarged*. New York: Macmillan, 1924.

Chapter V. FOREIGN PICTURE BOOKS IN A CHILDREN'S LIBRARY. MARIA CIMINO

[See List of Picture Books beginning on page 145]

Chapter VII. ILLUSTRATORS OF CHILDREN'S CLASSICS

AMERICAN INSTITUTE OF GRAPHIC ARTS. *An Exhibition of Books Made for Children*. New York, 1944.

BOLTON, THEODORE. *American Book Illustrators; Biographical Check List of 123 Artists*. New York: Bowker, 1938.

BRUNET, J. C. *Manuel du Libraire et de l'Amateur de Livres*. 5e Édition. Paris, 1860-80. 8 Vols.

COHEN, H. *Guide de l'Amateur de Livres à Gravures du XVIIIe Siècle*. 6e Édition, augmentée par S. de Ricci, Paris, 1912.

DARTON, F. J. HARVEY. *Children's Books in England; Five Centuries of Social Life*. London: Cambridge University Press, 1932.

DARTON, F. J. HARVEY. *Modern Book Illustration in Great Britain and America*. Special Winter Number, *The Studio*, London, 1931.

DAVIES, H. W. *Catalogue of a Collection of Early French Books in the Library of C. F. Murray*. 2 Vols. London, 1910.

DAVIES, H. W. *Catalogue of a Collection of Early German Books in the Library of C. F. Murray*. 2 Vols. London, 1913.

GUMUCHIAN ET CIE. *Les Livres de l'Enfance du XVe au XIXe Siècle*. Preface de Paul Gavault. Catalogue XIII. 2 Vols. Paris, 1930.

HIND, ARTHUR M. *A History of Engraving and Etching from the 15th Century to the Year 1914*. London: Constable, 1923.

HIND, ARTHUR M. *An Introduction to a History of Woodcut, with a Detailed Survey of Work Done in the XVth Century*. 2 Vols. London, 1935.

JAMES, PHILIP. *Children's Books of Yesterday*. Special Autumn Number, *The Studio*, London, 1933.

MOORE, ANNE CARROLL. *Children's Books of Yesterday: An Exhibition from Many Countries*. New York Public Library, 1933.

NEW YORK PUBLIC LIBRARY. *Children's Books Suggested as Holiday Gifts*. An Exhibition in the Central Children's Room, 1933

POLLARD, ALFRED W. *Italian Book Illustrations and Early Printing. A Catalogue of . . . the Library of C. W. Dyson-Perrins*. London: B. Quaritch, 1914.

REID, FORREST. *Illustrators of the Sixties*. London: Faber & Gwyer, 1928.

RÜMANN, ARTHUR. *Das Illustrierte Buch des XIX Jahrhunderts in England, Frankreich, und Deutschland, 1790-1860*. Leipzig: Insel-Verlag, 1930.

RÜMANN, ARTHUR. *Die Illustrierten Deutschen Bücher des XIX Jahrhunderts.* (Taschenbibliographien für Büchersammler, IV.) Stuttgart: J. Hoffmann, 1925.

SANDER, M. *Die Illustrierten Französischen Bücher des 19 Jahrhunderts.* (Taschenbibliographien für Büchersammler, I.) Stuttgart: J. Hoffmann, 1924.

SCHATZKI, WALTER. *Children's Books, Old and Rare.* Catalogue No. 1. New York, 1941.

THORPE, JAMES. *English Illustration: The Nineties.* London: Faber & Faber, 1935.

VICAIRE, G. *Manuel de l'Amateur: Livres du XIXe Siècle, 1801-1893.* 8 Vols. Paris, 1894-1920.

VICTORIA AND ALBERT MUSEUM, SOUTH KENSINGTON. *Exhibition of Illustrated Books for Children* (Historical Section). Catalogue. London, 1932.

WEITENKAMPF, FRANK. *The Illustrated Book.* Cambridge: Harvard University Press, 1938.

WHITE, GLEESON. *Children's Books and Their Illustrators.* Winter Number, *The Studio*, 1897-1898. London, 1897.

WHITE, GLEESON. *English Illustration: The Sixties.* 1855-'70. London: Constable, 1906.

WATT, H. A., and HOLZKNECHT, K. J. *Children's Books of Long Ago; A Garland of Pages and Pictures.* New York: Dryden Press, 1941.

Chapter VIII. ANIMATED DRAWING

GAINES, M. C. "Narrative Illustration, The Story of the Comics" in *Print, A Quarterly Journal of the Graphic Arts*, Vol. III, No. 2, Summer 1942.

GAINES, M. C. "Good Triumphs Over Evil — More About the Comics," in *Print, A Quarterly Journal of the Graphic Arts*, Vol. III, No. 3, 1943.

HERBERT, J. A. *Illuminated Manuscripts.* 2nd Edition. London: Methuen, 1912.

LEHMANN-HAUPT, HELLMUT. *The Terrible Gustave Doré.* New York: the Marchbanks Press, 1943.

RÜMANN, ARTHUR. *Das Illustrierte Buch des XIX Jahrhunderts in England, Frankreich, und Deutschland, 1790-1860.* Leipzig: Insel-Verlag, 1930.

SHERIDAN, MARTIN. *Comics and Their Creators: Life Stories of American Cartoonists.* Boston: R. T. Hale & Co., 1944.

WEITENKAMPF, FRANK. *The Illustrated Book.* Cambridge: Harvard University Press, 1928.

PART II: *BRIEF BIOGRAPHIES OF LIVING ILLUSTRATORS*

As noted in the introduction to Part II, sources for biographical material (when other than the artists themselves, their families, or publishers) are given at the close of the individual biographies.

PART III: *BIBLIOGRAPHIES*

ABBOTT, CHARLES D. *Howard Pyle.* New York: Harper & Brothers, 1925.

AESOP. *Fables of Aesop as first printed by William Caxton in 1484 with those of Avian, Alfonso and Poggio, now again edited and induced by Joseph Jacobs*, 2 Vols. Vol. 1, *History of the Aesopic Fable;* Vol. 2, *Text and Glossary.* London: David Nutt, 1889.

ALLIBONE, S. AUSTIN. *Critical Dictionary of English Literature and British and American Authors*, 3 Vols. Philadelphia: J. B. Lippincott & Co., 1874. *Supplement to Allibone's*, 2 Vols. Philadelphia: J. B. Lippincott & Co., 1891.

American Art Annual. Vols. X-XXXV (1913-1941). Washington, D. C.: American Federation of Arts.

American Catalogue of Books, 1876-1910. 9 Vols. in 13. New York: *Publisher's Weekly.*

AMERICAN LIBRARY ASSOCIATION. *Booklist.* Vol. 1 (January 1905) — date. Chicago: American Library Association.

ANDERSON GALLERIES, INC. *Rare & Valuable Colored Plate Books & an Extensive Cruikshank Collection.* New York: American Art Association, 1930.

Art Index. January 1929 – date. New York: H. W. Wilson Co.

BEWICK, THOMAS. *Memoir of Thomas Bewick, Written by Himself.* London: Longman, Green, Longman and Roberts, 1862.

BLACKBURN, HENRY. *Art of Illustration.* Edinburgh: John Grant, 1901.

BLACKBURN, HENRY. *Randolph Caldecott.* London: Sampson Low, Marston, Searle and Rivington, 1886.

BLACKBURN, PHILIP C., and LANGFELD, WILLIAM R. *Washington Irving, a Bibliography.* New York: New York Public Library, 1933.

BLANCK, JACOB. *Peter Parley to Penrod.* New York: R. R. Bowker Co., 1938.

BOLTON, THEODORE. *American Book Illustrators.* New York: R. R. Bowker Co., 1938.

BOWEN, MARJORIE. *William Hogarth.* New York: D. Appleton-Century Co., 1936.

BRAY, ANNA ELIZA. *Life of Thomas Stothard.* London: John Murray, 1851.

BRITISH MUSEUM. *Charles Dickens: An excerpt from the general catalogue of printed books in the British Museum.* London: William Clowes and Sons, Ltd., 1926.

BRITISH MUSEUM. DEPARTMENT OF PRINTED BOOKS. *Catalogue of Printed Books.* London: Printed by Clowes, 1881-1900. *Supplement.* 1900-1905. *General Catalogue of Printed Books.* London: W. Clowes, 1931 – date. (Vols. 1-37.)

BROWNE, NINA ELIZA. *Bibliography of Nathaniel Hawthorne.* Boston: Houghton Mifflin Co., 1905.

BRYAN, MICHAEL. *Bryan's Dictionary of Painters and Engravers: New edition revised and enlarged under supervision of George C. Williamson.* 5 Vols. New York: Macmillan Co., 1903.

Cambridge Bibliography of English Literature (600-1900), 4 Vols. New York: Macmillan Co., 1941.

Cambridge History of American Literature, Vol. 2. New York: Macmillan Co., 1931.

Cambridge History of English Literature, Vols. 11 and 13. New York: G. P. Putnam's Sons, 1928.

CARNEGIE LIBRARY OF PITTSBURGH. *Catalogue of Books in the Children's Department.* Pittsburgh: Carnegie Library, 1920.

Catalog of Works Illustrated by Thomas and John Bewick. London: John Gray Bell, 1851.

Century Cyclopedia of Names. New York: Century Co., 1914.

CHESSON, WILFRID HUGH. *George Cruikshank.* London: Duckworth and Co., *n.d.*

Chi È. Roma: Formeggini, 1936.

Children's Catalog, 1930 – date. New York: H. W. Wilson Co.

CHILDREN'S LIBRARIANS SECTION. *Children's Library Yearbook* (1929-32), 4 Vols. Chicago: American Library Association.

CLEMENT, CLARA ERSKINE, and HUTTON, LAURENCE. *Artists of the 19th Century.* Boston: Houghton Mifflin Co., Revised Edition. 1884.

COLE, SIR HENRY. *Fifty Years of Public Work,* 2 Vols. London: George Bell and Sons, 1884.

COOPER, ANICE PAGE. *About Artists.* Garden City, N. Y.: Doubleday, Page and Co., 1926.

COOPER, SUSAN FENIMORE. *Pages and Pictures from the Writings of James Fenimore Cooper.* New York: James Miller, 1861.

CRANE, WALTER. *Artist's Reminiscences.* New York: Macmillan Co., 1907.

CRANE, WALTER. *Of the Decorative Illustration of Books Old and New.* London: George Bell and Sons, 1896.

CUNDALL, HERBERT MINTON. *Birket Foster.* London: Adam and Charles Black, 1906.

CUNDALL, JOSEPH. *Brief History of Wood-engraving.* London: Sampson Low, Marston and Co., 1895.

CURRENT BIOGRAPHY (1940 – date). New York: H. W. Wilson Co.

DALZIEL BROTHERS. *Brothers Dalziel: A Record of Fifty Years' Work, 1840-90.* London: Methuen and Co., 1901.

DARTON, FREDERICK JOSEPH HARVEY. *Children's Books in England.* Cambridge at the University Press, 1932.

DARTON, FREDERICK JOSEPH HARVEY. *Modern Book Illustration in Great Britain and America.* London: The Studio Limited, 1931.

DAVENPORT, CYRIL JAMES HUMPHRIES. *Byways Among English Books*. New York: Frederick A. Stokes Co., *n.d.*

DAVIDSON, ANGUS. *Edward Lear*. London: John Murray, 1938.

Dictionary of American Biography, 20 Vols. New York: Charles Scribner's Sons, 1943.

Dictionary of National Biography, 63 Vols. London: Smith, Elder and Co., 1900. *First Supplement*, 3 Vols. London: Smith, Elder and Co., 1901. *Second Supplement*, 3 Vols. London: Smith, Elder and Co., 1912. *Third Supplement* (1912-1921), 1 Vol. London: Oxford University Press, 1927. *Fourth Supplement* (1922-1930), 1 Vol. London: Oxford University Press, 1937.

DISTRICT OF COLUMBIA PUBLIC LIBRARY. *Card Index to Books, on Illustrators and Illustration, in the Children's Department*. (Analyzed by illustrator.)

DISTRICT OF COLUMBIA PUBLIC LIBRARY. *General Catalog*.

DOBSON, AUSTIN. *Thomas Bewick and His Pupils*. London: Chatto and Windus, 1884.

DUYCKINCK, EVERT AUGUSTUS. *Brief Catalog of Books Illustrated with Engravings by Dr. Alexander Anderson*. New York: Printed by Thompson Moreau, 1885.

ELLIS, JESSIE CROFT. *General Index to Illustrations*. Boston: F. W. Faxon Company, 1931.

Encyclopaedia Britannica, 14th Edition, 24 Vols. New York: Encyclopaedia Britannica, Inc., 1929.

English Catalog of Books Published 1801-1930, 13 Vols. London: Sampson Low, 1864-1905. London: Publisher's Circular, 1912-1931.

EVERITT, GRAHAM. *English Caricaturists and Graphic Humourists*. London: Swan Sonnenschein & Co., 1893.

FIELD, LOUISE FRANCES. *Child and His Book*. London: Wells Gardner, Darton and Co., 1891.

FIELDING, MANTLE. *Dictionary of American Painters, Sculptors and Engravers*. Philadelphia: Printed for the Subscribers, *n.d.*

FRITH, WILLIAM POWELL. *John Leech, His Life and Work*, 2 Vols. London: Richard Bentley and Son, 1891.

GILCHRIST, ALEXANDER. *Life of William Blake*, 2 Vols. London: Macmillan & Co., 1863.

GOSSOP, ROBERT PERCY. *Book Illustration, a Review of the Art as It Is Today*. London: J. M. Dent and Sons, Ltd., 1937.

Grande Encyclopédie, 31 Vols. Paris: H. LaMirault et Cⁱᵉ., 1886-1902.

GROLIER CLUB. *Catalog of an Exhibition of Works by John Leech (1817-1864) Held at the Grolier Club from January 22 until March 8, 1914*. New York: Grolier Club, 1914.

GULLIVER, LUCILLE. *Louisa May Alcott, a Bibliography*. Boston: Little, Brown and Co., 1932.

GUMUCHIAN & Cⁱᴱ. *Les Livres de l'Enfance* (Catalogue XIII), 2 Vols. Paris: Gumuchian & Cⁱᵉ., 1930.

HAMILTON, SINCLAIR. *Early American Book Illustration* in *The Princeton University Library Chronicle*. Volume VI, Number 3, April 1945.

HAMILTON, WALTER. *A Memoir of George Cruikshank, Artist and Humourist, with numerous illustrations, and a bank note, not to be imitated*. London: Elliot Stock, 1878.

HARDIE, MARTIN. *English Coloured Books*. London: Methuen and Co., 1906.

Harper's Monthly Magazine, 1850 – date.

Harper's Young People, Vols. 1-20 (November 4, 1879-October 1899). Named changed to *Harper's Round Table*, April 30, 1895. New York: Harper & Brothers.

HILL, RUTH A., and BONDELI, ELSA DE. *Children's Books from Foreign Languages*. New York: H. W. Wilson Co., 1937.

HIND, ARTHUR MAYGER. *Short History of Engraving and Etching*. Boston: Houghton Mifflin Company, 1908.

Horn Book Magazine, Vol. I (October 1924) – date.

HOUSMAN, LAURENCE. *Arthur Boyd Houghton*. London: Kegan Paul, Trench, Trübner & Co., 1896.

HUGO, THOMAS. *Bewick Collector. A Descriptive Catalog of the Works of Thomas and John Bewick*. London: Lovell, Reeve and Co., 1866.

HUGO, THOMAS. *Catalog of the Choice and Valuable Collection of Books, etc. by or relating to John and Thomas Bewick*. London: Sotheby, Wilkinson & Hodge, 1877.

IVES, GEORGE BURNHAM. *Bibliography of Oliver Wendell Holmes*. Boston: Houghton Mifflin Co., 1907.

JACKSON, JOHN. *Treatise on Wood Engraving*. London: Charles Knight and Co., 1839.

JAMES, PHILIP. *Children's Books of Yesterday* (Special Autumn Number of *The Studio*). London: The Studio Limited, 1933.

JERROLD, BLANCHARD. *Life of George Cruikshank*. London: Chatto and Windus, 1898.

KELLY, JAMES. *American Catalogue of Books Published in the United States from Jan. 1861 to Jan. 1871*, 2 Vols. New York: Wiley, 1866-71.

KONODY, PAUL GEORGE. *Art of Walter Crane*. London: George Bell and Sons, 1902.

KUNITZ, STANLEY JASSPON. *Authors Today and Yesterday*. New York: H. W. Wilson Co., 1933.

KUNITZ, STANLEY JASSPON. *Living Authors*. New York: H. W. Wilson Co., 1931.

KUNITZ, STANLEY JASSPON, and HAYCRAFT, HOWARD. *American Authors, 1600-1900*. New York: H. W. Wilson Co., 1938.

KUNITZ, STANLEY JASSPON, and HAYCRAFT, HOWARD. *British Authors of the Nineteenth Century*. New York: H. W. Wilson Co., 1936.

KUNITZ, STANLEY JASSPON, and HAYCRAFT, HOWARD. *Junior Book of Authors*. New York: H. W. Wilson Co., 1934.

Lamb's Biographical Dictionary of the United States, 7 Vols. Boston: Federal Book Company of Boston, 1903.

LANG, ANDREW. *Library*. London: Macmillan and Co., 1892.

LAROUSSE, PIERRE ATHANASE. *Grand Dictionnaire Universel du XIXᵉ Siècle*, 17 Vols. Paris: Vᵛᵉ P. Larousse & Cⁱᵉ., 1866-90.

LATIMER, LOUISE PAYSON. *Illustrators*. Boston: F. W. Faxon Co., 1927, 1929.

LETHERBROW, T. *Warwick Brooke's Pencil-pictures of Child Life*. Boston: D. Lothrop Company, 1888.

LIBRARY OF CONGRESS. *General Catalog*

LINTON, WILLIAM JAMES. *Three Score and Ten Years (1820-1890)*. New York: Charles Scribner's Sons, 1894.

LOW, DAVID. *British Cartoonists, Caricaturists and Comic Artists*. London: William Collins, 1942.

LUCAS, EDWARD VERRALL. *Edwin Austin Abbey*, 2 Vols. New York: Charles Scribner's Sons, 1921.

MACFALL, HALDANE. *Book of Lovat Claud Fraser*. London: J. M. Dent & Sons, 1923.

MAHONY, BERTHA E., and WHITNEY, ELINOR. *Contemporary Illustrators of Children's Books*. Boston: Bookshop for Boys and Girls, 1930.

MAHONY, BERTHA E., and WHITNEY, ELINOR. *Five Years of Children's Books, a Supplement to Realms of Gold*. Garden City, N. Y.: Doubleday, Doran & Co., 1936.

MAHONY, BERTHA E., and WHITNEY, ELINOR. *Realms of Gold in Children's Books*. Garden City, N. Y.: Doubleday, Doran & Co., 1929.

MALLETT, DANIEL TROWBRIDGE. *Mallett's Index of Artists*. New York: R. R. Bowker Company, 1935. *Supplement to Mallett's Index of Artists*. New York: R. R. Bowker Company, 1940.

MARKS, JOHN GEORGE. *Life and Letters of Frederick Walker, A.R.A.* London: Macmillan and Co., Ltd., 1896.

Men and Women of America, a Biographical Dictionary of Contemporaries. New York: L. R. Hamersly and Co., 1910.

MILLARD, CHRISTOPHER SCLATER. *Printed Work of Claud Lovat Fraser*. London: Henry Danielson, 1923.

MOORE, ANNE CARROLL. *Three Owls*. Vol. 1. New York: Macmillan Co., 1925. Vol. 2. New York: Coward-McCann, 1928. Vol. 3. New York: Coward-McCann, 1931.

MORRILL, EDWARD. *American Children's Books, 1723-1939 (Catalogue Six)*. Boston: Edward Morrill and Son.

New International Encyclopedia, Second Edition. New York: Dodd, Mead and Company, Inc., 1925.

NONESUCH PRESS. *Nonesuch Dickensiana*. Bloomsbury: Nonesuch Press, 1937.

Our Young Folks. Vols. 1-9 (1865-1873).

Pageant of America. Vols. 11 and 12. New Haven: Yale University Press, 1926.

PAINE, ALBERT BIGELOW. *Mark Twain*, 3 Vols. New York: Harper & Brothers, 1912.

PALMER, A. H. *Life of Joseph Wolf, Animal Painter*. London: Longmans, Green & Co., 1895.

PENNELL, JOSEPH. *Graphic Arts*. Chicago: University of Chicago Press, 1921.

PENNELL, JOSEPH. *Modern Illustration*. London: George Bell and Sons, 1895.

PENNELL, JOSEPH. *Pen Drawing and Pen Draughtsmen*. New York: Macmillan Co., 1897.

PLARR, VICTOR G. *Men and Women of the Time*. London: George Routledge and Sons, Ltd., 1899.

POLLARD, ALFRED WILLIAM. *Early Illustrated Books*. New York: Empire State Book Co., 1927.

Princeton University Library Chronicle, Vol. IV, Nos. 2 and 3, February-April 1943. (George Cruikshank.)

Publisher's Trade List Annual. New York: R. R. Bowker Co.

Reference Catalogue of Current Literature. London: Whitaker, 1932, 1940. *Whitaker's Cumulative Book List, 1940-43*, and *Current Quarterly Supplements*. London: Whitaker and Sons, Ltd.

REID, FORREST. *Illustrators of the Sixties*. London: Faber and Gwyer Limited, 1928.

ROORBACH, ORVILLE AUGUSTUS. *Bibliotheca Americana, 1820-61*, 4 Vols. New York: Roorbach, 1852-61.

ROSENBACH, ABRAHAM SIMON WOLF. *Early American Children's Books*. Portland, Maine: Southworth Press, 1933.

RUZICKA, RUDOLPH. *Thomas Bewick, Engraver*. New York: The Typophiles, 1943.

SADLEIR, MICHAEL. *Excursions in Victorian Bibliography*. London: Chaundy and Cox, 1922.

St. Nicholas Magazine, Vols. 1-66 (November 1873-October 1939).

SALAMAN, MALCOLM CHARLES. *British Book Illustration Yesterday and Today*. London: The Studio Limited, 1923.

SALAMAN, MALCOLM CHARLES. *Modern Book Illustrators*. London: The Studio Limited, 1914.

SALAMAN, MALCOLM CHARLES. *Modern Woodcuts and Lithographs by British and French Artists*. London: The Studio Limited, 1919.

SHARP, ROBERT FARQUHARSON. *Dictionary of English Authors*. London: George Redway, 1897.

SHEPHERD, RICHARD HERNE. *Bibliography of Thackeray*. London: Elliot Stock, *n.d.*

SIMON, HOWARD. *500 Years of Art and Illustration*. Cleveland: World Publishing Co., 1942.

SITWELL, OSBERT. *Thomas Rowlandson*. London: The Studio Limited, 1929.

SITWELL, SACHEVERELL. *Narrative Pictures*. London: B. T. Batsford, Ltd., 1937.

SKETCHLEY, ROSE ESTHER DOROTHEA. *English Book Illustration of Today*. London: Kegan Paul, Trench, Trübner and Co., Ltd., 1903.

SMITH, ELVA SOPHRONIA. *History of Children's Literature*. Chicago: American Library Association, 1937.

SMITH, FRANCIS HOPKINSON. *American Illustrators*. New York: Charles Scribner's Sons, 1893.

SMITH, RALPH CLIFTON. *Biographical Index of American Artists*. Baltimore: Williams and Wilkins Co., 1930.

SPARROW, WALTER SHAW. *Book of British Etching*. New York: Dodd, Mead and Co., 1926.

SPIELMANN, MARION HARRY. *Hugh Thomson*. London: Adam and Charles Black, Ltd., 1931.

SPIELMANN, MARION HARRY. *Kate Greenaway*. London: Adam and Charles Black, Ltd., 1905.

STEPHENS, FREDERIC GEORGE. *Memoir of George Cruikshank*. New York: Scribner and Welford, 1891.

STEPHENS, FREDERIC GEORGE. *Memorials of William Mulready, R.A.* New York: Scribner and Welford, 1890.

SULLIVAN, EDMUND JOSEPH. *Art of Illustration*. London: Chapman and Hall, Ltd., 1932.

Ten Years and William Shakespeare: A Survey of the Publishing Activities of the Limited Editions Club from October 1929 to October 1940. New York: Limited Editions Club, Inc., 1940.

THACKERAY, WILLIAM MAKEPEACE. *Essay on the Genius of George Cruikshank*. London: George Redway, 1884.

THOMSON, DAVID CROAL. *Life and Works of Thomas Bewick*. London: The Art Journal Office, 1882.

THORPE, JAMES. *English Illustration: The Nineties*. London: Faber and Faber, 1935

TIDY, GORDON. *A Little about Leech*. London: Constable and Co., Ltd., 1931.

TUER, ANDREW W. *History of the Horn-book*. London: Leadenhall Press, Ltd., 1897.

TYTLER, SARAH. *Modern Painters and Their Paintings*. Boston: Roberts Brothers, 1893.

United States Catalog. Books in Print, 1912, 1928 (Editions 3-4). New York: H. W. Wilson Co.
    Cumulative Book Index (Supplements to United States Catalog). New York: H. W. Wilson Co.

VENABLES, EDMUND. *Life of John Bunyan*. London: Walter Scott, 1888.

WEITENKAMPF, FRANK. *American Graphic Art* (New Edition Revised and Enlarged). New York:
    Macmillan Co., 1924.

WEITENKAMPF, FRANK. *Illustrated Book*. Cambridge: Harvard University Press, 1938.

WELSH, CHARLES. *Bookseller of the Last Century*. London: Griffith, Farran, Okeden & Welsh, 1885.

WELSH, CHARLES. *On Coloured Books for Children*. London: C. W. H. Wyman, 1887.

WHITE, GLEESON. *Children's Books and Their Illustrators*. The Special Winter Number of *International Studio*, 1897-98. New York: The Studio Limited.

WHITE, GLEESON. *English Illustration, "The Sixties": 1855-70*. London: Archibald Constable and
    Co., Ltd., 1897.

Who Was Who, 3 Vols. (1897-1940). London: Adam and Charles Black.

Who Was Who in America, 1897-1942. Chicago: A. N. Marquis Co.

Who's Who, 1898 — date. London: Adam and Charles Black.

Who's Who in America, 1899 — date. Chicago: A. N. Marquis Co.

Who's Who in America Current Biographical Service. December 1939—date. Chicago: A. N. Marquis
    Co.

Who's Who in American Art, 3 Vols. (1935-1940). Washington, D. C.: American Federation of Arts.

Who's Who in Art, Second Edition. London: Art Trade Press, Ltd., 1929.

*Wood Engraving: 3 Essays by A. V. S. Anthony, Timothy Cole and Elbridge Kingsley with a List
    of American Books Illustrated by Wood Cuts*. New York: Grolier Club, 1916.

WOODBERRY, GEORGE E. *History of Wood-engraving*. New York: Harper and Brothers, 1883.

YOUNG, ART. *Thomas Rowlandson*. New York: Willey Book Co., 1938.

YOUNG, W. ARTHUR. *Dictionary of the Characters and Scenes in Stories and Poems of Rudyard
    Kipling, 1886-1911*. London: G. Routledge and Sons, Ltd., 1911.

ERNEST GRISET : *Good-Natured Bear*

THOMAS BEWICK : *Select Fables*

Notes and References

TEXT REFERENCES—*Part* I

1. *(p. 37) German Popular Stories, Vol. 1*, published by Baldwin, London 1824, contained twelve etchings by Cruikshank. Vol. 2, published by Robins, London 1826, contained ten of his etchings.

2. *(p. 38)* Frederic G. Stephens. *A Memoir of George Cruikshank*. Scribner and Welford.

3. *(p. 39)* M. H. Spielmann. *History of Punch*. Adam and Charles Black.

4. *(p. 40)* M. H. Spielmann. *History of Punch*. Adam and Charles Black.

5. *(p. 41)* Frederic G. Stephens. *A Memoir of George Cruikshank*. Scribner and Welford.

6. *(p. 68)* Henry Blackburn. *Harz Mountains, a Tour of the Toy Country*. Sampson Low.

7. *(p. 68)* Henry Blackburn. *Randolph Caldecott, His Early Art Career*. Sampson Low.

8. *(p. 74)* Henry Blackburn. *Breton Folk*. Sampson Low.

9. *(p. 76)* M. H. Spielmann and G. S. Layard. *Kate Greenaway*. Adam and Charles Black. Other quoted material in the section about Kate Greenaway is from the same source.

10. *(p. 168)* The material for most of this brief survey has come out of the author's working experience in printing, and many years' reading of trade literature and periodicals. The historical data has been verified by consulting *Encyclopædia Britannica*, 14th edition; *Colour Printing and Colour Printers* by R. M. Burch (Pitman); *A Chronology of Books and Printing* by David Greenhood and Helen Gentry (Macmillan).

There are no books generally available which explain the graphic processes for the layman, but two sources can be recommended for obtaining additional information: *The Processes of Graphic Reproduction in Printing*, by Harold Curwen (Faber and Faber), a book which is not too technical in vocabulary and in which the pictorial diagrams are illuminating; *Encyclopædia*
Britannica*, 14th edition. See articles on separate aspects of the subject. The one entitled "Color Printing" is a rich summary of all the processes.

11. *(p. 195)* "Narrative Illustration: The Story of the Comics," by M. C. Gaines, in *Print*, Vol. III, No. 2, and "More About Comics," by M. C. Gaines, in *Print*, Vol. III, No. 3.

12. *(p. 212)* See M. C. Gaines, "Narrative Illustration, The Story of the Comics," in *Print*, A Quarterly Journal of the Graphic Arts, Vol. III, No. 2, 1942. This article is based on an exhibition of the American Institute of Graphic Arts, to which I contributed some ideas and materials. The purpose of this note is to explain the similarity between some of the manuscripts and books selected for discussion in both Mr. Gaines' article and this chapter. H. L.-H.

13. *(p. 213)* A new publication called *The Eternal Bible* and published by Authentic Publications, Inc., is a conspicuous attempt to avoid the usual mistakes. The drawings are fresh and more personal, not so much the stereotyped people of the ordinary comics. The speech balloons have been eliminated and the color scheme departs from the usual commercial routine, such as we find it in *Picture Stories From the Bible*, in spite of a formidable Advisory Council of Education and Community Leaders.

TEXT REFERENCES—*Part* III

1. *(p. 379)* Viscount Grey. *Fallodon Papers:* Recreation.

2. *(p. 381)* Walter Crane. *Of the Decorative Illustration of Books Old and New*.

NOTES ON SPECIAL ILLUSTRATIONS

As noted in the Preface, information about most of the illustrations in this book is given in Part III, A Bibliography of Illustrators and Their Works. Some few exceptions, for which the text itself does not supply information, are covered by the notes which follow.

Cover. By T. M. Cleland. See page X in Preface.

Title page. Illustration by J. E. Millais, reproduced from Wordsworth's *Poems for the Young.* London: Alexander Strahan & Co., 1863.

Pages 1–15 inclusive. The woodcuts are by early and unidentified artists. The horn-book on page 10 was reproduced from Tuer's *History of the Horn-book.* London: Leadenhall Press, Ltd., 1897. The battledores on page 11 were photographed from reproductions of originals in the Boston Public Library.

Page 22. Illustration for *Comus* is from *Illustrations of Milton's Comus; Eight Drawings by William Blake Reproduced by William Griggs. Facsimiles from Mss. in possession of Bernard Quaritch.* London: Bernard Quaritch, 1890.

The illustration from *Songs of Innocence* was taken from the facsimile reproduction of a copy in the British Museum. London: Ernest Benn, Ltd., 1926.

Page 68. The Caldecott drawing for *Harz Mountains: A Tour of the Toy Country* is from a book of the same name by Henry Blackburn. London: Sampson Low, 1873.

Pages 123–156 inclusive. Information as to the books from which illustrations on these pages were reproduced will be found in the Selected List beginning on page 145.

Page 158. Diagram reproduced by permission of The Limited Editions Club from an article by Harry A. Groesbeck, Jr., in *The Dolphin, a Journal of the Making of Books,* Number One.

Page 174. Reproduced from a page in the 12th Century manuscript Winchester School Bible which is in the Pierpont Morgan Library.

Page 181. The Bilibin illustration is from Pushkin's *Volga,* a fairy tale in Russian, published in 1904, presumably in St. Petersburg, on the last Tsar's (Nicholas II) order.

Page 183. "Samson and the Lion" from a wood-engraving by Dalziel after Frederick Leighton, from *The Bible Gallery.* London, 1881.

Page 185. "The Eagle's Nest," mixed etching and engraving by Francis Barlow in his edition of Æsop, London, 1665. This is the first edition in which these illustrations appear.

Page 186. The wood-engraving by Eric Gill is from the opening page of Volume 4 of Chaucer's *Canterbury Tales.* London: The Golden Cockerel Press, 1931.

Page 188. The painting of Don Quixote and Sancho Panza was made by Honoré Daumier, but no edition of Cervantes' masterpiece was ever illustrated by this artist. The painting belongs to a private collection (Reinhardt) in Switzerland.

Page 189. The Boutet de Monvel illustration is from the title page of his edition of *Jeanne d'Arc.* Paris: Plon, Nourrit, 1900.

Page 206. The broadside is from *Les angues,* plate XLVII, No. 84.

Page 208. The illustration by Doré is reproduced from a modern Swiss reprint of *Les Travaux d'Hercule.*

Page 210. The page from Doré's *Histoire pittoresque, dramatique et caricaturale de la Sainte Russie* is reproduced from a modern German reprint.

The *Struwwelpeter* illustration is from the first edition. Frankfurt: Insel Verlag, 1946.

Page 211. Der verlorene Pfennig, illustrated by Arpad Schmidhammer, was published in Mainz by Joseph Scholz.

Page 227. The Merry Puppy Book for which Cecil Aldin drew the illustrations is by M. Byron. London: Oxford University Press.

Page 262. The woodcut by Lynd Ward is from *Contemporary Illustrators of Children's Books,* by Bertha E. Mahony and Elinor Whitney. Boston: The Bookshop for Boys and Girls, 1930.

Page 324. Theatre Shoes, illustrated by Richard Floethe, is by Noel Streatfeild. New York: Random House, 1945.

Page 384. Illustration from *Birket Foster's Pictures of English Landscape with Pictures in Words by Tom Taylor.* London: Routledge, Warne & Routledge, 1863.

Page 519. The illustration by Ernest Griset is from *The Good-Natured Bear* by R. Hengist Horne. London: Alexander Strahan & Co., Ltd. *n.d.*

THOMAS BEWICK: *History of Quadrupeds*

EDMUND DULAC: *Treasure Island*

List of Artists Represented by Illustrations

522

Index to Part I

Titles of books and magazines are in italic type.

Italic *figures* indicate illustrations. As noted in the preface, this index covers Part I
(pages 1-262) only. Material on the remaining pages is arranged alphabetically.

L. LESLIE BROOKE: *Nursery Rhyme Book*

This book, issued in a first edition of 5000 copies, has been set in Linotype Janson, with hand-set Garamond for display, by The Thomas Todd Company of Boston by whom it was also printed. The paper, special Enfield Ivory wove, was made by The Curtis Paper Company and supplied by The Stevens-Nelson Paper Corporation. Plates for the cover and text-page illustrations were made, with some few exceptions, by The Lincoln Engraving Company, Boston. The book was bound by The Boston Bookbinding Company. Beulah Folmsbee was the designer.

DATE DUE

PRINTED IN U.S.A.